Ōoku

THE INNER CHAMBERS

by **Fumi Yoshinaga**

VOL. **13**

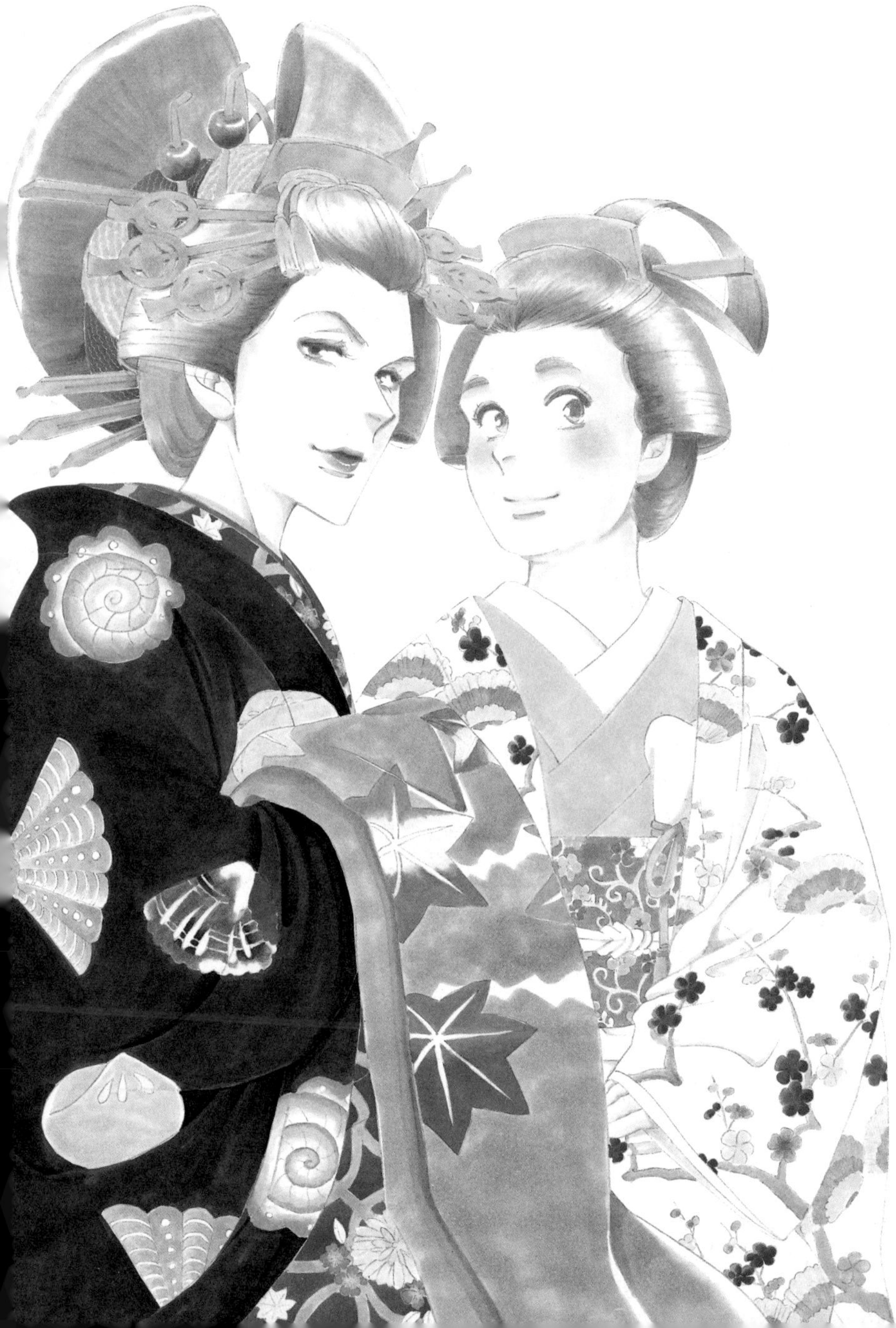

TABLE *of* CONTENTS

CHAPTER FIFTY-TWO
· *page* 9 ·

CHAPTER FIFTY-THREE
· *page* 59 ·

CHAPTER FIFTY-FOUR
· *page* 104 ·

CHAPTER FIFTY-FIVE
· *page* 162 ·

END NOTES
· *page* 241 ·

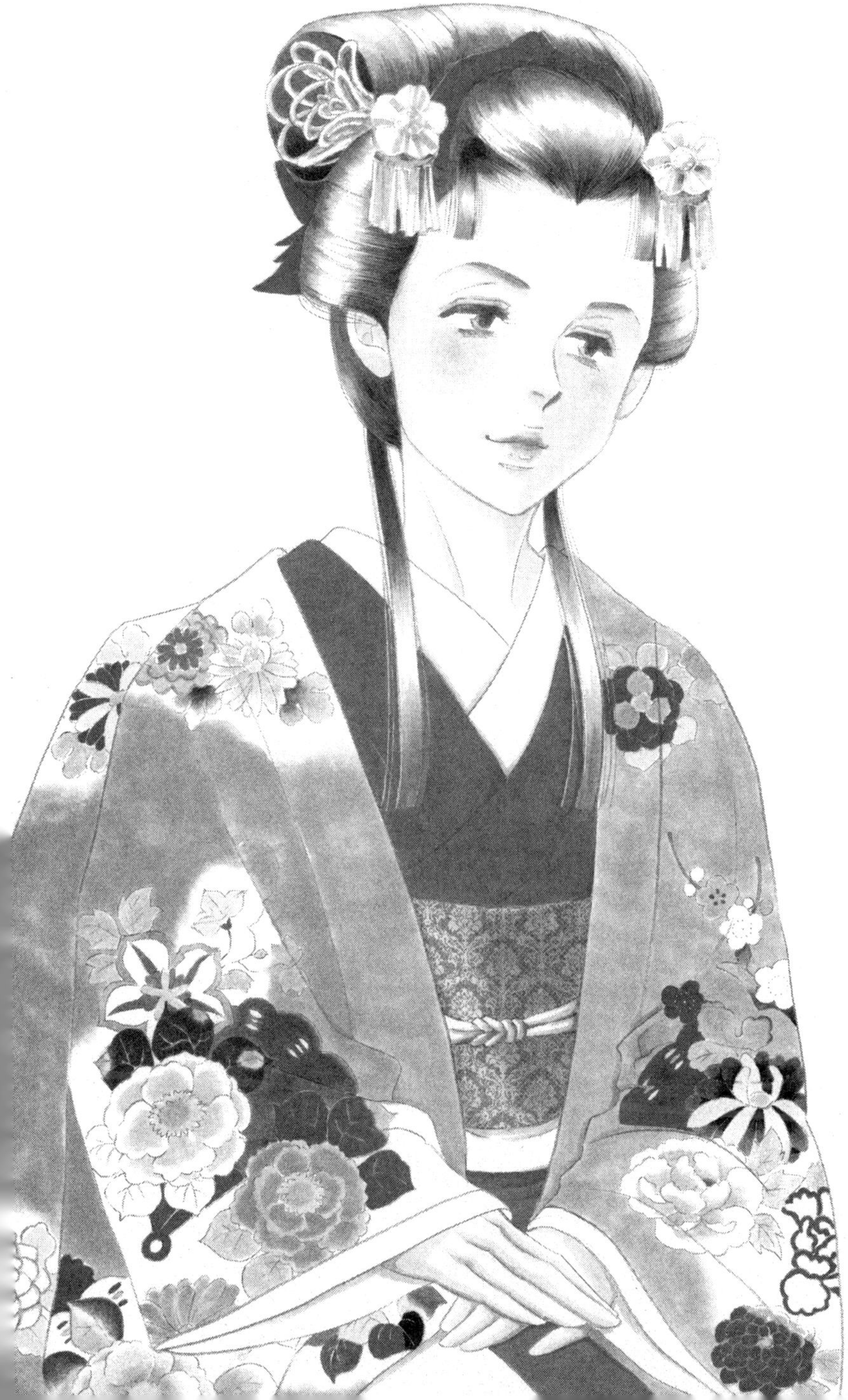

THE INNER CHAMBERS

CAST *of* CHARACTERS

From the birth of the "inverse Inner Chambers" to its zenith, to eradicating the Redface Pox, and now...?

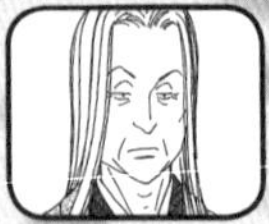

SENIOR CHAMBERLAIN

LADY KASUGA

↓

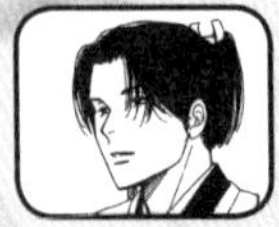

MADE-NOKOJI ARIKOTO

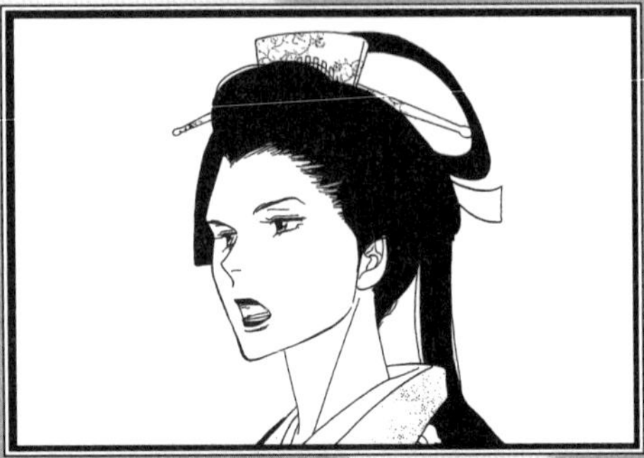

TOKUGAWA IEMITSU (III)

Impersonated her father, Iemitsu, at Lady Kasuga's urging after he died of the Redface Pox. Later became the first female shogun.

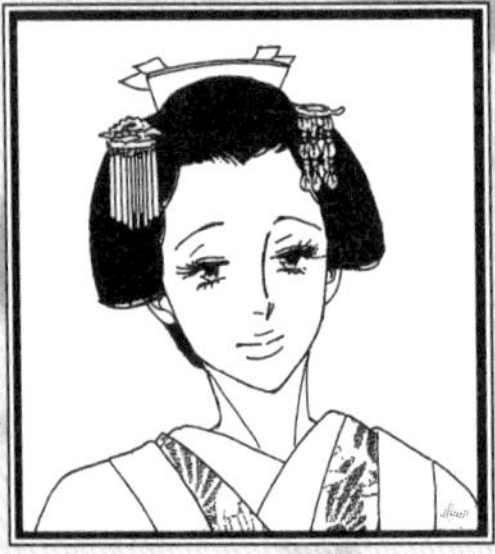

TOKUGAWA TSUNAYOSHI (V)

Endowed with both intellect and beauty, she did her best to rule wisely, but became known as "the Dog Shogun" due to unpopular policy mistakes later in her reign.

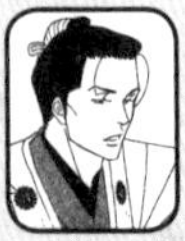

SENIOR CHAMBERLAIN

EMONNOSUKE

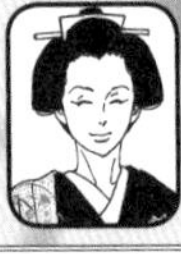

PRIVY COUNCILLOR

YANAGISAWA YOSHIYASU

TOKUGAWA TSUNASHIGE

TOKUGAWA IENOBU (VI)

A ruler of sterling character but poor health, who died soon after assuming office.

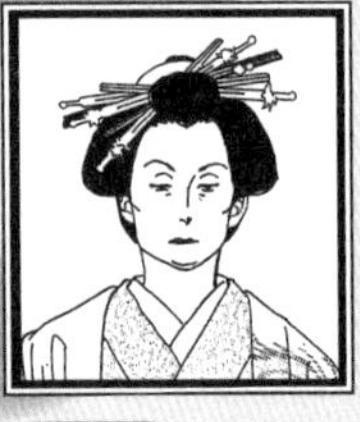

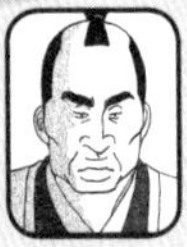

SENIOR CHAMBERLAIN

EJIMA

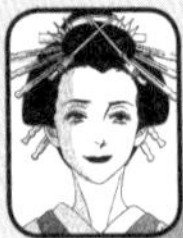

PRIVY COUNCILLOR

MANABE AKIFUSA

TOKUGAWA IETSUNA (IV)

Iemitsu's eldest daughter, known as "Lord Aye-do-so."

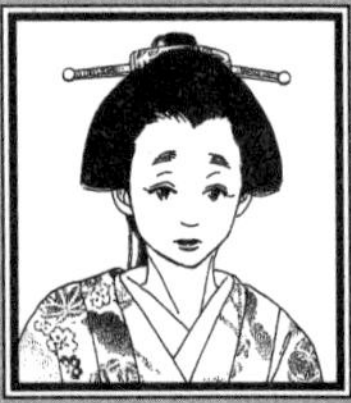

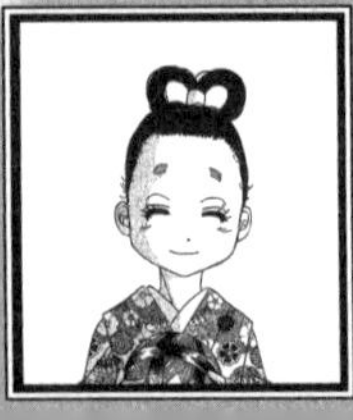

TOKUGAWA IETSUGU (VII)

Died in childhood.

THE REDFACE POX BUSTERS

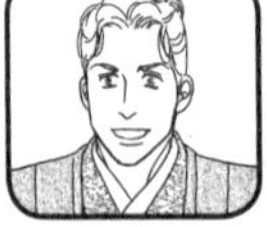

AONUMA

Mixed-race physician of Western medicine called to the Inner ambers. Succeeded in vaccinating ients against the Redface Pox, but was sentenced to death.

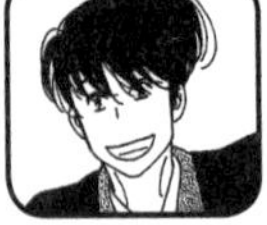

HIRAGA GENNAI

Multitalented genius and deep admirer of Tanuma. Devoted to finding a solution to the Redface Pox. Deceased.

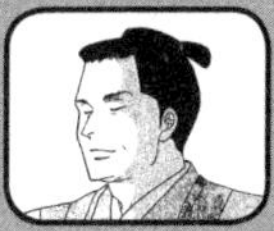

SENIOR CHAMBERLAIN

FUJINAMI

↓

SUGISHITA

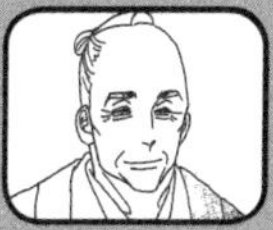

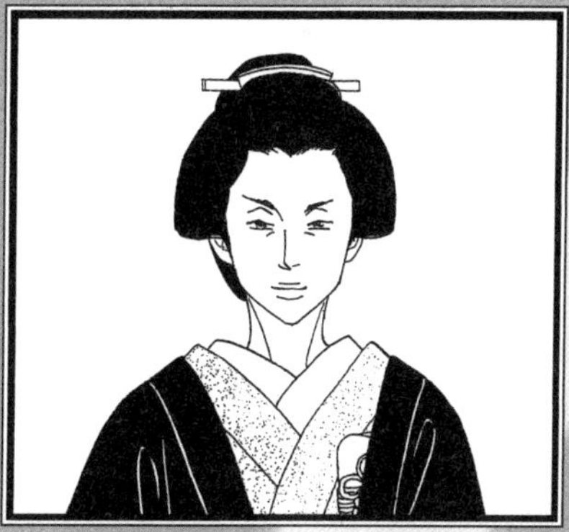

TOKUGAWA YOSHIMUNE (VIII)

Third daughter of Mitsusada, the second head of the Kii branch of the Tokugawa family. Acceded to domain lord and then, upon the death of Ietsugu, to shogun. Imposed and lived by a strict policy of austerity, dismissing large numbers of Inner Chamber courtiers and pursuing policies designed to increase income to the treasury.

PRIVY COUNCILLOR

KANO HISAMICHI

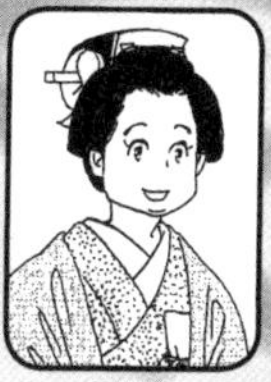

MUNETADA (HITOTSUBASHI BRANCH)

Yoshimune's third daughter

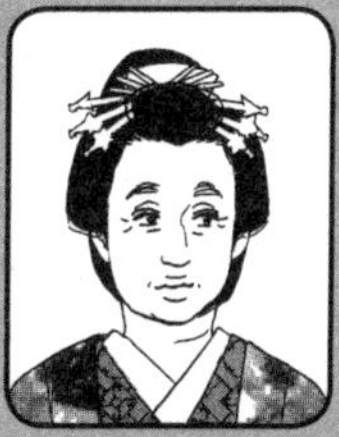

TOKUGAWA HARUSADA

"Monster" who ruled Edo Castle from behind the scenes for many years, and murdered many of its residents with poison, purely for her own ends.

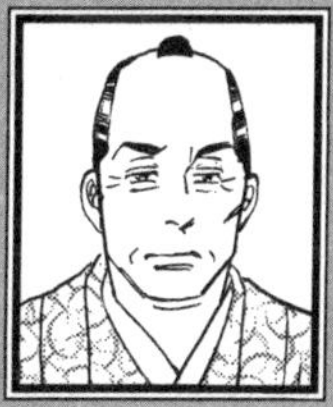

TOKUGAWA IENARI (XI)

Son of Harusada. Obedient, but slightly weak and timid.

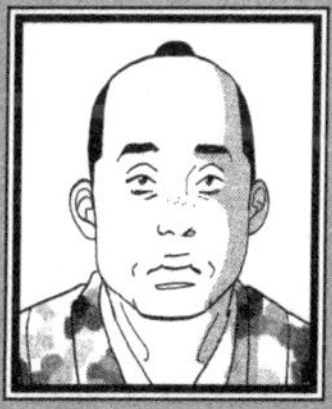

TOKUGAWA IEYOSHI (XII)

Made shogun at age 45 by his father Ienari.

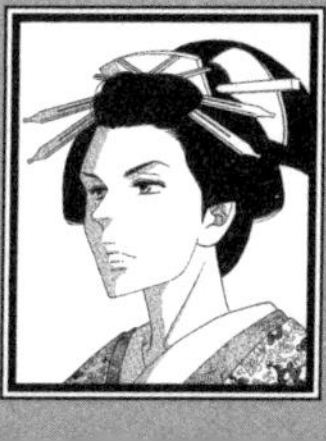

TOKUGAWA IESADA (XIII)

MUNETAKE (TAYASU BRANCH)

Yoshimune's second daughter

MATSUDAIRA SADANOBU

Although made a Senior Councillor after Tanuma's downfall, she was dismissed from this post after clashing with Harusada.

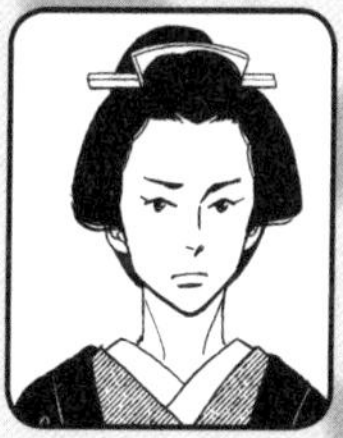

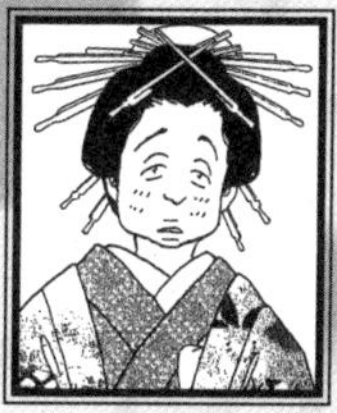

TOKUGAWA IESHIGE (IX)

Yoshimune's eldest daughter. Afflicted with a speech impediment, but not mentally disabled.

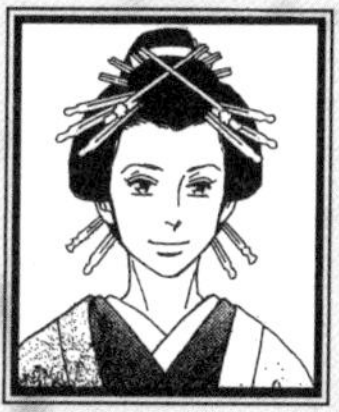

TOKUGAWA IEHARU (X)

Intelligent but brittle, she died of arsenic poisoning.

CHAMBERLAIN
↓
SENIOR COUNCILLOR

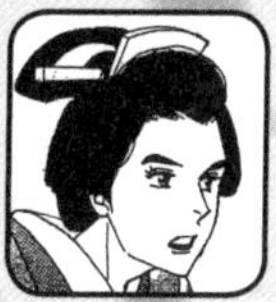

TANUMA OKITSUGU

Served Ieshige and later Ieharu as Senior Councillor.

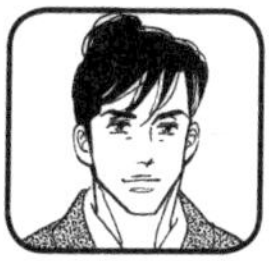

OUMI IHEI

Studied with Ryojun under Aonuma, and later became a doctor in town.

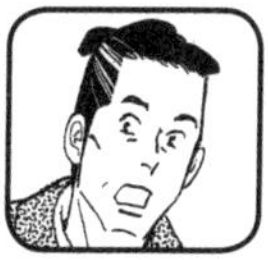

KUROKI SEIJUN

Ryojun's son. He took over his father's infirmary.

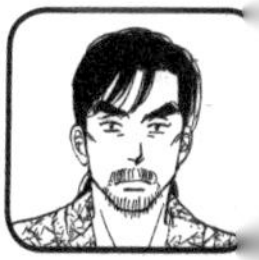

KUROKI RYO

Studied Hollander mec
under Aonuma. Later o
a medical clinic to se
townspeople and conti
researching the Redfac

Ōoku

THE INNER CHAMBERS

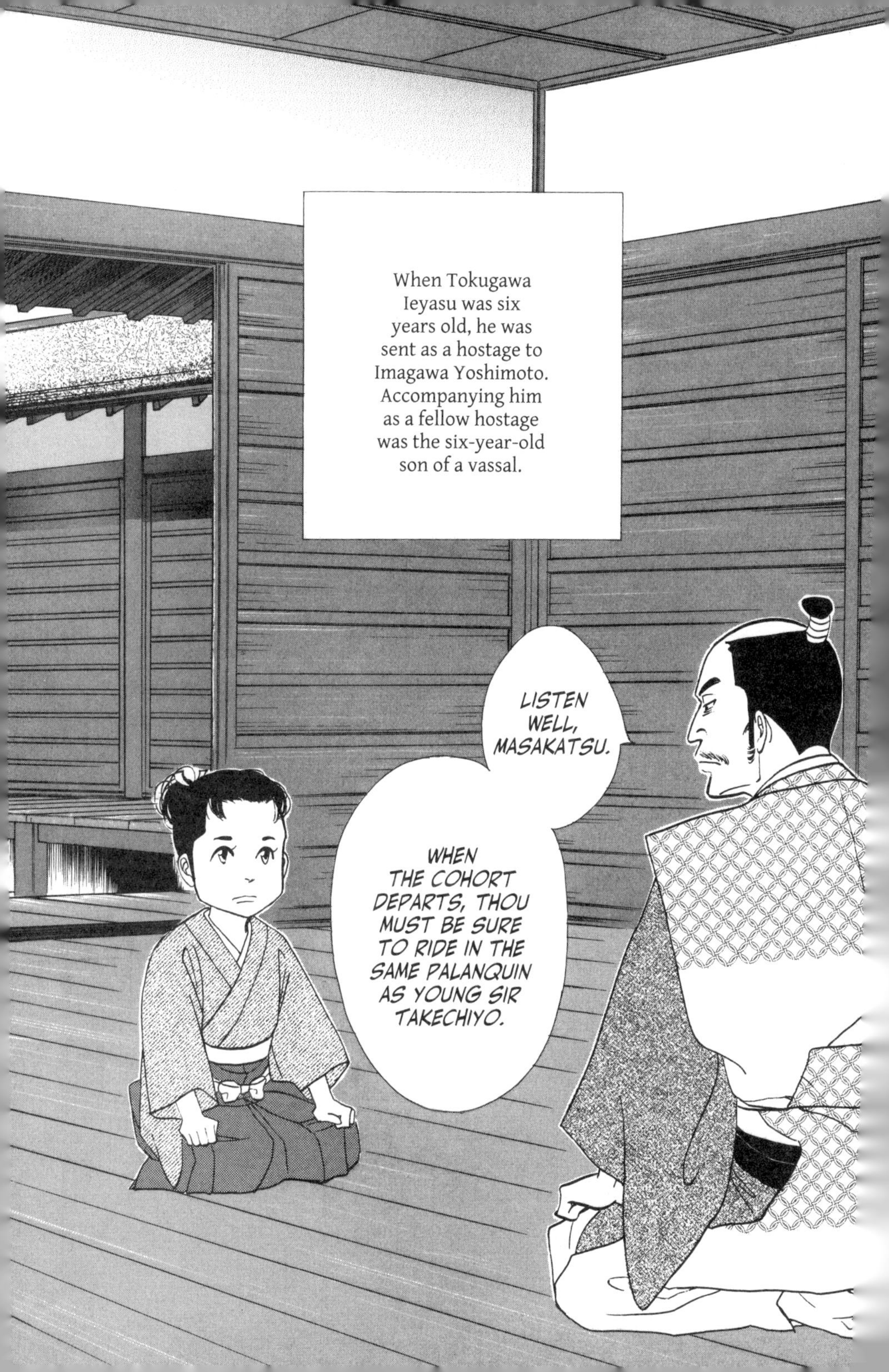
When Tokugawa Ieyasu was six years old, he was sent as a hostage to Imagawa Yoshimoto. Accompanying him as a fellow hostage was the six-year-old son of a vassal.
LISTEN WELL, MASAKATSU.
WHEN THE COHORT DEPARTS, THOU MUST BE SURE TO RIDE IN THE SAME PALANQUIN AS YOUNG SIR TAKECHIYO.

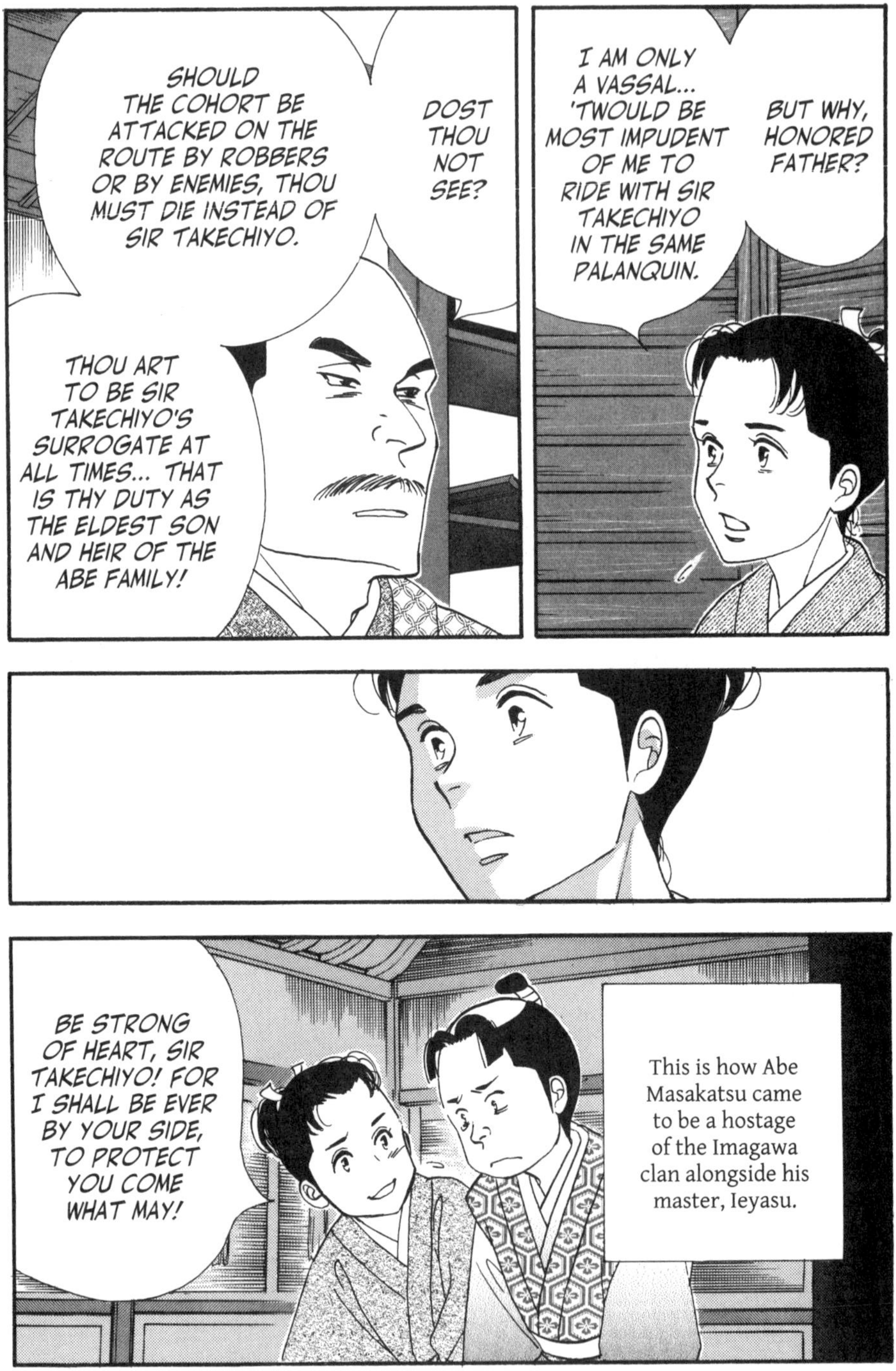
BUT WHY, HONORED FATHER?
I AM ONLY A VASSAL... 'TWOULD BE MOST IMPUDENT OF ME TO RIDE WITH SIR TAKECHIYO IN THE SAME PALANQUIN.
DOST THOU NOT SEE?
SHOULD THE COHORT BE ATTACKED ON THE ROUTE BY ROBBERS OR BY ENEMIES, THOU MUST DIE INSTEAD OF SIR TAKECHIYO.
THOU ART TO BE SIR TAKECHIYO'S SURROGATE AT ALL TIMES... THAT IS THY DUTY AS THE ELDEST SON AND HEIR OF THE ABE FAMILY!
This is how Abe Masakatsu came to be a hostage of the Imagawa clan alongside his master, Ieyasu.
BE STRONG OF HEART, SIR TAKECHIYO! FOR I SHALL BE EVER BY YOUR SIDE, TO PROTECT YOU COME WHAT MAY!

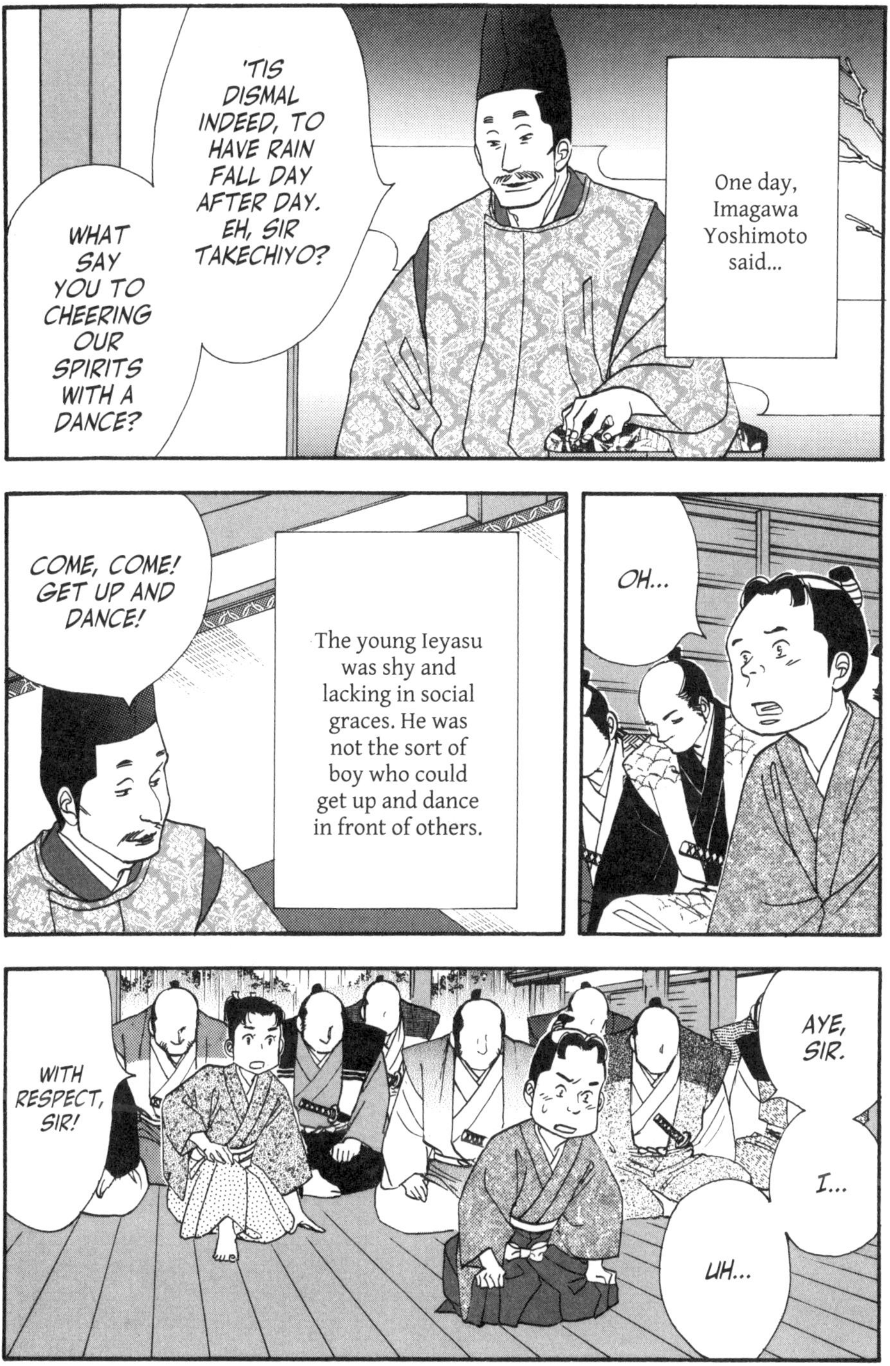
One day, Imagawa Yoshimoto said...
'TIS DISMAL INDEED, TO HAVE RAIN FALL DAY AFTER DAY. EH, SIR TAKECHIYO?
WHAT SAY YOU TO CHEERING OUR SPIRITS WITH A DANCE?
OH...
COME, COME! GET UP AND DANCE!
The young Ieyasu was shy and lacking in social graces. He was not the sort of boy who could get up and dance in front of others.
AYE, SIR.
I...
UH...
WITH RESPECT, SIR!

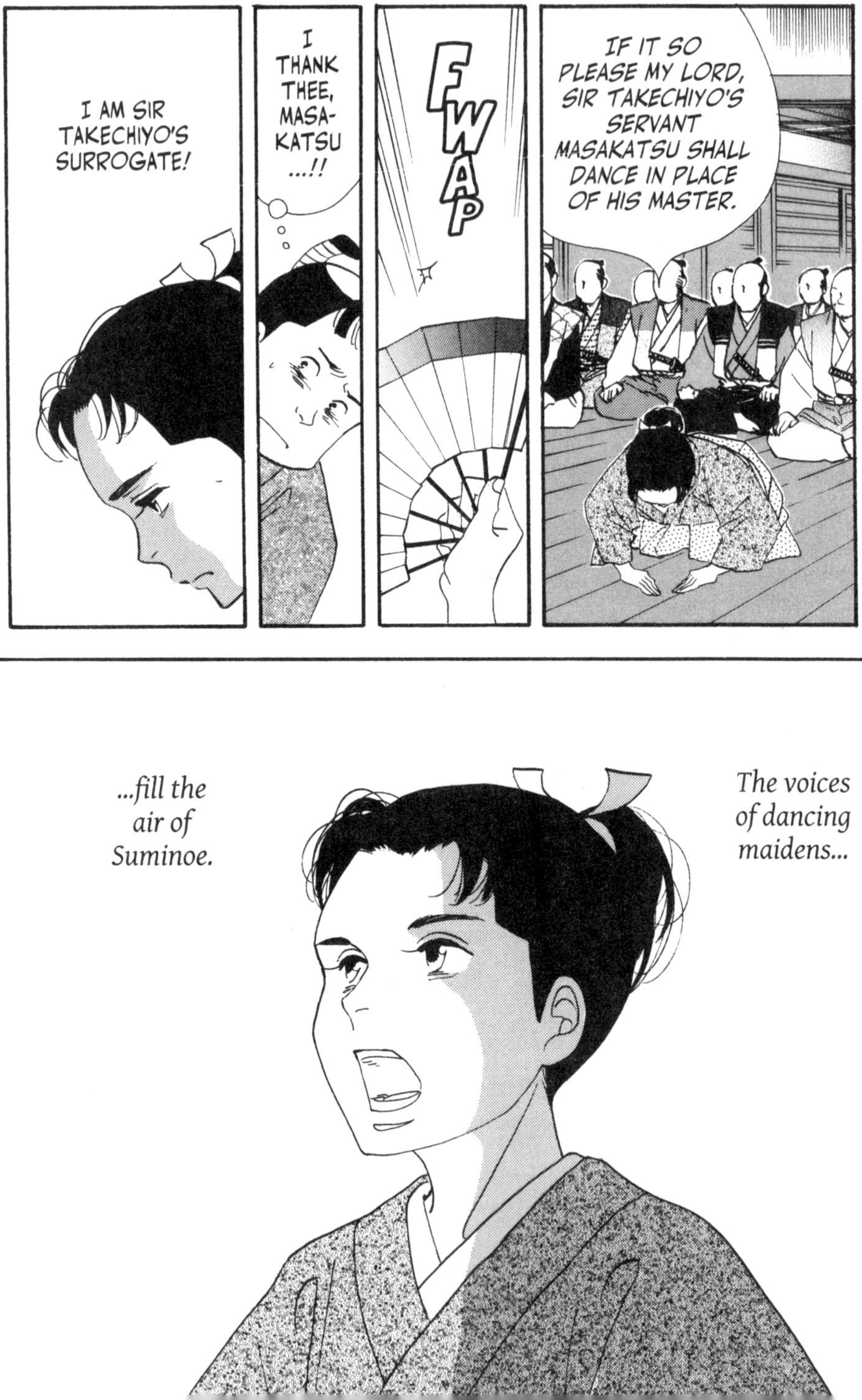

IF IT SO PLEASE MY LORD, SIR TAKECHIYO'S SERVANT MASAKATSU SHALL DANCE IN PLACE OF HIS MASTER.
FWAP
I THANK THEE, MASA-KATSU ...!!
I AM SIR TAKECHIYO'S SURROGATE!
The voices of dancing maidens...
...fill the air of Suminoe.

*The green of the
pine and the blue
of the sea...*

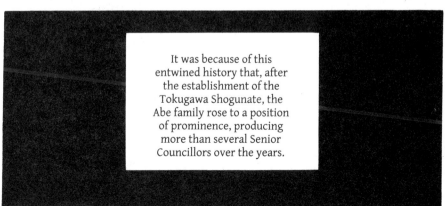

It was because of this
entwined history that, after
the establishment of the
Tokugawa Shogunate, the
Abe family rose to a position
of prominence, producing
more than several Senior
Councillors over the years.

And now, let
us go back,
seventeen
years before
Commodore
Perry's ships
sailed into
Uraga Bay...

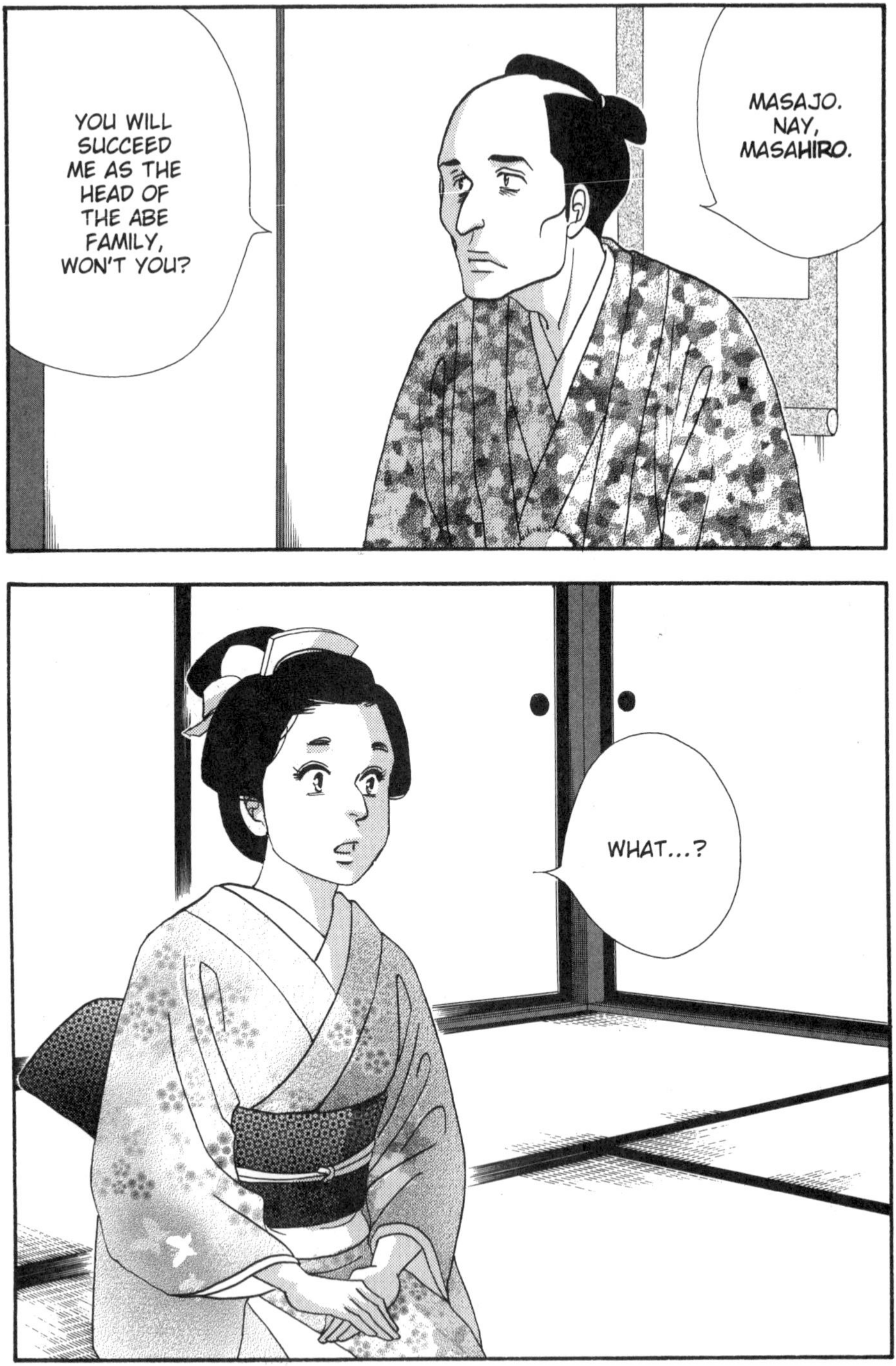
MASAJO. NAY, MASAHIRO.
YOU WILL SUCCEED ME AS THE HEAD OF THE ABE FAMILY, WON'T YOU?
WHAT...?

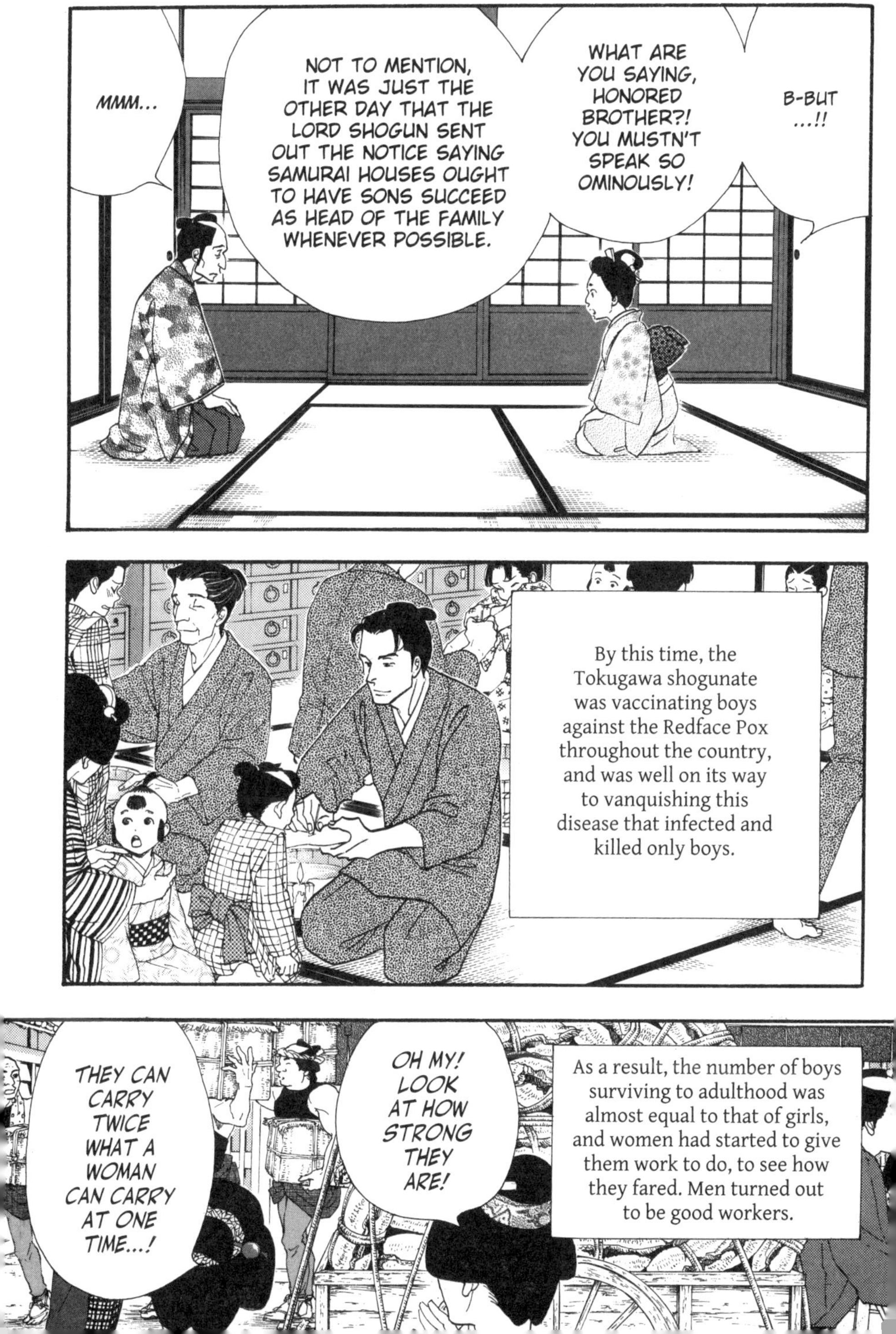
B-BUT ...!!
WHAT ARE YOU SAYING, HONORED BROTHER?! YOU MUSTN'T SPEAK SO OMINOUSLY!
NOT TO MENTION, IT WAS JUST THE OTHER DAY THAT THE LORD SHOGUN SENT OUT THE NOTICE SAYING SAMURAI HOUSES OUGHT TO HAVE SONS SUCCEED AS HEAD OF THE FAMILY WHENEVER POSSIBLE.
MMM...
By this time, the Tokugawa shogunate was vaccinating boys against the Redface Pox throughout the country, and was well on its way to vanquishing this disease that infected and killed only boys.
As a result, the number of boys surviving to adulthood was almost equal to that of girls, and women had started to give them work to do, to see how they fared. Men turned out to be good workers.
OH MY! LOOK AT HOW STRONG THEY ARE!
THEY CAN CARRY TWICE WHAT A WOMAN CAN CARRY AT ONE TIME...!

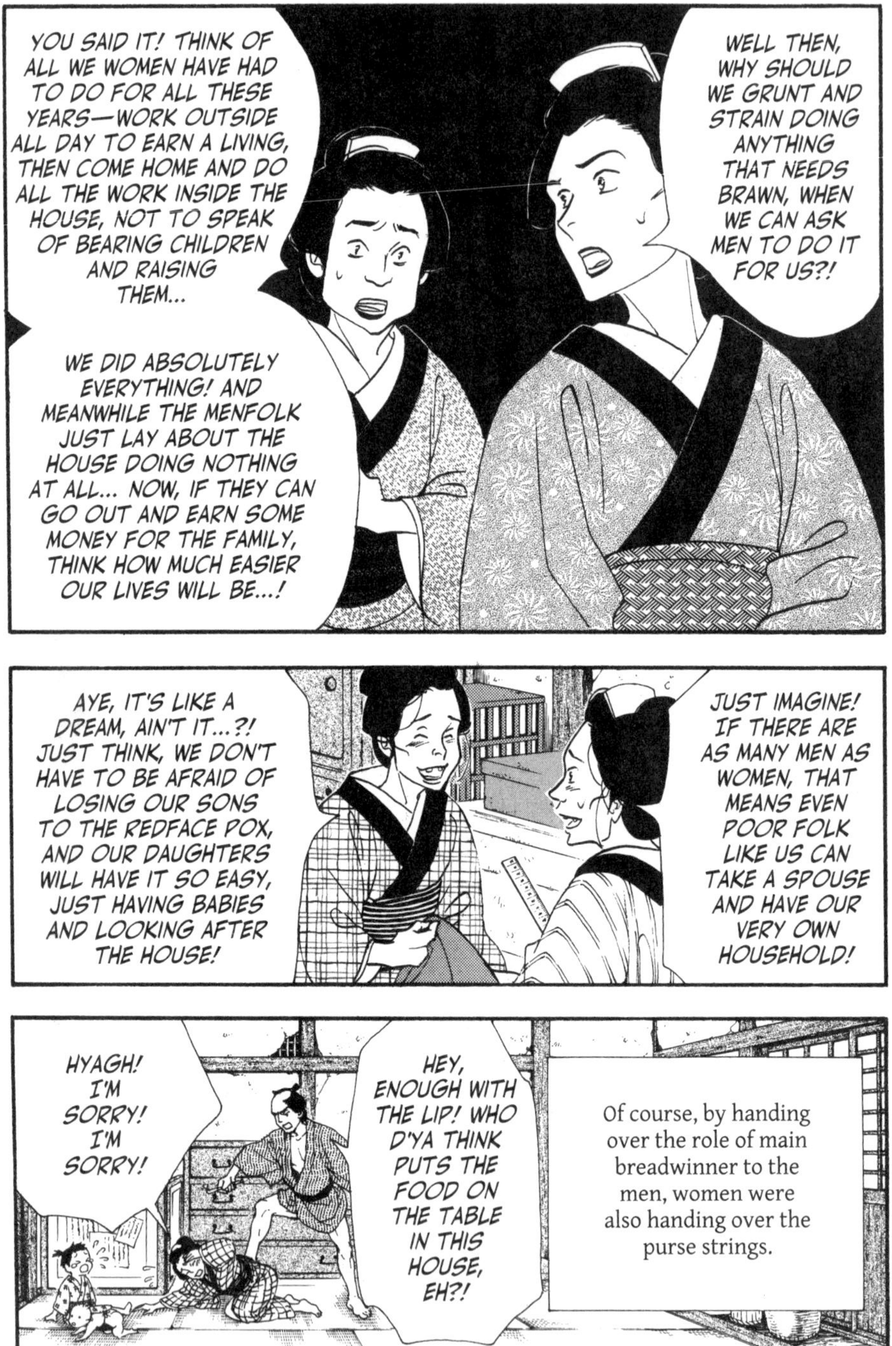
WELL THEN, WHY SHOULD WE GRUNT AND STRAIN DOING ANYTHING THAT NEEDS BRAWN, WHEN WE CAN ASK MEN TO DO IT FOR US?!
YOU SAID IT! THINK OF ALL WE WOMEN HAVE HAD TO DO FOR ALL THESE YEARS—WORK OUTSIDE ALL DAY TO EARN A LIVING, THEN COME HOME AND DO ALL THE WORK INSIDE THE HOUSE, NOT TO SPEAK OF BEARING CHILDREN AND RAISING THEM...
WE DID ABSOLUTELY EVERYTHING! AND MEANWHILE THE MENFOLK JUST LAY ABOUT THE HOUSE DOING NOTHING AT ALL... NOW, IF THEY CAN GO OUT AND EARN SOME MONEY FOR THE FAMILY, THINK HOW MUCH EASIER OUR LIVES WILL BE...!
JUST IMAGINE! IF THERE ARE AS MANY MEN AS WOMEN, THAT MEANS EVEN POOR FOLK LIKE US CAN TAKE A SPOUSE AND HAVE OUR VERY OWN HOUSEHOLD!
AYE, IT'S LIKE A DREAM, AIN'T IT...?! JUST THINK, WE DON'T HAVE TO BE AFRAID OF LOSING OUR SONS TO THE REDFACE POX, AND OUR DAUGHTERS WILL HAVE IT SO EASY, JUST HAVING BABIES AND LOOKING AFTER THE HOUSE!
Of course, by handing over the role of main breadwinner to the men, women were also handing over the purse strings.
HEY, ENOUGH WITH THE LIP! WHO D'YA THINK PUTS THE FOOD ON THE TABLE IN THIS HOUSE, EH?!
HYAGH! I'M SORRY! I'M SORRY!

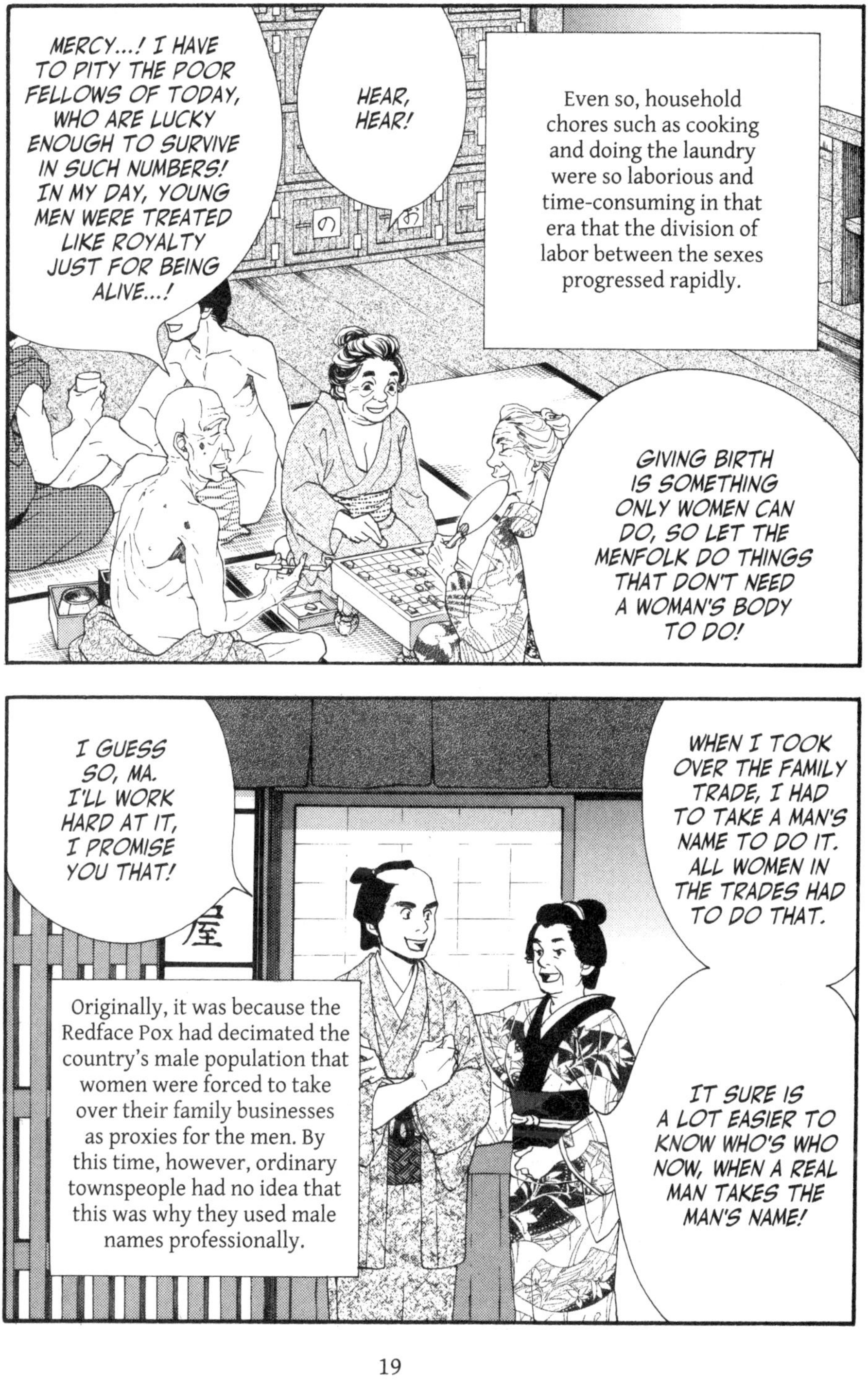
Even so, household chores such as cooking and doing the laundry were so laborious and time-consuming in that era that the division of labor between the sexes progressed rapidly.
GIVING BIRTH IS SOMETHING ONLY WOMEN CAN DO, SO LET THE MENFOLK DO THINGS THAT DON'T NEED A WOMAN'S BODY TO DO!
MERCY...! I HAVE TO PITY THE POOR FELLOWS OF TODAY, WHO ARE LUCKY ENOUGH TO SURVIVE IN SUCH NUMBERS! IN MY DAY, YOUNG MEN WERE TREATED LIKE ROYALTY JUST FOR BEING ALIVE...!
HEAR, HEAR!
WHEN I TOOK OVER THE FAMILY TRADE, I HAD TO TAKE A MAN'S NAME TO DO IT. ALL WOMEN IN THE TRADES HAD TO DO THAT.
IT SURE IS A LOT EASIER TO KNOW WHO'S WHO NOW, WHEN A REAL MAN TAKES THE MAN'S NAME!
I GUESS SO, MA. I'LL WORK HARD AT IT, I PROMISE YOU THAT!
Originally, it was because the Redface Pox had decimated the country's male population that women were forced to take over their family businesses as proxies for the men. By this time, however, ordinary townspeople had no idea that this was why they used male names professionally.

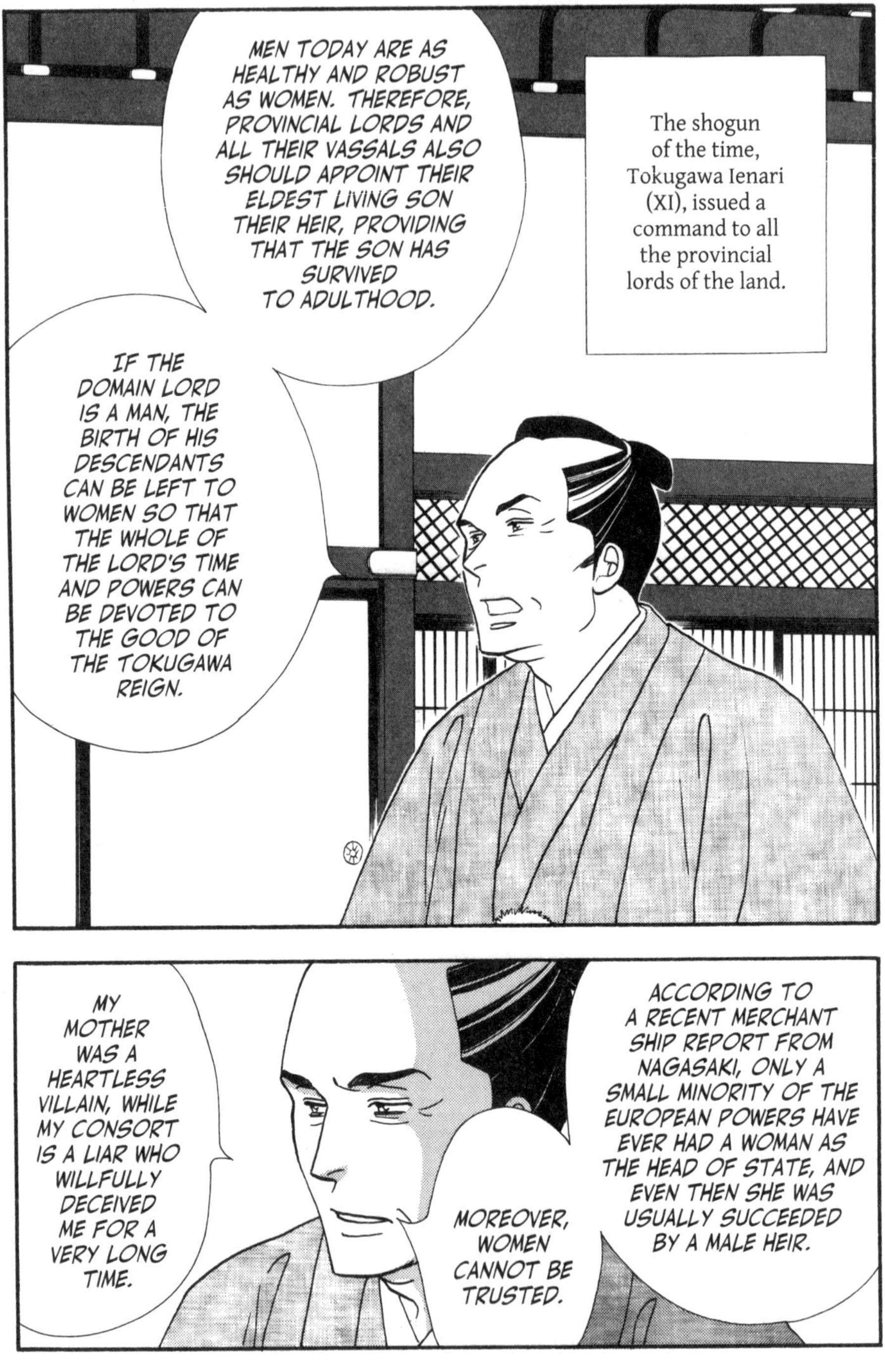
The shogun of the time, Tokugawa Ienari (XI), issued a command to all the provincial lords of the land.
MEN TODAY ARE AS HEALTHY AND ROBUST AS WOMEN. THEREFORE, PROVINCIAL LORDS AND ALL THEIR VASSALS ALSO SHOULD APPOINT THEIR ELDEST LIVING SON THEIR HEIR, PROVIDING THAT THE SON HAS SURVIVED TO ADULTHOOD.
IF THE DOMAIN LORD IS A MAN, THE BIRTH OF HIS DESCENDANTS CAN BE LEFT TO WOMEN SO THAT THE WHOLE OF THE LORD'S TIME AND POWERS CAN BE DEVOTED TO THE GOOD OF THE TOKUGAWA REIGN.
ACCORDING TO A RECENT MERCHANT SHIP REPORT FROM NAGASAKI, ONLY A SMALL MINORITY OF THE EUROPEAN POWERS HAVE EVER HAD A WOMAN AS THE HEAD OF STATE, AND EVEN THEN SHE WAS USUALLY SUCCEEDED BY A MALE HEIR.
MOREOVER, WOMEN CANNOT BE TRUSTED.
MY MOTHER WAS A HEARTLESS VILLAIN, WHILE MY CONSORT IS A LIAR WHO WILLFULLY DECEIVED ME FOR A VERY LONG TIME.

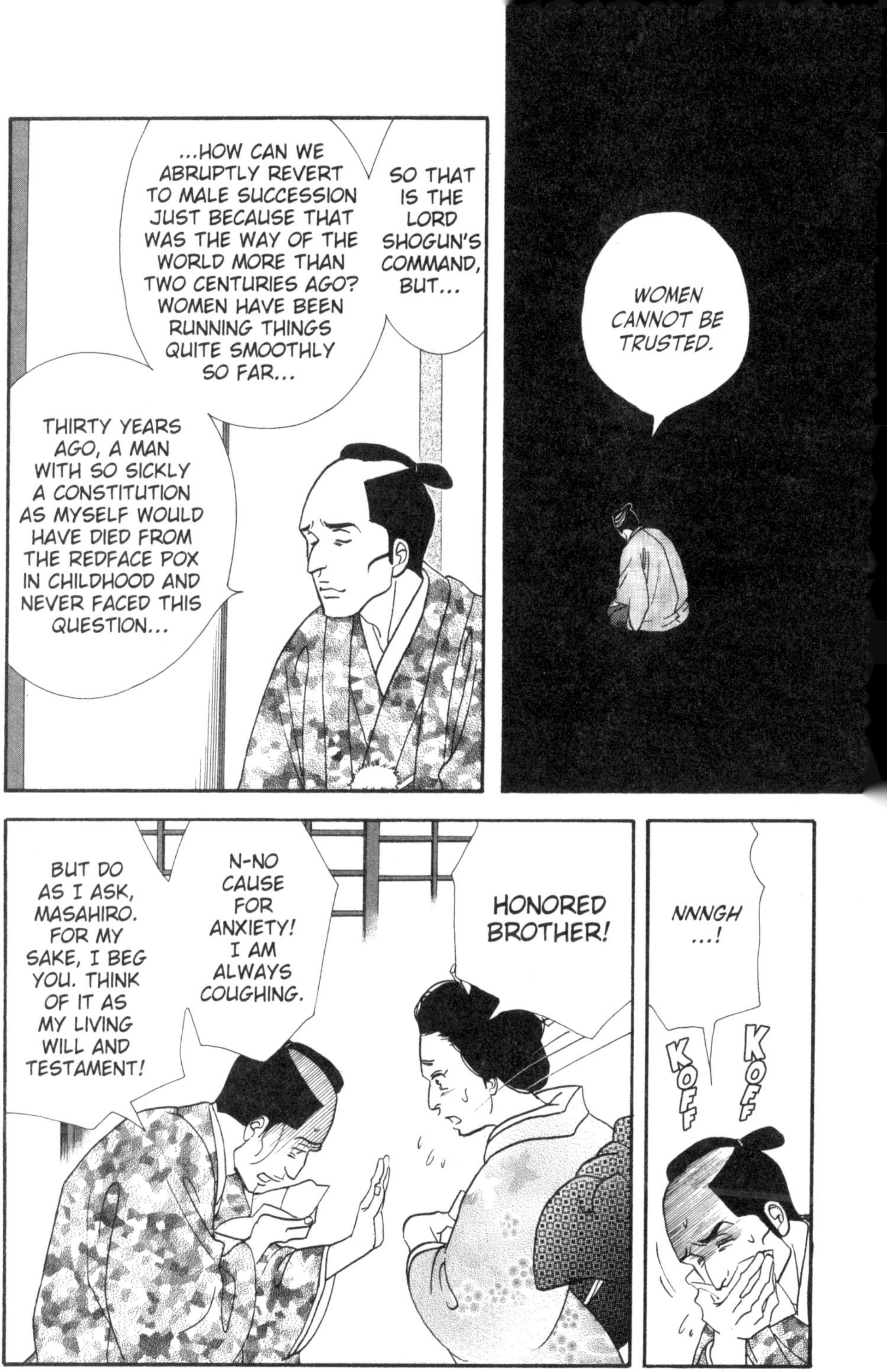
WOMEN CANNOT BE TRUSTED.
SO THAT IS THE LORD SHOGUN'S COMMAND, BUT...
...HOW CAN WE ABRUPTLY REVERT TO MALE SUCCESSION JUST BECAUSE THAT WAS THE WAY OF THE WORLD MORE THAN TWO CENTURIES AGO? WOMEN HAVE BEEN RUNNING THINGS QUITE SMOOTHLY SO FAR...
THIRTY YEARS AGO, A MAN WITH SO SICKLY A CONSTITUTION AS MYSELF WOULD HAVE DIED FROM THE REDFACE POX IN CHILDHOOD AND NEVER FACED THIS QUESTION...
NNNGH ...!
KOFF
KOFF
HONORED BROTHER!
N-NO CAUSE FOR ANXIETY! I AM ALWAYS COUGHING.
BUT DO AS I ASK, MASAHIRO. FOR MY SAKE, I BEG YOU. THINK OF IT AS MY LIVING WILL AND TESTAMENT!

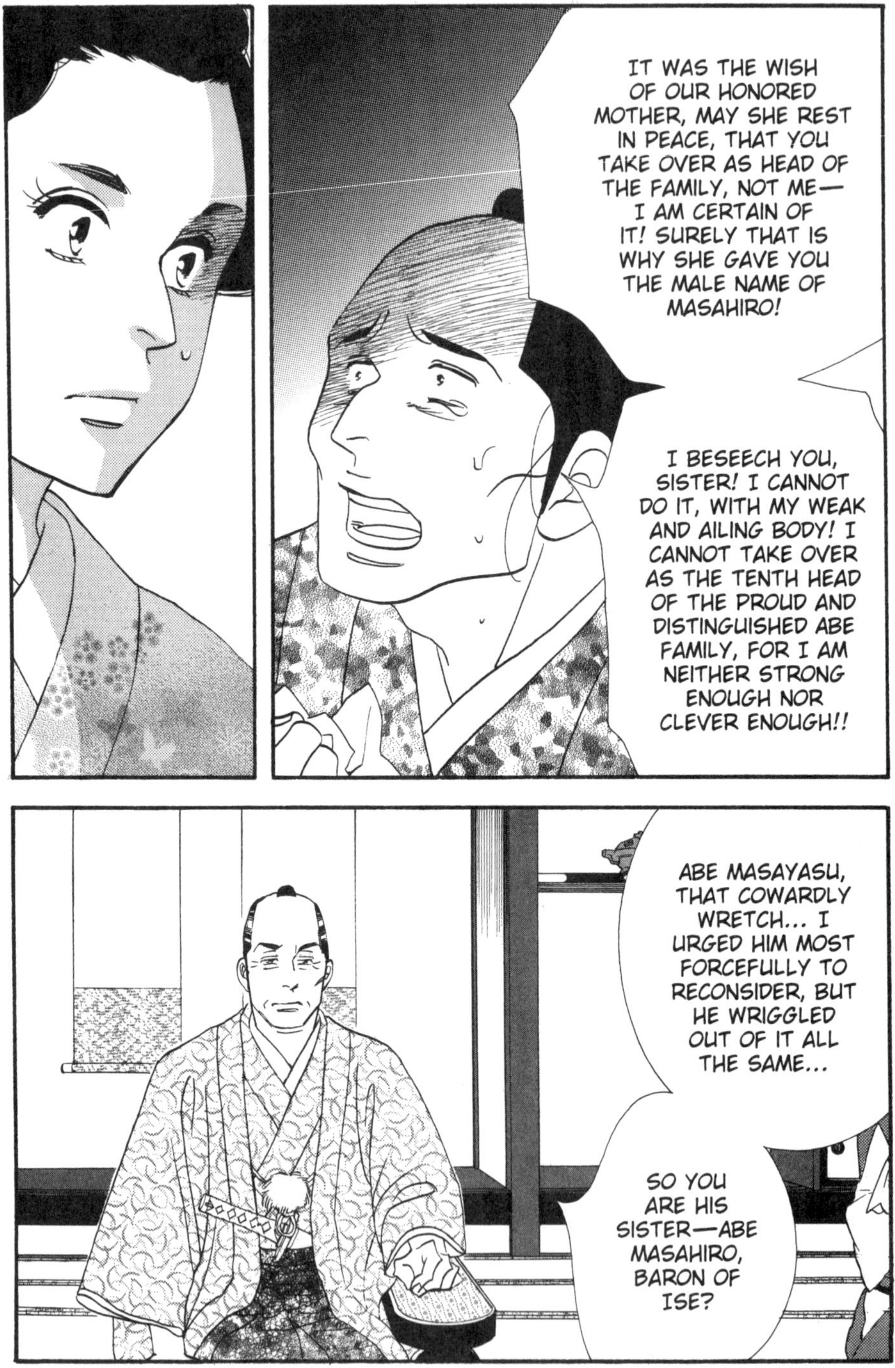
IT WAS THE WISH OF OUR HONORED MOTHER, MAY SHE REST IN PEACE, THAT YOU TAKE OVER AS HEAD OF THE FAMILY, NOT ME— I AM CERTAIN OF IT! SURELY THAT IS WHY SHE GAVE YOU THE MALE NAME OF MASAHIRO!
I BESEECH YOU, SISTER! I CANNOT DO IT, WITH MY WEAK AND AILING BODY! I CANNOT TAKE OVER AS THE TENTH HEAD OF THE PROUD AND DISTINGUISHED ABE FAMILY, FOR I AM NEITHER STRONG ENOUGH NOR CLEVER ENOUGH!!
ABE MASAYASU, THAT COWARDLY WRETCH... I URGED HIM MOST FORCEFULLY TO RECONSIDER, BUT HE WRIGGLED OUT OF IT ALL THE SAME...
SO YOU ARE HIS SISTER—ABE MASAHIRO, BARON OF ISE?

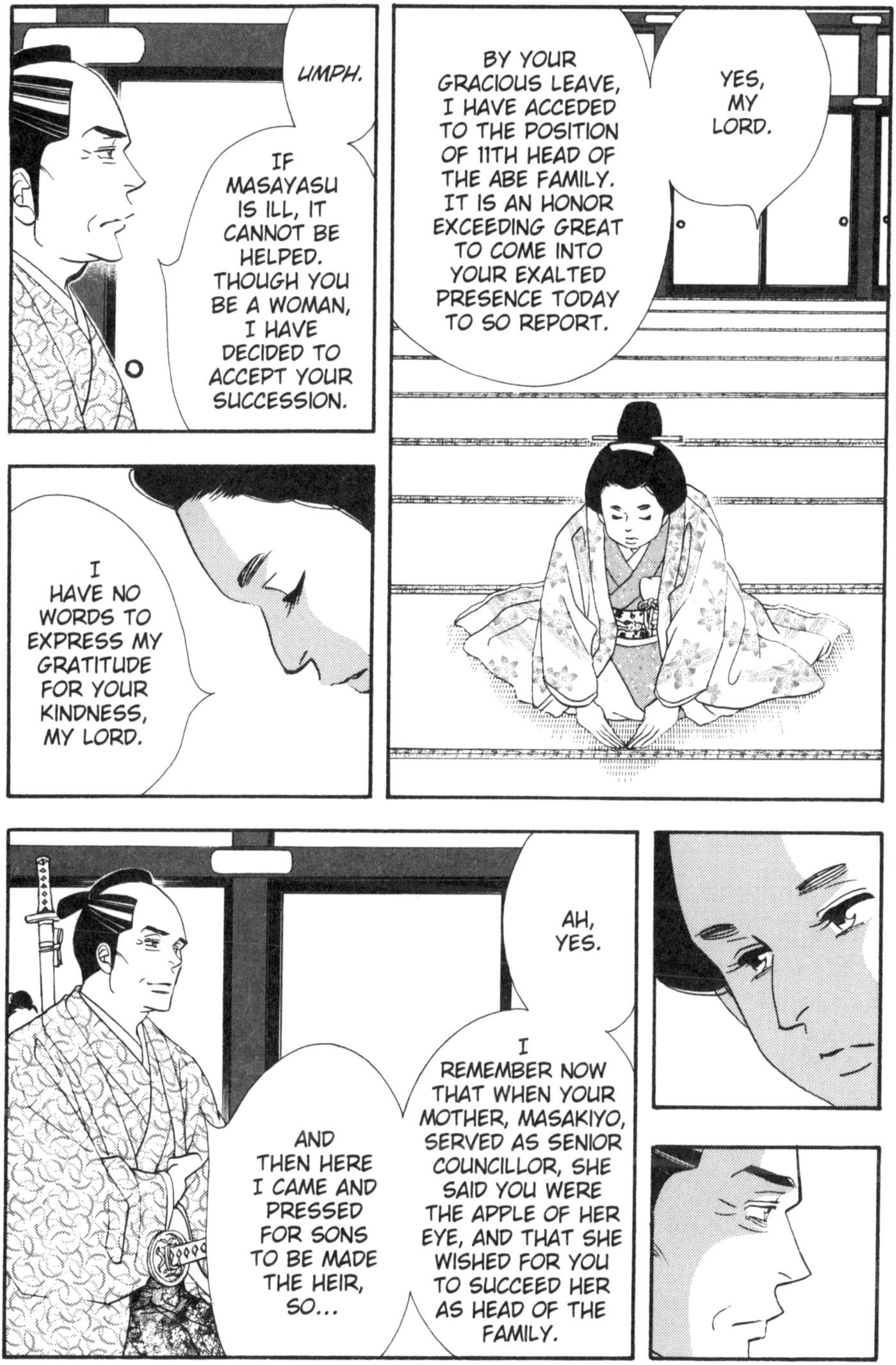
YES, MY LORD.
BY YOUR GRACIOUS LEAVE, I HAVE ACCEDED TO THE POSITION OF 11TH HEAD OF THE ABE FAMILY. IT IS AN HONOR EXCEEDING GREAT TO COME INTO YOUR EXALTED PRESENCE TODAY TO SO REPORT.
UMPH.
IF MASAYASU IS ILL, IT CANNOT BE HELPED. THOUGH YOU BE A WOMAN, I HAVE DECIDED TO ACCEPT YOUR SUCCESSION.
I HAVE NO WORDS TO EXPRESS MY GRATITUDE FOR YOUR KINDNESS, MY LORD.
AH, YES.
I REMEMBER NOW THAT WHEN YOUR MOTHER, MASAKIYO, SERVED AS SENIOR COUNCILLOR, SHE SAID YOU WERE THE APPLE OF HER EYE, AND THAT SHE WISHED FOR YOU TO SUCCEED HER AS HEAD OF THE FAMILY.
AND THEN HERE I CAME AND PRESSED FOR SONS TO BE MADE THE HEIR, SO...

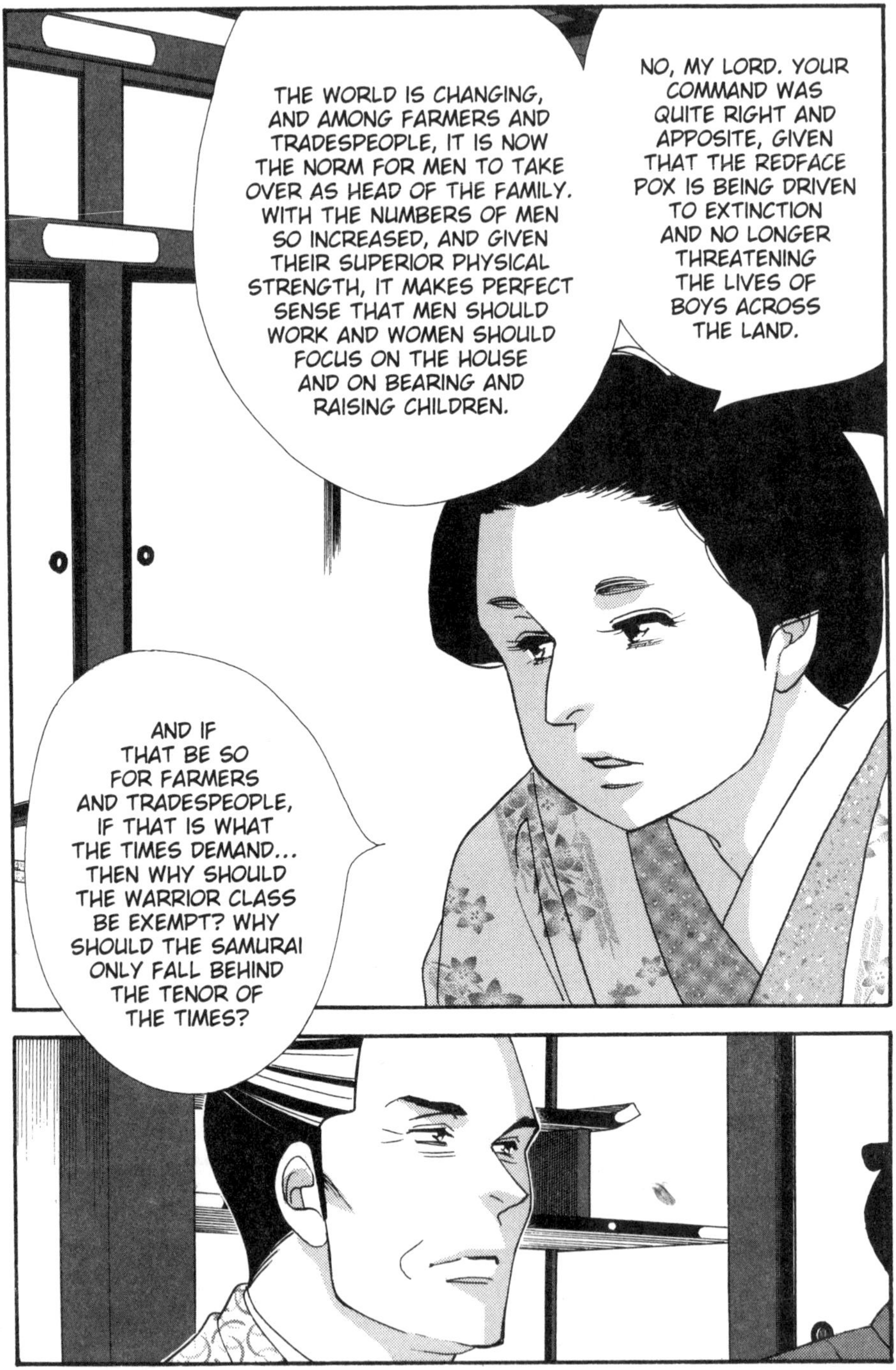
NO, MY LORD. YOUR COMMAND WAS QUITE RIGHT AND APPOSITE, GIVEN THAT THE REDFACE POX IS BEING DRIVEN TO EXTINCTION AND NO LONGER THREATENING THE LIVES OF BOYS ACROSS THE LAND.
THE WORLD IS CHANGING, AND AMONG FARMERS AND TRADESPEOPLE, IT IS NOW THE NORM FOR MEN TO TAKE OVER AS HEAD OF THE FAMILY. WITH THE NUMBERS OF MEN SO INCREASED, AND GIVEN THEIR SUPERIOR PHYSICAL STRENGTH, IT MAKES PERFECT SENSE THAT MEN SHOULD WORK AND WOMEN SHOULD FOCUS ON THE HOUSE AND ON BEARING AND RAISING CHILDREN.
AND IF THAT BE SO FOR FARMERS AND TRADESPEOPLE, IF THAT IS WHAT THE TIMES DEMAND... THEN WHY SHOULD THE WARRIOR CLASS BE EXEMPT? WHY SHOULD THE SAMURAI ONLY FALL BEHIND THE TENOR OF THE TIMES?

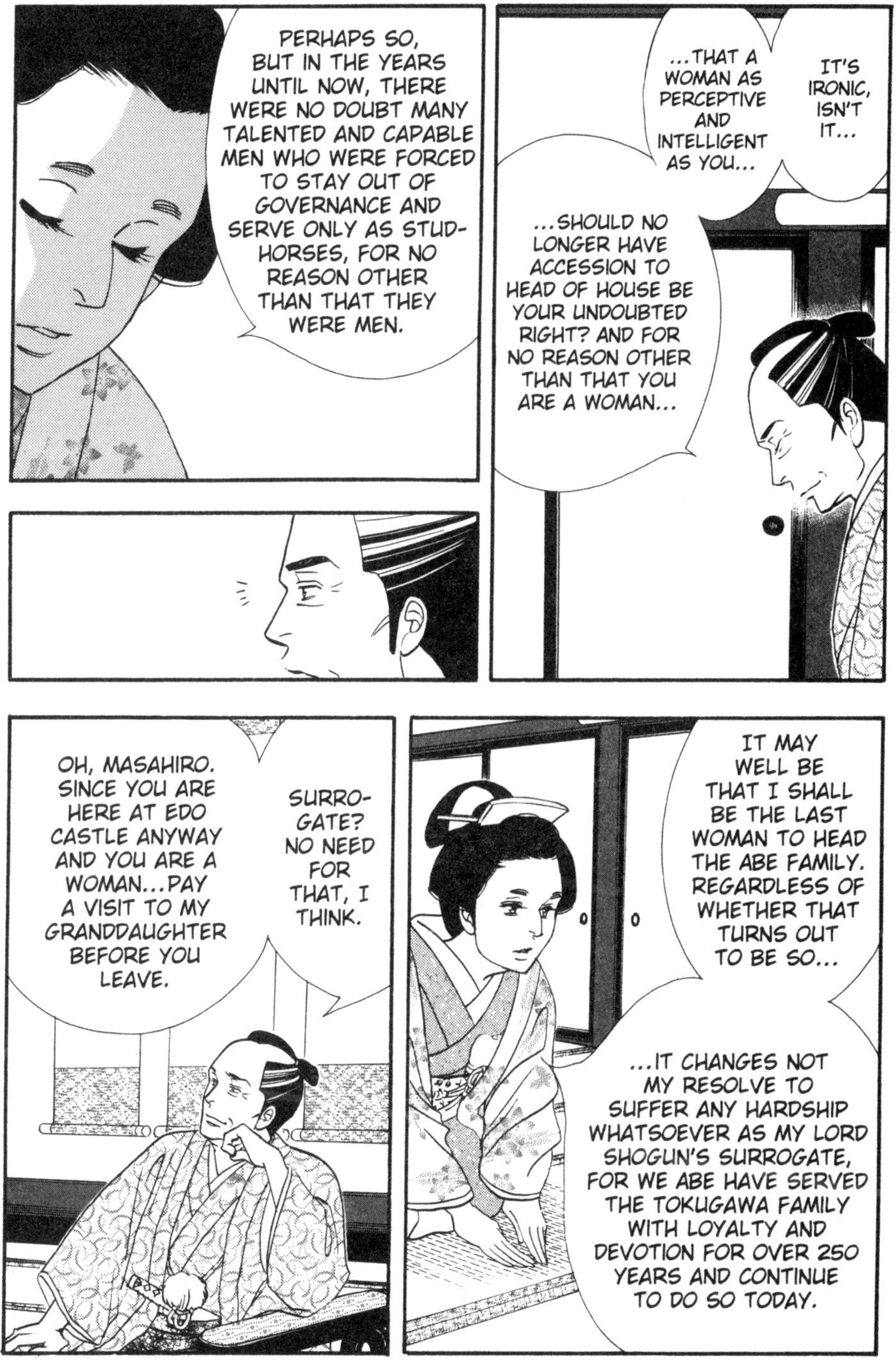
IT'S IRONIC, ISN'T IT...
...THAT A WOMAN AS PERCEPTIVE AND INTELLIGENT AS YOU...
...SHOULD NO LONGER HAVE ACCESSION TO HEAD OF HOUSE BE YOUR UNDOUBTED RIGHT? AND FOR NO REASON OTHER THAN THAT YOU ARE A WOMAN...
PERHAPS SO, BUT IN THE YEARS UNTIL NOW, THERE WERE NO DOUBT MANY TALENTED AND CAPABLE MEN WHO WERE FORCED TO STAY OUT OF GOVERNANCE AND SERVE ONLY AS STUD-HORSES, FOR NO REASON OTHER THAN THAT THEY WERE MEN.
IT MAY WELL BE THAT I SHALL BE THE LAST WOMAN TO HEAD THE ABE FAMILY. REGARDLESS OF WHETHER THAT TURNS OUT TO BE SO...
...IT CHANGES NOT MY RESOLVE TO SUFFER ANY HARDSHIP WHATSOEVER AS MY LORD SHOGUN'S SURROGATE, FOR WE ABE HAVE SERVED THE TOKUGAWA FAMILY WITH LOYALTY AND DEVOTION FOR OVER 250 YEARS AND CONTINUE TO DO SO TODAY.
SURROGATE? NO NEED FOR THAT, I THINK.
OH, MASAHIRO. SINCE YOU ARE HERE AT EDO CASTLE ANYWAY AND YOU ARE A WOMAN...PAY A VISIT TO MY GRANDDAUGHTER BEFORE YOU LEAVE.

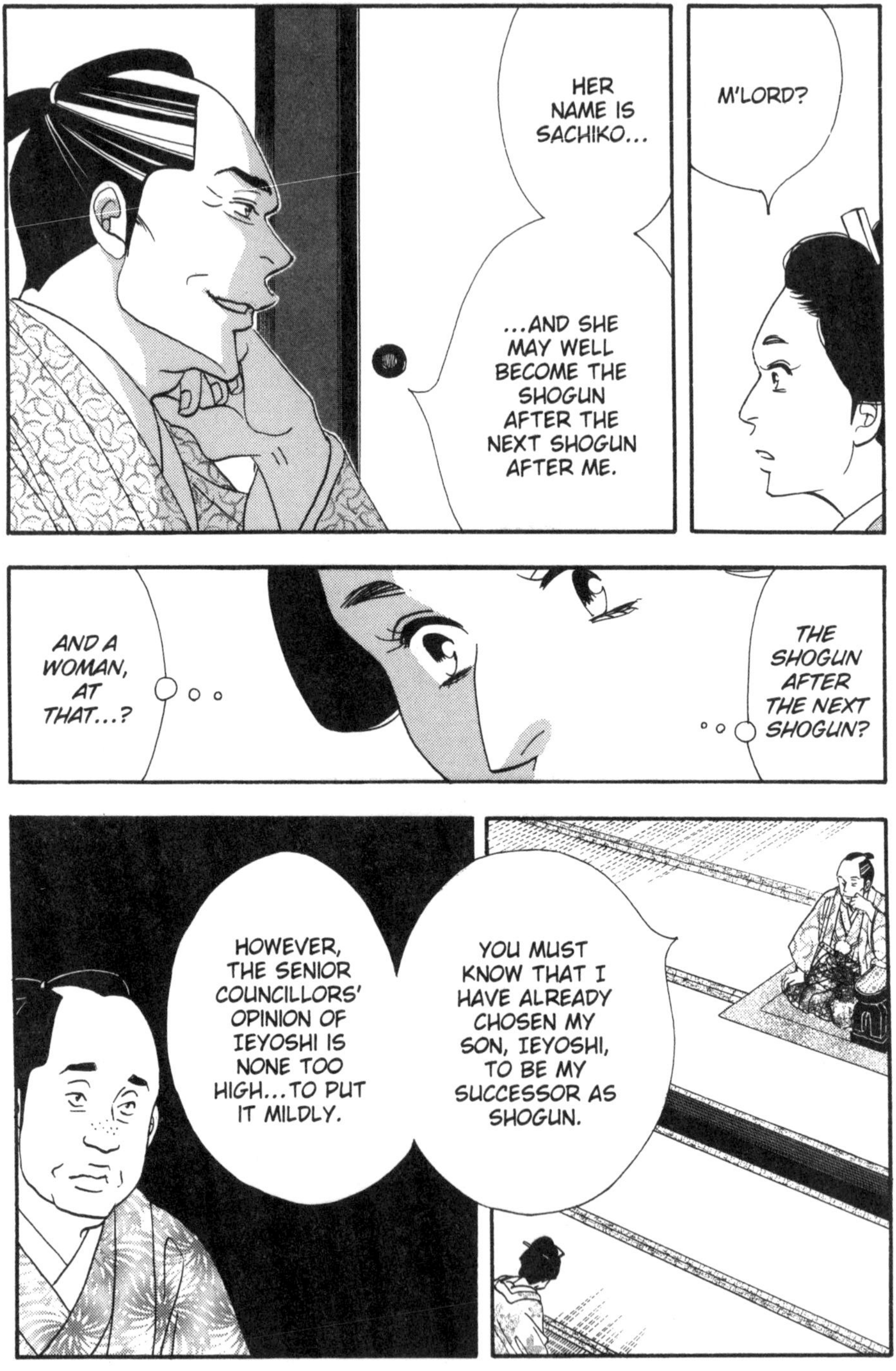
M'LORD?
HER NAME IS SACHIKO...
...AND SHE MAY WELL BECOME THE SHOGUN AFTER THE NEXT SHOGUN AFTER ME.
THE SHOGUN AFTER THE NEXT SHOGUN?
AND A WOMAN, AT THAT...?
YOU MUST KNOW THAT I HAVE ALREADY CHOSEN MY SON, IEYOSHI, TO BE MY SUCCESSOR AS SHOGUN.
HOWEVER, THE SENIOR COUNCILLORS' OPINION OF IEYOSHI IS NONE TOO HIGH...TO PUT IT MILDLY.

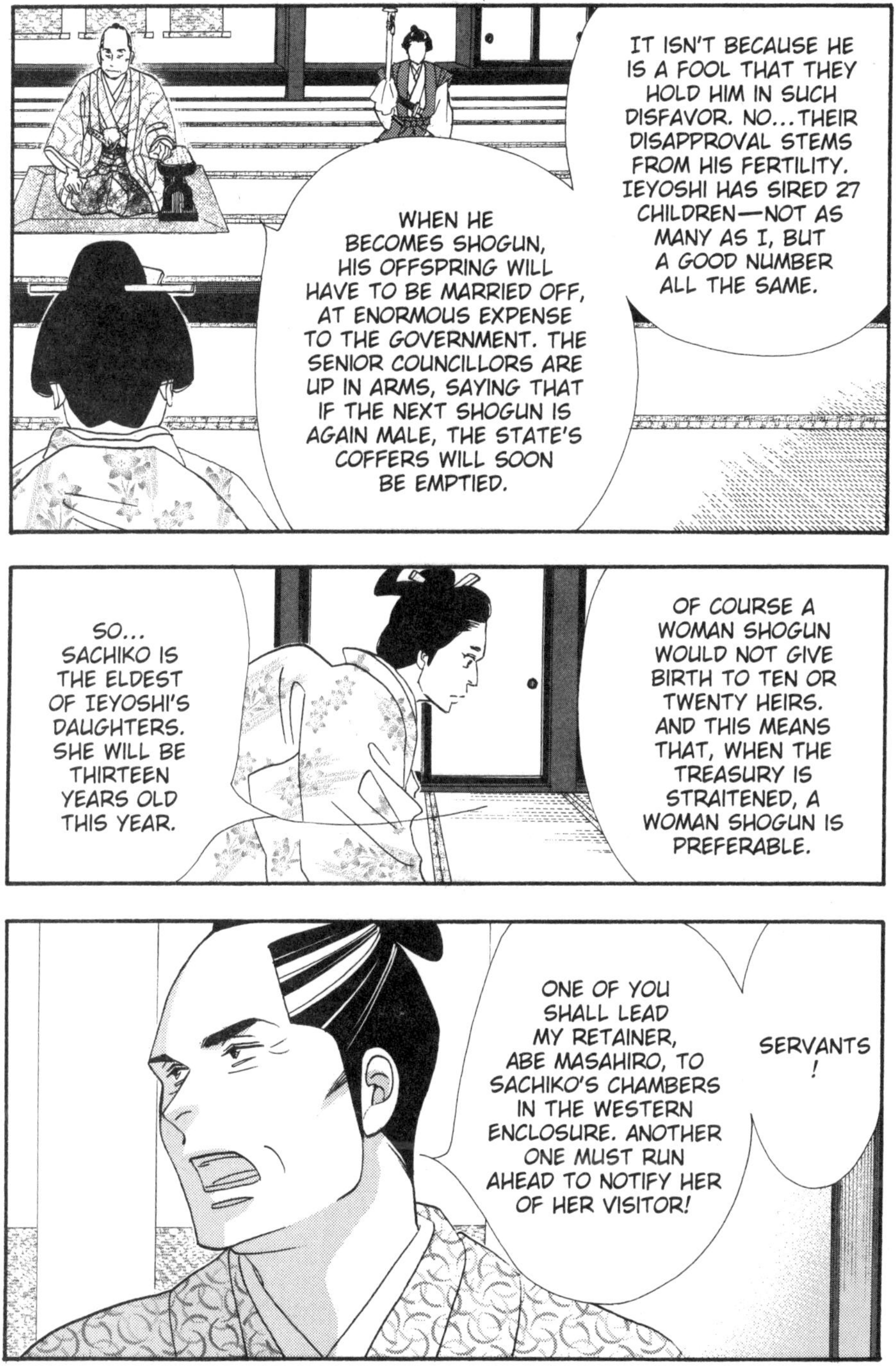
IT ISN'T BECAUSE HE IS A FOOL THAT THEY HOLD HIM IN SUCH DISFAVOR. NO...THEIR DISAPPROVAL STEMS FROM HIS FERTILITY. IEYOSHI HAS SIRED 27 CHILDREN—NOT AS MANY AS I, BUT A GOOD NUMBER ALL THE SAME.
WHEN HE BECOMES SHOGUN, HIS OFFSPRING WILL HAVE TO BE MARRIED OFF, AT ENORMOUS EXPENSE TO THE GOVERNMENT. THE SENIOR COUNCILLORS ARE UP IN ARMS, SAYING THAT IF THE NEXT SHOGUN IS AGAIN MALE, THE STATE'S COFFERS WILL SOON BE EMPTIED.
OF COURSE A WOMAN SHOGUN WOULD NOT GIVE BIRTH TO TEN OR TWENTY HEIRS. AND THIS MEANS THAT, WHEN THE TREASURY IS STRAITENED, A WOMAN SHOGUN IS PREFERABLE.
SO... SACHIKO IS THE ELDEST OF IEYOSHI'S DAUGHTERS. SHE WILL BE THIRTEEN YEARS OLD THIS YEAR.
SERVANTS!
ONE OF YOU SHALL LEAD MY RETAINER, ABE MASAHIRO, TO SACHIKO'S CHAMBERS IN THE WESTERN ENCLOSURE. ANOTHER ONE MUST RUN AHEAD TO NOTIFY HER OF HER VISITOR!

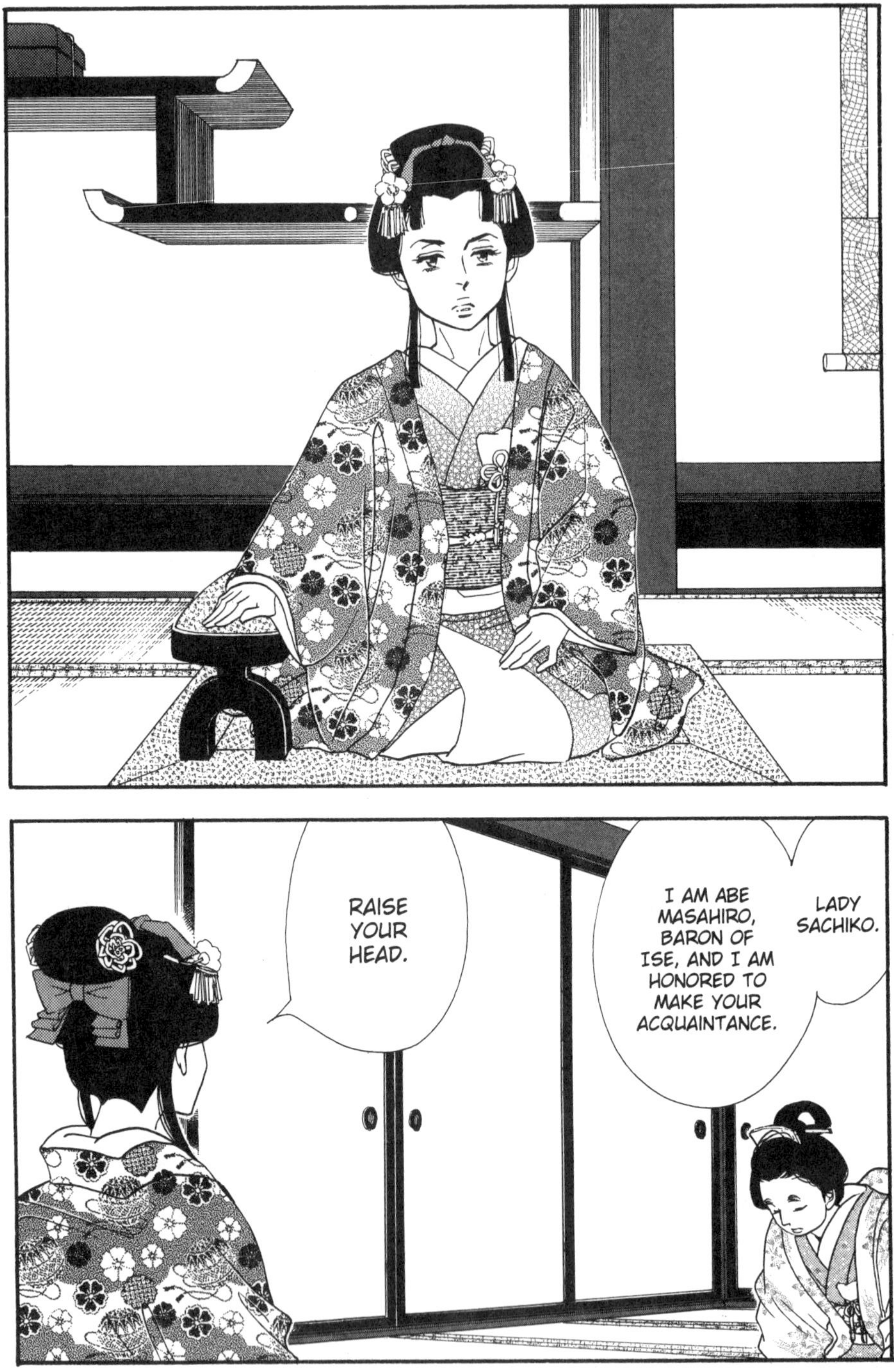
LADY SACHIKO.
I AM ABE MASAHIRO, BARON OF ISE, AND I AM HONORED TO MAKE YOUR ACQUAINTANCE.
RAISE YOUR HEAD.

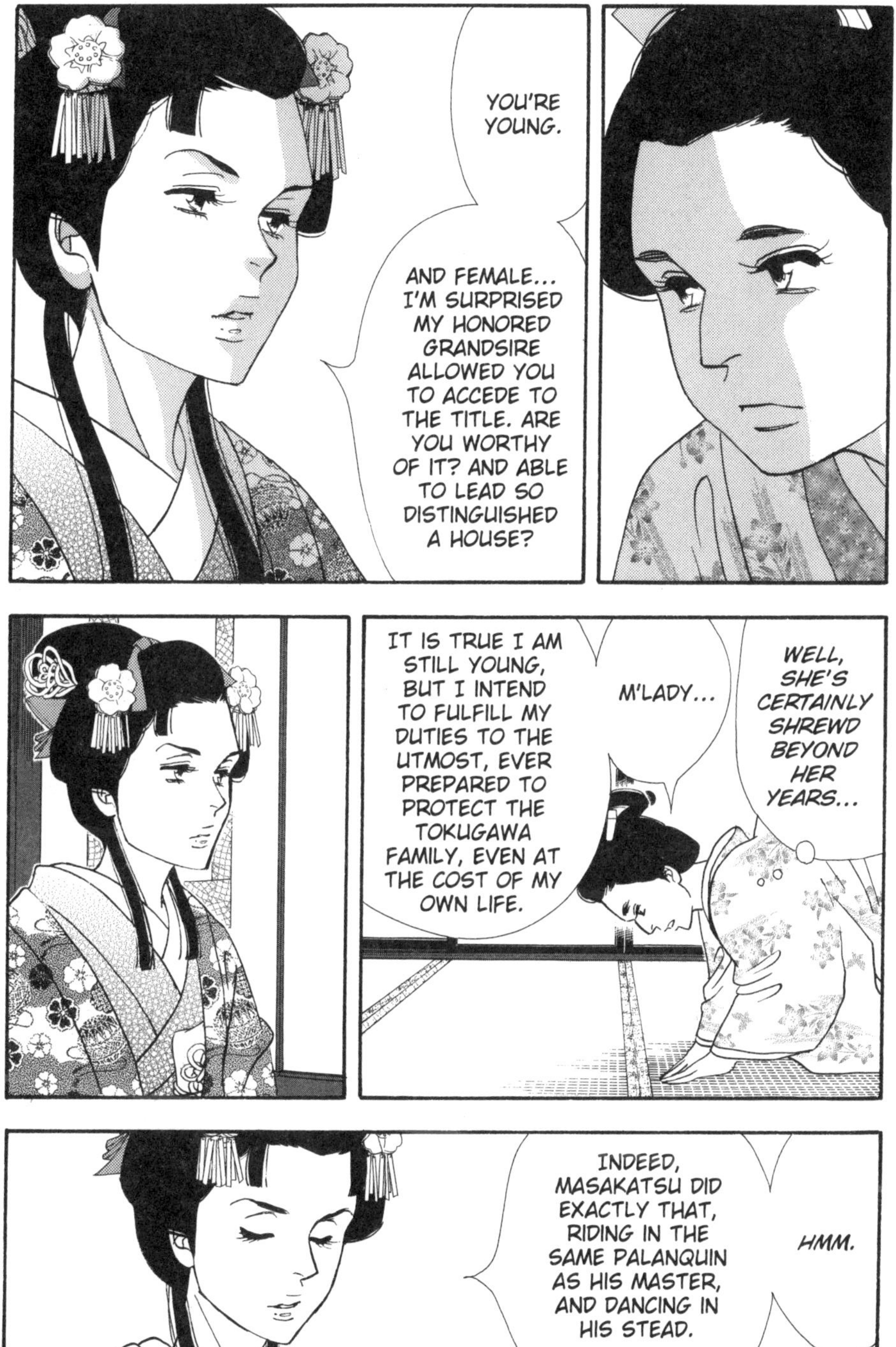
YOU'RE YOUNG.
AND FEMALE... I'M SURPRISED MY HONORED GRANDSIRE ALLOWED YOU TO ACCEDE TO THE TITLE. ARE YOU WORTHY OF IT? AND ABLE TO LEAD SO DISTINGUISHED A HOUSE?
WELL, SHE'S CERTAINLY SHREWD BEYOND HER YEARS...
M'LADY...
IT IS TRUE I AM STILL YOUNG, BUT I INTEND TO FULFILL MY DUTIES TO THE UTMOST, EVER PREPARED TO PROTECT THE TOKUGAWA FAMILY, EVEN AT THE COST OF MY OWN LIFE.
HMM.
INDEED, MASAKATSU DID EXACTLY THAT, RIDING IN THE SAME PALANQUIN AS HIS MASTER, AND DANCING IN HIS STEAD.

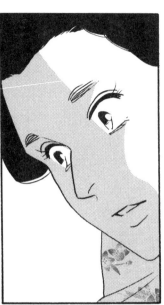

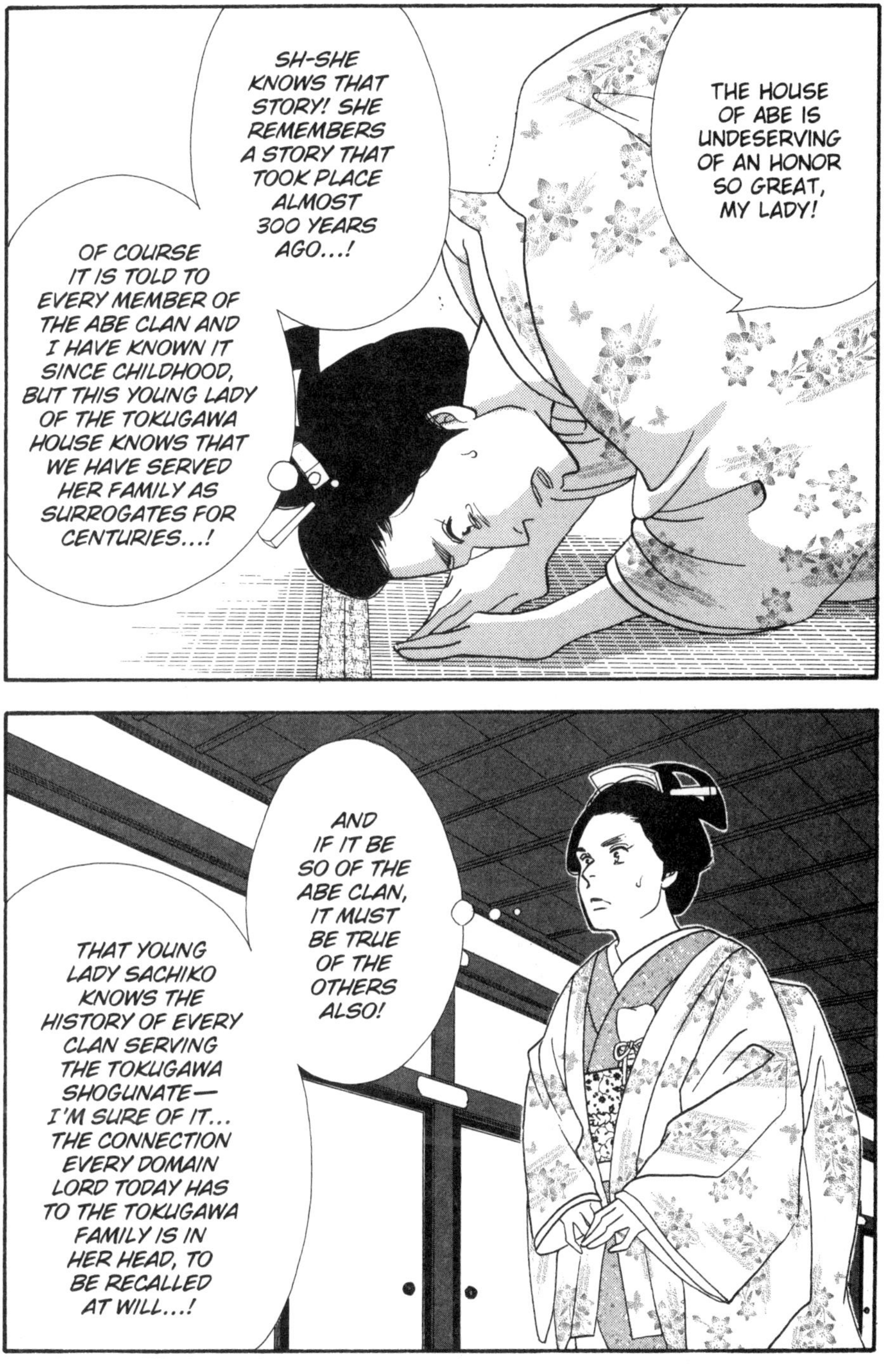
THE HOUSE OF ABE IS UNDESERVING OF AN HONOR SO GREAT, MY LADY!
SH-SHE KNOWS THAT STORY! SHE REMEMBERS A STORY THAT TOOK PLACE ALMOST 300 YEARS AGO...!
OF COURSE IT IS TOLD TO EVERY MEMBER OF THE ABE CLAN AND I HAVE KNOWN IT SINCE CHILDHOOD, BUT THIS YOUNG LADY OF THE TOKUGAWA HOUSE KNOWS THAT WE HAVE SERVED HER FAMILY AS SURROGATES FOR CENTURIES...!
AND IF IT BE SO OF THE ABE CLAN, IT MUST BE TRUE OF THE OTHERS ALSO!
THAT YOUNG LADY SACHIKO KNOWS THE HISTORY OF EVERY CLAN SERVING THE TOKUGAWA SHOGUNATE— I'M SURE OF IT... THE CONNECTION EVERY DOMAIN LORD TODAY HAS TO THE TOKUGAWA FAMILY IS IN HER HEAD, TO BE RECALLED AT WILL...!

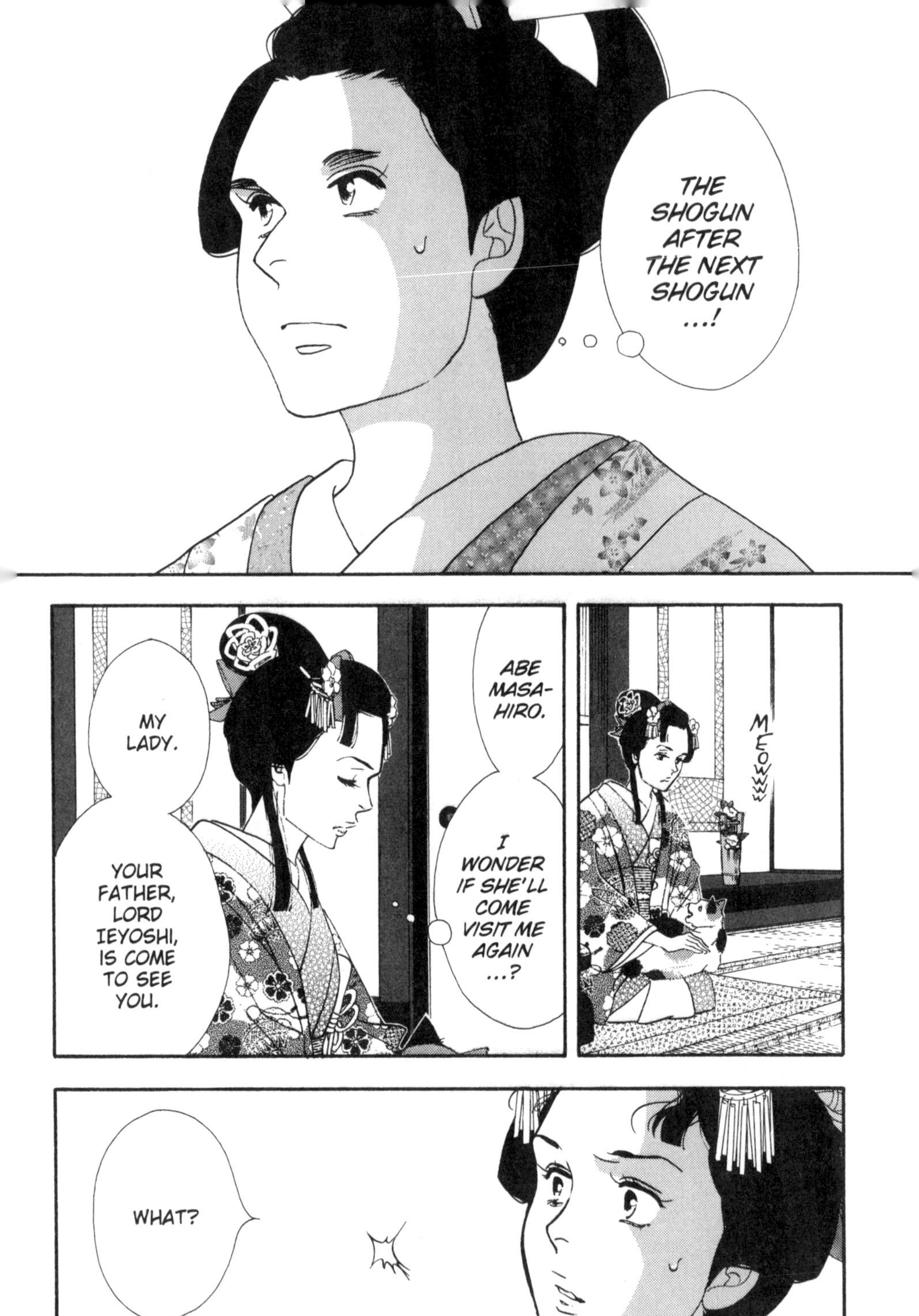
THE SHOGUN AFTER THE NEXT SHOGUN ...!
MEOWWW
ABE MASA-HIRO.
I WONDER IF SHE'LL COME VISIT ME AGAIN ...?
MY LADY.
YOUR FATHER, LORD IEYOSHI, IS COME TO SEE YOU.
WHAT?

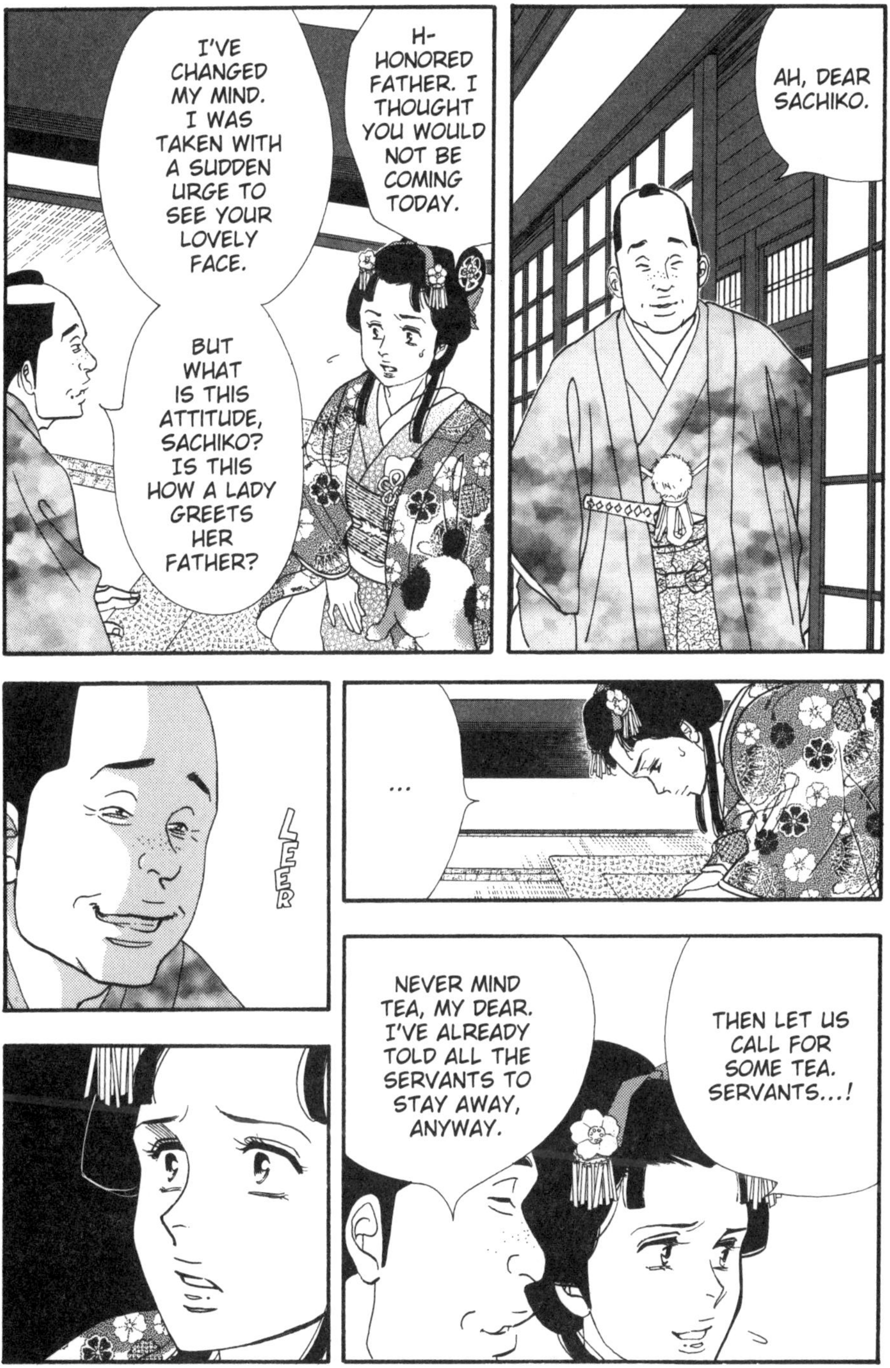
AH, DEAR SACHIKO.
H- HONORED FATHER. I THOUGHT YOU WOULD NOT BE COMING TODAY.
I'VE CHANGED MY MIND. I WAS TAKEN WITH A SUDDEN URGE TO SEE YOUR LOVELY FACE.
BUT WHAT IS THIS ATTITUDE, SACHIKO? IS THIS HOW A LADY GREETS HER FATHER?
...
LEER
THEN LET US CALL FOR SOME TEA. SERVANTS...!
NEVER MIND TEA, MY DEAR. I'VE ALREADY TOLD ALL THE SERVANTS TO STAY AWAY, ANYWAY.

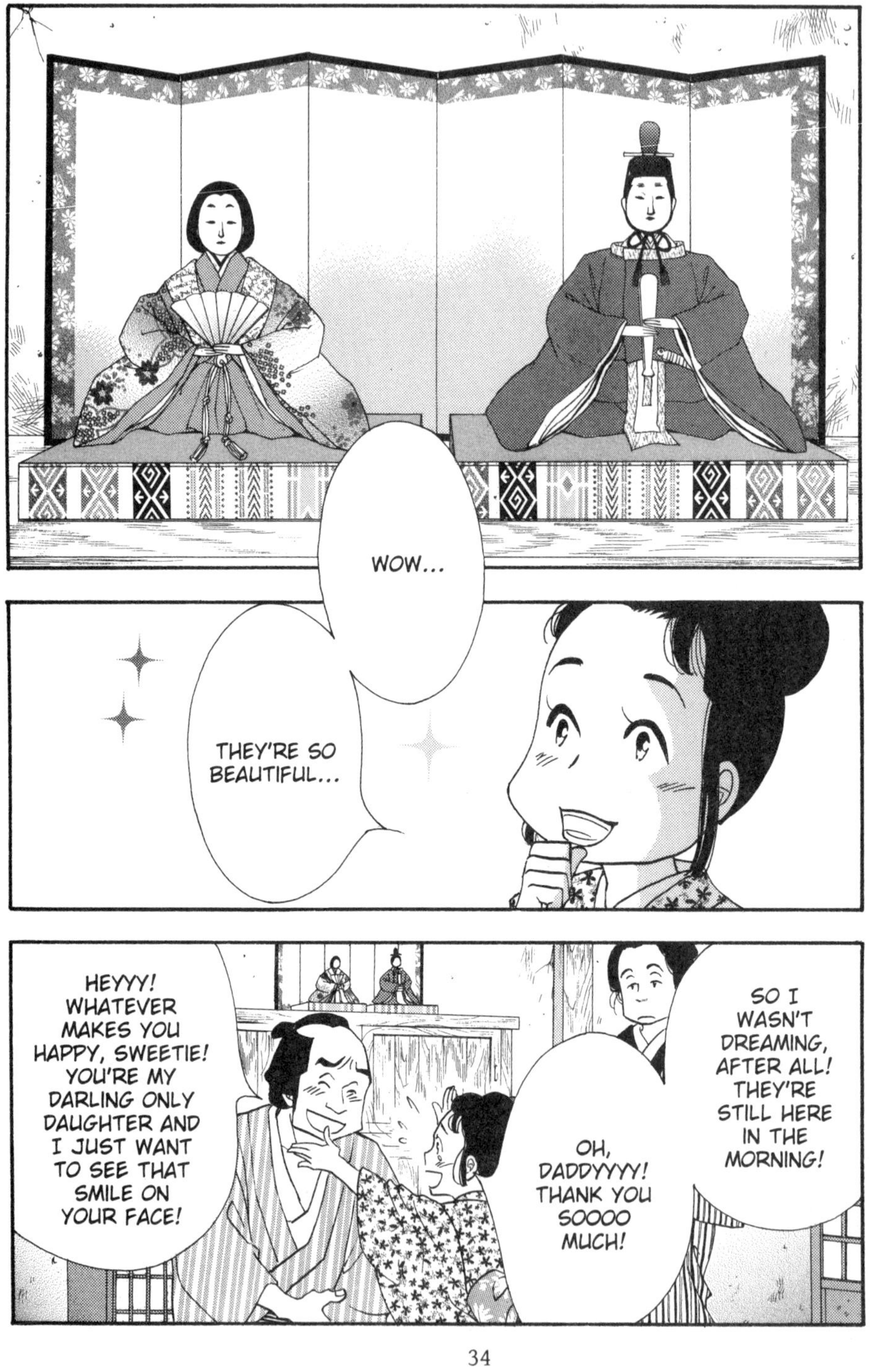
WOW...
THEY'RE SO BEAUTIFUL...
SO I WASN'T DREAMING, AFTER ALL! THEY'RE STILL HERE IN THE MORNING!
OH, DADDYYYY! THANK YOU SOOOO MUCH!
HEYYY! WHATEVER MAKES YOU HAPPY, SWEETIE! YOU'RE MY DARLING ONLY DAUGHTER AND I JUST WANT TO SEE THAT SMILE ON YOUR FACE!

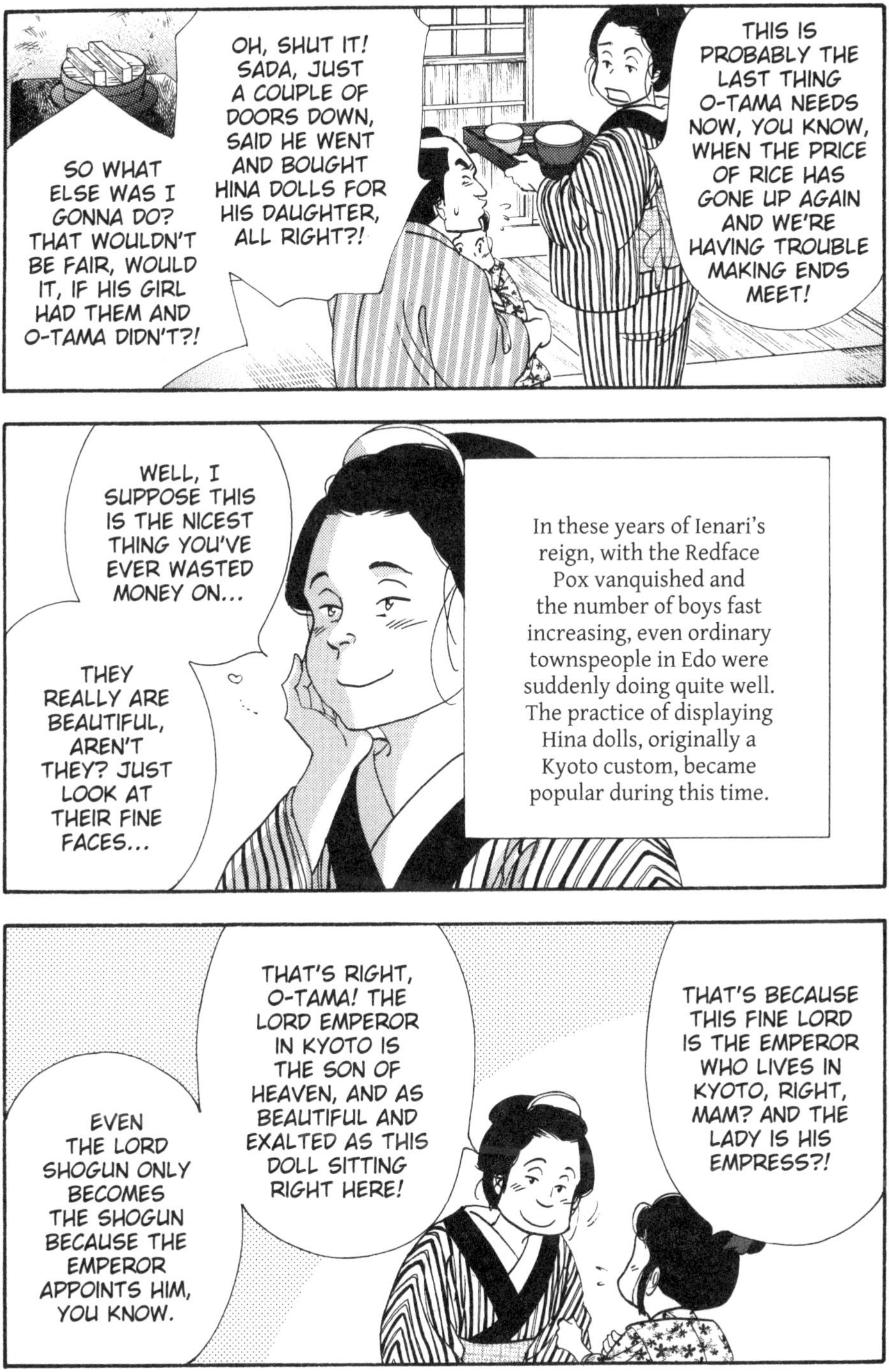
THIS IS PROBABLY THE LAST THING O-TAMA NEEDS NOW, YOU KNOW, WHEN THE PRICE OF RICE HAS GONE UP AGAIN AND WE'RE HAVING TROUBLE MAKING ENDS MEET!
OH, SHUT IT! SADA, JUST A COUPLE OF DOORS DOWN, SAID HE WENT AND BOUGHT HINA DOLLS FOR HIS DAUGHTER, ALL RIGHT?!
SO WHAT ELSE WAS I GONNA DO? THAT WOULDN'T BE FAIR, WOULD IT, IF HIS GIRL HAD THEM AND O-TAMA DIDN'T?!
In these years of Ienari's reign, with the Redface Pox vanquished and the number of boys fast increasing, even ordinary townspeople in Edo were suddenly doing quite well. The practice of displaying Hina dolls, originally a Kyoto custom, became popular during this time.
WELL, I SUPPOSE THIS IS THE NICEST THING YOU'VE EVER WASTED MONEY ON...
THEY REALLY ARE BEAUTIFUL, AREN'T THEY? JUST LOOK AT THEIR FINE FACES...
THAT'S BECAUSE THIS FINE LORD IS THE EMPEROR WHO LIVES IN KYOTO, RIGHT, MAM? AND THE LADY IS HIS EMPRESS?!
THAT'S RIGHT, O-TAMA! THE LORD EMPEROR IN KYOTO IS THE SON OF HEAVEN, AND AS BEAUTIFUL AND EXALTED AS THIS DOLL SITTING RIGHT HERE!
EVEN THE LORD SHOGUN ONLY BECOMES THE SHOGUN BECAUSE THE EMPEROR APPOINTS HIM, YOU KNOW.

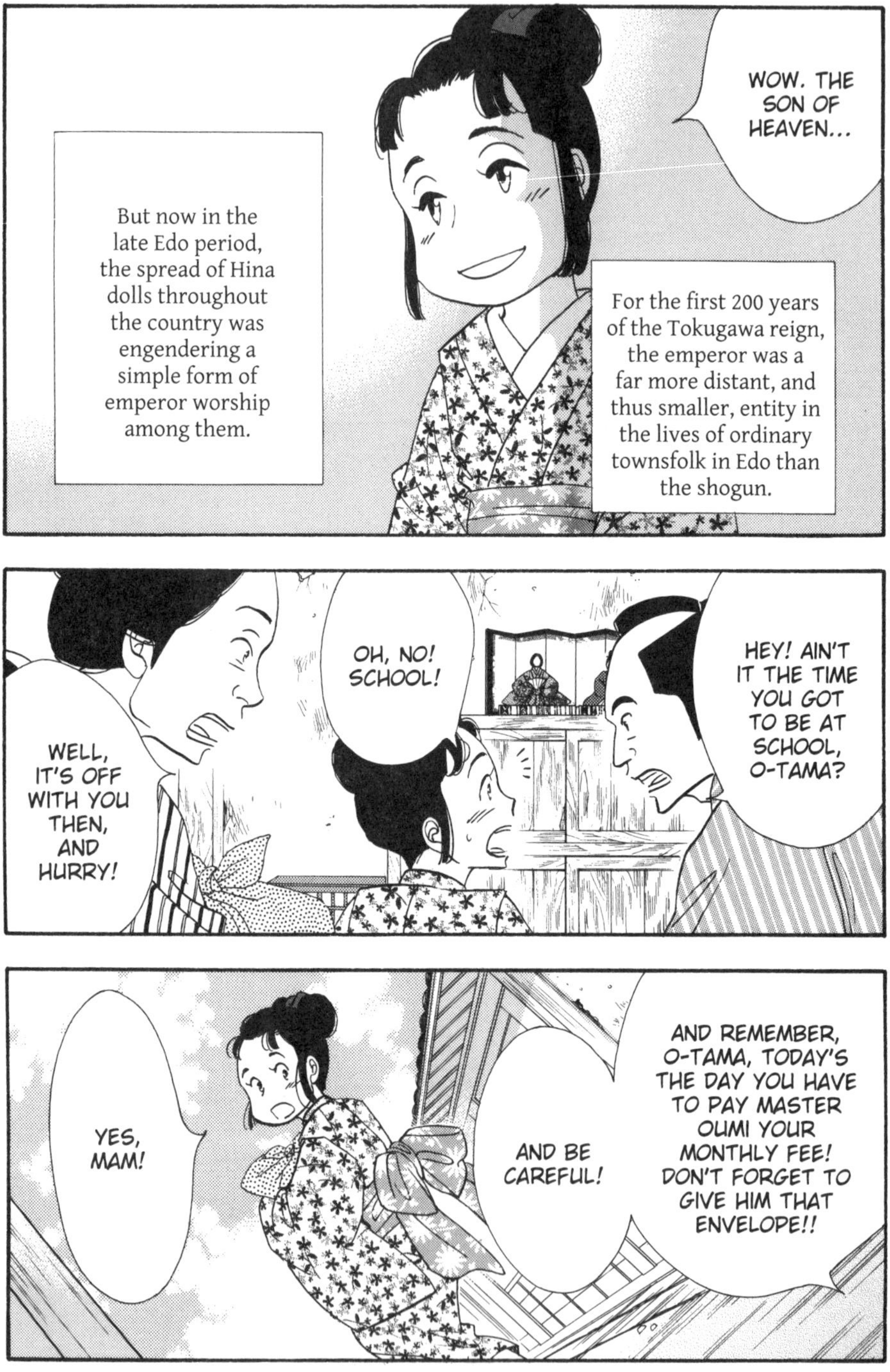
WOW. THE SON OF HEAVEN...
For the first 200 years of the Tokugawa reign, the emperor was a far more distant, and thus smaller, entity in the lives of ordinary townsfolk in Edo than the shogun.
But now in the late Edo period, the spread of Hina dolls throughout the country was engendering a simple form of emperor worship among them.
HEY! AIN'T IT THE TIME YOU GOT TO BE AT SCHOOL, O-TAMA?
OH, NO! SCHOOL!
WELL, IT'S OFF WITH YOU THEN, AND HURRY!
AND REMEMBER, O-TAMA, TODAY'S THE DAY YOU HAVE TO PAY MASTER OUMI YOUR MONTHLY FEE! DON'T FORGET TO GIVE HIM THAT ENVELOPE!!
AND BE CAREFUL!
YES, MAM!

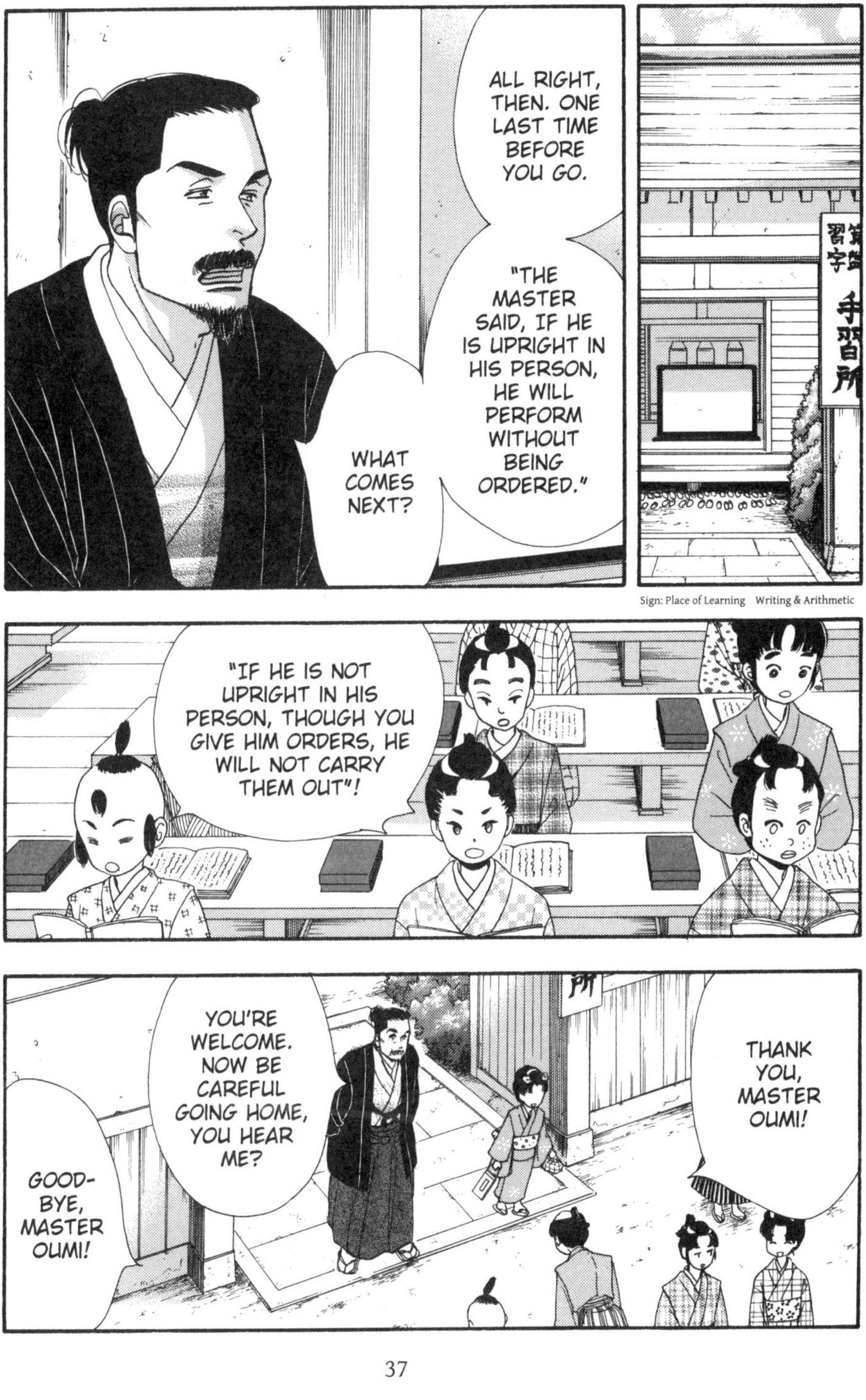
算盤 習字
手習所
ALL RIGHT, THEN. ONE LAST TIME BEFORE YOU GO.
"THE MASTER SAID, IF HE IS UPRIGHT IN HIS PERSON, HE WILL PERFORM WITHOUT BEING ORDERED."
WHAT COMES NEXT?
"IF HE IS NOT UPRIGHT IN HIS PERSON, THOUGH YOU GIVE HIM ORDERS, HE WILL NOT CARRY THEM OUT"!
THANK YOU, MASTER OUMI!
YOU'RE WELCOME. NOW BE CAREFUL GOING HOME, YOU HEAR ME?
GOOD-BYE, MASTER OUMI!

Sign: Place of Learning Writing & Arithmetic

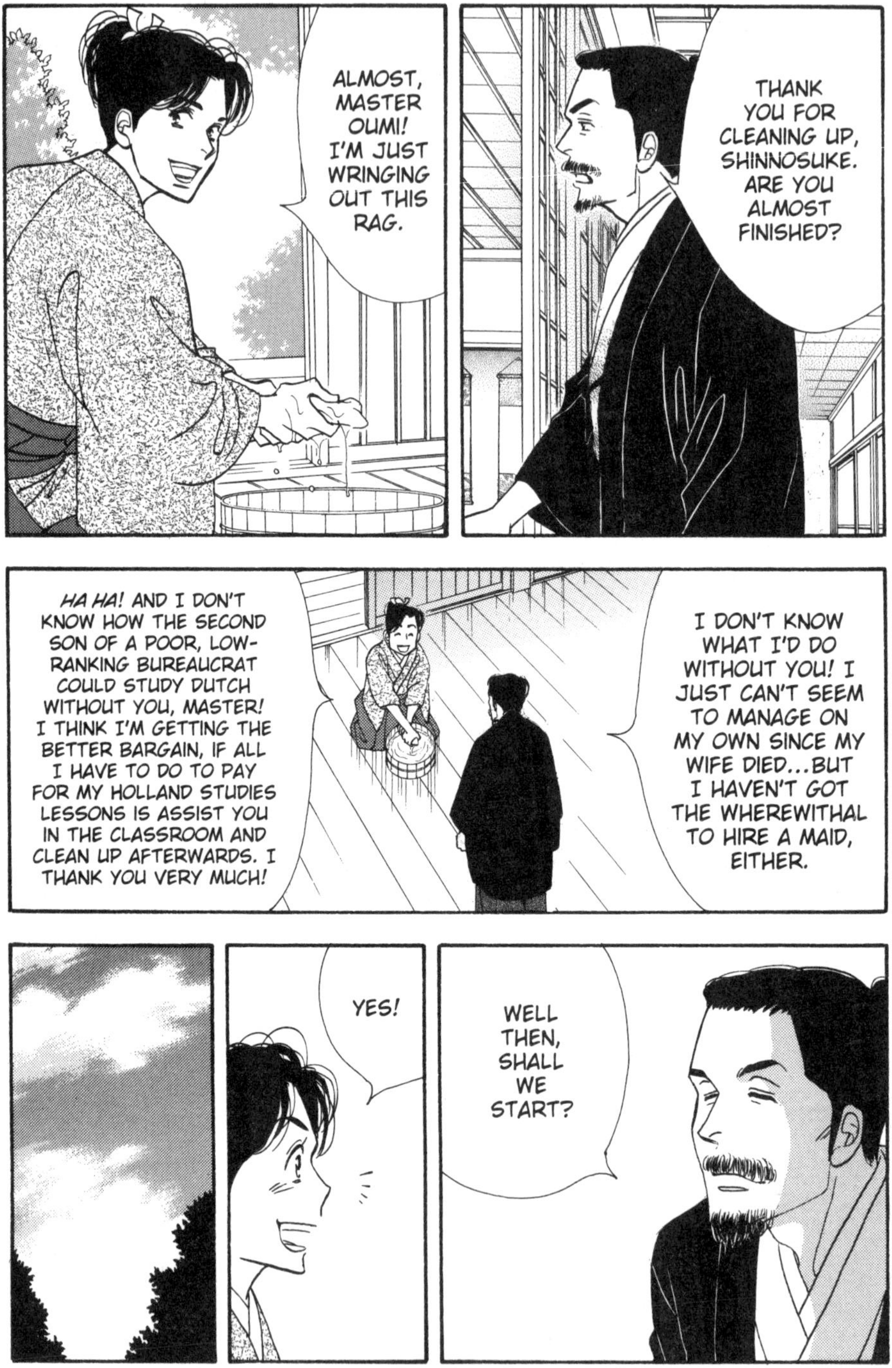
THANK YOU FOR CLEANING UP, SHINNOSUKE. ARE YOU ALMOST FINISHED?
ALMOST, MASTER OUMI! I'M JUST WRINGING OUT THIS RAG.
I DON'T KNOW WHAT I'D DO WITHOUT YOU! I JUST CAN'T SEEM TO MANAGE ON MY OWN SINCE MY WIFE DIED...BUT I HAVEN'T GOT THE WHEREWITHAL TO HIRE A MAID, EITHER.
HA HA! AND I DON'T KNOW HOW THE SECOND SON OF A POOR, LOW-RANKING BUREAUCRAT COULD STUDY DUTCH WITHOUT YOU, MASTER! I THINK I'M GETTING THE BETTER BARGAIN, IF ALL I HAVE TO DO TO PAY FOR MY HOLLAND STUDIES LESSONS IS ASSIST YOU IN THE CLASSROOM AND CLEAN UP AFTERWARDS. I THANK YOU VERY MUCH!
WELL THEN, SHALL WE START?
YES!

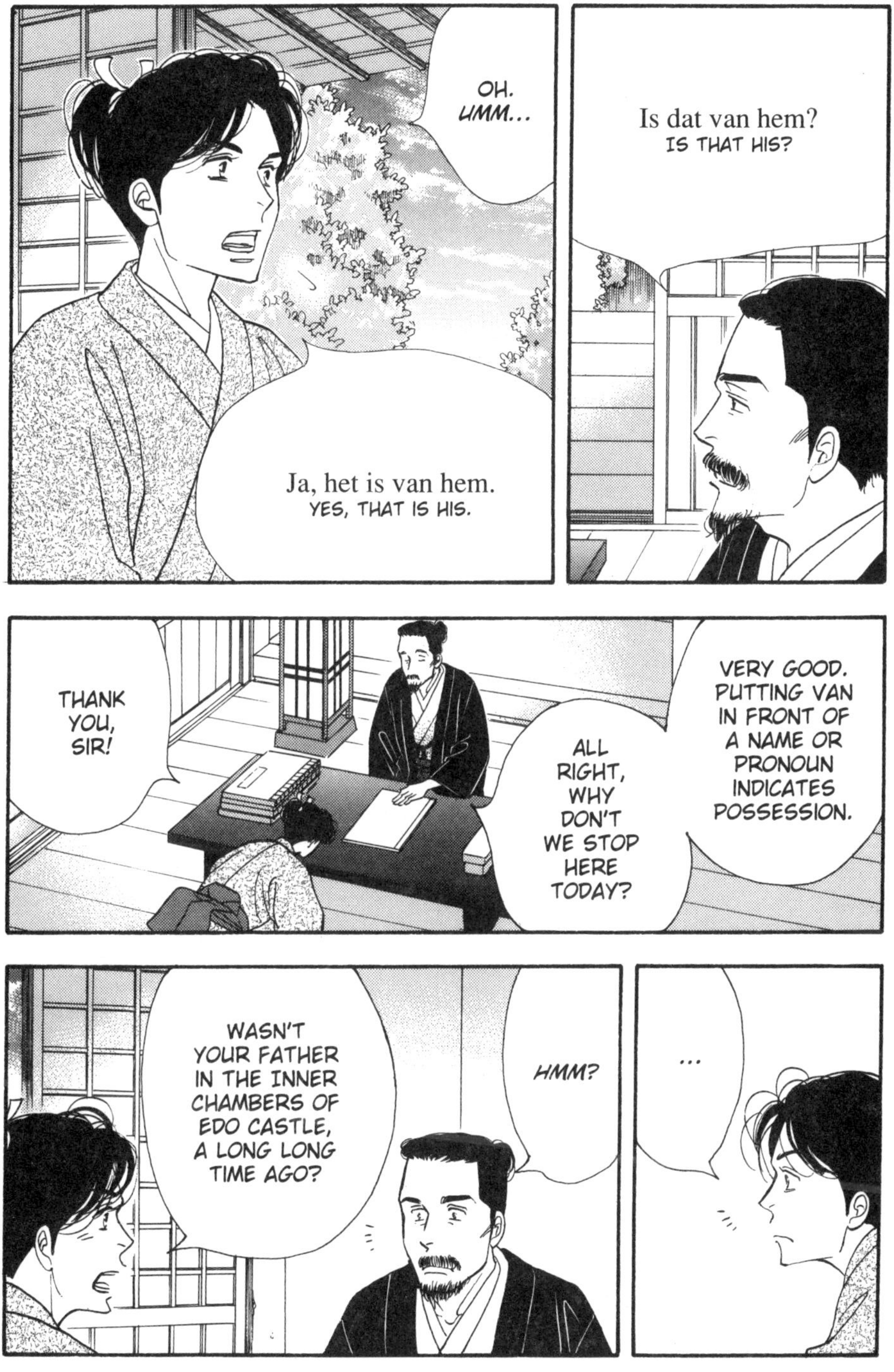
Is dat van hem?
IS THAT HIS?
OH. UMM...
Ja, het is van hem.
YES, THAT IS HIS.
VERY GOOD. PUTTING VAN IN FRONT OF A NAME OR PRONOUN INDICATES POSSESSION.
ALL RIGHT, WHY DON'T WE STOP HERE TODAY?
THANK YOU, SIR!
...
HMM?
WASN'T YOUR FATHER IN THE INNER CHAMBERS OF EDO CASTLE, A LONG LONG TIME AGO?

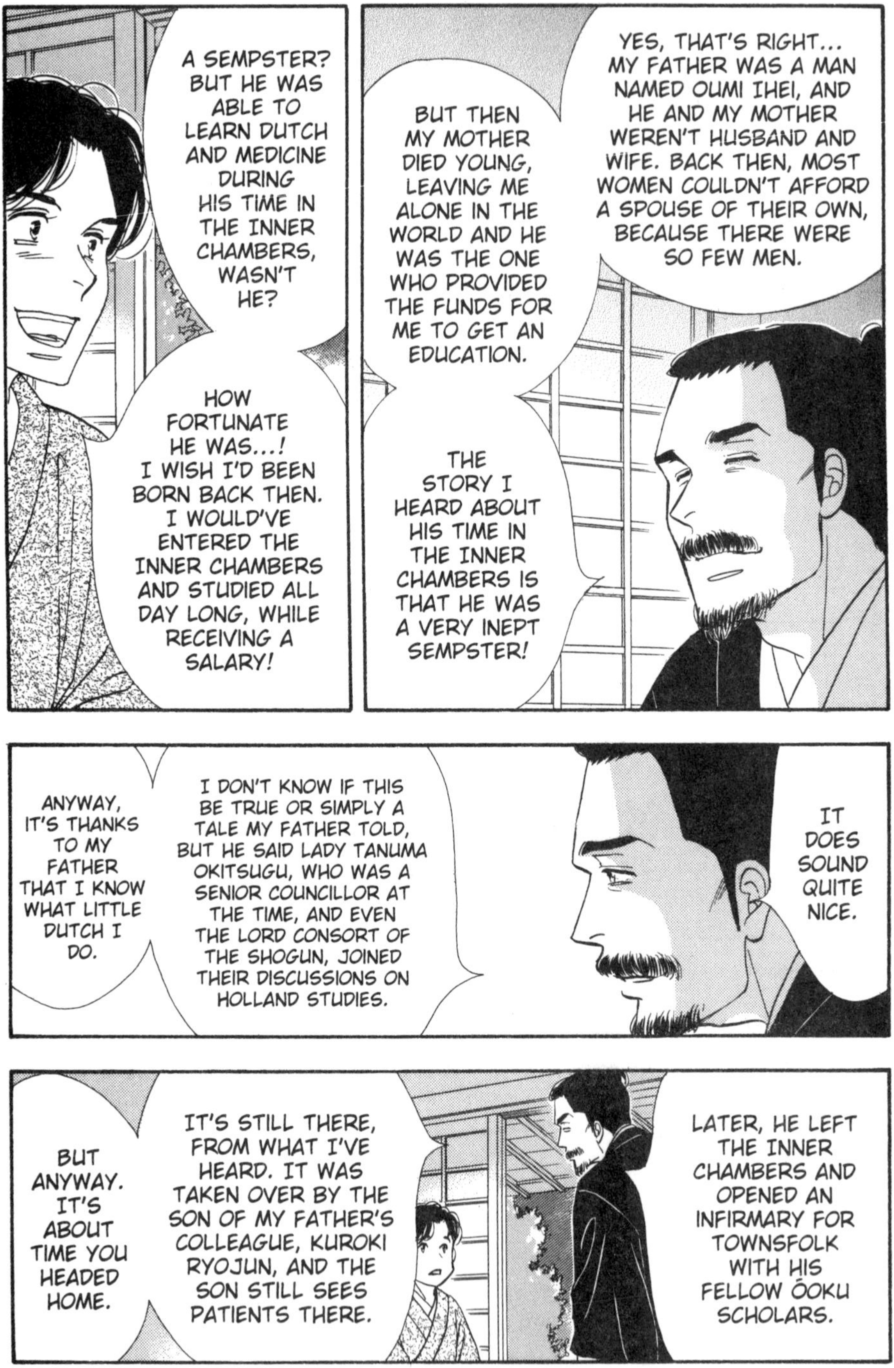
YES, THAT'S RIGHT... MY FATHER WAS A MAN NAMED OUMI IHEI, AND HE AND MY MOTHER WEREN'T HUSBAND AND WIFE. BACK THEN, MOST WOMEN COULDN'T AFFORD A SPOUSE OF THEIR OWN, BECAUSE THERE WERE SO FEW MEN.
BUT THEN MY MOTHER DIED YOUNG, LEAVING ME ALONE IN THE WORLD AND HE WAS THE ONE WHO PROVIDED THE FUNDS FOR ME TO GET AN EDUCATION.
THE STORY I HEARD ABOUT HIS TIME IN THE INNER CHAMBERS IS THAT HE WAS A VERY INEPT SEMPSTER!
A SEMPSTER? BUT HE WAS ABLE TO LEARN DUTCH AND MEDICINE DURING HIS TIME IN THE INNER CHAMBERS, WASN'T HE?
HOW FORTUNATE HE WAS...! I WISH I'D BEEN BORN BACK THEN. I WOULD'VE ENTERED THE INNER CHAMBERS AND STUDIED ALL DAY LONG, WHILE RECEIVING A SALARY!
IT DOES SOUND QUITE NICE.
I DON'T KNOW IF THIS BE TRUE OR SIMPLY A TALE MY FATHER TOLD, BUT HE SAID LADY TANUMA OKITSUGU, WHO WAS A SENIOR COUNCILLOR AT THE TIME, AND EVEN THE LORD CONSORT OF THE SHOGUN, JOINED THEIR DISCUSSIONS ON HOLLAND STUDIES.
ANYWAY, IT'S THANKS TO MY FATHER THAT I KNOW WHAT LITTLE DUTCH I DO.
LATER, HE LEFT THE INNER CHAMBERS AND OPENED AN INFIRMARY FOR TOWNSFOLK WITH HIS FELLOW ŌOKU SCHOLARS.
IT'S STILL THERE, FROM WHAT I'VE HEARD. IT WAS TAKEN OVER BY THE SON OF MY FATHER'S COLLEAGUE, KUROKI RYOJUN, AND THE SON STILL SEES PATIENTS THERE.
BUT ANYWAY. IT'S ABOUT TIME YOU HEADED HOME.

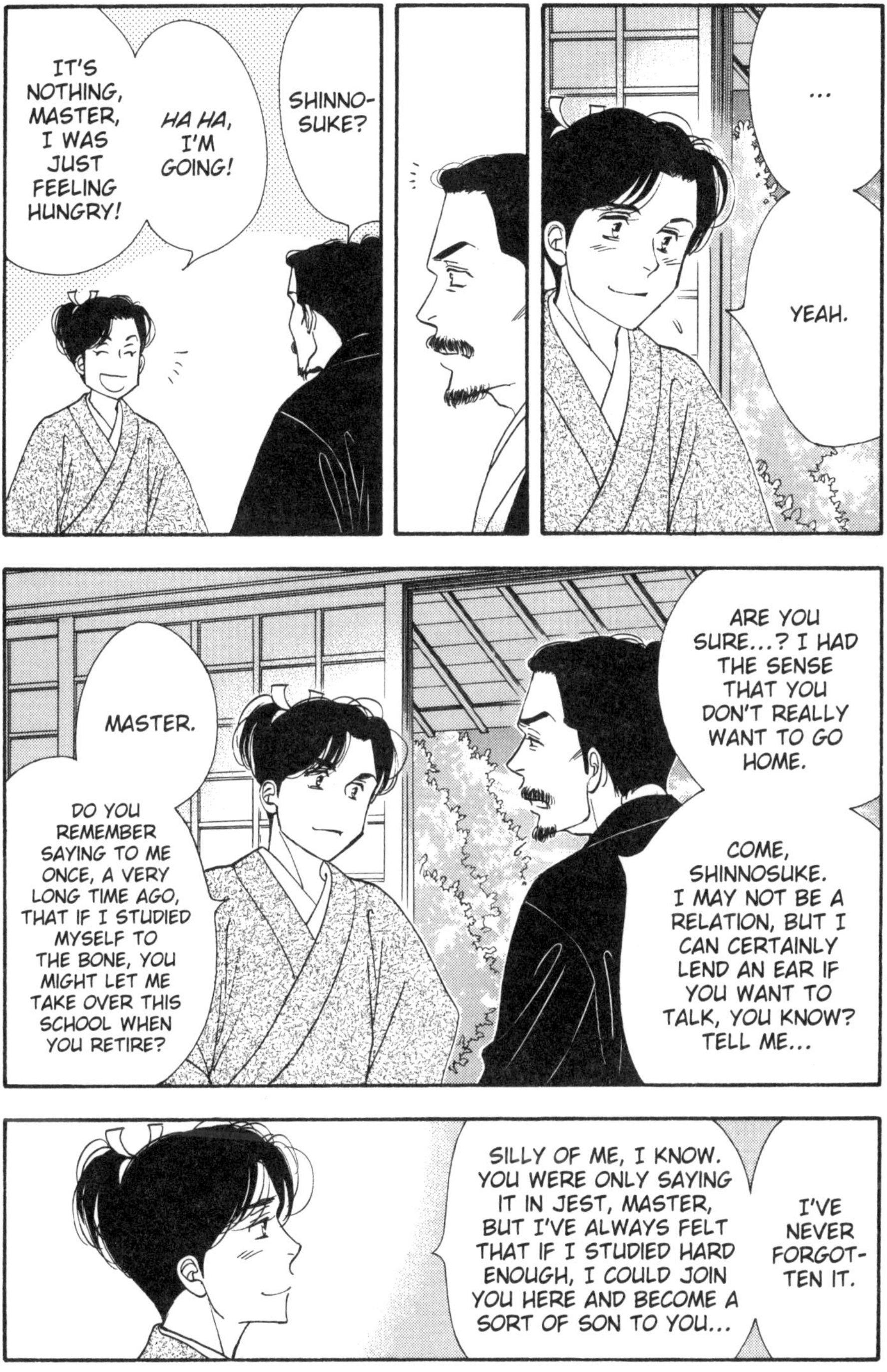
...
YEAH.
SHINNO-SUKE?
HA HA, I'M GOING!
IT'S NOTHING, MASTER, I WAS JUST FEELING HUNGRY!
ARE YOU SURE...? I HAD THE SENSE THAT YOU DON'T REALLY WANT TO GO HOME.
COME, SHINNOSUKE. I MAY NOT BE A RELATION, BUT I CAN CERTAINLY LEND AN EAR IF YOU WANT TO TALK, YOU KNOW? TELL ME...
MASTER.
DO YOU REMEMBER SAYING TO ME ONCE, A VERY LONG TIME AGO, THAT IF I STUDIED MYSELF TO THE BONE, YOU MIGHT LET ME TAKE OVER THIS SCHOOL WHEN YOU RETIRE?
I'VE NEVER FORGOT-TEN IT.
SILLY OF ME, I KNOW. YOU WERE ONLY SAYING IT IN JEST, MASTER, BUT I'VE ALWAYS FELT THAT IF I STUDIED HARD ENOUGH, I COULD JOIN YOU HERE AND BECOME A SORT OF SON TO YOU...

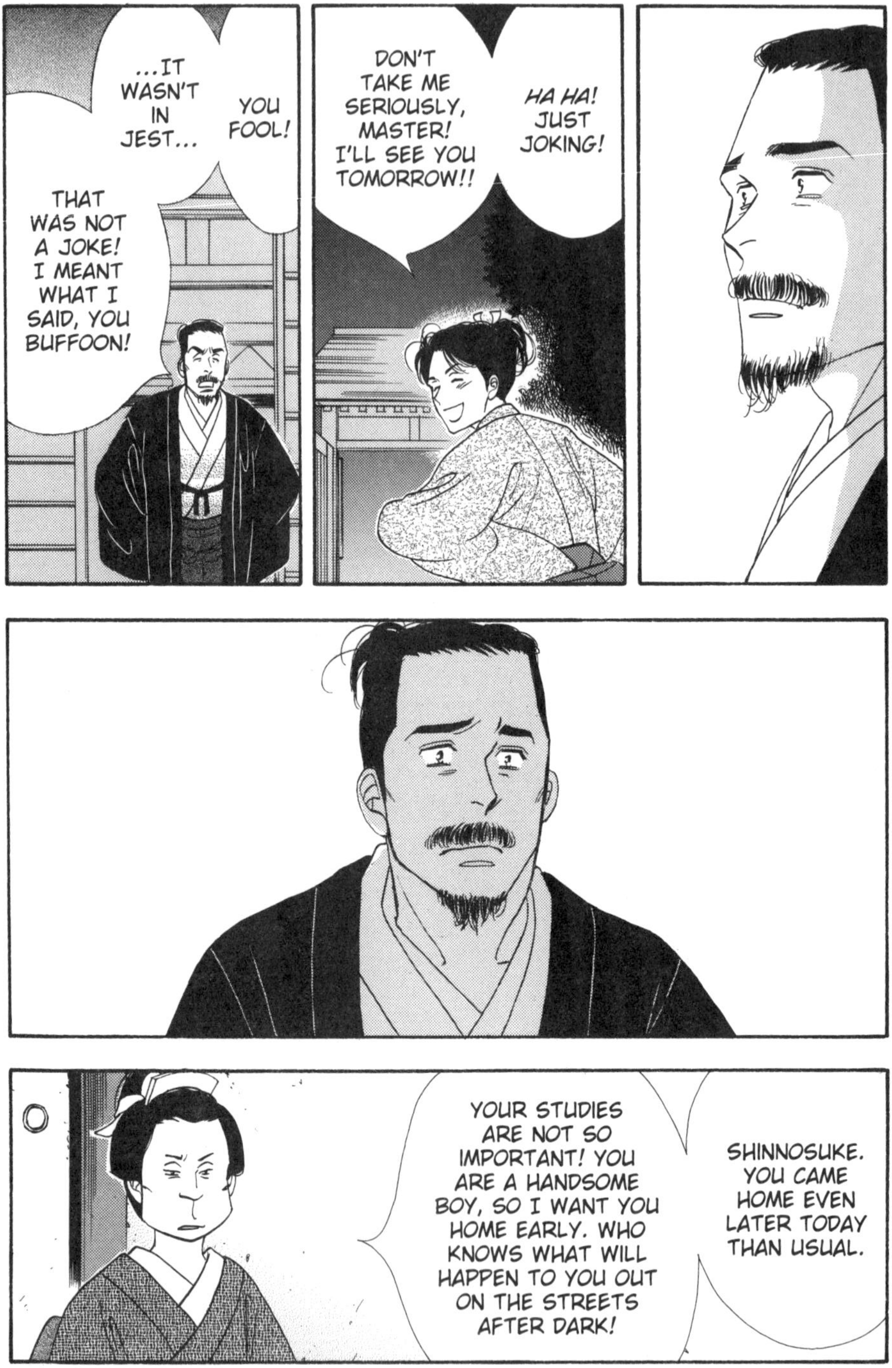
HA HA! JUST JOKING!
DON'T TAKE ME SERIOUSLY, MASTER! I'LL SEE YOU TOMORROW!!
YOU FOOL!
...IT WASN'T IN JEST...
THAT WAS NOT A JOKE! I MEANT WHAT I SAID, YOU BUFFOON!
SHINNOSUKE. YOU CAME HOME EVEN LATER TODAY THAN USUAL.
YOUR STUDIES ARE NOT SO IMPORTANT! YOU ARE A HANDSOME BOY, SO I WANT YOU HOME EARLY. WHO KNOWS WHAT WILL HAPPEN TO YOU OUT ON THE STREETS AFTER DARK!

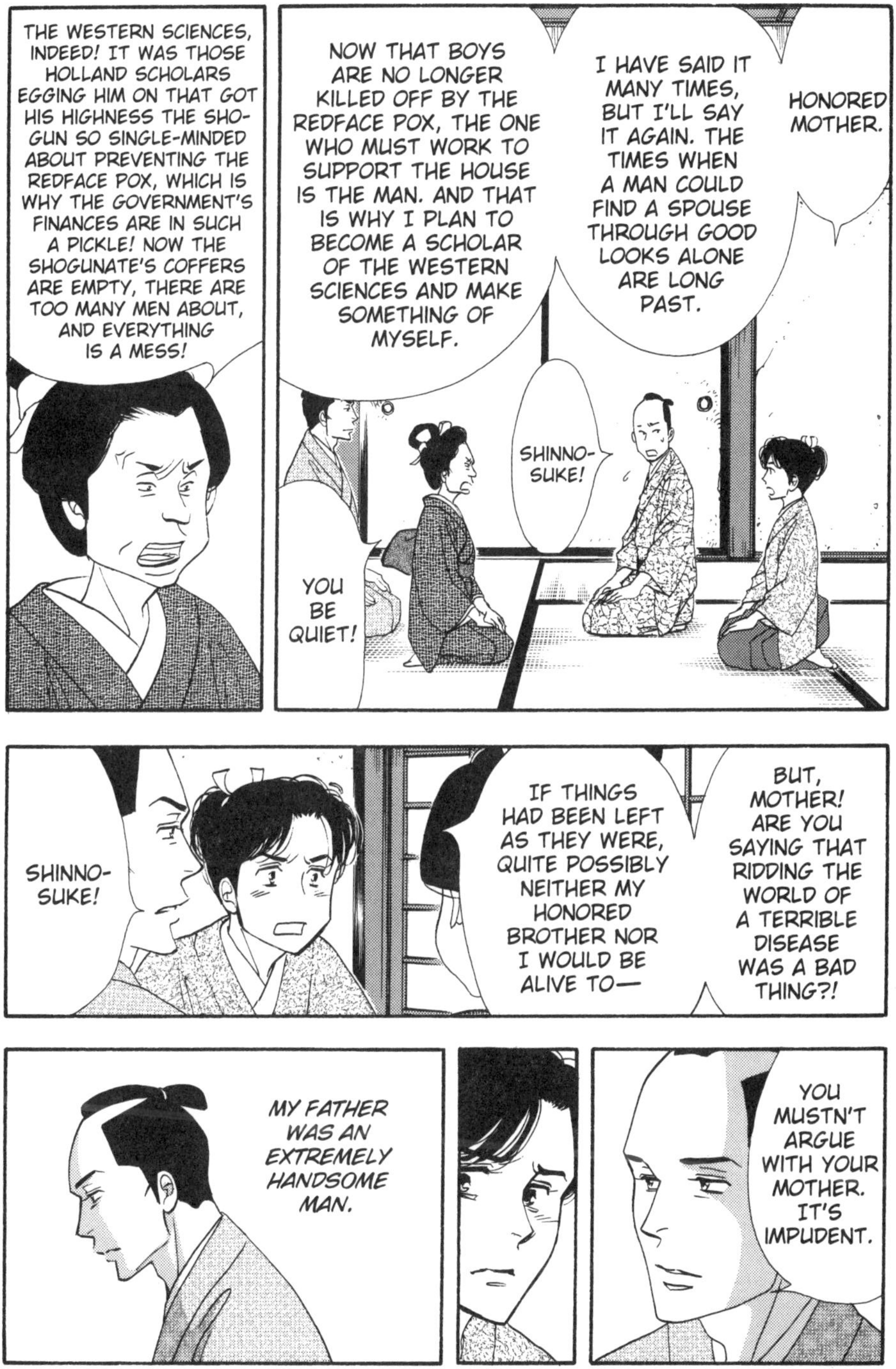
HONORED MOTHER.
I HAVE SAID IT MANY TIMES, BUT I'LL SAY IT AGAIN. THE TIMES WHEN A MAN COULD FIND A SPOUSE THROUGH GOOD LOOKS ALONE ARE LONG PAST.
NOW THAT BOYS ARE NO LONGER KILLED OFF BY THE REDFACE POX, THE ONE WHO MUST WORK TO SUPPORT THE HOUSE IS THE MAN. AND THAT IS WHY I PLAN TO BECOME A SCHOLAR OF THE WESTERN SCIENCES AND MAKE SOMETHING OF MYSELF.
SHINNO-SUKE!
YOU BE QUIET!
THE WESTERN SCIENCES, INDEED! IT WAS THOSE HOLLAND SCHOLARS EGGING HIM ON THAT GOT HIS HIGHNESS THE SHO-GUN SO SINGLE-MINDED ABOUT PREVENTING THE REDFACE POX, WHICH IS WHY THE GOVERNMENT'S FINANCES ARE IN SUCH A PICKLE! NOW THE SHOGUNATE'S COFFERS ARE EMPTY, THERE ARE TOO MANY MEN ABOUT, AND EVERYTHING IS A MESS!
BUT, MOTHER! ARE YOU SAYING THAT RIDDING THE WORLD OF A TERRIBLE DISEASE WAS A BAD THING?!
IF THINGS HAD BEEN LEFT AS THEY WERE, QUITE POSSIBLY NEITHER MY HONORED BROTHER NOR I WOULD BE ALIVE TO—
SHINNO-SUKE!
YOU MUSTN'T ARGUE WITH YOUR MOTHER. IT'S IMPUDENT.
MY FATHER WAS AN EXTREMELY HANDSOME MAN.

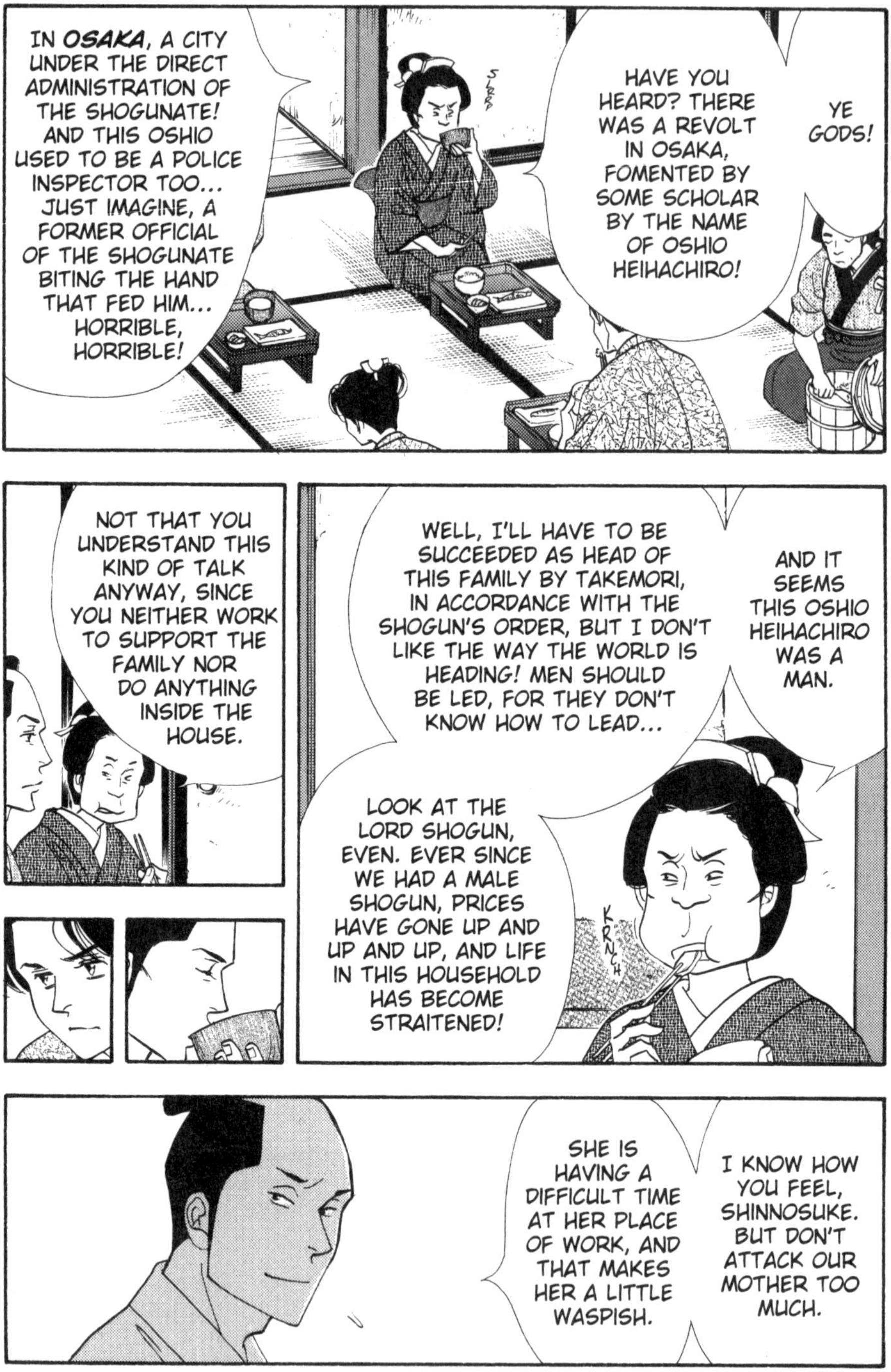
YE GODS!
HAVE YOU HEARD? THERE WAS A REVOLT IN OSAKA, FOMENTED BY SOME SCHOLAR BY THE NAME OF OSHIO HEIHACHIRO!
SLRRP
IN OSAKA, A CITY UNDER THE DIRECT ADMINISTRATION OF THE SHOGUNATE! AND THIS OSHIO USED TO BE A POLICE INSPECTOR TOO... JUST IMAGINE, A FORMER OFFICIAL OF THE SHOGUNATE BITING THE HAND THAT FED HIM... HORRIBLE, HORRIBLE!
AND IT SEEMS THIS OSHIO HEIHACHIRO WAS A MAN.
WELL, I'LL HAVE TO BE SUCCEEDED AS HEAD OF THIS FAMILY BY TAKEMORI, IN ACCORDANCE WITH THE SHOGUN'S ORDER, BUT I DON'T LIKE THE WAY THE WORLD IS HEADING! MEN SHOULD BE LED, FOR THEY DON'T KNOW HOW TO LEAD...
LOOK AT THE LORD SHOGUN, EVEN. EVER SINCE WE HAD A MALE SHOGUN, PRICES HAVE GONE UP AND UP AND UP, AND LIFE IN THIS HOUSEHOLD HAS BECOME STRAITENED!
KRNCH
NOT THAT YOU UNDERSTAND THIS KIND OF TALK ANYWAY, SINCE YOU NEITHER WORK TO SUPPORT THE FAMILY NOR DO ANYTHING INSIDE THE HOUSE.
I KNOW HOW YOU FEEL, SHINNOSUKE. BUT DON'T ATTACK OUR MOTHER TOO MUCH.
SHE IS HAVING A DIFFICULT TIME AT HER PLACE OF WORK, AND THAT MAKES HER A LITTLE WASPISH.

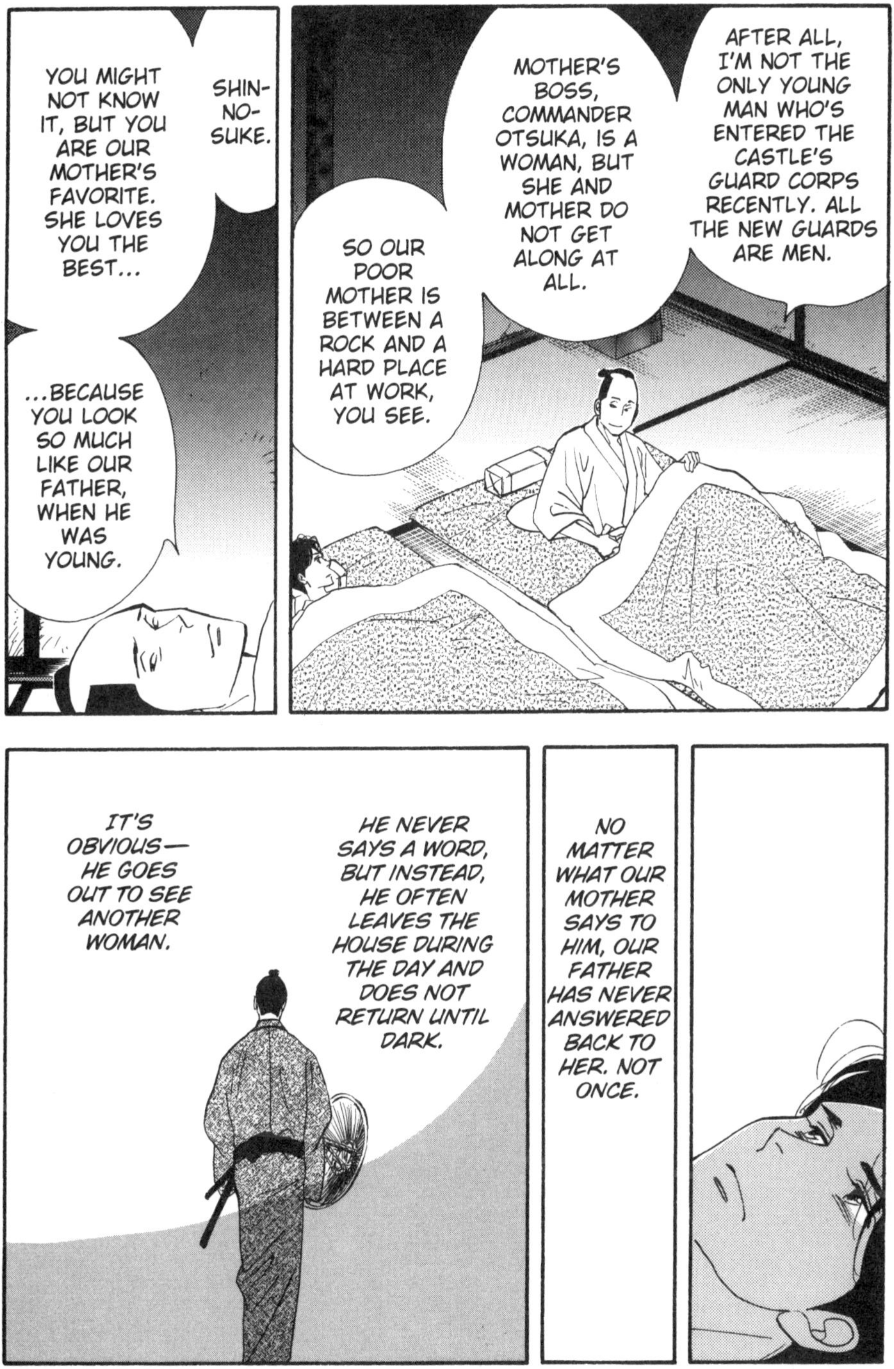
AFTER ALL, I'M NOT THE ONLY YOUNG MAN WHO'S ENTERED THE CASTLE'S GUARD CORPS RECENTLY. ALL THE NEW GUARDS ARE MEN.
MOTHER'S BOSS, COMMANDER OTSUKA, IS A WOMAN, BUT SHE AND MOTHER DO NOT GET ALONG AT ALL.
SO OUR POOR MOTHER IS BETWEEN A ROCK AND A HARD PLACE AT WORK, YOU SEE.
SHIN-NO-SUKE.
YOU MIGHT NOT KNOW IT, BUT YOU ARE OUR MOTHER'S FAVORITE. SHE LOVES YOU THE BEST...
...BECAUSE YOU LOOK SO MUCH LIKE OUR FATHER, WHEN HE WAS YOUNG.
NO MATTER WHAT OUR MOTHER SAYS TO HIM, OUR FATHER HAS NEVER ANSWERED BACK TO HER. NOT ONCE.
HE NEVER SAYS A WORD, BUT INSTEAD, HE OFTEN LEAVES THE HOUSE DURING THE DAY AND DOES NOT RETURN UNTIL DARK.
IT'S OBVIOUS— HE GOES OUT TO SEE ANOTHER WOMAN.

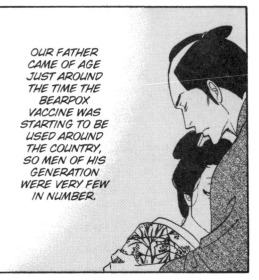

OUR FATHER CAME OF AGE JUST AROUND THE TIME THE BEARPOX VACCINE WAS STARTING TO BE USED AROUND THE COUNTRY, SO MEN OF HIS GENERATION WERE VERY FEW IN NUMBER.
AND ON TOP OF THAT, WITH HIS GOOD LOOKS... THERE WAS NO CHANCE WOMEN HIS AGE WOULD JUST LEAVE HIM ALONE.
I DON'T LIKE WOMEN LIKE MY MOTHER, BUT I DON'T WANT TO BECOME A MAN LIKE MY FATHER, EITHER.

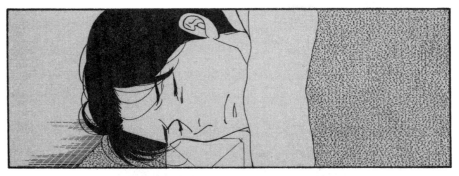

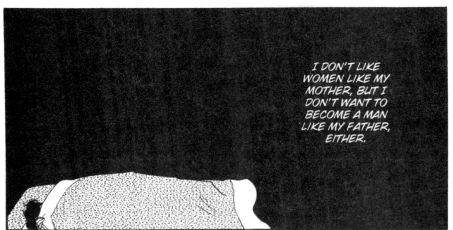

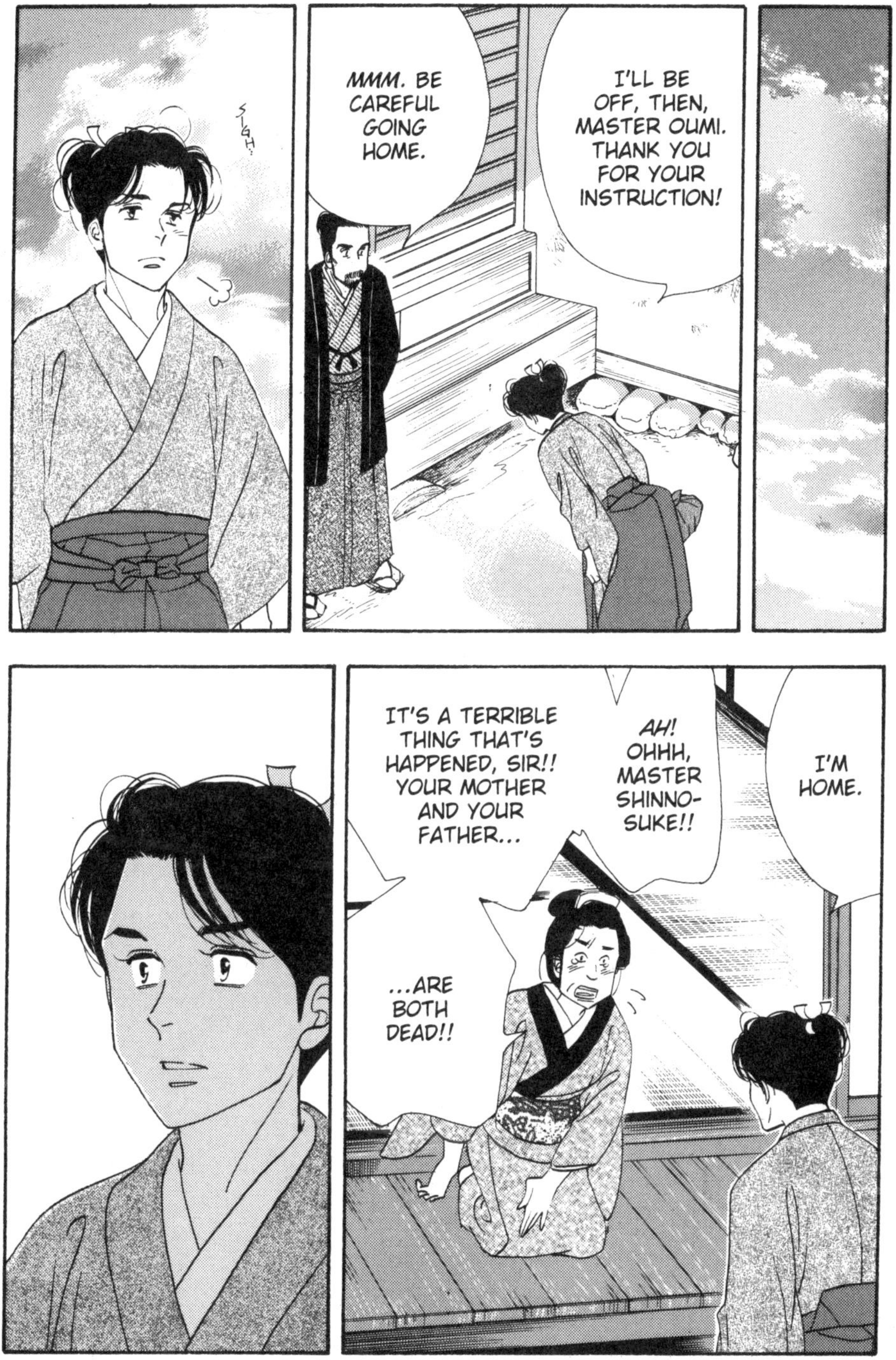
I'LL BE OFF, THEN, MASTER OUMI. THANK YOU FOR YOUR INSTRUCTION!
MMM. BE CAREFUL GOING HOME.
SIGH
I'M HOME.
AH! OHHH, MASTER SHINNO-SUKE!!
IT'S A TERRIBLE THING THAT'S HAPPENED, SIR!! YOUR MOTHER AND YOUR FATHER...
...ARE BOTH DEAD!!

THIS IS WHAT HAPPENED.

...WAS WITH ANOTHER WOMAN IN A TRYSTING INN, WHEN OUR MOTHER BURST IN UPON THEM. SHE GREW QUITE FRENZIED WHEN SHE SAW THEM, AND STABBED BOTH OUR FATHER AND HIS LOVER TO DEATH.

OUR FATHER...

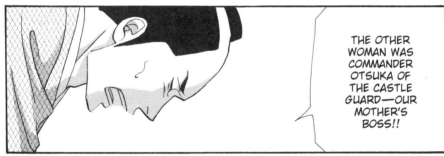

THE OTHER WOMAN WAS COMMANDER OTSUKA OF THE CASTLE GUARD—OUR MOTHER'S BOSS!!

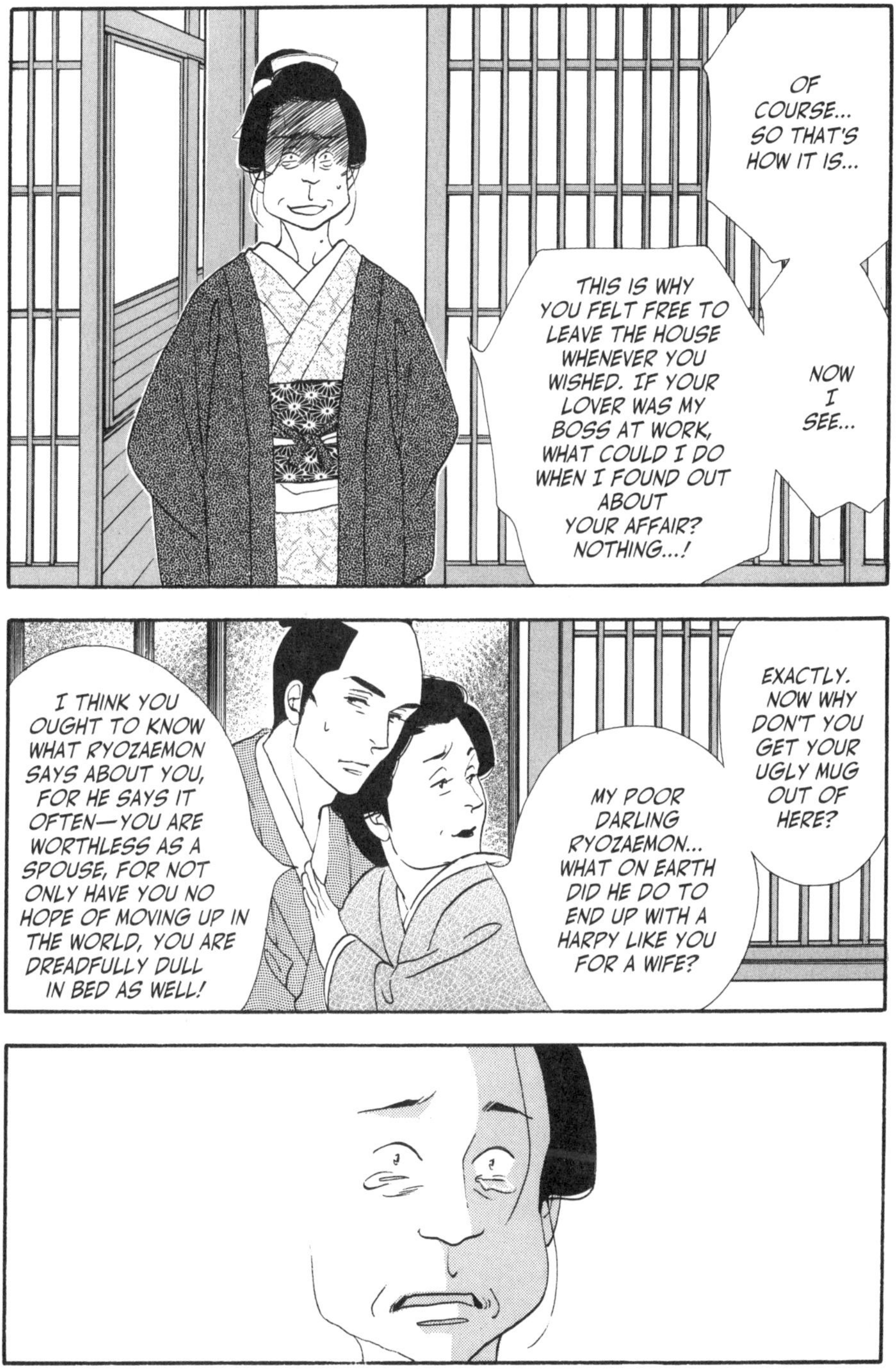
OF COURSE... SO THAT'S HOW IT IS...
NOW I SEE...
THIS IS WHY YOU FELT FREE TO LEAVE THE HOUSE WHENEVER YOU WISHED. IF YOUR LOVER WAS MY BOSS AT WORK, WHAT COULD I DO WHEN I FOUND OUT ABOUT YOUR AFFAIR? NOTHING...!
EXACTLY. NOW WHY DON'T YOU GET YOUR UGLY MUG OUT OF HERE?
MY POOR DARLING RYOZAEMON... WHAT ON EARTH DID HE DO TO END UP WITH A HARPY LIKE YOU FOR A WIFE?
I THINK YOU OUGHT TO KNOW WHAT RYOZAEMON SAYS ABOUT YOU, FOR HE SAYS IT OFTEN—YOU ARE WORTHLESS AS A SPOUSE, FOR NOT ONLY HAVE YOU NO HOPE OF MOVING UP IN THE WORLD, YOU ARE DREADFULLY DULL IN BED AS WELL!

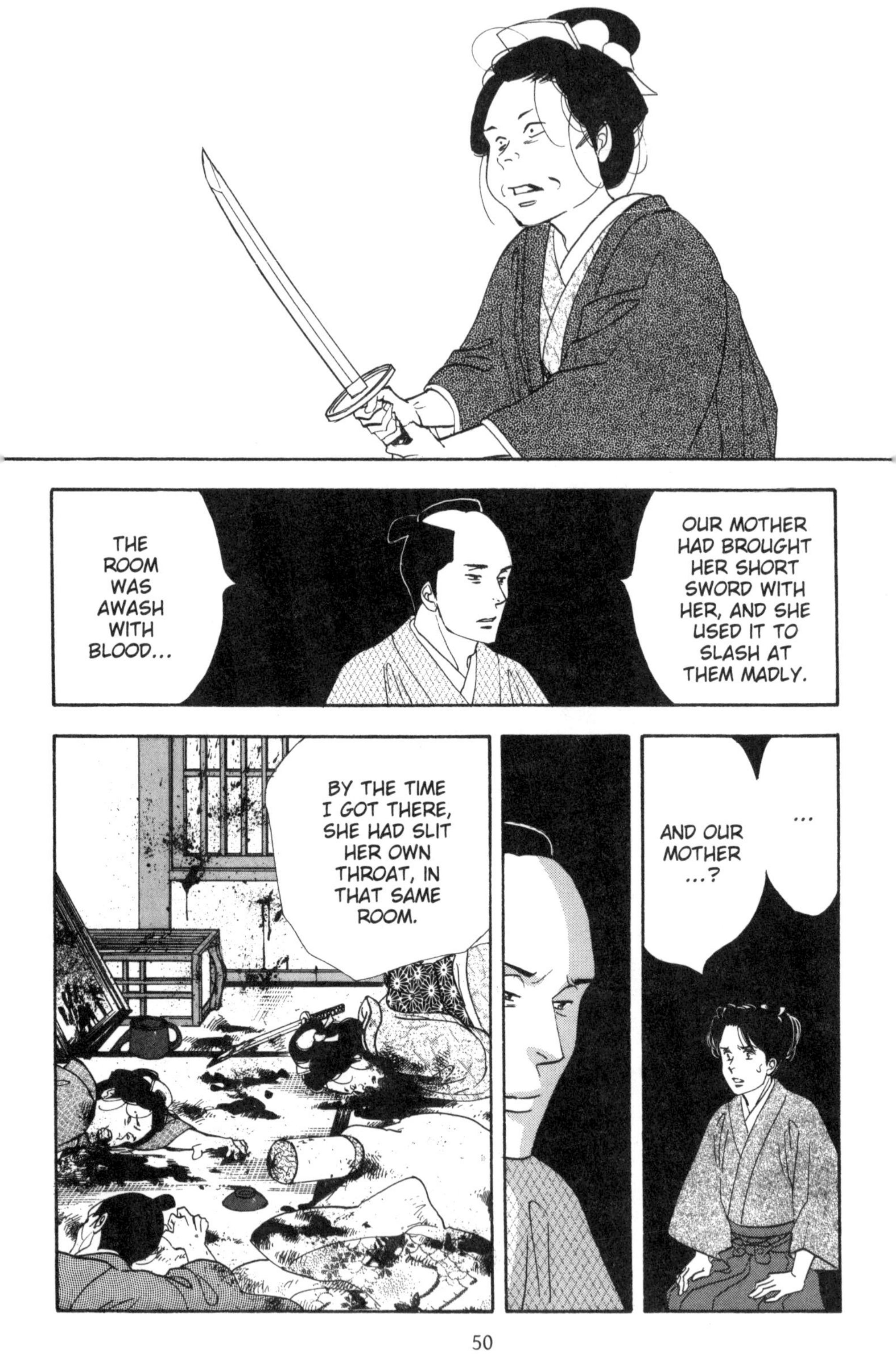
OUR MOTHER HAD BROUGHT HER SHORT SWORD WITH HER, AND SHE USED IT TO SLASH AT THEM MADLY.
THE ROOM WAS AWASH WITH BLOOD...
...
AND OUR MOTHER ...?
BY THE TIME I GOT THERE, SHE HAD SLIT HER OWN THROAT, IN THAT SAME ROOM.

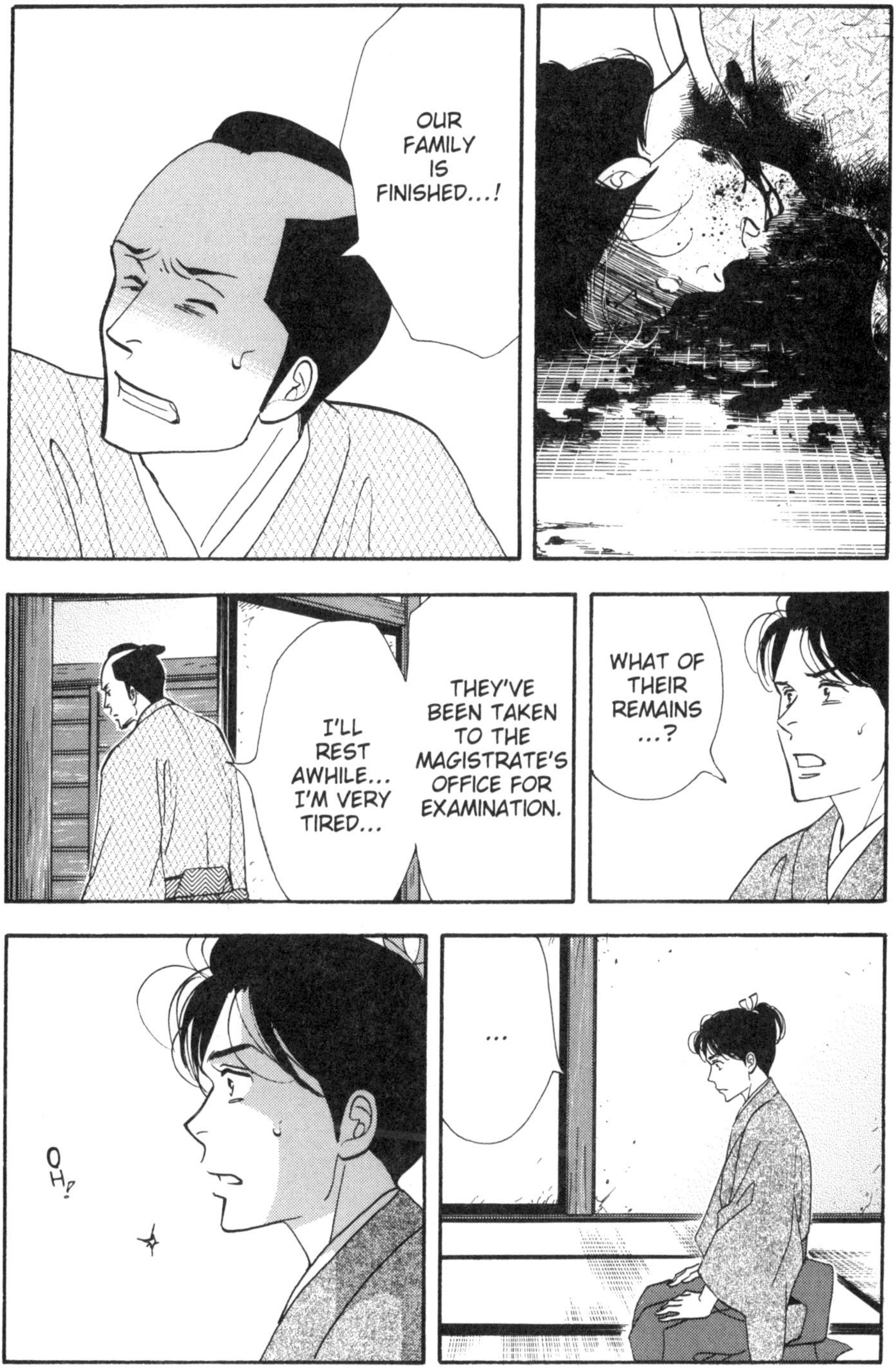
OUR FAMILY IS FINISHED...!
WHAT OF THEIR REMAINS ...?
THEY'VE BEEN TAKEN TO THE MAGISTRATE'S OFFICE FOR EXAMINATION.
I'LL REST AWHILE... I'M VERY TIRED...
...
OH!

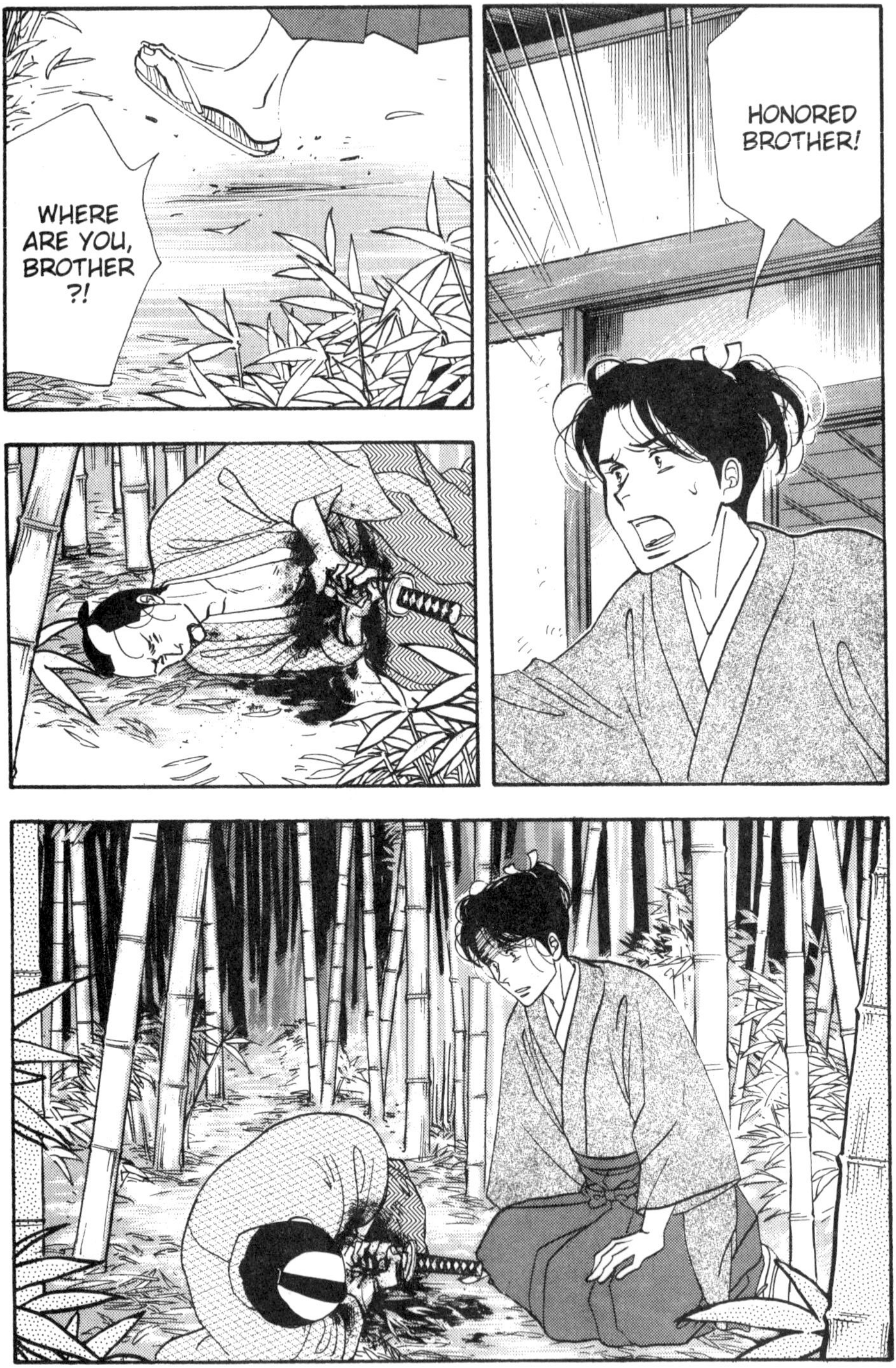
HONORED BROTHER!
WHERE ARE YOU, BROTHER ?!

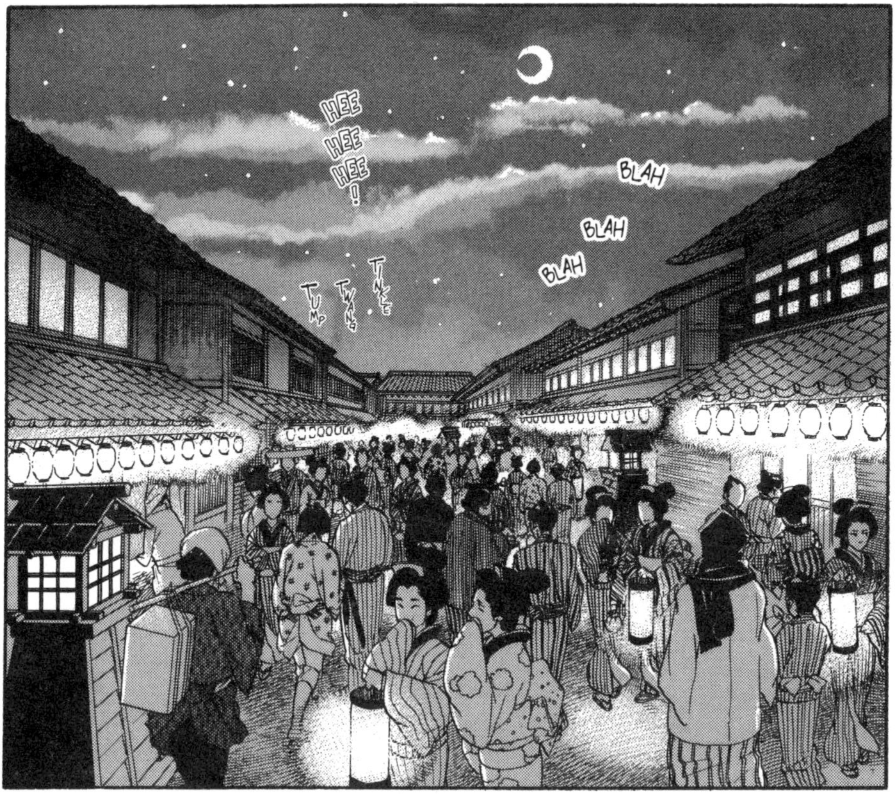
HEE HEE HEE!
BLAH
BLAH
BLAH
TINKLE
TWANG
TUMP

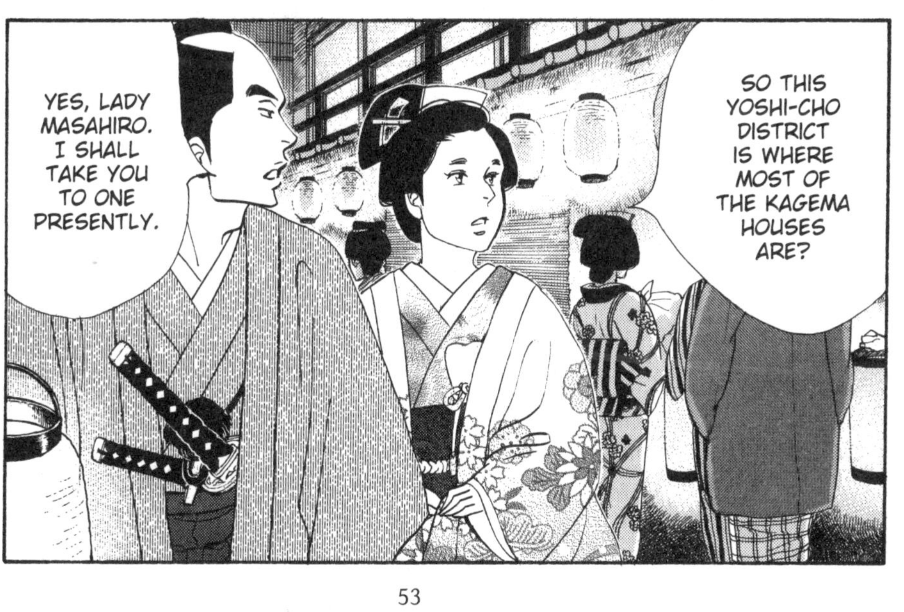
SO THIS YOSHI-CHO DISTRICT IS WHERE MOST OF THE KAGEMA HOUSES ARE?
YES, LADY MASAHIRO. I SHALL TAKE YOU TO ONE PRESENTLY.

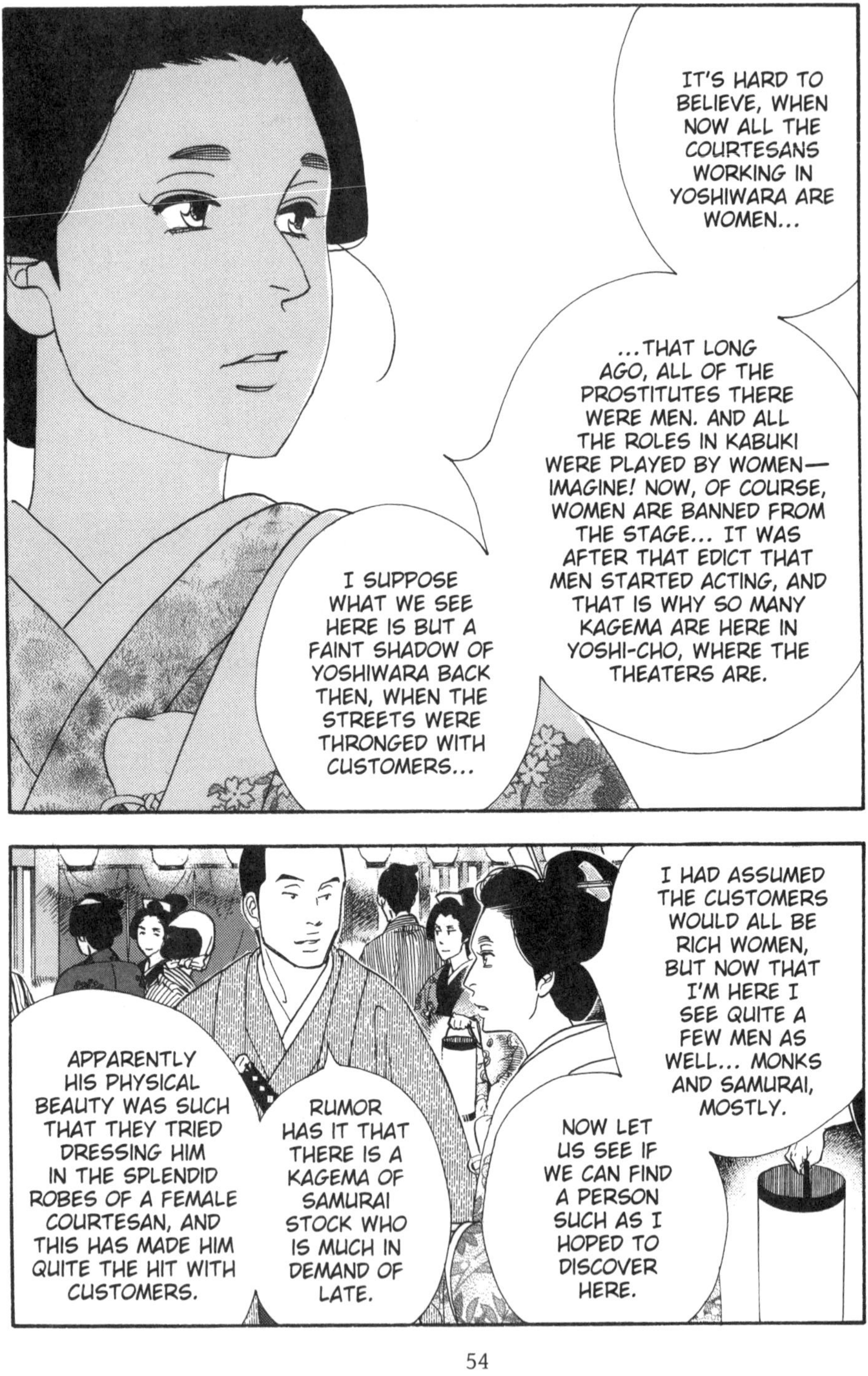
IT'S HARD TO BELIEVE, WHEN NOW ALL THE COURTESANS WORKING IN YOSHIWARA ARE WOMEN...
...THAT LONG AGO, ALL OF THE PROSTITUTES THERE WERE MEN. AND ALL THE ROLES IN KABUKI WERE PLAYED BY WOMEN—IMAGINE! NOW, OF COURSE, WOMEN ARE BANNED FROM THE STAGE... IT WAS AFTER THAT EDICT THAT MEN STARTED ACTING, AND THAT IS WHY SO MANY KAGEMA ARE HERE IN YOSHI-CHO, WHERE THE THEATERS ARE.
I SUPPOSE WHAT WE SEE HERE IS BUT A FAINT SHADOW OF YOSHIWARA BACK THEN, WHEN THE STREETS WERE THRONGED WITH CUSTOMERS...
I HAD ASSUMED THE CUSTOMERS WOULD ALL BE RICH WOMEN, BUT NOW THAT I'M HERE I SEE QUITE A FEW MEN AS WELL... MONKS AND SAMURAI, MOSTLY.
NOW LET US SEE IF WE CAN FIND A PERSON SUCH AS I HOPED TO DISCOVER HERE.
RUMOR HAS IT THAT THERE IS A KAGEMA OF SAMURAI STOCK WHO IS MUCH IN DEMAND OF LATE.
APPARENTLY HIS PHYSICAL BEAUTY WAS SUCH THAT THEY TRIED DRESSING HIM IN THE SPLENDID ROBES OF A FEMALE COURTESAN, AND THIS HAS MADE HIM QUITE THE HIT WITH CUSTOMERS.

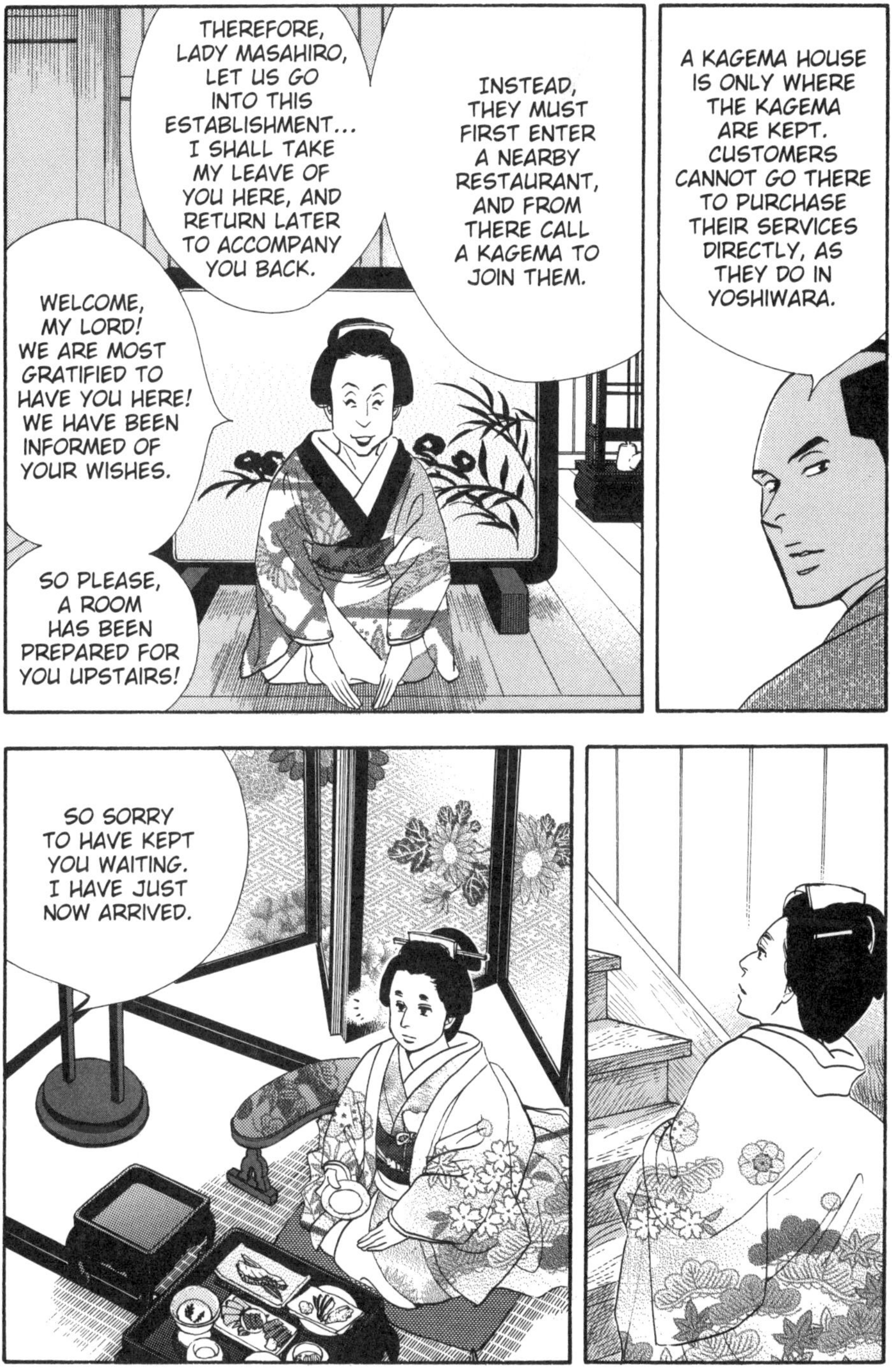
A KAGEMA HOUSE IS ONLY WHERE THE KAGEMA ARE KEPT. CUSTOMERS CANNOT GO THERE TO PURCHASE THEIR SERVICES DIRECTLY, AS THEY DO IN YOSHIWARA.
INSTEAD, THEY MUST FIRST ENTER A NEARBY RESTAURANT, AND FROM THERE CALL A KAGEMA TO JOIN THEM.
THEREFORE, LADY MASAHIRO, LET US GO INTO THIS ESTABLISHMENT... I SHALL TAKE MY LEAVE OF YOU HERE, AND RETURN LATER TO ACCOMPANY YOU BACK.
WELCOME, MY LORD! WE ARE MOST GRATIFIED TO HAVE YOU HERE! WE HAVE BEEN INFORMED OF YOUR WISHES.
SO PLEASE, A ROOM HAS BEEN PREPARED FOR YOU UPSTAIRS!
SO SORRY TO HAVE KEPT YOU WAITING. I HAVE JUST NOW ARRIVED.

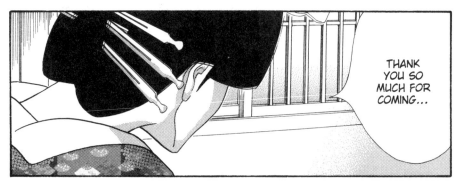

THANK YOU SO MUCH FOR COMING...

!

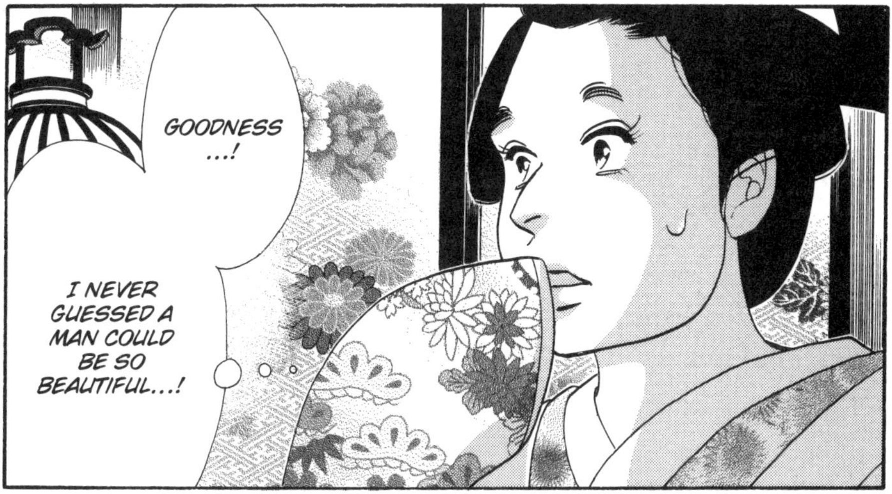
GOODNESS ...!
I NEVER GUESSED A MAN COULD BE SO BEAUTIFUL...!

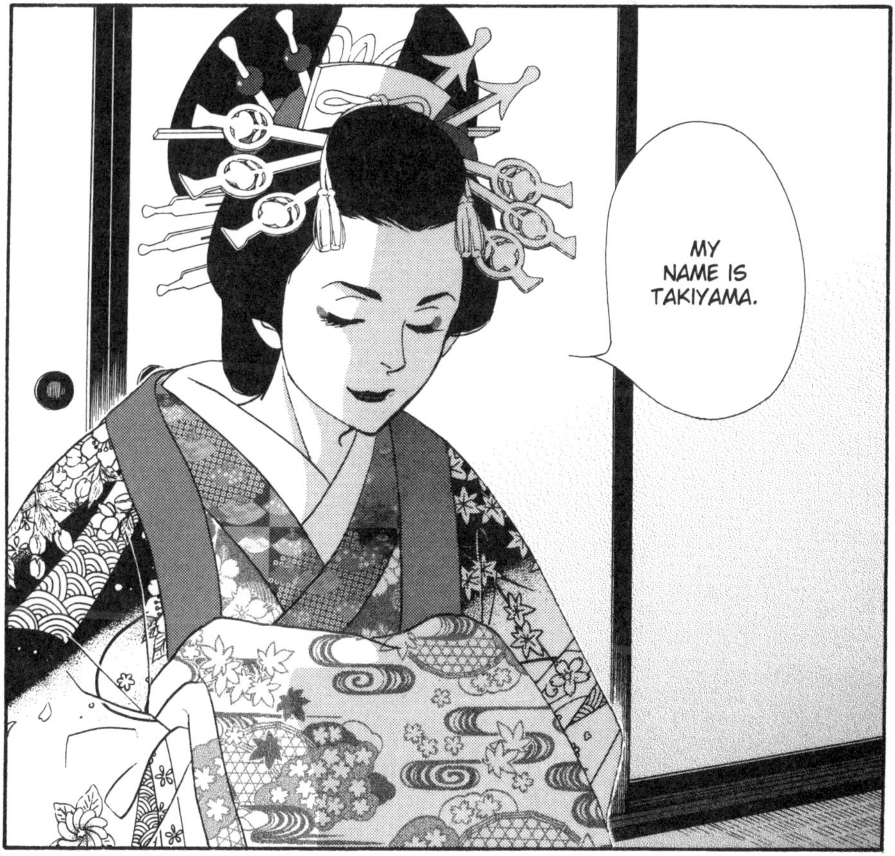
MY NAME IS TAKIYAMA.

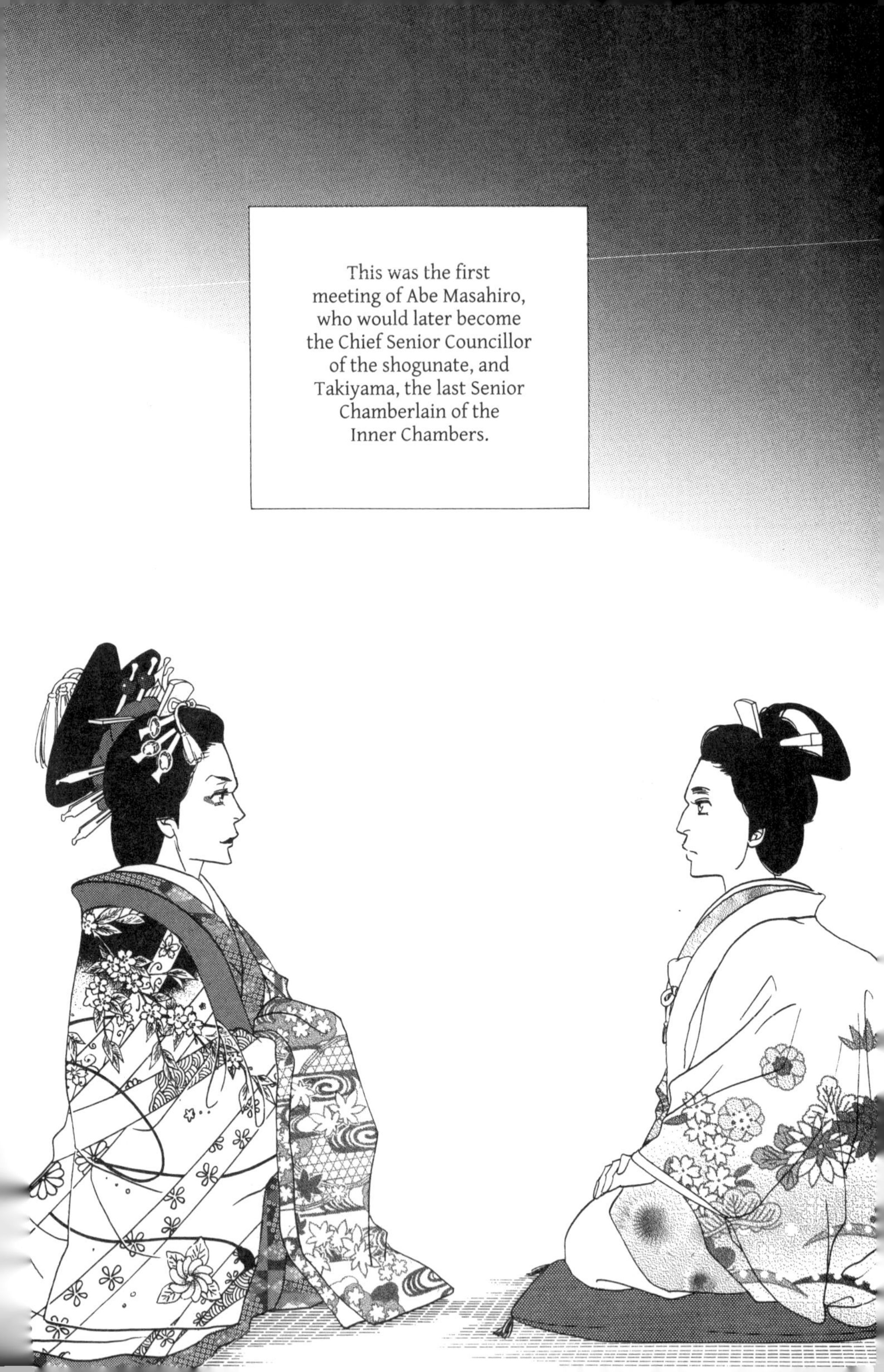
This was the first meeting of Abe Masahiro, who would later become the Chief Senior Councillor of the shogunate, and Takiyama, the last Senior Chamberlain of the Inner Chambers.

Ōoku

THE INNER CHAMBERS

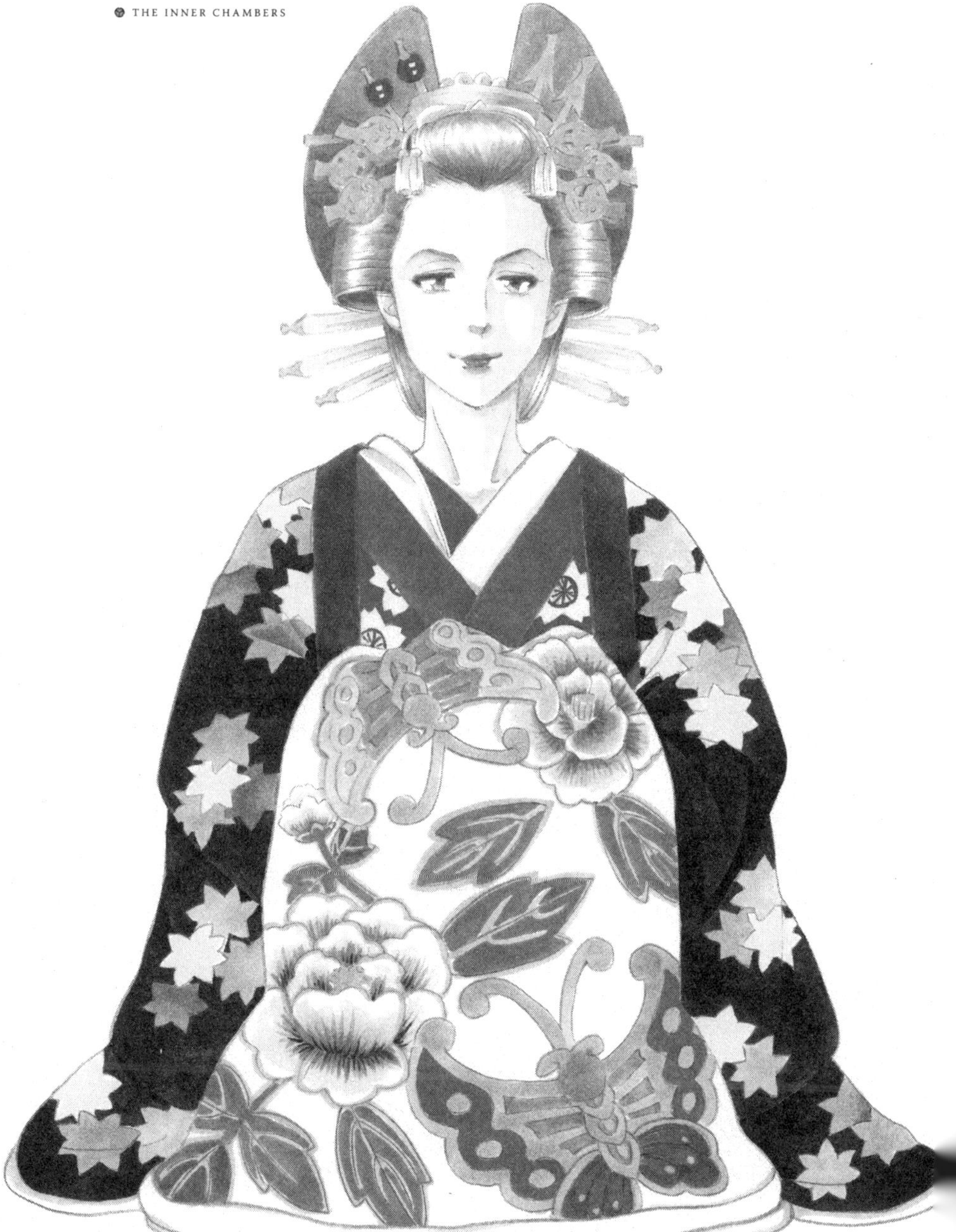

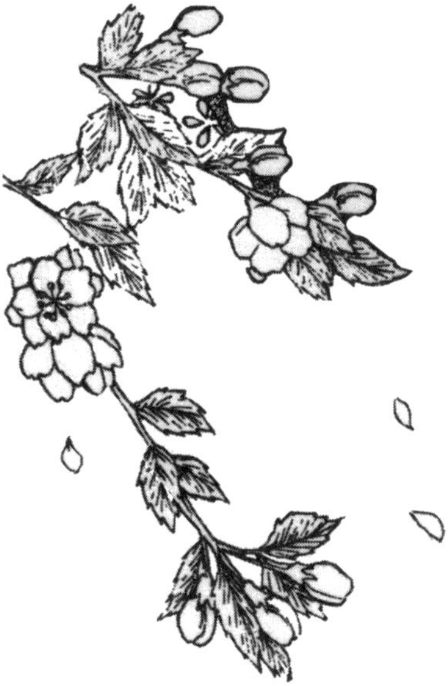

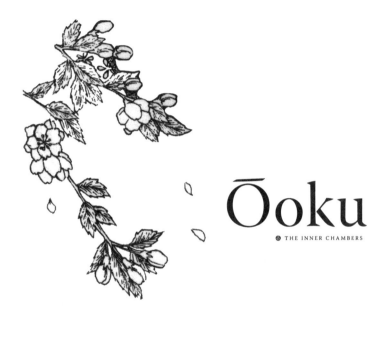

Ōoku

THE INNER CHAMBERS

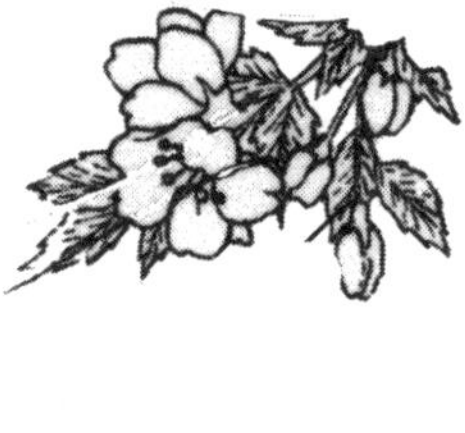

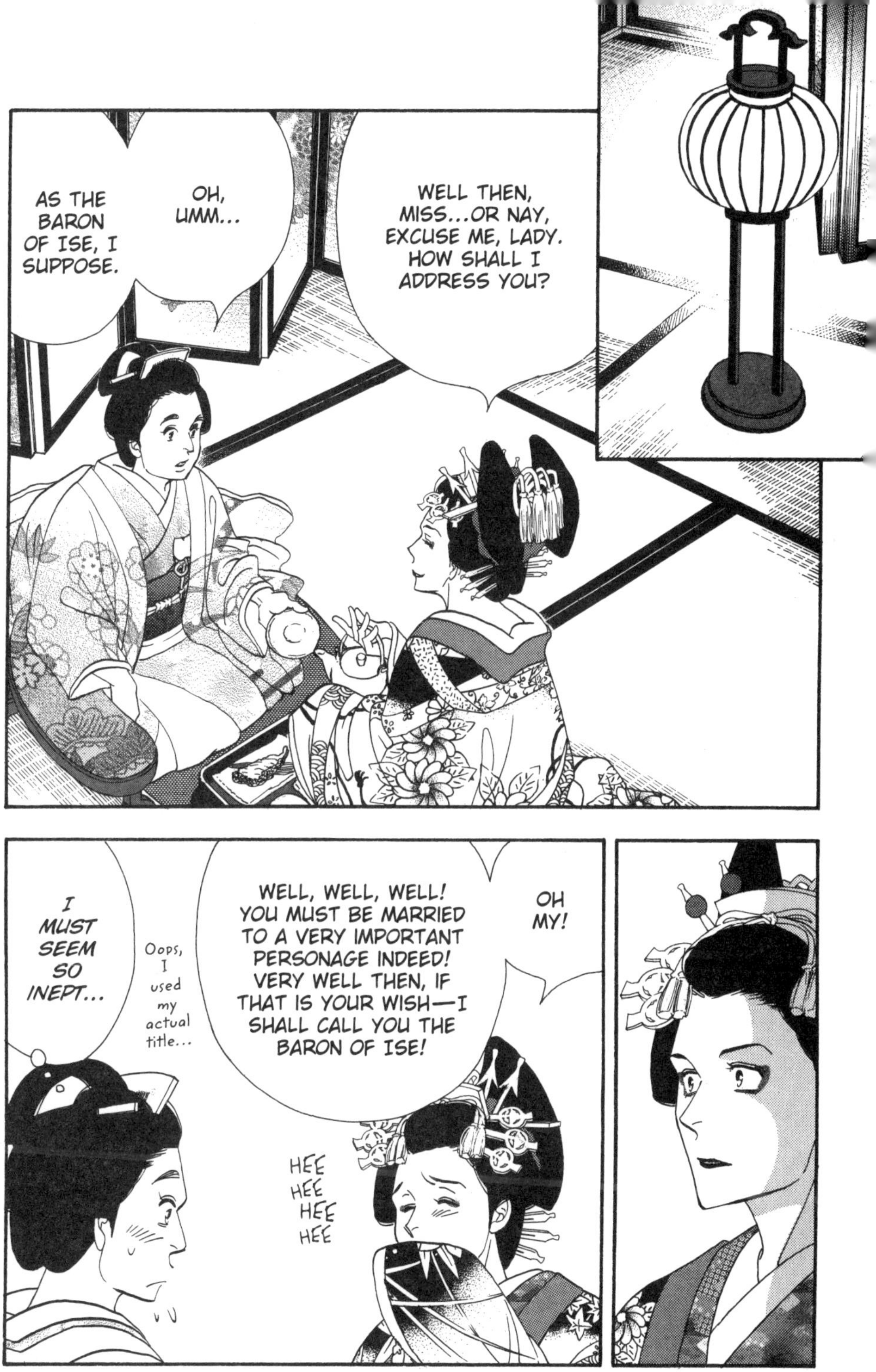
WELL THEN, MISS...OR NAY, EXCUSE ME, LADY. HOW SHALL I ADDRESS YOU?
OH, UMM...
AS THE BARON OF ISE, I SUPPOSE.
OH MY!
WELL, WELL, WELL! YOU MUST BE MARRIED TO A VERY IMPORTANT PERSONAGE INDEED! VERY WELL THEN, IF THAT IS YOUR WISH—I SHALL CALL YOU THE BARON OF ISE!
HEE HEE HEE HEE
Oops, I used my actual title...
I MUST SEEM SO INEPT...

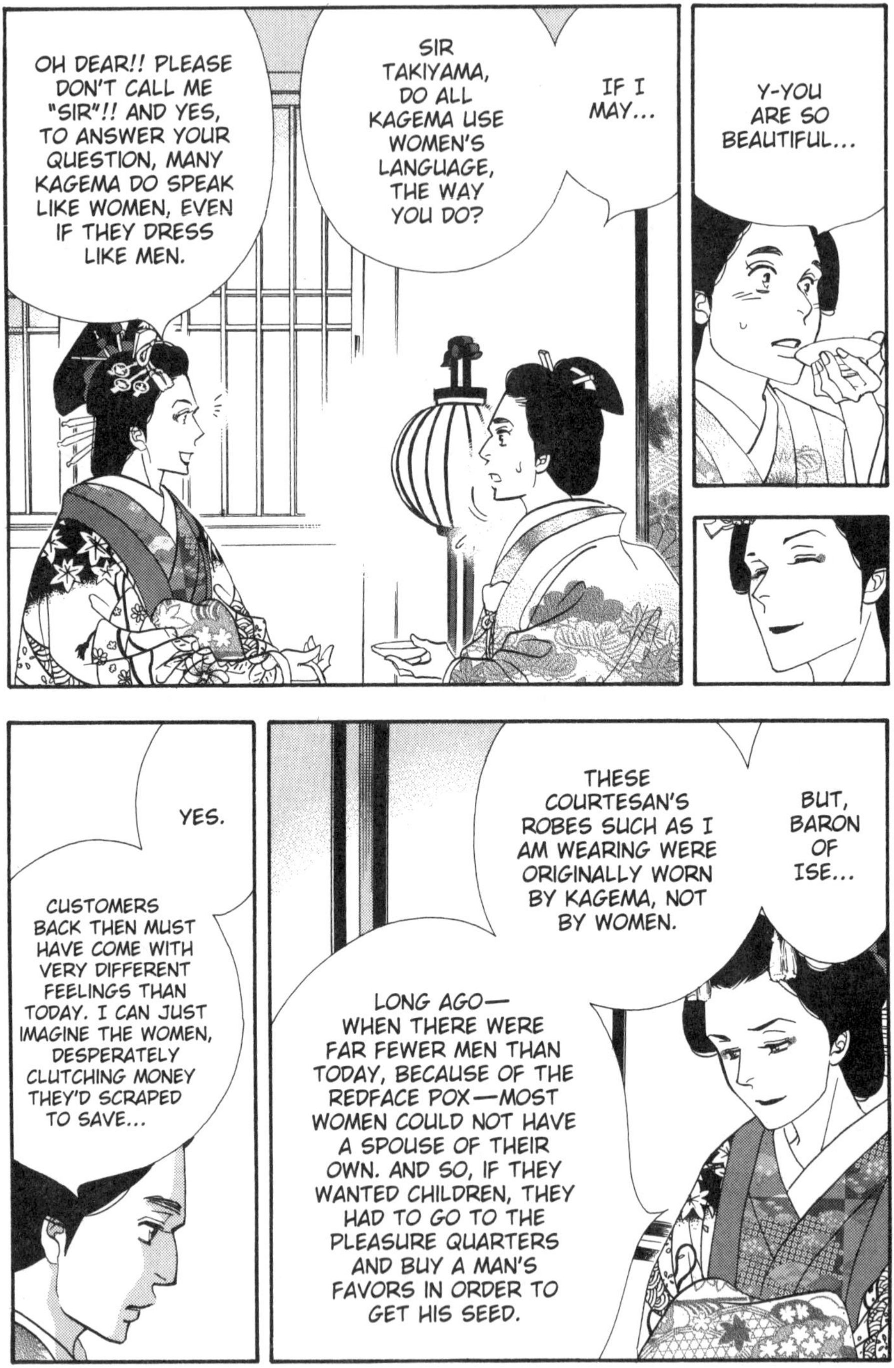
Y-YOU ARE SO BEAUTIFUL...
IF I MAY...
SIR TAKIYAMA, DO ALL KAGEMA USE WOMEN'S LANGUAGE, THE WAY YOU DO?
OH DEAR!! PLEASE DON'T CALL ME "SIR"!! AND YES, TO ANSWER YOUR QUESTION, MANY KAGEMA DO SPEAK LIKE WOMEN, EVEN IF THEY DRESS LIKE MEN.
BUT, BARON OF ISE...
THESE COURTESAN'S ROBES SUCH AS I AM WEARING WERE ORIGINALLY WORN BY KAGEMA, NOT BY WOMEN.
LONG AGO—WHEN THERE WERE FAR FEWER MEN THAN TODAY, BECAUSE OF THE REDFACE POX—MOST WOMEN COULD NOT HAVE A SPOUSE OF THEIR OWN. AND SO, IF THEY WANTED CHILDREN, THEY HAD TO GO TO THE PLEASURE QUARTERS AND BUY A MAN'S FAVORS IN ORDER TO GET HIS SEED.
YES.
CUSTOMERS BACK THEN MUST HAVE COME WITH VERY DIFFERENT FEELINGS THAN TODAY. I CAN JUST IMAGINE THE WOMEN, DESPERATELY CLUTCHING MONEY THEY'D SCRAPED TO SAVE...

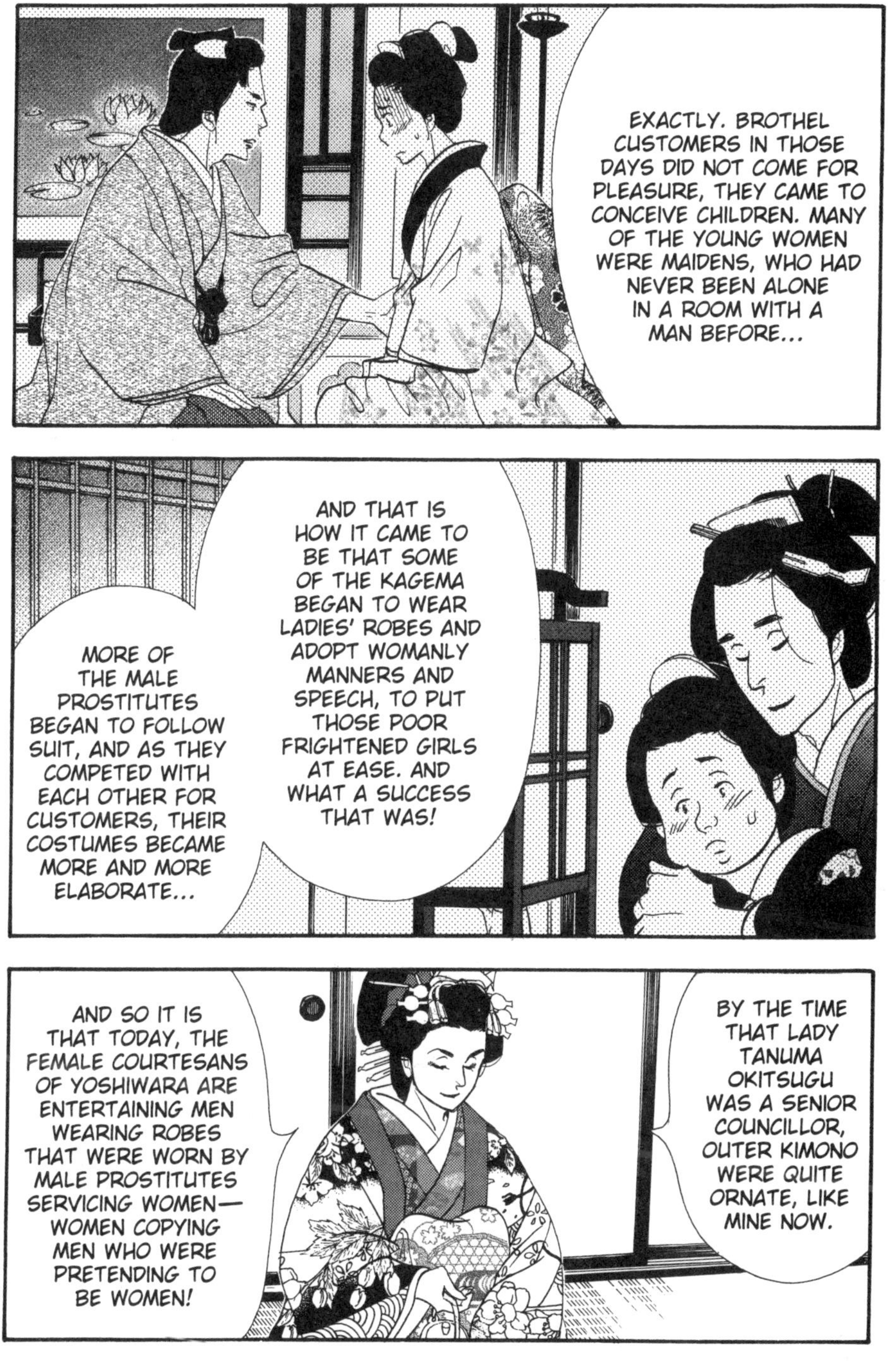
EXACTLY. BROTHEL CUSTOMERS IN THOSE DAYS DID NOT COME FOR PLEASURE, THEY CAME TO CONCEIVE CHILDREN. MANY OF THE YOUNG WOMEN WERE MAIDENS, WHO HAD NEVER BEEN ALONE IN A ROOM WITH A MAN BEFORE...
AND THAT IS HOW IT CAME TO BE THAT SOME OF THE KAGEMA BEGAN TO WEAR LADIES' ROBES AND ADOPT WOMANLY MANNERS AND SPEECH, TO PUT THOSE POOR FRIGHTENED GIRLS AT EASE. AND WHAT A SUCCESS THAT WAS!
MORE OF THE MALE PROSTITUTES BEGAN TO FOLLOW SUIT, AND AS THEY COMPETED WITH EACH OTHER FOR CUSTOMERS, THEIR COSTUMES BECAME MORE AND MORE ELABORATE...
BY THE TIME THAT LADY TANUMA OKITSUGU WAS A SENIOR COUNCILLOR, OUTER KIMONO WERE QUITE ORNATE, LIKE MINE NOW.
AND SO IT IS THAT TODAY, THE FEMALE COURTESANS OF YOSHIWARA ARE ENTERTAINING MEN WEARING ROBES THAT WERE WORN BY MALE PROSTITUTES SERVICING WOMEN—WOMEN COPYING MEN WHO WERE PRETENDING TO BE WOMEN!

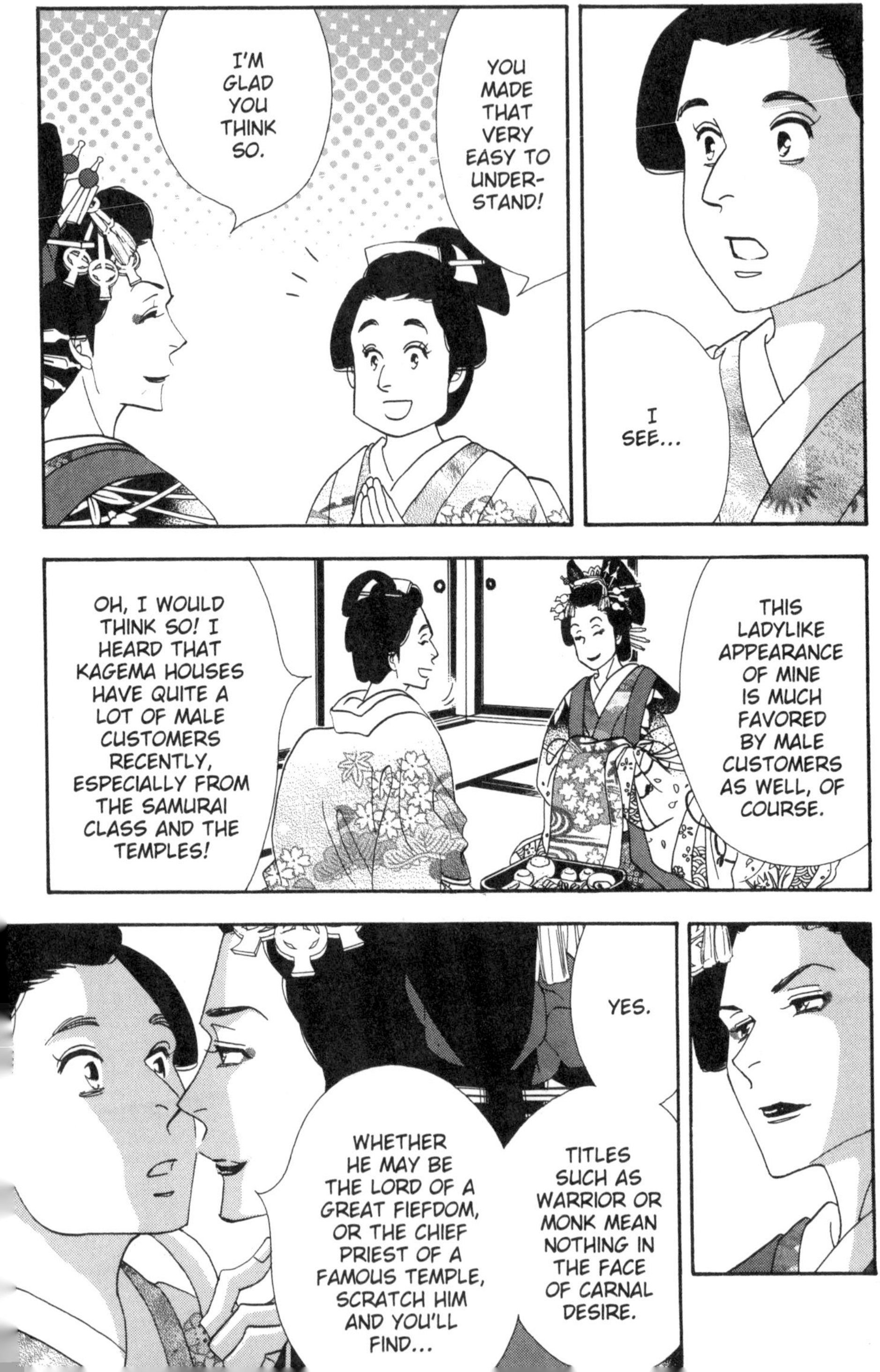
I SEE...
YOU MADE THAT VERY EASY TO UNDERSTAND!
I'M GLAD YOU THINK SO.
THIS LADYLIKE APPEARANCE OF MINE IS MUCH FAVORED BY MALE CUSTOMERS AS WELL, OF COURSE.
OH, I WOULD THINK SO! I HEARD THAT KAGEMA HOUSES HAVE QUITE A LOT OF MALE CUSTOMERS RECENTLY, ESPECIALLY FROM THE SAMURAI CLASS AND THE TEMPLES!
YES.
TITLES SUCH AS WARRIOR OR MONK MEAN NOTHING IN THE FACE OF CARNAL DESIRE.
WHETHER HE MAY BE THE LORD OF A GREAT FIEFDOM, OR THE CHIEF PRIEST OF A FAMOUS TEMPLE, SCRATCH HIM AND YOU'LL FIND...

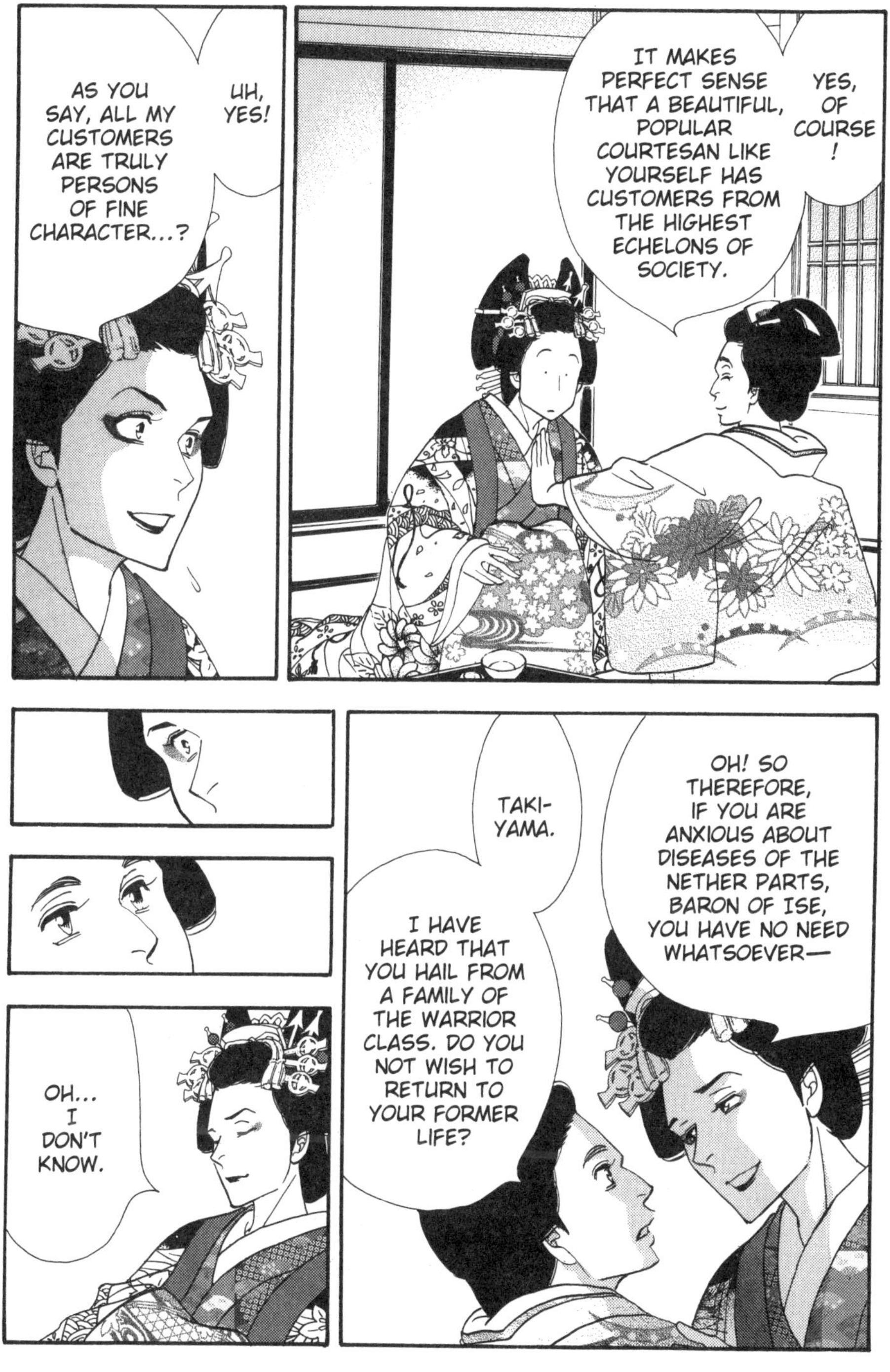
YES, OF COURSE!
IT MAKES PERFECT SENSE THAT A BEAUTIFUL, POPULAR COURTESAN LIKE YOURSELF HAS CUSTOMERS FROM THE HIGHEST ECHELONS OF SOCIETY.
UH, YES!
AS YOU SAY, ALL MY CUSTOMERS ARE TRULY PERSONS OF FINE CHARACTER...?
OH! SO THEREFORE, IF YOU ARE ANXIOUS ABOUT DISEASES OF THE NETHER PARTS, BARON OF ISE, YOU HAVE NO NEED WHATSOEVER—
TAKI-YAMA.
I HAVE HEARD THAT YOU HAIL FROM A FAMILY OF THE WARRIOR CLASS. DO YOU NOT WISH TO RETURN TO YOUR FORMER LIFE?
OH... I DON'T KNOW.

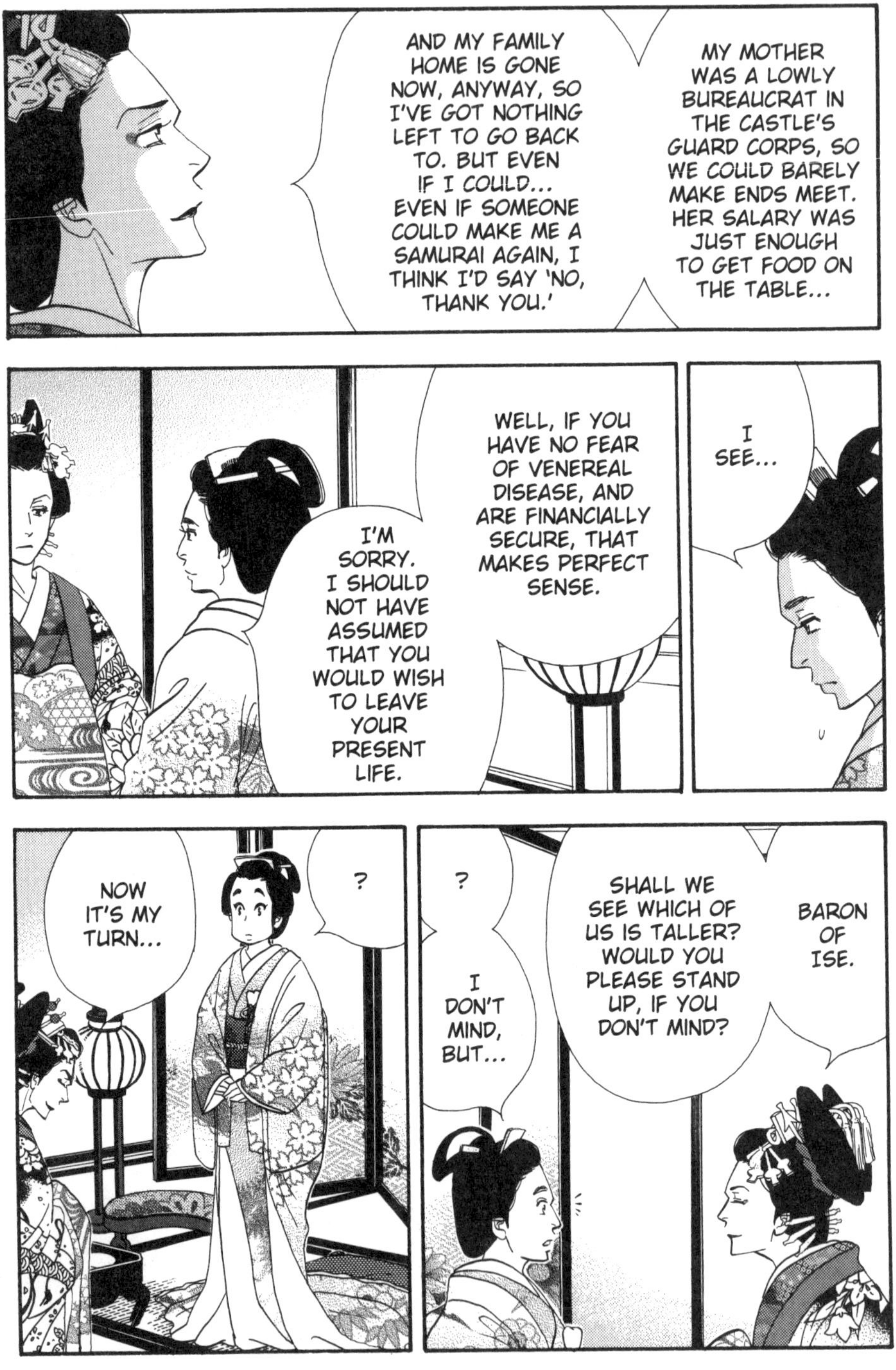
MY MOTHER WAS A LOWLY BUREAUCRAT IN THE CASTLE'S GUARD CORPS, SO WE COULD BARELY MAKE ENDS MEET. HER SALARY WAS JUST ENOUGH TO GET FOOD ON THE TABLE...
AND MY FAMILY HOME IS GONE NOW, ANYWAY, SO I'VE GOT NOTHING LEFT TO GO BACK TO. BUT EVEN IF I COULD... EVEN IF SOMEONE COULD MAKE ME A SAMURAI AGAIN, I THINK I'D SAY 'NO, THANK YOU.'
I SEE...
WELL, IF YOU HAVE NO FEAR OF VENEREAL DISEASE, AND ARE FINANCIALLY SECURE, THAT MAKES PERFECT SENSE.
I'M SORRY. I SHOULD NOT HAVE ASSUMED THAT YOU WOULD WISH TO LEAVE YOUR PRESENT LIFE.
BARON OF ISE.
SHALL WE SEE WHICH OF US IS TALLER? WOULD YOU PLEASE STAND UP, IF YOU DON'T MIND?
?
I DON'T MIND, BUT...
?
NOW IT'S MY TURN...

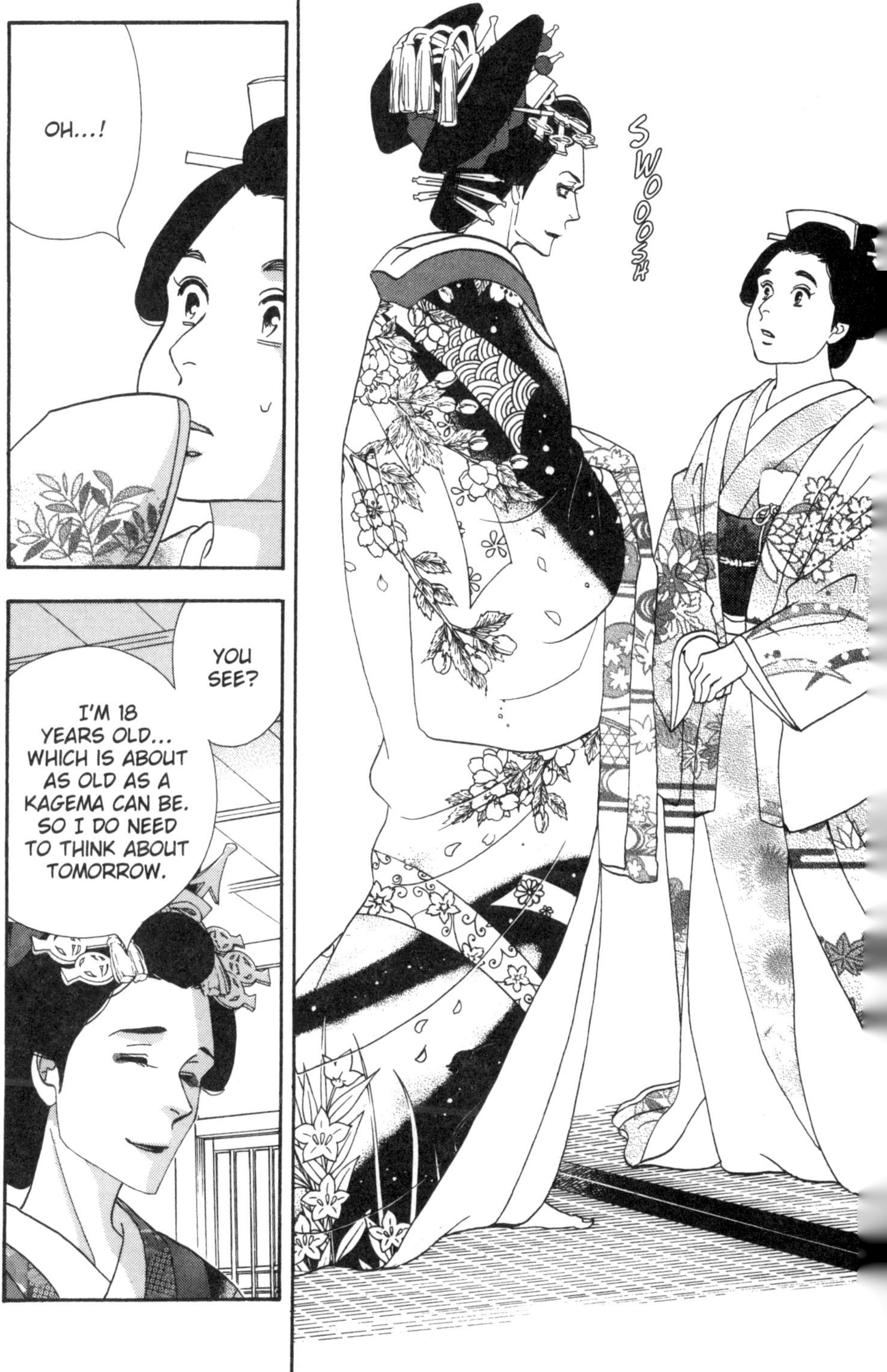
SWOOOSH
OH...!
YOU SEE?
I'M 18 YEARS OLD... WHICH IS ABOUT AS OLD AS A KAGEMA CAN BE. SO I DO NEED TO THINK ABOUT TOMORROW.

WHEN BOYS BECOME MEN, THEIR BODIES HARDEN AND BECOME BRAWNY. THEIR ANUSES GET MORE RIGID AND TIGHT AS WELL, AND THEN THEY'VE BECOME USELESS AS KAGEMA.

IN THE OLD DAYS, WHEN MEN WERE PRECIOUS FROM SCARCITY, SOMEONE LIKE ME COULD HAVE CAUGHT THE NOTICE OF A RICH MERCHANT'S DAUGHTER OR A PROVINCIAL LADY-LORD, AND BEEN MADE THEIR SPOUSE... BUT THERE'S NO CHANCE OF THAT NOW.

NOW, WHEN A KAGEMA HITS THE AGE OF TWENTY AND GETS KICKED OUT OF THE TEAHOUSES, HE'LL STAY INSIDE THE PLEASURE DISTRICT AND GET WORK AS AN ENTERTAINER. NOBODY EVER GETS A STRAIGHT JOB AFTER THIS.

...AND THAT'S WHY I WANT TO MAKE AS MUCH MONEY AS I CAN WHILE I CAN, SO I CAN PAY OFF MY DEBT AND LEAVE THIS PLACE.

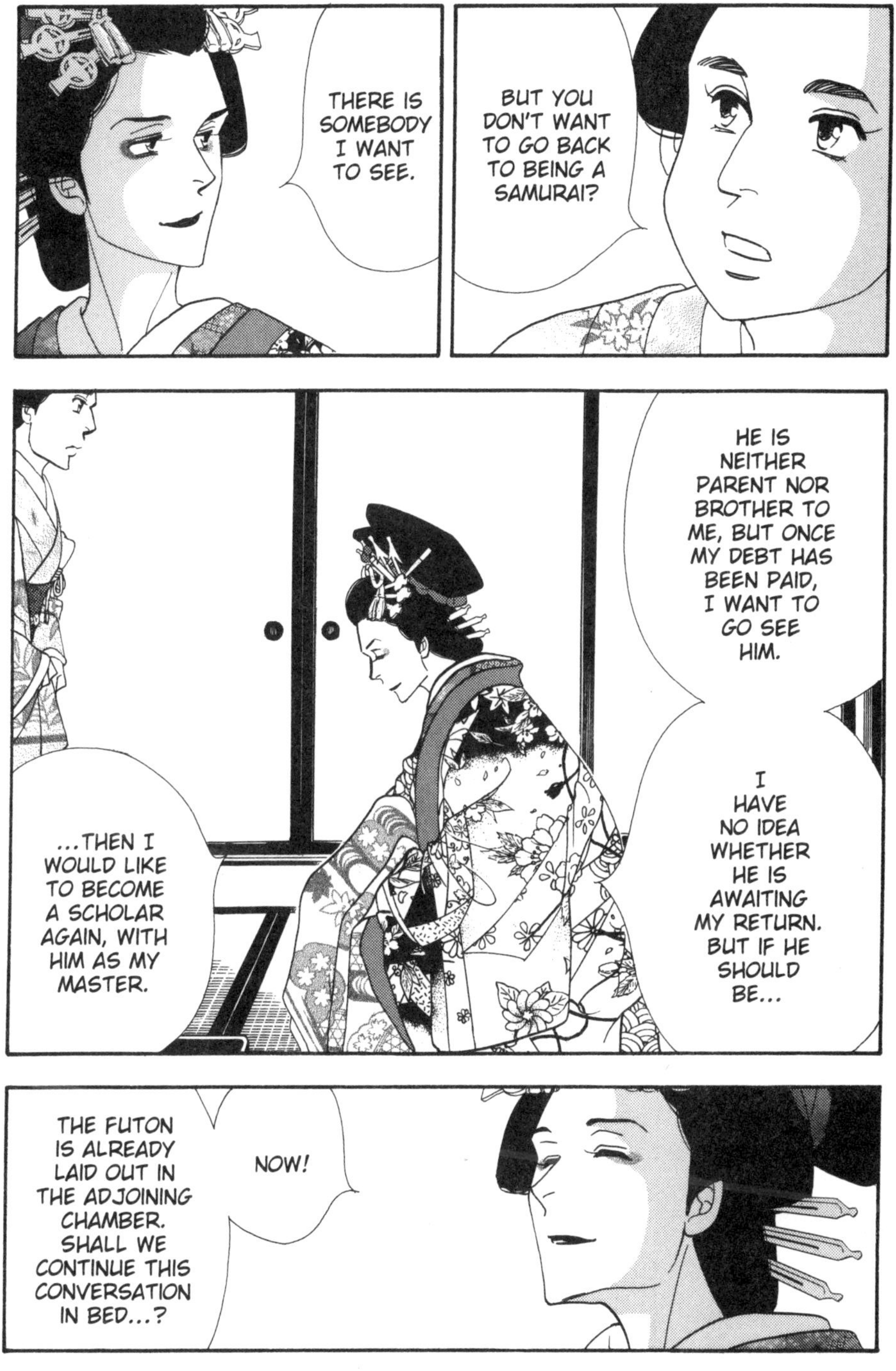
BUT YOU DON'T WANT TO GO BACK TO BEING A SAMURAI?
THERE IS SOMEBODY I WANT TO SEE.
HE IS NEITHER PARENT NOR BROTHER TO ME, BUT ONCE MY DEBT HAS BEEN PAID, I WANT TO GO SEE HIM.
I HAVE NO IDEA WHETHER HE IS AWAITING MY RETURN. BUT IF HE SHOULD BE...
...THEN I WOULD LIKE TO BECOME A SCHOLAR AGAIN, WITH HIM AS MY MASTER.
NOW!
THE FUTON IS ALREADY LAID OUT IN THE ADJOINING CHAMBER. SHALL WE CONTINUE THIS CONVERSATION IN BED...?

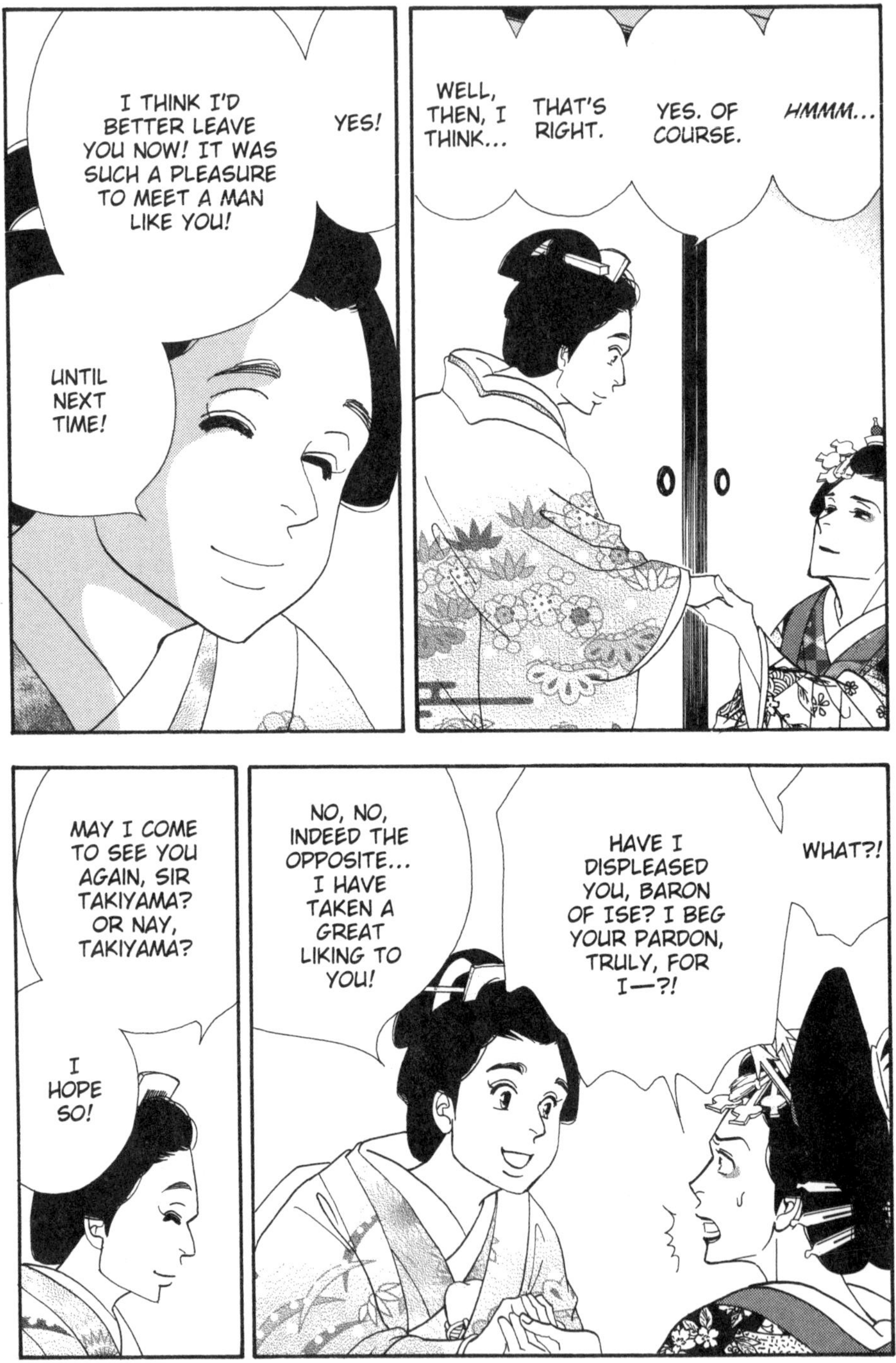
HMMM...
YES. OF COURSE.
THAT'S RIGHT.
WELL, THEN, I THINK...
YES!
I THINK I'D BETTER LEAVE YOU NOW! IT WAS SUCH A PLEASURE TO MEET A MAN LIKE YOU!
UNTIL NEXT TIME!
WHAT?!
HAVE I DISPLEASED YOU, BARON OF ISE? I BEG YOUR PARDON, TRULY, FOR I—?!
NO, NO, INDEED THE OPPOSITE... I HAVE TAKEN A GREAT LIKING TO YOU!
MAY I COME TO SEE YOU AGAIN, SIR TAKIYAMA? OR NAY, TAKIYAMA?
I HOPE SO!

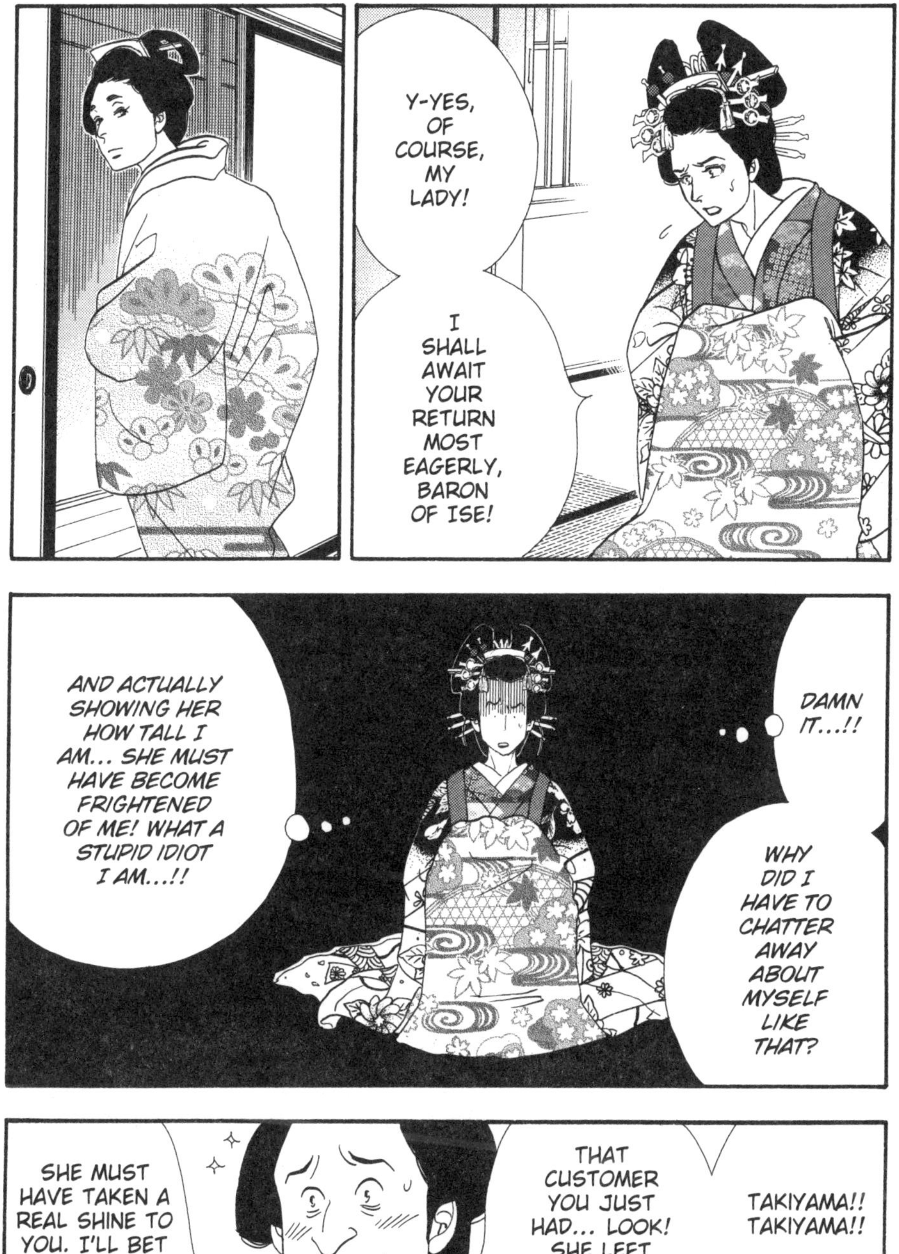
Y-YES, OF COURSE, MY LADY!
I SHALL AWAIT YOUR RETURN MOST EAGERLY, BARON OF ISE!
DAMN IT...!!
WHY DID I HAVE TO CHATTER AWAY ABOUT MYSELF LIKE THAT?
AND ACTUALLY SHOWING HER HOW TALL I AM... SHE MUST HAVE BECOME FRIGHTENED OF ME! WHAT A STUPID IDIOT I AM...!!
TAKIYAMA!! TAKIYAMA!!
THAT CUSTOMER YOU JUST HAD... LOOK! SHE LEFT YOU ALL OF THIS, AS A BONUS...!!
SHE MUST HAVE TAKEN A REAL SHINE TO YOU. I'LL BET SHE BECOMES A REGULAR PATRON!!

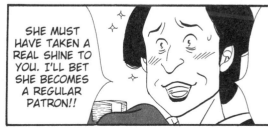

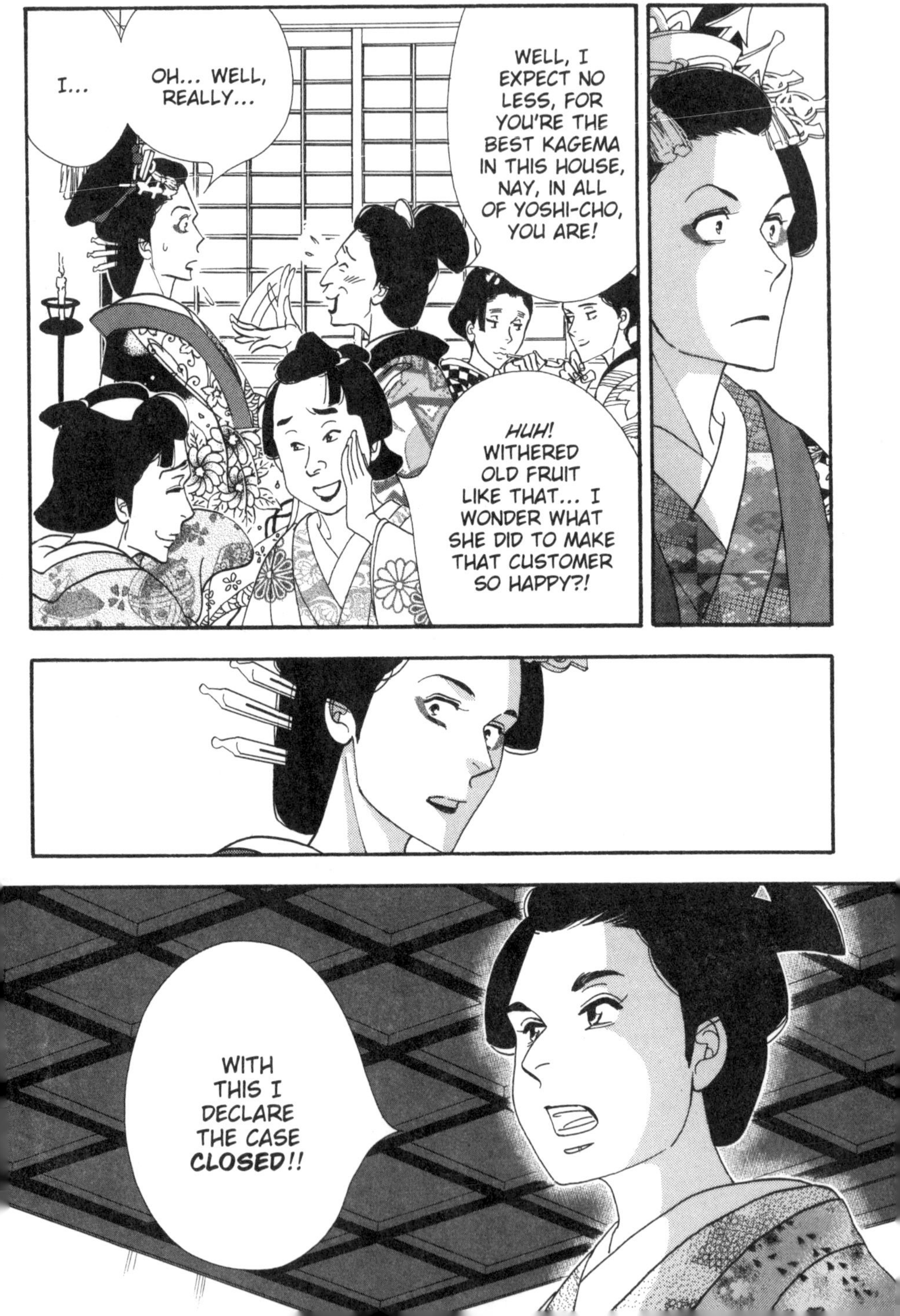
WELL, I EXPECT NO LESS, FOR YOU'RE THE BEST KAGEMA IN THIS HOUSE, NAY, IN ALL OF YOSHI-CHO, YOU ARE!
OH... WELL, REALLY...
I...
HUH! WITHERED OLD FRUIT LIKE THAT... I WONDER WHAT SHE DID TO MAKE THAT CUSTOMER SO HAPPY?!
WITH THIS I DECLARE THE CASE **CLOSED**!!

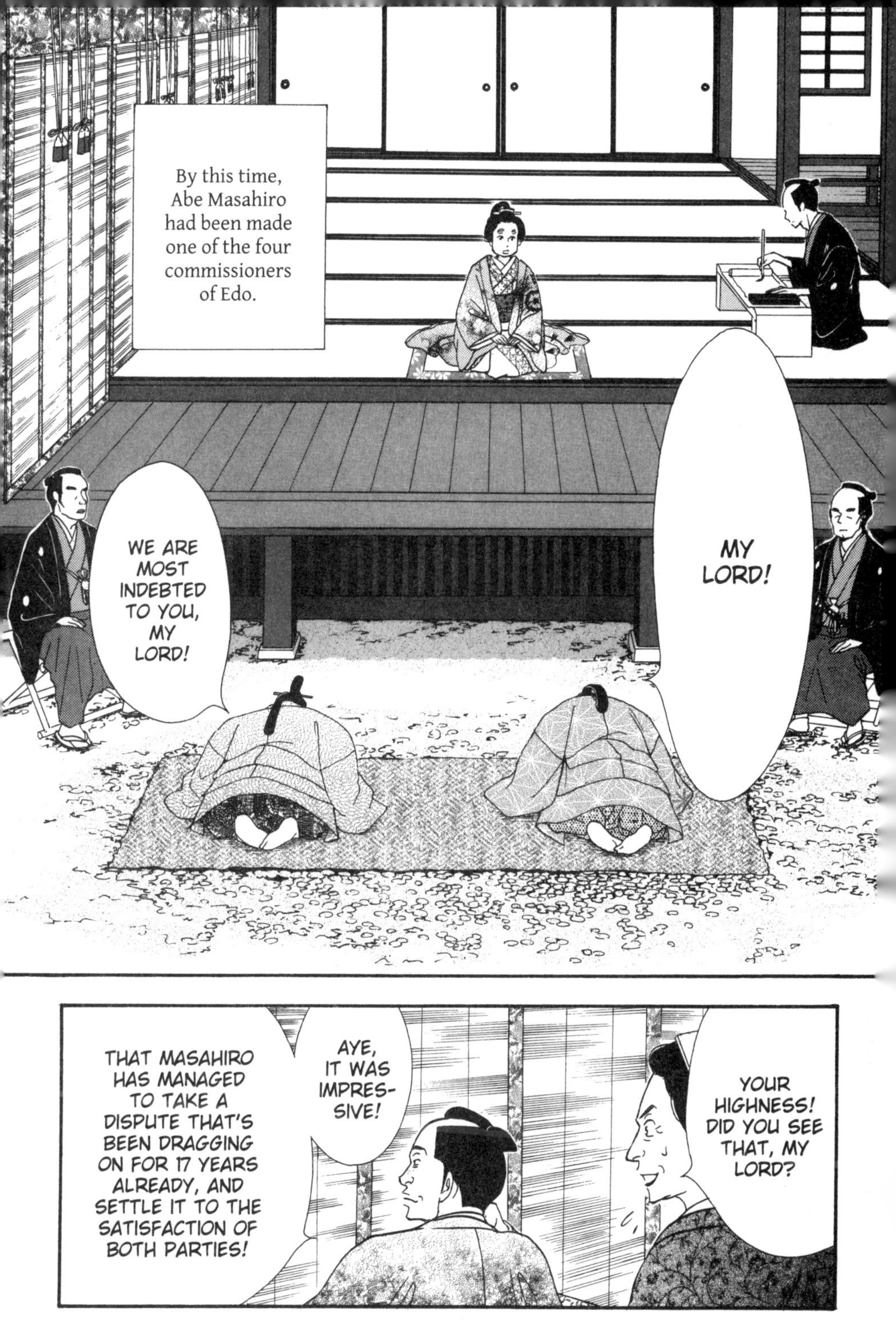
By this time, Abe Masahiro had been made one of the four commissioners of Edo.
MY LORD!
WE ARE MOST INDEBTED TO YOU, MY LORD!
YOUR HIGHNESS! DID YOU SEE THAT, MY LORD?
AYE, IT WAS IMPRES-SIVE!
THAT MASAHIRO HAS MANAGED TO TAKE A DISPUTE THAT'S BEEN DRAGGING ON FOR 17 YEARS ALREADY, AND SETTLE IT TO THE SATISFACTION OF BOTH PARTIES!

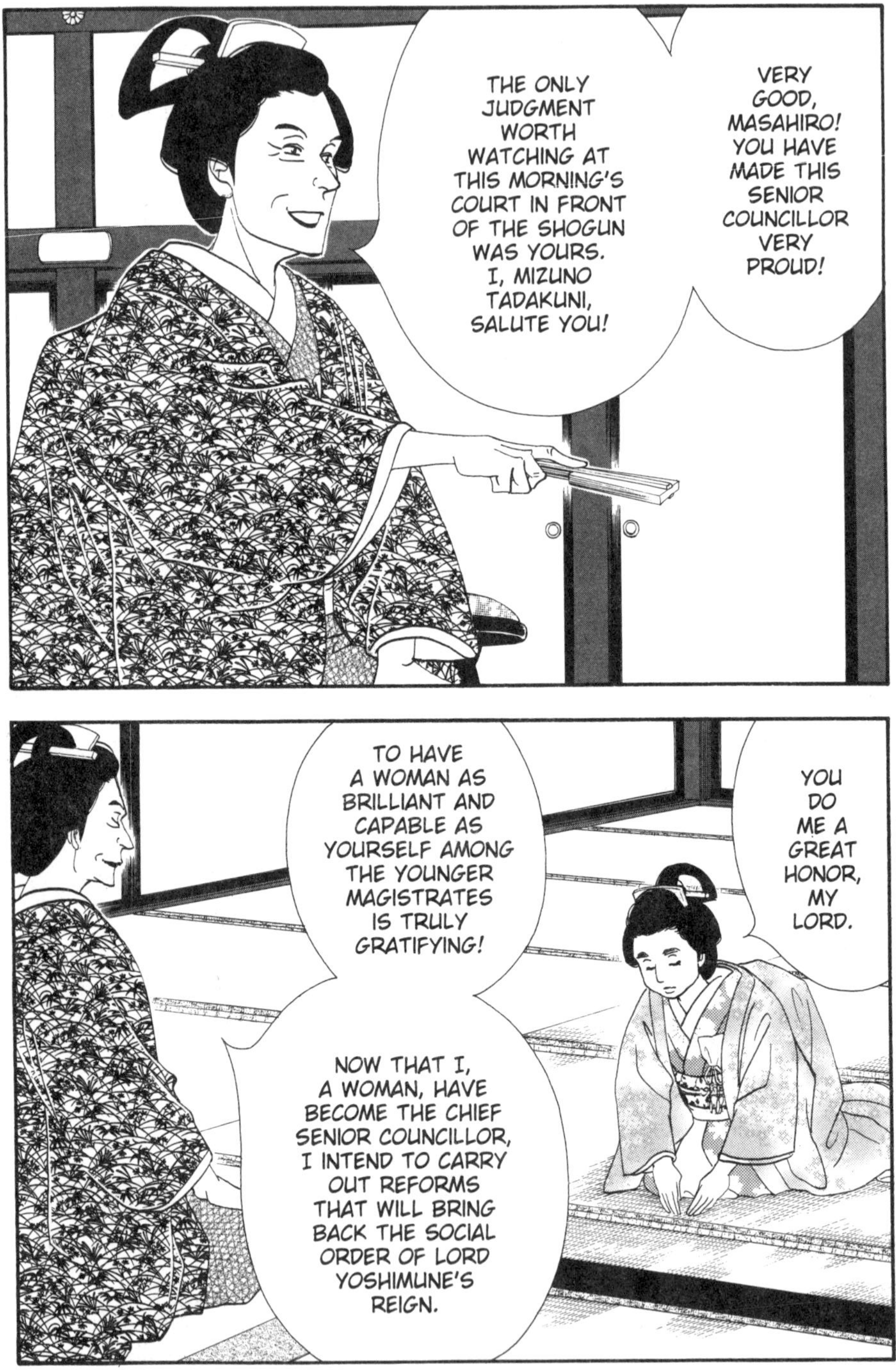
VERY GOOD, MASAHIRO! YOU HAVE MADE THIS SENIOR COUNCILLOR VERY PROUD!
THE ONLY JUDGMENT WORTH WATCHING AT THIS MORNING'S COURT IN FRONT OF THE SHOGUN WAS YOURS. I, MIZUNO TADAKUNI, SALUTE YOU!
YOU DO ME A GREAT HONOR, MY LORD.
TO HAVE A WOMAN AS BRILLIANT AND CAPABLE AS YOURSELF AMONG THE YOUNGER MAGISTRATES IS TRULY GRATIFYING!
NOW THAT I, A WOMAN, HAVE BECOME THE CHIEF SENIOR COUNCILLOR, I INTEND TO CARRY OUT REFORMS THAT WILL BRING BACK THE SOCIAL ORDER OF LORD YOSHIMUNE'S REIGN.

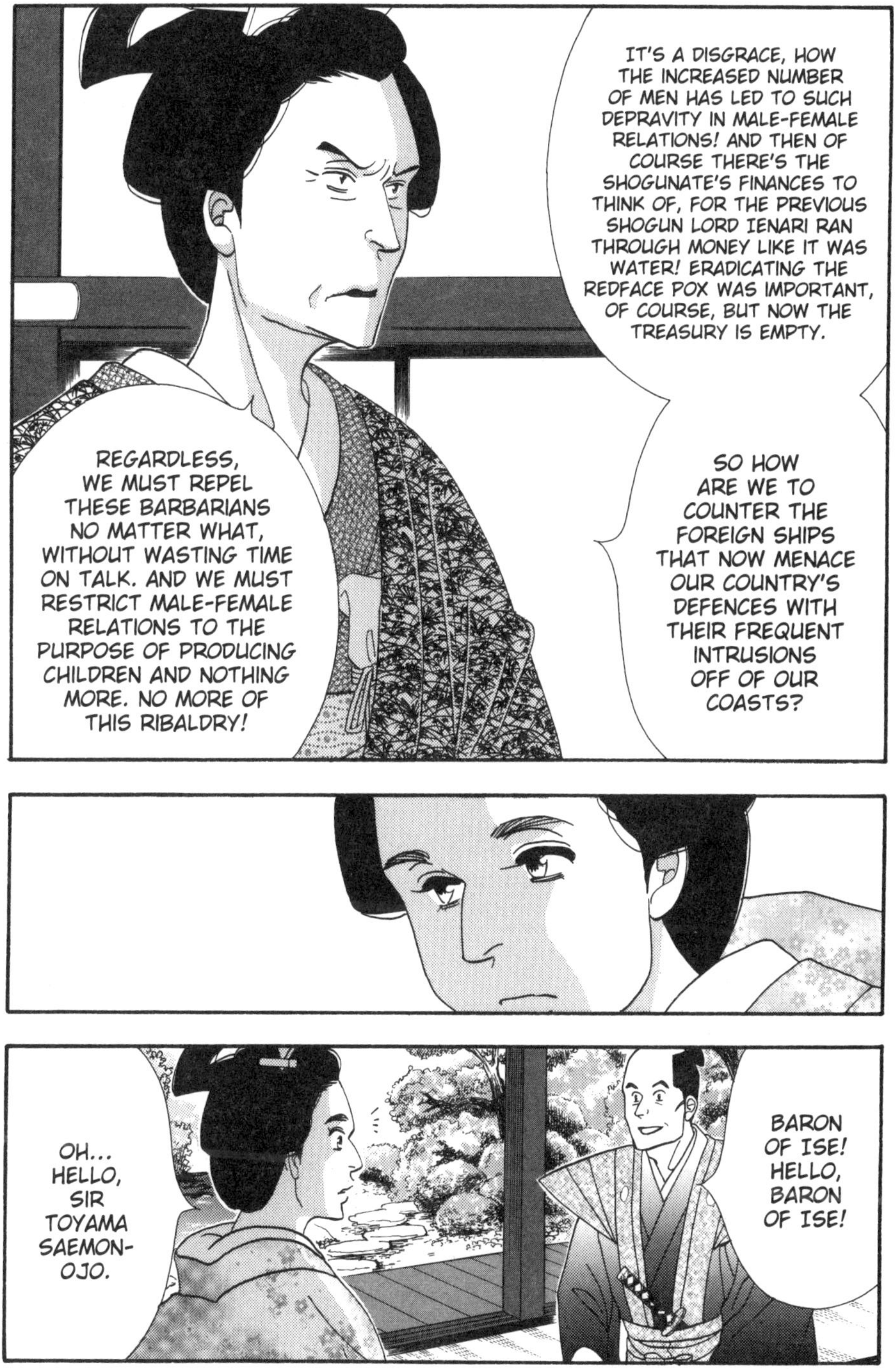
IT'S A DISGRACE, HOW THE INCREASED NUMBER OF MEN HAS LED TO SUCH DEPRAVITY IN MALE-FEMALE RELATIONS! AND THEN OF COURSE THERE'S THE SHOGUNATE'S FINANCES TO THINK OF, FOR THE PREVIOUS SHOGUN LORD IENARI RAN THROUGH MONEY LIKE IT WAS WATER! ERADICATING THE REDFACE POX WAS IMPORTANT, OF COURSE, BUT NOW THE TREASURY IS EMPTY.
SO HOW ARE WE TO COUNTER THE FOREIGN SHIPS THAT NOW MENACE OUR COUNTRY'S DEFENCES WITH THEIR FREQUENT INTRUSIONS OFF OF OUR COASTS?
REGARDLESS, WE MUST REPEL THESE BARBARIANS NO MATTER WHAT, WITHOUT WASTING TIME ON TALK. AND WE MUST RESTRICT MALE-FEMALE RELATIONS TO THE PURPOSE OF PRODUCING CHILDREN AND NOTHING MORE. NO MORE OF THIS RIBALDRY!
BARON OF ISE! HELLO, BARON OF ISE!
OH... HELLO, SIR TOYAMA SAEMON-OJO.

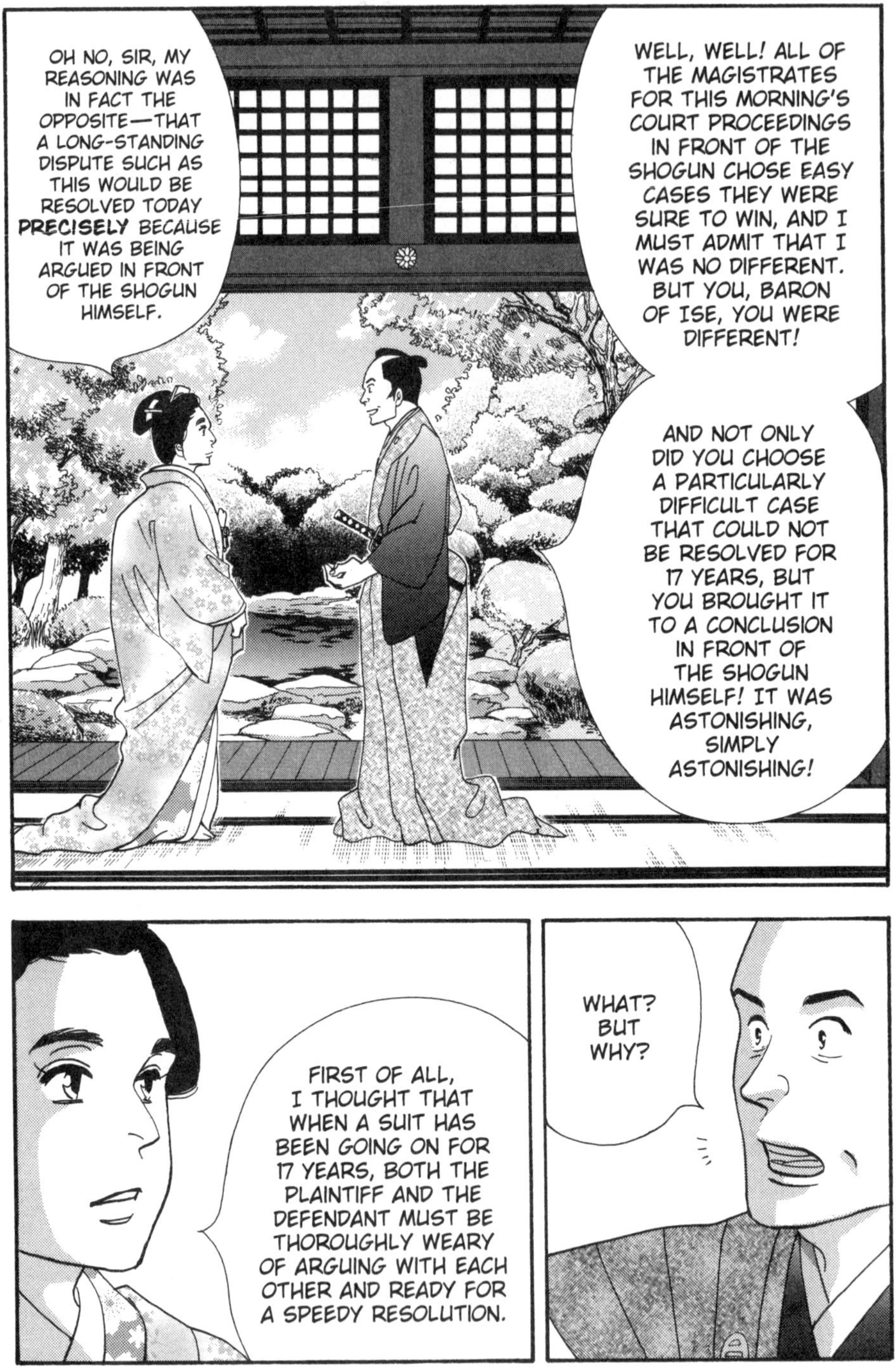
WELL, WELL! ALL OF THE MAGISTRATES FOR THIS MORNING'S COURT PROCEEDINGS IN FRONT OF THE SHOGUN CHOSE EASY CASES THEY WERE SURE TO WIN, AND I MUST ADMIT THAT I WAS NO DIFFERENT. BUT YOU, BARON OF ISE, YOU WERE DIFFERENT!
AND NOT ONLY DID YOU CHOOSE A PARTICULARLY DIFFICULT CASE THAT COULD NOT BE RESOLVED FOR 17 YEARS, BUT YOU BROUGHT IT TO A CONCLUSION IN FRONT OF THE SHOGUN HIMSELF! IT WAS ASTONISHING, SIMPLY ASTONISHING!
OH NO, SIR, MY REASONING WAS IN FACT THE OPPOSITE—THAT A LONG-STANDING DISPUTE SUCH AS THIS WOULD BE RESOLVED TODAY **PRECISELY** BECAUSE IT WAS BEING ARGUED IN FRONT OF THE SHOGUN HIMSELF.
WHAT? BUT WHY?
FIRST OF ALL, I THOUGHT THAT WHEN A SUIT HAS BEEN GOING ON FOR 17 YEARS, BOTH THE PLAINTIFF AND THE DEFENDANT MUST BE THOROUGHLY WEARY OF ARGUING WITH EACH OTHER AND READY FOR A SPEEDY RESOLUTION.

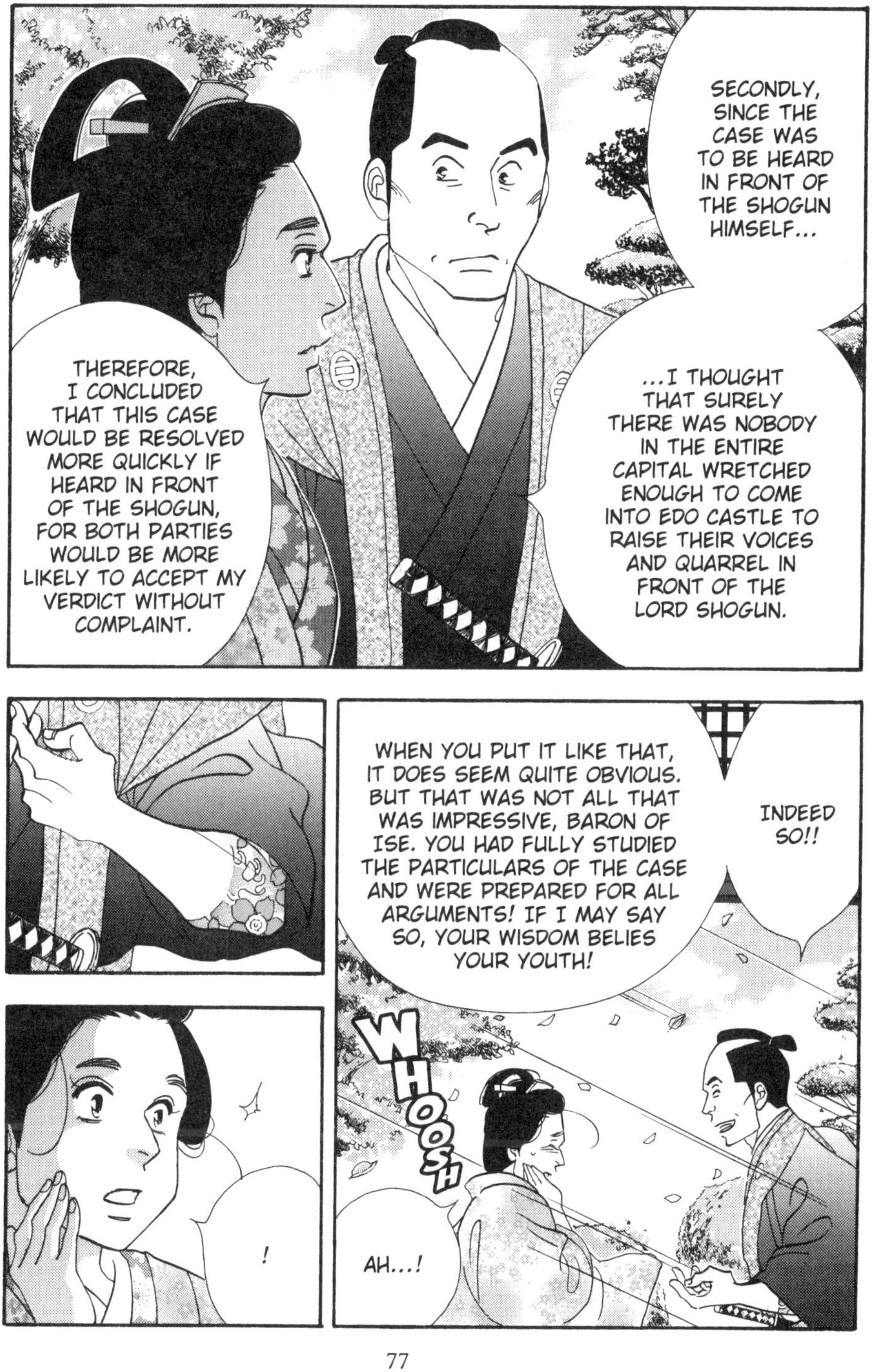
SECONDLY, SINCE THE CASE WAS TO BE HEARD IN FRONT OF THE SHOGUN HIMSELF...
...I THOUGHT THAT SURELY THERE WAS NOBODY IN THE ENTIRE CAPITAL WRETCHED ENOUGH TO COME INTO EDO CASTLE TO RAISE THEIR VOICES AND QUARREL IN FRONT OF THE LORD SHOGUN.
THEREFORE, I CONCLUDED THAT THIS CASE WOULD BE RESOLVED MORE QUICKLY IF HEARD IN FRONT OF THE SHOGUN, FOR BOTH PARTIES WOULD BE MORE LIKELY TO ACCEPT MY VERDICT WITHOUT COMPLAINT.
INDEED SO!!
WHEN YOU PUT IT LIKE THAT, IT DOES SEEM QUITE OBVIOUS. BUT THAT WAS NOT ALL THAT WAS IMPRESSIVE, BARON OF ISE. YOU HAD FULLY STUDIED THE PARTICULARS OF THE CASE AND WERE PREPARED FOR ALL ARGUMENTS! IF I MAY SAY SO, YOUR WISDOM BELIES YOUR YOUTH!
WHOOSH
AH...!
!

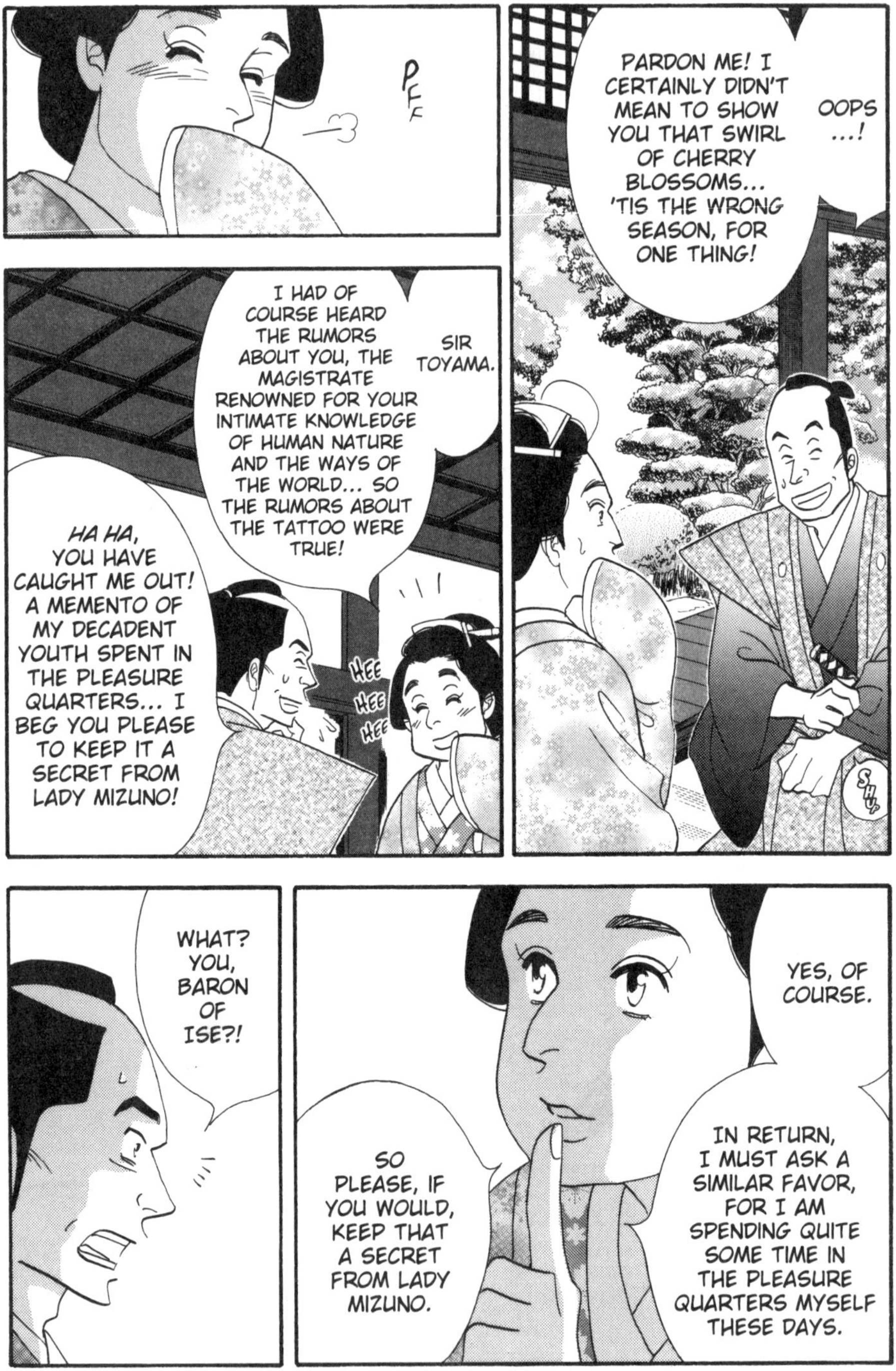
OOPS ...!
PARDON ME! I CERTAINLY DIDN'T MEAN TO SHOW YOU THAT SWIRL OF CHERRY BLOSSOMS... 'TIS THE WRONG SEASON, FOR ONE THING!
SHUP
PFF
SIR TOYAMA.
I HAD OF COURSE HEARD THE RUMORS ABOUT YOU, THE MAGISTRATE RENOWNED FOR YOUR INTIMATE KNOWLEDGE OF HUMAN NATURE AND THE WAYS OF THE WORLD... SO THE RUMORS ABOUT THE TATTOO WERE TRUE!
HEE HEE HEE
HA HA, YOU HAVE CAUGHT ME OUT! A MEMENTO OF MY DECADENT YOUTH SPENT IN THE PLEASURE QUARTERS... I BEG YOU PLEASE TO KEEP IT A SECRET FROM LADY MIZUNO!
YES, OF COURSE.
IN RETURN, I MUST ASK A SIMILAR FAVOR, FOR I AM SPENDING QUITE SOME TIME IN THE PLEASURE QUARTERS MYSELF THESE DAYS.
SO PLEASE, IF YOU WOULD, KEEP THAT A SECRET FROM LADY MIZUNO.
WHAT? YOU, BARON OF ISE?!

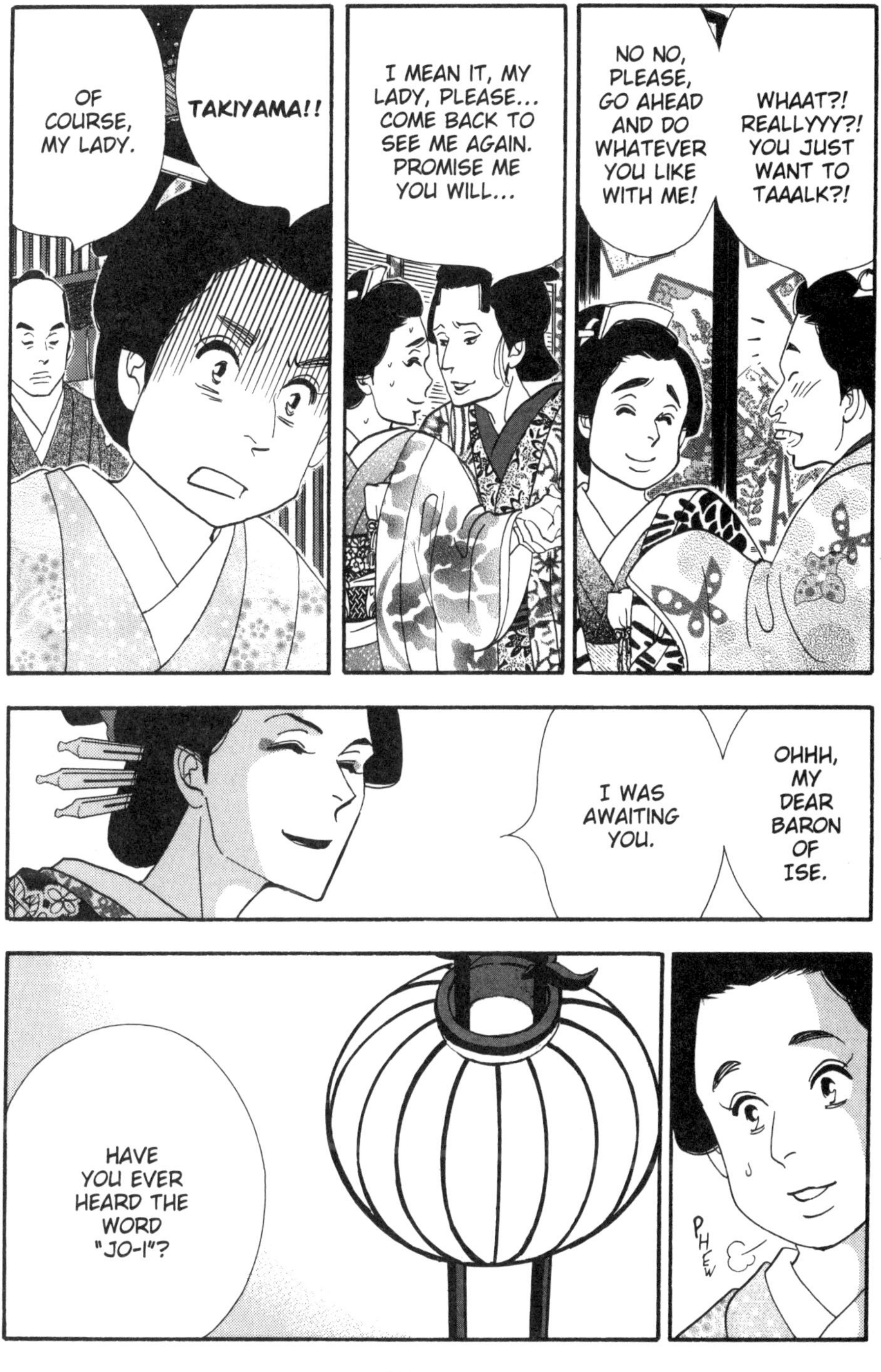
WHAAT?! REALLYYY?! YOU JUST WANT TO TAAALK?!
NO NO, PLEASE, GO AHEAD AND DO WHATEVER YOU LIKE WITH ME!
I MEAN IT, MY LADY, PLEASE... COME BACK TO SEE ME AGAIN. PROMISE ME YOU WILL...
TAKIYAMA!!
OF COURSE, MY LADY.
OHHH, MY DEAR BARON OF ISE.
I WAS AWAITING YOU.
PHEW
HAVE YOU EVER HEARD THE WORD "JO-I"?

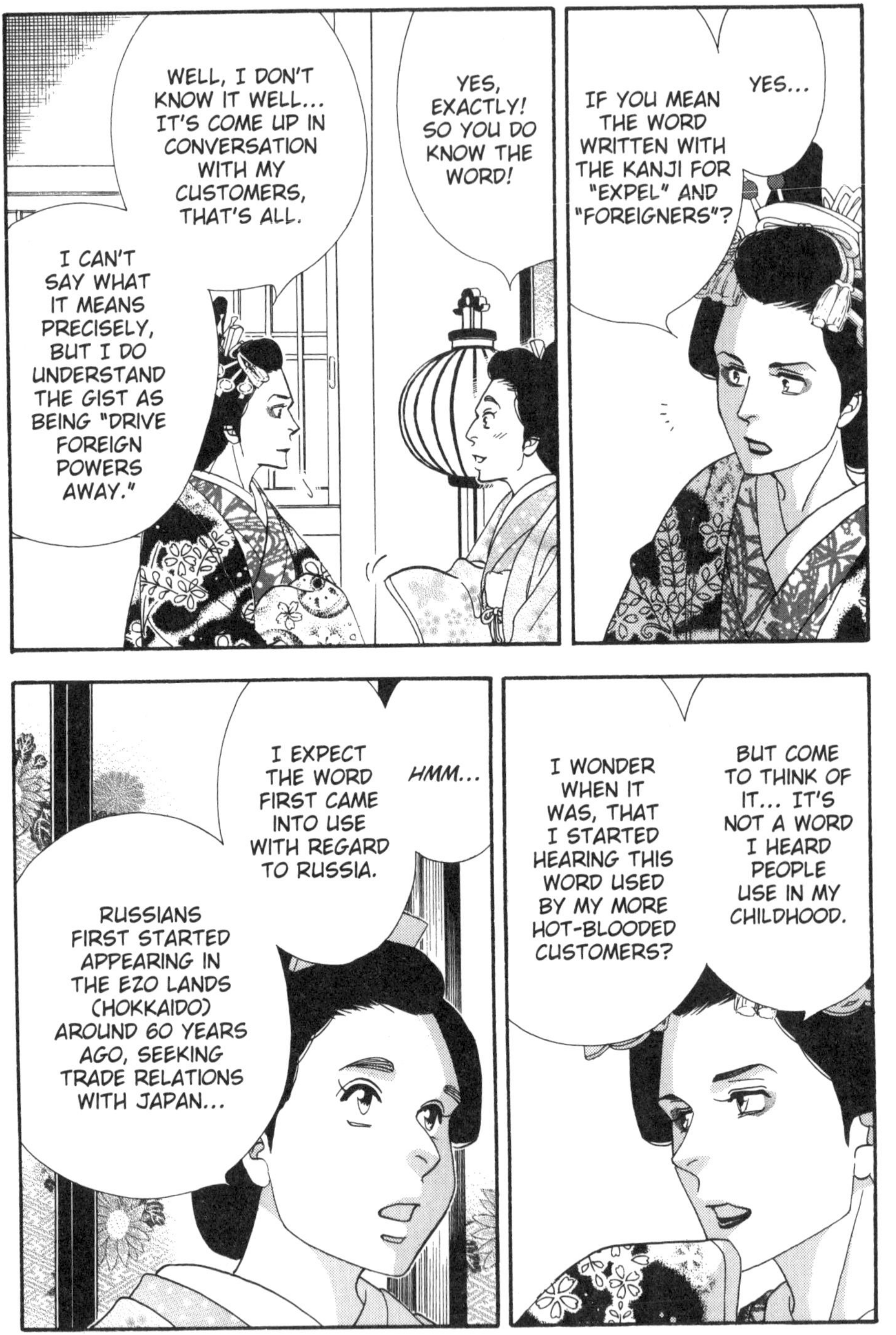
YES...
IF YOU MEAN THE WORD WRITTEN WITH THE KANJI FOR "EXPEL" AND "FOREIGNERS"?
YES, EXACTLY! SO YOU DO KNOW THE WORD!
WELL, I DON'T KNOW IT WELL... IT'S COME UP IN CONVERSATION WITH MY CUSTOMERS, THAT'S ALL.
I CAN'T SAY WHAT IT MEANS PRECISELY, BUT I DO UNDERSTAND THE GIST AS BEING "DRIVE FOREIGN POWERS AWAY."
BUT COME TO THINK OF IT... IT'S NOT A WORD I HEARD PEOPLE USE IN MY CHILDHOOD.
I WONDER WHEN IT WAS, THAT I STARTED HEARING THIS WORD USED BY MY MORE HOT-BLOODED CUSTOMERS?
HMM...
I EXPECT THE WORD FIRST CAME INTO USE WITH REGARD TO RUSSIA.
RUSSIANS FIRST STARTED APPEARING IN THE EZO LANDS (HOKKAIDO) AROUND 60 YEARS AGO, SEEKING TRADE RELATIONS WITH JAPAN...

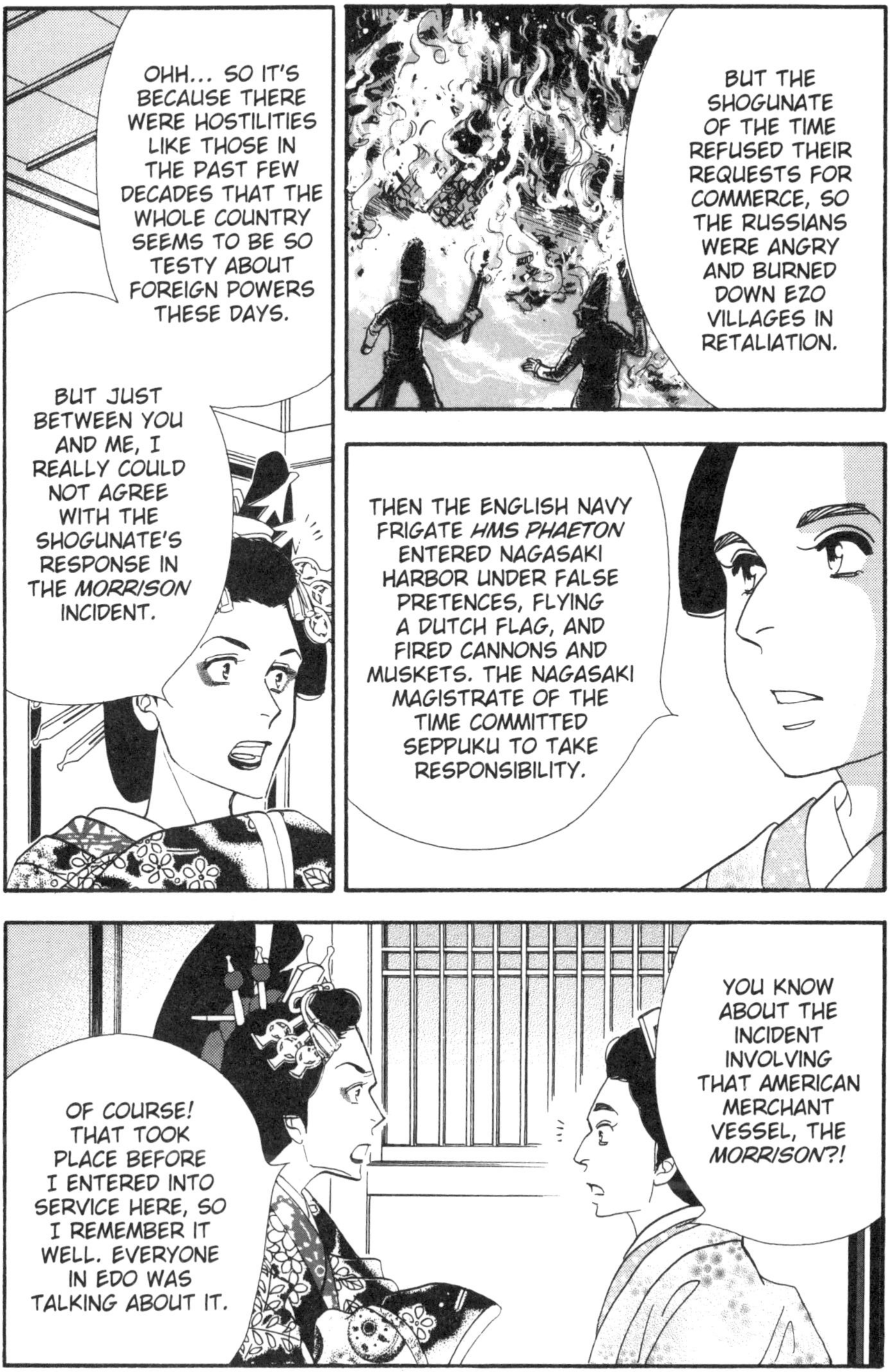
BUT THE SHOGUNATE OF THE TIME REFUSED THEIR REQUESTS FOR COMMERCE, SO THE RUSSIANS WERE ANGRY AND BURNED DOWN EZO VILLAGES IN RETALIATION.
THEN THE ENGLISH NAVY FRIGATE *HMS PHAETON* ENTERED NAGASAKI HARBOR UNDER FALSE PRETENCES, FLYING A DUTCH FLAG, AND FIRED CANNONS AND MUSKETS. THE NAGASAKI MAGISTRATE OF THE TIME COMMITTED SEPPUKU TO TAKE RESPONSIBILITY.
OHH... SO IT'S BECAUSE THERE WERE HOSTILITIES LIKE THOSE IN THE PAST FEW DECADES THAT THE WHOLE COUNTRY SEEMS TO BE SO TESTY ABOUT FOREIGN POWERS THESE DAYS.
BUT JUST BETWEEN YOU AND ME, I REALLY COULD NOT AGREE WITH THE SHOGUNATE'S RESPONSE IN THE *MORRISON* INCIDENT.
YOU KNOW ABOUT THE INCIDENT INVOLVING THAT AMERICAN MERCHANT VESSEL, THE *MORRISON*?!
OF COURSE! THAT TOOK PLACE BEFORE I ENTERED INTO SERVICE HERE, SO I REMEMBER IT WELL. EVERYONE IN EDO WAS TALKING ABOUT IT.

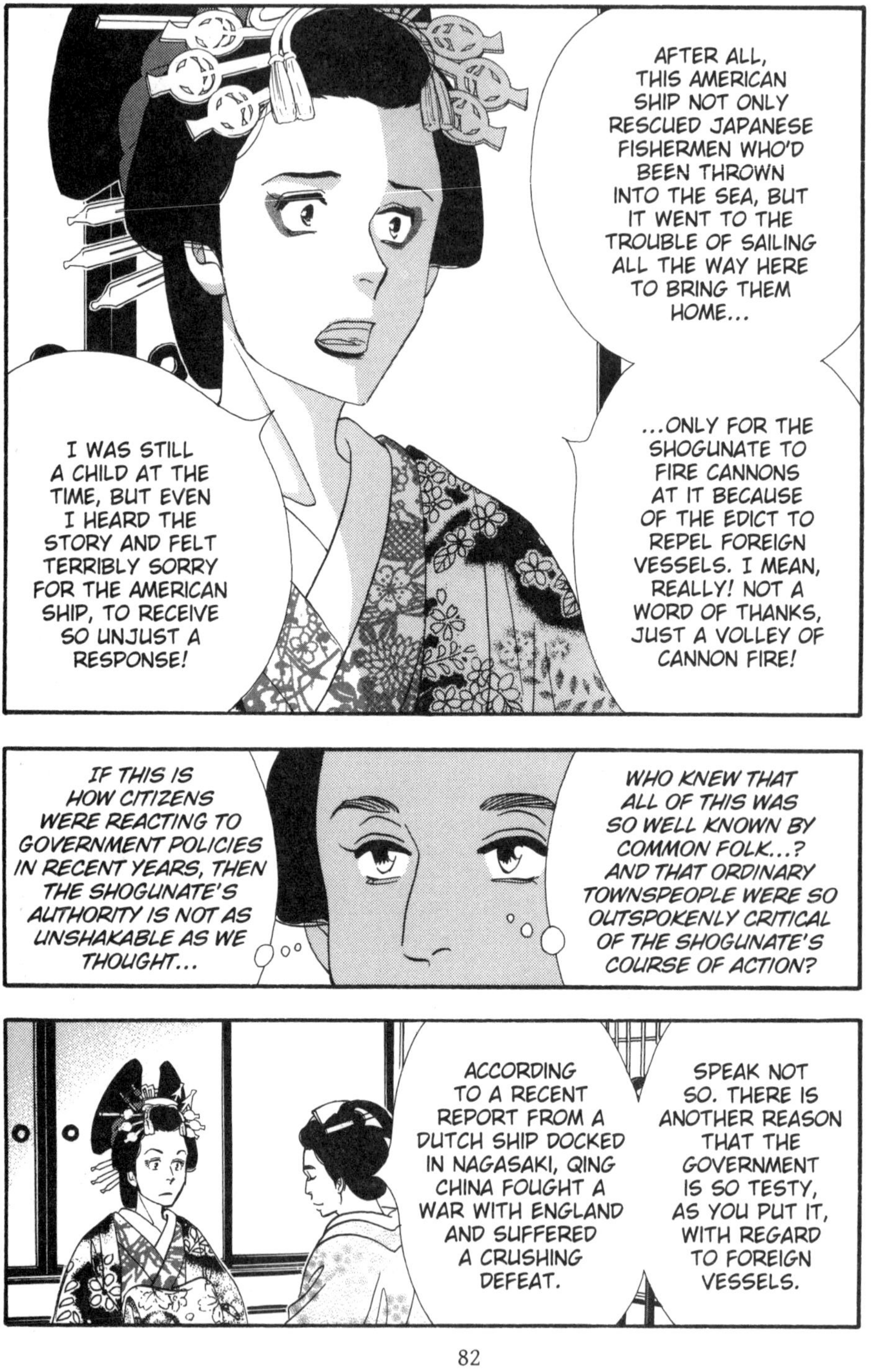
AFTER ALL, THIS AMERICAN SHIP NOT ONLY RESCUED JAPANESE FISHERMEN WHO'D BEEN THROWN INTO THE SEA, BUT IT WENT TO THE TROUBLE OF SAILING ALL THE WAY HERE TO BRING THEM HOME...
...ONLY FOR THE SHOGUNATE TO FIRE CANNONS AT IT BECAUSE OF THE EDICT TO REPEL FOREIGN VESSELS. I MEAN, REALLY! NOT A WORD OF THANKS, JUST A VOLLEY OF CANNON FIRE!
I WAS STILL A CHILD AT THE TIME, BUT EVEN I HEARD THE STORY AND FELT TERRIBLY SORRY FOR THE AMERICAN SHIP, TO RECEIVE SO UNJUST A RESPONSE!
WHO KNEW THAT ALL OF THIS WAS SO WELL KNOWN BY COMMON FOLK...? AND THAT ORDINARY TOWNSPEOPLE WERE SO OUTSPOKENLY CRITICAL OF THE SHOGUNATE'S COURSE OF ACTION?
IF THIS IS HOW CITIZENS WERE REACTING TO GOVERNMENT POLICIES IN RECENT YEARS, THEN THE SHOGUNATE'S AUTHORITY IS NOT AS UNSHAKABLE AS WE THOUGHT...
SPEAK NOT SO. THERE IS ANOTHER REASON THAT THE GOVERNMENT IS SO TESTY, AS YOU PUT IT, WITH REGARD TO FOREIGN VESSELS.
ACCORDING TO A RECENT REPORT FROM A DUTCH SHIP DOCKED IN NAGASAKI, QING CHINA FOUGHT A WAR WITH ENGLAND AND SUFFERED A CRUSHING DEFEAT.

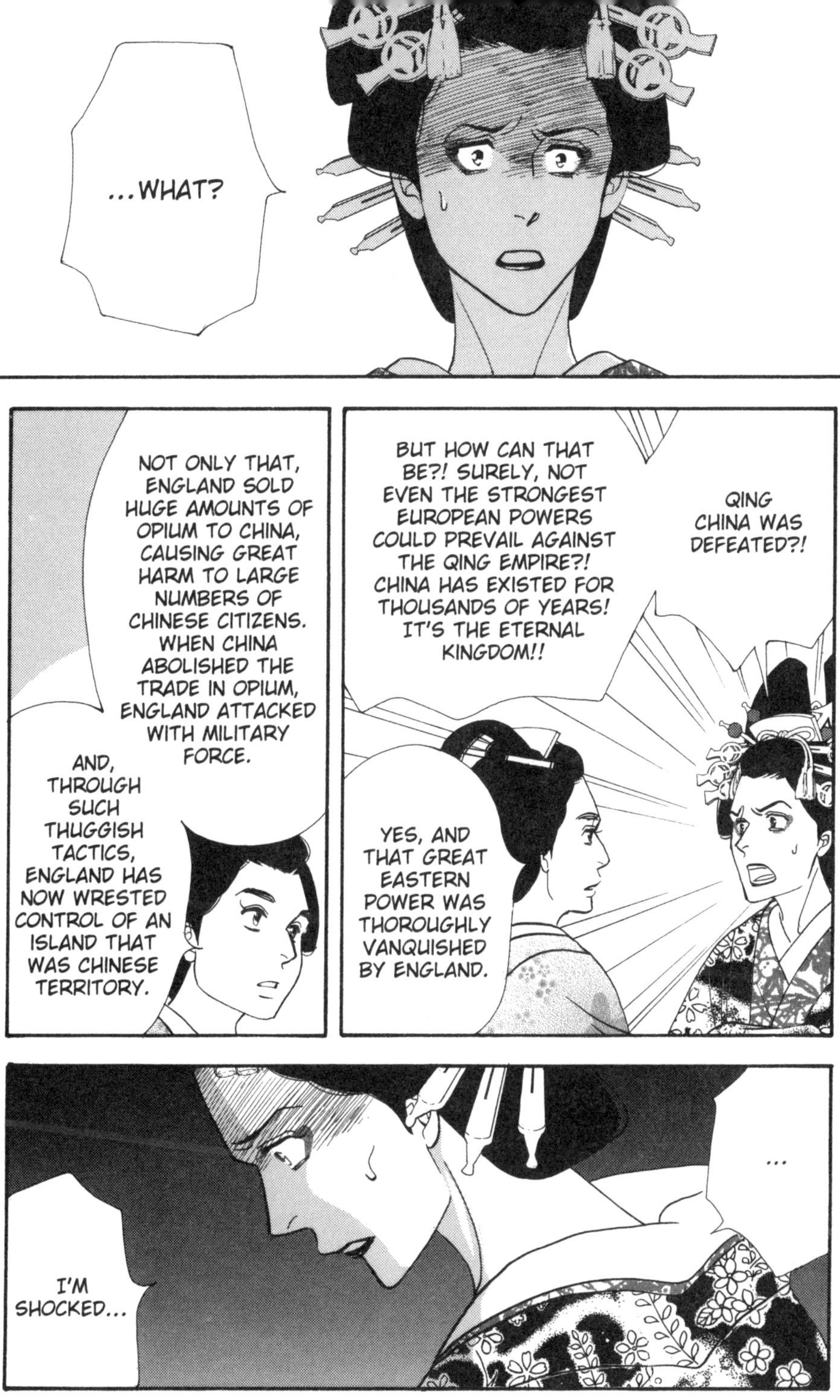
...WHAT?
QING CHINA WAS DEFEATED?!
BUT HOW CAN THAT BE?! SURELY, NOT EVEN THE STRONGEST EUROPEAN POWERS COULD PREVAIL AGAINST THE QING EMPIRE?! CHINA HAS EXISTED FOR THOUSANDS OF YEARS! IT'S THE ETERNAL KINGDOM!!
YES, AND THAT GREAT EASTERN POWER WAS THOROUGHLY VANQUISHED BY ENGLAND.
NOT ONLY THAT, ENGLAND SOLD HUGE AMOUNTS OF OPIUM TO CHINA, CAUSING GREAT HARM TO LARGE NUMBERS OF CHINESE CITIZENS. WHEN CHINA ABOLISHED THE TRADE IN OPIUM, ENGLAND ATTACKED WITH MILITARY FORCE.
AND, THROUGH SUCH THUGGISH TACTICS, ENGLAND HAS NOW WRESTED CONTROL OF AN ISLAND THAT WAS CHINESE TERRITORY.
...
I'M SHOCKED...

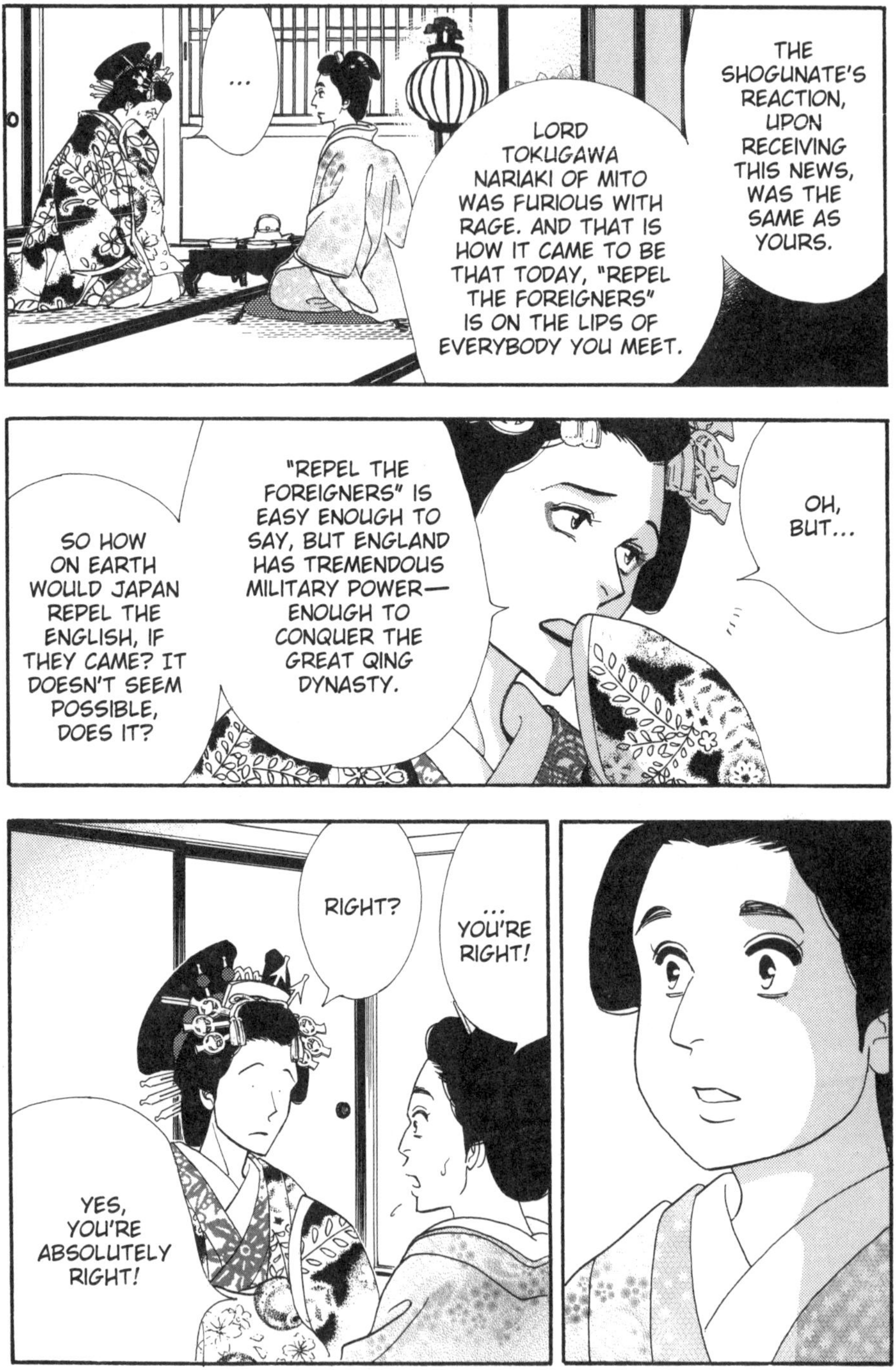
THE SHOGUNATE'S REACTION, UPON RECEIVING THIS NEWS, WAS THE SAME AS YOURS.
LORD TOKUGAWA NARIAKI OF MITO WAS FURIOUS WITH RAGE. AND THAT IS HOW IT CAME TO BE THAT TODAY, "REPEL THE FOREIGNERS" IS ON THE LIPS OF EVERYBODY YOU MEET.
...
OH, BUT...
"REPEL THE FOREIGNERS" IS EASY ENOUGH TO SAY, BUT ENGLAND HAS TREMENDOUS MILITARY POWER—ENOUGH TO CONQUER THE GREAT QING DYNASTY.
SO HOW ON EARTH WOULD JAPAN REPEL THE ENGLISH, IF THEY CAME? IT DOESN'T SEEM POSSIBLE, DOES IT?
RIGHT?
... YOU'RE RIGHT!
YES, YOU'RE ABSOLUTELY RIGHT!

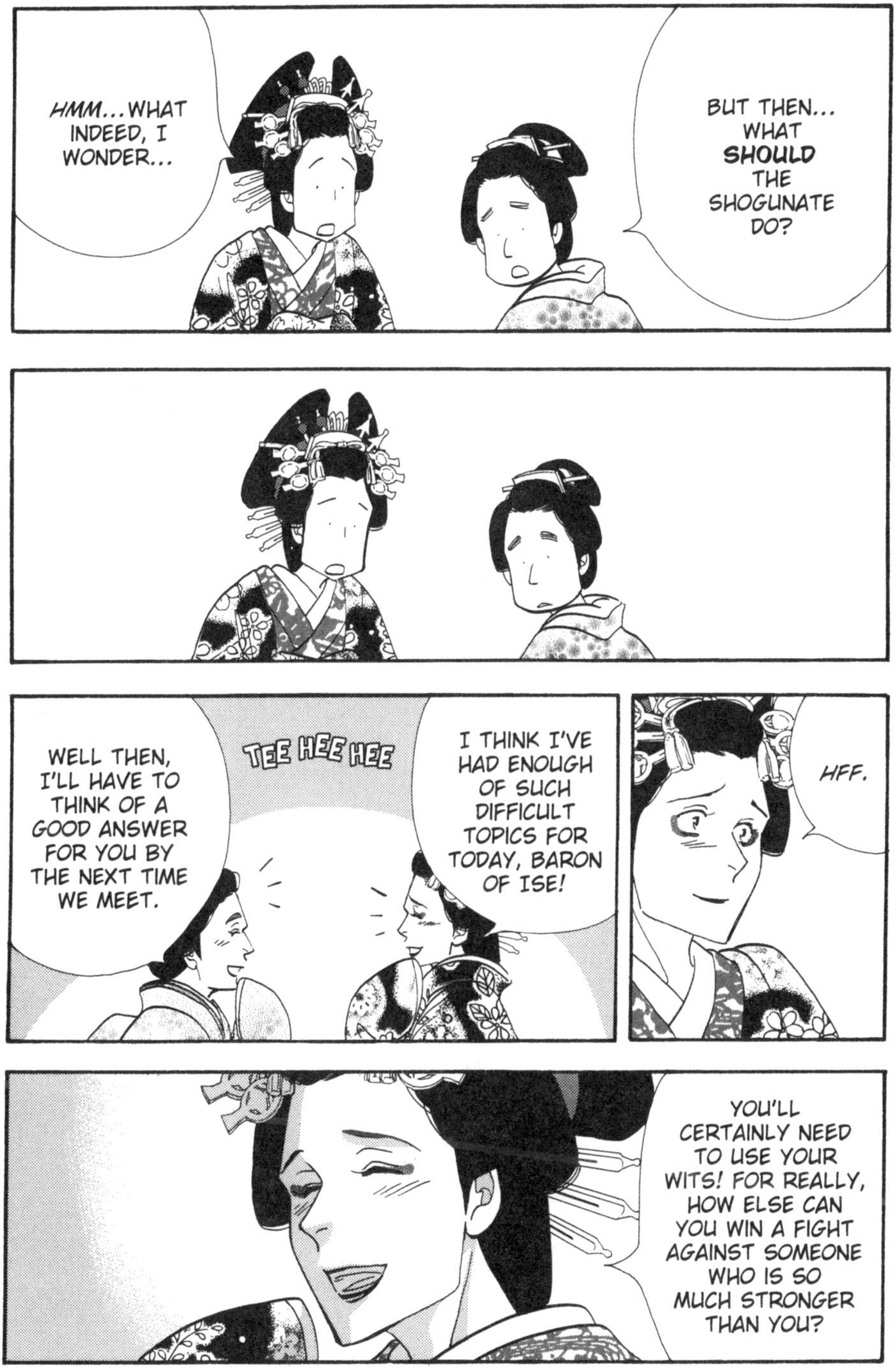
BUT THEN... WHAT **SHOULD** THE SHOGUNATE DO?
HMM...WHAT INDEED, I WONDER...
HFF.
I THINK I'VE HAD ENOUGH OF SUCH DIFFICULT TOPICS FOR TODAY, BARON OF ISE!
TEE HEE HEE
WELL THEN, I'LL HAVE TO THINK OF A GOOD ANSWER FOR YOU BY THE NEXT TIME WE MEET.
YOU'LL CERTAINLY NEED TO USE YOUR WITS! FOR REALLY, HOW ELSE CAN YOU WIN A FIGHT AGAINST SOMEONE WHO IS SO MUCH STRONGER THAN YOU?

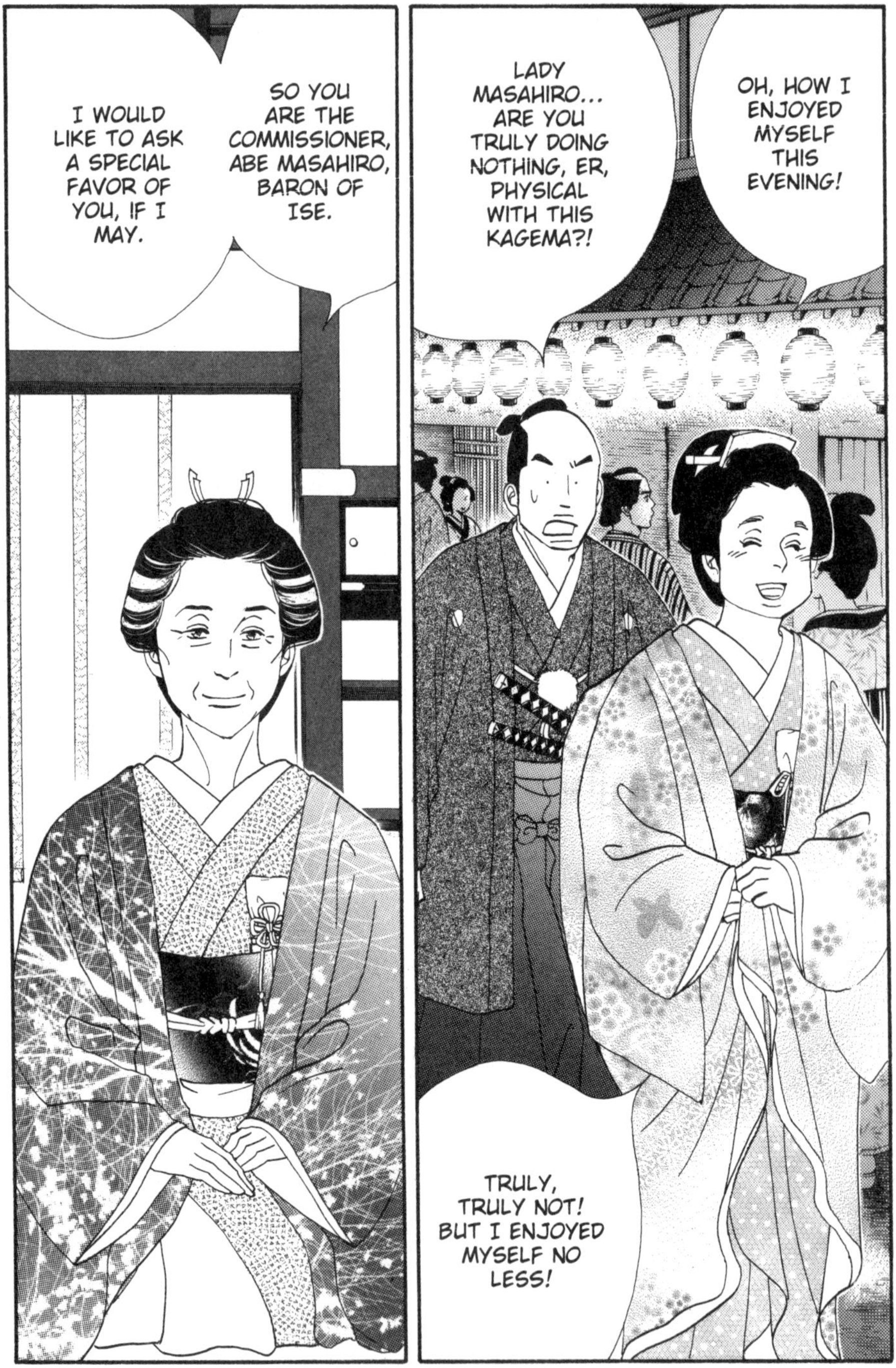
OH, HOW I ENJOYED MYSELF THIS EVENING!
LADY MASAHIRO... ARE YOU TRULY DOING NOTHING, ER, PHYSICAL WITH THIS KAGEMA?!
TRULY, TRULY NOT! BUT I ENJOYED MYSELF NO LESS!
SO YOU ARE THE COMMISSIONER, ABE MASAHIRO, BARON OF ISE.
I WOULD LIKE TO ASK A SPECIAL FAVOR OF YOU, IF I MAY.

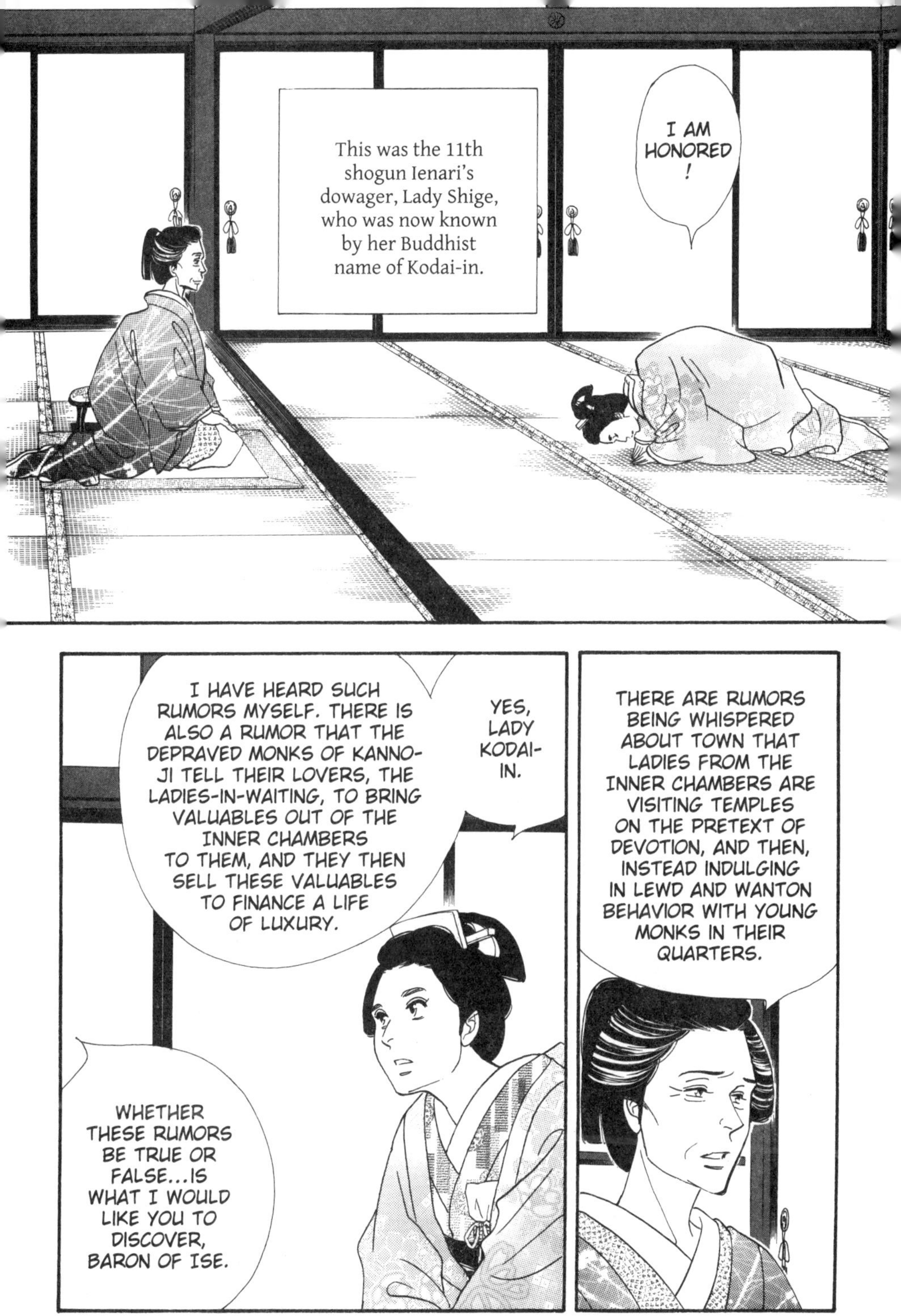
I AM HONORED!
This was the 11th shogun Ienari's dowager, Lady Shige, who was now known by her Buddhist name of Kodai-in.
THERE ARE RUMORS BEING WHISPERED ABOUT TOWN THAT LADIES FROM THE INNER CHAMBERS ARE VISITING TEMPLES ON THE PRETEXT OF DEVOTION, AND THEN, INSTEAD INDULGING IN LEWD AND WANTON BEHAVIOR WITH YOUNG MONKS IN THEIR QUARTERS.
YES, LADY KODAI-IN.
I HAVE HEARD SUCH RUMORS MYSELF. THERE IS ALSO A RUMOR THAT THE DEPRAVED MONKS OF KANNO-JI TELL THEIR LOVERS, THE LADIES-IN-WAITING, TO BRING VALUABLES OUT OF THE INNER CHAMBERS TO THEM, AND THEY THEN SELL THESE VALUABLES TO FINANCE A LIFE OF LUXURY.
WHETHER THESE RUMORS BE TRUE OR FALSE...IS WHAT I WOULD LIKE YOU TO DISCOVER, BARON OF ISE.

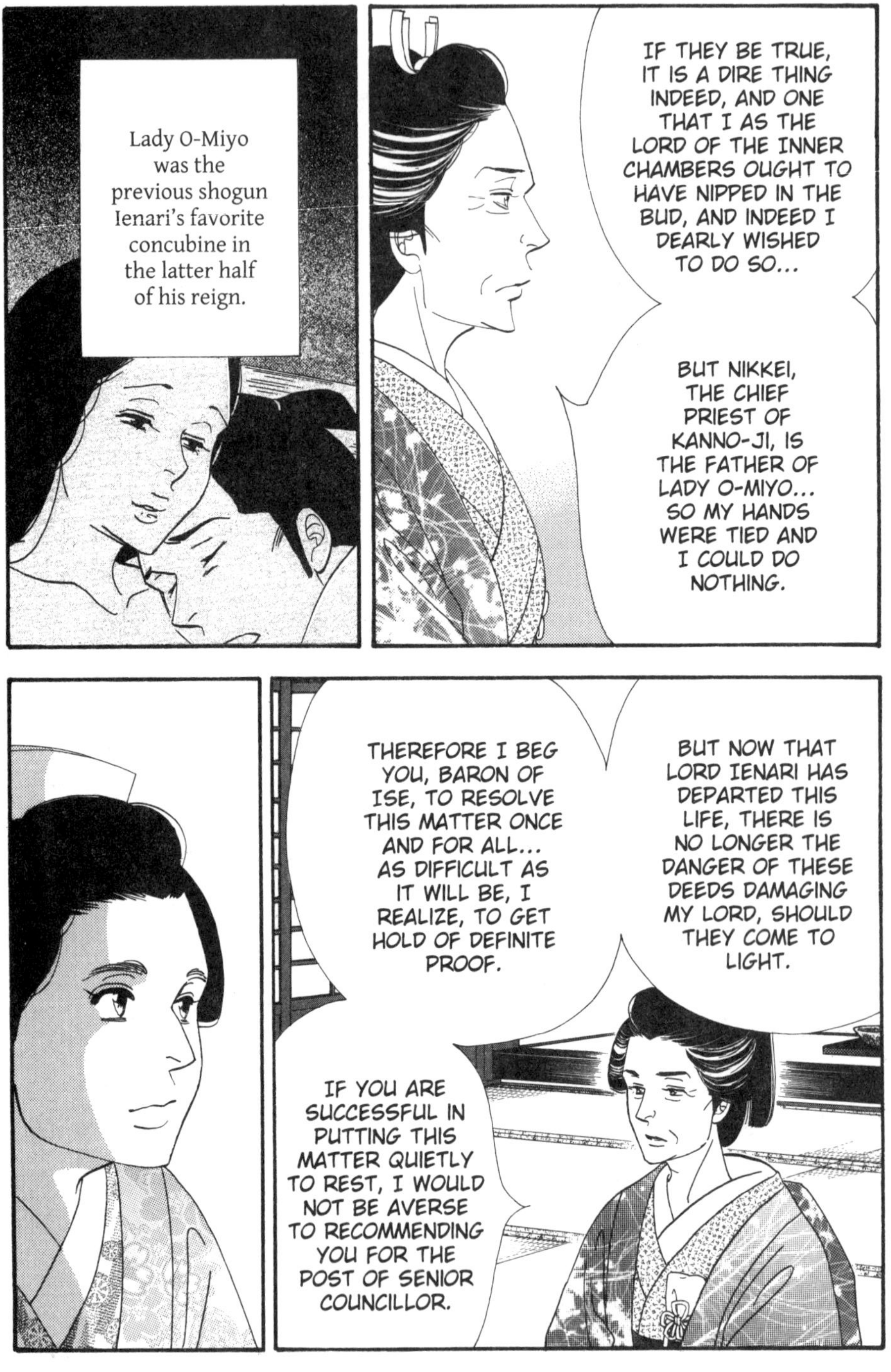
IF THEY BE TRUE, IT IS A DIRE THING INDEED, AND ONE THAT I AS THE LORD OF THE INNER CHAMBERS OUGHT TO HAVE NIPPED IN THE BUD, AND INDEED I DEARLY WISHED TO DO SO...
BUT NIKKEI, THE CHIEF PRIEST OF KANNO-JI, IS THE FATHER OF LADY O-MIYO... SO MY HANDS WERE TIED AND I COULD DO NOTHING.
Lady O-Miyo was the previous shogun Ienari's favorite concubine in the latter half of his reign.
BUT NOW THAT LORD IENARI HAS DEPARTED THIS LIFE, THERE IS NO LONGER THE DANGER OF THESE DEEDS DAMAGING MY LORD, SHOULD THEY COME TO LIGHT.
THEREFORE I BEG YOU, BARON OF ISE, TO RESOLVE THIS MATTER ONCE AND FOR ALL... AS DIFFICULT AS IT WILL BE, I REALIZE, TO GET HOLD OF DEFINITE PROOF.
IF YOU ARE SUCCESSFUL IN PUTTING THIS MATTER QUIETLY TO REST, I WOULD NOT BE AVERSE TO RECOMMENDING YOU FOR THE POST OF SENIOR COUNCILLOR.

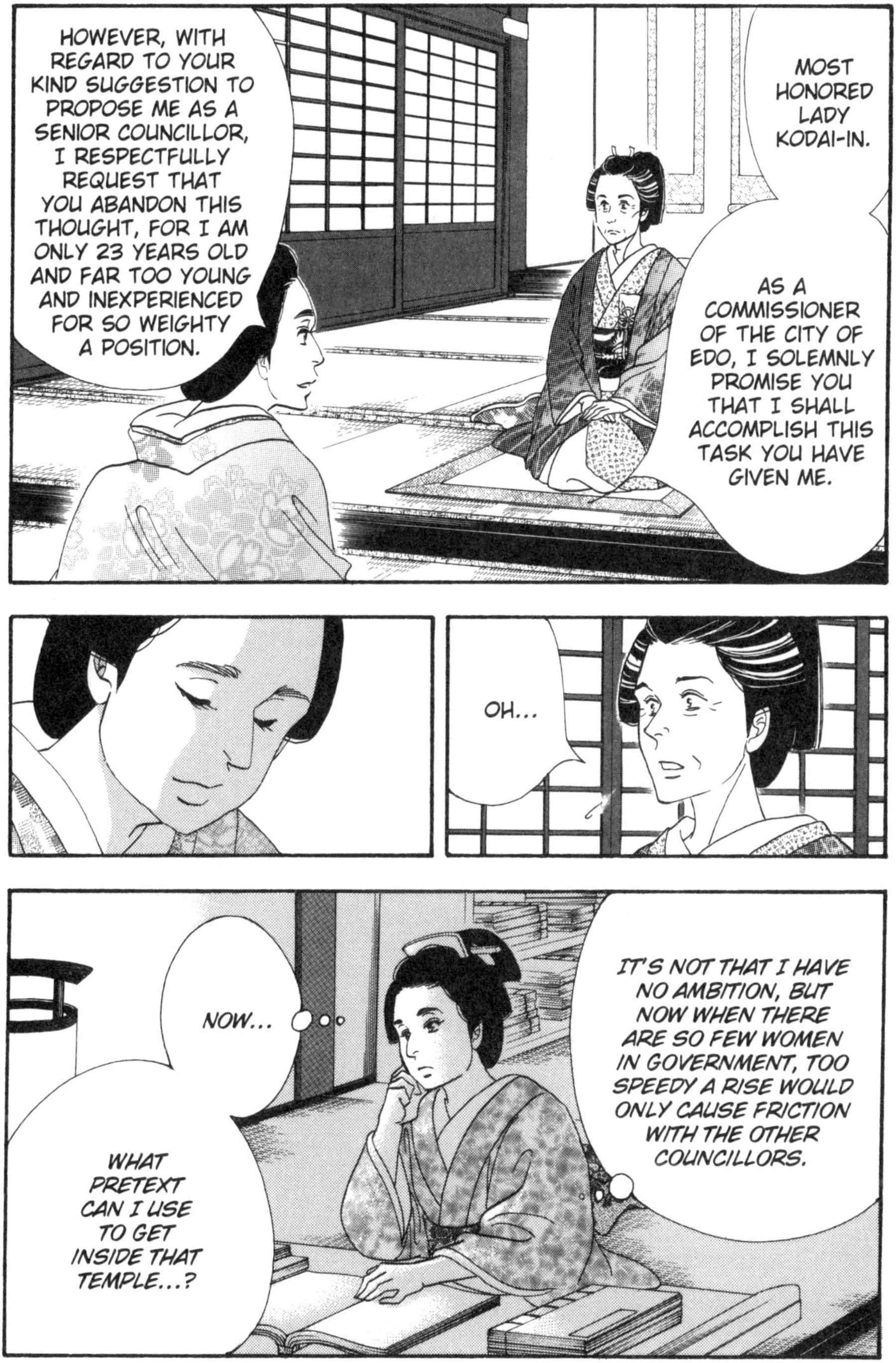
MOST HONORED LADY KODAI-IN.
AS A COMMISSIONER OF THE CITY OF EDO, I SOLEMNLY PROMISE YOU THAT I SHALL ACCOMPLISH THIS TASK YOU HAVE GIVEN ME.
HOWEVER, WITH REGARD TO YOUR KIND SUGGESTION TO PROPOSE ME AS A SENIOR COUNCILLOR, I RESPECTFULLY REQUEST THAT YOU ABANDON THIS THOUGHT, FOR I AM ONLY 23 YEARS OLD AND FAR TOO YOUNG AND INEXPERIENCED FOR SO WEIGHTY A POSITION.
OH...
IT'S NOT THAT I HAVE NO AMBITION, BUT NOW WHEN THERE ARE SO FEW WOMEN IN GOVERNMENT, TOO SPEEDY A RISE WOULD ONLY CAUSE FRICTION WITH THE OTHER COUNCILLORS.
NOW...
WHAT PRETEXT CAN I USE TO GET INSIDE THAT TEMPLE...?

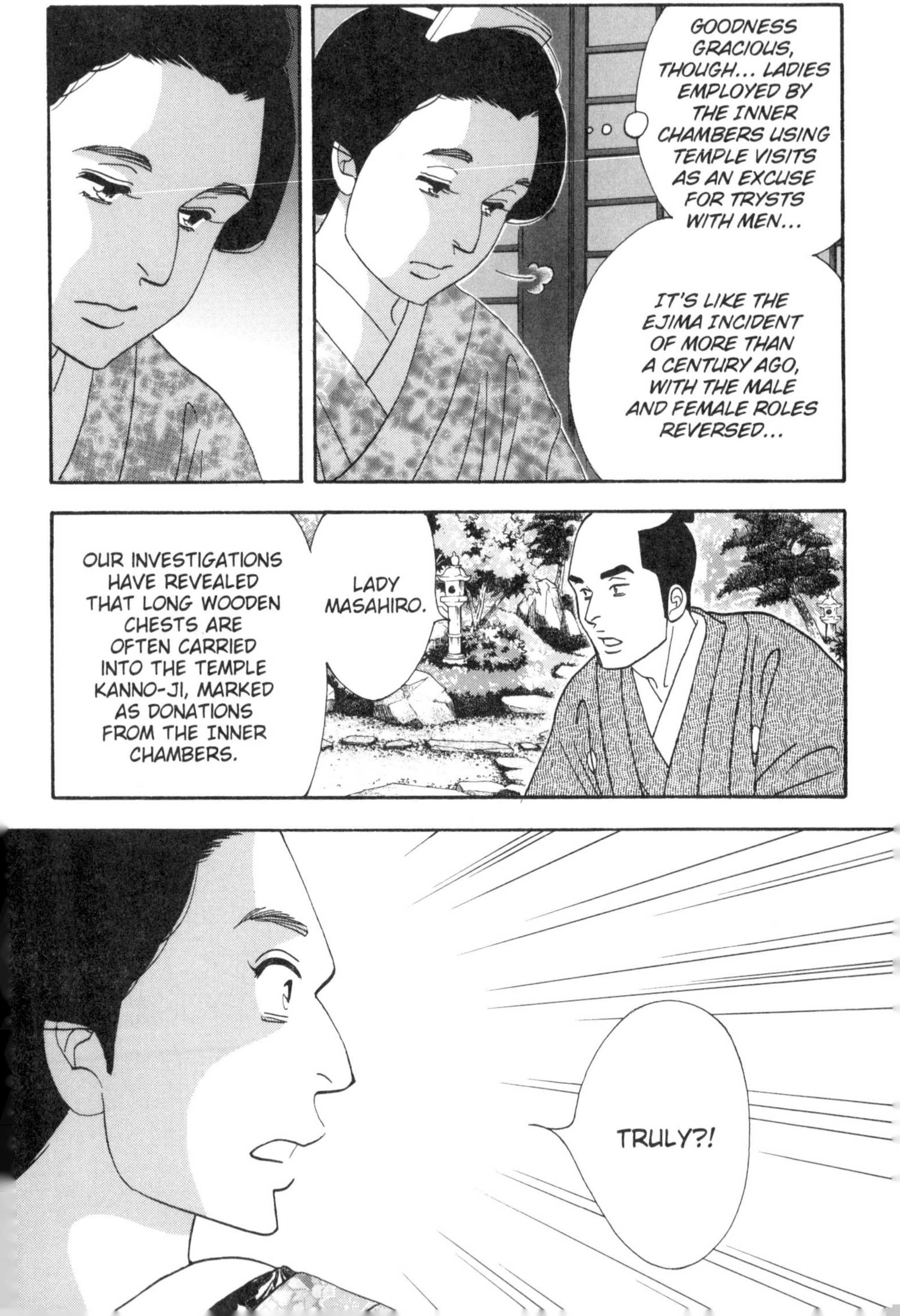
GOODNESS GRACIOUS, THOUGH... LADIES EMPLOYED BY THE INNER CHAMBERS USING TEMPLE VISITS AS AN EXCUSE FOR TRYSTS WITH MEN...
IT'S LIKE THE EJIMA INCIDENT OF MORE THAN A CENTURY AGO, WITH THE MALE AND FEMALE ROLES REVERSED...
LADY MASAHIRO.
OUR INVESTIGATIONS HAVE REVEALED THAT LONG WOODEN CHESTS ARE OFTEN CARRIED INTO THE TEMPLE KANNO-JI, MARKED AS DONATIONS FROM THE INNER CHAMBERS.
TRULY?!

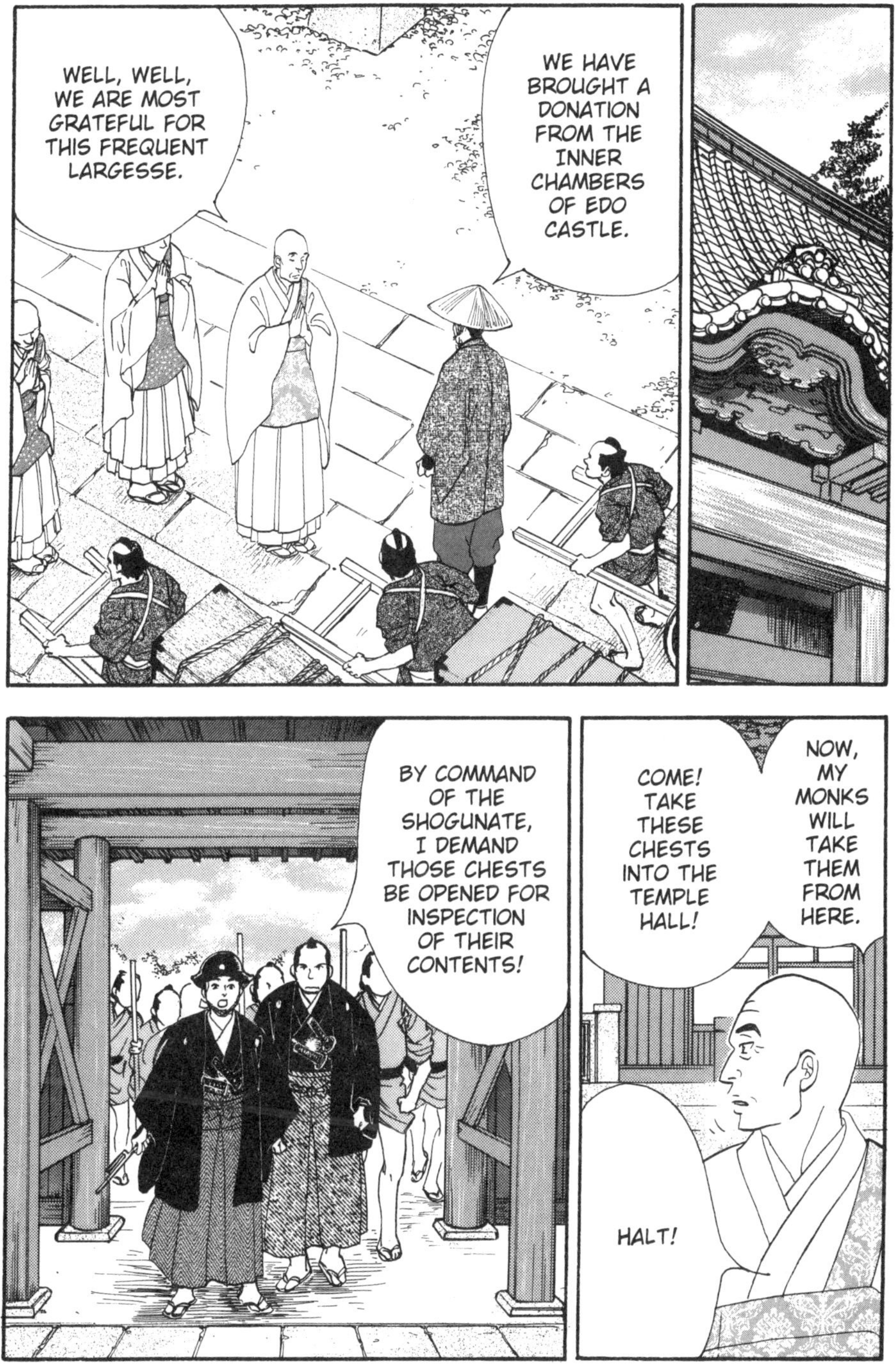
WE HAVE BROUGHT A DONATION FROM THE INNER CHAMBERS OF EDO CASTLE.
WELL, WELL, WE ARE MOST GRATEFUL FOR THIS FREQUENT LARGESSE.
NOW, MY MONKS WILL TAKE THEM FROM HERE.
COME! TAKE THESE CHESTS INTO THE TEMPLE HALL!
HALT!
BY COMMAND OF THE SHOGUNATE, I DEMAND THOSE CHESTS BE OPENED FOR INSPECTION OF THEIR CONTENTS!

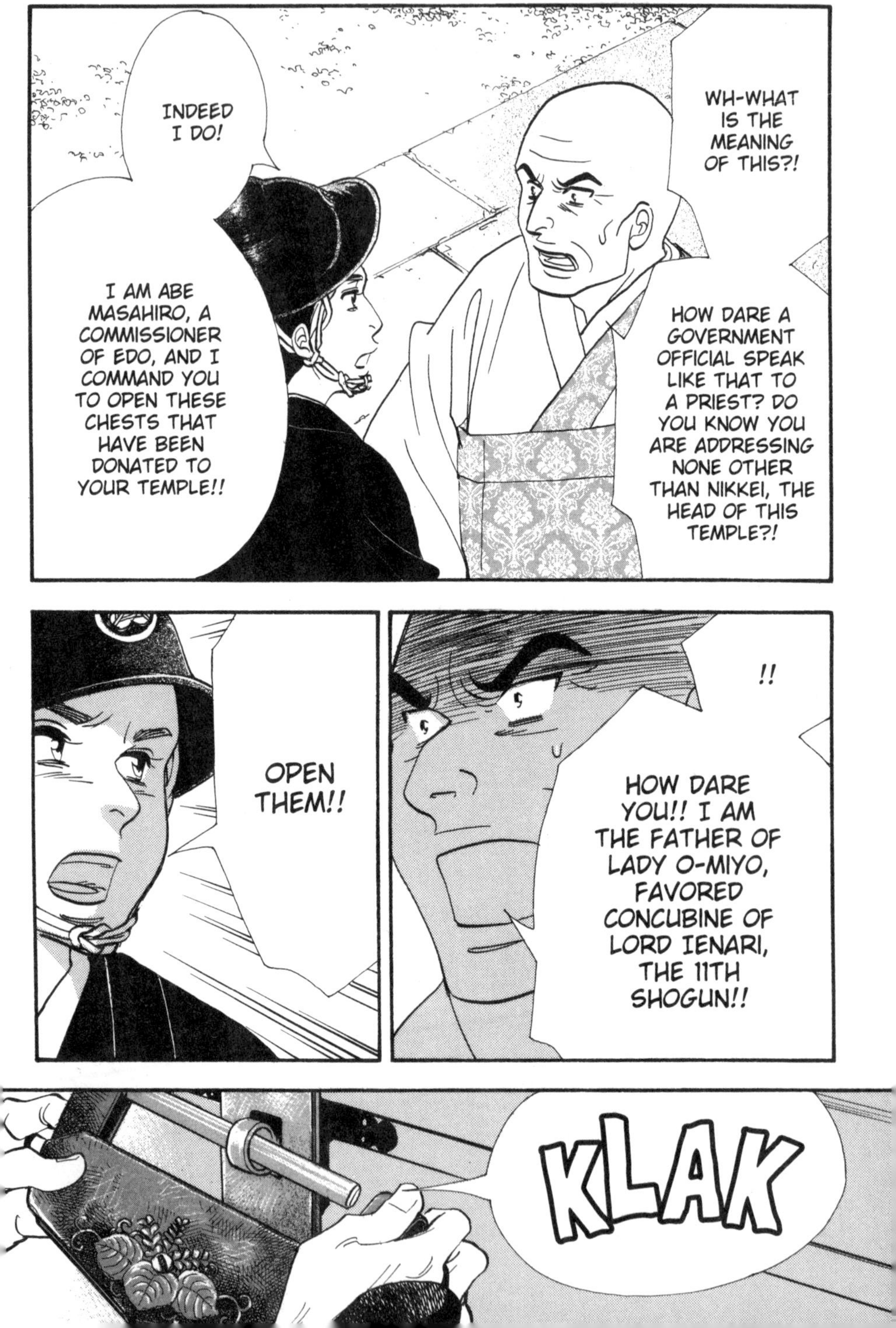
WH-WHAT IS THE MEANING OF THIS?!
HOW DARE A GOVERNMENT OFFICIAL SPEAK LIKE THAT TO A PRIEST? DO YOU KNOW YOU ARE ADDRESSING NONE OTHER THAN NIKKEI, THE HEAD OF THIS TEMPLE?!
INDEED I DO!
I AM ABE MASAHIRO, A COMMISSIONER OF EDO, AND I COMMAND YOU TO OPEN THESE CHESTS THAT HAVE BEEN DONATED TO YOUR TEMPLE!!
!!
HOW DARE YOU!! I AM THE FATHER OF LADY O-MIYO, FAVORED CONCUBINE OF LORD IENARI, THE 11TH SHOGUN!!
OPEN THEM!!
KLAK

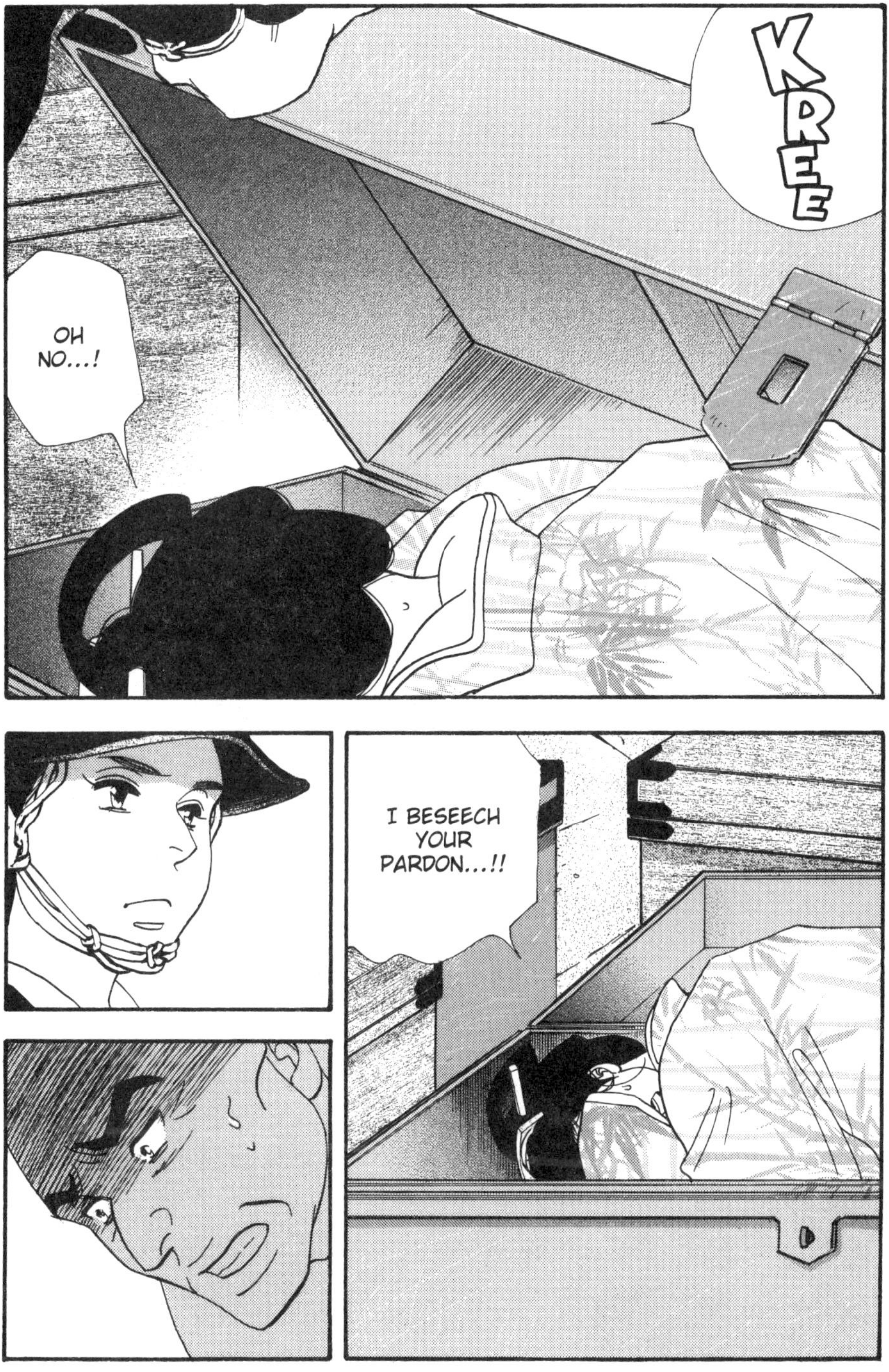
KREE
OH NO...!
I BESEECH YOUR PARDON...!!

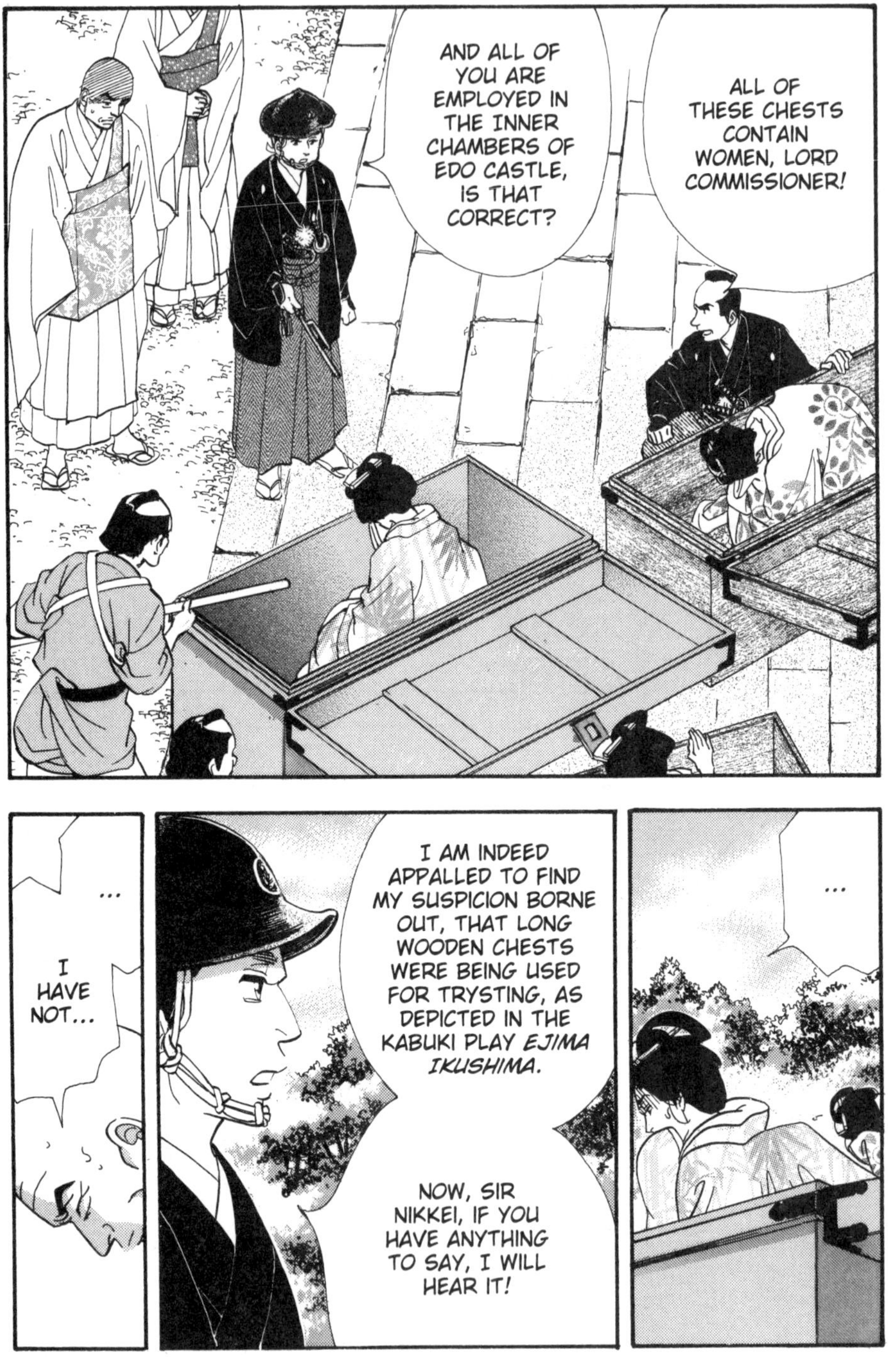
ALL OF THESE CHESTS CONTAIN WOMEN, LORD COMMISSIONER!
AND ALL OF YOU ARE EMPLOYED IN THE INNER CHAMBERS OF EDO CASTLE, IS THAT CORRECT?
...
I AM INDEED APPALLED TO FIND MY SUSPICION BORNE OUT, THAT LONG WOODEN CHESTS WERE BEING USED FOR TRYSTING, AS DEPICTED IN THE KABUKI PLAY *EJIMA IKUSHIMA*.
NOW, SIR NIKKEI, IF YOU HAVE ANYTHING TO SAY, I WILL HEAR IT!
...
I HAVE NOT...

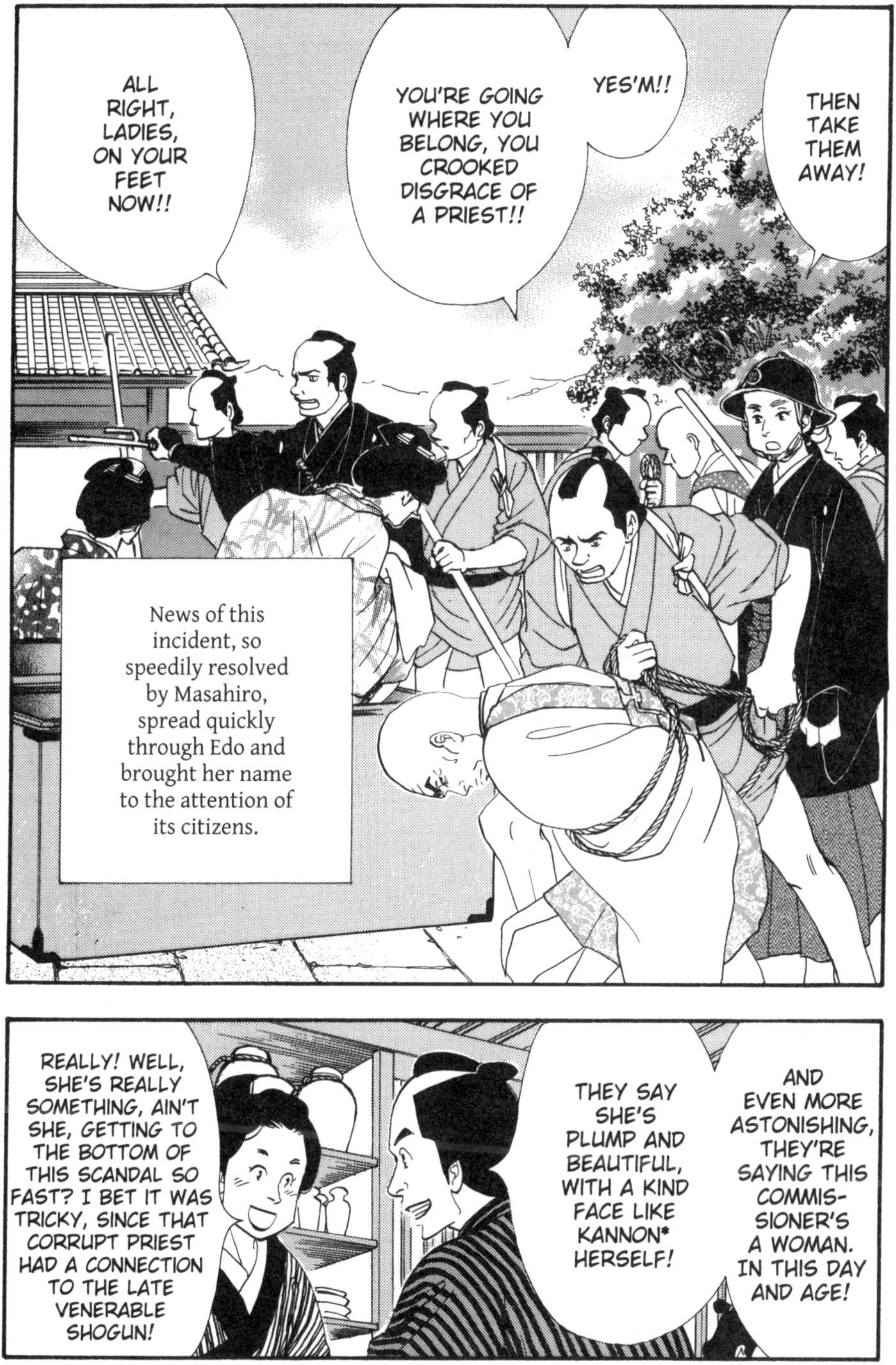
THEN TAKE THEM AWAY!
YES'M!!
YOU'RE GOING WHERE YOU BELONG, YOU CROOKED DISGRACE OF A PRIEST!!
ALL RIGHT, LADIES, ON YOUR FEET NOW!!
News of this incident, so speedily resolved by Masahiro, spread quickly through Edo and brought her name to the attention of its citizens.
AND EVEN MORE ASTONISHING, THEY'RE SAYING THIS COMMIS-SIONER'S A WOMAN. IN THIS DAY AND AGE!
THEY SAY SHE'S PLUMP AND BEAUTIFUL, WITH A KIND FACE LIKE KANNON* HERSELF!
REALLY! WELL, SHE'S REALLY SOMETHING, AIN'T SHE, GETTING TO THE BOTTOM OF THIS SCANDAL SO FAST? I BET IT WAS TRICKY, SINCE THAT CORRUPT PRIEST HAD A CONNECTION TO THE LATE VENERABLE SHOGUN!

*Kannon/Guanyin = the goddess of mercy

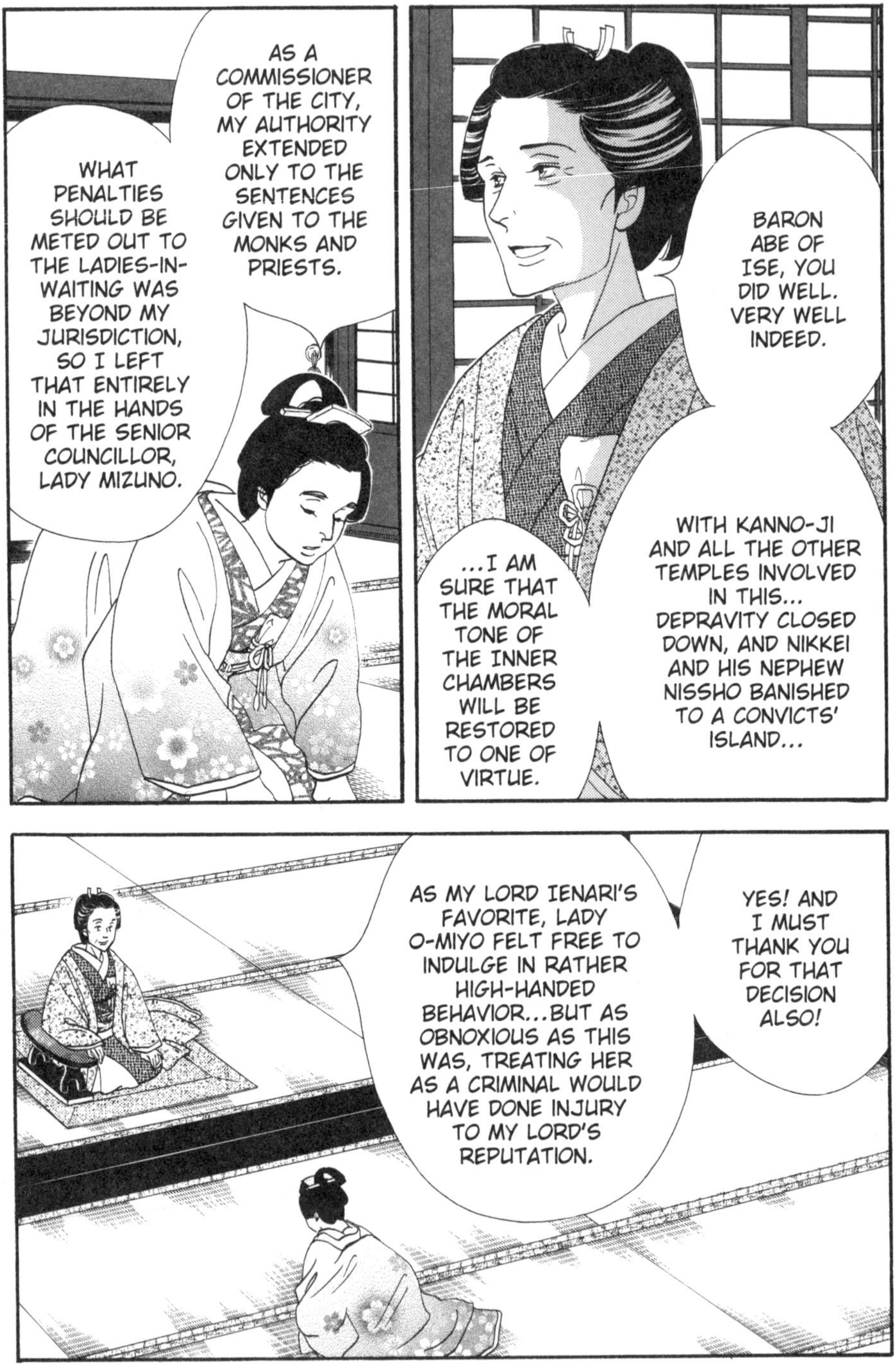
BARON ABE OF ISE, YOU DID WELL. VERY WELL INDEED.
WITH KANNO-JI AND ALL THE OTHER TEMPLES INVOLVED IN THIS... DEPRAVITY CLOSED DOWN, AND NIKKEI AND HIS NEPHEW NISSHO BANISHED TO A CONVICTS' ISLAND...
...I AM SURE THAT THE MORAL TONE OF THE INNER CHAMBERS WILL BE RESTORED TO ONE OF VIRTUE.
AS A COMMISSIONER OF THE CITY, MY AUTHORITY EXTENDED ONLY TO THE SENTENCES GIVEN TO THE MONKS AND PRIESTS.
WHAT PENALTIES SHOULD BE METED OUT TO THE LADIES-IN-WAITING WAS BEYOND MY JURISDICTION, SO I LEFT THAT ENTIRELY IN THE HANDS OF THE SENIOR COUNCILLOR, LADY MIZUNO.
YES! AND I MUST THANK YOU FOR THAT DECISION ALSO!
AS MY LORD IENARI'S FAVORITE, LADY O-MIYO FELT FREE TO INDULGE IN RATHER HIGH-HANDED BEHAVIOR...BUT AS OBNOXIOUS AS THIS WAS, TREATING HER AS A CRIMINAL WOULD HAVE DONE INJURY TO MY LORD'S REPUTATION.

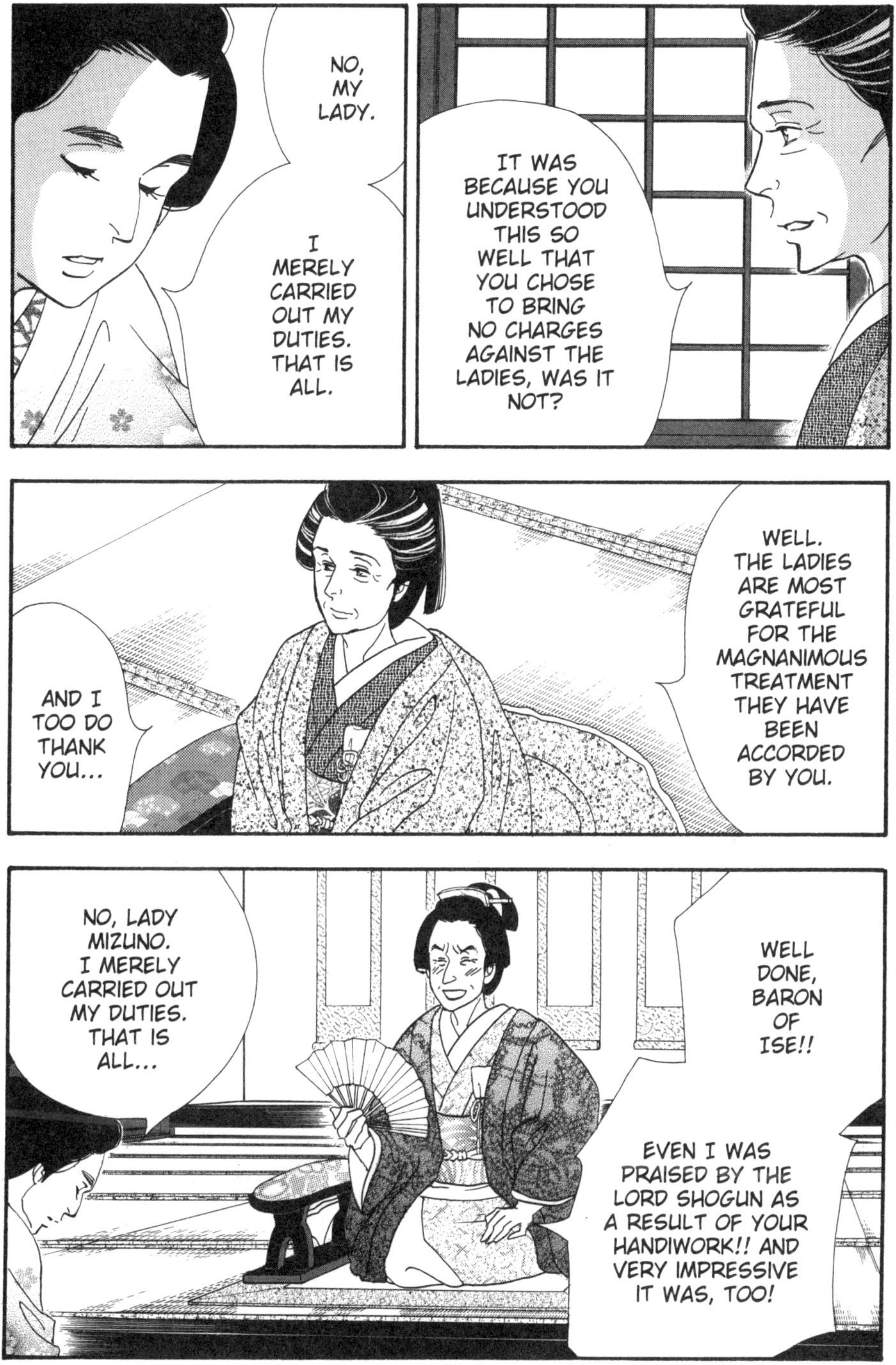
IT WAS BECAUSE YOU UNDERSTOOD THIS SO WELL THAT YOU CHOSE TO BRING NO CHARGES AGAINST THE LADIES, WAS IT NOT?
NO, MY LADY.
I MERELY CARRIED OUT MY DUTIES. THAT IS ALL.
WELL. THE LADIES ARE MOST GRATEFUL FOR THE MAGNANIMOUS TREATMENT THEY HAVE BEEN ACCORDED BY YOU.
AND I TOO DO THANK YOU...
WELL DONE, BARON OF ISE!!
EVEN I WAS PRAISED BY THE LORD SHOGUN AS A RESULT OF YOUR HANDIWORK!! AND VERY IMPRESSIVE IT WAS, TOO!
NO, LADY MIZUNO. I MERELY CARRIED OUT MY DUTIES. THAT IS ALL...

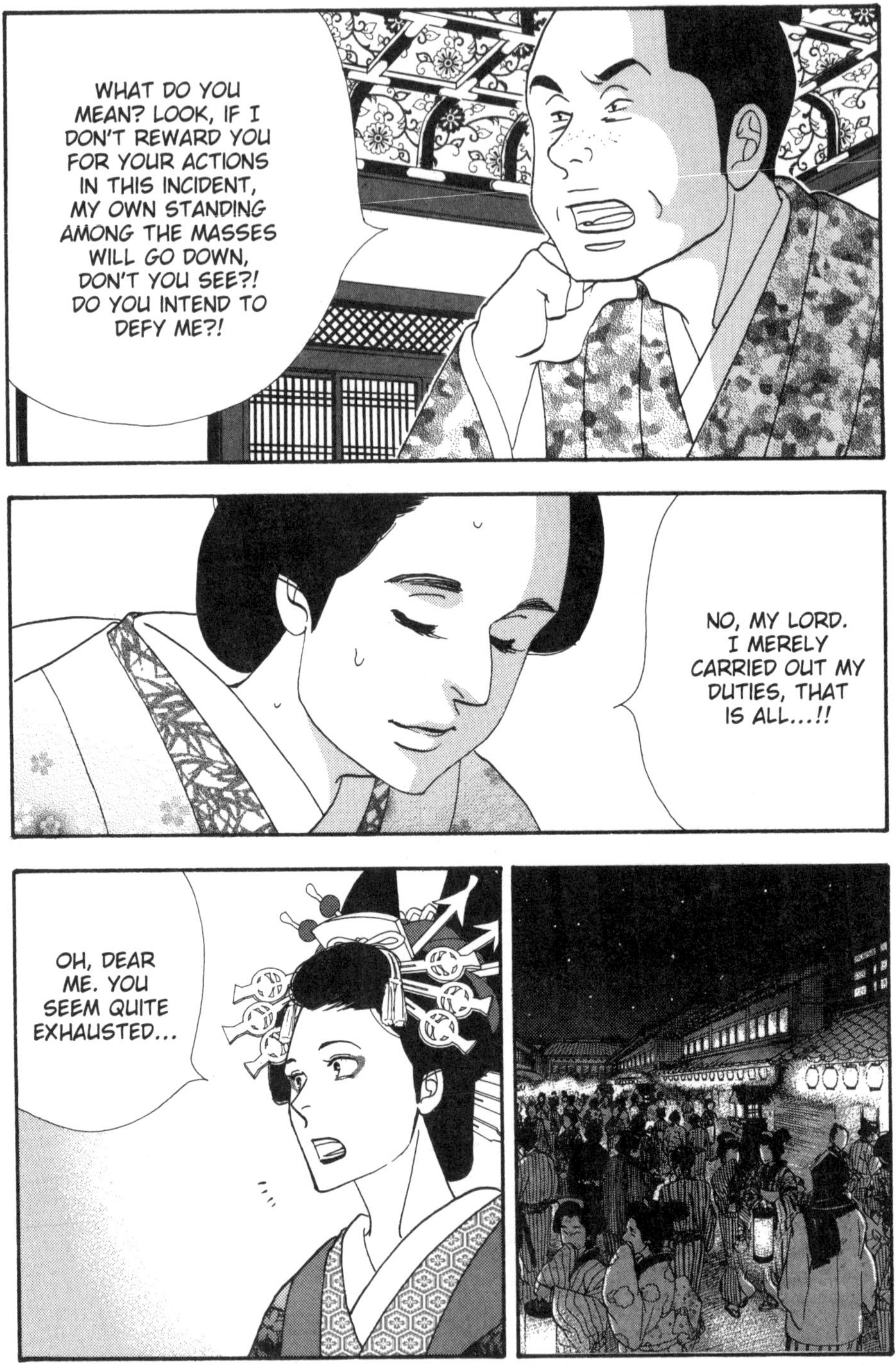
WHAT DO YOU MEAN? LOOK, IF I DON'T REWARD YOU FOR YOUR ACTIONS IN THIS INCIDENT, MY OWN STANDING AMONG THE MASSES WILL GO DOWN, DON'T YOU SEE?! DO YOU INTEND TO DEFY ME?!
NO, MY LORD. I MERELY CARRIED OUT MY DUTIES, THAT IS ALL...!!
OH, DEAR ME. YOU SEEM QUITE EXHAUSTED...

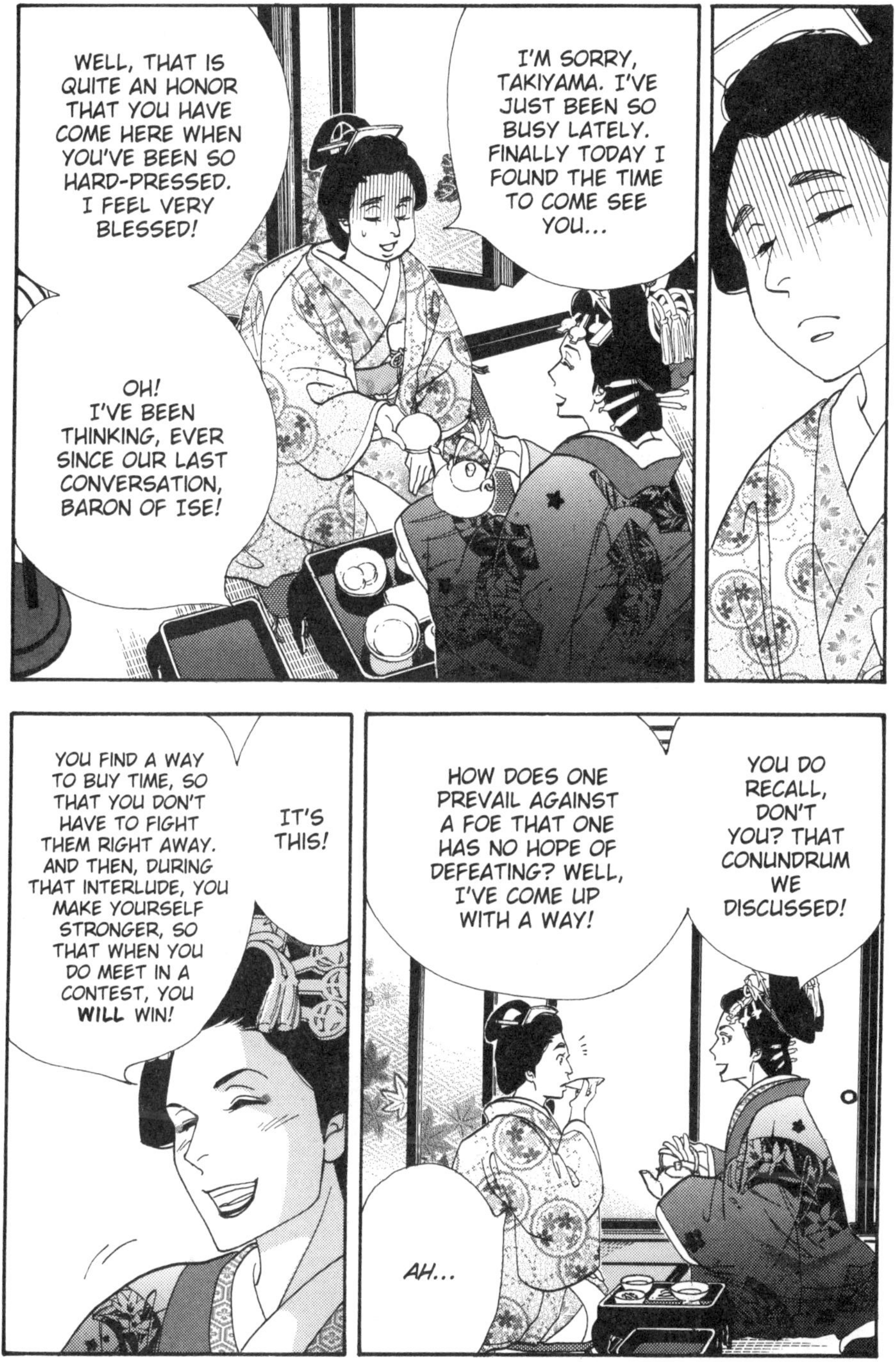
I'M SORRY, TAKIYAMA. I'VE JUST BEEN SO BUSY LATELY. FINALLY TODAY I FOUND THE TIME TO COME SEE YOU...
WELL, THAT IS QUITE AN HONOR THAT YOU HAVE COME HERE WHEN YOU'VE BEEN SO HARD-PRESSED. I FEEL VERY BLESSED!
OH! I'VE BEEN THINKING, EVER SINCE OUR LAST CONVERSATION, BARON OF ISE!
YOU DO RECALL, DON'T YOU? THAT CONUNDRUM WE DISCUSSED!
HOW DOES ONE PREVAIL AGAINST A FOE THAT ONE HAS NO HOPE OF DEFEATING? WELL, I'VE COME UP WITH A WAY!
AH...
IT'S THIS!
YOU FIND A WAY TO BUY TIME, SO THAT YOU DON'T HAVE TO FIGHT THEM RIGHT AWAY. AND THEN, DURING THAT INTERLUDE, YOU MAKE YOURSELF STRONGER, SO THAT WHEN YOU DO MEET IN A CONTEST, YOU **WILL** WIN!

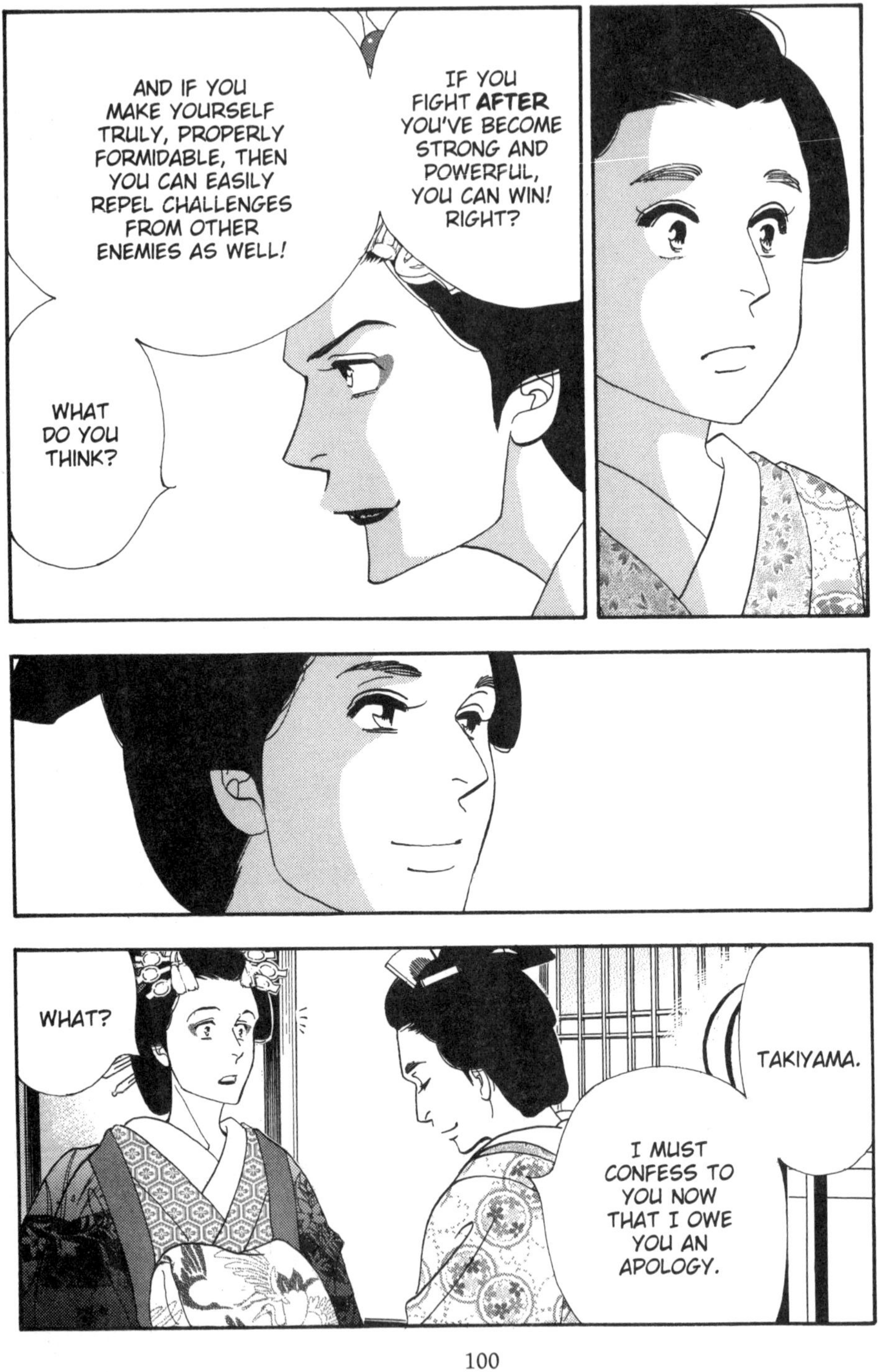
IF YOU FIGHT **AFTER** YOU'VE BECOME STRONG AND POWERFUL, YOU CAN WIN! RIGHT?
AND IF YOU MAKE YOURSELF TRULY, PROPERLY FORMIDABLE, THEN YOU CAN EASILY REPEL CHALLENGES FROM OTHER ENEMIES AS WELL!
WHAT DO YOU THINK?
TAKIYAMA.
WHAT?
I MUST CONFESS TO YOU NOW THAT I OWE YOU AN APOLOGY.

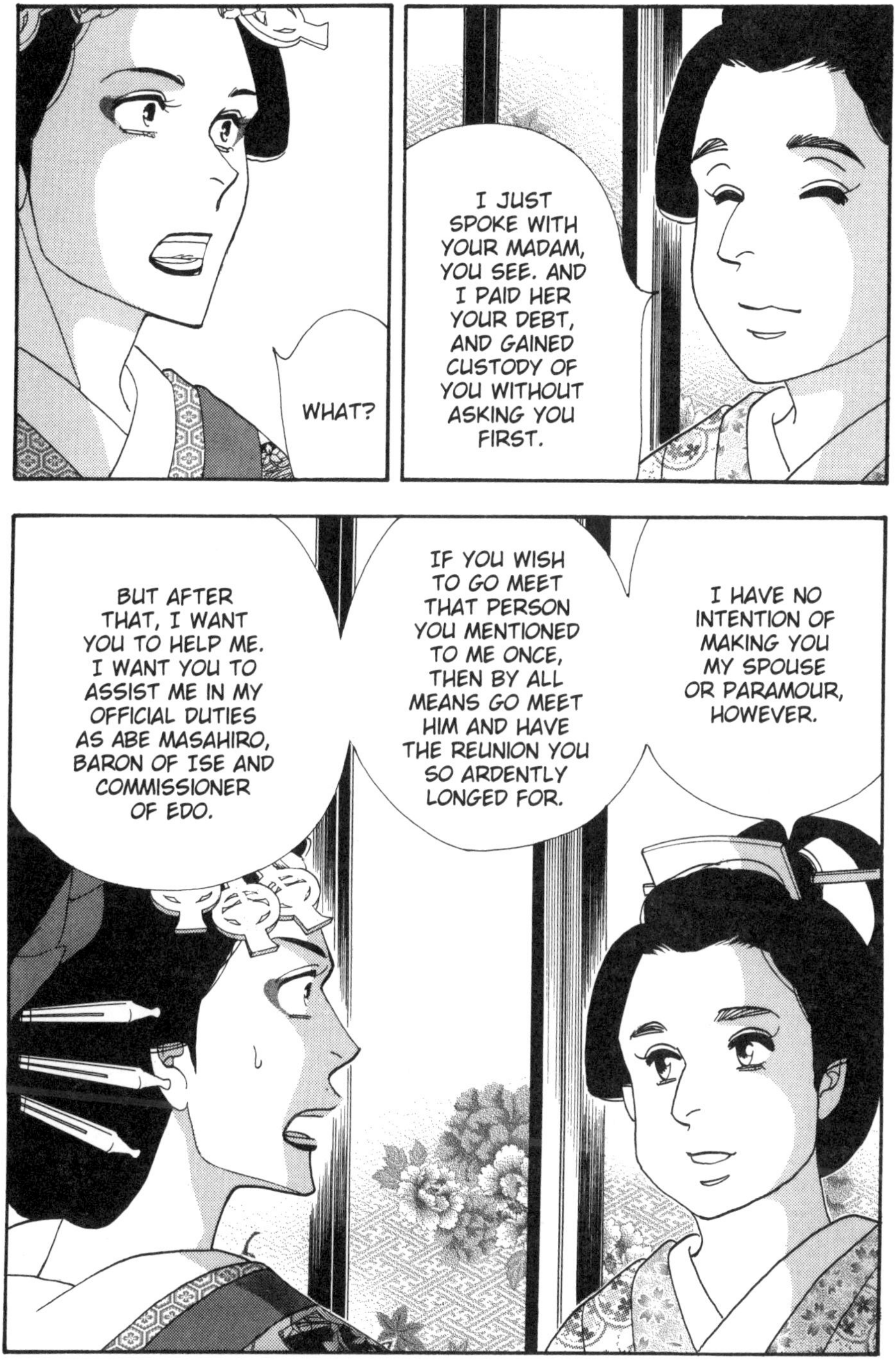
I JUST SPOKE WITH YOUR MADAM, YOU SEE. AND I PAID HER YOUR DEBT, AND GAINED CUSTODY OF YOU WITHOUT ASKING YOU FIRST.
WHAT?
I HAVE NO INTENTION OF MAKING YOU MY SPOUSE OR PARAMOUR, HOWEVER.
IF YOU WISH TO GO MEET THAT PERSON YOU MENTIONED TO ME ONCE, THEN BY ALL MEANS GO MEET HIM AND HAVE THE REUNION YOU SO ARDENTLY LONGED FOR.
BUT AFTER THAT, I WANT YOU TO HELP ME. I WANT YOU TO ASSIST ME IN MY OFFICIAL DUTIES AS ABE MASAHIRO, BARON OF ISE AND COMMISSIONER OF EDO.

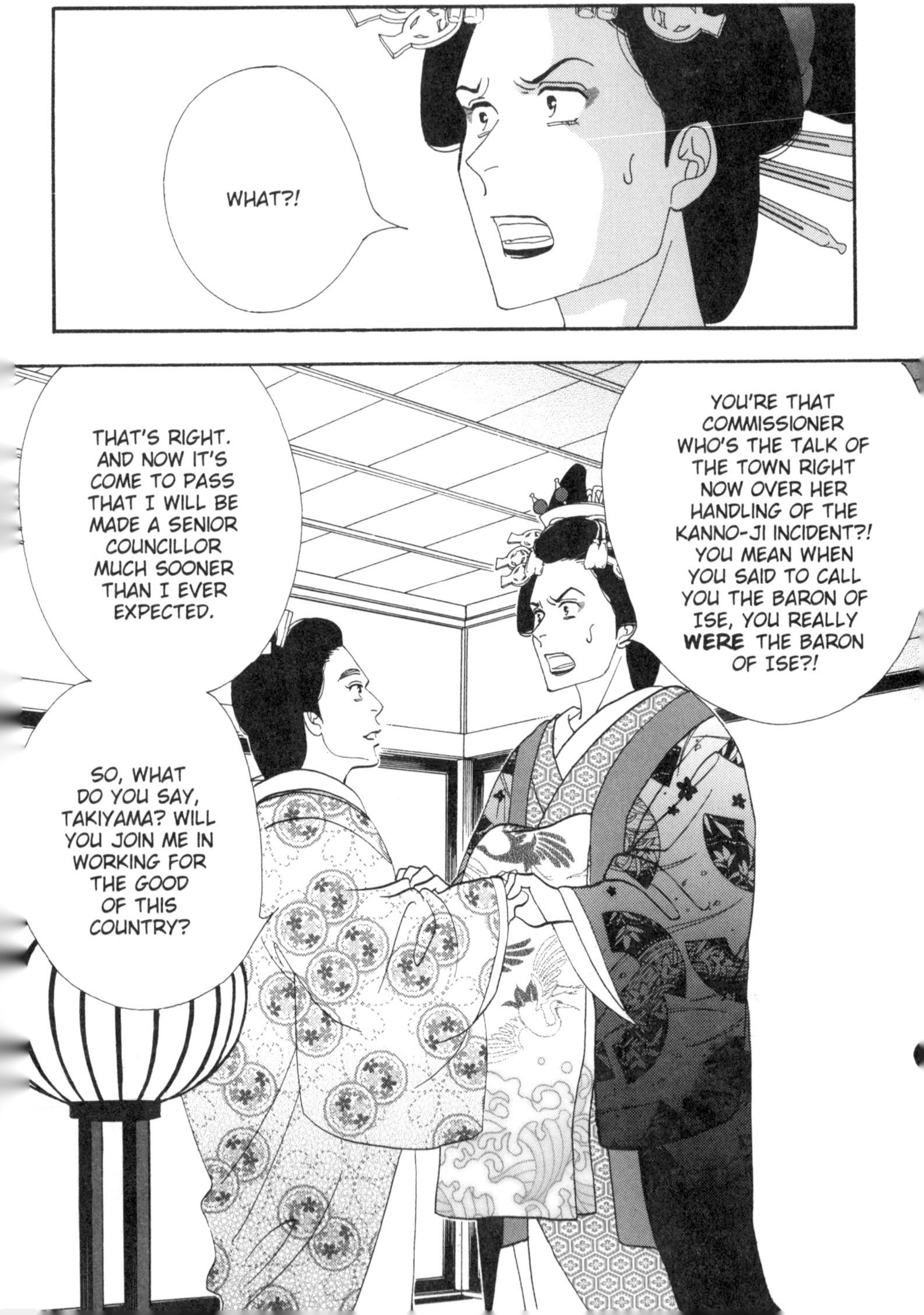
WHAT?!
YOU'RE THAT COMMISSIONER WHO'S THE TALK OF THE TOWN RIGHT NOW OVER HER HANDLING OF THE KANNO-JI INCIDENT?! YOU MEAN WHEN YOU SAID TO CALL YOU THE BARON OF ISE, YOU REALLY **WERE** THE BARON OF ISE?!
THAT'S RIGHT. AND NOW IT'S COME TO PASS THAT I WILL BE MADE A SENIOR COUNCILLOR MUCH SOONER THAN I EVER EXPECTED.
SO, WHAT DO YOU SAY, TAKIYAMA? WILL YOU JOIN ME IN WORKING FOR THE GOOD OF THIS COUNTRY?

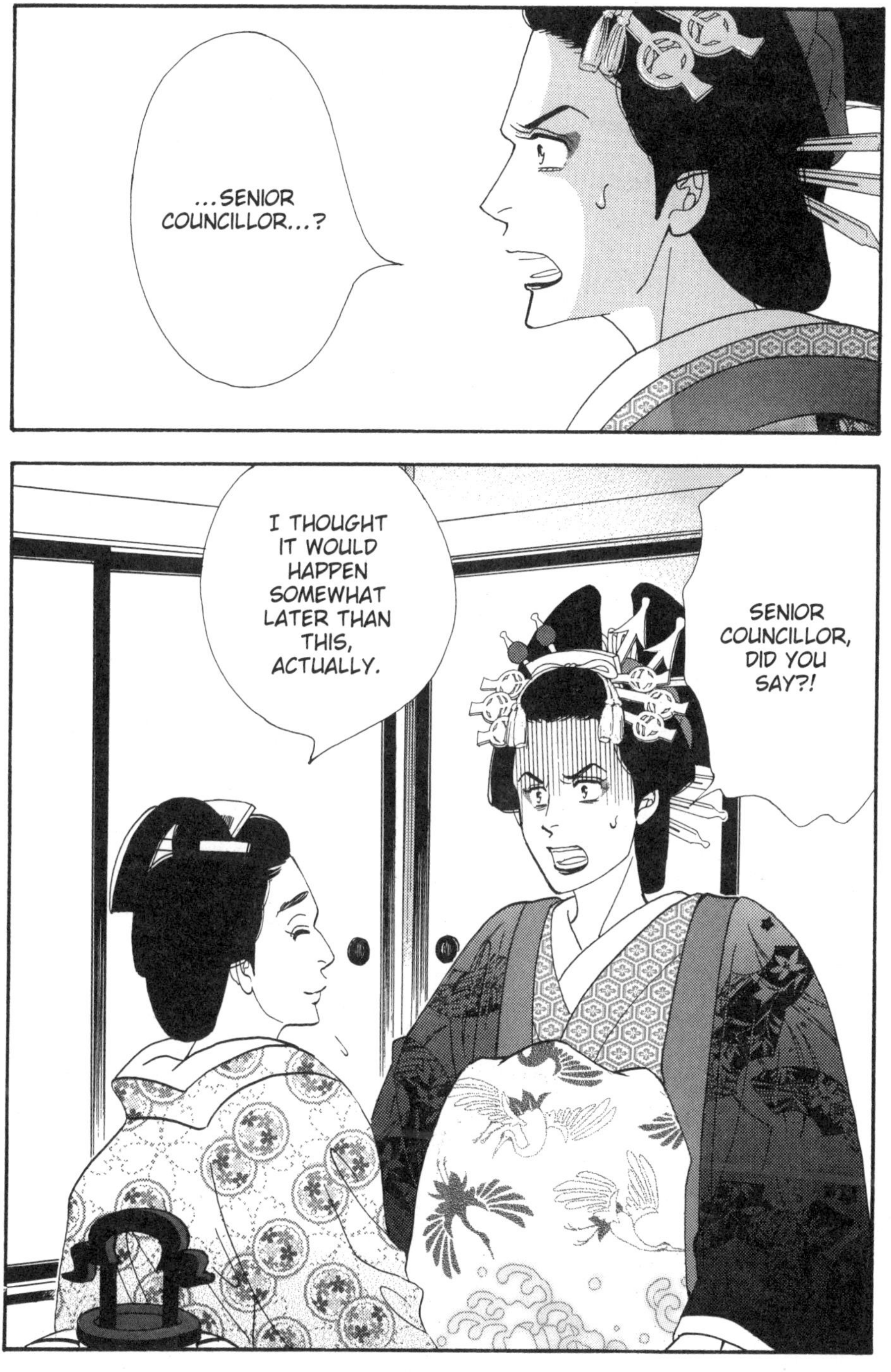
...SENIOR COUNCILLOR...?
SENIOR COUNCILLOR, DID YOU SAY?!
I THOUGHT IT WOULD HAPPEN SOMEWHAT LATER THAN THIS, ACTUALLY.

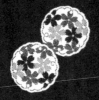

Ōoku

❀ THE INNER CHAMBERS

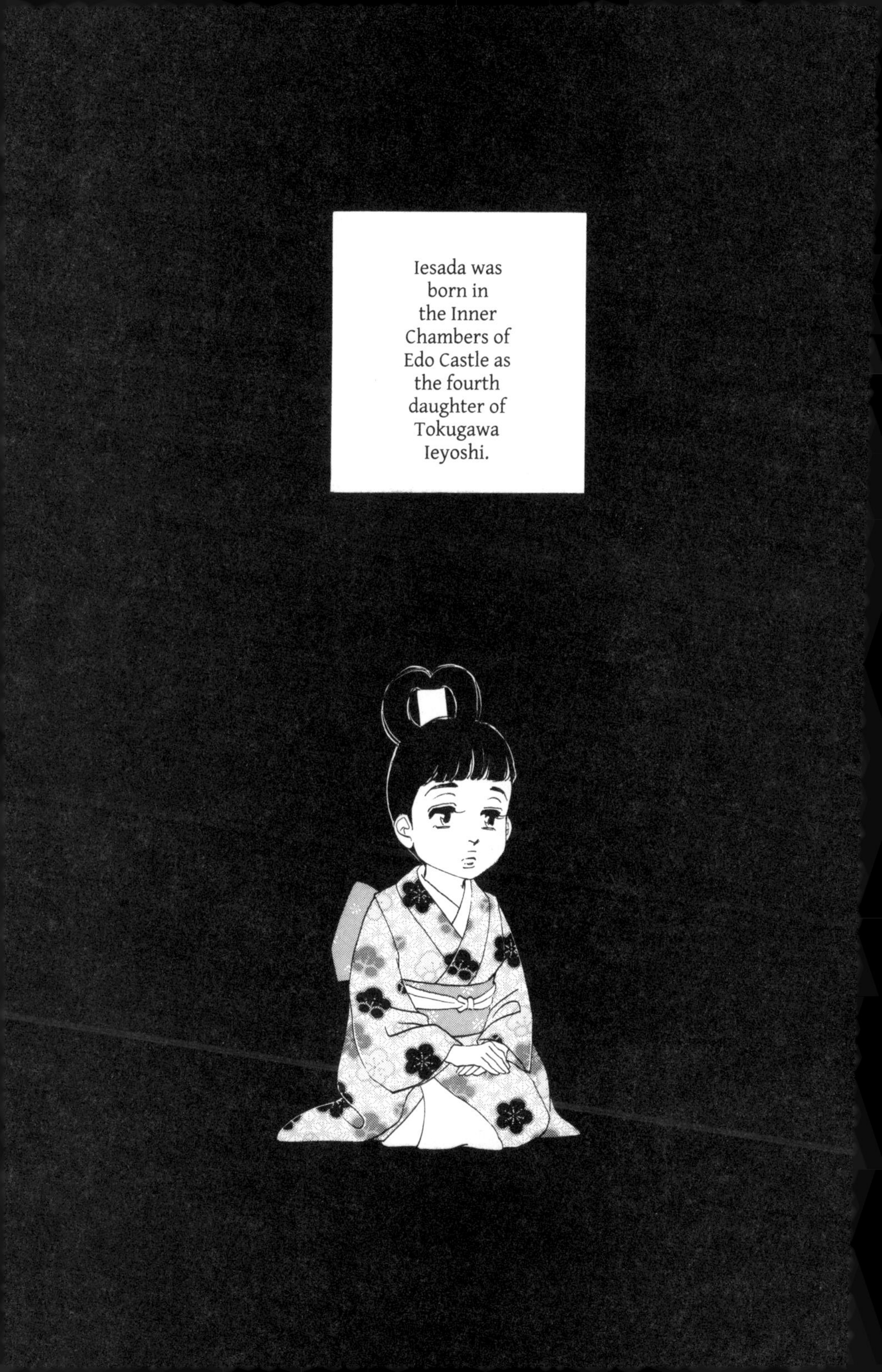
Iesada was born in the Inner Chambers of Edo Castle as the fourth daughter of Tokugawa Ieyoshi.

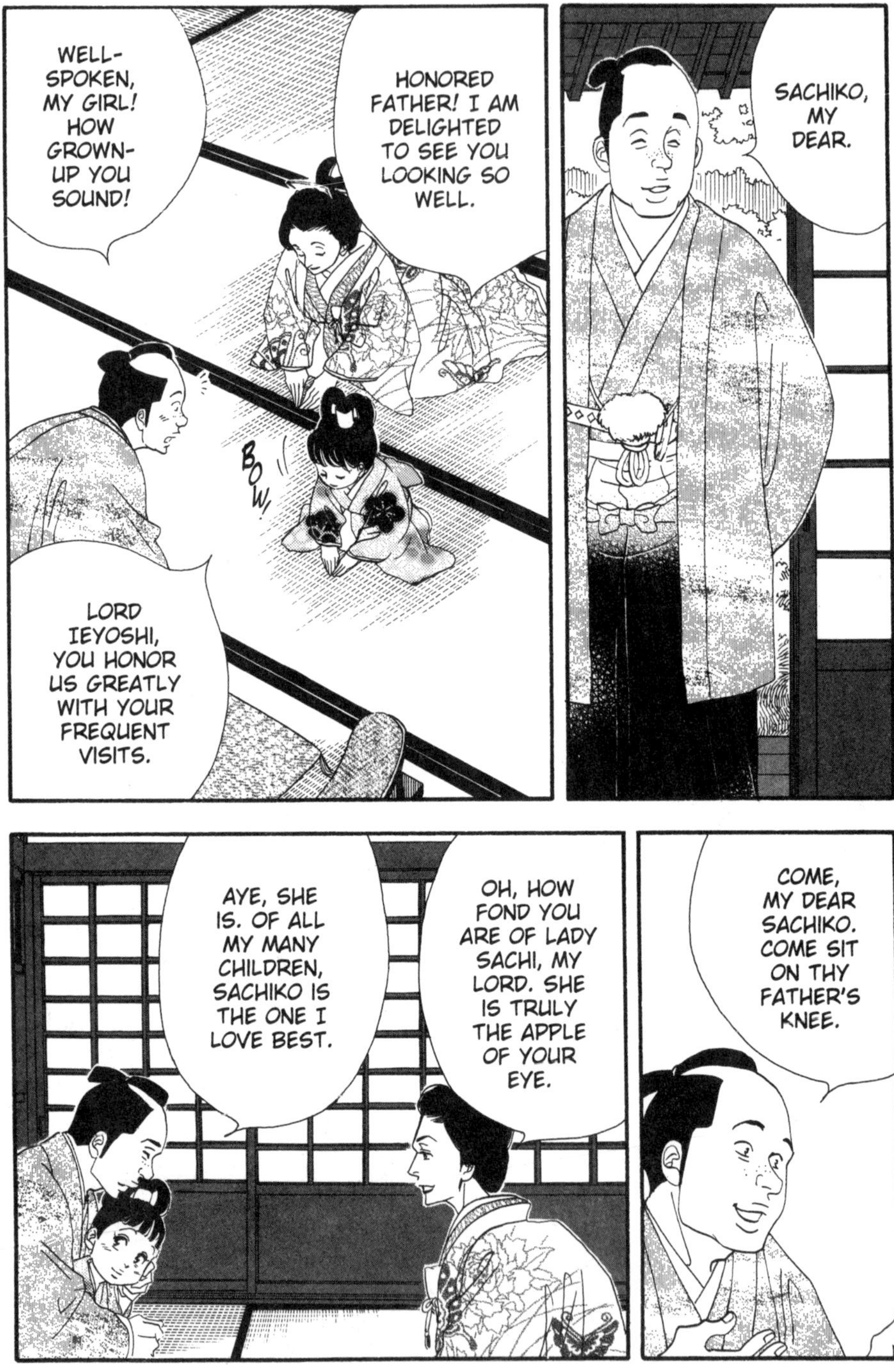
SACHIKO, MY DEAR.
HONORED FATHER! I AM DELIGHTED TO SEE YOU LOOKING SO WELL.
WELL-SPOKEN, MY GIRL! HOW GROWN-UP YOU SOUND!
BOW!
LORD IEYOSHI, YOU HONOR US GREATLY WITH YOUR FREQUENT VISITS.
COME, MY DEAR SACHIKO. COME SIT ON THY FATHER'S KNEE.
OH, HOW FOND YOU ARE OF LADY SACHI, MY LORD. SHE IS TRULY THE APPLE OF YOUR EYE.
AYE, SHE IS. OF ALL MY MANY CHILDREN, SACHIKO IS THE ONE I LOVE BEST.

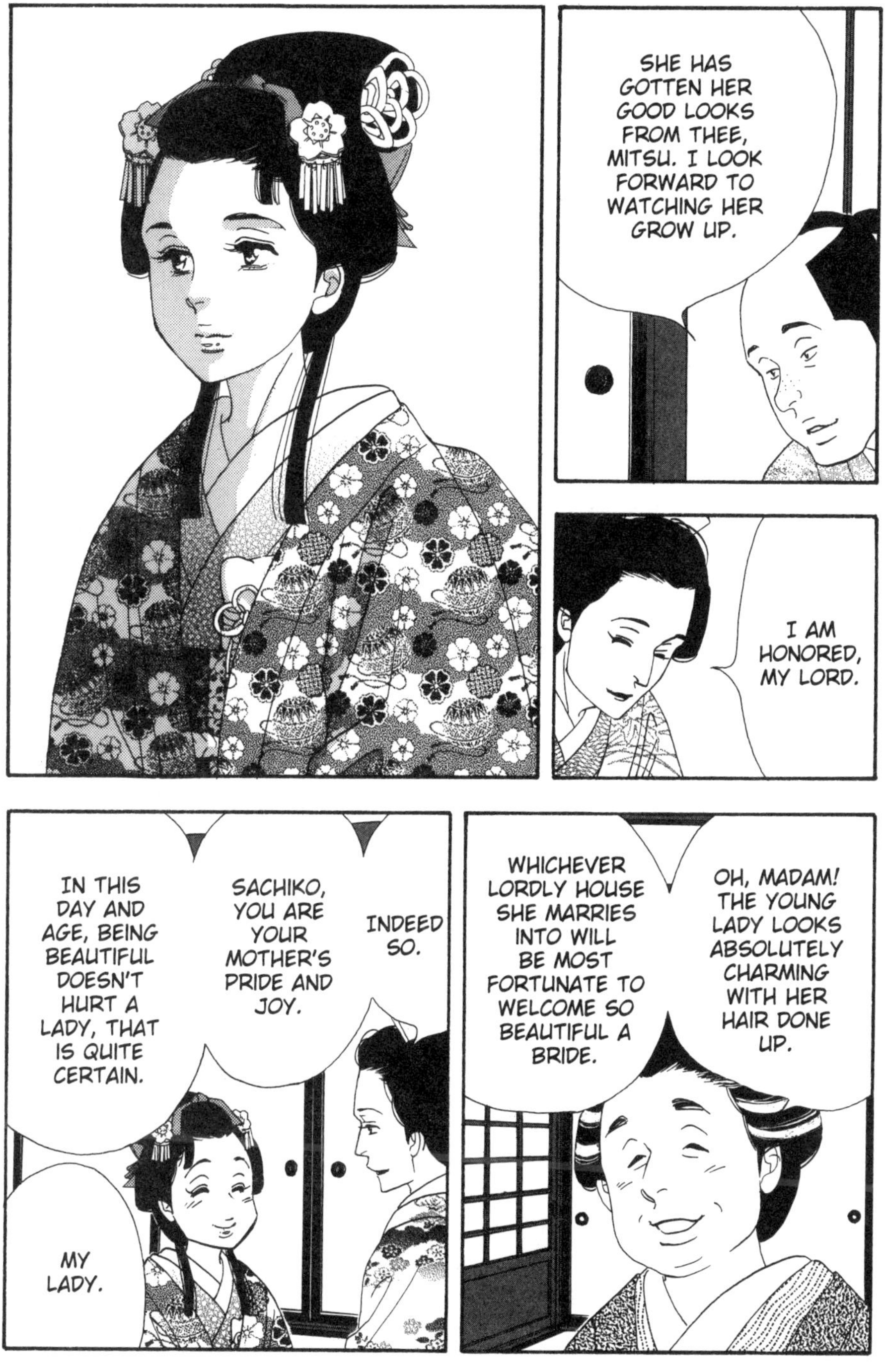
SHE HAS GOTTEN HER GOOD LOOKS FROM THEE, MITSU. I LOOK FORWARD TO WATCHING HER GROW UP.
I AM HONORED, MY LORD.
OH, MADAM! THE YOUNG LADY LOOKS ABSOLUTELY CHARMING WITH HER HAIR DONE UP.
WHICHEVER LORDLY HOUSE SHE MARRIES INTO WILL BE MOST FORTUNATE TO WELCOME SO BEAUTIFUL A BRIDE.
INDEED SO.
SACHIKO, YOU ARE YOUR MOTHER'S PRIDE AND JOY.
IN THIS DAY AND AGE, BEING BEAUTIFUL DOESN'T HURT A LADY, THAT IS QUITE CERTAIN.
MY LADY.

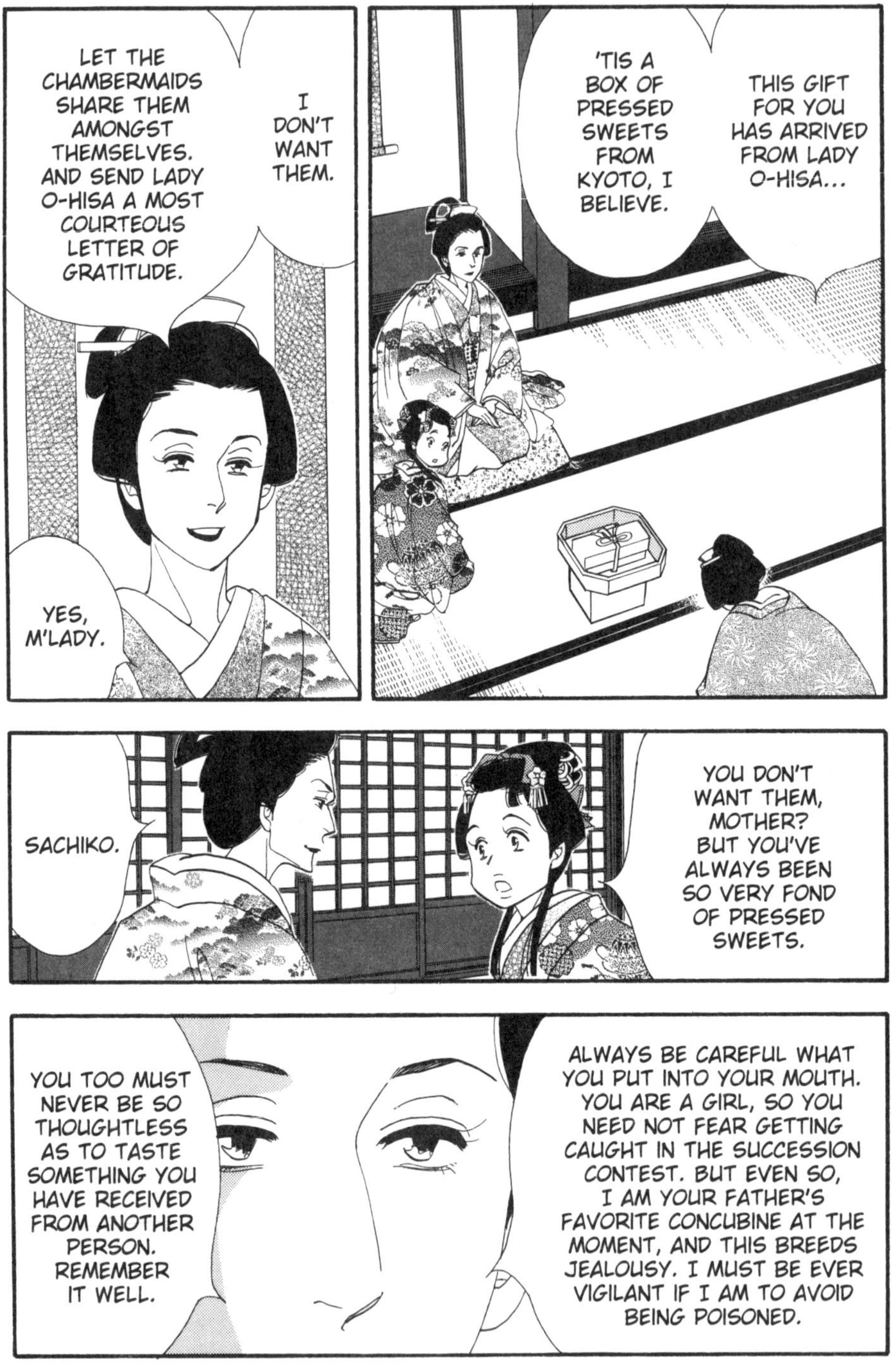
THIS GIFT FOR YOU HAS ARRIVED FROM LADY O-HISA...
'TIS A BOX OF PRESSED SWEETS FROM KYOTO, I BELIEVE.
I DON'T WANT THEM.
LET THE CHAMBERMAIDS SHARE THEM AMONGST THEMSELVES. AND SEND LADY O-HISA A MOST COURTEOUS LETTER OF GRATITUDE.
YES, M'LADY.
YOU DON'T WANT THEM, MOTHER? BUT YOU'VE ALWAYS BEEN SO VERY FOND OF PRESSED SWEETS.
SACHIKO.
ALWAYS BE CAREFUL WHAT YOU PUT INTO YOUR MOUTH. YOU ARE A GIRL, SO YOU NEED NOT FEAR GETTING CAUGHT IN THE SUCCESSION CONTEST. BUT EVEN SO, I AM YOUR FATHER'S FAVORITE CONCUBINE AT THE MOMENT, AND THIS BREEDS JEALOUSY. I MUST BE EVER VIGILANT IF I AM TO AVOID BEING POISONED.
YOU TOO MUST NEVER BE SO THOUGHTLESS AS TO TASTE SOMETHING YOU HAVE RECEIVED FROM ANOTHER PERSON. REMEMBER IT WELL.

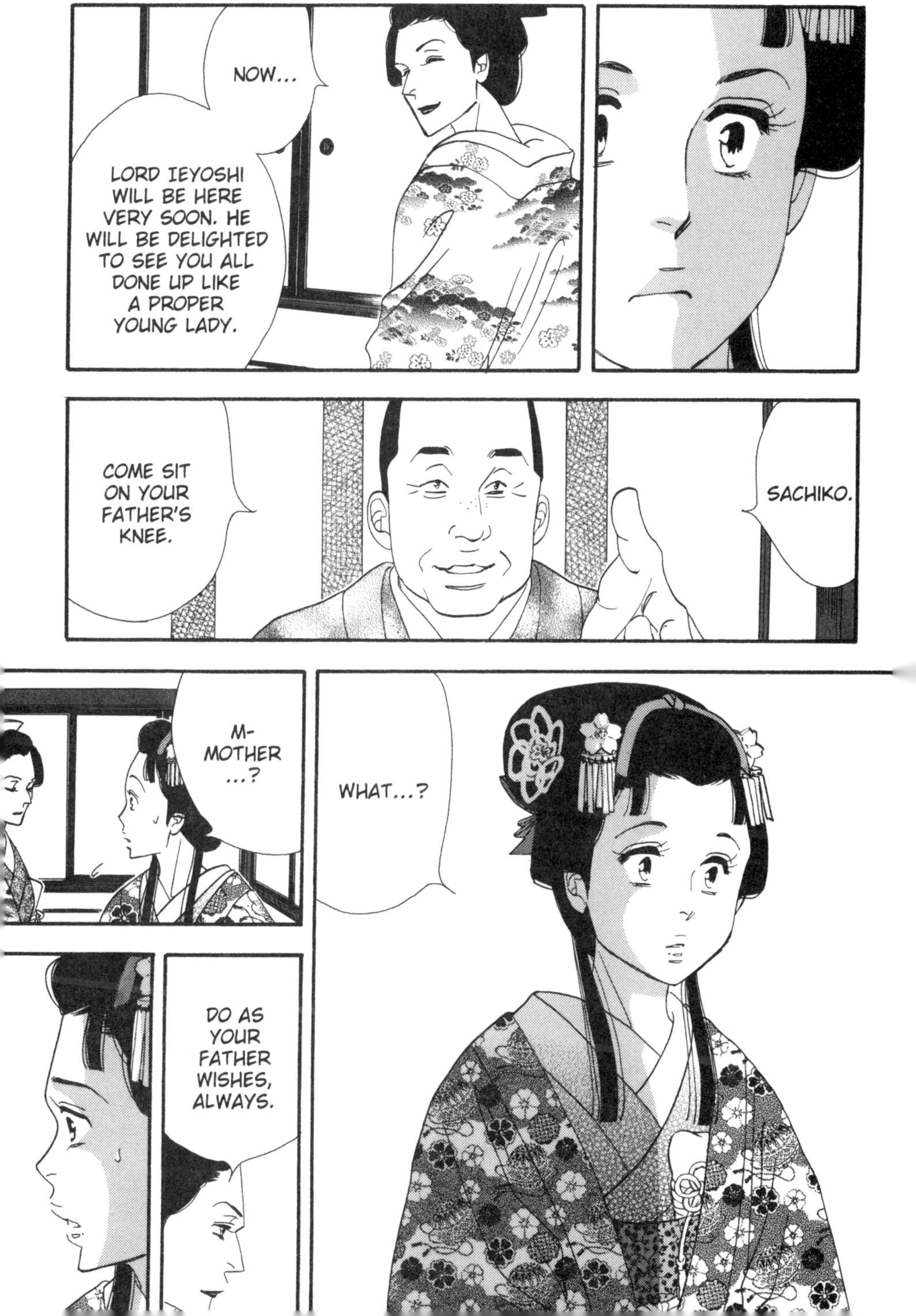
NOW...
LORD IEYOSHI WILL BE HERE VERY SOON. HE WILL BE DELIGHTED TO SEE YOU ALL DONE UP LIKE A PROPER YOUNG LADY.
SACHIKO.
COME SIT ON YOUR FATHER'S KNEE.
WHAT...?
M-MOTHER ...?
DO AS YOUR FATHER WISHES, ALWAYS.

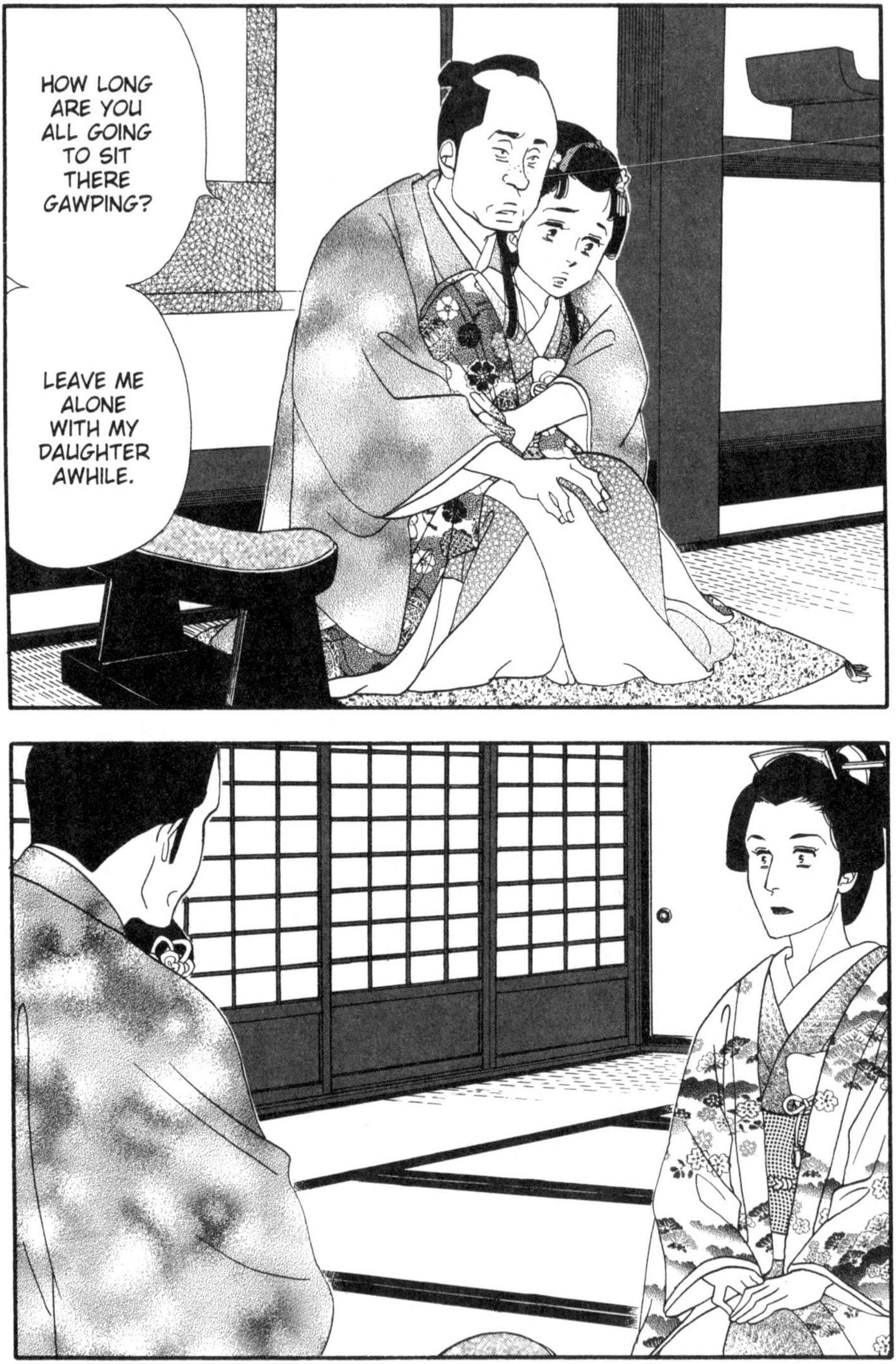
HOW LONG ARE YOU ALL GOING TO SIT THERE GAWPING?
LEAVE ME ALONE WITH MY DAUGHTER AWHILE.

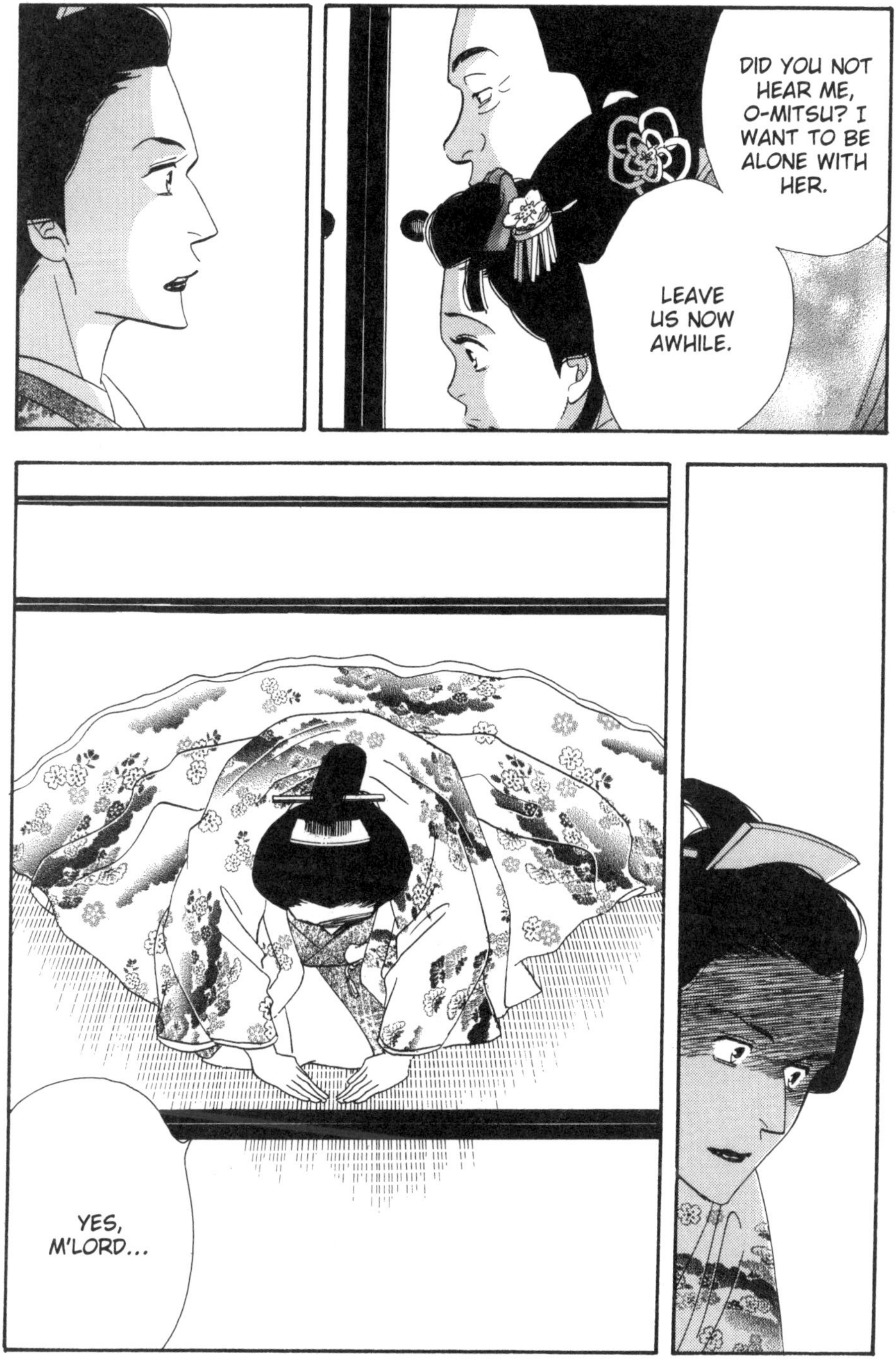
DID YOU NOT HEAR ME, O-MITSU? I WANT TO BE ALONE WITH HER.
LEAVE US NOW AWHILE.
YES, M'LORD...

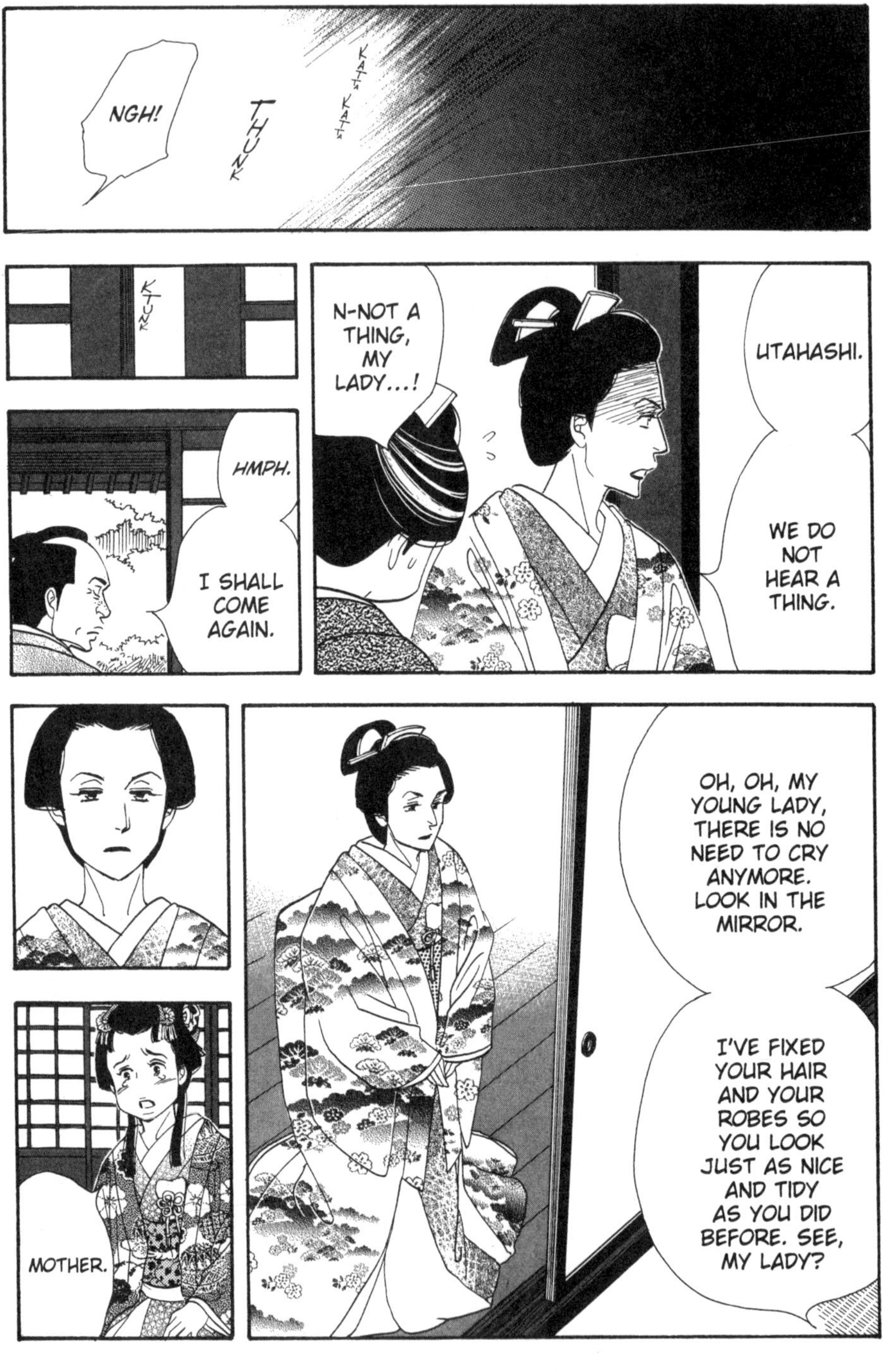
KATA KATA
THUNK
NGH!
UTAHASHI.
WE DO NOT HEAR A THING.
N-NOT A THING, MY LADY...!
KTUNK
HMPH.
I SHALL COME AGAIN.
OH, OH, MY YOUNG LADY, THERE IS NO NEED TO CRY ANYMORE. LOOK IN THE MIRROR.
I'VE FIXED YOUR HAIR AND YOUR ROBES SO YOU LOOK JUST AS NICE AND TIDY AS YOU DID BEFORE. SEE, MY LADY?
MOTHER.

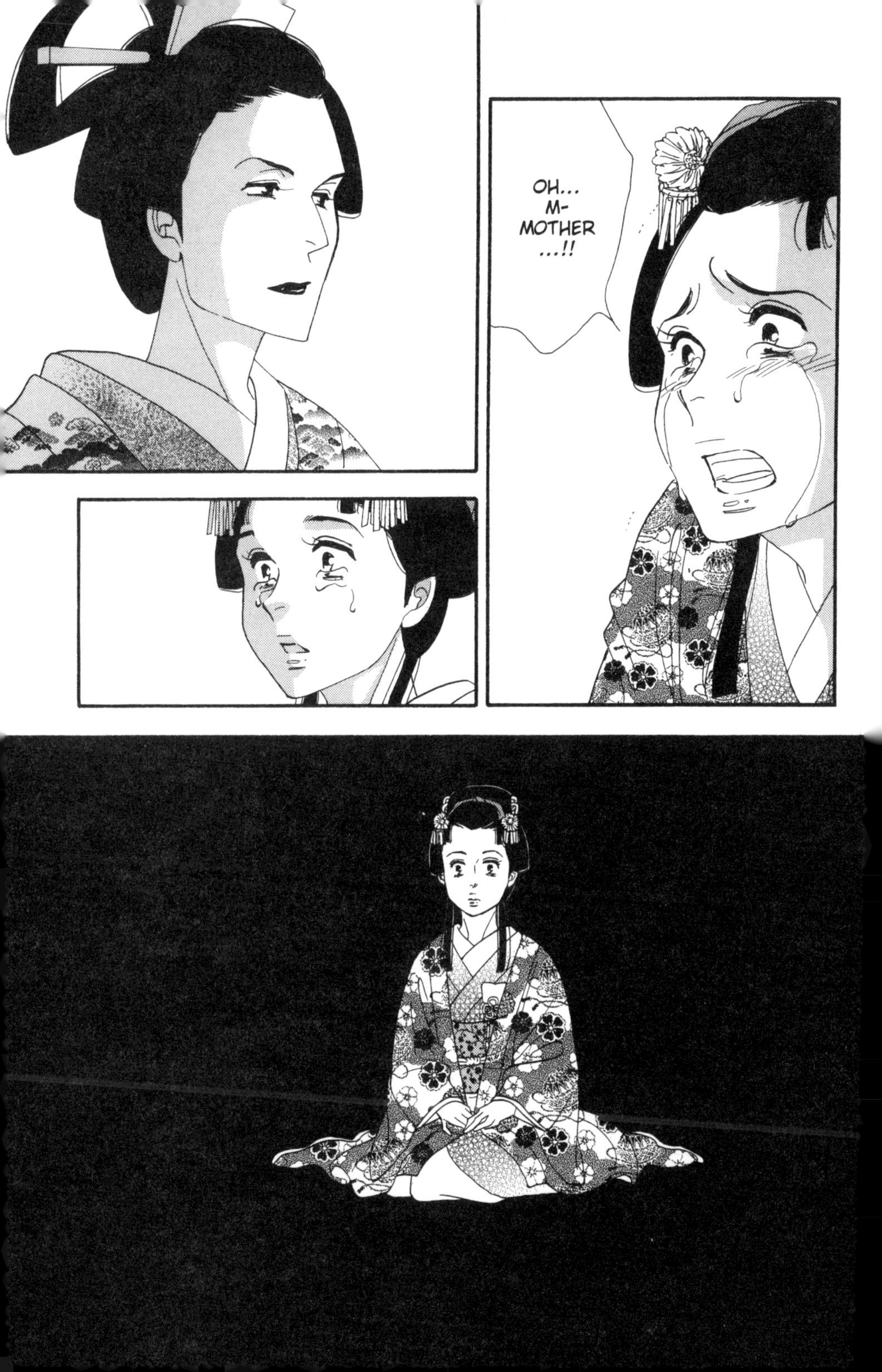
OH... M-MOTHER ...!!

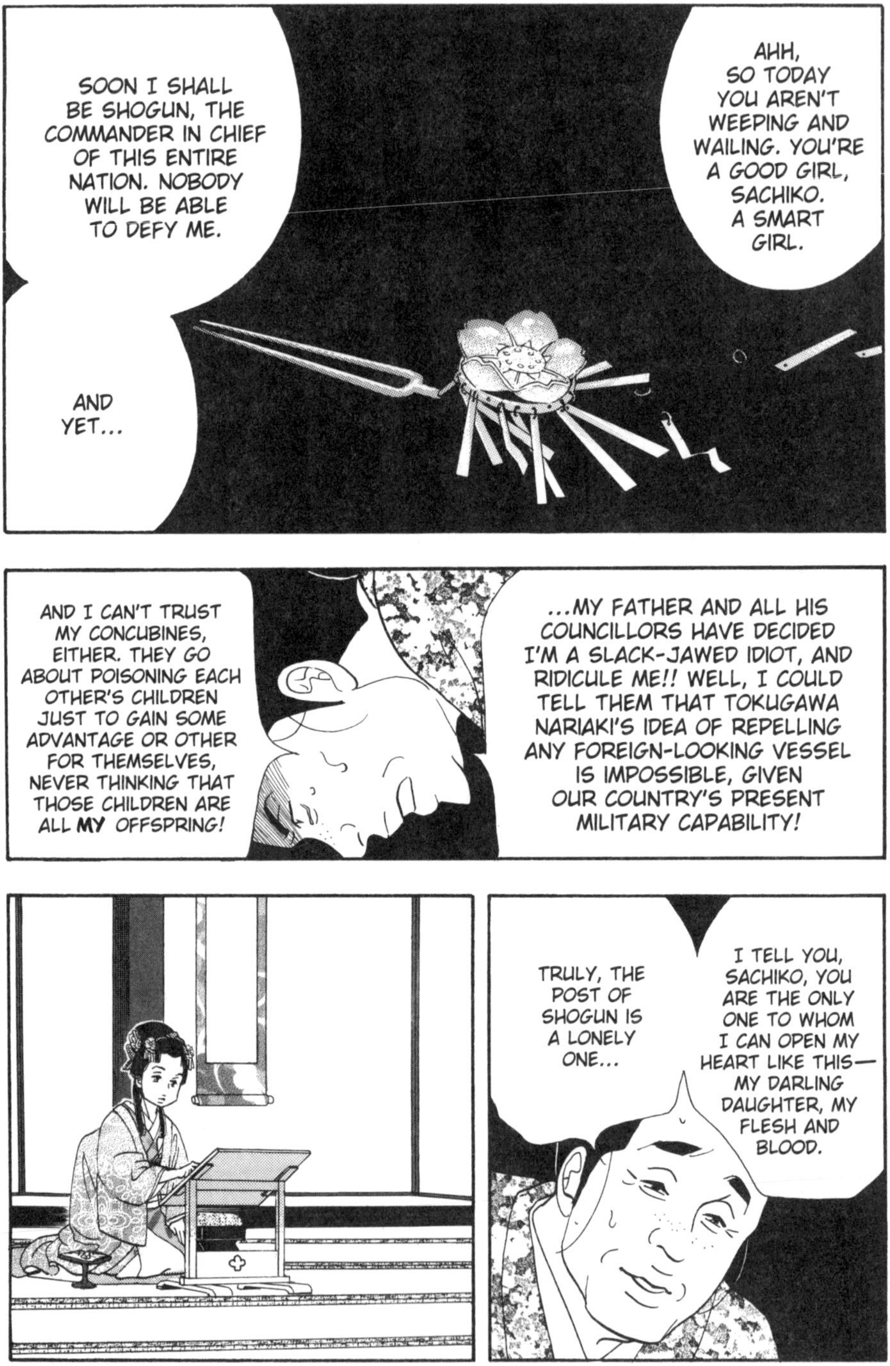
AHH, SO TODAY YOU AREN'T WEEPING AND WAILING. YOU'RE A GOOD GIRL, SACHIKO. A SMART GIRL.
SOON I SHALL BE SHOGUN, THE COMMANDER IN CHIEF OF THIS ENTIRE NATION. NOBODY WILL BE ABLE TO DEFY ME.
AND YET...
...MY FATHER AND ALL HIS COUNCILLORS HAVE DECIDED I'M A SLACK-JAWED IDIOT, AND RIDICULE ME!! WELL, I COULD TELL THEM THAT TOKUGAWA NARIAKI'S IDEA OF REPELLING ANY FOREIGN-LOOKING VESSEL IS IMPOSSIBLE, GIVEN OUR COUNTRY'S PRESENT MILITARY CAPABILITY!
AND I CAN'T TRUST MY CONCUBINES, EITHER. THEY GO ABOUT POISONING EACH OTHER'S CHILDREN JUST TO GAIN SOME ADVANTAGE OR OTHER FOR THEMSELVES, NEVER THINKING THAT THOSE CHILDREN ARE ALL **MY** OFFSPRING!
I TELL YOU, SACHIKO, YOU ARE THE ONLY ONE TO WHOM I CAN OPEN MY HEART LIKE THIS— MY DARLING DAUGHTER, MY FLESH AND BLOOD.
TRULY, THE POST OF SHOGUN IS A LONELY ONE...

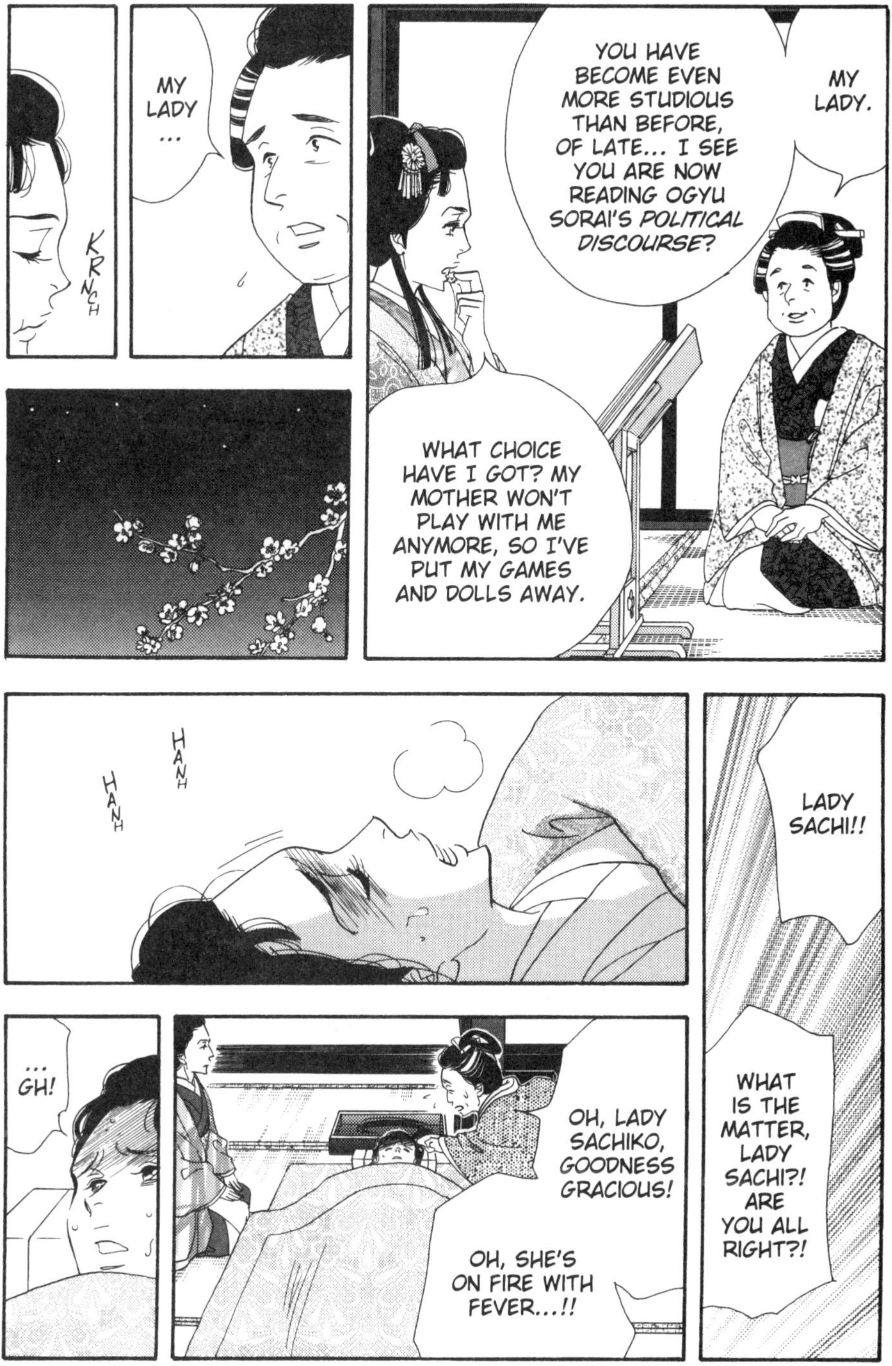
MY LADY.
YOU HAVE BECOME EVEN MORE STUDIOUS THAN BEFORE, OF LATE... I SEE YOU ARE NOW READING OGYU SORAI'S *POLITICAL DISCOURSE*?
WHAT CHOICE HAVE I GOT? MY MOTHER WON'T PLAY WITH ME ANYMORE, SO I'VE PUT MY GAMES AND DOLLS AWAY.
MY LADY ...
KRNCH
LADY SACHI!!
WHAT IS THE MATTER, LADY SACHI?! ARE YOU ALL RIGHT?!
HANH
HANH
OH, LADY SACHIKO, GOODNESS GRACIOUS!
OH, SHE'S ON FIRE WITH FEVER...!!
... GH!

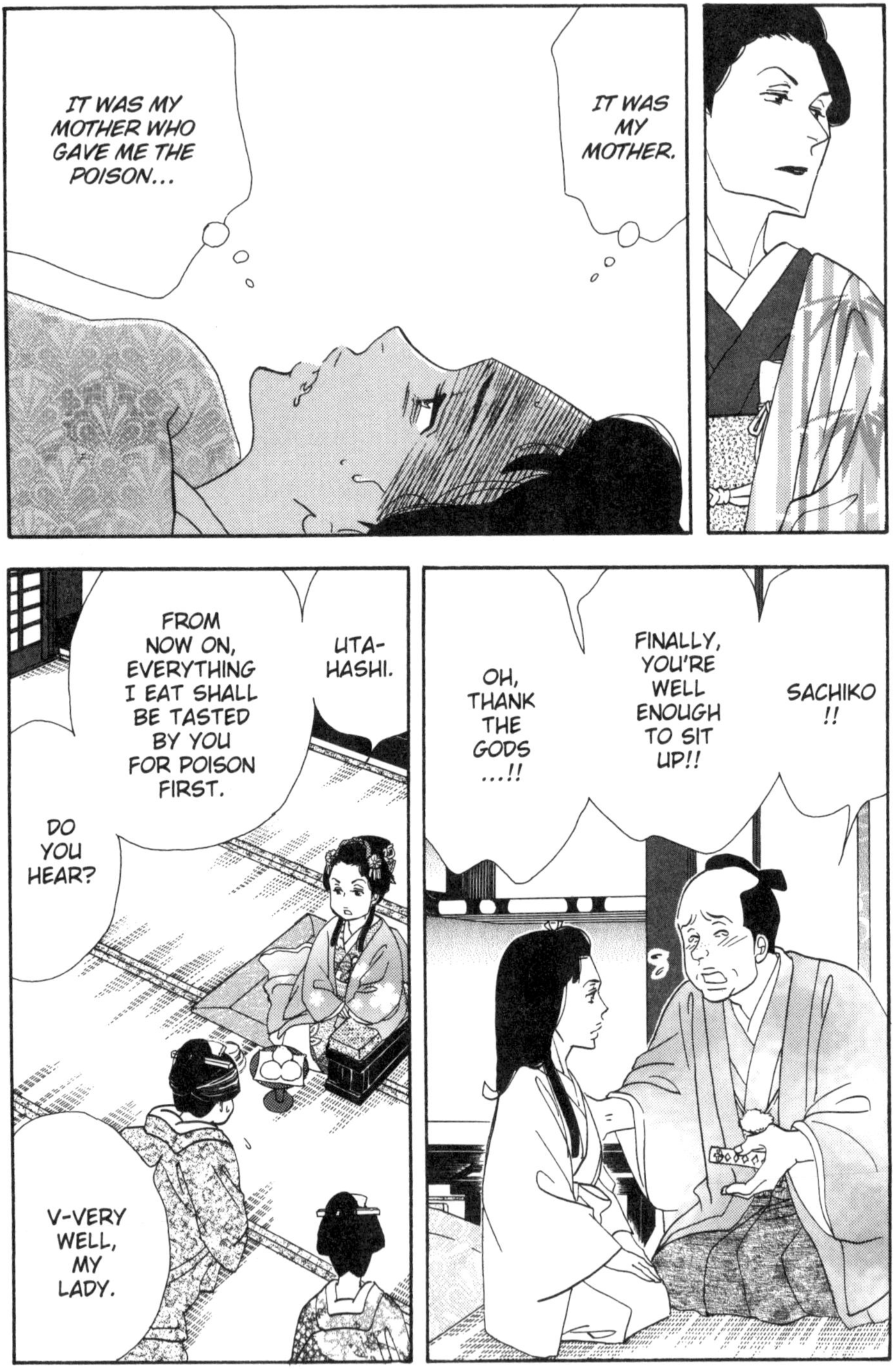
IT WAS MY MOTHER.
IT WAS MY MOTHER WHO GAVE ME THE POISON...
SACHIKO!!
FINALLY, YOU'RE WELL ENOUGH TO SIT UP!!
OH, THANK THE GODS ...!!
UTA-HASHI.
FROM NOW ON, EVERYTHING I EAT SHALL BE TASTED BY YOU FOR POISON FIRST.
DO YOU HEAR?
V-VERY WELL, MY LADY.

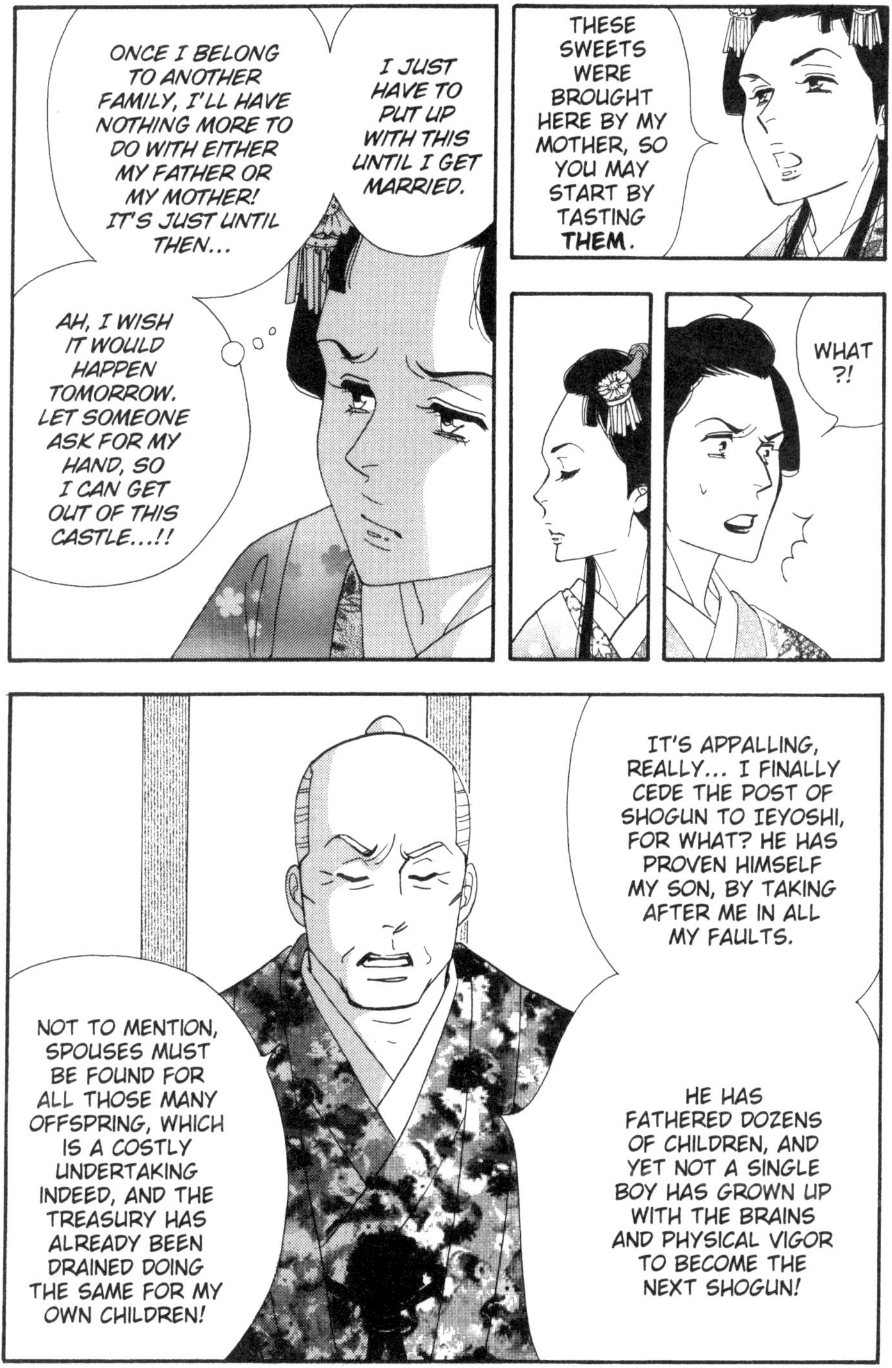
THESE SWEETS WERE BROUGHT HERE BY MY MOTHER, SO YOU MAY START BY TASTING **THEM**.
WHAT ?!
I JUST HAVE TO PUT UP WITH THIS UNTIL I GET MARRIED.
ONCE I BELONG TO ANOTHER FAMILY, I'LL HAVE NOTHING MORE TO DO WITH EITHER MY FATHER OR MY MOTHER! IT'S JUST UNTIL THEN...
AH, I WISH IT WOULD HAPPEN TOMORROW. LET SOMEONE ASK FOR MY HAND, SO I CAN GET OUT OF THIS CASTLE...!!
IT'S APPALLING, REALLY... I FINALLY CEDE THE POST OF SHOGUN TO IEYOSHI, FOR WHAT? HE HAS PROVEN HIMSELF MY SON, BY TAKING AFTER ME IN ALL MY FAULTS.
HE HAS FATHERED DOZENS OF CHILDREN, AND YET NOT A SINGLE BOY HAS GROWN UP WITH THE BRAINS AND PHYSICAL VIGOR TO BECOME THE NEXT SHOGUN!
NOT TO MENTION, SPOUSES MUST BE FOUND FOR ALL THOSE MANY OFFSPRING, WHICH IS A COSTLY UNDERTAKING INDEED, AND THE TREASURY HAS ALREADY BEEN DRAINED DOING THE SAME FOR MY OWN CHILDREN!

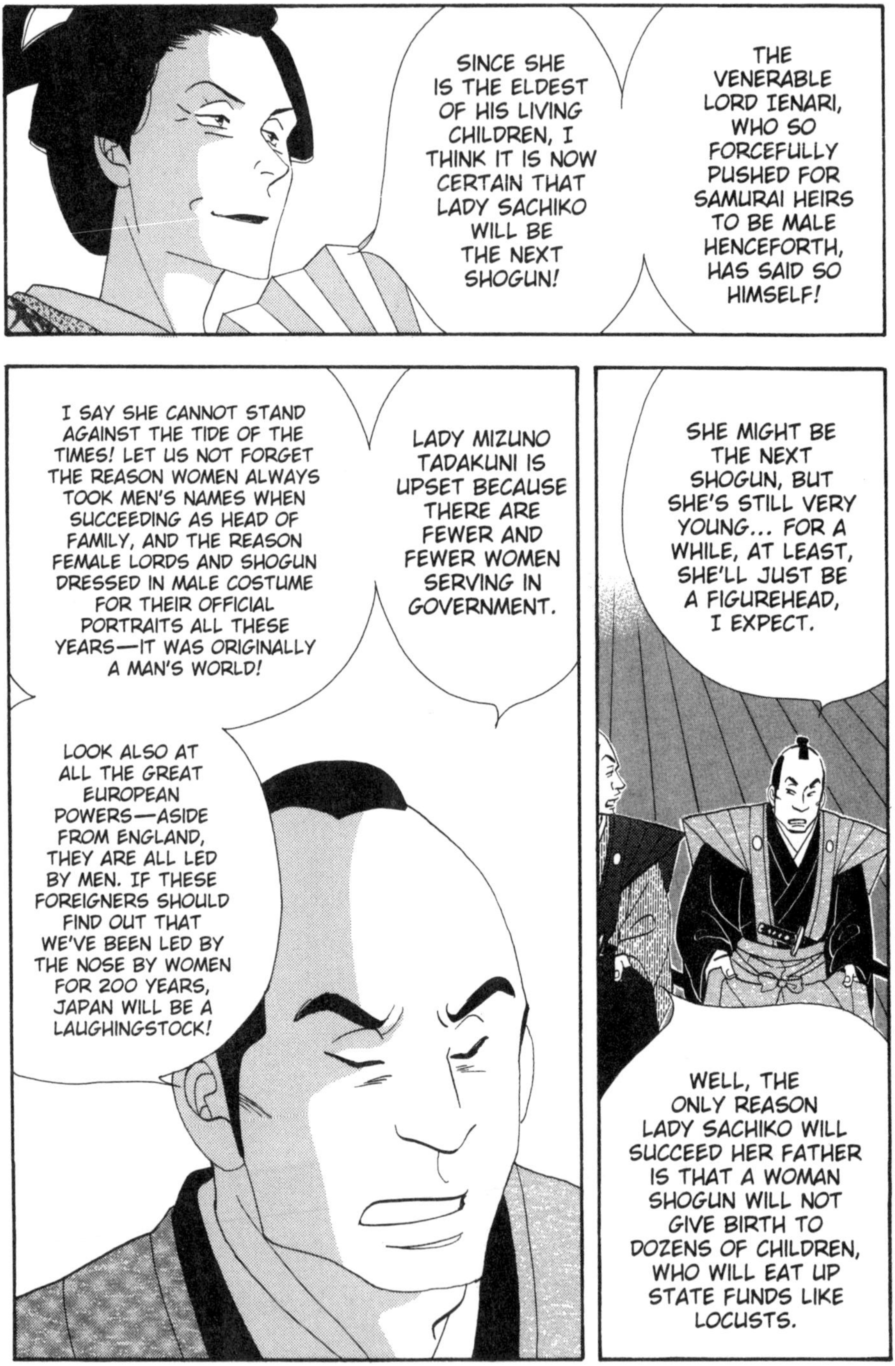
THE VENERABLE LORD IENARI, WHO SO FORCEFULLY PUSHED FOR SAMURAI HEIRS TO BE MALE HENCEFORTH, HAS SAID SO HIMSELF!
SINCE SHE IS THE ELDEST OF HIS LIVING CHILDREN, I THINK IT IS NOW CERTAIN THAT LADY SACHIKO WILL BE THE NEXT SHOGUN!
SHE MIGHT BE THE NEXT SHOGUN, BUT SHE'S STILL VERY YOUNG... FOR A WHILE, AT LEAST, SHE'LL JUST BE A FIGUREHEAD, I EXPECT.
WELL, THE ONLY REASON LADY SACHIKO WILL SUCCEED HER FATHER IS THAT A WOMAN SHOGUN WILL NOT GIVE BIRTH TO DOZENS OF CHILDREN, WHO WILL EAT UP STATE FUNDS LIKE LOCUSTS.
LADY MIZUNO TADAKUNI IS UPSET BECAUSE THERE ARE FEWER AND FEWER WOMEN SERVING IN GOVERNMENT.
I SAY SHE CANNOT STAND AGAINST THE TIDE OF THE TIMES! LET US NOT FORGET THE REASON WOMEN ALWAYS TOOK MEN'S NAMES WHEN SUCCEEDING AS HEAD OF FAMILY, AND THE REASON FEMALE LORDS AND SHOGUN DRESSED IN MALE COSTUME FOR THEIR OFFICIAL PORTRAITS ALL THESE YEARS—IT WAS ORIGINALLY A MAN'S WORLD!
LOOK ALSO AT ALL THE GREAT EUROPEAN POWERS—ASIDE FROM ENGLAND, THEY ARE ALL LED BY MEN. IF THESE FOREIGNERS SHOULD FIND OUT THAT WE'VE BEEN LED BY THE NOSE BY WOMEN FOR 200 YEARS, JAPAN WILL BE A LAUGHINGSTOCK!

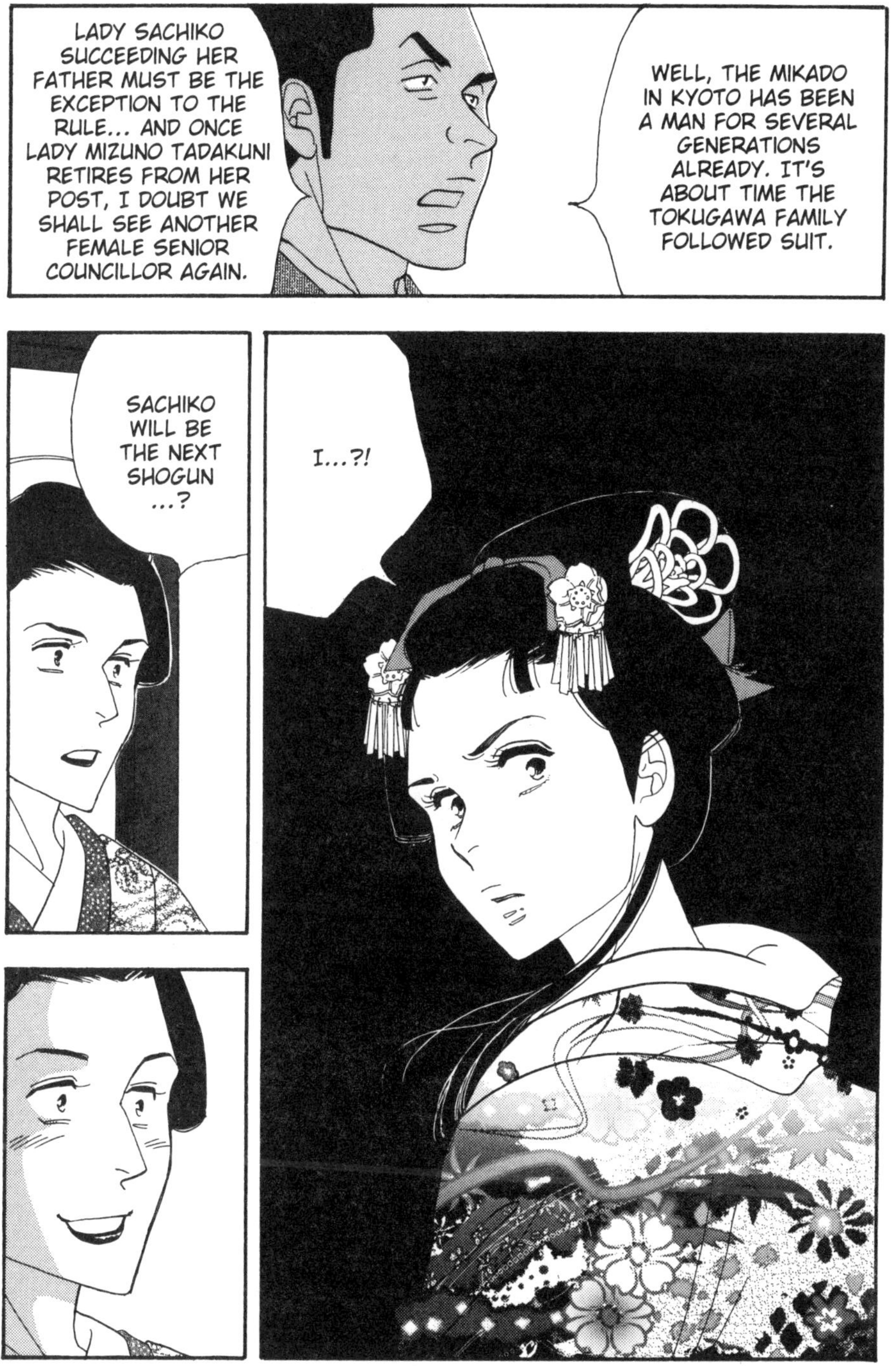
WELL, THE MIKADO IN KYOTO HAS BEEN A MAN FOR SEVERAL GENERATIONS ALREADY. IT'S ABOUT TIME THE TOKUGAWA FAMILY FOLLOWED SUIT.
LADY SACHIKO SUCCEEDING HER FATHER MUST BE THE EXCEPTION TO THE RULE... AND ONCE LADY MIZUNO TADAKUNI RETIRES FROM HER POST, I DOUBT WE SHALL SEE ANOTHER FEMALE SENIOR COUNCILLOR AGAIN.
I...?!
SACHIKO WILL BE THE NEXT SHOGUN ...?

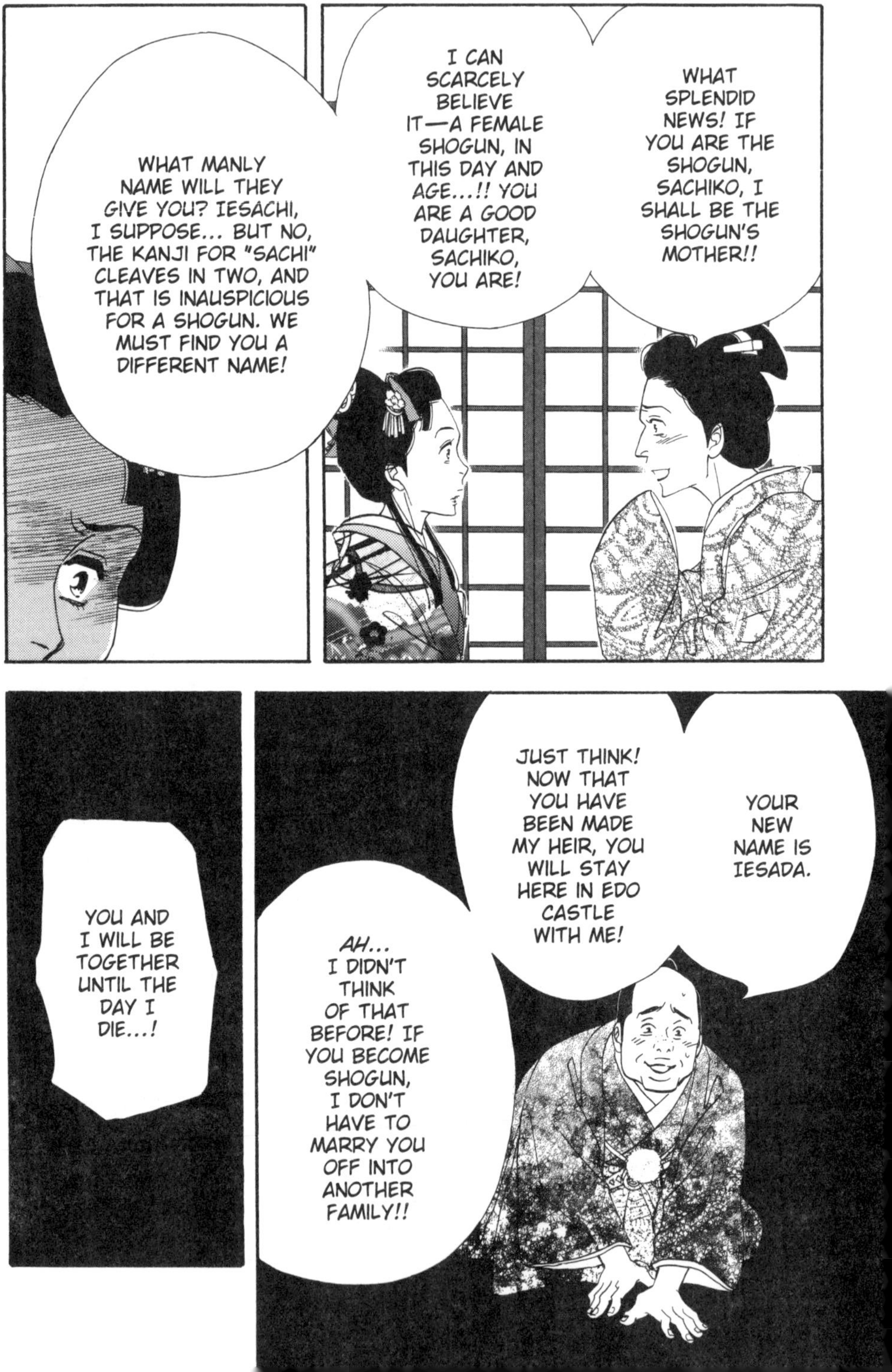
WHAT SPLENDID NEWS! IF YOU ARE THE SHOGUN, SACHIKO, I SHALL BE THE SHOGUN'S MOTHER!!
I CAN SCARCELY BELIEVE IT—A FEMALE SHOGUN, IN THIS DAY AND AGE...!! YOU ARE A GOOD DAUGHTER, SACHIKO, YOU ARE!
WHAT MANLY NAME WILL THEY GIVE YOU? IESACHI, I SUPPOSE... BUT NO, THE KANJI FOR "SACHI" CLEAVES IN TWO, AND THAT IS INAUSPICIOUS FOR A SHOGUN. WE MUST FIND YOU A DIFFERENT NAME!
YOUR NEW NAME IS IESADA.
JUST THINK! NOW THAT YOU HAVE BEEN MADE MY HEIR, YOU WILL STAY HERE IN EDO CASTLE WITH ME!
AH... I DIDN'T THINK OF THAT BEFORE! IF YOU BECOME SHOGUN, I DON'T HAVE TO MARRY YOU OFF INTO ANOTHER FAMILY!!
YOU AND I WILL BE TOGETHER UNTIL THE DAY I DIE...!

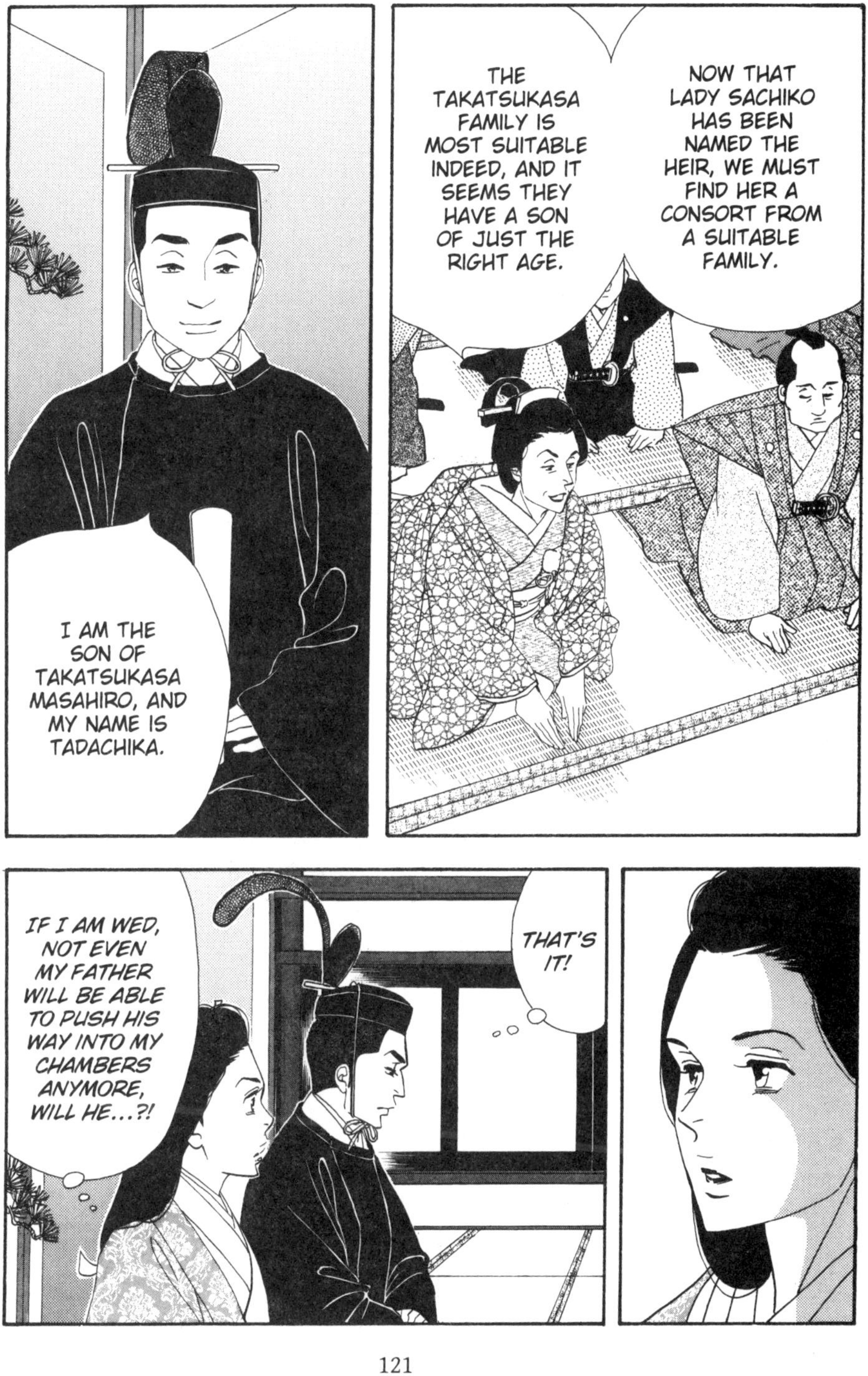
NOW THAT LADY SACHIKO HAS BEEN NAMED THE HEIR, WE MUST FIND HER A CONSORT FROM A SUITABLE FAMILY.
THE TAKATSUKASA FAMILY IS MOST SUITABLE INDEED, AND IT SEEMS THEY HAVE A SON OF JUST THE RIGHT AGE.
I AM THE SON OF TAKATSUKASA MASAHIRO, AND MY NAME IS TADACHIKA.
THAT'S IT!
IF I AM WED, NOT EVEN MY FATHER WILL BE ABLE TO PUSH HIS WAY INTO MY CHAMBERS ANYMORE, WILL HE...?!

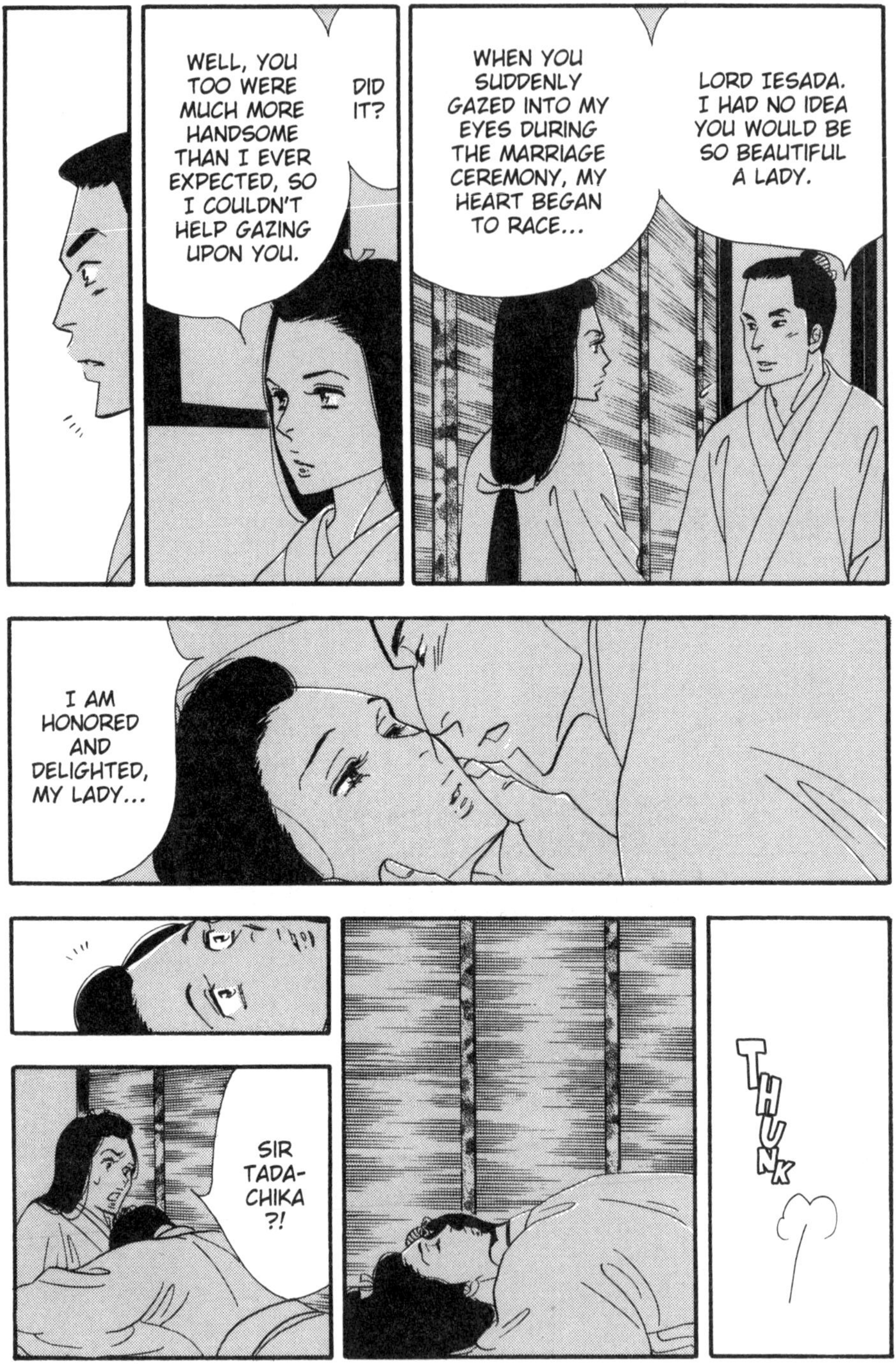
LORD IESADA. I HAD NO IDEA YOU WOULD BE SO BEAUTIFUL A LADY.
WHEN YOU SUDDENLY GAZED INTO MY EYES DURING THE MARRIAGE CEREMONY, MY HEART BEGAN TO RACE...
DID IT?
WELL, YOU TOO WERE MUCH MORE HANDSOME THAN I EVER EXPECTED, SO I COULDN'T HELP GAZING UPON YOU.
I AM HONORED AND DELIGHTED, MY LADY...
THUNK
SIR TADA-CHIKA?!

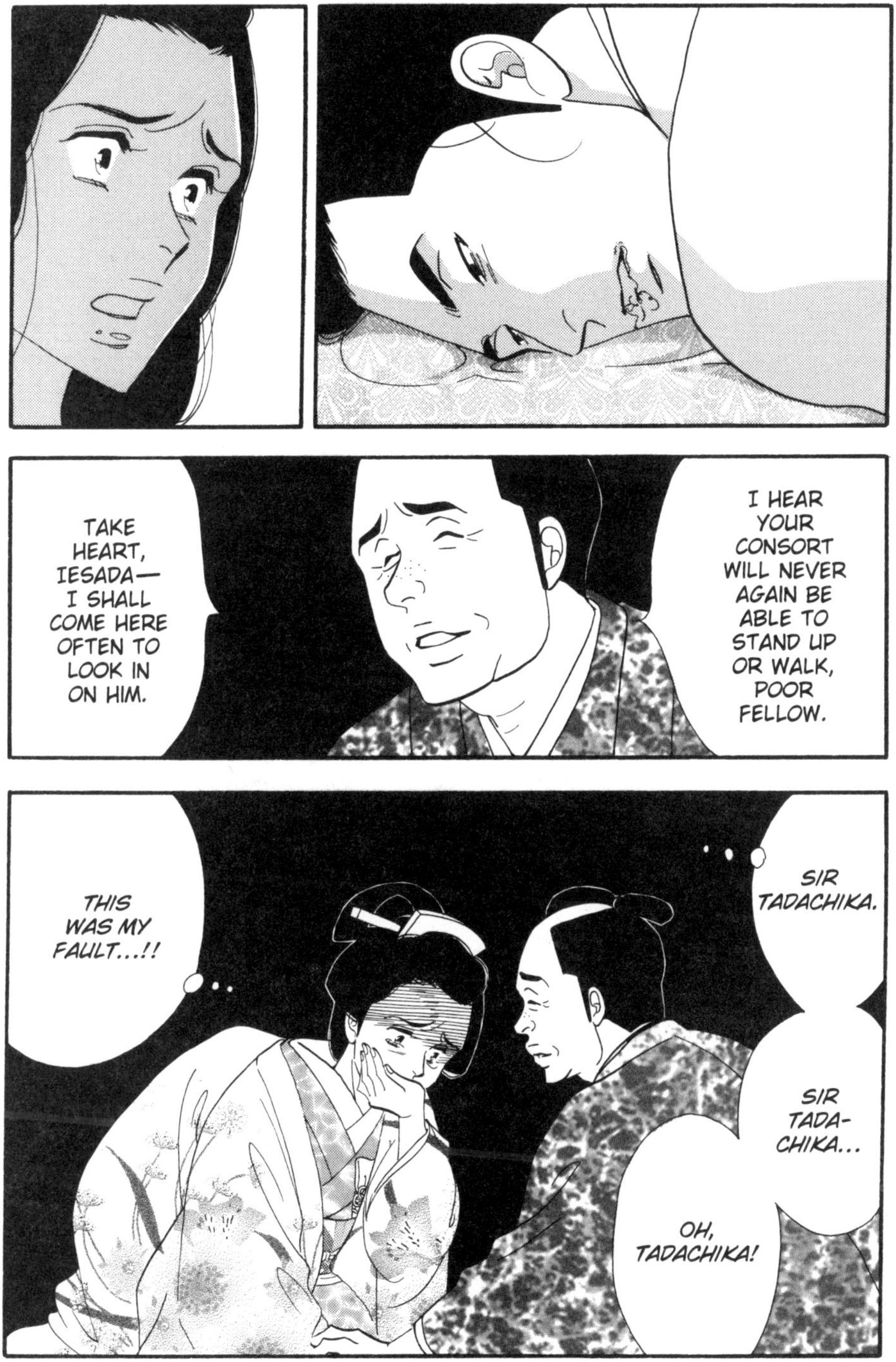
I HEAR YOUR CONSORT WILL NEVER AGAIN BE ABLE TO STAND UP OR WALK, POOR FELLOW.
TAKE HEART, IESADA— I SHALL COME HERE OFTEN TO LOOK IN ON HIM.
SIR TADACHIKA.
THIS WAS MY FAULT...!!
SIR TADA-CHIKA...
OH, TADACHIKA!

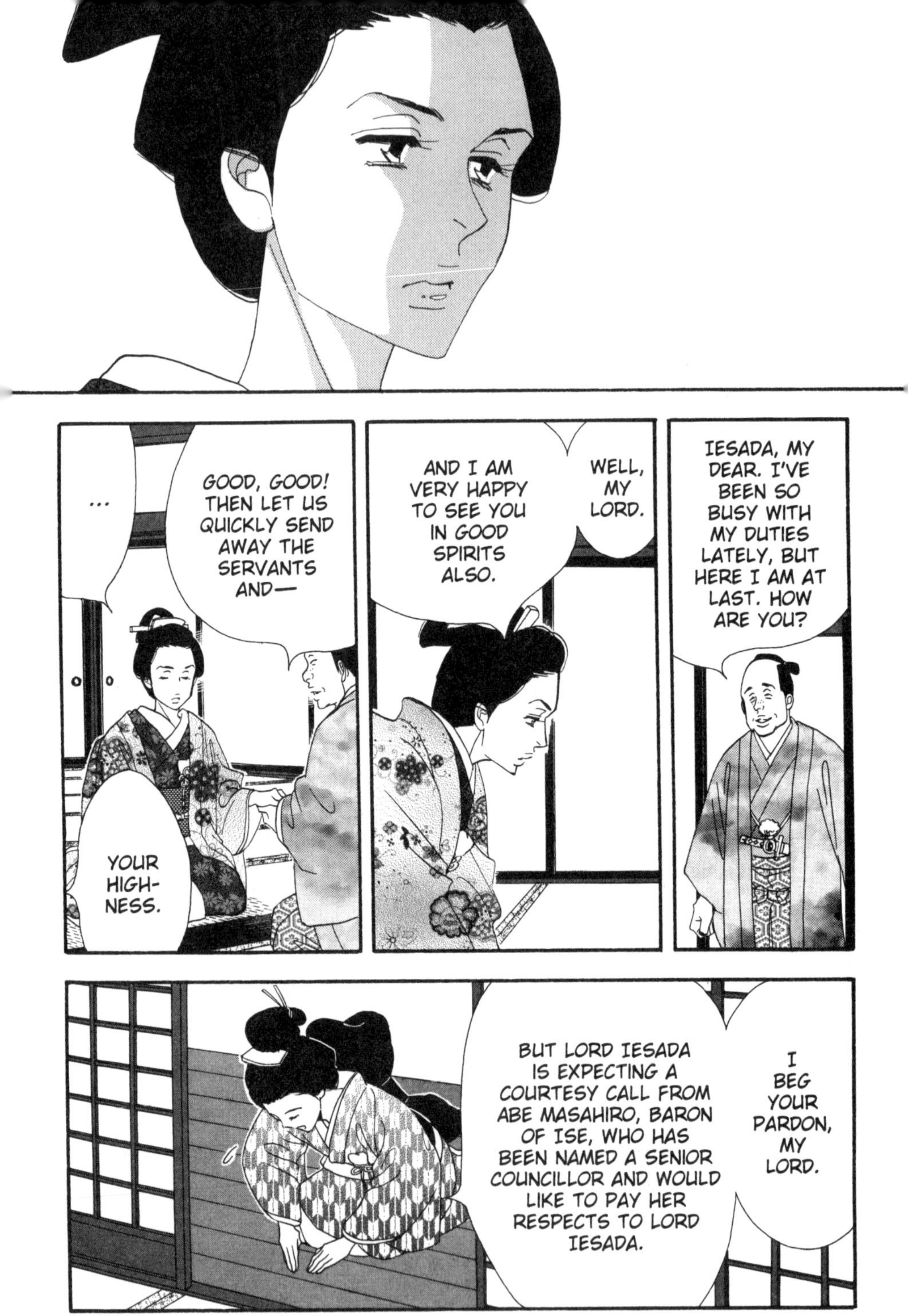
IESADA, MY DEAR. I'VE BEEN SO BUSY WITH MY DUTIES LATELY, BUT HERE I AM AT LAST. HOW ARE YOU?
WELL, MY LORD.
AND I AM VERY HAPPY TO SEE YOU IN GOOD SPIRITS ALSO.
GOOD, GOOD! THEN LET US QUICKLY SEND AWAY THE SERVANTS AND—
...
YOUR HIGHNESS.
I BEG YOUR PARDON, MY LORD.
BUT LORD IESADA IS EXPECTING A COURTESY CALL FROM ABE MASAHIRO, BARON OF ISE, WHO HAS BEEN NAMED A SENIOR COUNCILLOR AND WOULD LIKE TO PAY HER RESPECTS TO LORD IESADA.

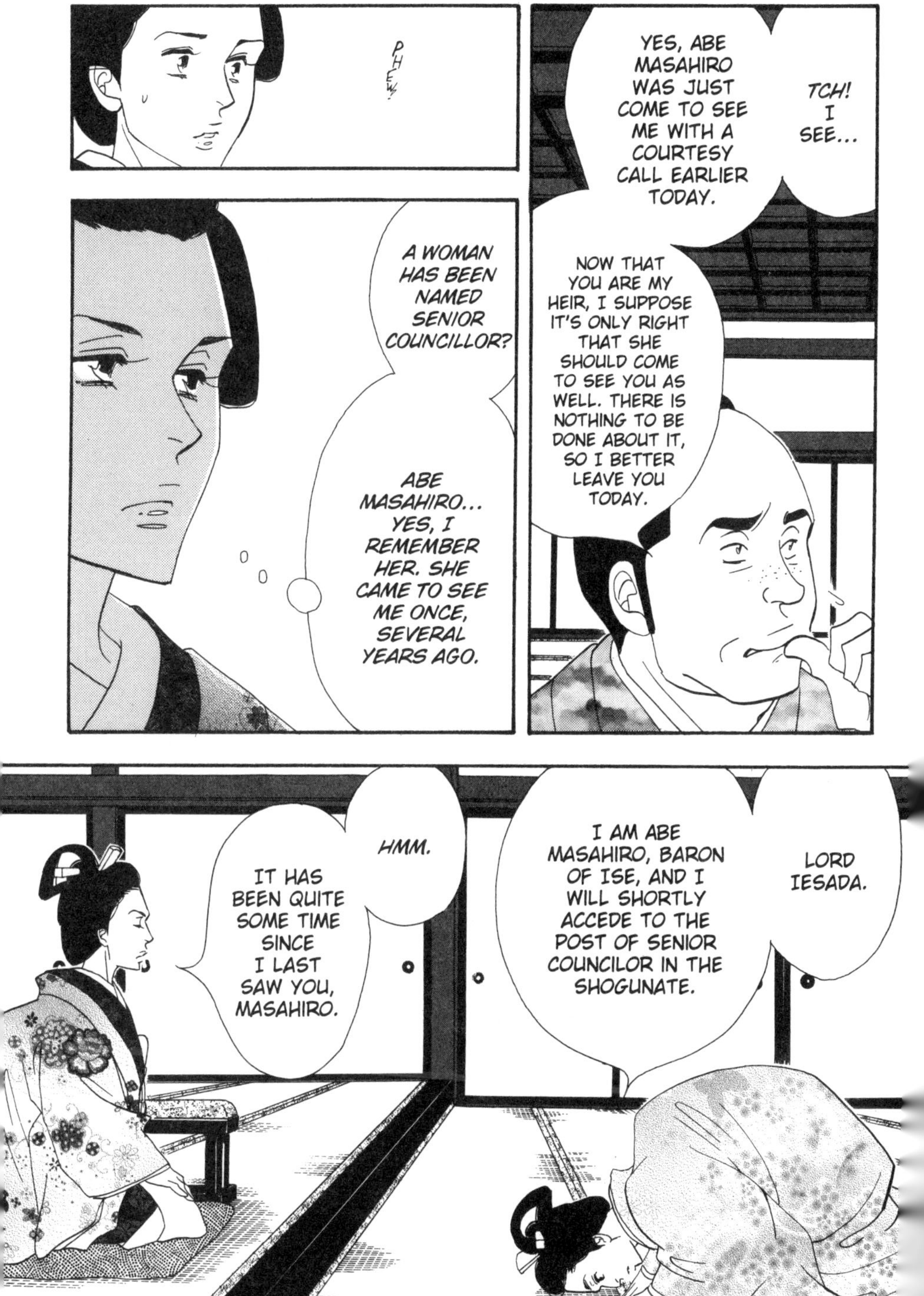
TCH! I SEE...
YES, ABE MASAHIRO WAS JUST COME TO SEE ME WITH A COURTESY CALL EARLIER TODAY.
NOW THAT YOU ARE MY HEIR, I SUPPOSE IT'S ONLY RIGHT THAT SHE SHOULD COME TO SEE YOU AS WELL. THERE IS NOTHING TO BE DONE ABOUT IT, SO I BETTER LEAVE YOU TODAY.
PHEW
A WOMAN HAS BEEN NAMED SENIOR COUNCILLOR?
ABE MASAHIRO... YES, I REMEMBER HER. SHE CAME TO SEE ME ONCE, SEVERAL YEARS AGO.
LORD IESADA.
I AM ABE MASAHIRO, BARON OF ISE, AND I WILL SHORTLY ACCEDE TO THE POST OF SENIOR COUNCILOR IN THE SHOGUNATE.
HMM.
IT HAS BEEN QUITE SOME TIME SINCE I LAST SAW YOU, MASAHIRO.

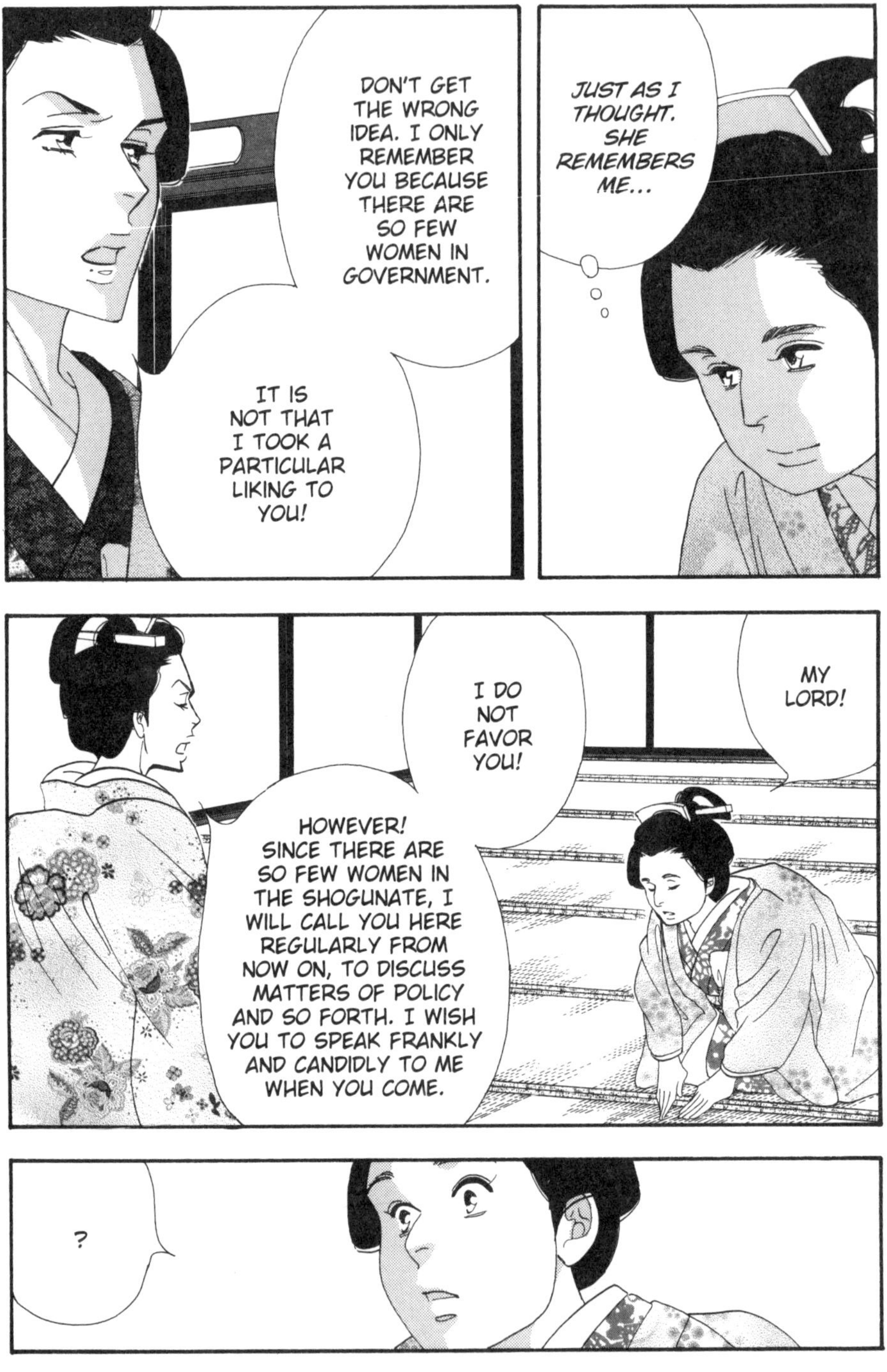
JUST AS I THOUGHT. SHE REMEMBERS ME...
DON'T GET THE WRONG IDEA. I ONLY REMEMBER YOU BECAUSE THERE ARE SO FEW WOMEN IN GOVERNMENT.
IT IS NOT THAT I TOOK A PARTICULAR LIKING TO YOU!
MY LORD!
I DO NOT FAVOR YOU!
HOWEVER! SINCE THERE ARE SO FEW WOMEN IN THE SHOGUNATE, I WILL CALL YOU HERE REGULARLY FROM NOW ON, TO DISCUSS MATTERS OF POLICY AND SO FORTH. I WISH YOU TO SPEAK FRANKLY AND CANDIDLY TO ME WHEN YOU COME.
?

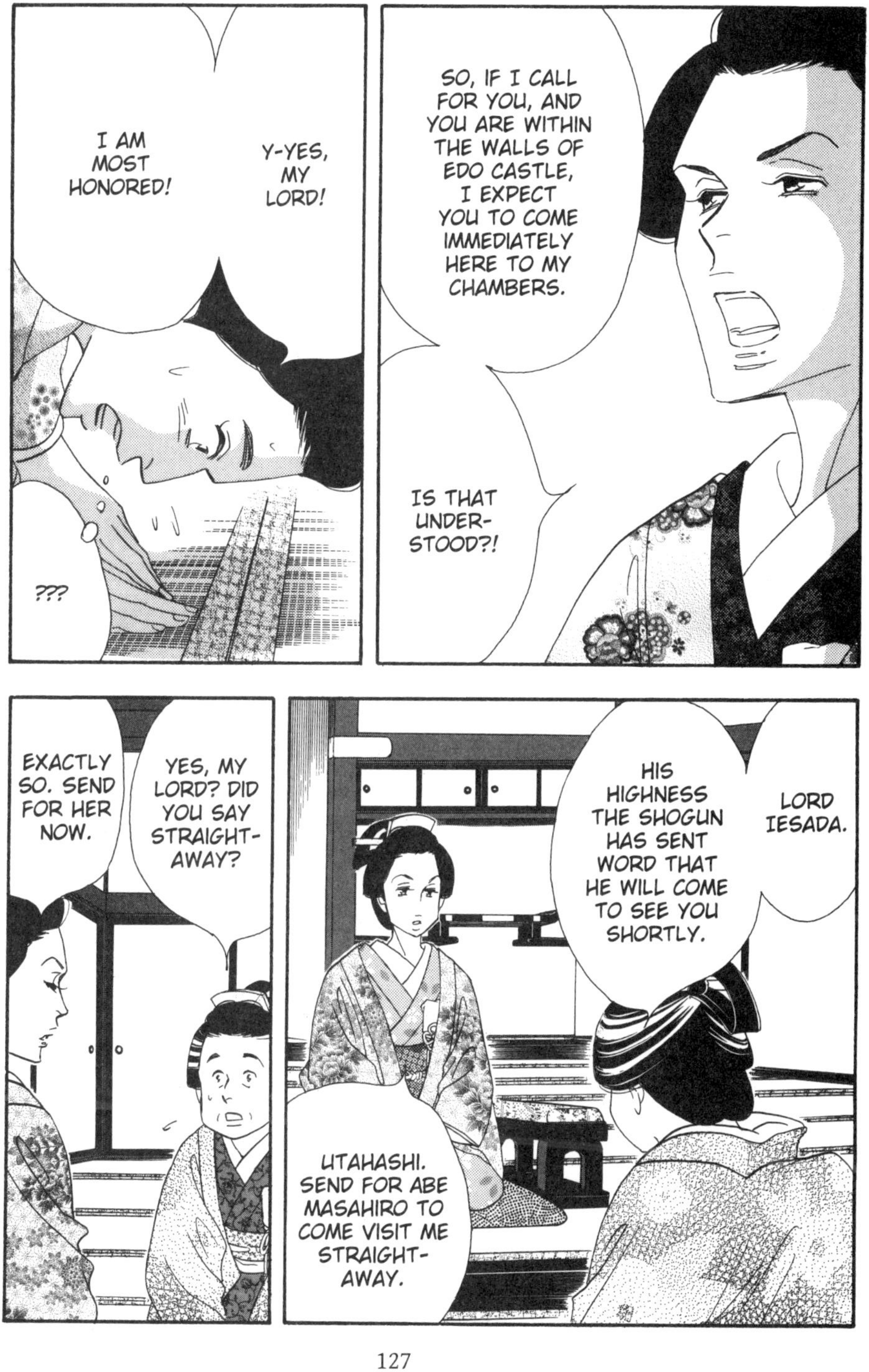
SO, IF I CALL FOR YOU, AND YOU ARE WITHIN THE WALLS OF EDO CASTLE, I EXPECT YOU TO COME IMMEDIATELY HERE TO MY CHAMBERS.
IS THAT UNDER-STOOD?!
Y-YES, MY LORD!
I AM MOST HONORED!
???
LORD IESADA.
HIS HIGHNESS THE SHOGUN HAS SENT WORD THAT HE WILL COME TO SEE YOU SHORTLY.
UTAHASHI. SEND FOR ABE MASAHIRO TO COME VISIT ME STRAIGHT-AWAY.
YES, MY LORD? DID YOU SAY STRAIGHT-AWAY?
EXACTLY SO. SEND FOR HER NOW.

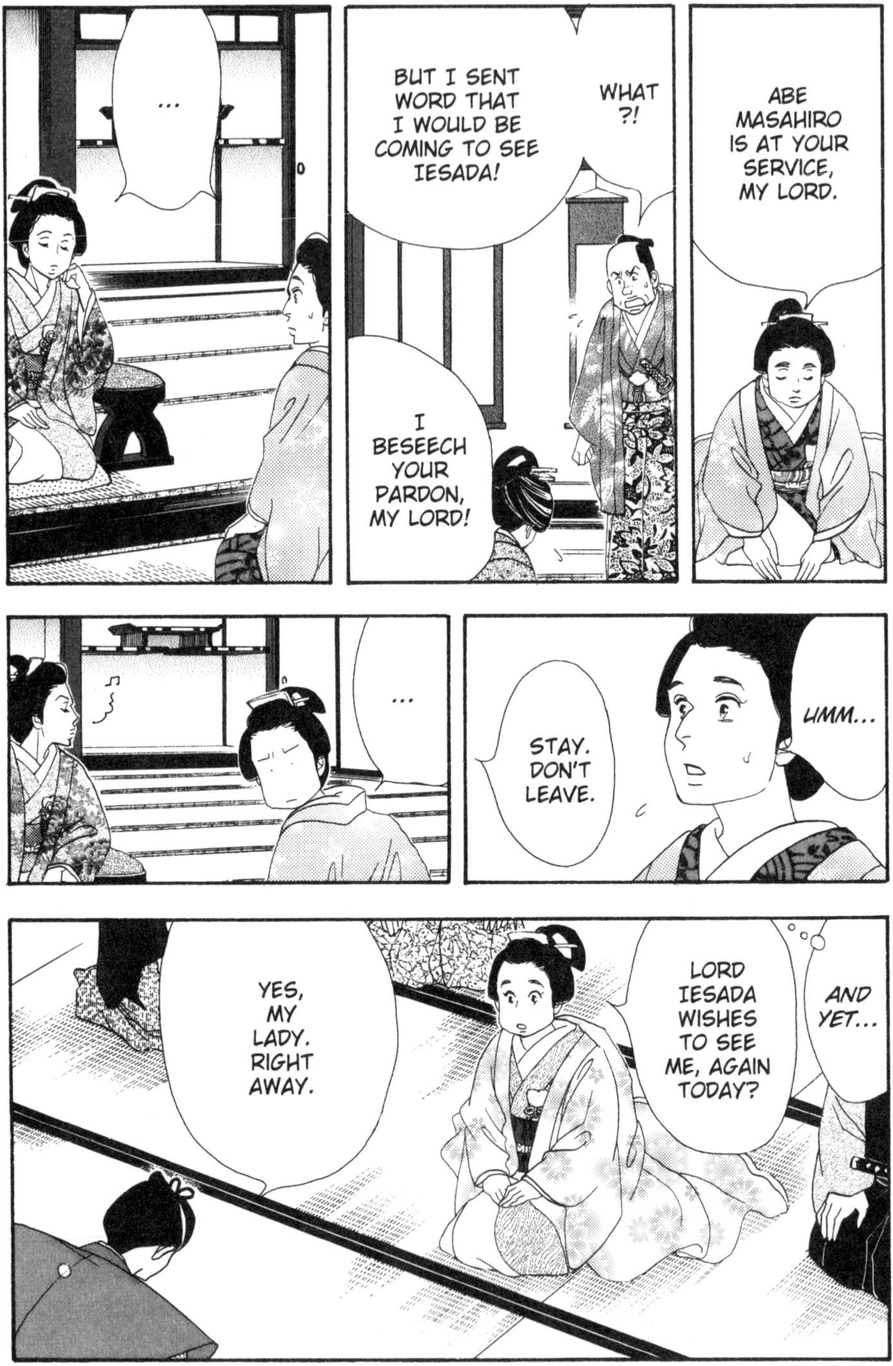
ABE MASAHIRO IS AT YOUR SERVICE, MY LORD.
WHAT ?!
BUT I SENT WORD THAT I WOULD BE COMING TO SEE IESADA!
I BESEECH YOUR PARDON, MY LORD!
...
UMM...
STAY. DON'T LEAVE.
...
AND YET...
LORD IESADA WISHES TO SEE ME, AGAIN TODAY?
YES, MY LADY. RIGHT AWAY.

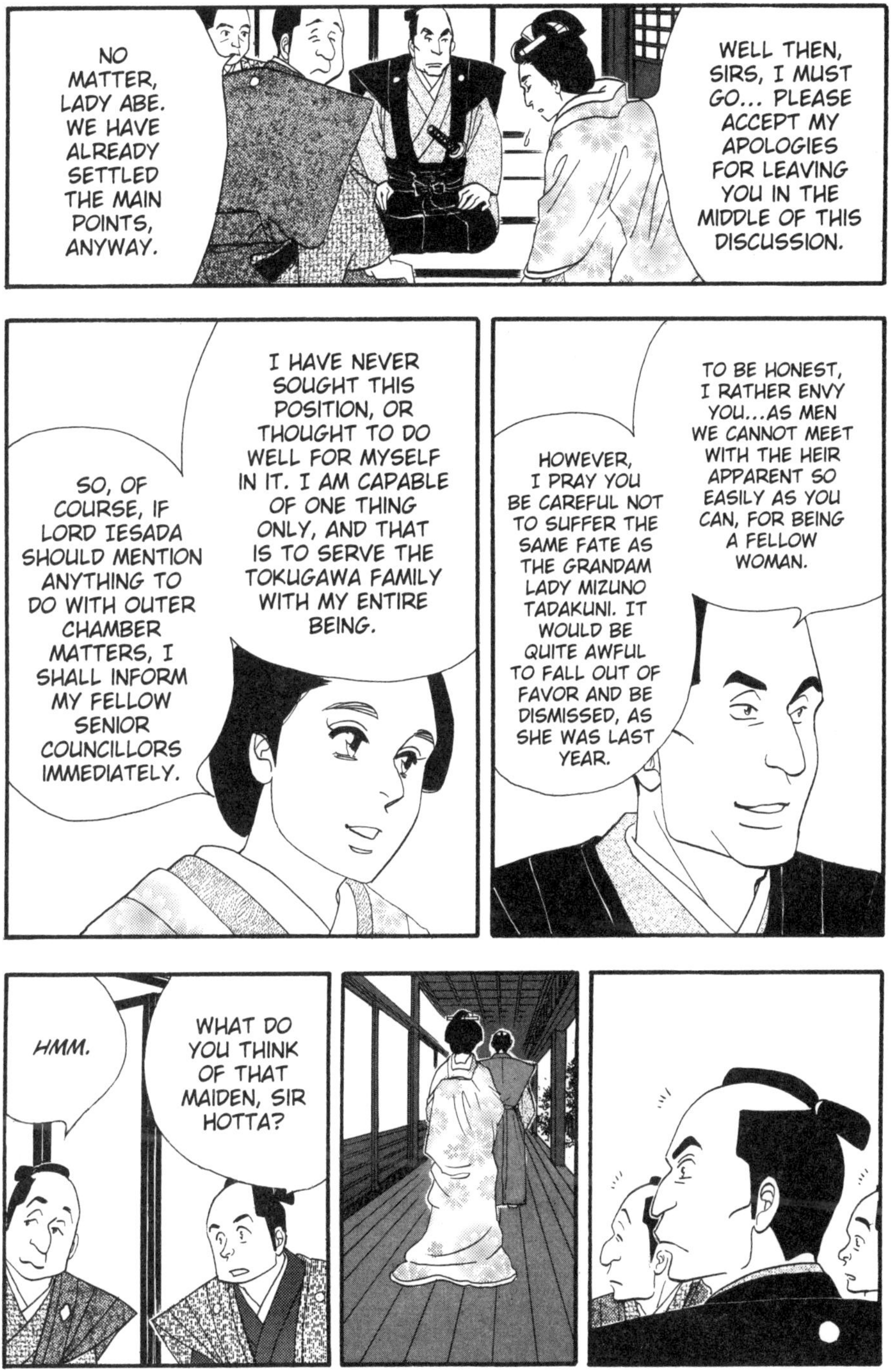
WELL THEN, SIRS, I MUST GO... PLEASE ACCEPT MY APOLOGIES FOR LEAVING YOU IN THE MIDDLE OF THIS DISCUSSION.
NO MATTER, LADY ABE. WE HAVE ALREADY SETTLED THE MAIN POINTS, ANYWAY.
TO BE HONEST, I RATHER ENVY YOU...AS MEN WE CANNOT MEET WITH THE HEIR APPARENT SO EASILY AS YOU CAN, FOR BEING A FELLOW WOMAN.
HOWEVER, I PRAY YOU BE CAREFUL NOT TO SUFFER THE SAME FATE AS THE GRANDAM LADY MIZUNO TADAKUNI. IT WOULD BE QUITE AWFUL TO FALL OUT OF FAVOR AND BE DISMISSED, AS SHE WAS LAST YEAR.
I HAVE NEVER SOUGHT THIS POSITION, OR THOUGHT TO DO WELL FOR MYSELF IN IT. I AM CAPABLE OF ONE THING ONLY, AND THAT IS TO SERVE THE TOKUGAWA FAMILY WITH MY ENTIRE BEING.
SO, OF COURSE, IF LORD IESADA SHOULD MENTION ANYTHING TO DO WITH OUTER CHAMBER MATTERS, I SHALL INFORM MY FELLOW SENIOR COUNCILLORS IMMEDIATELY.
WHAT DO YOU THINK OF THAT MAIDEN, SIR HOTTA?
HMM.

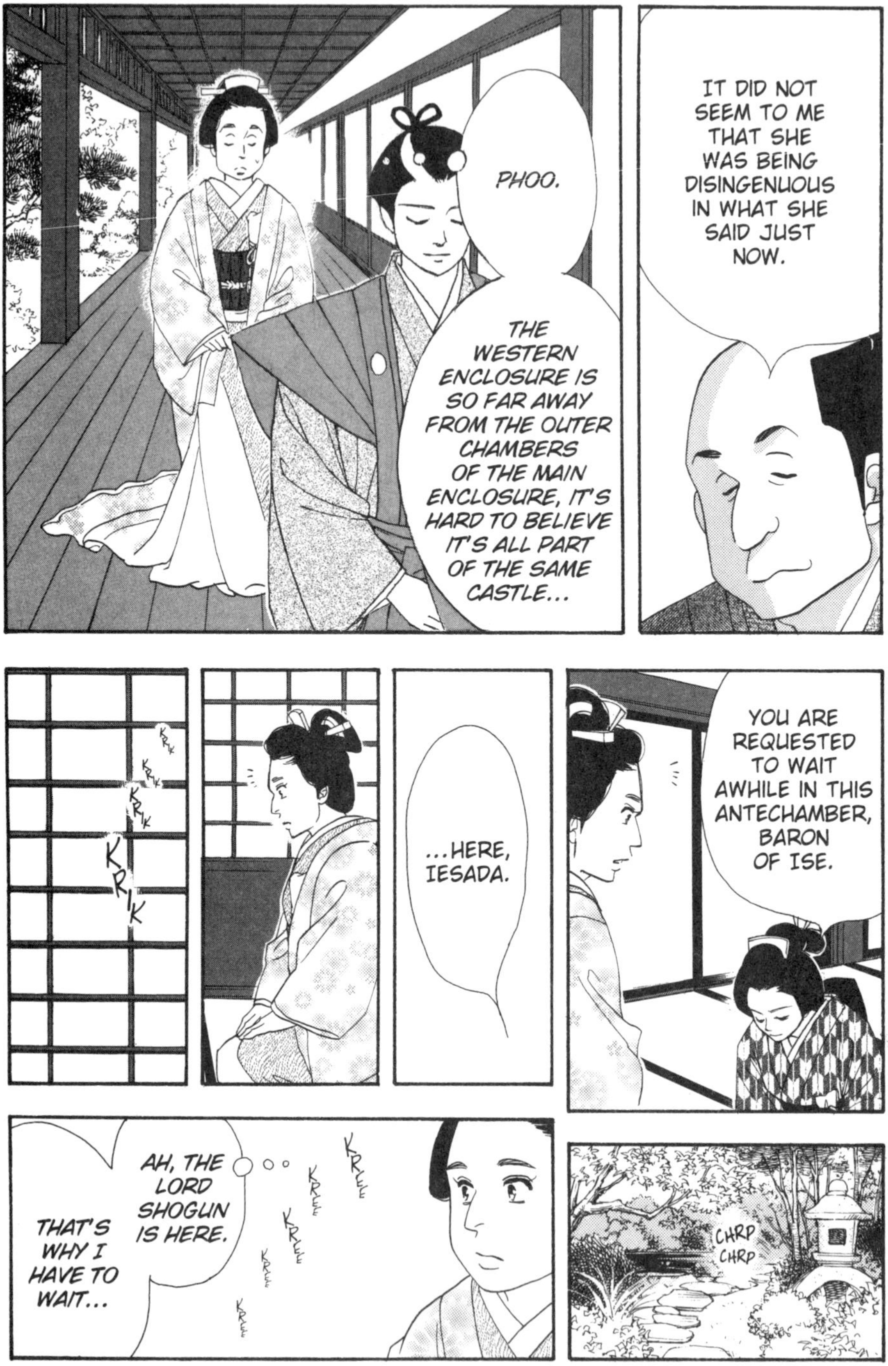
IT DID NOT SEEM TO ME THAT SHE WAS BEING DISINGENUOUS IN WHAT SHE SAID JUST NOW.
PHOO.
THE WESTERN ENCLOSURE IS SO FAR AWAY FROM THE OUTER CHAMBERS OF THE MAIN ENCLOSURE, IT'S HARD TO BELIEVE IT'S ALL PART OF THE SAME CASTLE...
YOU ARE REQUESTED TO WAIT AWHILE IN THIS ANTECHAMBER, BARON OF ISE.
...HERE, IESADA.
KRIK
KRIK
KRIK
KRIK
CHRP
CHRP
KREE
KREE
KREE
KREE
KREE
AH, THE LORD SHOGUN IS HERE.
THAT'S WHY I HAVE TO WAIT...

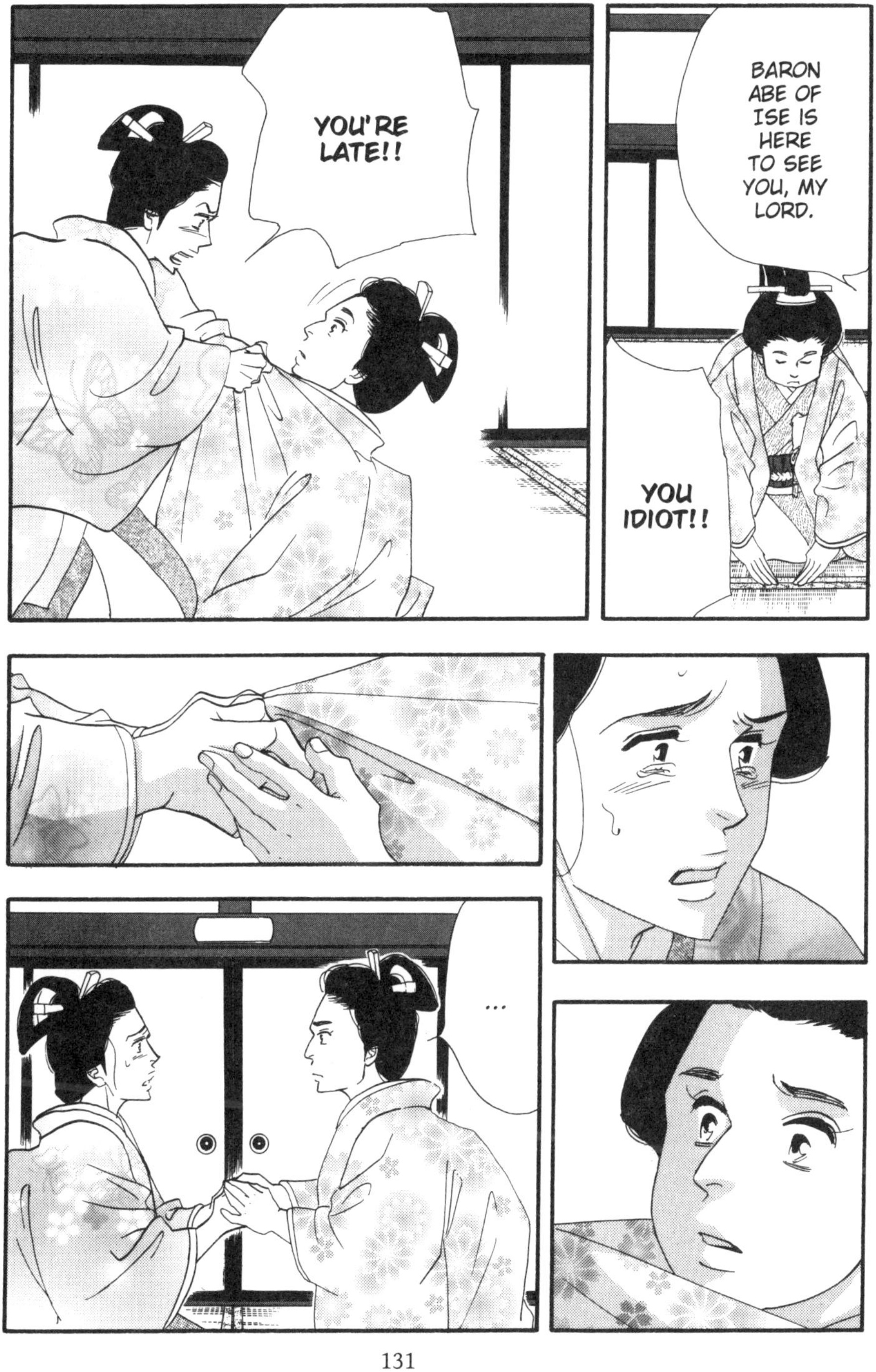
BARON ABE OF ISE IS HERE TO SEE YOU, MY LORD.
YOU IDIOT!!
YOU'RE LATE!!
...

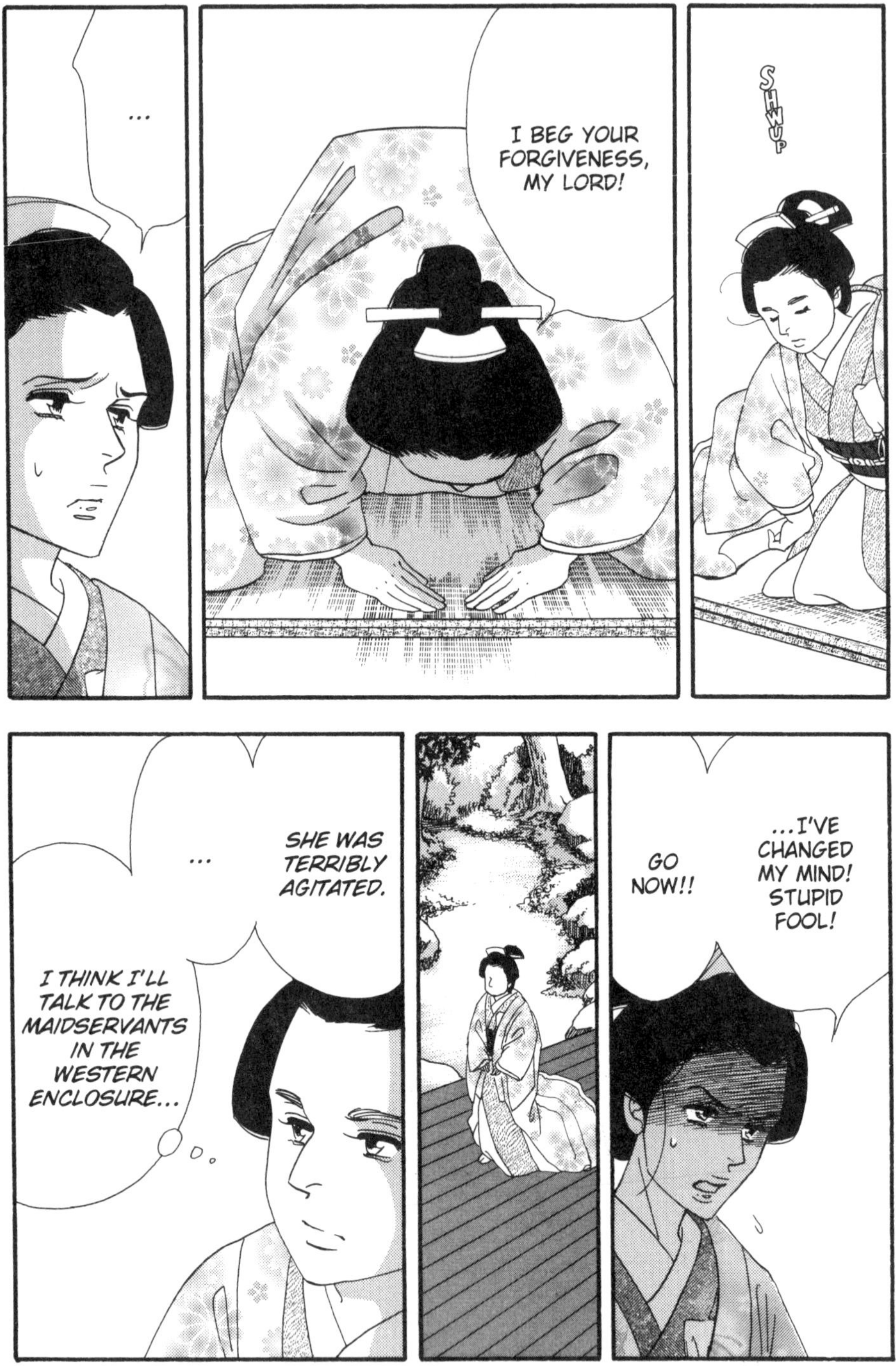
SHWUP
I BEG YOUR FORGIVENESS, MY LORD!
...
...I'VE CHANGED MY MIND! STUPID FOOL!
GO NOW!!
SHE WAS TERRIBLY AGITATED.
...
I THINK I'LL TALK TO THE MAIDSERVANTS IN THE WESTERN ENCLOSURE...

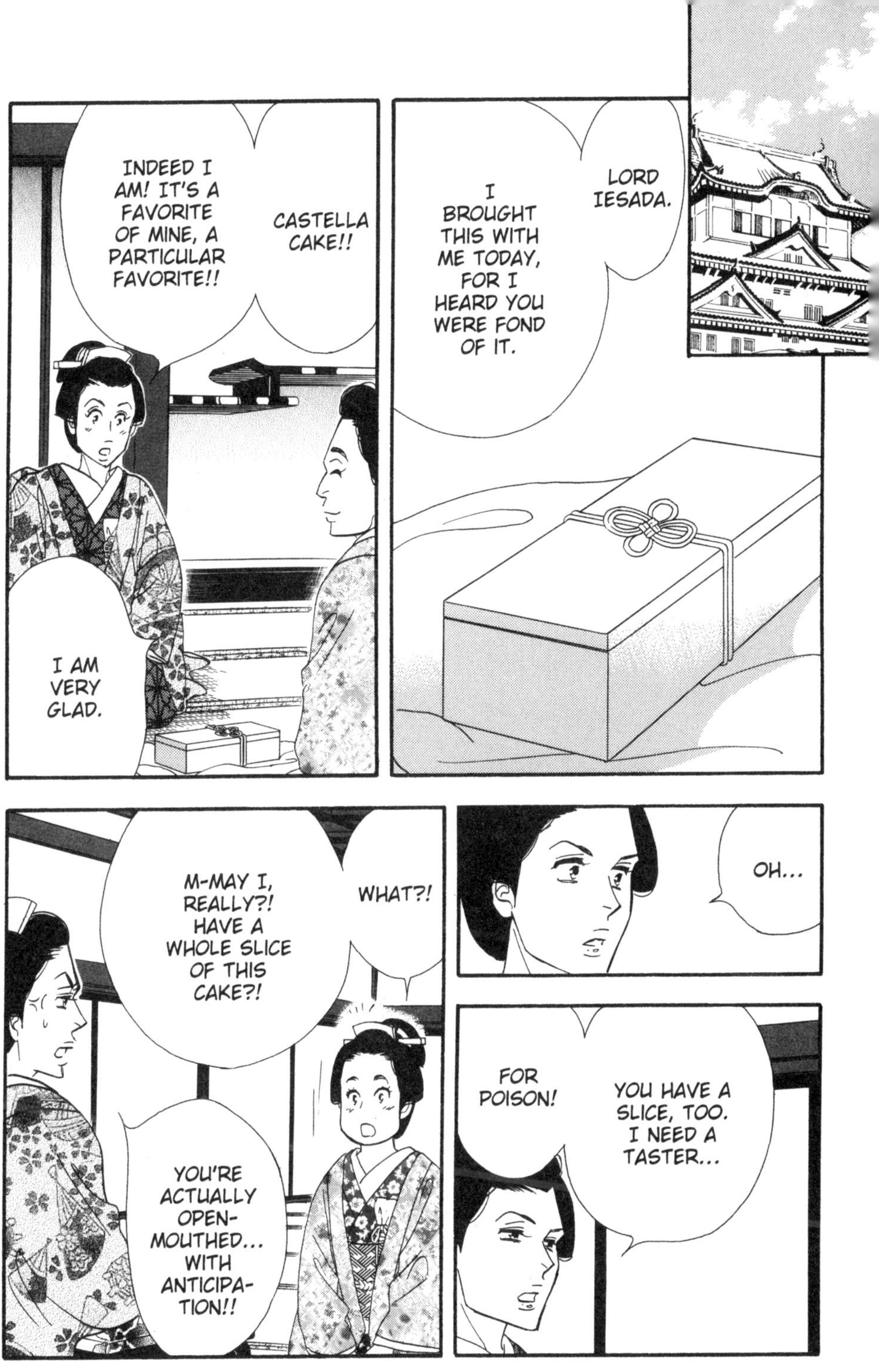
LORD IESADA.
I BROUGHT THIS WITH ME TODAY, FOR I HEARD YOU WERE FOND OF IT.
CASTELLA CAKE!!
INDEED I AM! IT'S A FAVORITE OF MINE, A PARTICULAR FAVORITE!!
I AM VERY GLAD.
OH...
YOU HAVE A SLICE, TOO. I NEED A TASTER...
FOR POISON!
WHAT?!
M-MAY I, REALLY?! HAVE A WHOLE SLICE OF THIS CAKE?!
YOU'RE ACTUALLY OPEN-MOUTHED... WITH ANTICIPA-TION!!

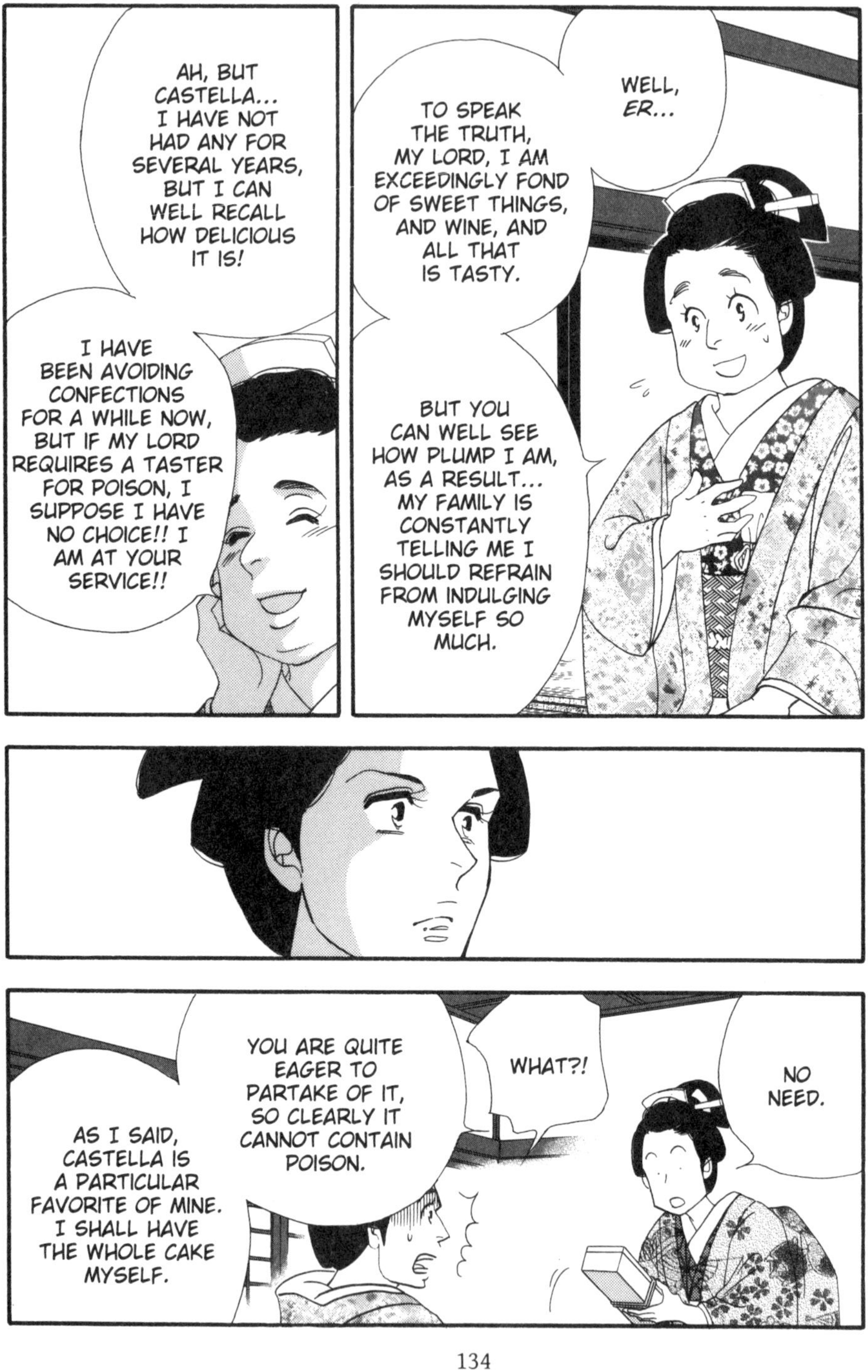
WELL, ER...
TO SPEAK THE TRUTH, MY LORD, I AM EXCEEDINGLY FOND OF SWEET THINGS, AND WINE, AND ALL THAT IS TASTY.
BUT YOU CAN WELL SEE HOW PLUMP I AM, AS A RESULT... MY FAMILY IS CONSTANTLY TELLING ME I SHOULD REFRAIN FROM INDULGING MYSELF SO MUCH.
AH, BUT CASTELLA... I HAVE NOT HAD ANY FOR SEVERAL YEARS, BUT I CAN WELL RECALL HOW DELICIOUS IT IS!
I HAVE BEEN AVOIDING CONFECTIONS FOR A WHILE NOW, BUT IF MY LORD REQUIRES A TASTER FOR POISON, I SUPPOSE I HAVE NO CHOICE!! I AM AT YOUR SERVICE!!
NO NEED.
WHAT?!
YOU ARE QUITE EAGER TO PARTAKE OF IT, SO CLEARLY IT CANNOT CONTAIN POISON.
AS I SAID, CASTELLA IS A PARTICULAR FAVORITE OF MINE. I SHALL HAVE THE WHOLE CAKE MYSELF.

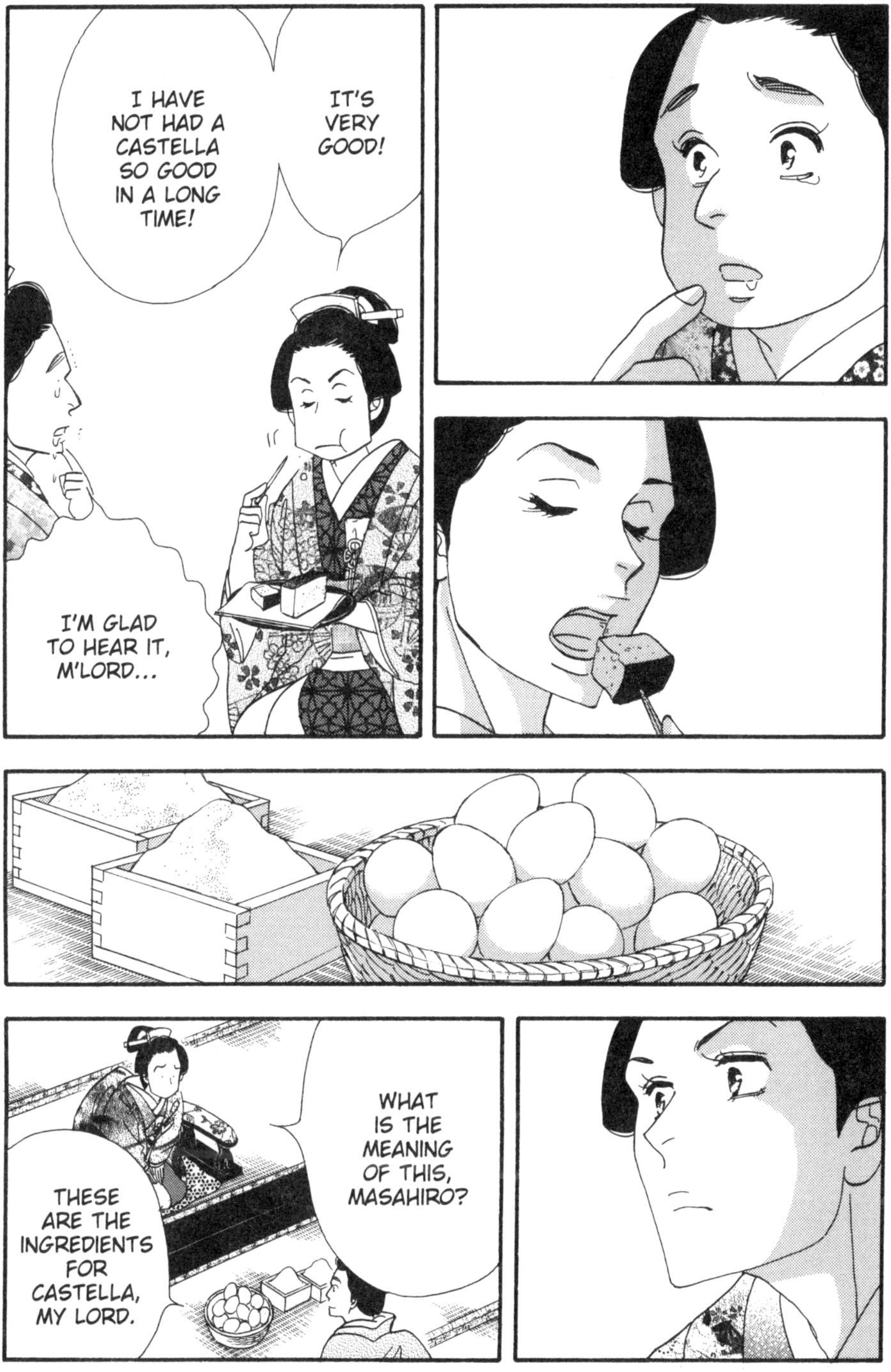
IT'S VERY GOOD!
I HAVE NOT HAD A CASTELLA SO GOOD IN A LONG TIME!
I'M GLAD TO HEAR IT, M'LORD...
WHAT IS THE MEANING OF THIS, MASAHIRO?
THESE ARE THE INGREDIENTS FOR CASTELLA, MY LORD.

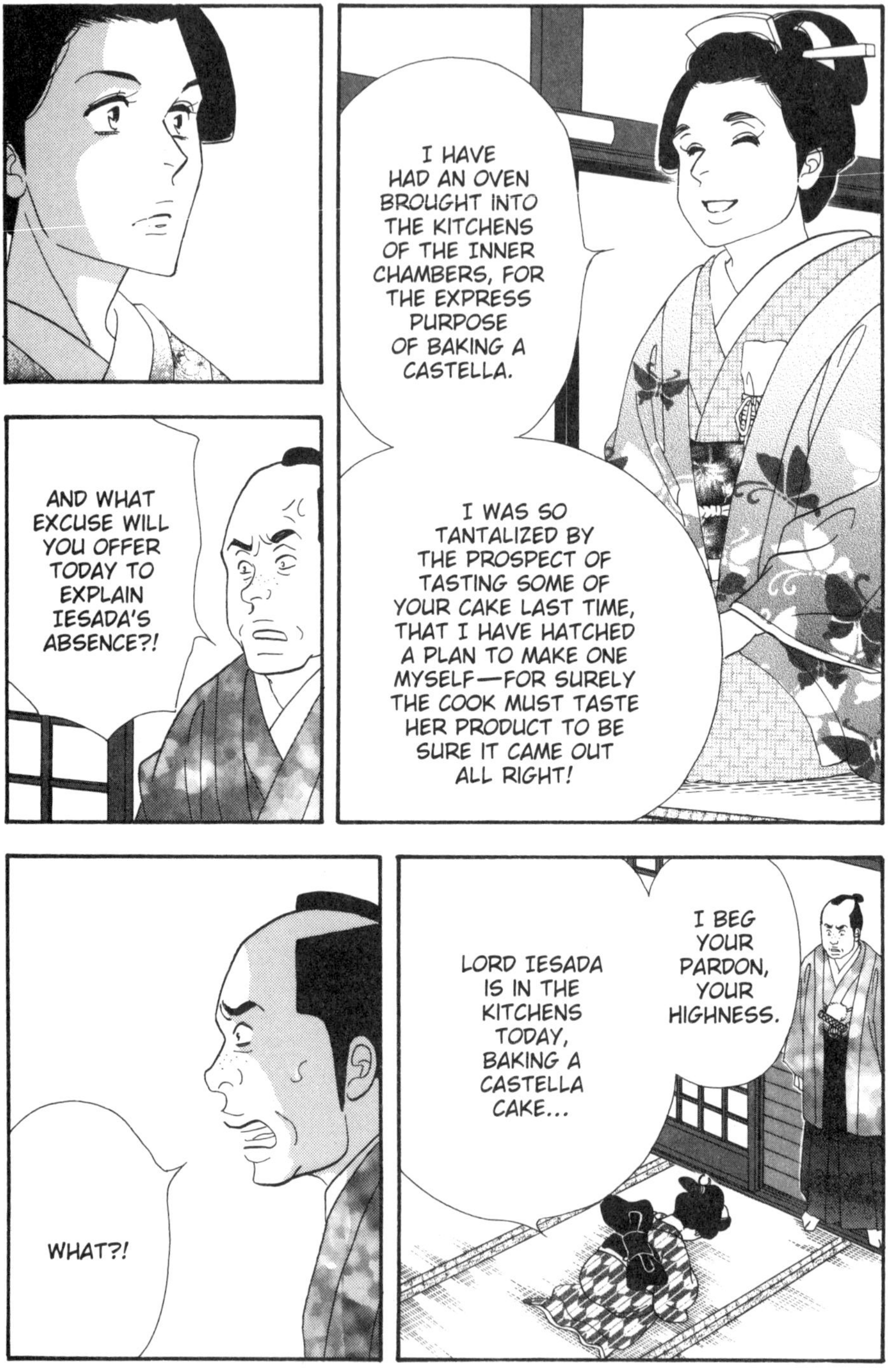
I HAVE HAD AN OVEN BROUGHT INTO THE KITCHENS OF THE INNER CHAMBERS, FOR THE EXPRESS PURPOSE OF BAKING A CASTELLA.
I WAS SO TANTALIZED BY THE PROSPECT OF TASTING SOME OF YOUR CAKE LAST TIME, THAT I HAVE HATCHED A PLAN TO MAKE ONE MYSELF—FOR SURELY THE COOK MUST TASTE HER PRODUCT TO BE SURE IT CAME OUT ALL RIGHT!
AND WHAT EXCUSE WILL YOU OFFER TODAY TO EXPLAIN IESADA'S ABSENCE?!
I BEG YOUR PARDON, YOUR HIGHNESS.
LORD IESADA IS IN THE KITCHENS TODAY, BAKING A CASTELLA CAKE...
WHAT?!

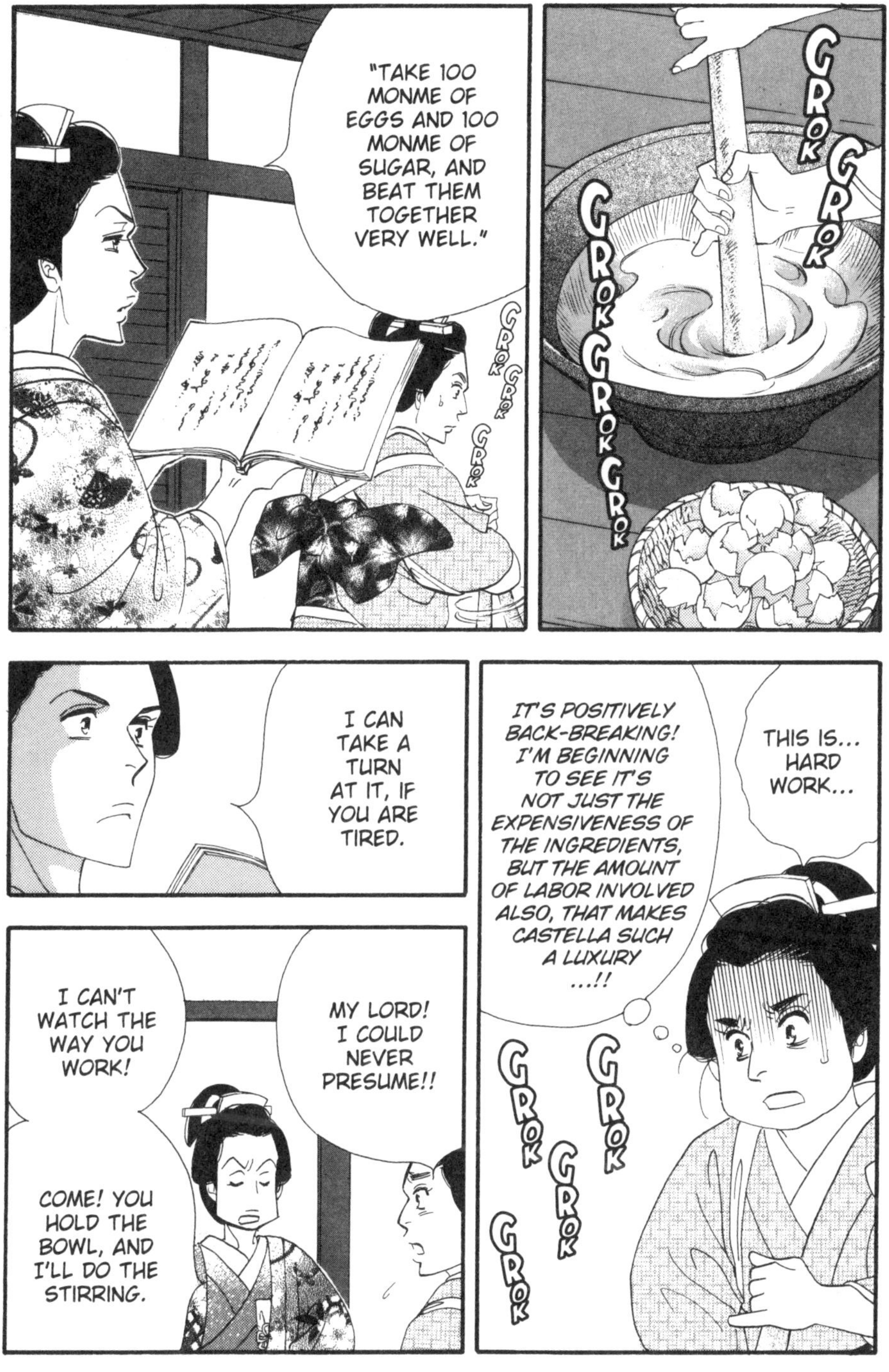
GROK GROK
GROK GROK GROK GROK
"TAKE 100 MONME OF EGGS AND 100 MONME OF SUGAR, AND BEAT THEM TOGETHER VERY WELL."
GROK GROK GROK
THIS IS... HARD WORK...
IT'S POSITIVELY BACK-BREAKING! I'M BEGINNING TO SEE IT'S NOT JUST THE EXPENSIVENESS OF THE INGREDIENTS, BUT THE AMOUNT OF LABOR INVOLVED ALSO, THAT MAKES CASTELLA SUCH A LUXURY ...!!
GROK GROK GROK
I CAN TAKE A TURN AT IT, IF YOU ARE TIRED.
MY LORD! I COULD NEVER PRESUME!!
I CAN'T WATCH THE WAY YOU WORK!
COME! YOU HOLD THE BOWL, AND I'LL DO THE STIRRING.

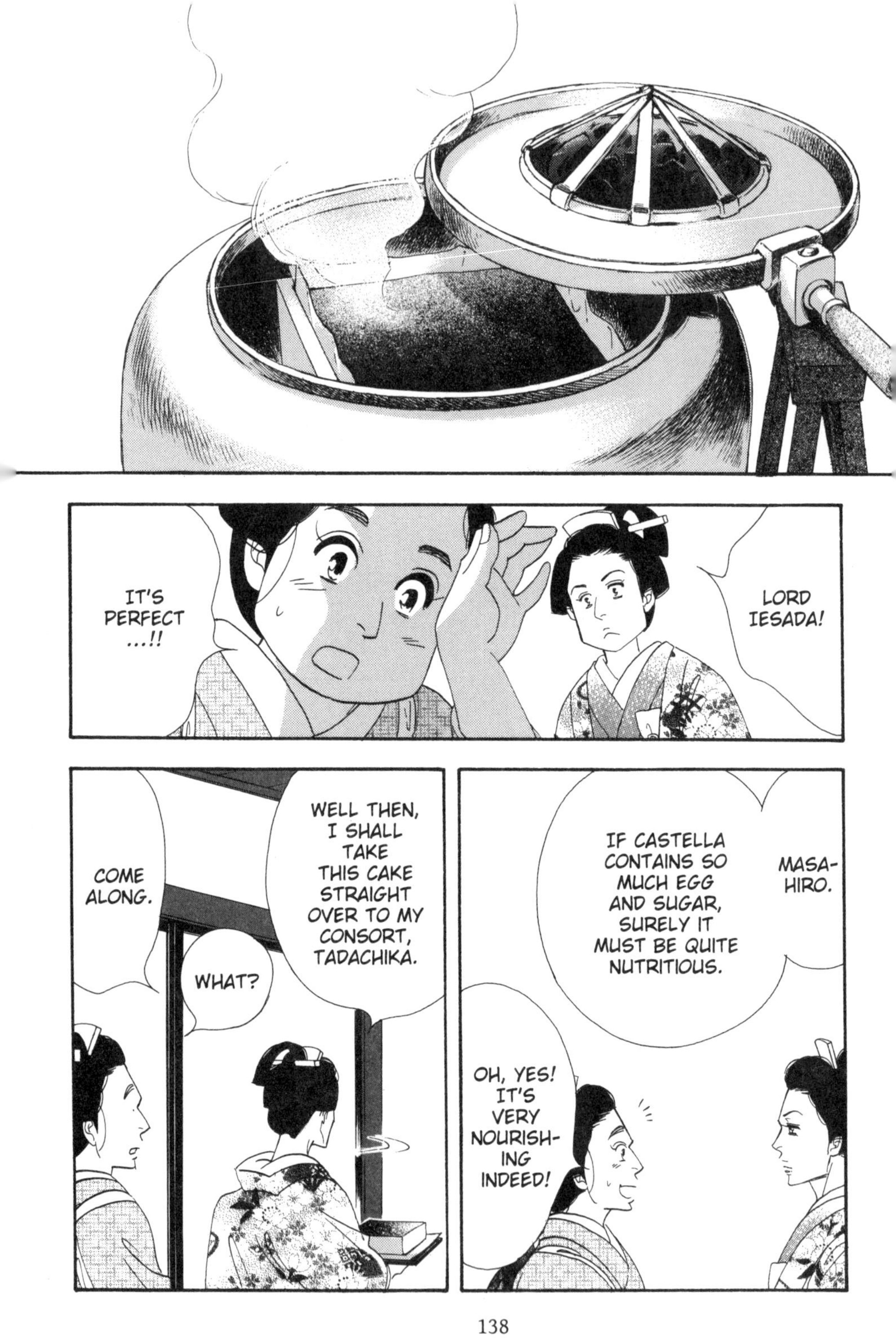
LORD IESADA!
IT'S PERFECT ...!!
MASA-HIRO.
IF CASTELLA CONTAINS SO MUCH EGG AND SUGAR, SURELY IT MUST BE QUITE NUTRITIOUS.
OH, YES! IT'S VERY NOURISH-ING INDEED!
WELL THEN, I SHALL TAKE THIS CAKE STRAIGHT OVER TO MY CONSORT, TADACHIKA.
WHAT?
COME ALONG.

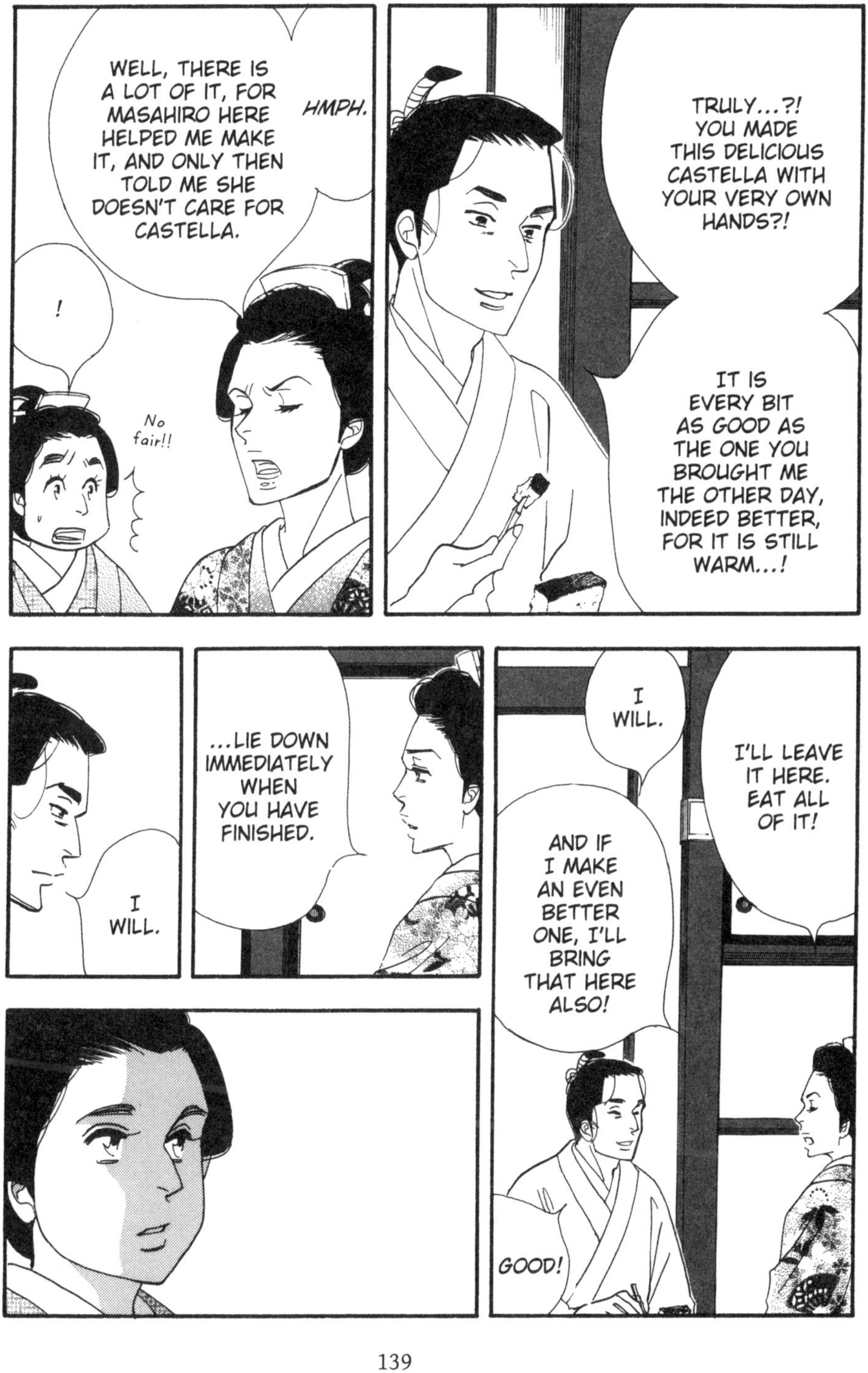
TRULY...?! YOU MADE THIS DELICIOUS CASTELLA WITH YOUR VERY OWN HANDS?!
IT IS EVERY BIT AS GOOD AS THE ONE YOU BROUGHT ME THE OTHER DAY, INDEED BETTER, FOR IT IS STILL WARM...!
HMPH.
WELL, THERE IS A LOT OF IT, FOR MASAHIRO HERE HELPED ME MAKE IT, AND ONLY THEN TOLD ME SHE DOESN'T CARE FOR CASTELLA.
!
No fair!!
I'LL LEAVE IT HERE. EAT ALL OF IT!
I WILL.
AND IF I MAKE AN EVEN BETTER ONE, I'LL BRING THAT HERE ALSO!
GOOD!
...LIE DOWN IMMEDIATELY WHEN YOU HAVE FINISHED.
I WILL.

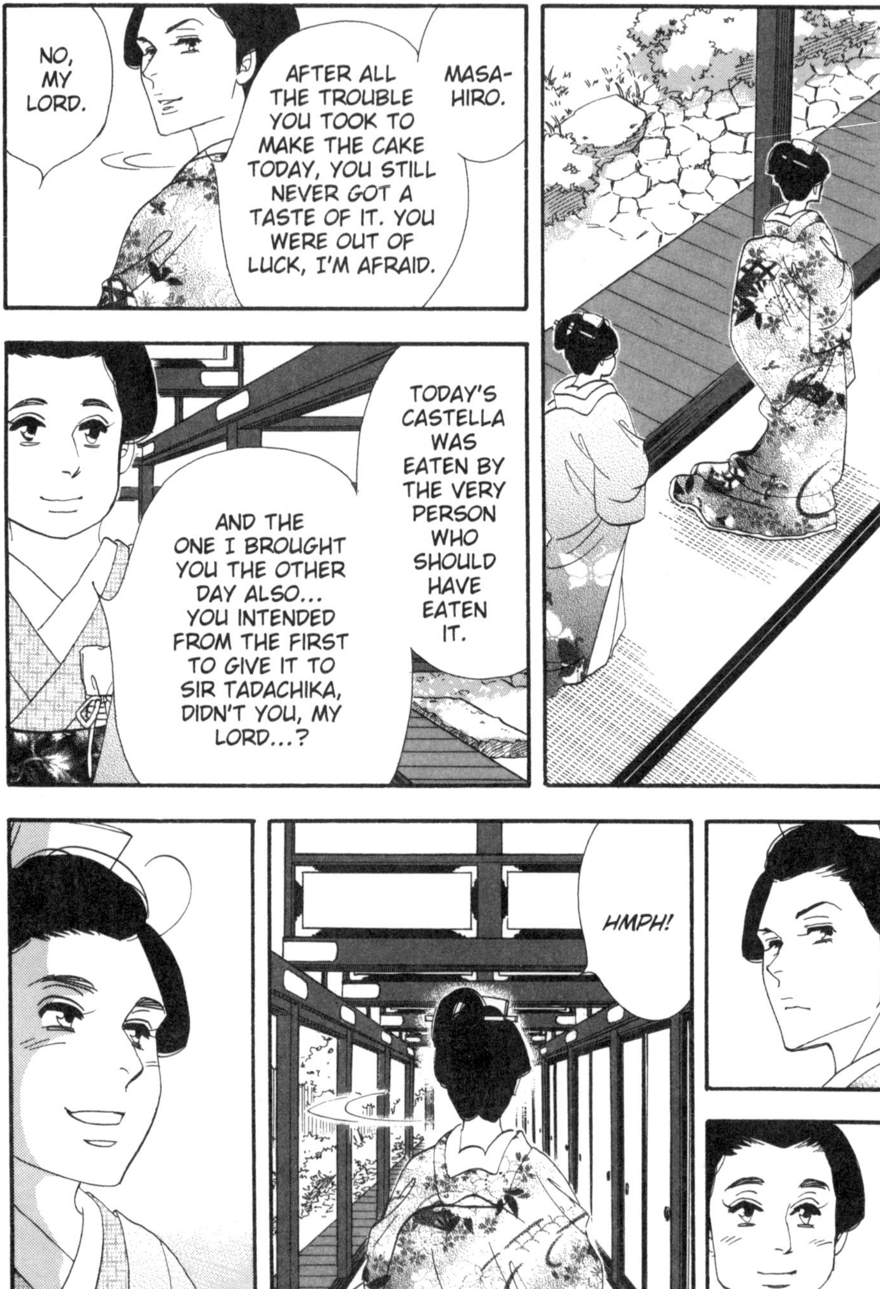
MASA-HIRO.
AFTER ALL THE TROUBLE YOU TOOK TO MAKE THE CAKE TODAY, YOU STILL NEVER GOT A TASTE OF IT. YOU WERE OUT OF LUCK, I'M AFRAID.
NO, MY LORD.
TODAY'S CASTELLA WAS EATEN BY THE VERY PERSON WHO SHOULD HAVE EATEN IT.
AND THE ONE I BROUGHT YOU THE OTHER DAY ALSO... YOU INTENDED FROM THE FIRST TO GIVE IT TO SIR TADACHIKA, DIDN'T YOU, MY LORD...?
HMPH!

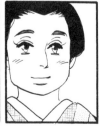

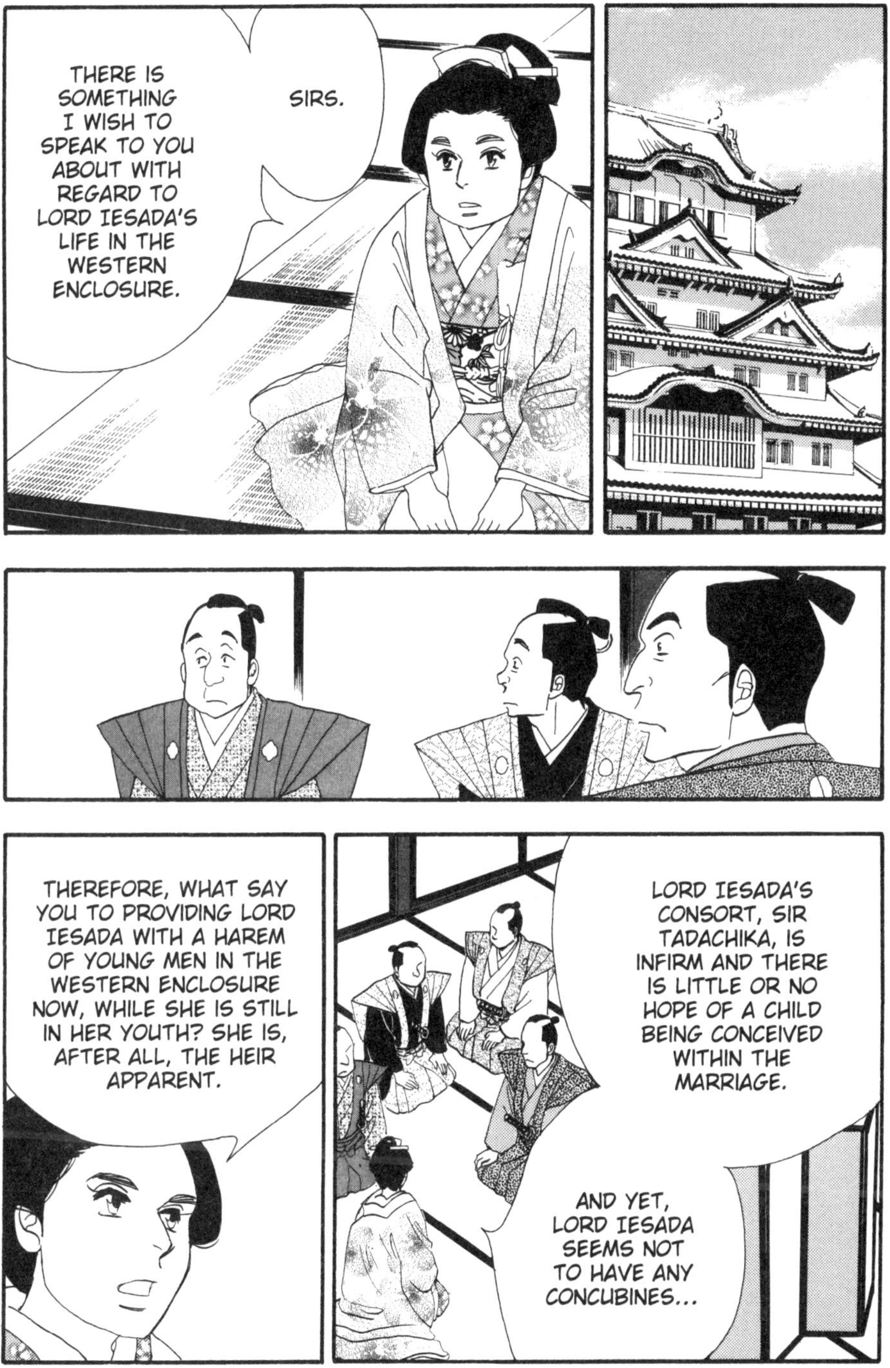
SIRS.
THERE IS SOMETHING I WISH TO SPEAK TO YOU ABOUT WITH REGARD TO LORD IESADA'S LIFE IN THE WESTERN ENCLOSURE.
LORD IESADA'S CONSORT, SIR TADACHIKA, IS INFIRM AND THERE IS LITTLE OR NO HOPE OF A CHILD BEING CONCEIVED WITHIN THE MARRIAGE.
AND YET, LORD IESADA SEEMS NOT TO HAVE ANY CONCUBINES...
THEREFORE, WHAT SAY YOU TO PROVIDING LORD IESADA WITH A HAREM OF YOUNG MEN IN THE WESTERN ENCLOSURE NOW, WHILE SHE IS STILL IN HER YOUTH? SHE IS, AFTER ALL, THE HEIR APPARENT.

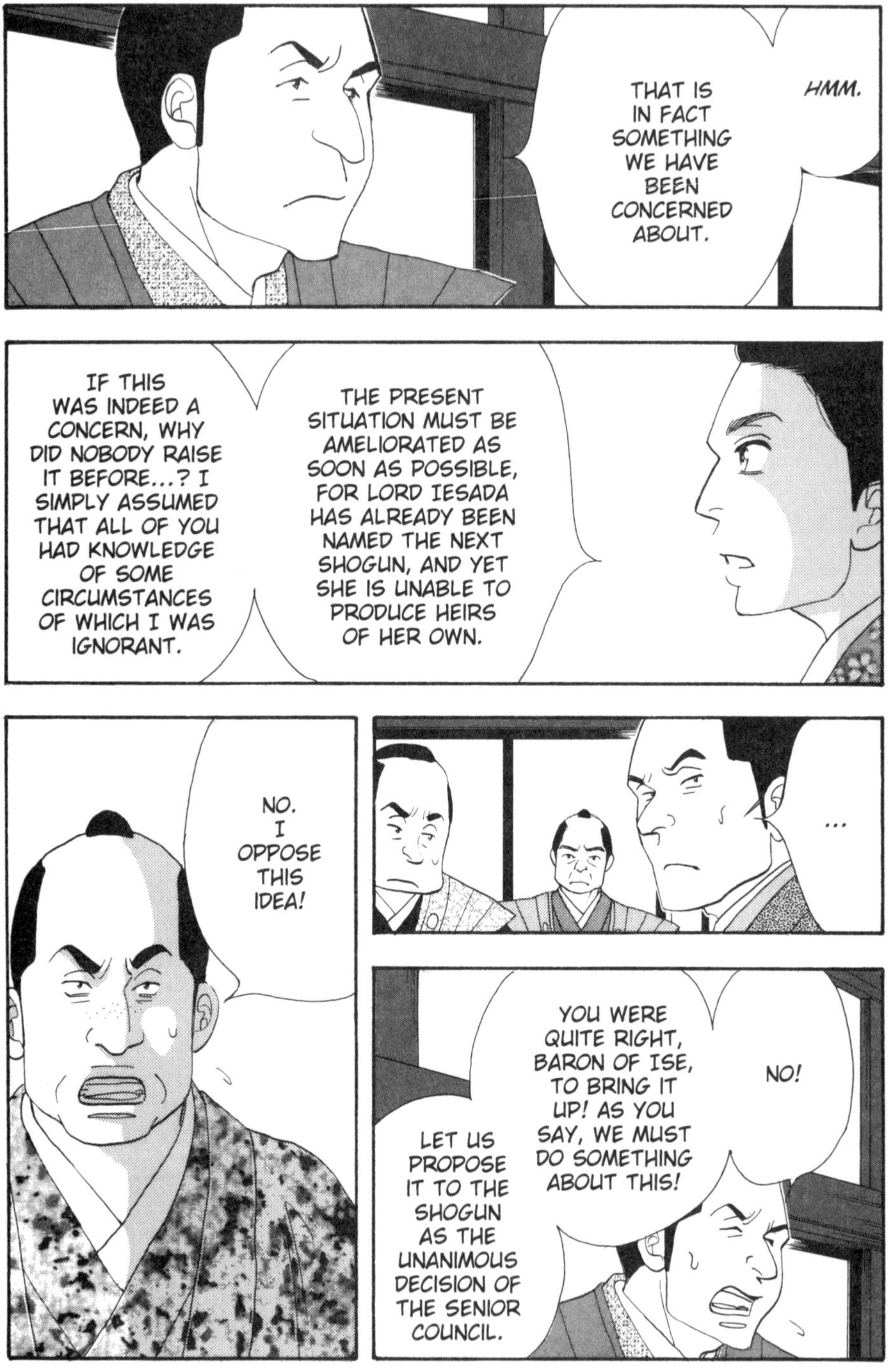
HMM.
THAT IS IN FACT SOMETHING WE HAVE BEEN CONCERNED ABOUT.
THE PRESENT SITUATION MUST BE AMELIORATED AS SOON AS POSSIBLE, FOR LORD IESADA HAS ALREADY BEEN NAMED THE NEXT SHOGUN, AND YET SHE IS UNABLE TO PRODUCE HEIRS OF HER OWN.
IF THIS WAS INDEED A CONCERN, WHY DID NOBODY RAISE IT BEFORE...? I SIMPLY ASSUMED THAT ALL OF YOU HAD KNOWLEDGE OF SOME CIRCUMSTANCES OF WHICH I WAS IGNORANT.
...
NO!
YOU WERE QUITE RIGHT, BARON OF ISE, TO BRING IT UP! AS YOU SAY, WE MUST DO SOMETHING ABOUT THIS!
LET US PROPOSE IT TO THE SHOGUN AS THE UNANIMOUS DECISION OF THE SENIOR COUNCIL.
NO. I OPPOSE THIS IDEA!

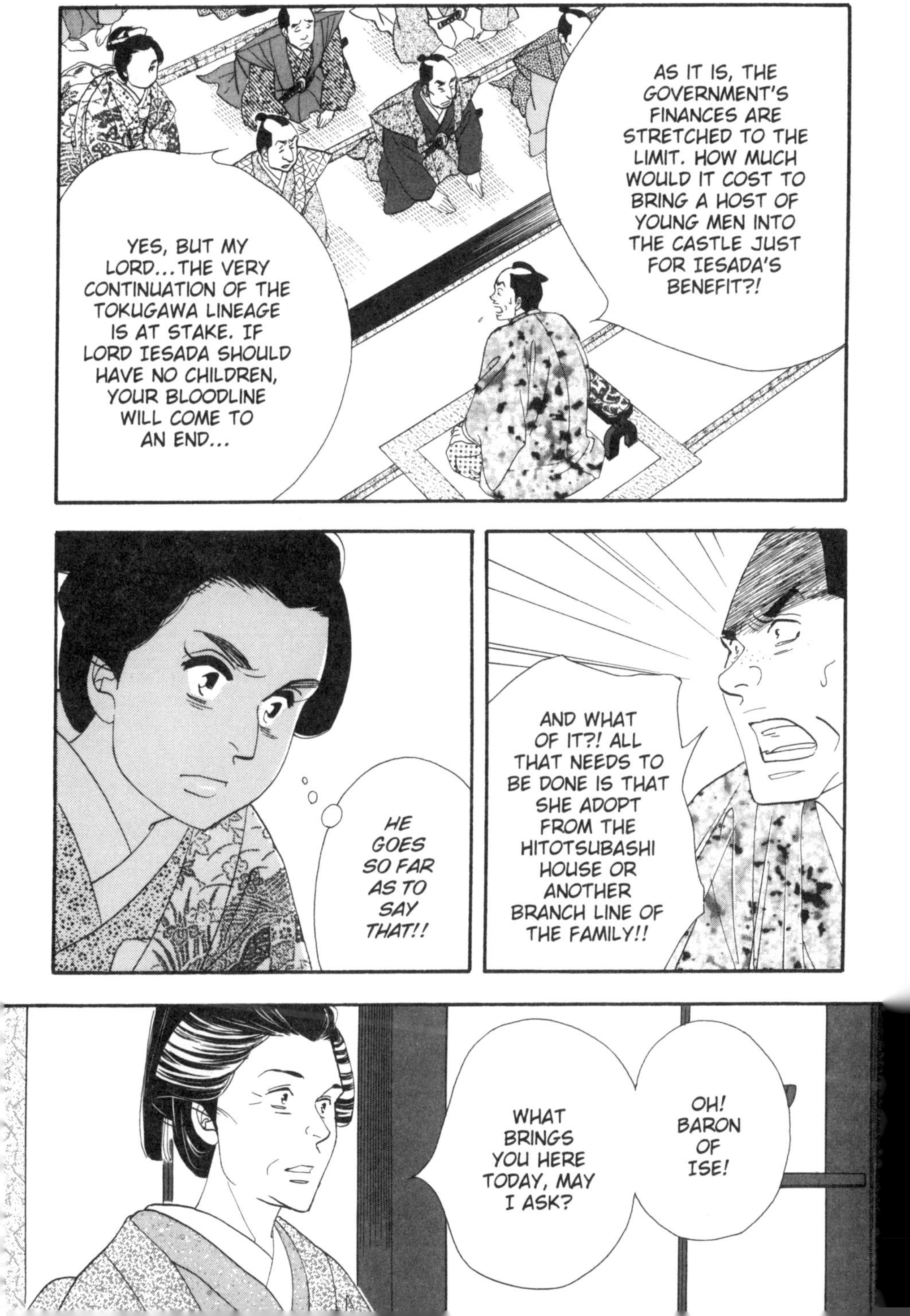
AS IT IS, THE GOVERNMENT'S FINANCES ARE STRETCHED TO THE LIMIT. HOW MUCH WOULD IT COST TO BRING A HOST OF YOUNG MEN INTO THE CASTLE JUST FOR IESADA'S BENEFIT?!
YES, BUT MY LORD...THE VERY CONTINUATION OF THE TOKUGAWA LINEAGE IS AT STAKE. IF LORD IESADA SHOULD HAVE NO CHILDREN, YOUR BLOODLINE WILL COME TO AN END...
AND WHAT OF IT?! ALL THAT NEEDS TO BE DONE IS THAT SHE ADOPT FROM THE HITOTSUBASHI HOUSE OR ANOTHER BRANCH LINE OF THE FAMILY!!
HE GOES SO FAR AS TO SAY THAT!!
OH! BARON OF ISE!
WHAT BRINGS YOU HERE TODAY, MAY I ASK?

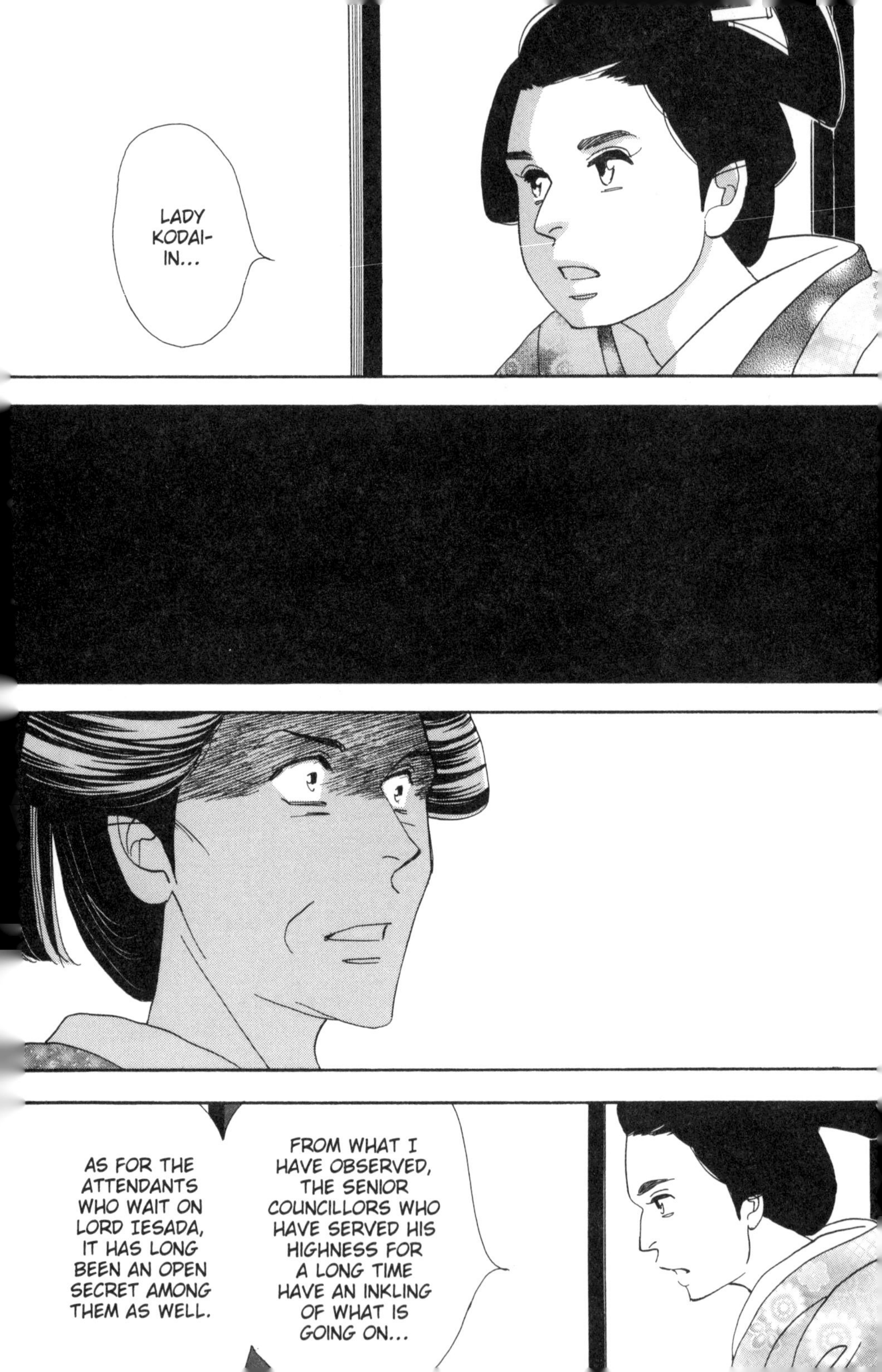
LADY KODAI-IN...
FROM WHAT I HAVE OBSERVED, THE SENIOR COUNCILLORS WHO HAVE SERVED HIS HIGHNESS FOR A LONG TIME HAVE AN INKLING OF WHAT IS GOING ON...
AS FOR THE ATTENDANTS WHO WAIT ON LORD IESADA, IT HAS LONG BEEN AN OPEN SECRET AMONG THEM AS WELL.

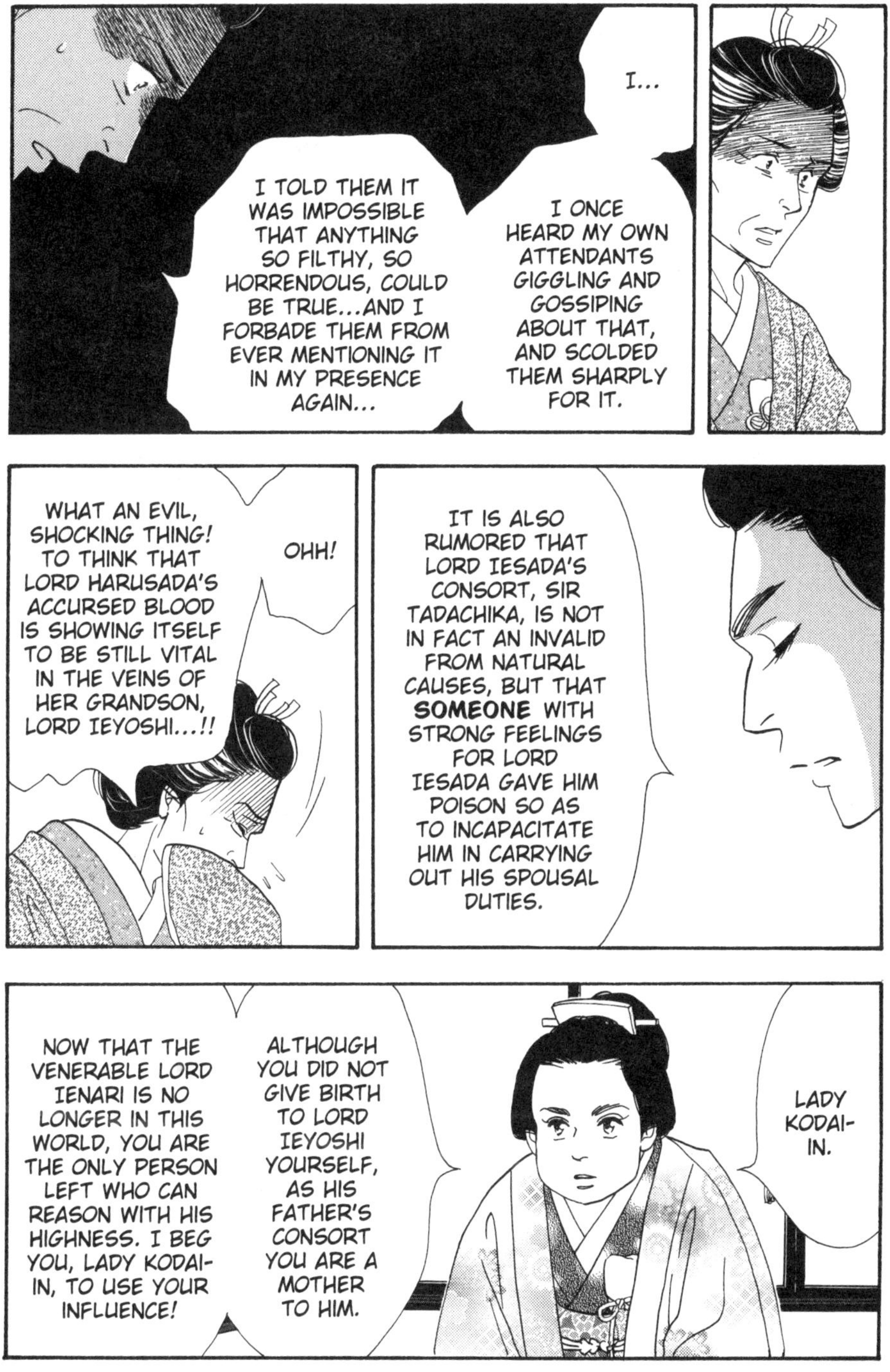
I...
I ONCE HEARD MY OWN ATTENDANTS GIGGLING AND GOSSIPING ABOUT THAT, AND SCOLDED THEM SHARPLY FOR IT.
I TOLD THEM IT WAS IMPOSSIBLE THAT ANYTHING SO FILTHY, SO HORRENDOUS, COULD BE TRUE...AND I FORBADE THEM FROM EVER MENTIONING IT IN MY PRESENCE AGAIN...
IT IS ALSO RUMORED THAT LORD IESADA'S CONSORT, SIR TADACHIKA, IS NOT IN FACT AN INVALID FROM NATURAL CAUSES, BUT THAT **SOMEONE** WITH STRONG FEELINGS FOR LORD IESADA GAVE HIM POISON SO AS TO INCAPACITATE HIM IN CARRYING OUT HIS SPOUSAL DUTIES.
OHH!
WHAT AN EVIL, SHOCKING THING! TO THINK THAT LORD HARUSADA'S ACCURSED BLOOD IS SHOWING ITSELF TO BE STILL VITAL IN THE VEINS OF HER GRANDSON, LORD IEYOSHI...!!
LADY KODAI-IN.
ALTHOUGH YOU DID NOT GIVE BIRTH TO LORD IEYOSHI YOURSELF, AS HIS FATHER'S CONSORT YOU ARE A MOTHER TO HIM.
NOW THAT THE VENERABLE LORD IENARI IS NO LONGER IN THIS WORLD, YOU ARE THE ONLY PERSON LEFT WHO CAN REASON WITH HIS HIGHNESS. I BEG YOU, LADY KODAI-IN, TO USE YOUR INFLUENCE!

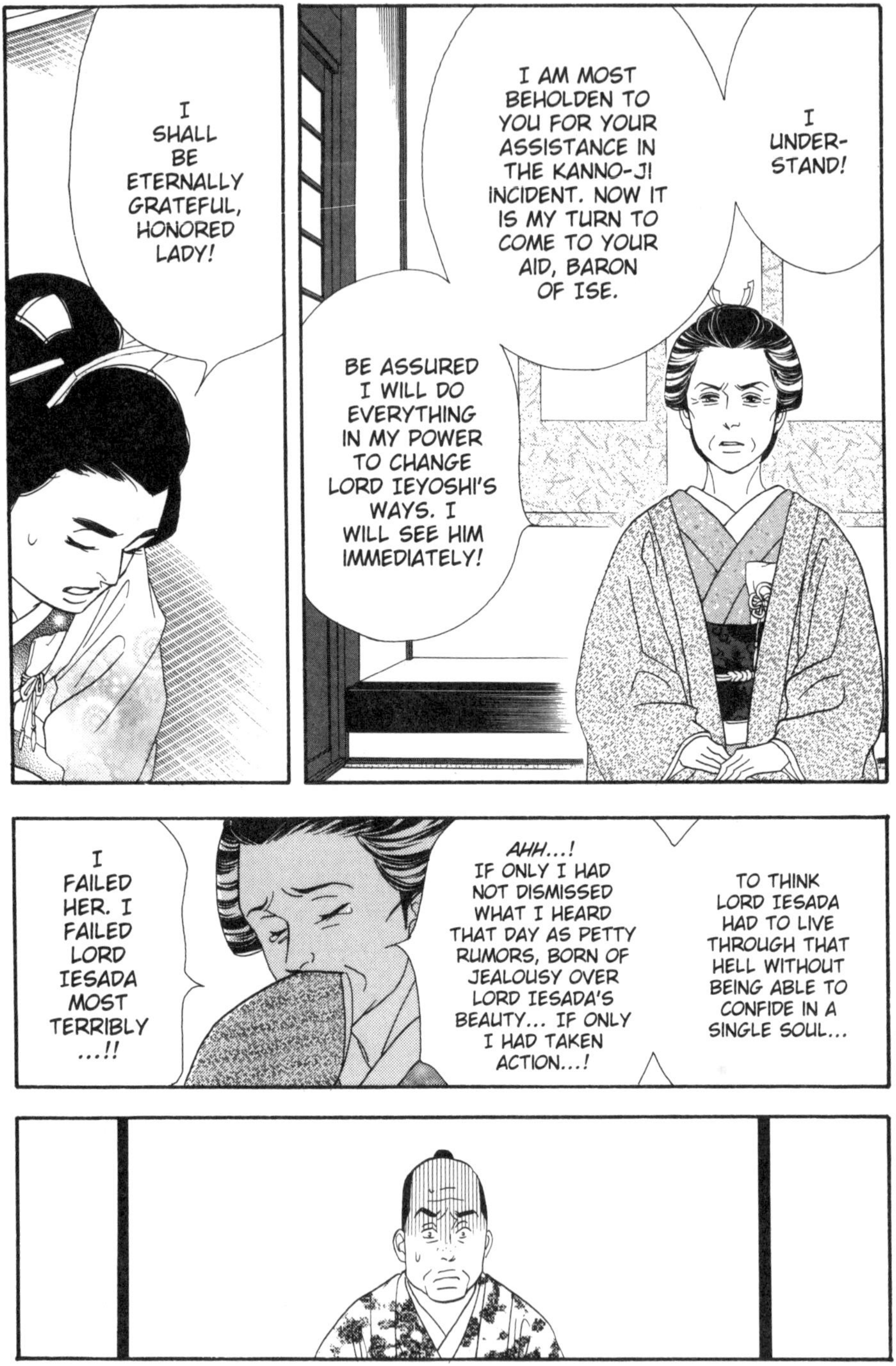
I UNDER-STAND!
I AM MOST BEHOLDEN TO YOU FOR YOUR ASSISTANCE IN THE KANNO-JI INCIDENT. NOW IT IS MY TURN TO COME TO YOUR AID, BARON OF ISE.
BE ASSURED I WILL DO EVERYTHING IN MY POWER TO CHANGE LORD IEYOSHI'S WAYS. I WILL SEE HIM IMMEDIATELY!
I SHALL BE ETERNALLY GRATEFUL, HONORED LADY!
TO THINK LORD IESADA HAD TO LIVE THROUGH THAT HELL WITHOUT BEING ABLE TO CONFIDE IN A SINGLE SOUL...
AHH...! IF ONLY I HAD NOT DISMISSED WHAT I HEARD THAT DAY AS PETTY RUMORS, BORN OF JEALOUSY OVER LORD IESADA'S BEAUTY... IF ONLY I HAD TAKEN ACTION...!
I FAILED HER. I FAILED LORD IESADA MOST TERRIBLY ...!!

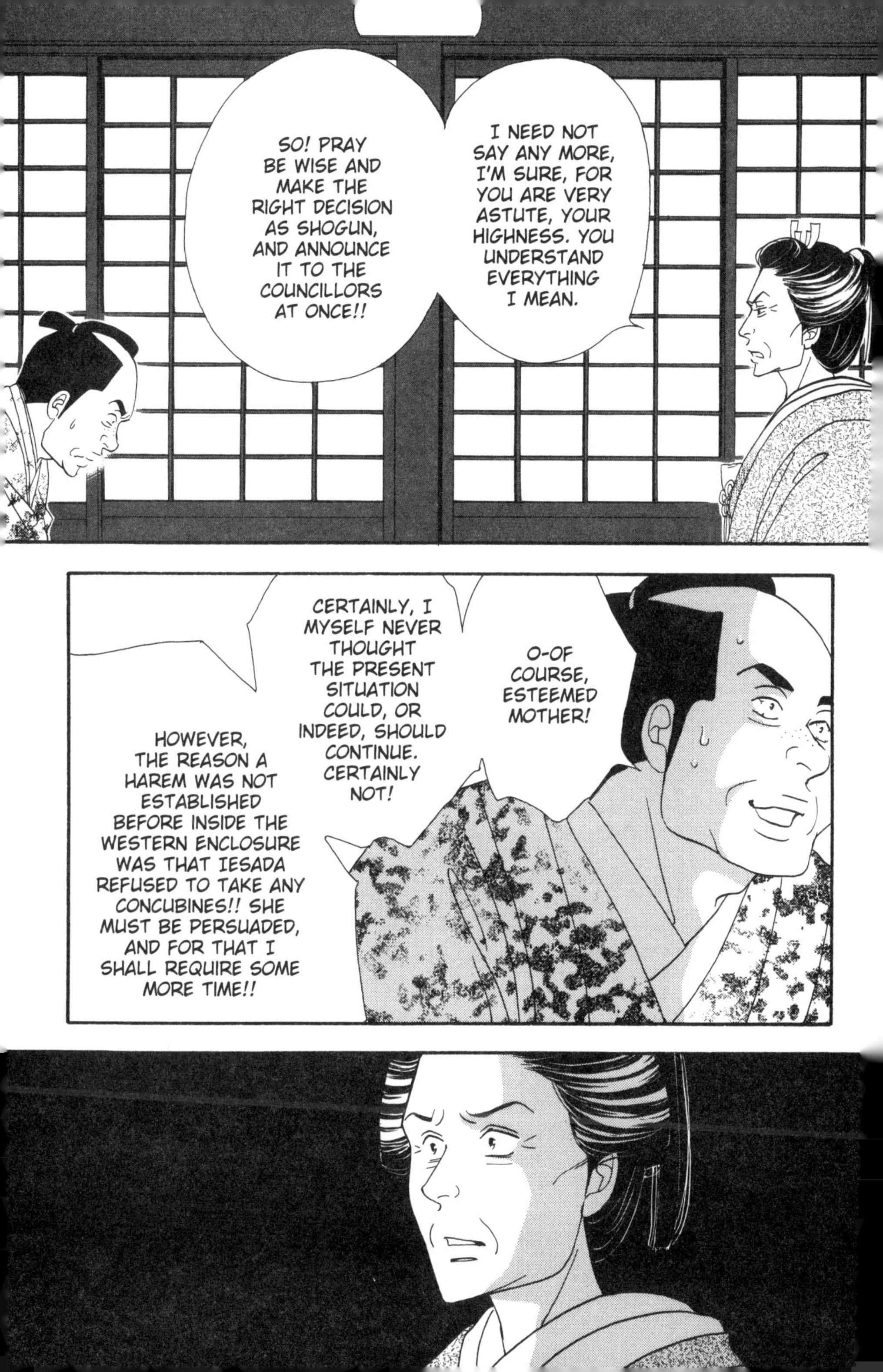
I NEED NOT SAY ANY MORE, I'M SURE, FOR YOU ARE VERY ASTUTE, YOUR HIGHNESS. YOU UNDERSTAND EVERYTHING I MEAN.
SO! PRAY BE WISE AND MAKE THE RIGHT DECISION AS SHOGUN, AND ANNOUNCE IT TO THE COUNCILLORS AT ONCE!!
O-OF COURSE, ESTEEMED MOTHER!
CERTAINLY, I MYSELF NEVER THOUGHT THE PRESENT SITUATION COULD, OR INDEED, SHOULD CONTINUE. CERTAINLY NOT!
HOWEVER, THE REASON A HAREM WAS NOT ESTABLISHED BEFORE INSIDE THE WESTERN ENCLOSURE WAS THAT IESADA REFUSED TO TAKE ANY CONCUBINES!! SHE MUST BE PERSUADED, AND FOR THAT I SHALL REQUIRE SOME MORE TIME!!

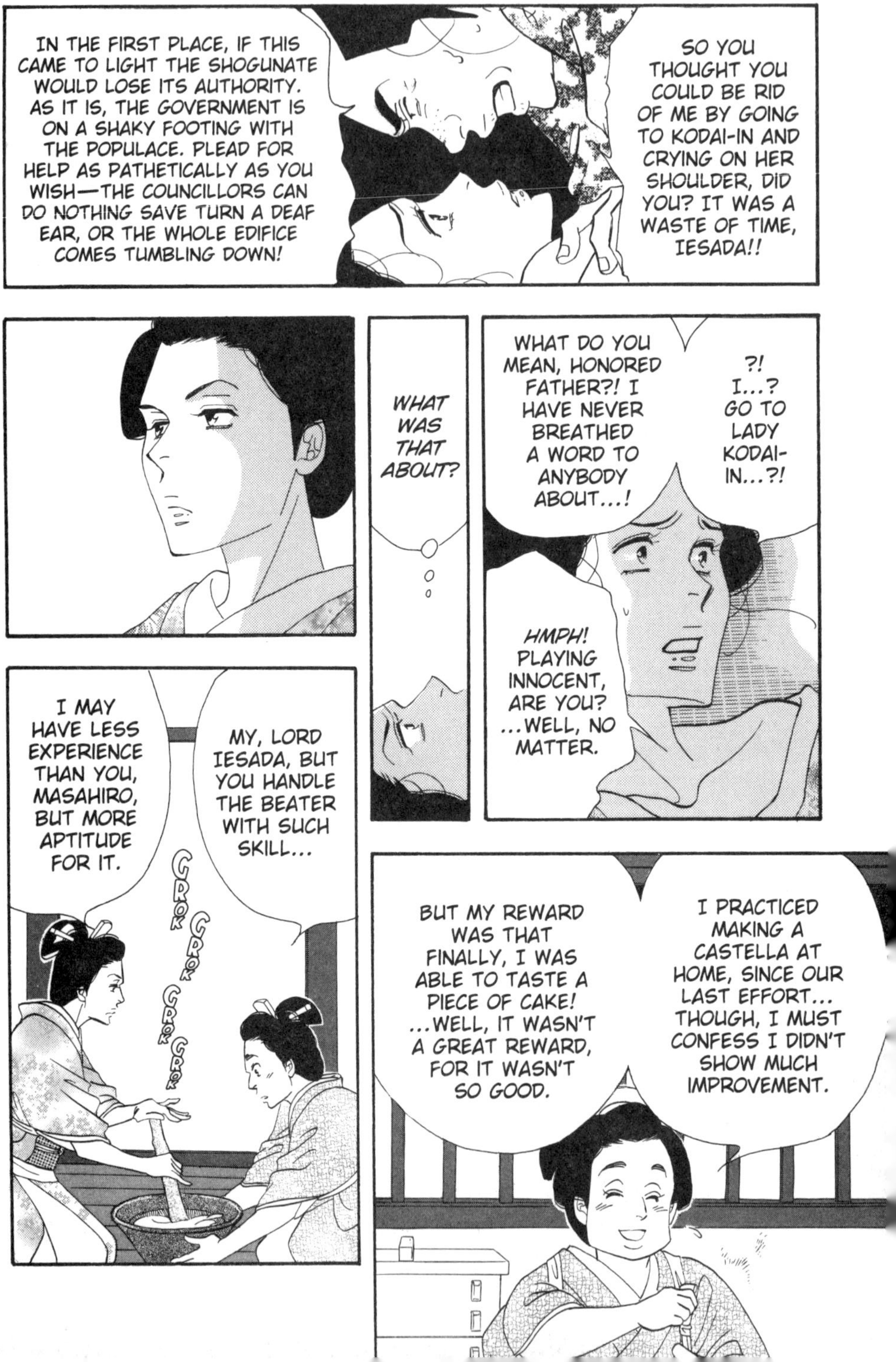
SO YOU THOUGHT YOU COULD BE RID OF ME BY GOING TO KODAI-IN AND CRYING ON HER SHOULDER, DID YOU? IT WAS A WASTE OF TIME, IESADA!!
IN THE FIRST PLACE, IF THIS CAME TO LIGHT THE SHOGUNATE WOULD LOSE ITS AUTHORITY. AS IT IS, THE GOVERNMENT IS ON A SHAKY FOOTING WITH THE POPULACE. PLEAD FOR HELP AS PATHETICALLY AS YOU WISH—THE COUNCILLORS CAN DO NOTHING SAVE TURN A DEAF EAR, OR THE WHOLE EDIFICE COMES TUMBLING DOWN!
?! I...? GO TO LADY KODAI-IN...?!
WHAT DO YOU MEAN, HONORED FATHER?! I HAVE NEVER BREATHED A WORD TO ANYBODY ABOUT...!
HMPH! PLAYING INNOCENT, ARE YOU? ...WELL, NO MATTER.
WHAT WAS THAT ABOUT?
MY, LORD IESADA, BUT YOU HANDLE THE BEATER WITH SUCH SKILL...
I MAY HAVE LESS EXPERIENCE THAN YOU, MASAHIRO, BUT MORE APTITUDE FOR IT.
GROK GROK GROK GROK
I PRACTICED MAKING A CASTELLA AT HOME, SINCE OUR LAST EFFORT... THOUGH, I MUST CONFESS I DIDN'T SHOW MUCH IMPROVEMENT.
BUT MY REWARD WAS THAT FINALLY, I WAS ABLE TO TASTE A PIECE OF CAKE! ...WELL, IT WASN'T A GREAT REWARD, FOR IT WASN'T SO GOOD.

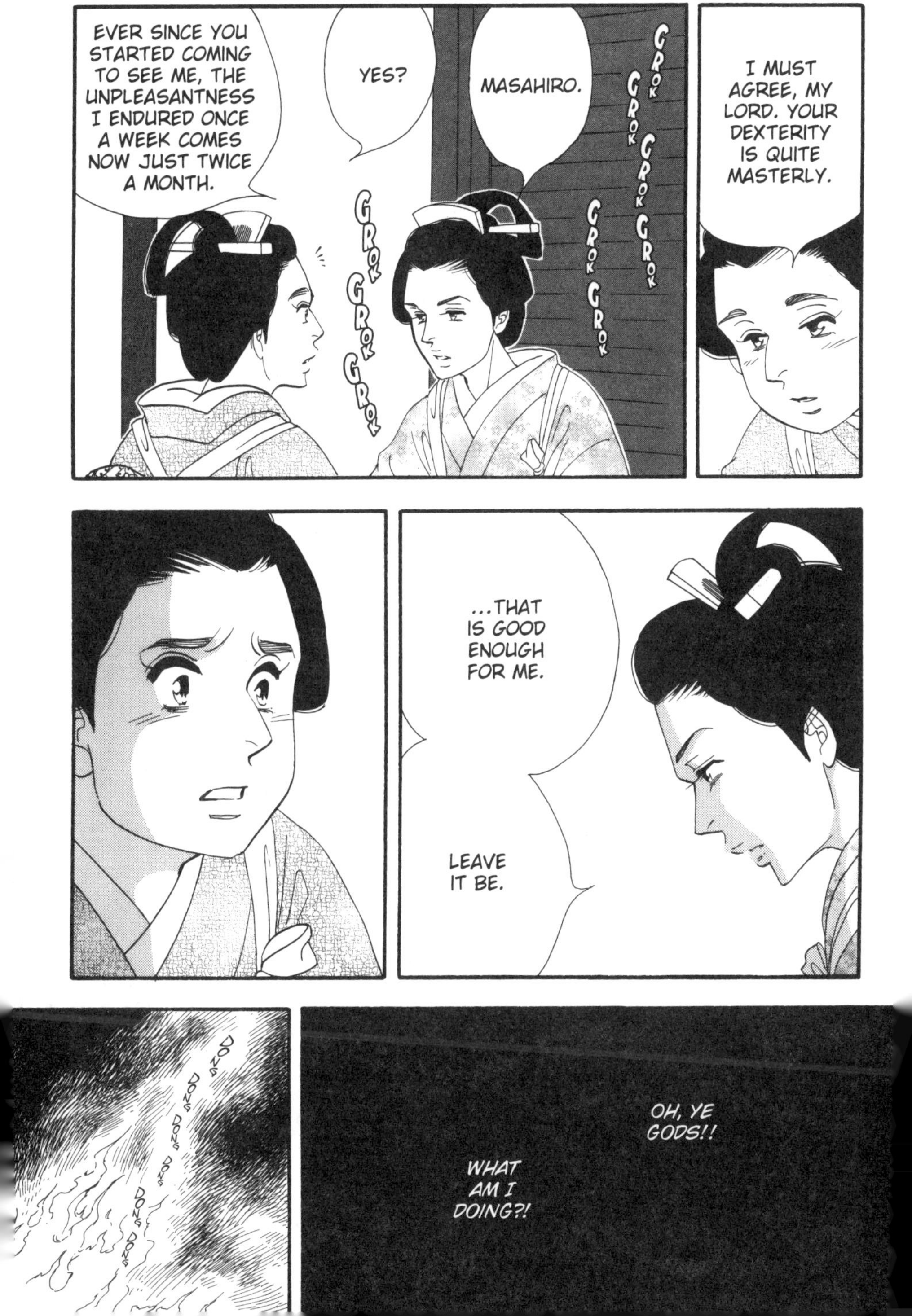
I MUST AGREE, MY LORD. YOUR DEXTERITY IS QUITE MASTERLY.
MASAHIRO.
GROK GROK GROK GROK GROK GROK
YES?
GROK GROK GROK
EVER SINCE YOU STARTED COMING TO SEE ME, THE UNPLEASANTNESS I ENDURED ONCE A WEEK COMES NOW JUST TWICE A MONTH.
...THAT IS GOOD ENOUGH FOR ME.
LEAVE IT BE.
OH, YE GODS!!
WHAT AM I DOING?!
DONS DONS DONS DONS DONS DONS DONS

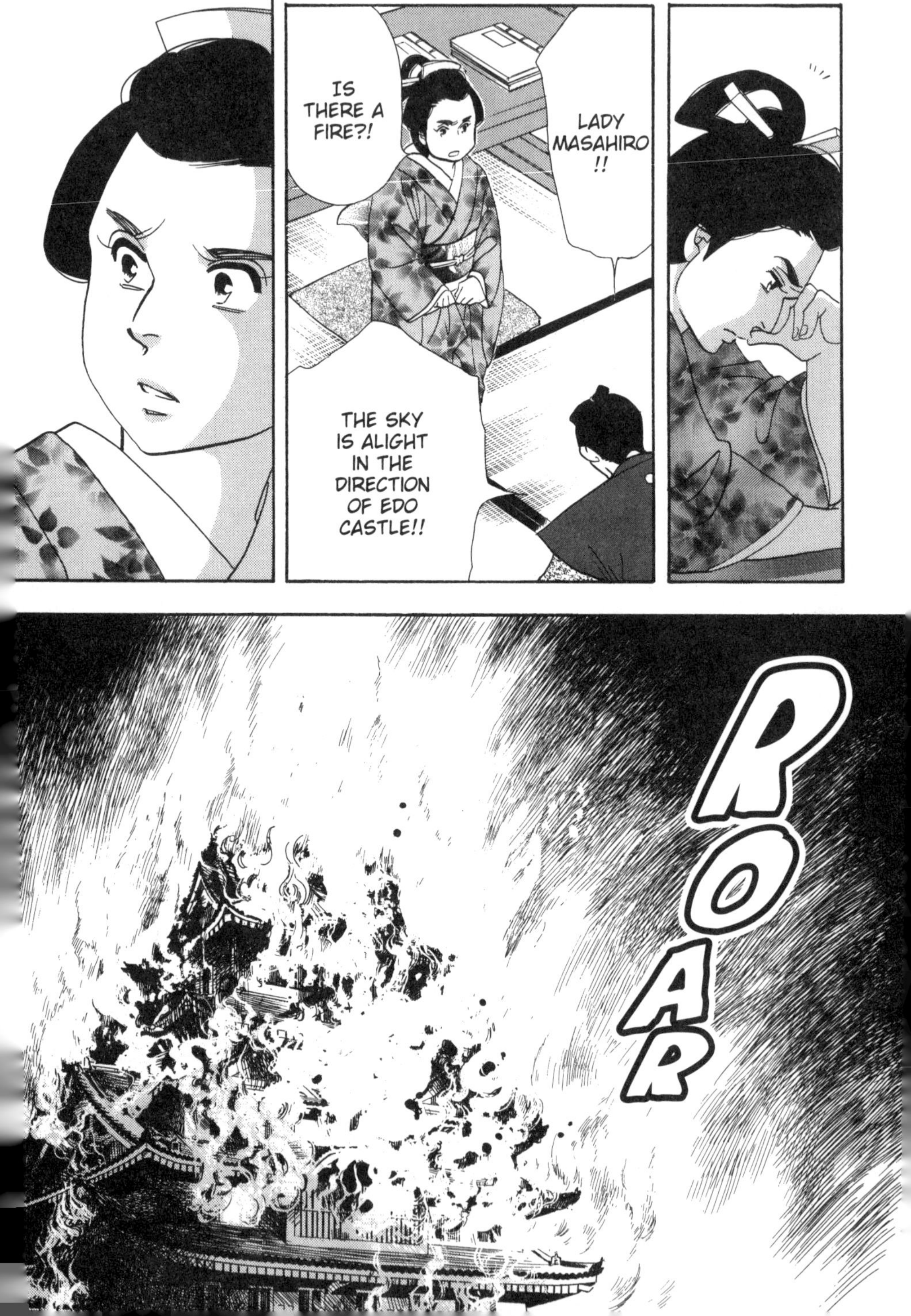
LADY MASAHIRO !!
IS THERE A FIRE?!
THE SKY IS ALIGHT IN THE DIRECTION OF EDO CASTLE!!
ROAR

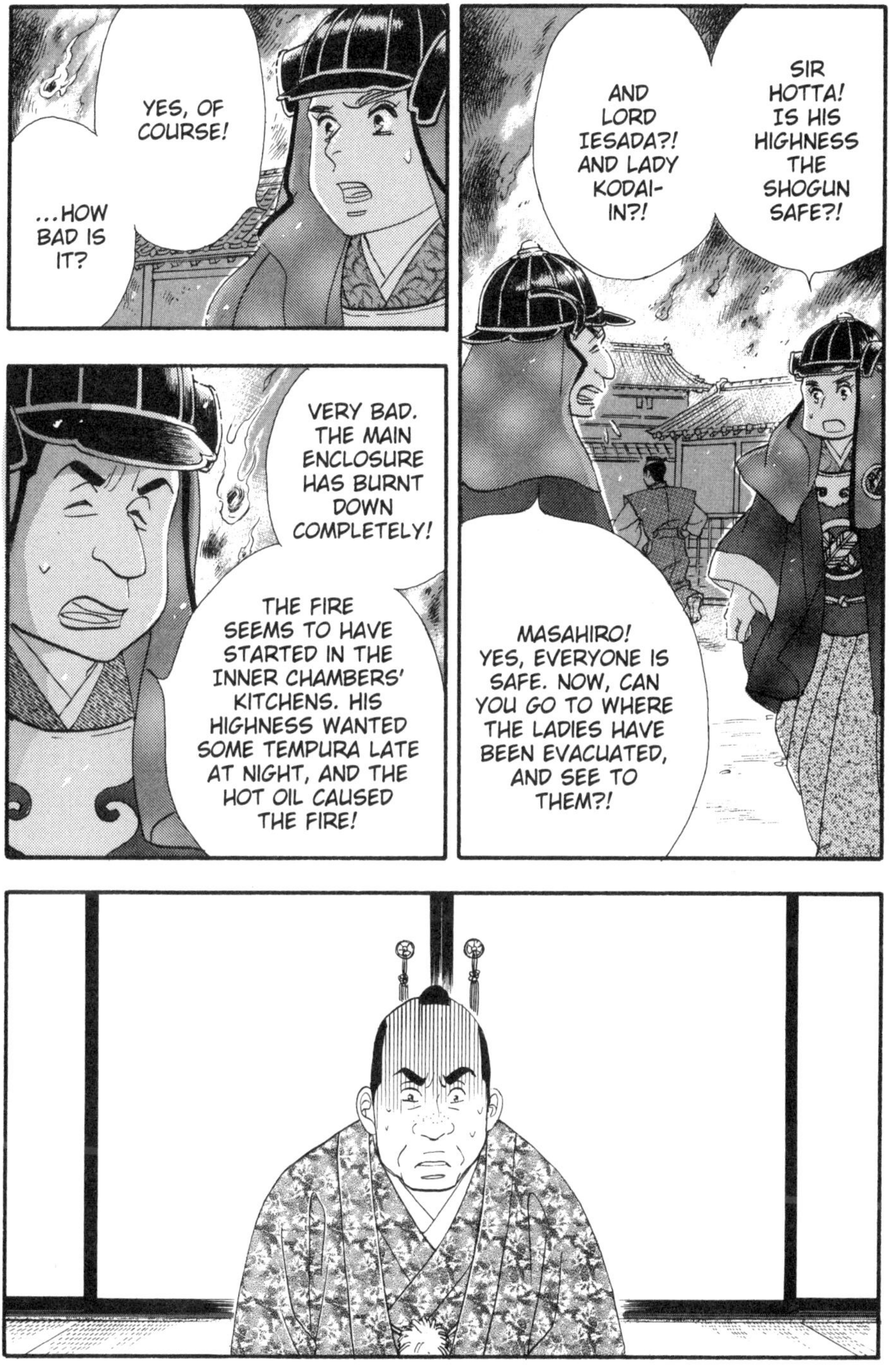
SIR HOTTA! IS HIS HIGHNESS THE SHOGUN SAFE?!
AND LORD IESADA?! AND LADY KODAI-IN?!
MASAHIRO! YES, EVERYONE IS SAFE. NOW, CAN YOU GO TO WHERE THE LADIES HAVE BEEN EVACUATED, AND SEE TO THEM?!
YES, OF COURSE!
...HOW BAD IS IT?
VERY BAD. THE MAIN ENCLOSURE HAS BURNT DOWN COMPLETELY!
THE FIRE SEEMS TO HAVE STARTED IN THE INNER CHAMBERS' KITCHENS. HIS HIGHNESS WANTED SOME TEMPURA LATE AT NIGHT, AND THE HOT OIL CAUSED THE FIRE!

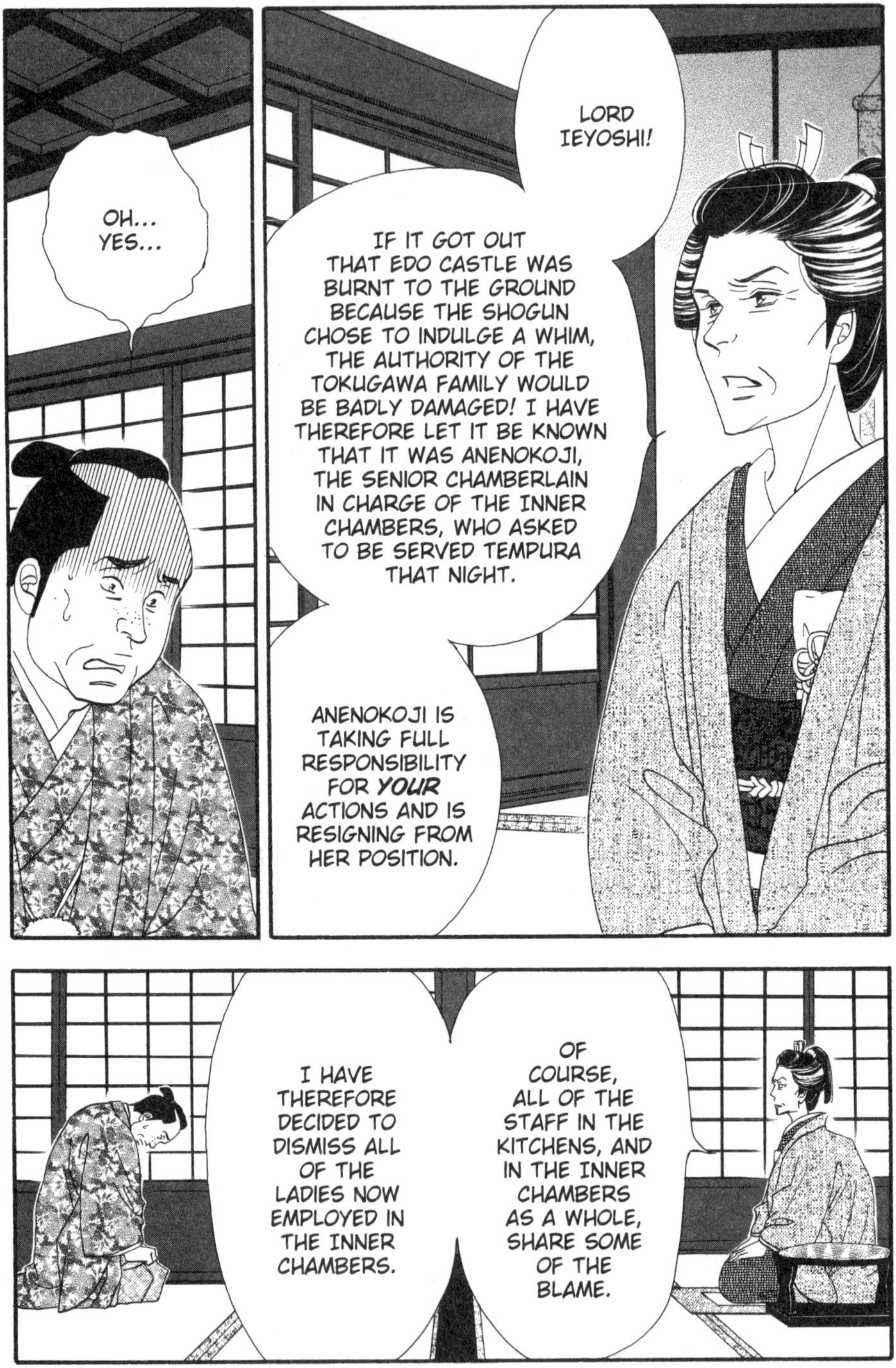
LORD IEYOSHI!
IF IT GOT OUT THAT EDO CASTLE WAS BURNT TO THE GROUND BECAUSE THE SHOGUN CHOSE TO INDULGE A WHIM, THE AUTHORITY OF THE TOKUGAWA FAMILY WOULD BE BADLY DAMAGED! I HAVE THEREFORE LET IT BE KNOWN THAT IT WAS ANENOKOJI, THE SENIOR CHAMBERLAIN IN CHARGE OF THE INNER CHAMBERS, WHO ASKED TO BE SERVED TEMPURA THAT NIGHT.
ANENOKOJI IS TAKING FULL RESPONSIBILITY FOR YOUR ACTIONS AND IS RESIGNING FROM HER POSITION.
OH... YES...
OF COURSE, ALL OF THE STAFF IN THE KITCHENS, AND IN THE INNER CHAMBERS AS A WHOLE, SHARE SOME OF THE BLAME.
I HAVE THEREFORE DECIDED TO DISMISS ALL OF THE LADIES NOW EMPLOYED IN THE INNER CHAMBERS.

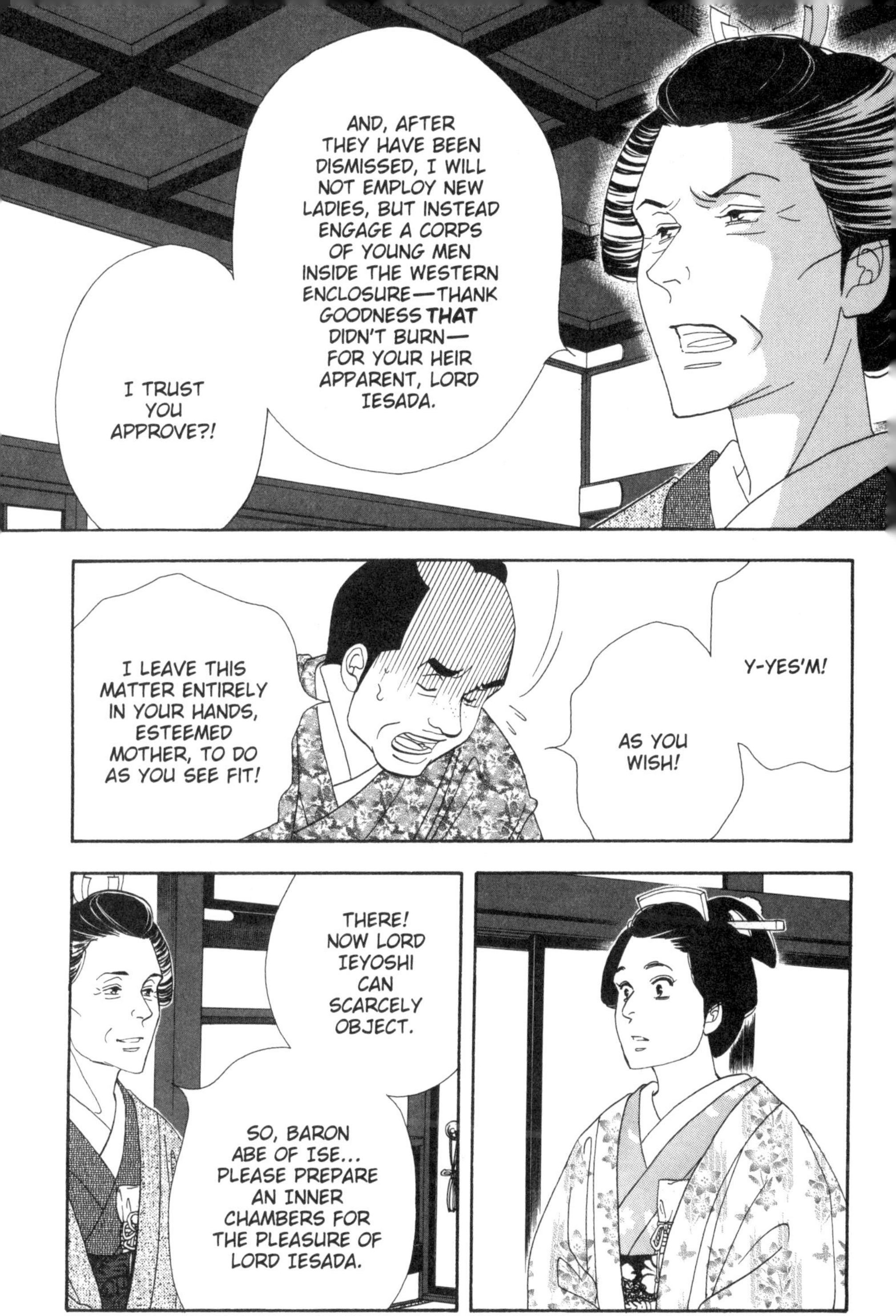
AND, AFTER THEY HAVE BEEN DISMISSED, I WILL NOT EMPLOY NEW LADIES, BUT INSTEAD ENGAGE A CORPS OF YOUNG MEN INSIDE THE WESTERN ENCLOSURE—THANK GOODNESS **THAT** DIDN'T BURN—FOR YOUR HEIR APPARENT, LORD IESADA.
I TRUST YOU APPROVE?!
Y-YES'M!
AS YOU WISH!
I LEAVE THIS MATTER ENTIRELY IN YOUR HANDS, ESTEEMED MOTHER, TO DO AS YOU SEE FIT!
THERE! NOW LORD IEYOSHI CAN SCARCELY OBJECT.
SO, BARON ABE OF ISE... PLEASE PREPARE AN INNER CHAMBERS FOR THE PLEASURE OF LORD IESADA.

I AM TRULY... TRULY GRATEFUL FOR YOUR MAGNIFICENT HANDLING OF THIS AFFAIR!

LADY KODAI-IN.

Kodai-in, the consort of the 11th Tokugawa shogun, Ienari, quietly drew her last breath at the end of that year. She was 72 years old.

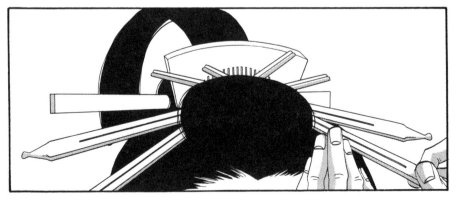

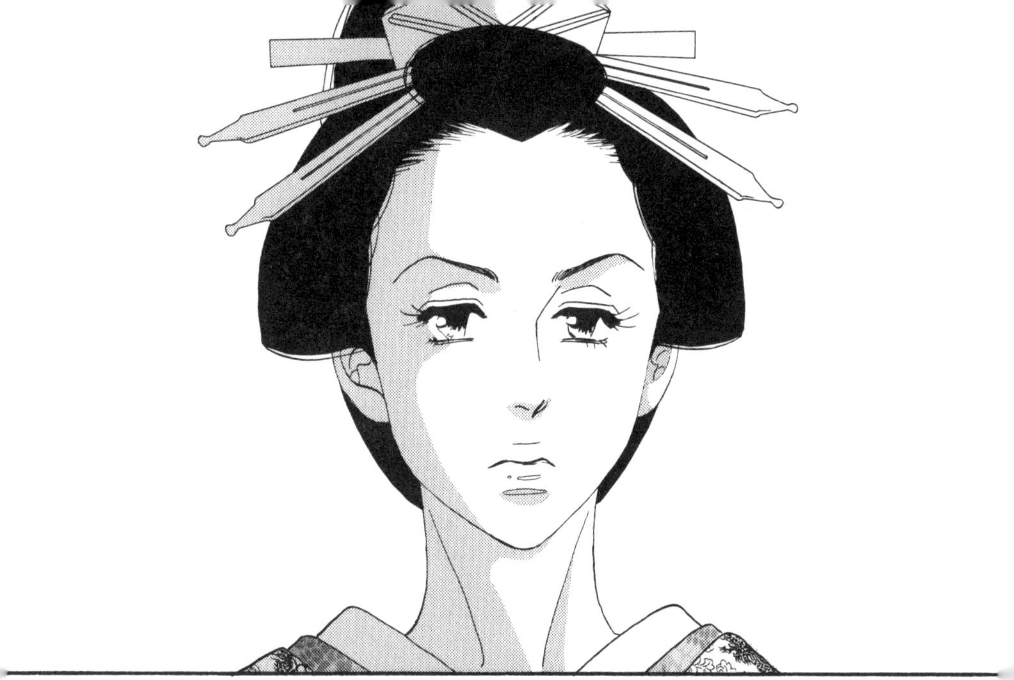
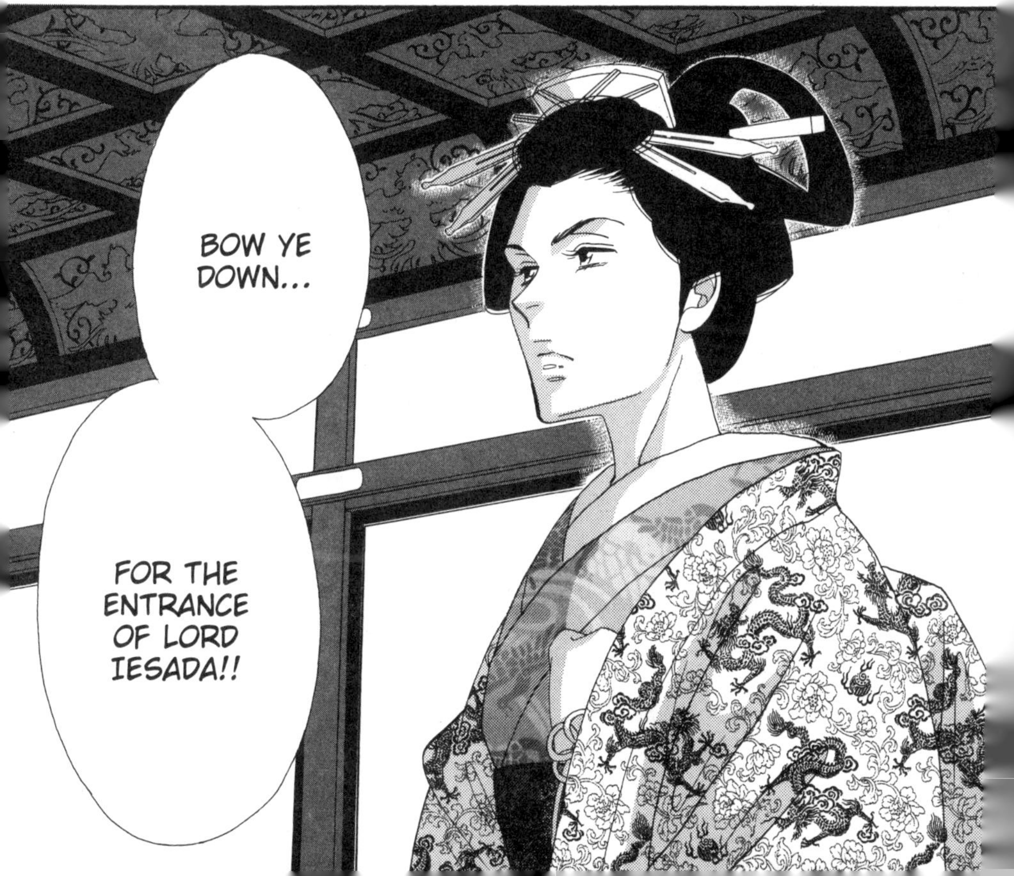
BOW YE DOWN...
FOR THE ENTRANCE OF LORD IESADA!!

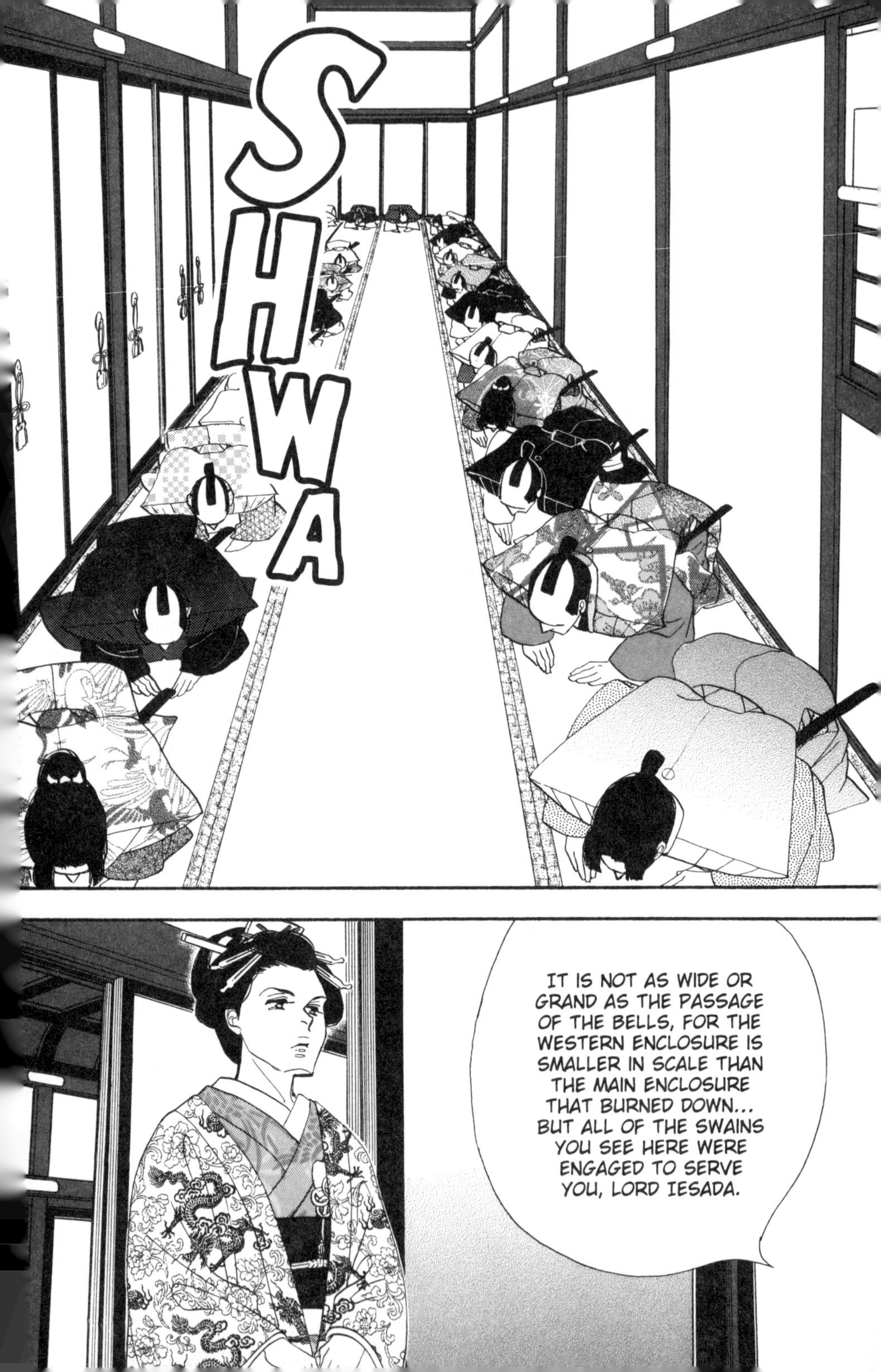
SHWA
IT IS NOT AS WIDE OR GRAND AS THE PASSAGE OF THE BELLS, FOR THE WESTERN ENCLOSURE IS SMALLER IN SCALE THAN THE MAIN ENCLOSURE THAT BURNED DOWN... BUT ALL OF THE SWAINS YOU SEE HERE WERE ENGAGED TO SERVE YOU, LORD IESADA.

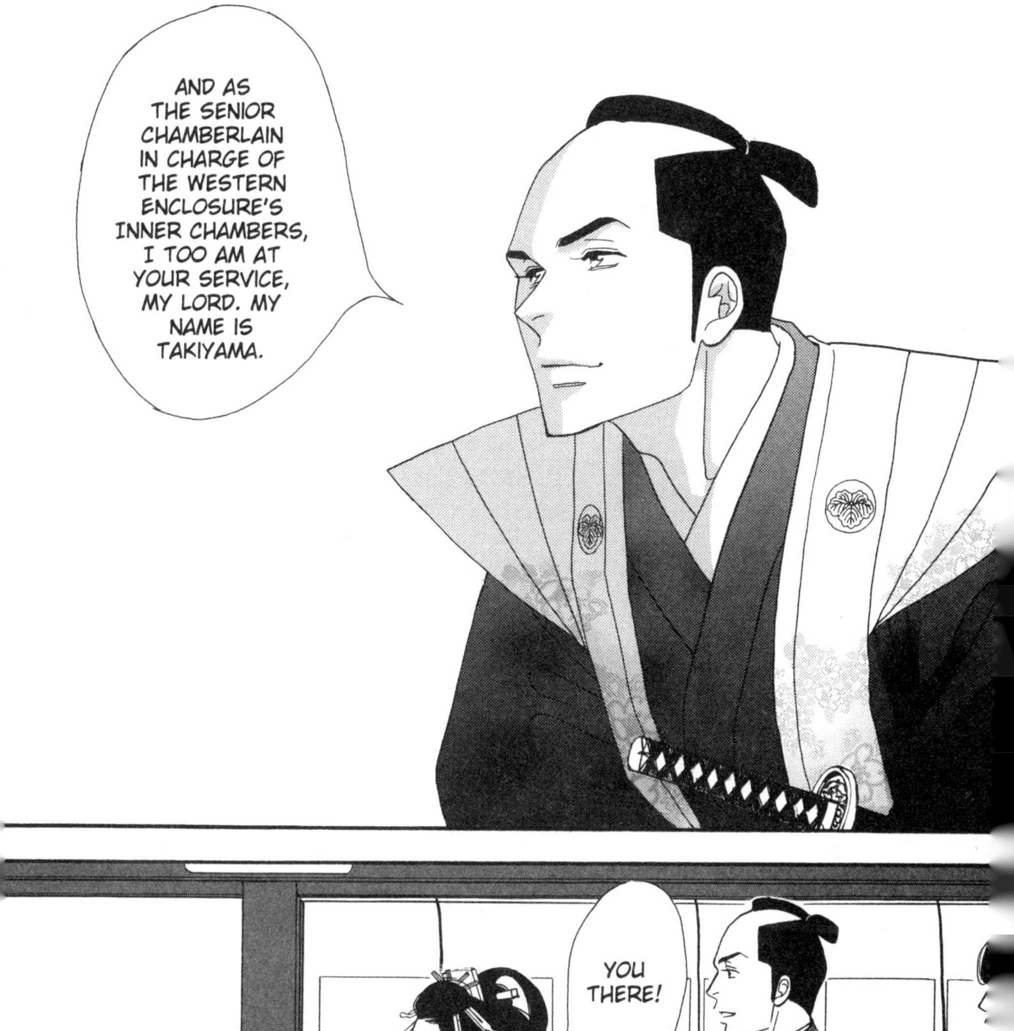
AND AS THE SENIOR CHAMBERLAIN IN CHARGE OF THE WESTERN ENCLOSURE'S INNER CHAMBERS, I TOO AM AT YOUR SERVICE, MY LORD. MY NAME IS TAKIYAMA.

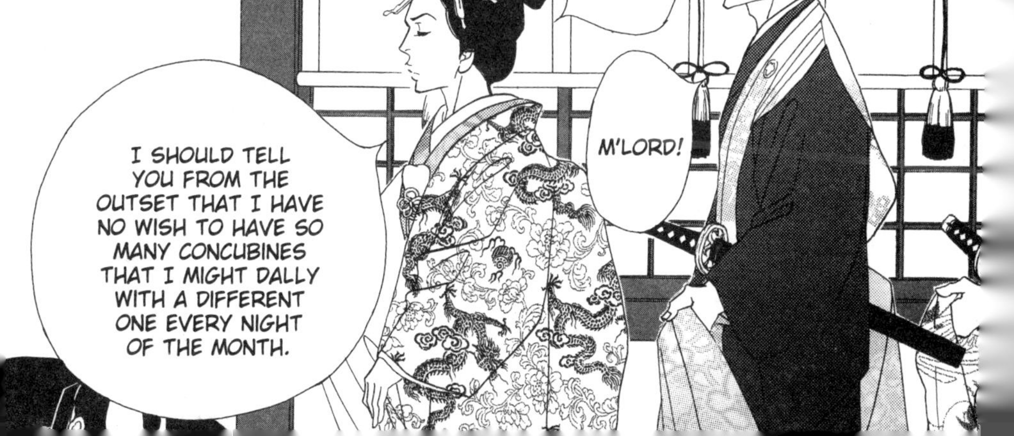
YOU THERE!
M'LORD!
I SHOULD TELL YOU FROM THE OUTSET THAT I HAVE NO WISH TO HAVE SO MANY CONCUBINES THAT I MIGHT DALLY WITH A DIFFERENT ONE EVERY NIGHT OF THE MONTH.

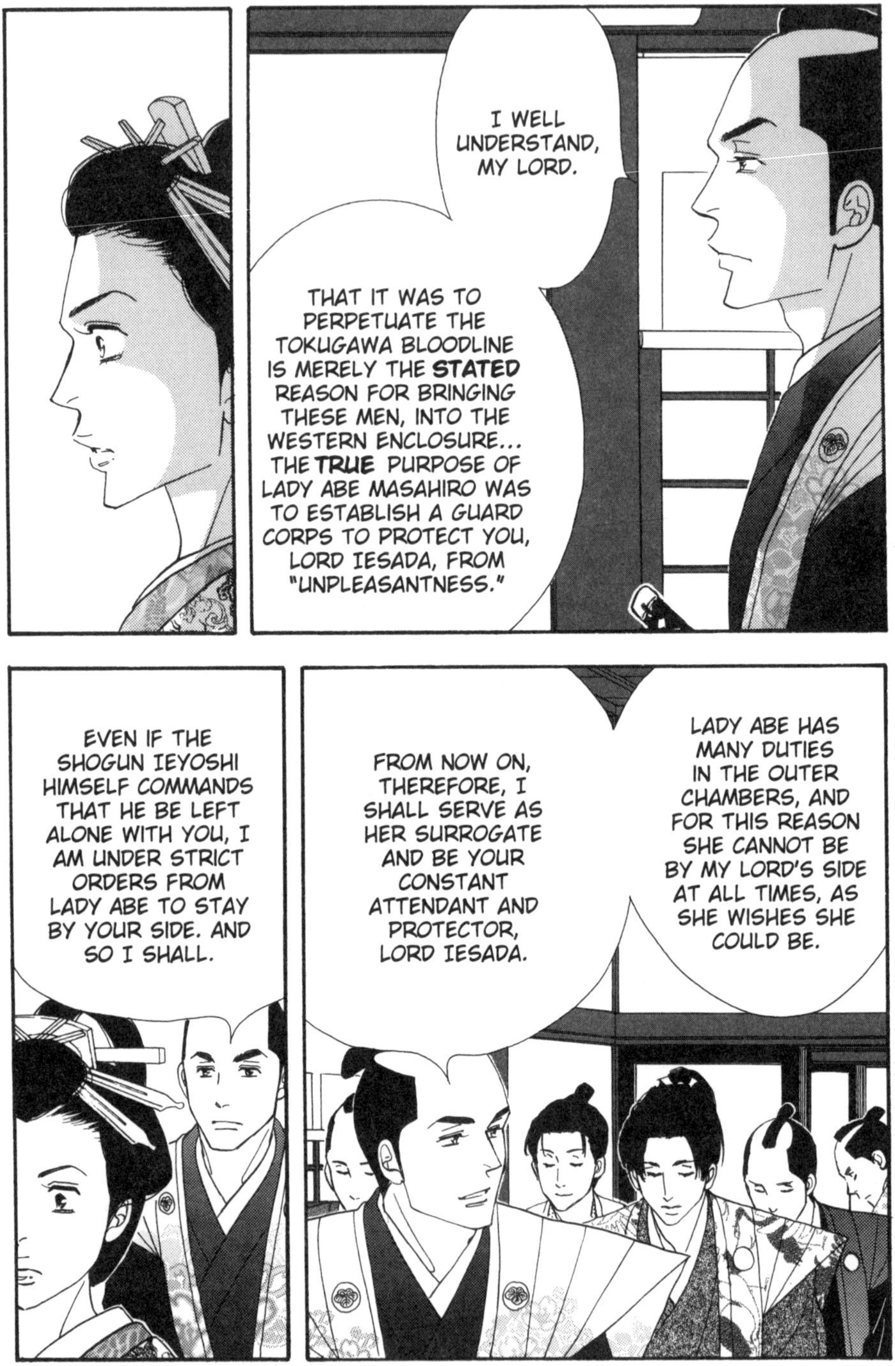
I WELL UNDERSTAND, MY LORD.
THAT IT WAS TO PERPETUATE THE TOKUGAWA BLOODLINE IS MERELY THE STATED REASON FOR BRINGING THESE MEN, INTO THE WESTERN ENCLOSURE... THE TRUE PURPOSE OF LADY ABE MASAHIRO WAS TO ESTABLISH A GUARD CORPS TO PROTECT YOU, LORD IESADA, FROM "UNPLEASANTNESS."
LADY ABE HAS MANY DUTIES IN THE OUTER CHAMBERS, AND FOR THIS REASON SHE CANNOT BE BY MY LORD'S SIDE AT ALL TIMES, AS SHE WISHES SHE COULD BE.
FROM NOW ON, THEREFORE, I SHALL SERVE AS HER SURROGATE AND BE YOUR CONSTANT ATTENDANT AND PROTECTOR, LORD IESADA.
EVEN IF THE SHOGUN IEYOSHI HIMSELF COMMANDS THAT HE BE LEFT ALONE WITH YOU, I AM UNDER STRICT ORDERS FROM LADY ABE TO STAY BY YOUR SIDE. AND SO I SHALL.

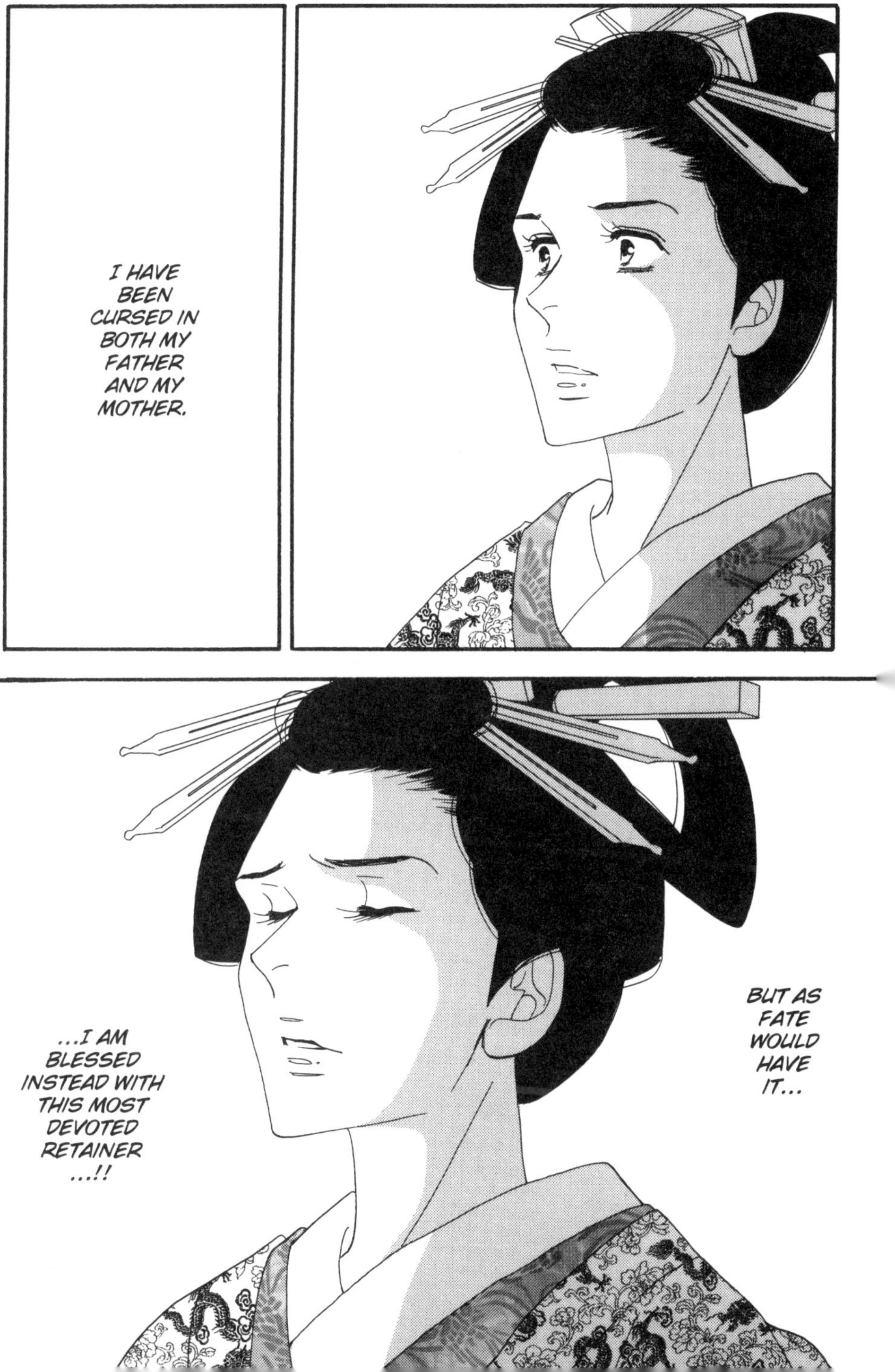
I HAVE BEEN CURSED IN BOTH MY FATHER AND MY MOTHER.
BUT AS FATE WOULD HAVE IT...
...I AM BLESSED INSTEAD WITH THIS MOST DEVOTED RETAINER ...!!

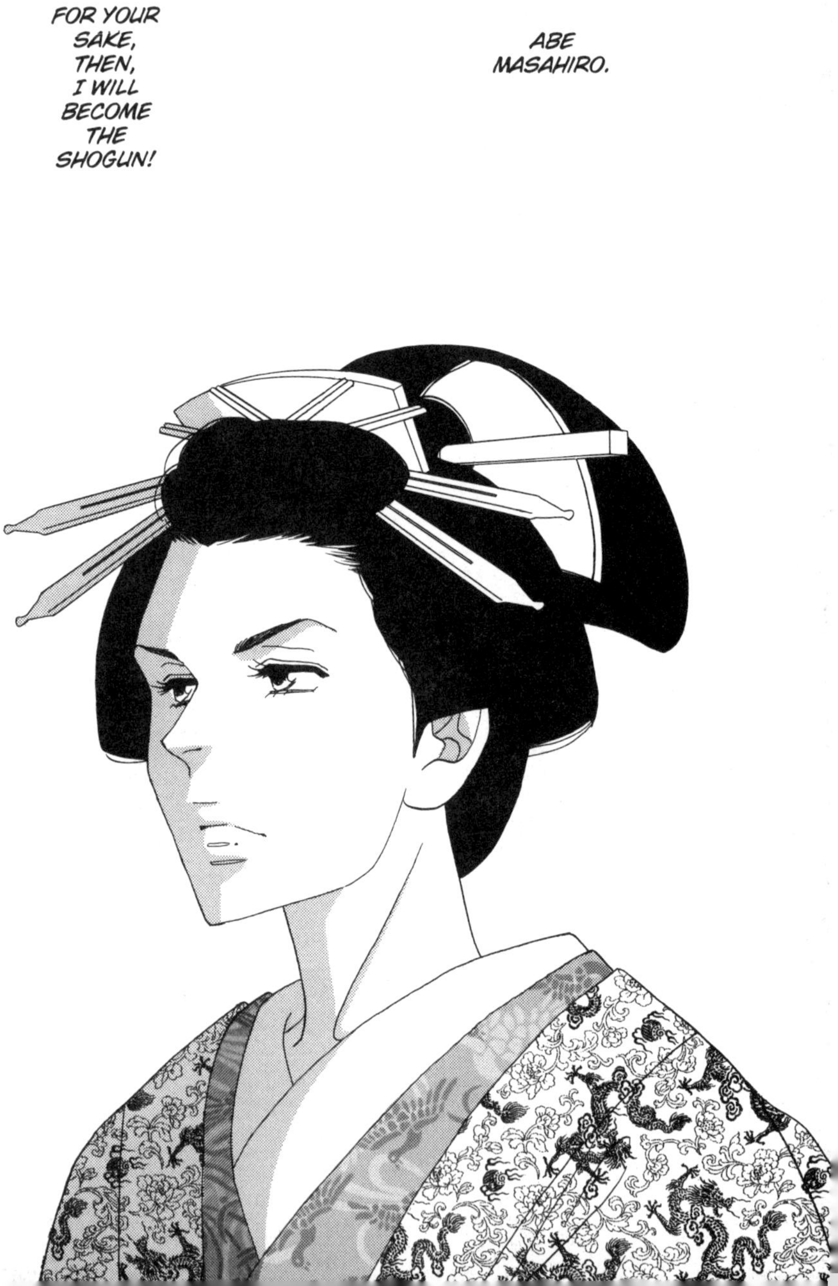
ABE MASAHIRO.
FOR YOUR SAKE, THEN, I WILL BECOME THE SHOGUN!

Ōoku

THE INNER CHAMBERS

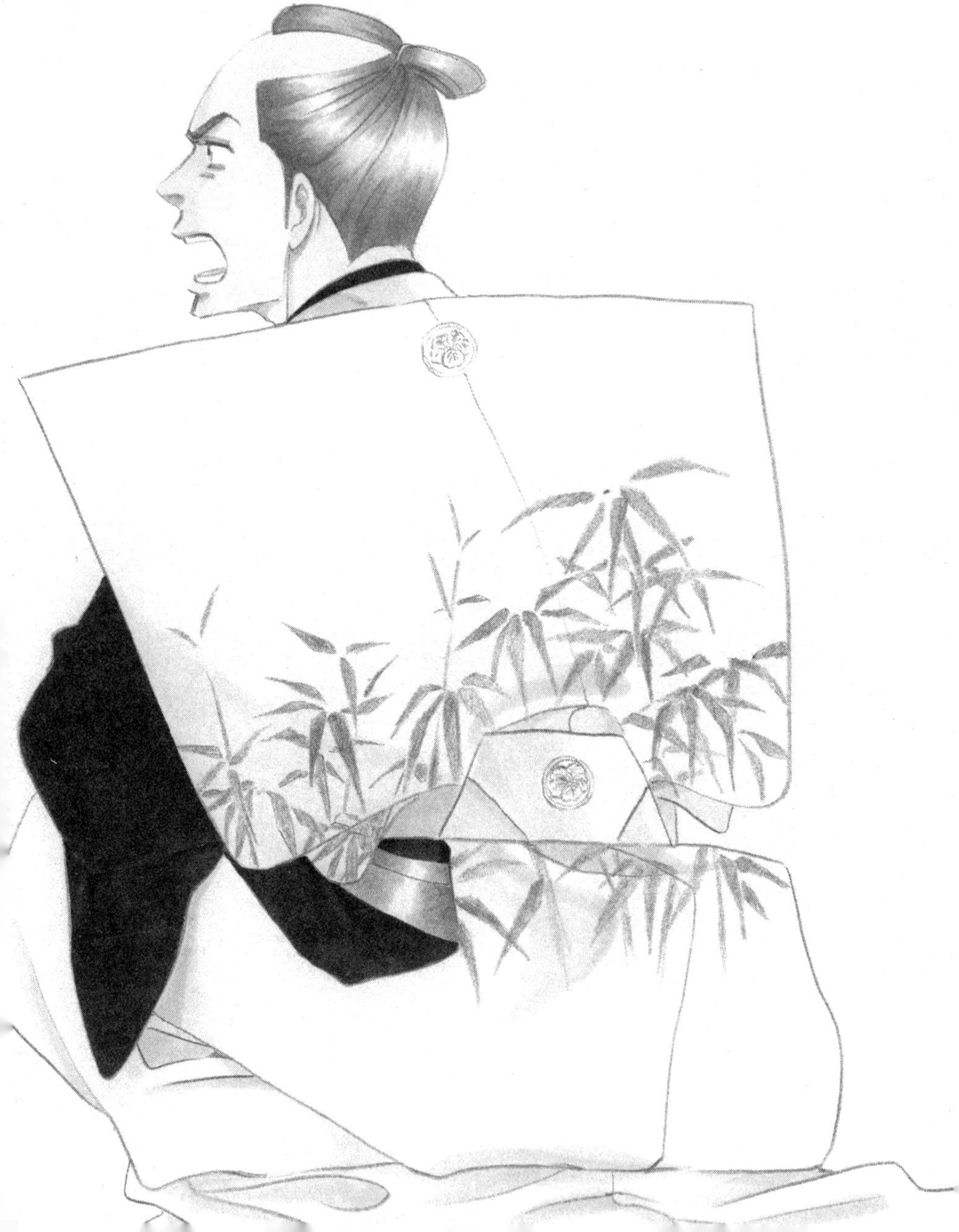

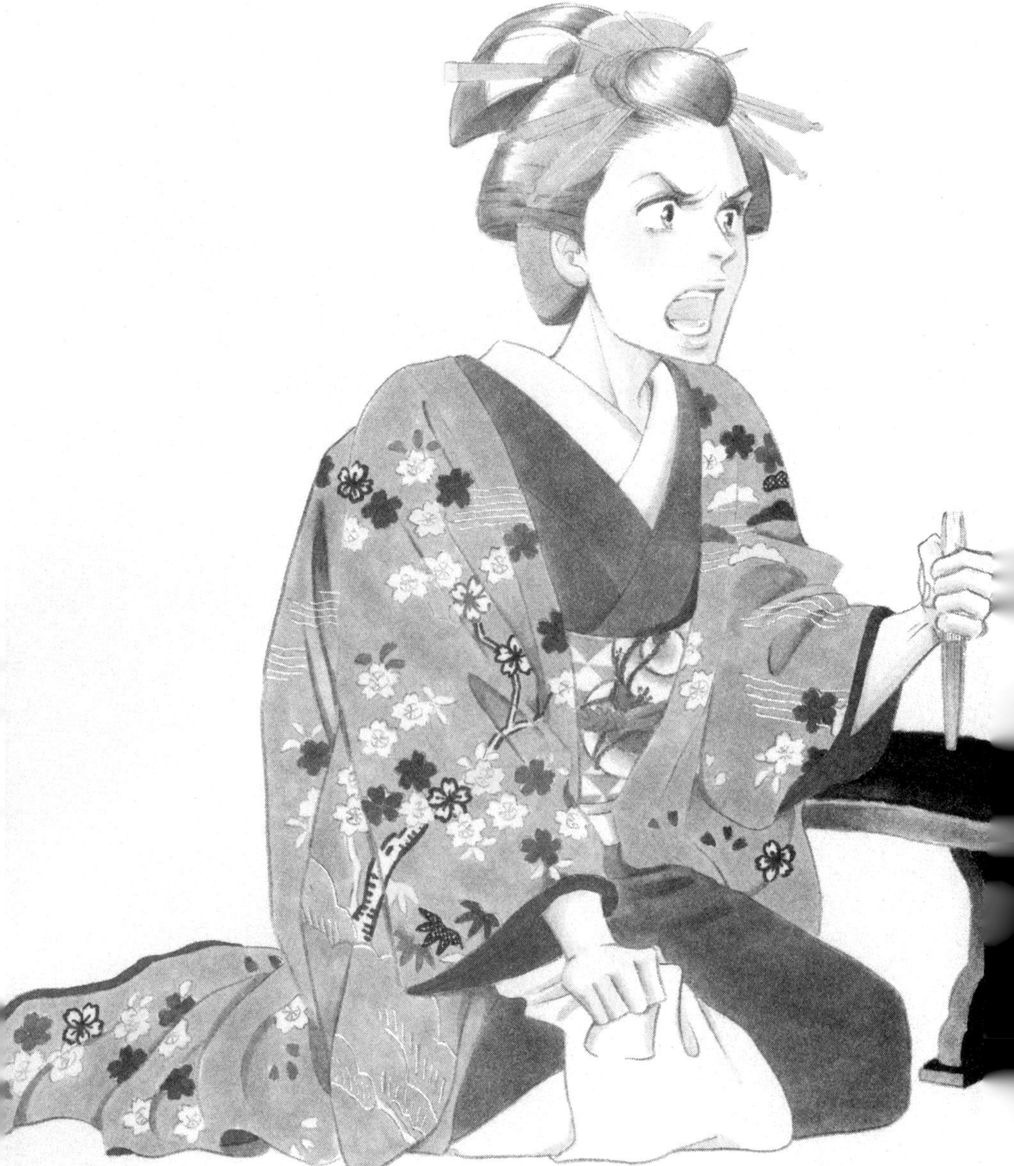

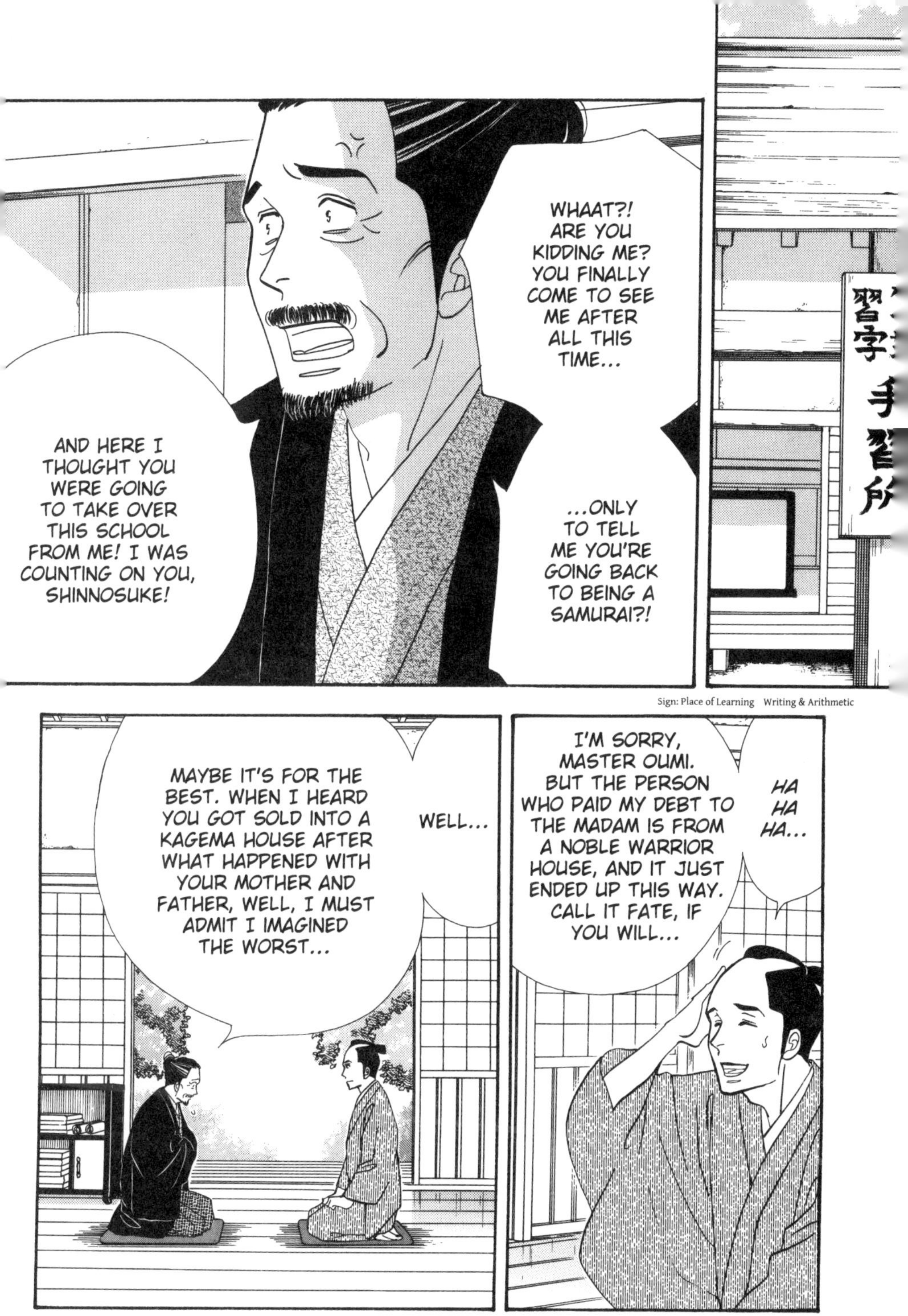
習字
手習所
WHAAT?! ARE YOU KIDDING ME? YOU FINALLY COME TO SEE ME AFTER ALL THIS TIME...
...ONLY TO TELL ME YOU'RE GOING BACK TO BEING A SAMURAI?!
AND HERE I THOUGHT YOU WERE GOING TO TAKE OVER THIS SCHOOL FROM ME! I WAS COUNTING ON YOU, SHINNOSUKE!
I'M SORRY, MASTER OUMI. BUT THE PERSON WHO PAID MY DEBT TO THE MADAM IS FROM A NOBLE WARRIOR HOUSE, AND IT JUST ENDED UP THIS WAY. CALL IT FATE, IF YOU WILL...
HA HA HA...
WELL...
MAYBE IT'S FOR THE BEST. WHEN I HEARD YOU GOT SOLD INTO A KAGEMA HOUSE AFTER WHAT HAPPENED WITH YOUR MOTHER AND FATHER, WELL, I MUST ADMIT I IMAGINED THE WORST...

Sign: Place of Learning Writing & Arithmetic

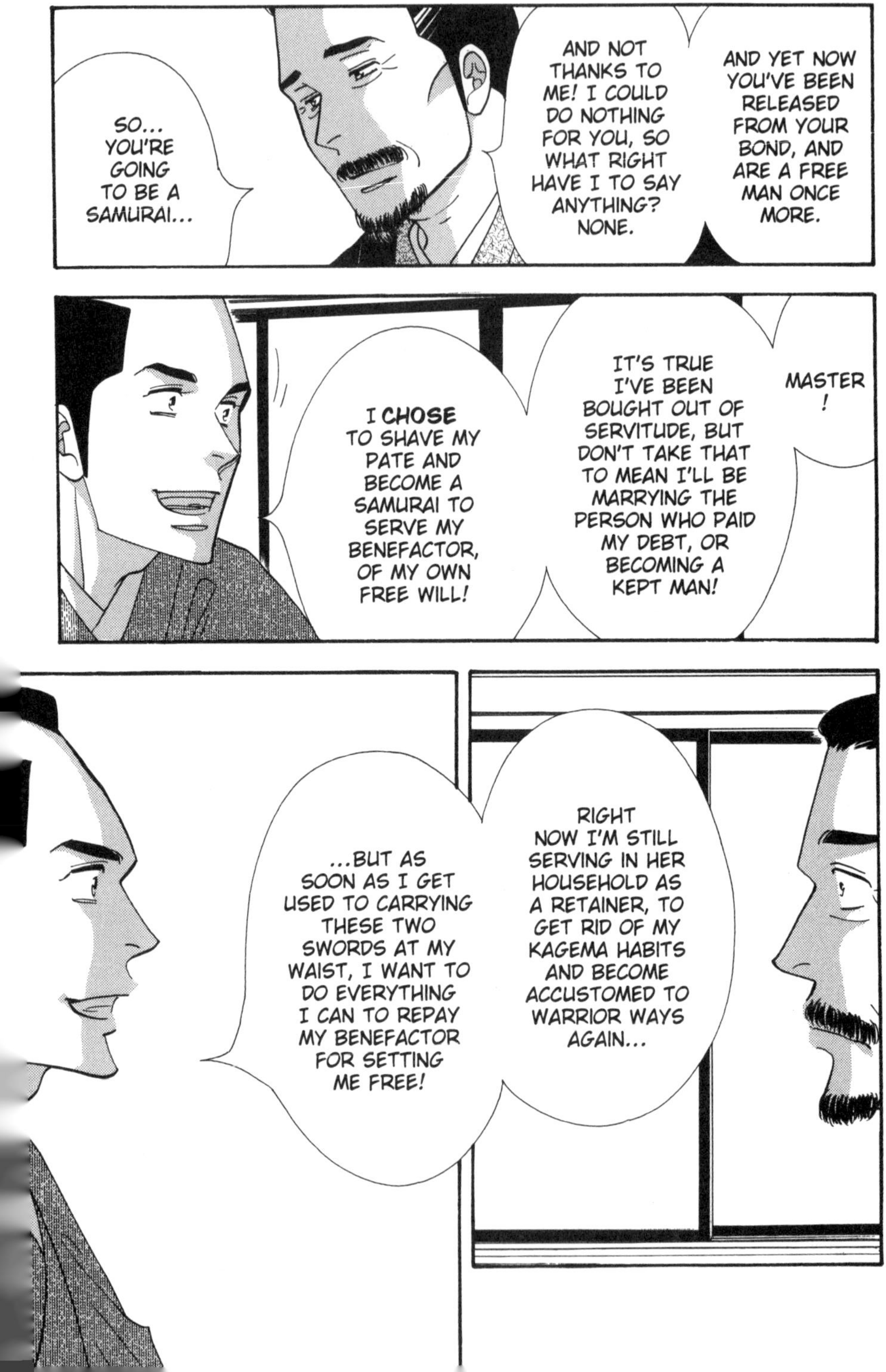
AND YET NOW YOU'VE BEEN RELEASED FROM YOUR BOND, AND ARE A FREE MAN ONCE MORE.
AND NOT THANKS TO ME! I COULD DO NOTHING FOR YOU, SO WHAT RIGHT HAVE I TO SAY ANYTHING? NONE.
SO... YOU'RE GOING TO BE A SAMURAI...
MASTER!
IT'S TRUE I'VE BEEN BOUGHT OUT OF SERVITUDE, BUT DON'T TAKE THAT TO MEAN I'LL BE MARRYING THE PERSON WHO PAID MY DEBT, OR BECOMING A KEPT MAN!
I **CHOSE** TO SHAVE MY PATE AND BECOME A SAMURAI TO SERVE MY BENEFACTOR, OF MY OWN FREE WILL!
RIGHT NOW I'M STILL SERVING IN HER HOUSEHOLD AS A RETAINER, TO GET RID OF MY KAGEMA HABITS AND BECOME ACCUSTOMED TO WARRIOR WAYS AGAIN...
...BUT AS SOON AS I GET USED TO CARRYING THESE TWO SWORDS AT MY WAIST, I WANT TO DO EVERYTHING I CAN TO REPAY MY BENEFACTOR FOR SETTING ME FREE!

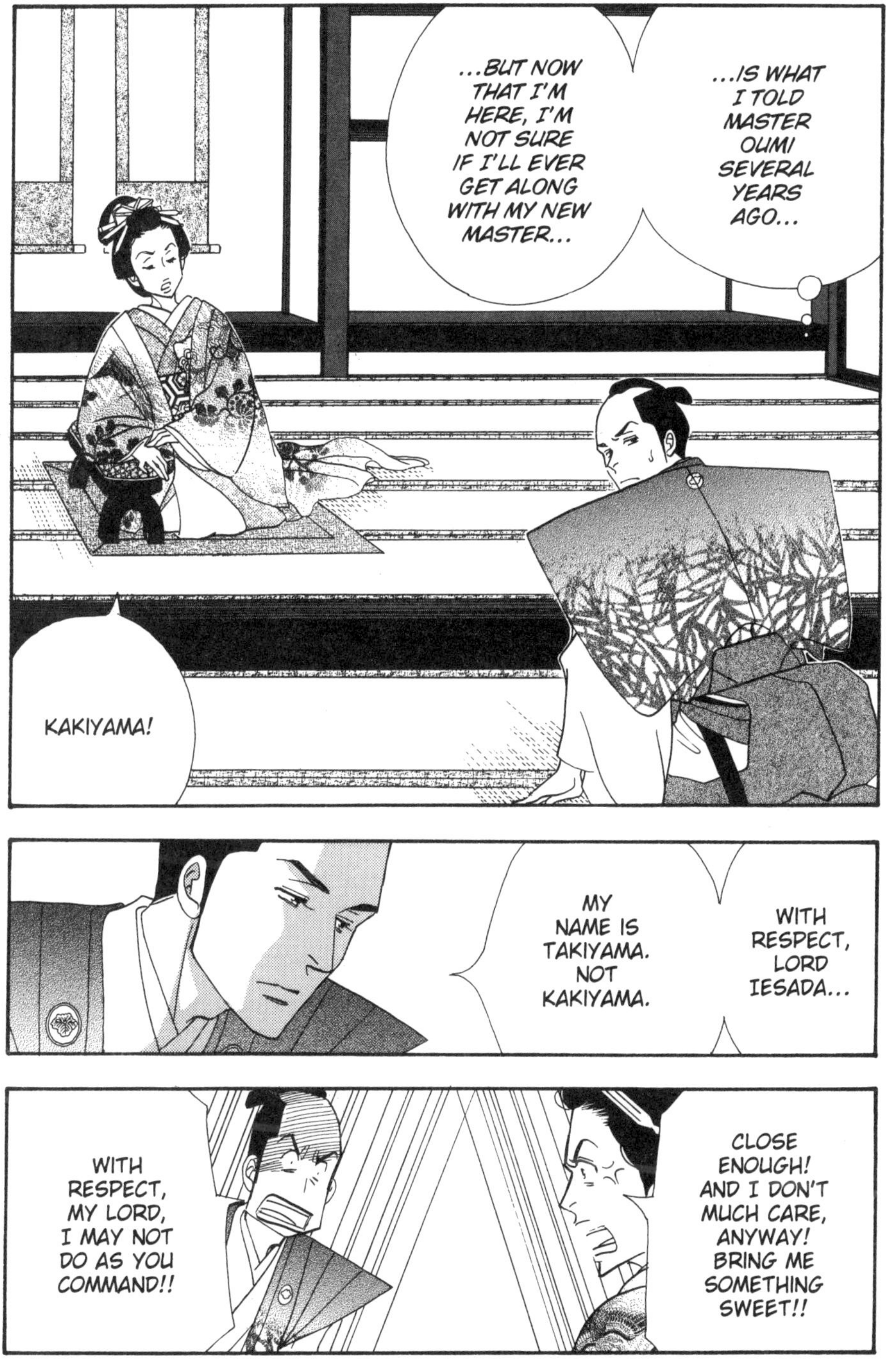
...IS WHAT I TOLD MASTER OUMI SEVERAL YEARS AGO...
...BUT NOW THAT I'M HERE, I'M NOT SURE IF I'LL EVER GET ALONG WITH MY NEW MASTER...
KAKIYAMA!
WITH RESPECT, LORD IESADA...
MY NAME IS TAKIYAMA. NOT KAKIYAMA.
CLOSE ENOUGH! AND I DON'T MUCH CARE, ANYWAY! BRING ME SOMETHING SWEET!!
WITH RESPECT, MY LORD, I MAY NOT DO AS YOU COMMAND!!

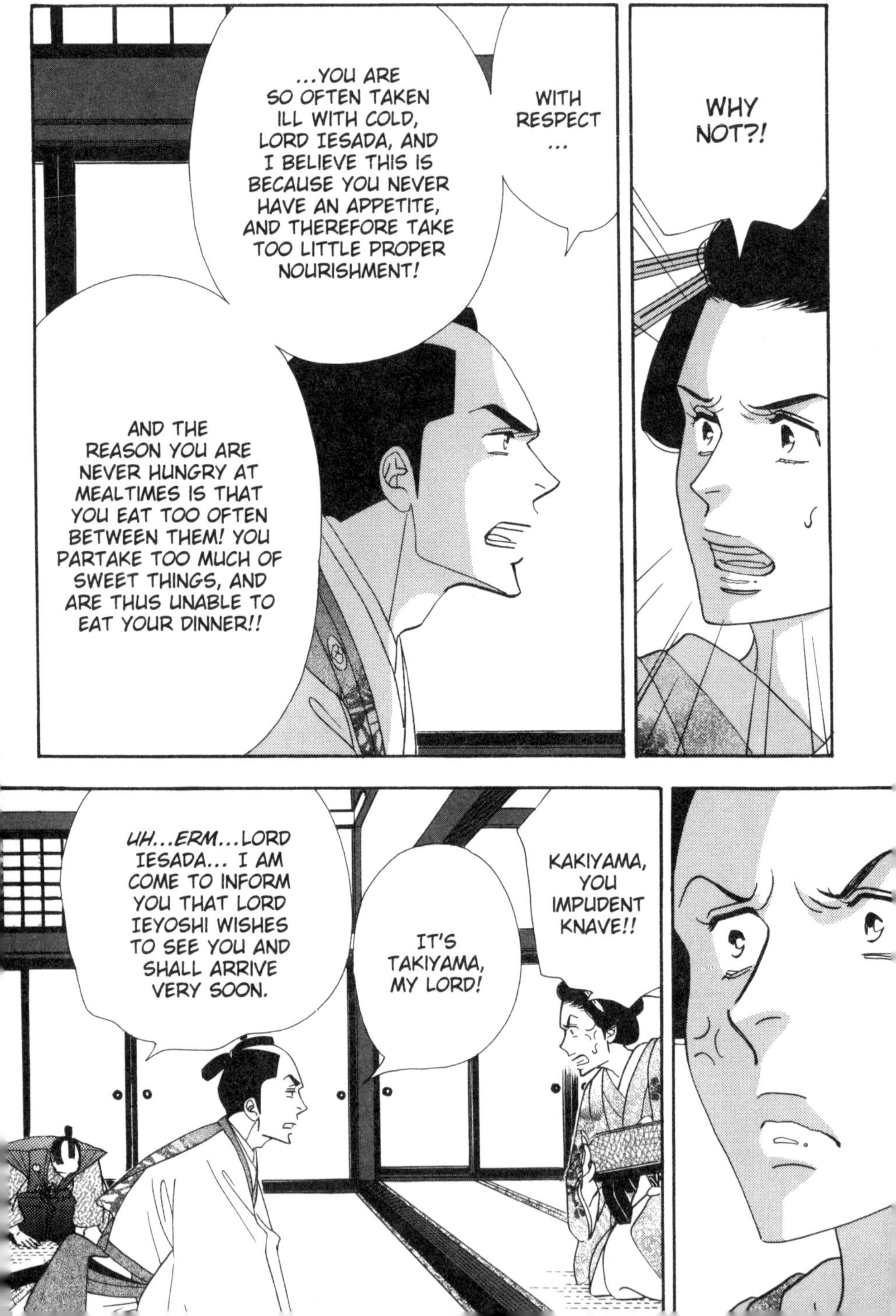
WHY NOT?!
WITH RESPECT ...
...YOU ARE SO OFTEN TAKEN ILL WITH COLD, LORD IESADA, AND I BELIEVE THIS IS BECAUSE YOU NEVER HAVE AN APPETITE, AND THEREFORE TAKE TOO LITTLE PROPER NOURISHMENT!
AND THE REASON YOU ARE NEVER HUNGRY AT MEALTIMES IS THAT YOU EAT TOO OFTEN BETWEEN THEM! YOU PARTAKE TOO MUCH OF SWEET THINGS, AND ARE THUS UNABLE TO EAT YOUR DINNER!!
KAKIYAMA, YOU IMPUDENT KNAVE!!
IT'S TAKIYAMA, MY LORD!
*UH...ERM...*LORD IESADA... I AM COME TO INFORM YOU THAT LORD IEYOSHI WISHES TO SEE YOU AND SHALL ARRIVE VERY SOON.

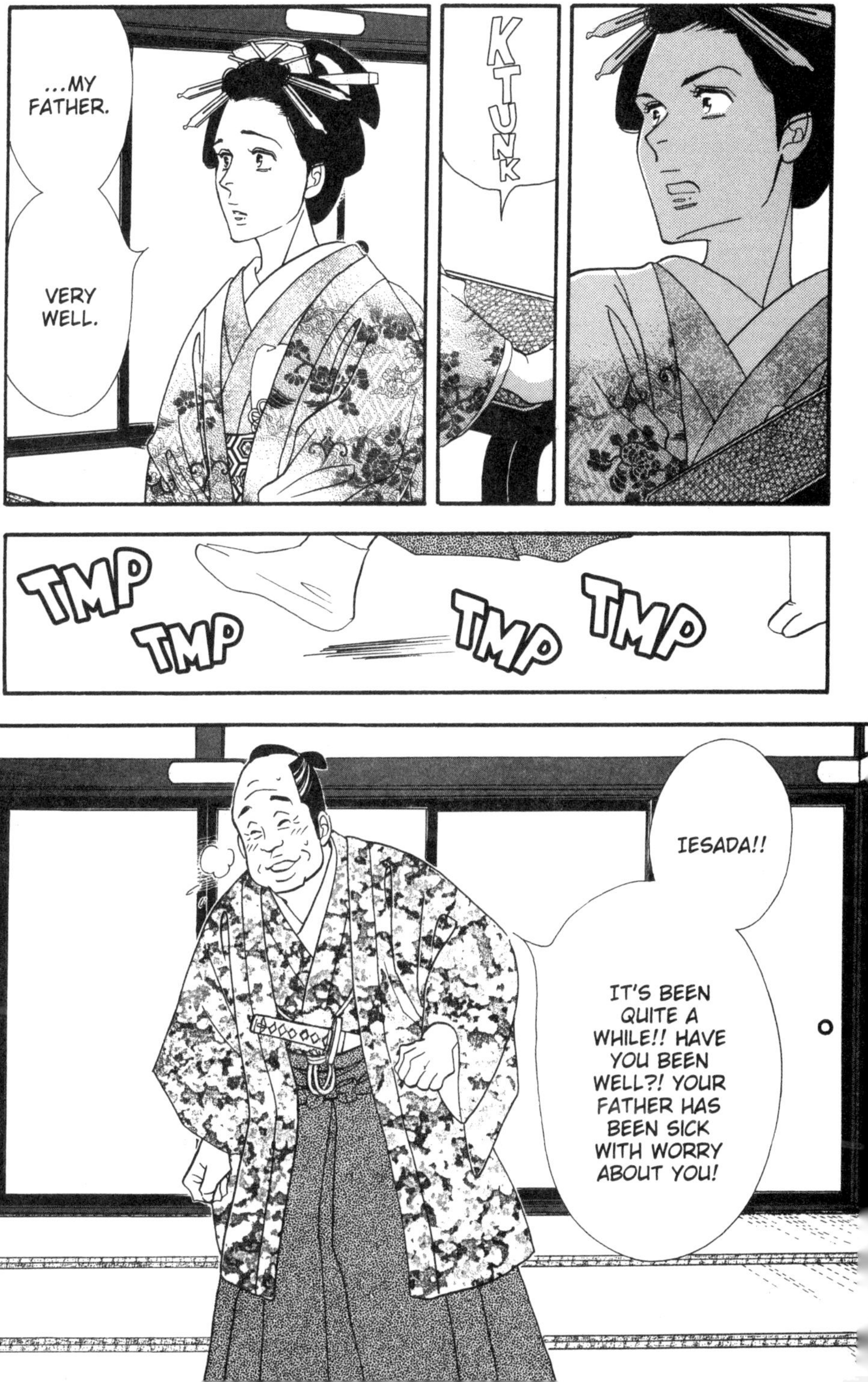
KTUNK
...MY FATHER.
VERY WELL.
TMP TMP TMP TMP
IESADA!!
IT'S BEEN QUITE A WHILE!! HAVE YOU BEEN WELL?! YOUR FATHER HAS BEEN SICK WITH WORRY ABOUT YOU!

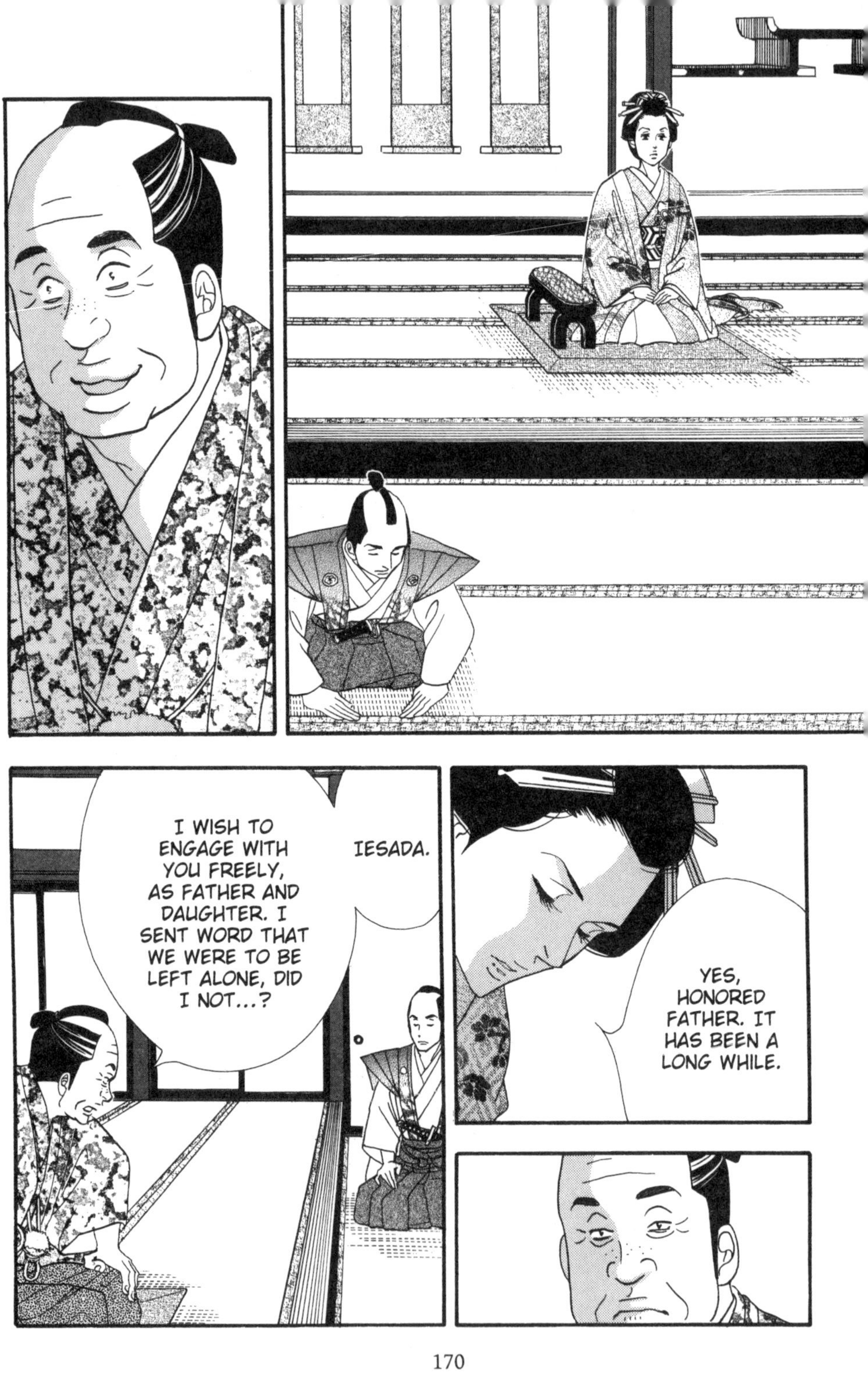
YES, HONORED FATHER. IT HAS BEEN A LONG WHILE.
IESADA.
I WISH TO ENGAGE WITH YOU FREELY, AS FATHER AND DAUGHTER. I SENT WORD THAT WE WERE TO BE LEFT ALONE, DID I NOT...?

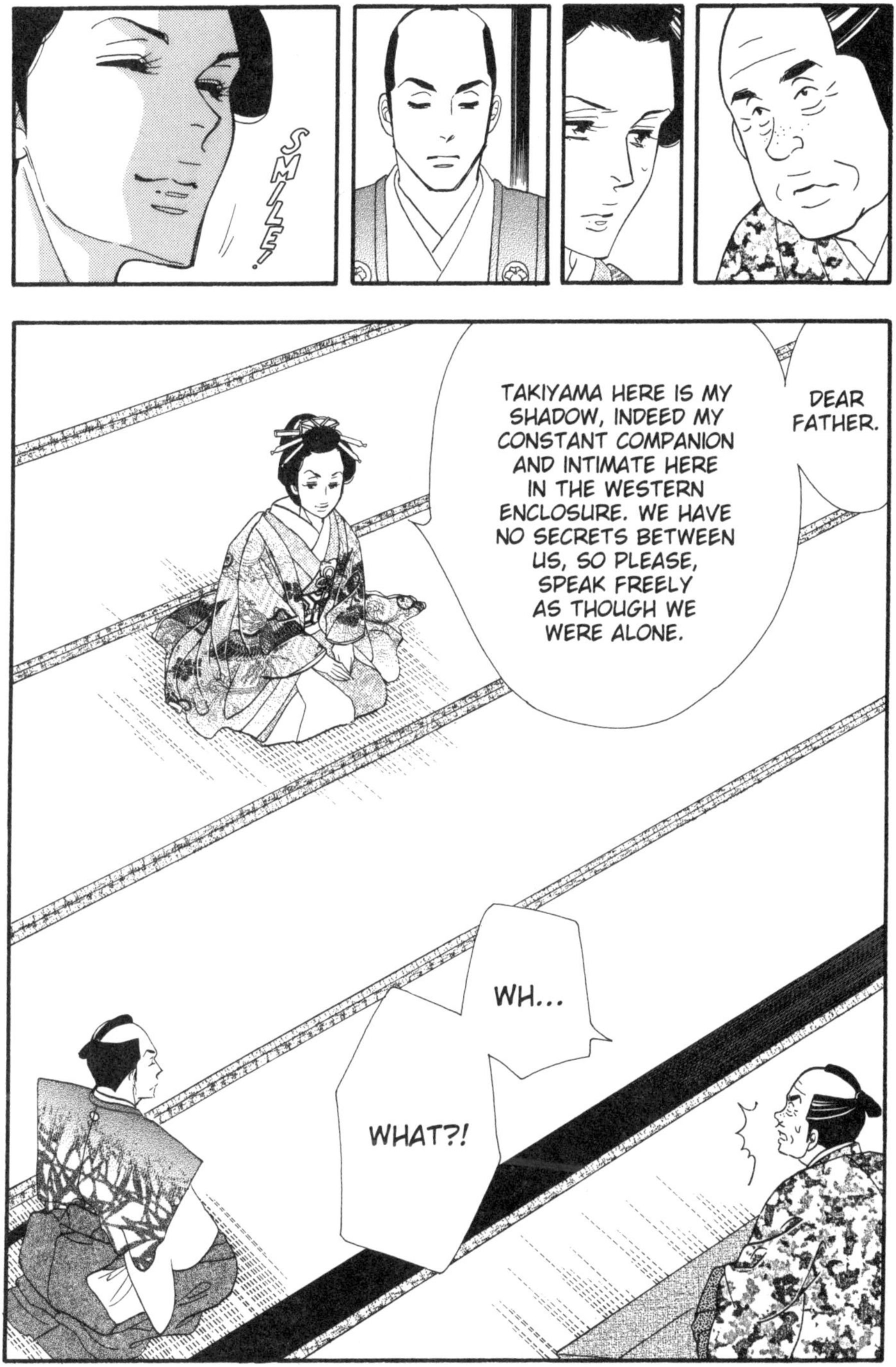
SMILE!
DEAR FATHER.
TAKIYAMA HERE IS MY SHADOW, INDEED MY CONSTANT COMPANION AND INTIMATE HERE IN THE WESTERN ENCLOSURE. WE HAVE NO SECRETS BETWEEN US, SO PLEASE, SPEAK FREELY AS THOUGH WE WERE ALONE.
WH...
WHAT?!

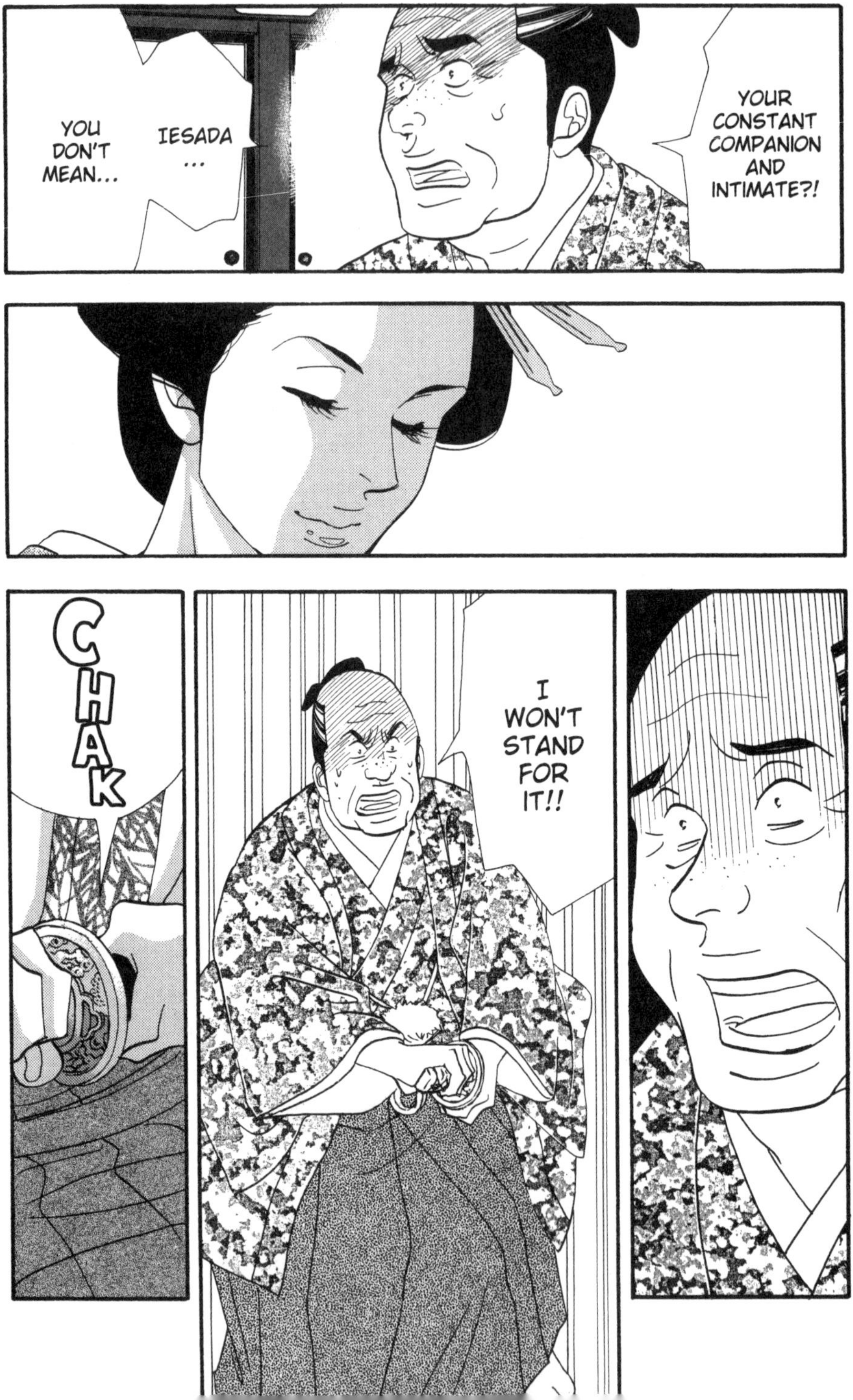
YOUR CONSTANT COMPANION AND INTIMATE?!
YOU DON'T MEAN... IESADA...
I WON'T STAND FOR IT!!
CHAK

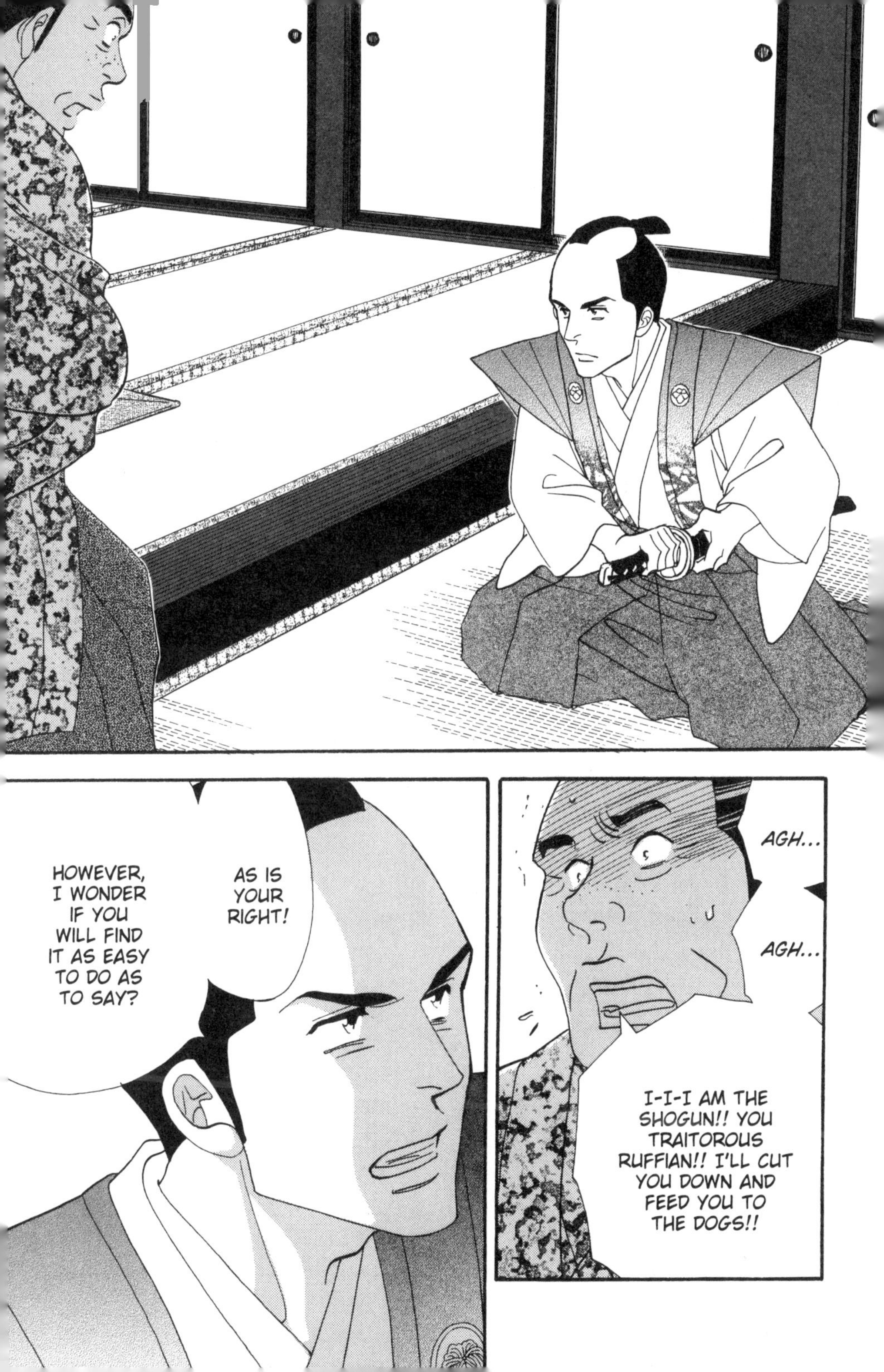
AGH...
AGH...
I-I-I AM THE SHOGUN!! YOU TRAITOROUS RUFFIAN!! I'LL CUT YOU DOWN AND FEED YOU TO THE DOGS!!
AS IS YOUR RIGHT!
HOWEVER, I WONDER IF YOU WILL FIND IT AS EASY TO DO AS TO SAY?

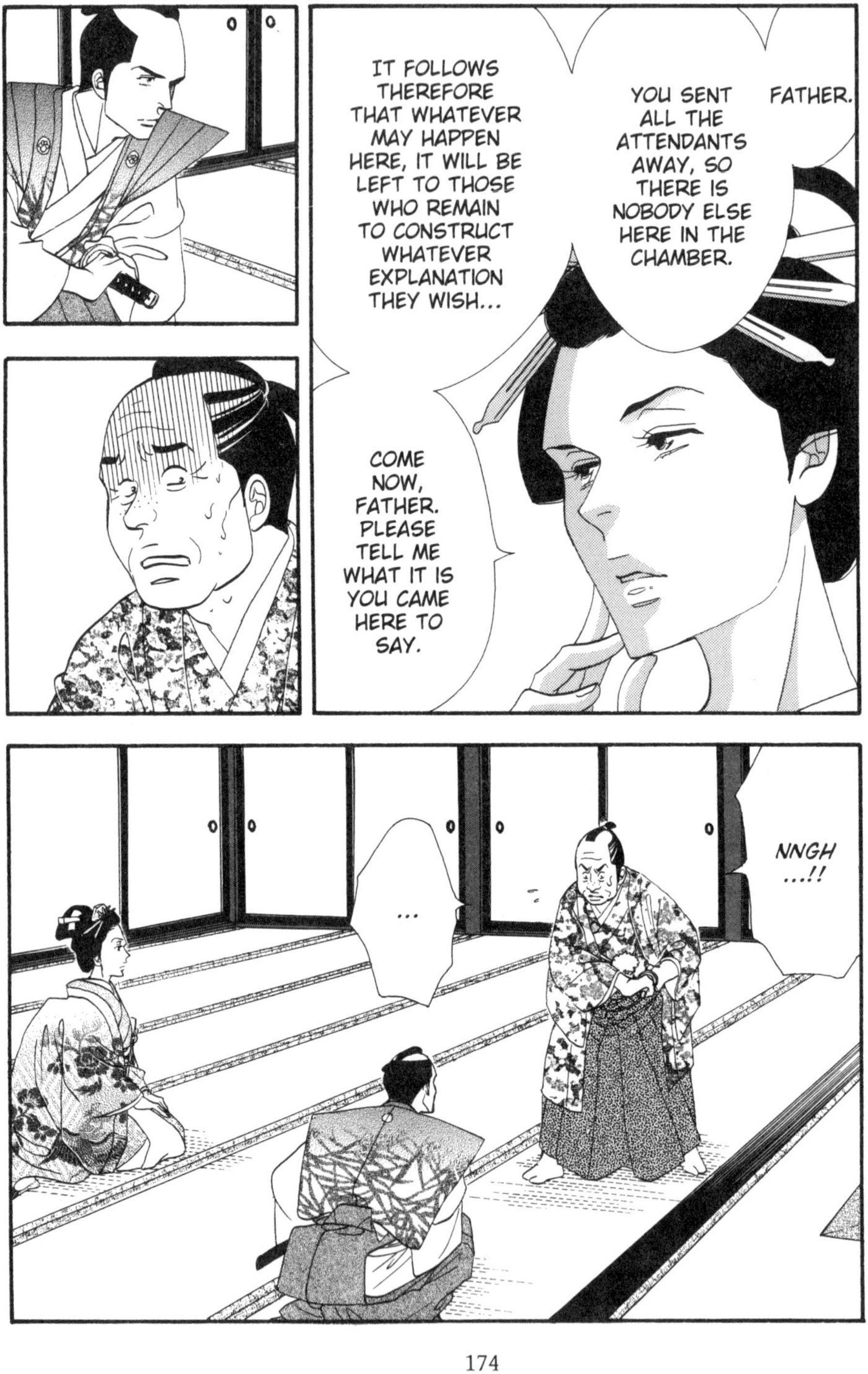
FATHER.
YOU SENT ALL THE ATTENDANTS AWAY, SO THERE IS NOBODY ELSE HERE IN THE CHAMBER.
IT FOLLOWS THEREFORE THAT WHATEVER MAY HAPPEN HERE, IT WILL BE LEFT TO THOSE WHO REMAIN TO CONSTRUCT WHATEVER EXPLANATION THEY WISH...
COME NOW, FATHER. PLEASE TELL ME WHAT IT IS YOU CAME HERE TO SAY.
NNGH ...!!
...

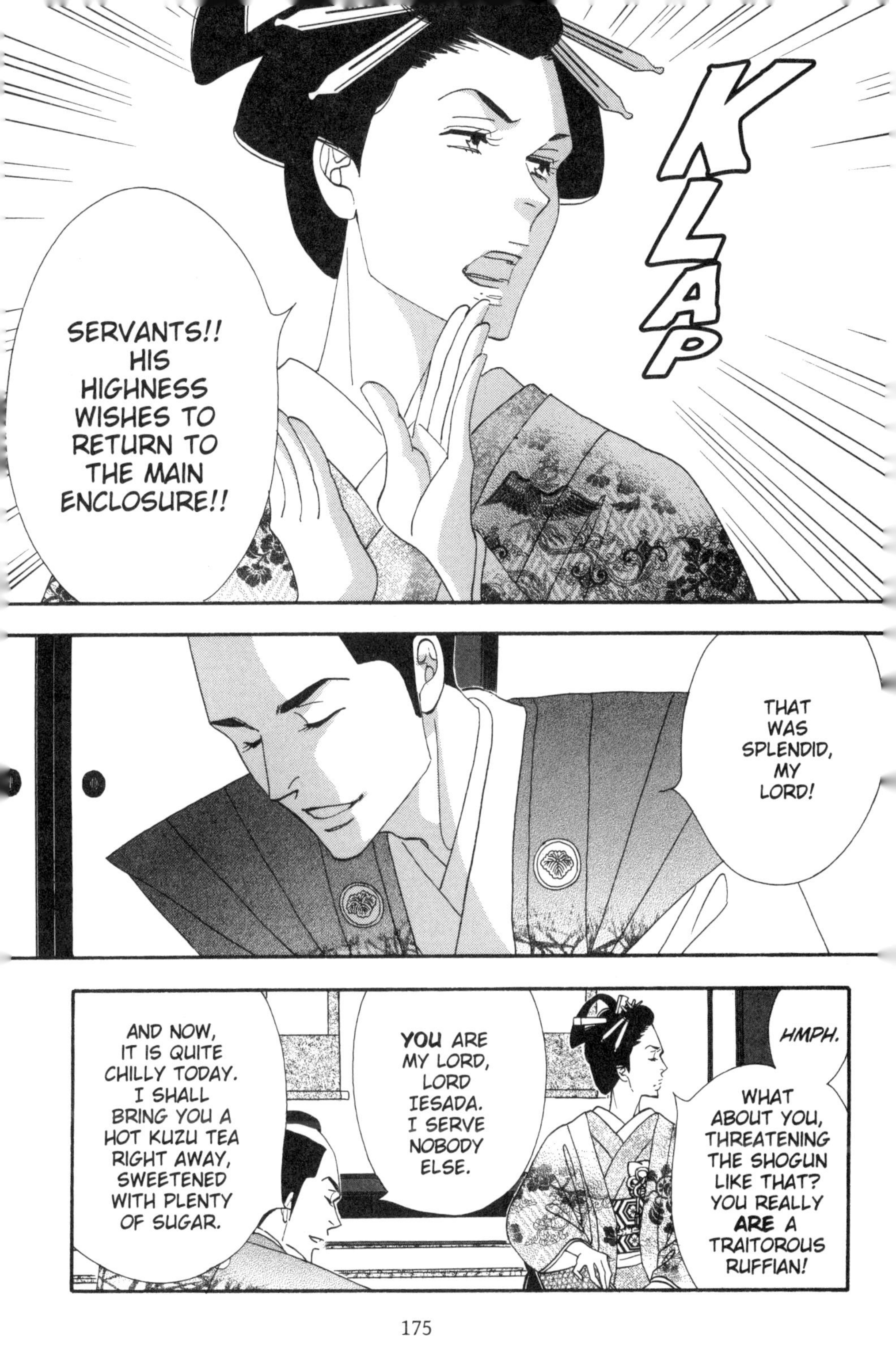
KLAP
SERVANTS!! HIS HIGHNESS WISHES TO RETURN TO THE MAIN ENCLOSURE!!
THAT WAS SPLENDID, MY LORD!
HMPH.
WHAT ABOUT YOU, THREATENING THE SHOGUN LIKE THAT? YOU REALLY **ARE** A TRAITOROUS RUFFIAN!
YOU ARE MY LORD, LORD IESADA. I SERVE NOBODY ELSE.
AND NOW, IT IS QUITE CHILLY TODAY. I SHALL BRING YOU A HOT KUZU TEA RIGHT AWAY, SWEETENED WITH PLENTY OF SUGAR.

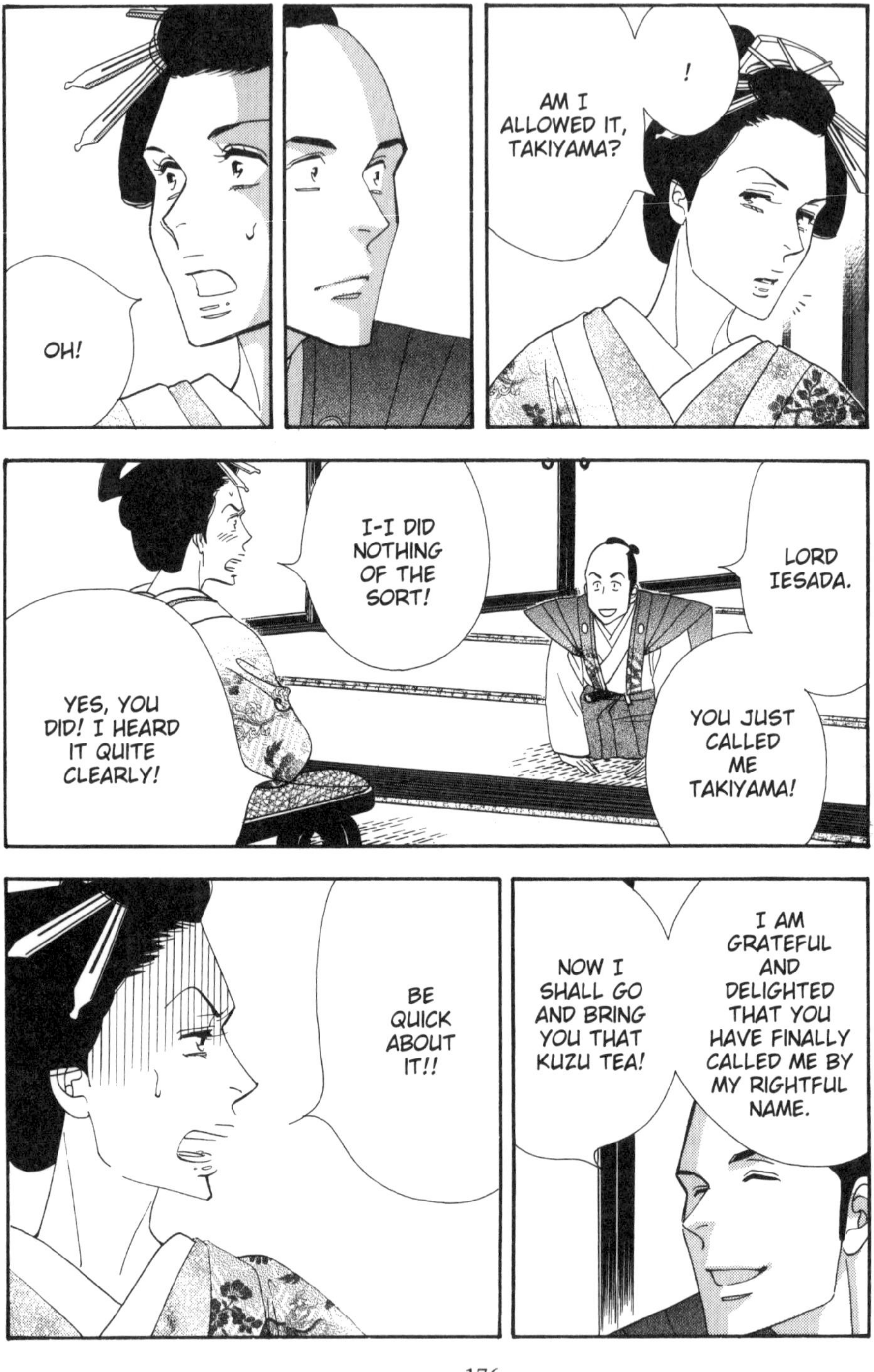
!
AM I ALLOWED IT, TAKIYAMA?
OH!
LORD IESADA.
YOU JUST CALLED ME TAKIYAMA!
I-I DID NOTHING OF THE SORT!
YES, YOU DID! I HEARD IT QUITE CLEARLY!
I AM GRATEFUL AND DELIGHTED THAT YOU HAVE FINALLY CALLED ME BY MY RIGHTFUL NAME.
NOW I SHALL GO AND BRING YOU THAT KUZU TEA!
BE QUICK ABOUT IT!!

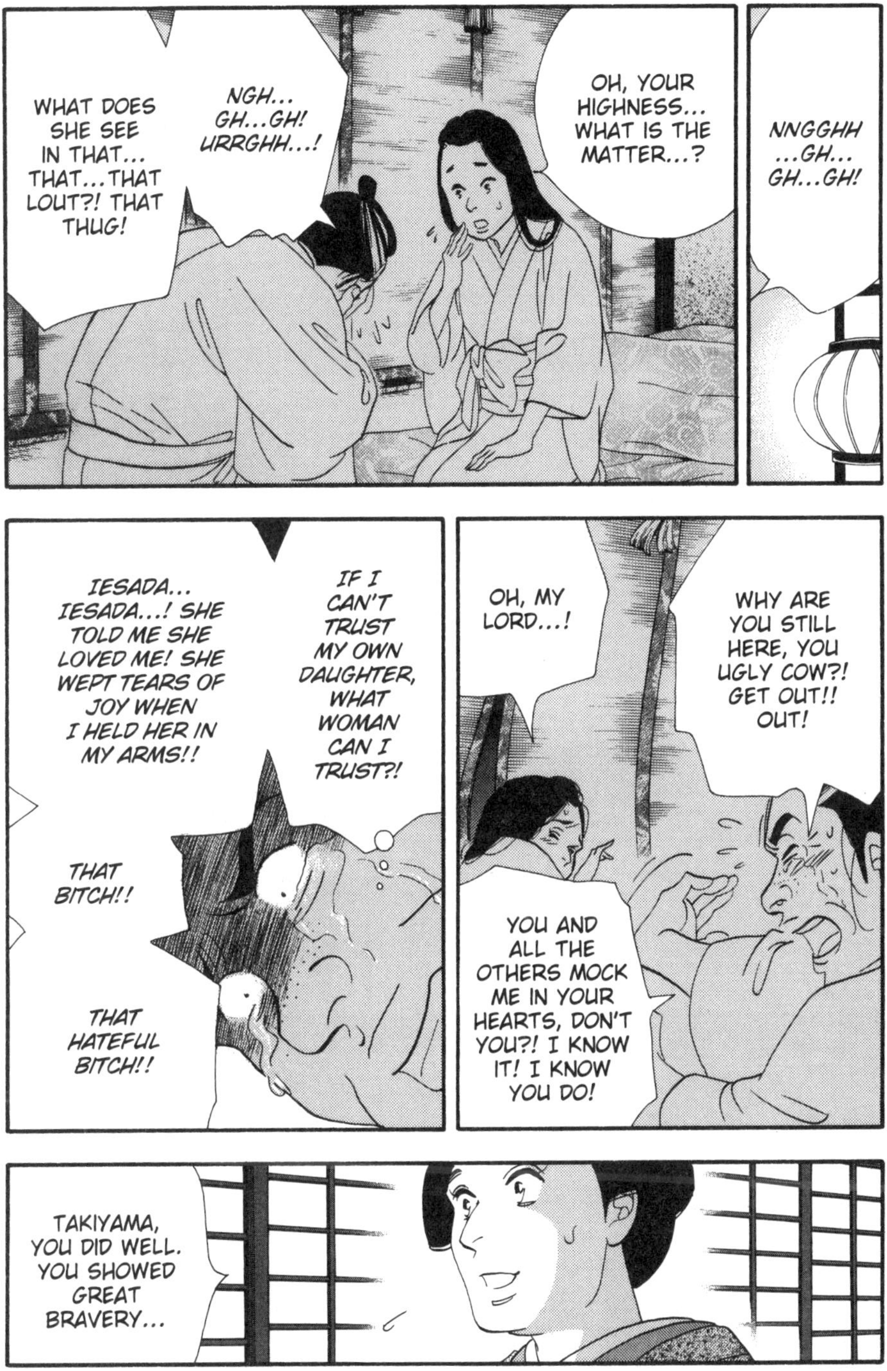
NNGGHH ...GH... GH...GH!
OH, YOUR HIGHNESS... WHAT IS THE MATTER...?
NGH... GH...GH! URRGHH...!
WHAT DOES SHE SEE IN THAT... THAT...THAT LOUT?! THAT THUG!
WHY ARE YOU STILL HERE, YOU UGLY COW?! GET OUT!! OUT!
OH, MY LORD...!
YOU AND ALL THE OTHERS MOCK ME IN YOUR HEARTS, DON'T YOU?! I KNOW IT! I KNOW YOU DO!
IF I CAN'T TRUST MY OWN DAUGHTER, WHAT WOMAN CAN I TRUST?!
IESADA... IESADA...! SHE TOLD ME SHE LOVED ME! SHE WEPT TEARS OF JOY WHEN I HELD HER IN MY ARMS!!
THAT BITCH!!
THAT HATEFUL BITCH!!
TAKIYAMA, YOU DID WELL. YOU SHOWED GREAT BRAVERY...

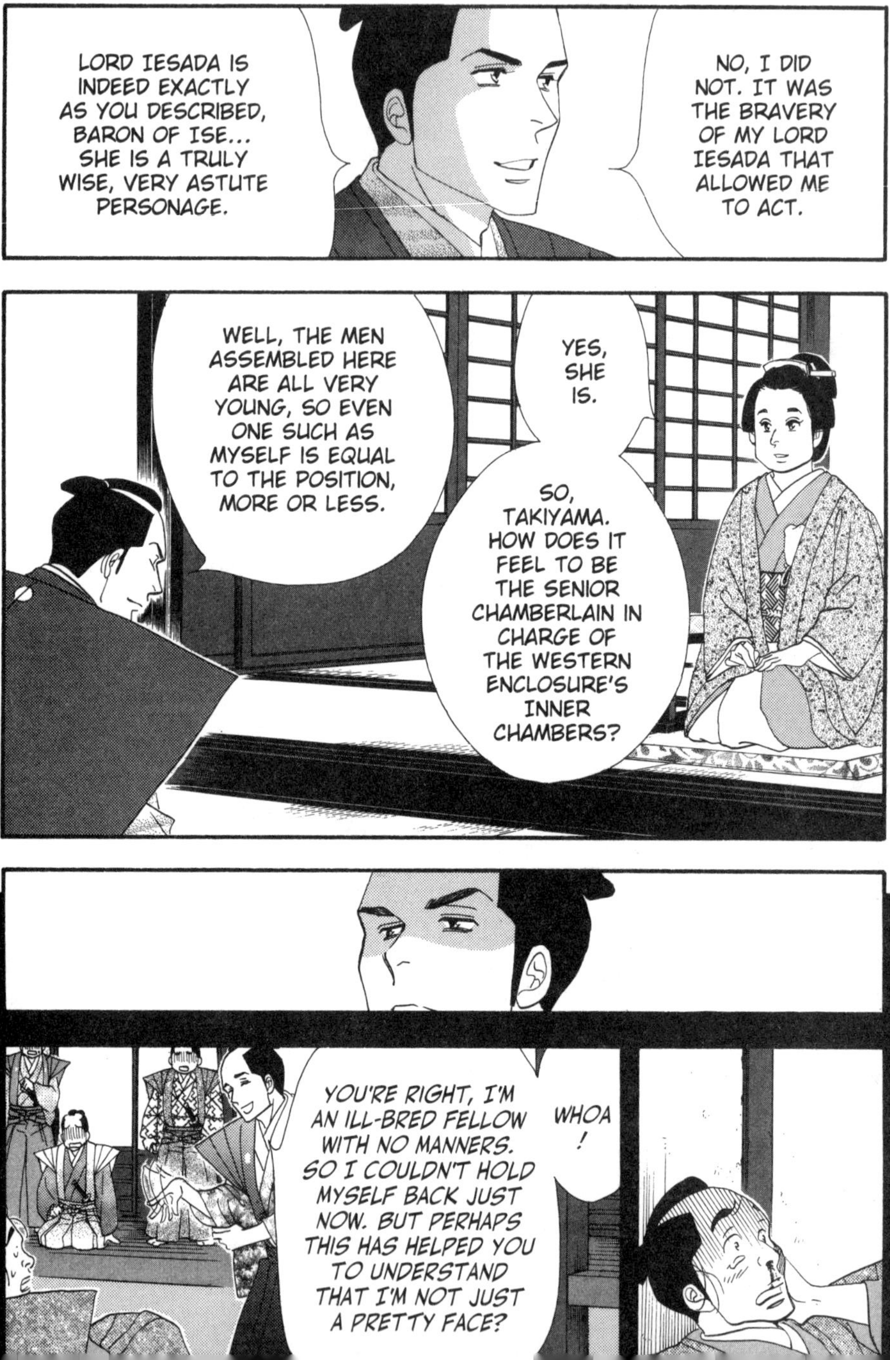
NO, I DID NOT. IT WAS THE BRAVERY OF MY LORD IESADA THAT ALLOWED ME TO ACT.
LORD IESADA IS INDEED EXACTLY AS YOU DESCRIBED, BARON OF ISE... SHE IS A TRULY WISE, VERY ASTUTE PERSONAGE.
YES, SHE IS.
SO, TAKIYAMA. HOW DOES IT FEEL TO BE THE SENIOR CHAMBERLAIN IN CHARGE OF THE WESTERN ENCLOSURE'S INNER CHAMBERS?
WELL, THE MEN ASSEMBLED HERE ARE ALL VERY YOUNG, SO EVEN ONE SUCH AS MYSELF IS EQUAL TO THE POSITION, MORE OR LESS.
WHOA!
YOU'RE RIGHT, I'M AN ILL-BRED FELLOW WITH NO MANNERS. SO I COULDN'T HOLD MYSELF BACK JUST NOW. BUT PERHAPS THIS HAS HELPED YOU TO UNDERSTAND THAT I'M NOT JUST A PRETTY FACE?

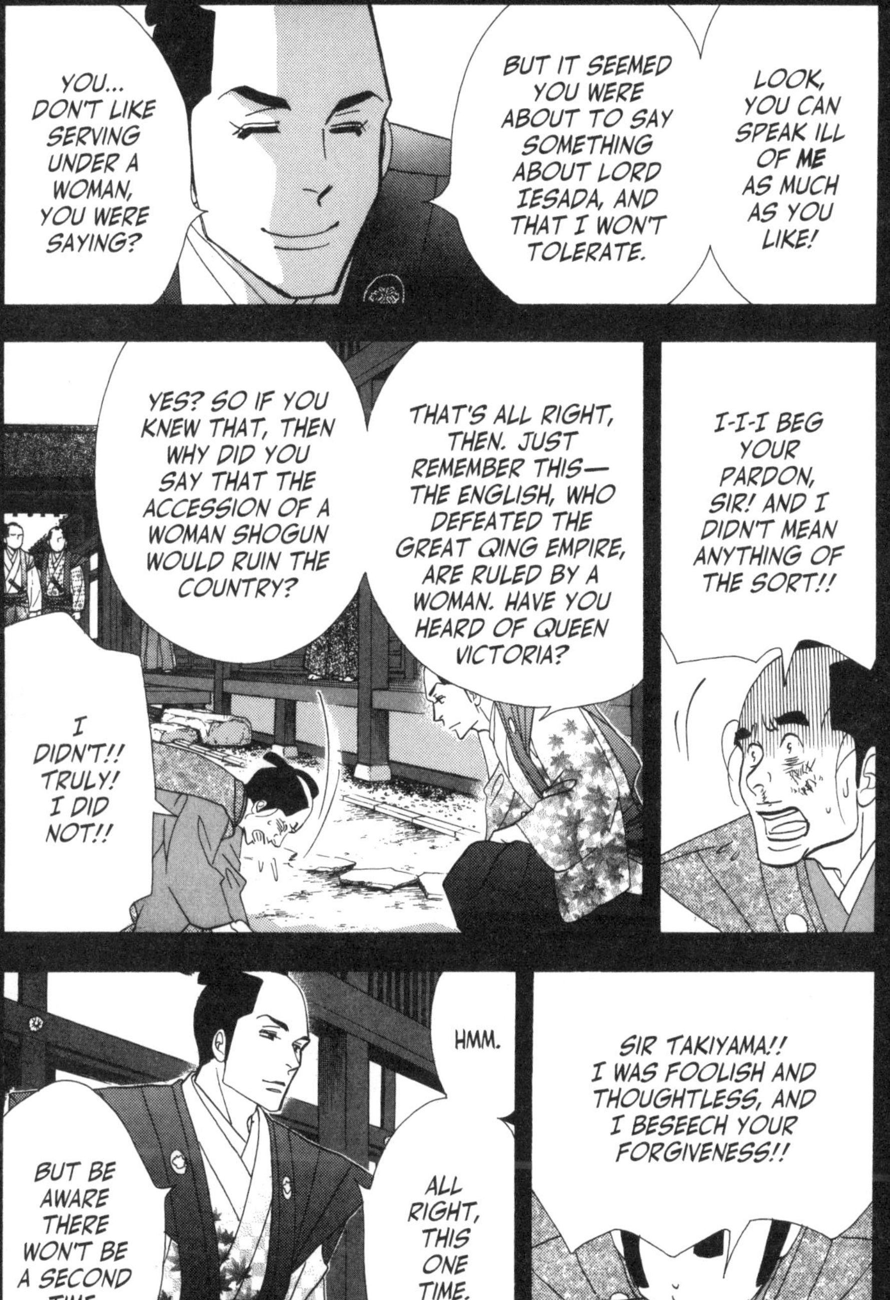
LOOK, YOU CAN SPEAK ILL OF ME AS MUCH AS YOU LIKE!
BUT IT SEEMED YOU WERE ABOUT TO SAY SOMETHING ABOUT LORD IESADA, AND THAT I WON'T TOLERATE.
YOU... DON'T LIKE SERVING UNDER A WOMAN, YOU WERE SAYING?
I-I-I BEG YOUR PARDON, SIR! AND I DIDN'T MEAN ANYTHING OF THE SORT!!
THAT'S ALL RIGHT, THEN. JUST REMEMBER THIS— THE ENGLISH, WHO DEFEATED THE GREAT QING EMPIRE, ARE RULED BY A WOMAN. HAVE YOU HEARD OF QUEEN VICTORIA?
YES? SO IF YOU KNEW THAT, THEN WHY DID YOU SAY THAT THE ACCESSION OF A WOMAN SHOGUN WOULD RUIN THE COUNTRY?
I DIDN'T!! TRULY! I DID NOT!!
SIR TAKIYAMA!! I WAS FOOLISH AND THOUGHTLESS, AND I BESEECH YOUR FORGIVENESS!!
HMM.
ALL RIGHT, THIS ONE TIME.
BUT BE AWARE THERE WON'T BE A SECOND TIME.

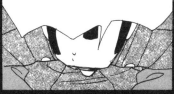

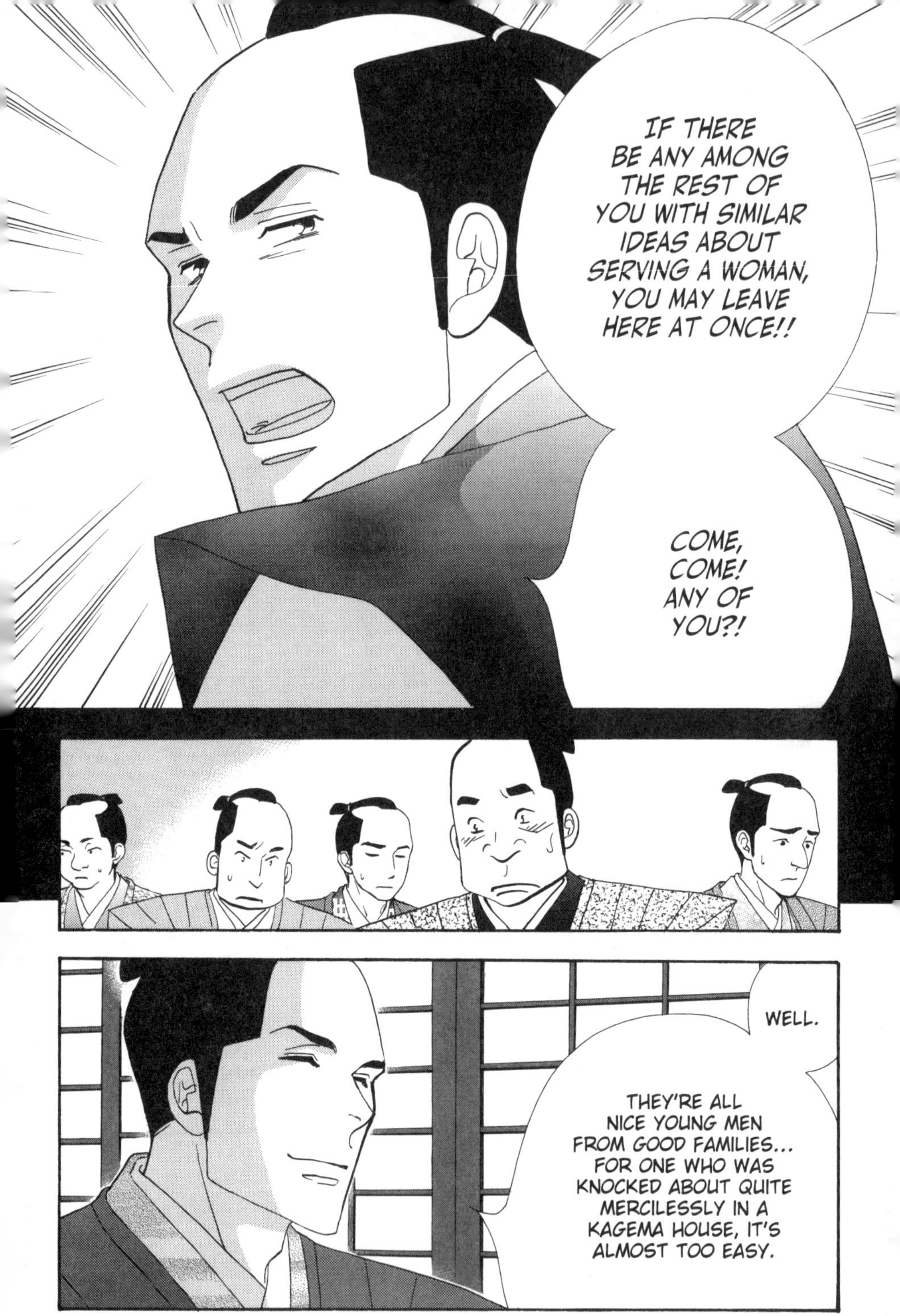
IF THERE BE ANY AMONG THE REST OF YOU WITH SIMILAR IDEAS ABOUT SERVING A WOMAN, YOU MAY LEAVE HERE AT ONCE!!
COME, COME! ANY OF YOU?!
WELL.
THEY'RE ALL NICE YOUNG MEN FROM GOOD FAMILIES... FOR ONE WHO WAS KNOCKED ABOUT QUITE MERCILESSLY IN A KAGEMA HOUSE, IT'S ALMOST TOO EASY.

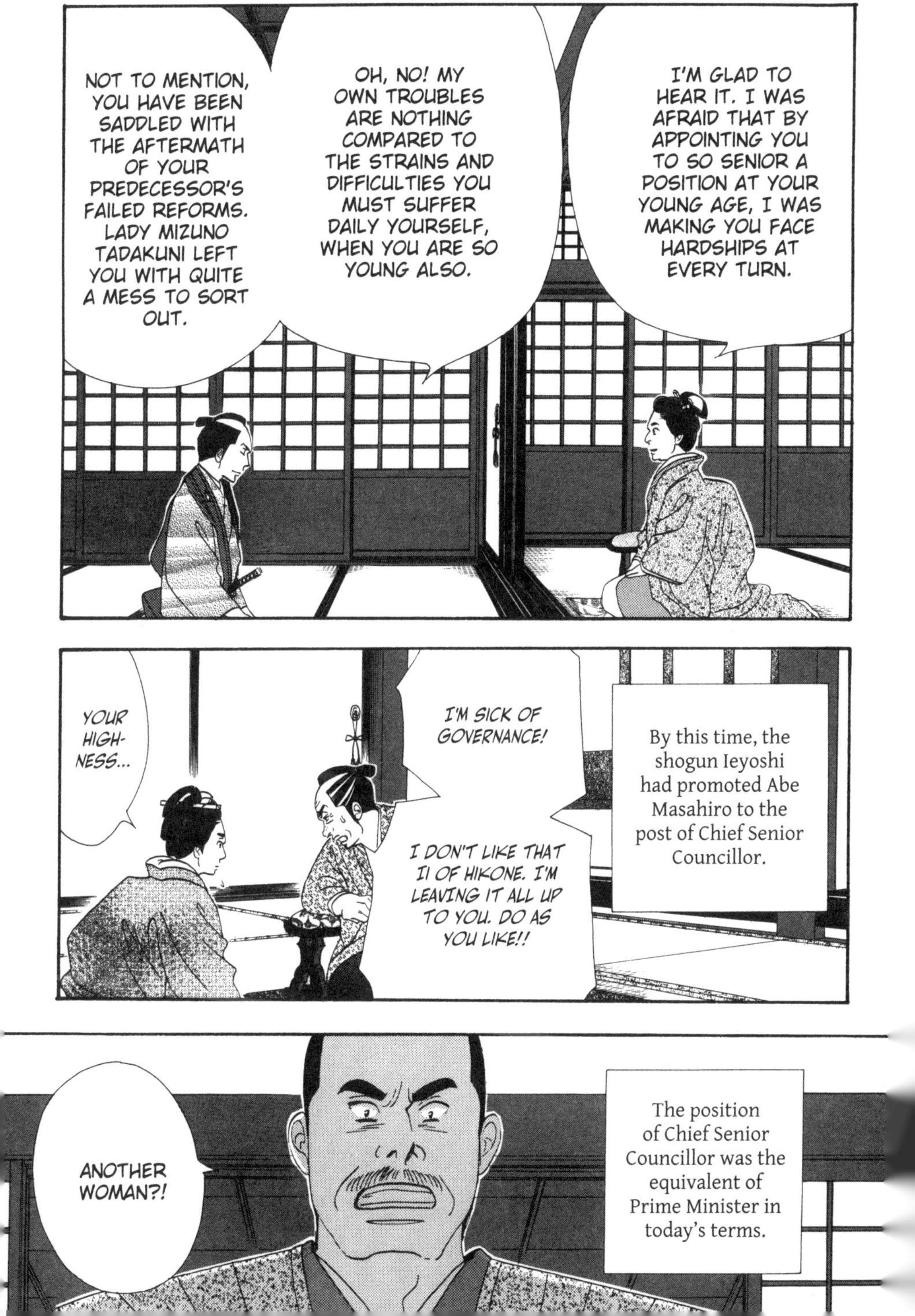
I'M GLAD TO HEAR IT. I WAS AFRAID THAT BY APPOINTING YOU TO SO SENIOR A POSITION AT YOUR YOUNG AGE, I WAS MAKING YOU FACE HARDSHIPS AT EVERY TURN.
OH, NO! MY OWN TROUBLES ARE NOTHING COMPARED TO THE STRAINS AND DIFFICULTIES YOU MUST SUFFER DAILY YOURSELF, WHEN YOU ARE SO YOUNG ALSO.
NOT TO MENTION, YOU HAVE BEEN SADDLED WITH THE AFTERMATH OF YOUR PREDECESSOR'S FAILED REFORMS. LADY MIZUNO TADAKUNI LEFT YOU WITH QUITE A MESS TO SORT OUT.
By this time, the shogun Ieyoshi had promoted Abe Masahiro to the post of Chief Senior Councillor.
I'M SICK OF GOVERNANCE!
I DON'T LIKE THAT II OF HIKONE. I'M LEAVING IT ALL UP TO YOU. DO AS YOU LIKE!!
YOUR HIGHNESS...
The position of Chief Senior Councillor was the equivalent of Prime Minister in today's terms.
ANOTHER WOMAN?!

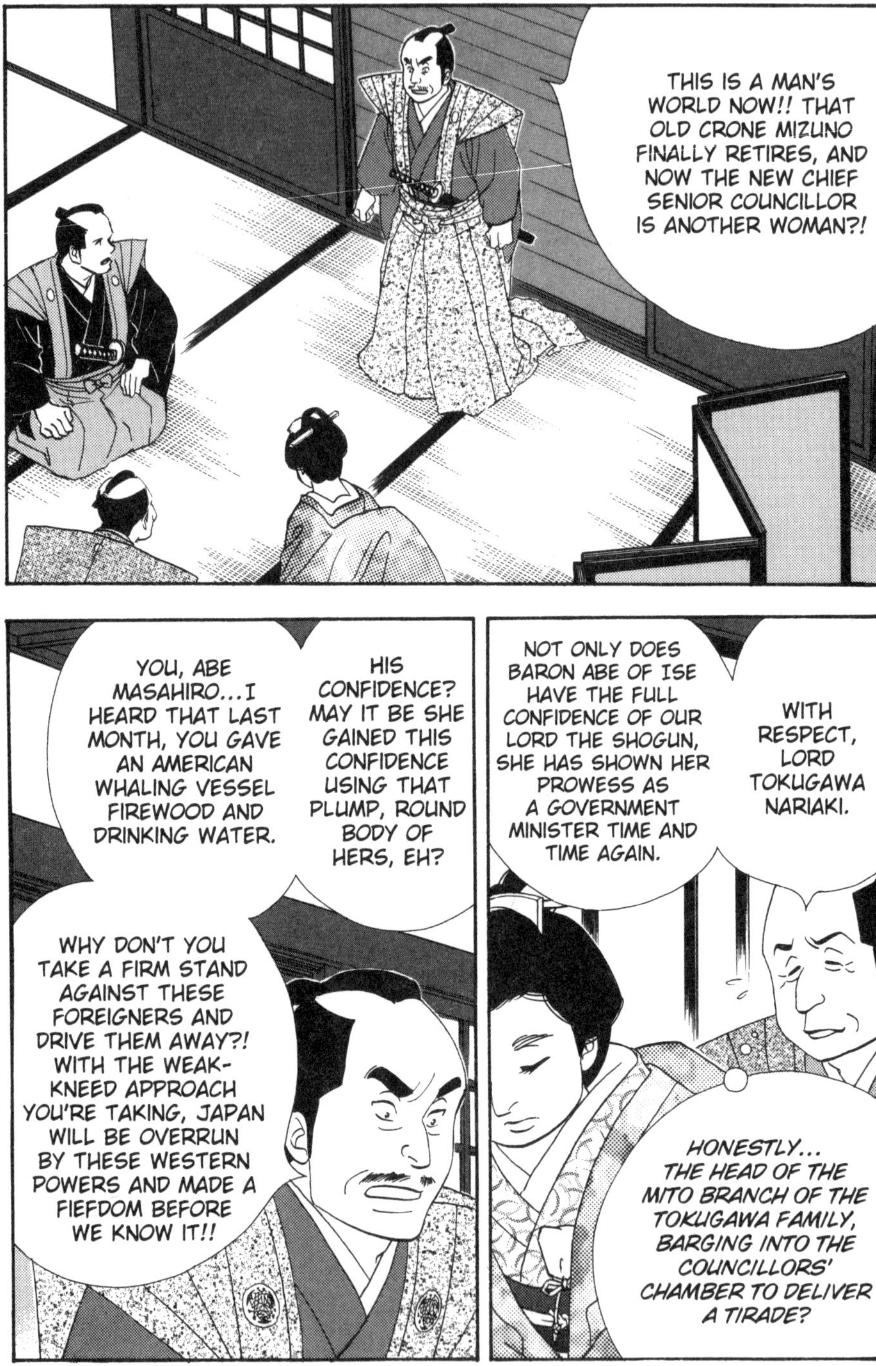
THIS IS A MAN'S WORLD NOW!! THAT OLD CRONE MIZUNO FINALLY RETIRES, AND NOW THE NEW CHIEF SENIOR COUNCILLOR IS ANOTHER WOMAN?!
WITH RESPECT, LORD TOKUGAWA NARIAKI.
NOT ONLY DOES BARON ABE OF ISE HAVE THE FULL CONFIDENCE OF OUR LORD THE SHOGUN, SHE HAS SHOWN HER PROWESS AS A GOVERNMENT MINISTER TIME AND TIME AGAIN.
HONESTLY... THE HEAD OF THE MITO BRANCH OF THE TOKUGAWA FAMILY, BARGING INTO THE COUNCILLORS' CHAMBER TO DELIVER A TIRADE?
HIS CONFIDENCE? MAY IT BE SHE GAINED THIS CONFIDENCE USING THAT PLUMP, ROUND BODY OF HERS, EH?
YOU, ABE MASAHIRO...I HEARD THAT LAST MONTH, YOU GAVE AN AMERICAN WHALING VESSEL FIREWOOD AND DRINKING WATER.
WHY DON'T YOU TAKE A FIRM STAND AGAINST THESE FOREIGNERS AND DRIVE THEM AWAY?! WITH THE WEAK-KNEED APPROACH YOU'RE TAKING, JAPAN WILL BE OVERRUN BY THESE WESTERN POWERS AND MADE A FIEFDOM BEFORE WE KNOW IT!!

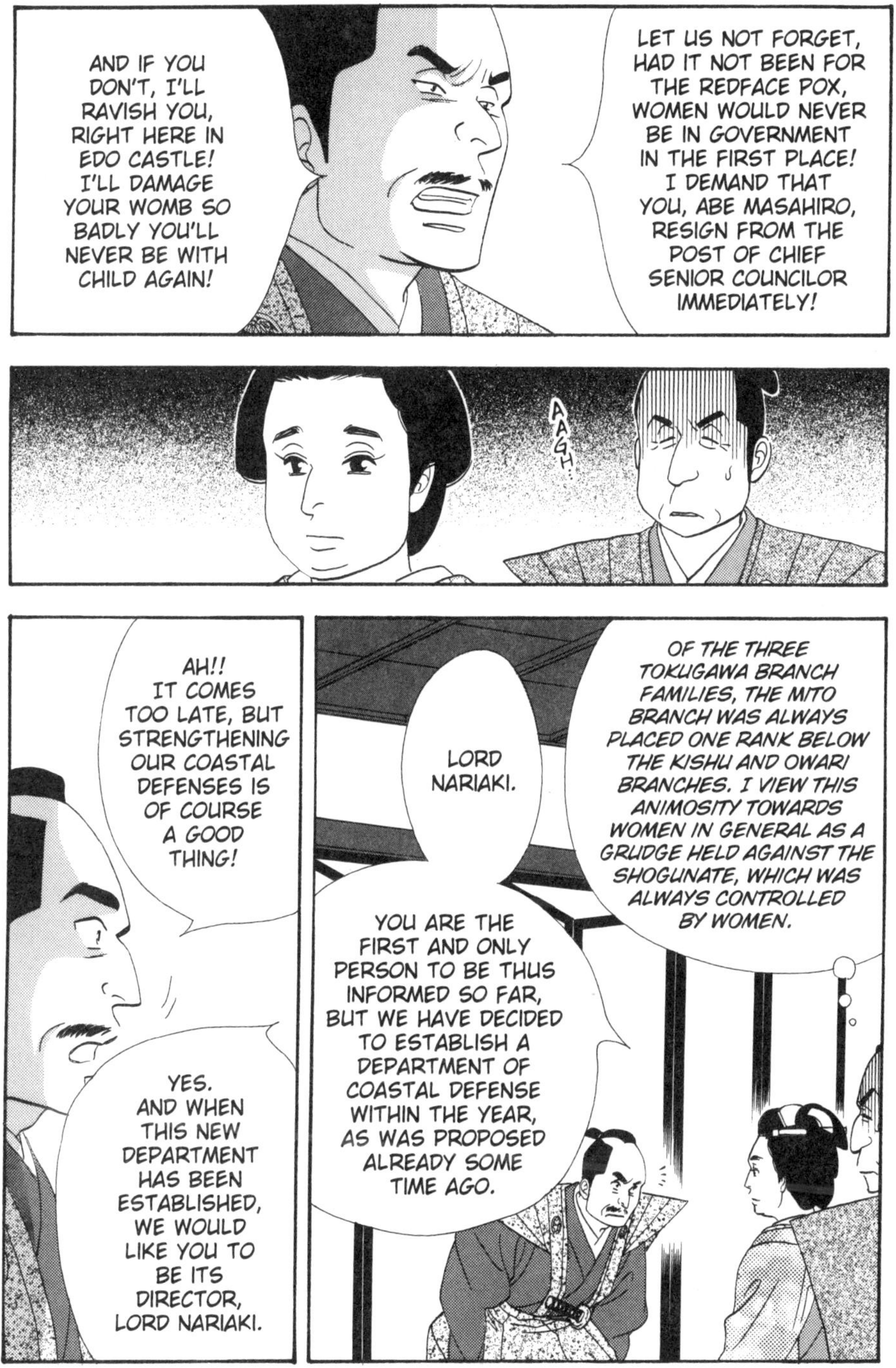
LET US NOT FORGET, HAD IT NOT BEEN FOR THE REDFACE POX, WOMEN WOULD NEVER BE IN GOVERNMENT IN THE FIRST PLACE! I DEMAND THAT YOU, ABE MASAHIRO, RESIGN FROM THE POST OF CHIEF SENIOR COUNCILOR IMMEDIATELY!
AND IF YOU DON'T, I'LL RAVISH YOU, RIGHT HERE IN EDO CASTLE! I'LL DAMAGE YOUR WOMB SO BADLY YOU'LL NEVER BE WITH CHILD AGAIN!
AAGH...
OF THE THREE TOKUGAWA BRANCH FAMILIES, THE MITO BRANCH WAS ALWAYS PLACED ONE RANK BELOW THE KISHU AND OWARI BRANCHES. I VIEW THIS ANIMOSITY TOWARDS WOMEN IN GENERAL AS A GRUDGE HELD AGAINST THE SHOGUNATE, WHICH WAS ALWAYS CONTROLLED BY WOMEN.
LORD NARIAKI.
YOU ARE THE FIRST AND ONLY PERSON TO BE THUS INFORMED SO FAR, BUT WE HAVE DECIDED TO ESTABLISH A DEPARTMENT OF COASTAL DEFENSE WITHIN THE YEAR, AS WAS PROPOSED ALREADY SOME TIME AGO.
AH!! IT COMES TOO LATE, BUT STRENGTHENING OUR COASTAL DEFENSES IS OF COURSE A GOOD THING!
YES. AND WHEN THIS NEW DEPARTMENT HAS BEEN ESTABLISHED, WE WOULD LIKE YOU TO BE ITS DIRECTOR, LORD NARIAKI.

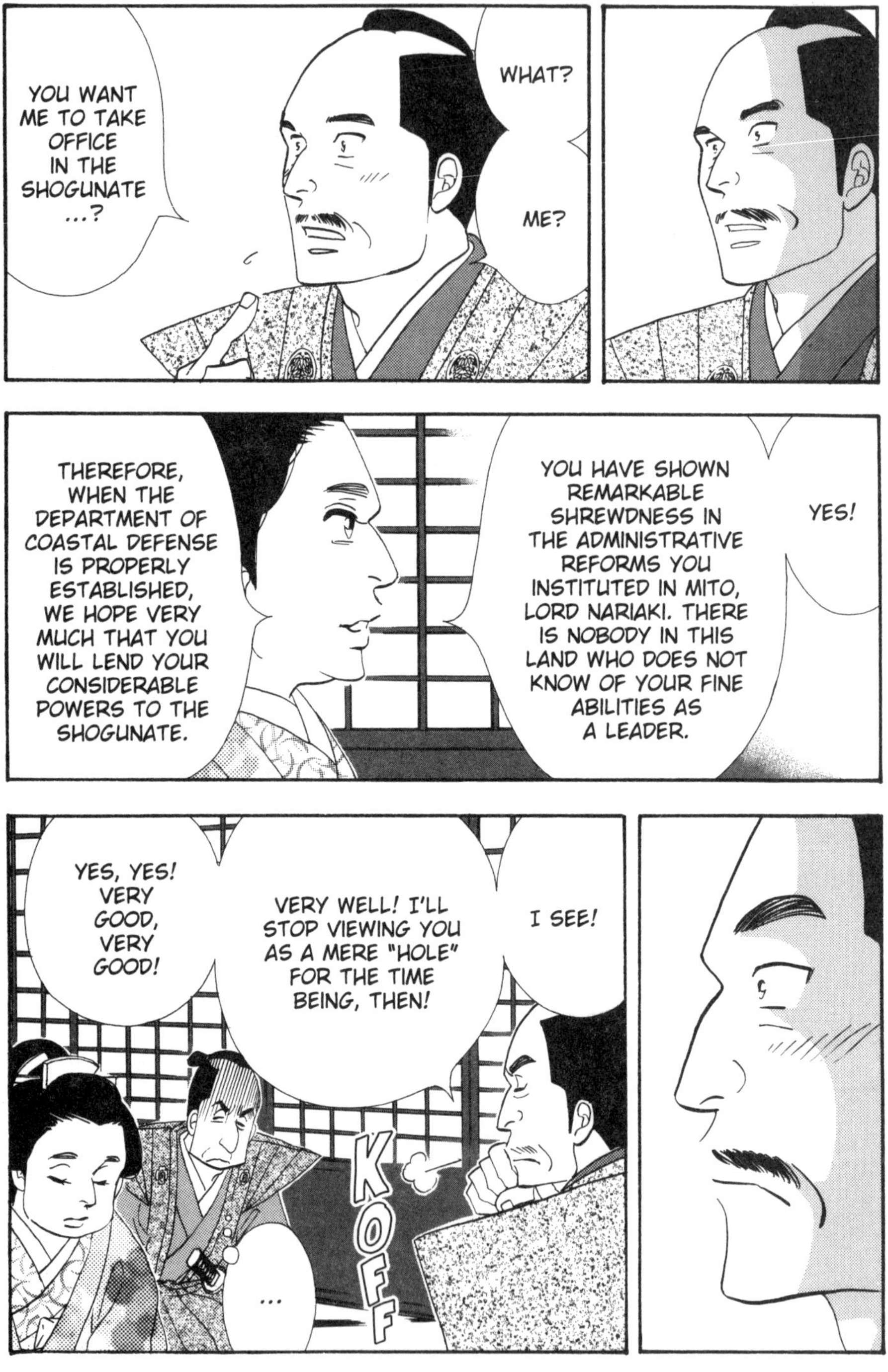
WHAT?
ME?
YOU WANT ME TO TAKE OFFICE IN THE SHOGUNATE ...?
YES!
YOU HAVE SHOWN REMARKABLE SHREWDNESS IN THE ADMINISTRATIVE REFORMS YOU INSTITUTED IN MITO, LORD NARIAKI. THERE IS NOBODY IN THIS LAND WHO DOES NOT KNOW OF YOUR FINE ABILITIES AS A LEADER.
THEREFORE, WHEN THE DEPARTMENT OF COASTAL DEFENSE IS PROPERLY ESTABLISHED, WE HOPE VERY MUCH THAT YOU WILL LEND YOUR CONSIDERABLE POWERS TO THE SHOGUNATE.
I SEE!
VERY WELL! I'LL STOP VIEWING YOU AS A MERE "HOLE" FOR THE TIME BEING, THEN!
YES, YES! VERY GOOD, VERY GOOD!
KOFF
...

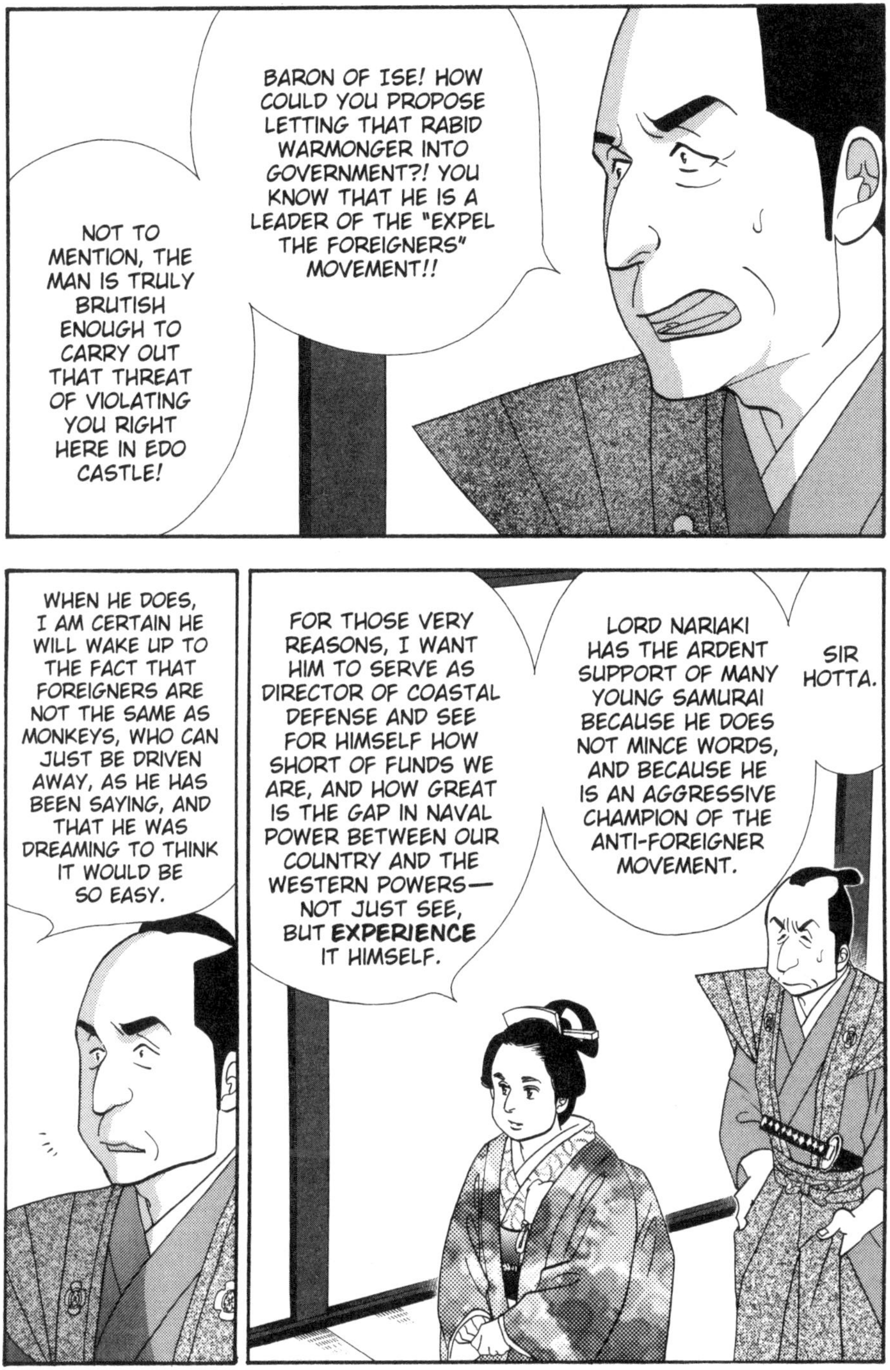
BARON OF ISE! HOW COULD YOU PROPOSE LETTING THAT RABID WARMONGER INTO GOVERNMENT?! YOU KNOW THAT HE IS A LEADER OF THE "EXPEL THE FOREIGNERS" MOVEMENT!!
NOT TO MENTION, THE MAN IS TRULY BRUTISH ENOUGH TO CARRY OUT THAT THREAT OF VIOLATING YOU RIGHT HERE IN EDO CASTLE!
SIR HOTTA.
LORD NARIAKI HAS THE ARDENT SUPPORT OF MANY YOUNG SAMURAI BECAUSE HE DOES NOT MINCE WORDS, AND BECAUSE HE IS AN AGGRESSIVE CHAMPION OF THE ANTI-FOREIGNER MOVEMENT.
FOR THOSE VERY REASONS, I WANT HIM TO SERVE AS DIRECTOR OF COASTAL DEFENSE AND SEE FOR HIMSELF HOW SHORT OF FUNDS WE ARE, AND HOW GREAT IS THE GAP IN NAVAL POWER BETWEEN OUR COUNTRY AND THE WESTERN POWERS— NOT JUST SEE, BUT **EXPERIENCE** IT HIMSELF.
WHEN HE DOES, I AM CERTAIN HE WILL WAKE UP TO THE FACT THAT FOREIGNERS ARE NOT THE SAME AS MONKEYS, WHO CAN JUST BE DRIVEN AWAY, AS HE HAS BEEN SAYING, AND THAT HE WAS DREAMING TO THINK IT WOULD BE SO EASY.

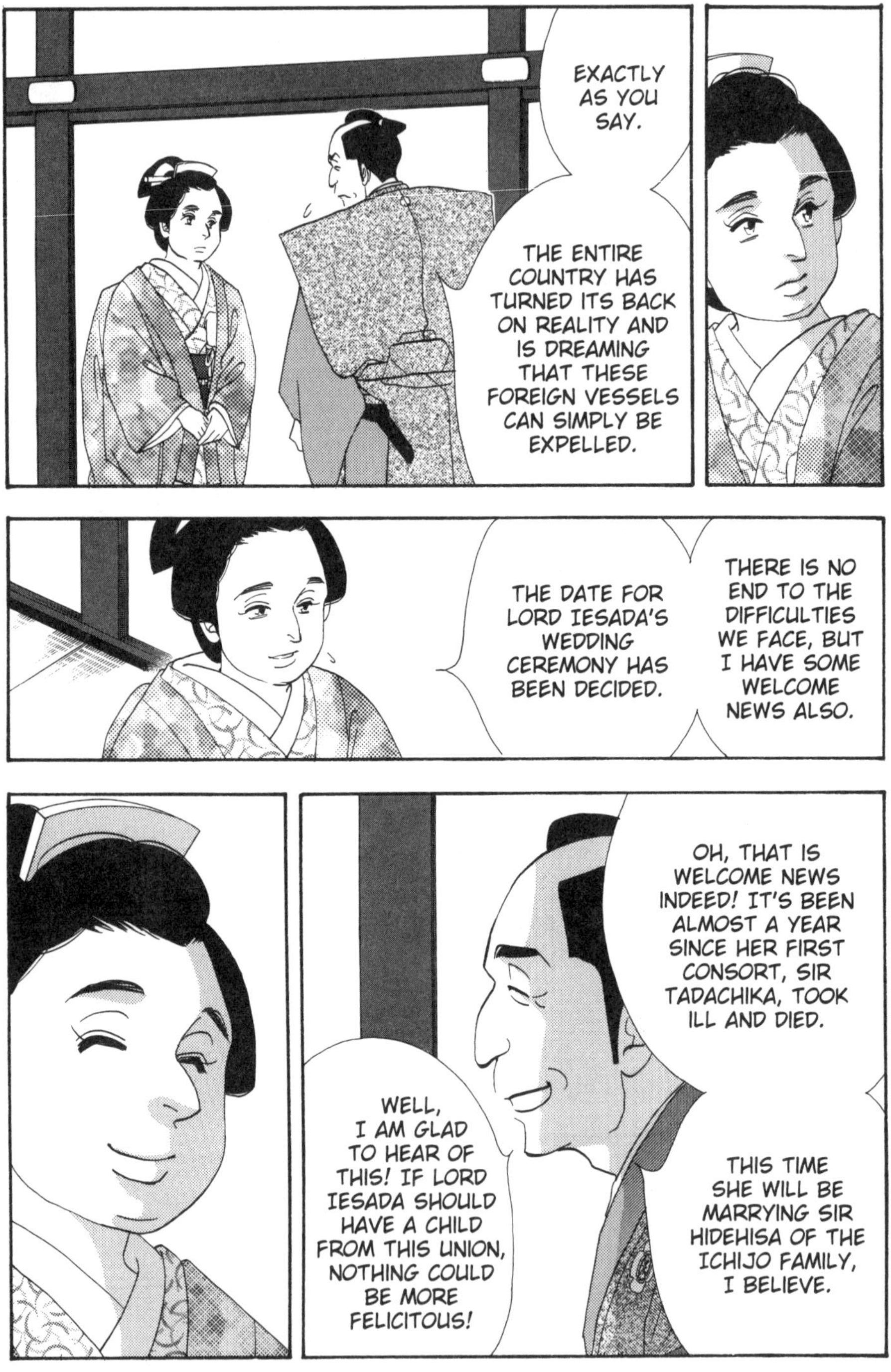
EXACTLY AS YOU SAY.
THE ENTIRE COUNTRY HAS TURNED ITS BACK ON REALITY AND IS DREAMING THAT THESE FOREIGN VESSELS CAN SIMPLY BE EXPELLED.
THERE IS NO END TO THE DIFFICULTIES WE FACE, BUT I HAVE SOME WELCOME NEWS ALSO.
THE DATE FOR LORD IESADA'S WEDDING CEREMONY HAS BEEN DECIDED.
OH, THAT IS WELCOME NEWS INDEED! IT'S BEEN ALMOST A YEAR SINCE HER FIRST CONSORT, SIR TADACHIKA, TOOK ILL AND DIED.
THIS TIME SHE WILL BE MARRYING SIR HIDEHISA OF THE ICHIJO FAMILY, I BELIEVE.
WELL, I AM GLAD TO HEAR OF THIS! IF LORD IESADA SHOULD HAVE A CHILD FROM THIS UNION, NOTHING COULD BE MORE FELICITOUS!

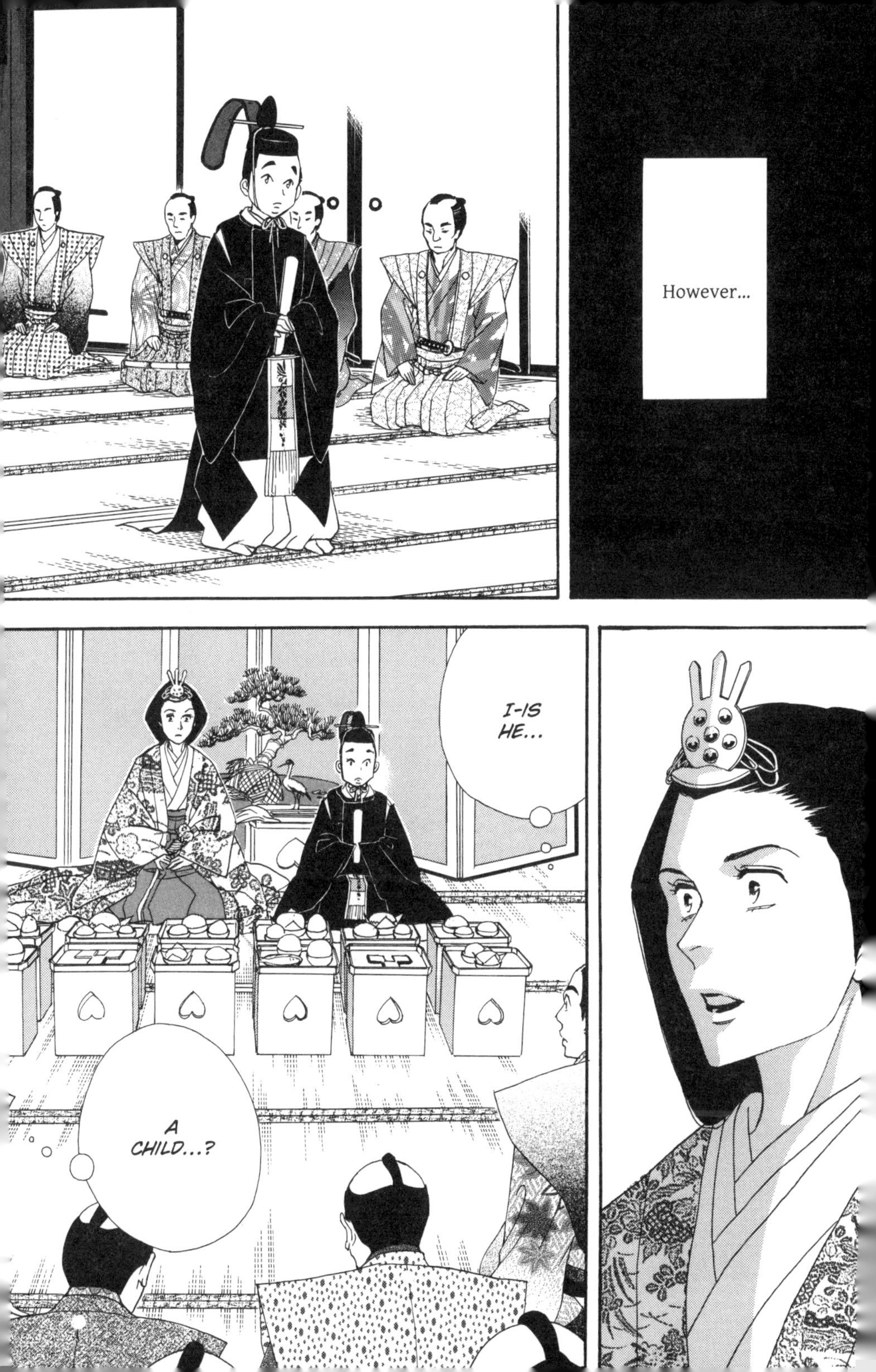
However...
I-IS HE...
A CHILD...?

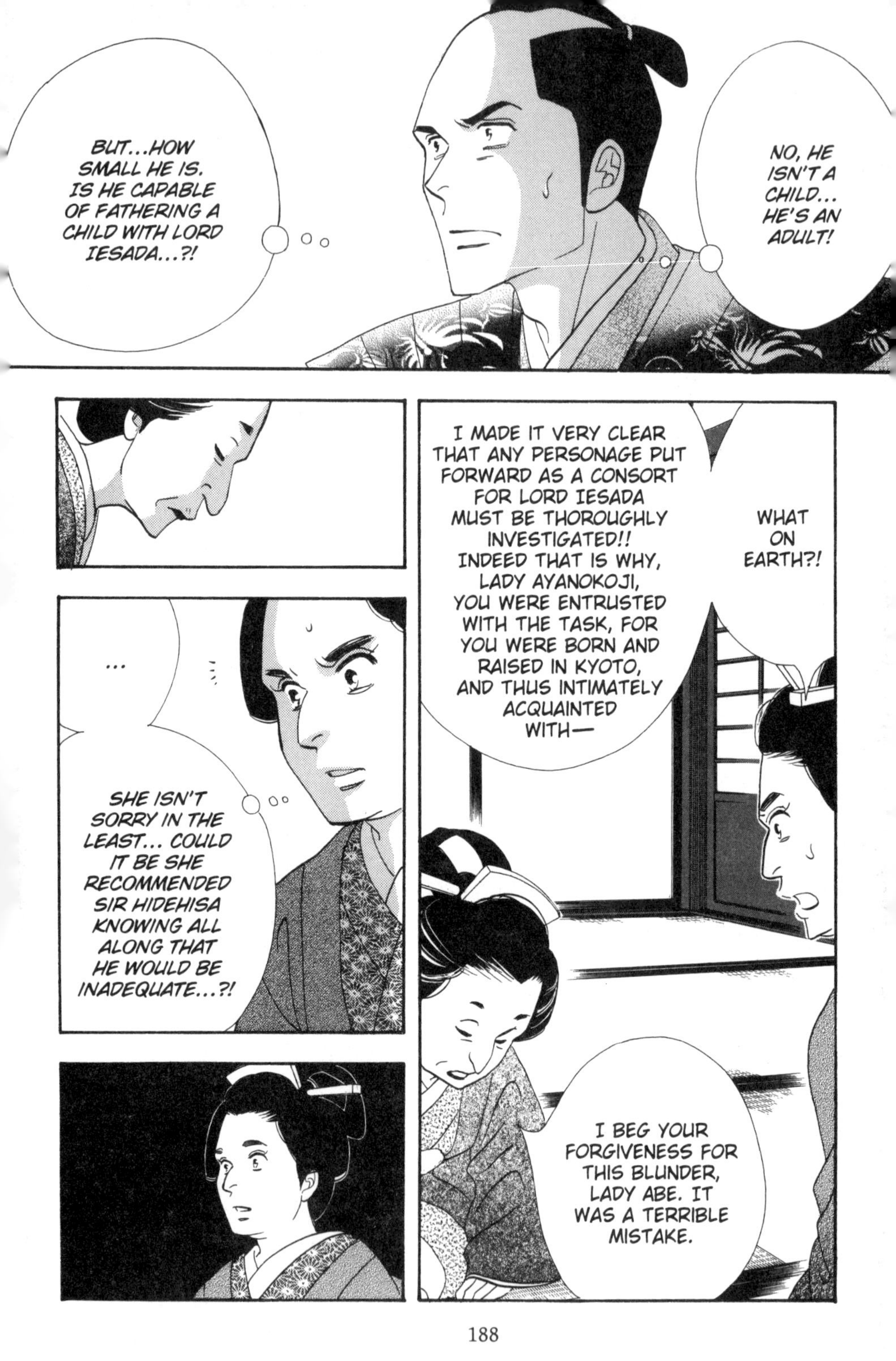
NO, HE ISN'T A CHILD... HE'S AN ADULT!
BUT...HOW SMALL HE IS. IS HE CAPABLE OF FATHERING A CHILD WITH LORD IESADA...?!
WHAT ON EARTH?!
I MADE IT VERY CLEAR THAT ANY PERSONAGE PUT FORWARD AS A CONSORT FOR LORD IESADA MUST BE THOROUGHLY INVESTIGATED!! INDEED THAT IS WHY, LADY AYANOKOJI, YOU WERE ENTRUSTED WITH THE TASK, FOR YOU WERE BORN AND RAISED IN KYOTO, AND THUS INTIMATELY ACQUAINTED WITH—
I BEG YOUR FORGIVENESS FOR THIS BLUNDER, LADY ABE. IT WAS A TERRIBLE MISTAKE.
...
SHE ISN'T SORRY IN THE LEAST... COULD IT BE SHE RECOMMENDED SIR HIDEHISA KNOWING ALL ALONG THAT HE WOULD BE INADEQUATE...?!

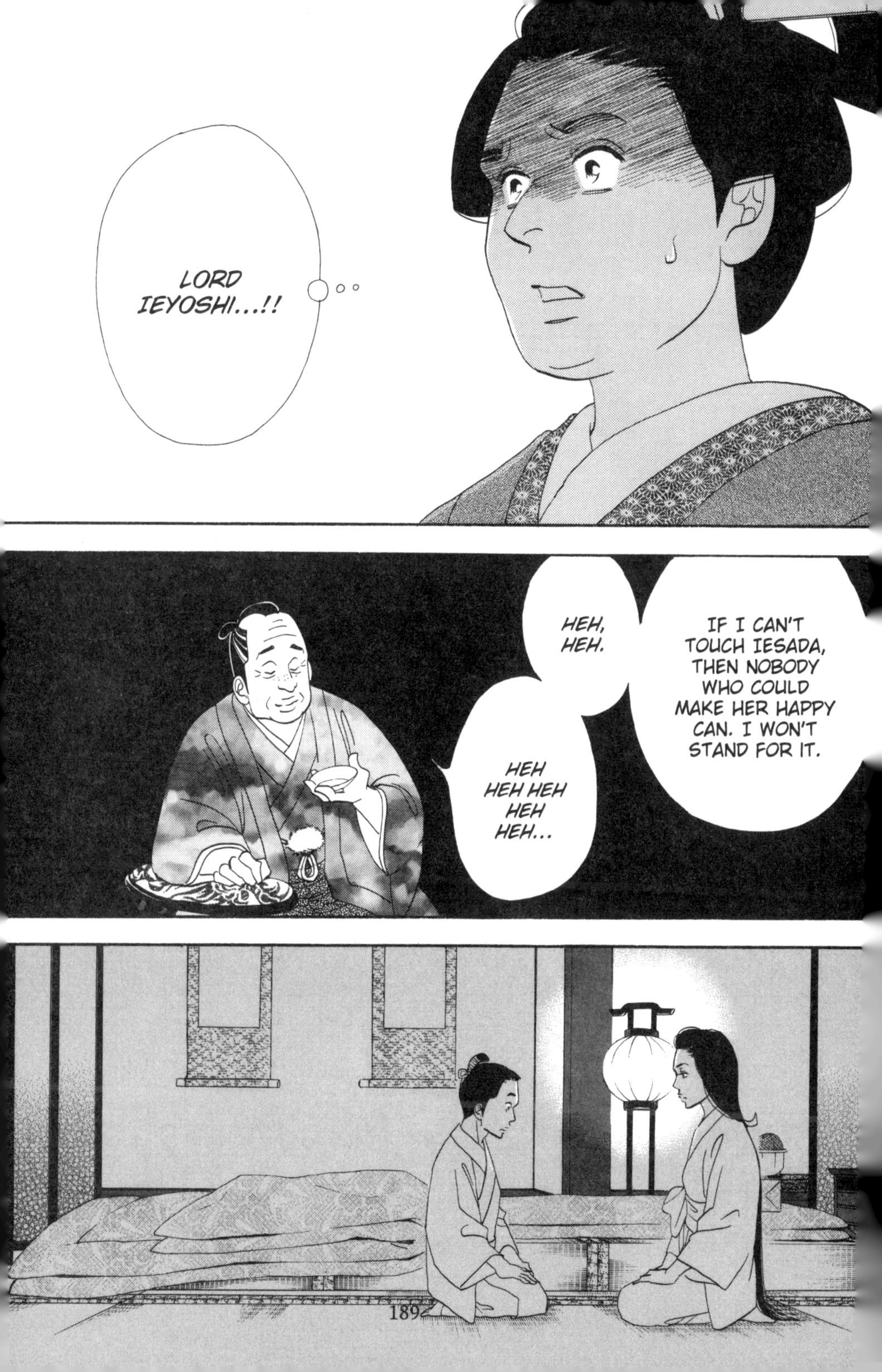
LORD IEYOSHI...!!
IF I CAN'T TOUCH IESADA, THEN NOBODY WHO COULD MAKE HER HAPPY CAN. I WON'T STAND FOR IT.
HEH, HEH.
HEH HEH HEH HEH HEH...

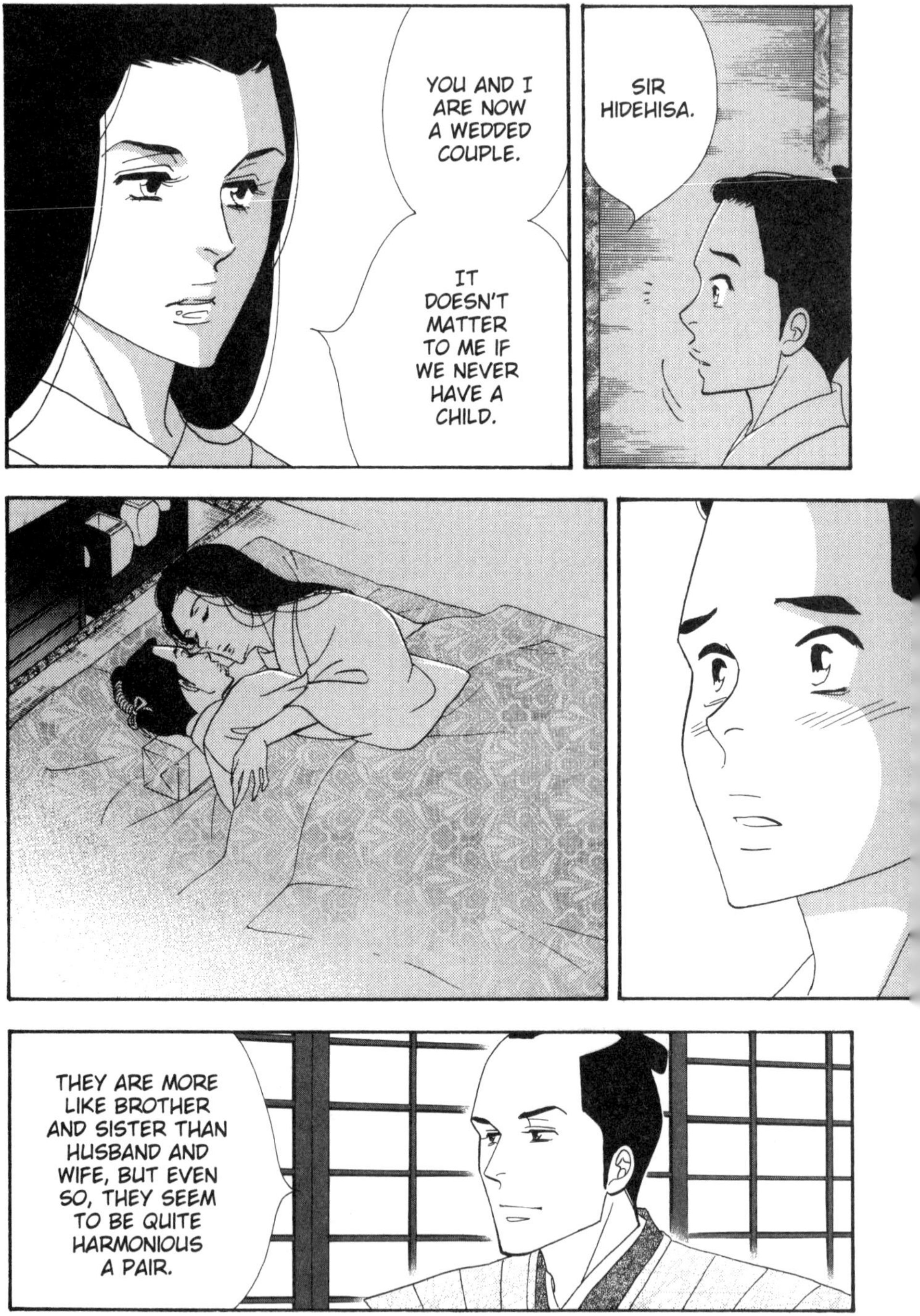
SIR HIDEHISA.
YOU AND I ARE NOW A WEDDED COUPLE.
IT DOESN'T MATTER TO ME IF WE NEVER HAVE A CHILD.
THEY ARE MORE LIKE BROTHER AND SISTER THAN HUSBAND AND WIFE, BUT EVEN SO, THEY SEEM TO BE QUITE HARMONIOUS A PAIR.

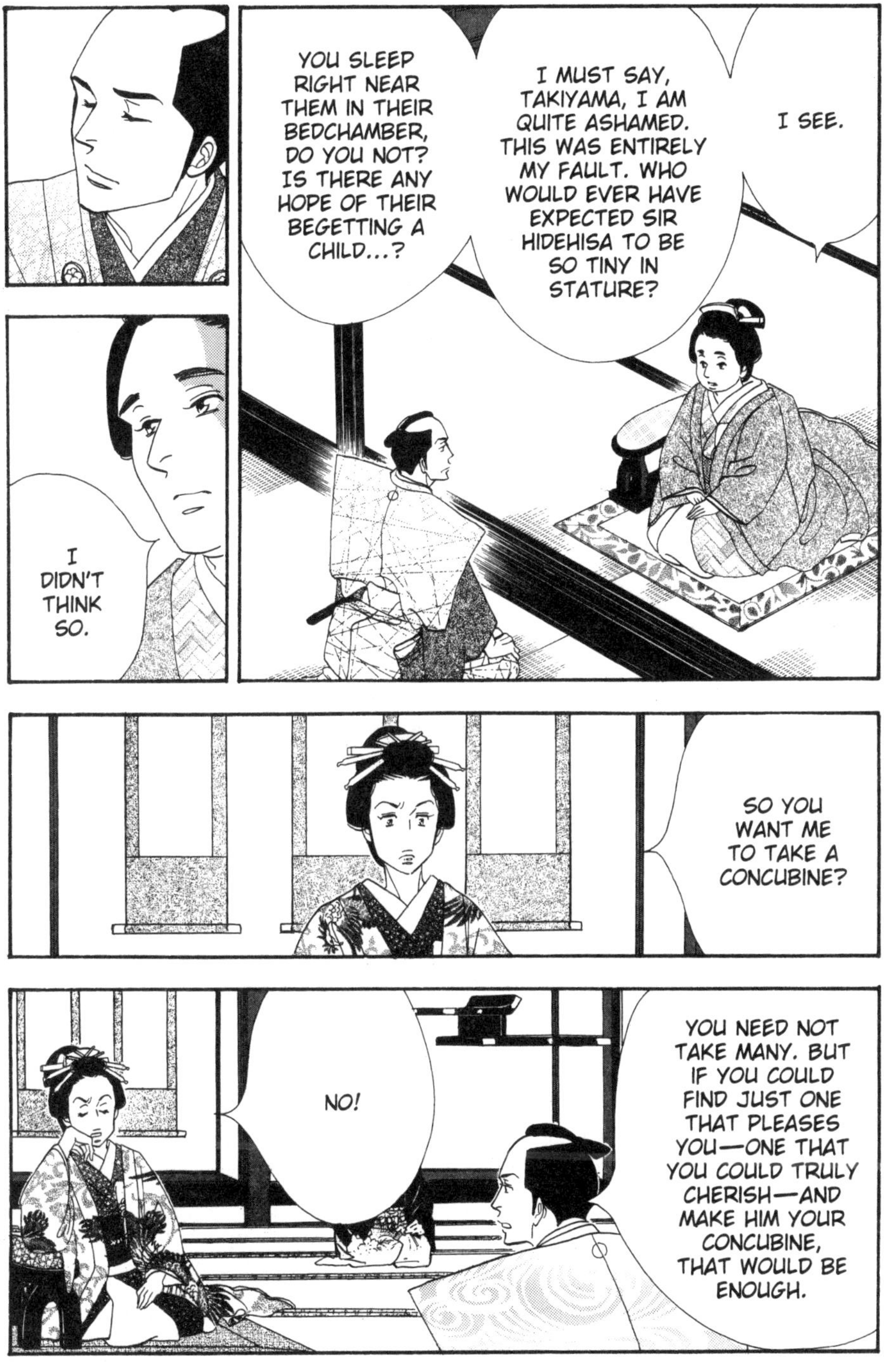
I SEE.
I MUST SAY, TAKIYAMA, I AM QUITE ASHAMED. THIS WAS ENTIRELY MY FAULT. WHO WOULD EVER HAVE EXPECTED SIR HIDEHISA TO BE SO TINY IN STATURE?
YOU SLEEP RIGHT NEAR THEM IN THEIR BEDCHAMBER, DO YOU NOT? IS THERE ANY HOPE OF THEIR BEGETTING A CHILD...?
I DIDN'T THINK SO.
SO YOU WANT ME TO TAKE A CONCUBINE?
YOU NEED NOT TAKE MANY. BUT IF YOU COULD FIND JUST ONE THAT PLEASES YOU—ONE THAT YOU COULD TRULY CHERISH—AND MAKE HIM YOUR CONCUBINE, THAT WOULD BE ENOUGH.
NO!

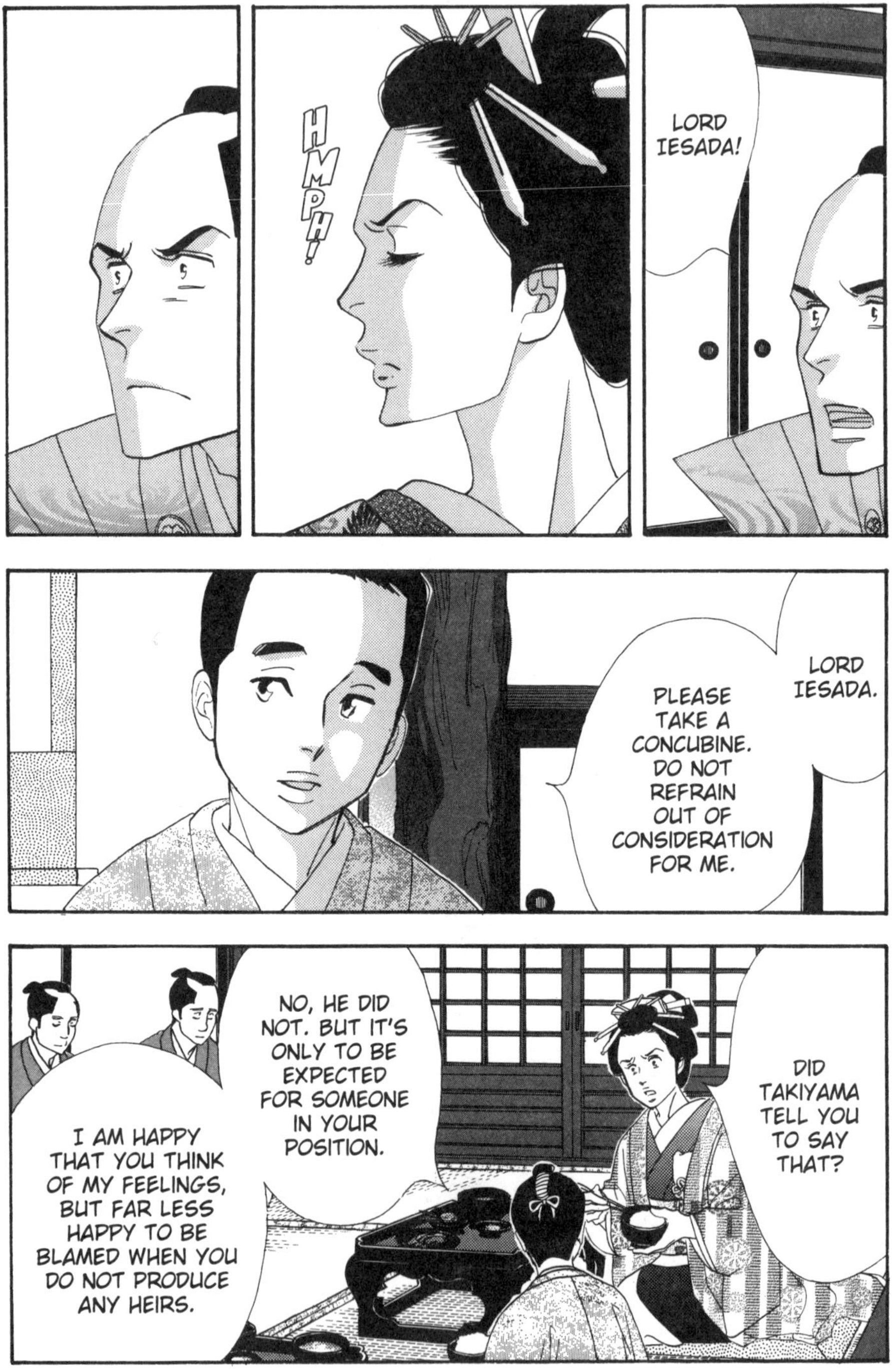
LORD IESADA!
HMMPH!
LORD IESADA.
PLEASE TAKE A CONCUBINE. DO NOT REFRAIN OUT OF CONSIDERATION FOR ME.
DID TAKIYAMA TELL YOU TO SAY THAT?
NO, HE DID NOT. BUT IT'S ONLY TO BE EXPECTED FOR SOMEONE IN YOUR POSITION.
I AM HAPPY THAT YOU THINK OF MY FEELINGS, BUT FAR LESS HAPPY TO BE BLAMED WHEN YOU DO NOT PRODUCE ANY HEIRS.

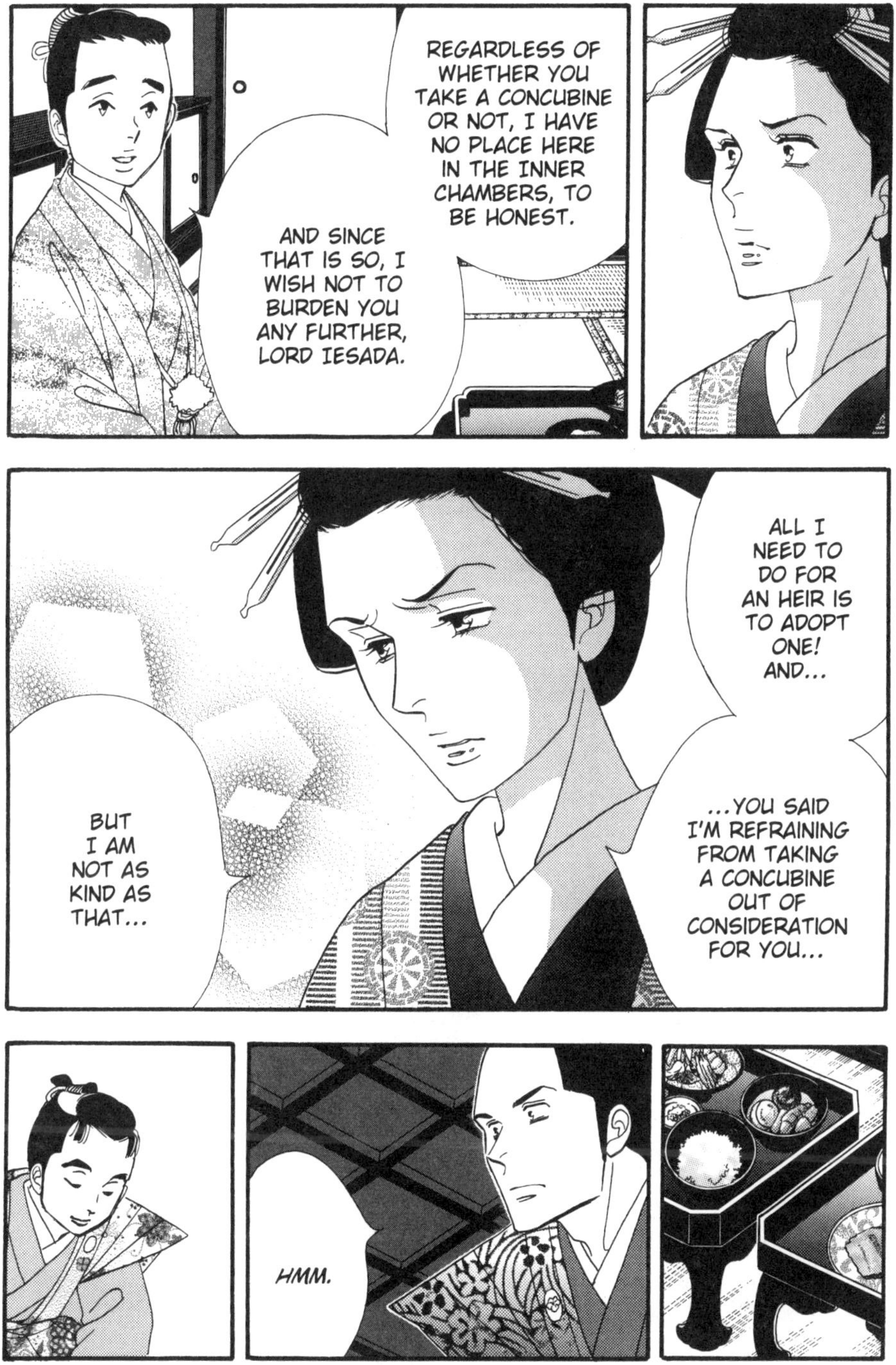
REGARDLESS OF WHETHER YOU TAKE A CONCUBINE OR NOT, I HAVE NO PLACE HERE IN THE INNER CHAMBERS, TO BE HONEST.
AND SINCE THAT IS SO, I WISH NOT TO BURDEN YOU ANY FURTHER, LORD IESADA.
ALL I NEED TO DO FOR AN HEIR IS TO ADOPT ONE! AND...
...YOU SAID I'M REFRAINING FROM TAKING A CONCUBINE OUT OF CONSIDERATION FOR YOU...
BUT I AM NOT AS KIND AS THAT...
HMM.

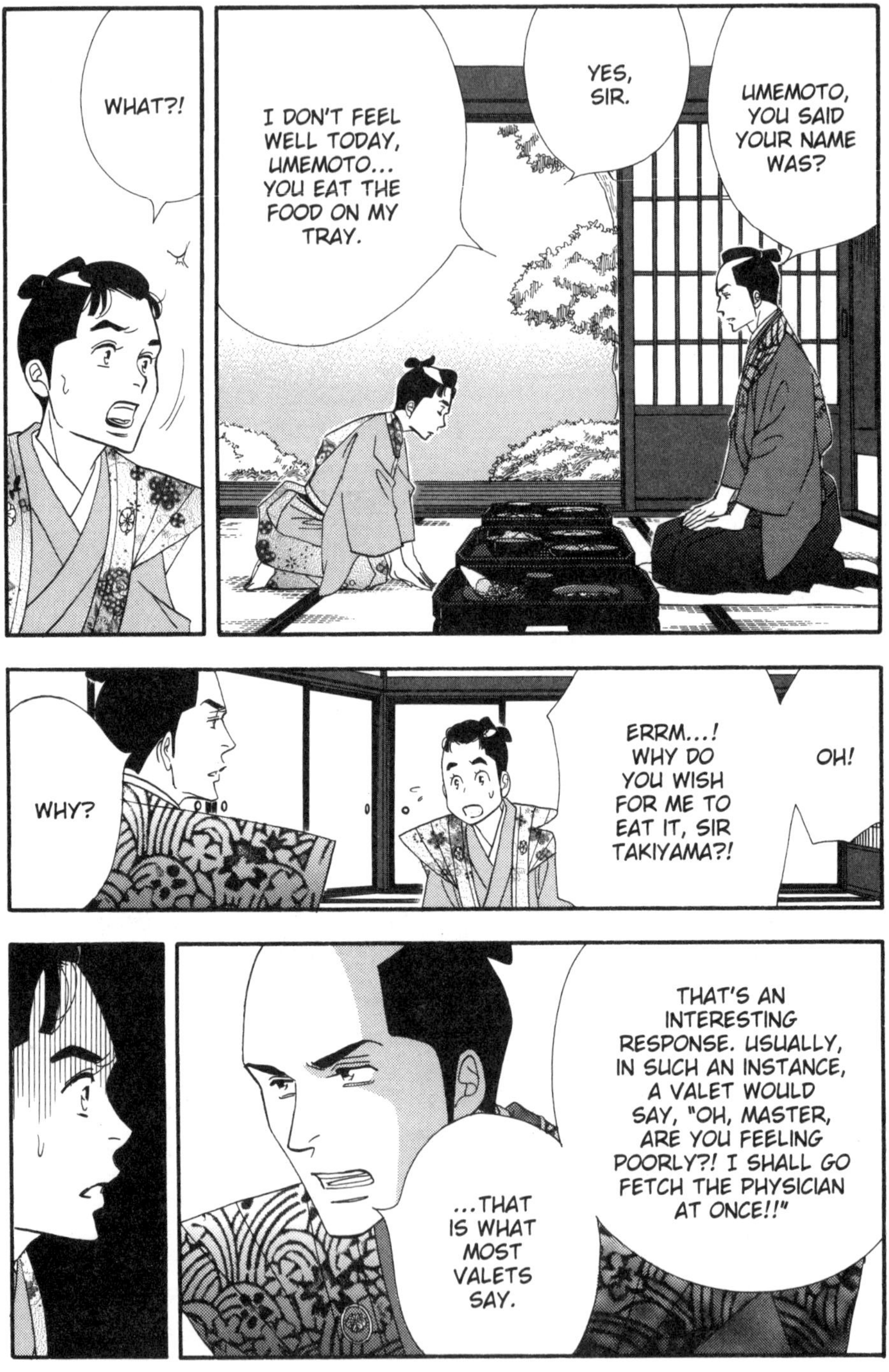
UMEMOTO, YOU SAID YOUR NAME WAS?
YES, SIR.
I DON'T FEEL WELL TODAY, UMEMOTO... YOU EAT THE FOOD ON MY TRAY.
WHAT?!
OH!
ERRM...! WHY DO YOU WISH FOR ME TO EAT IT, SIR TAKIYAMA?!
WHY?
THAT'S AN INTERESTING RESPONSE. USUALLY, IN SUCH AN INSTANCE, A VALET WOULD SAY, "OH, MASTER, ARE YOU FEELING POORLY?! I SHALL GO FETCH THE PHYSICIAN AT ONCE!!"
...THAT IS WHAT MOST VALETS SAY.

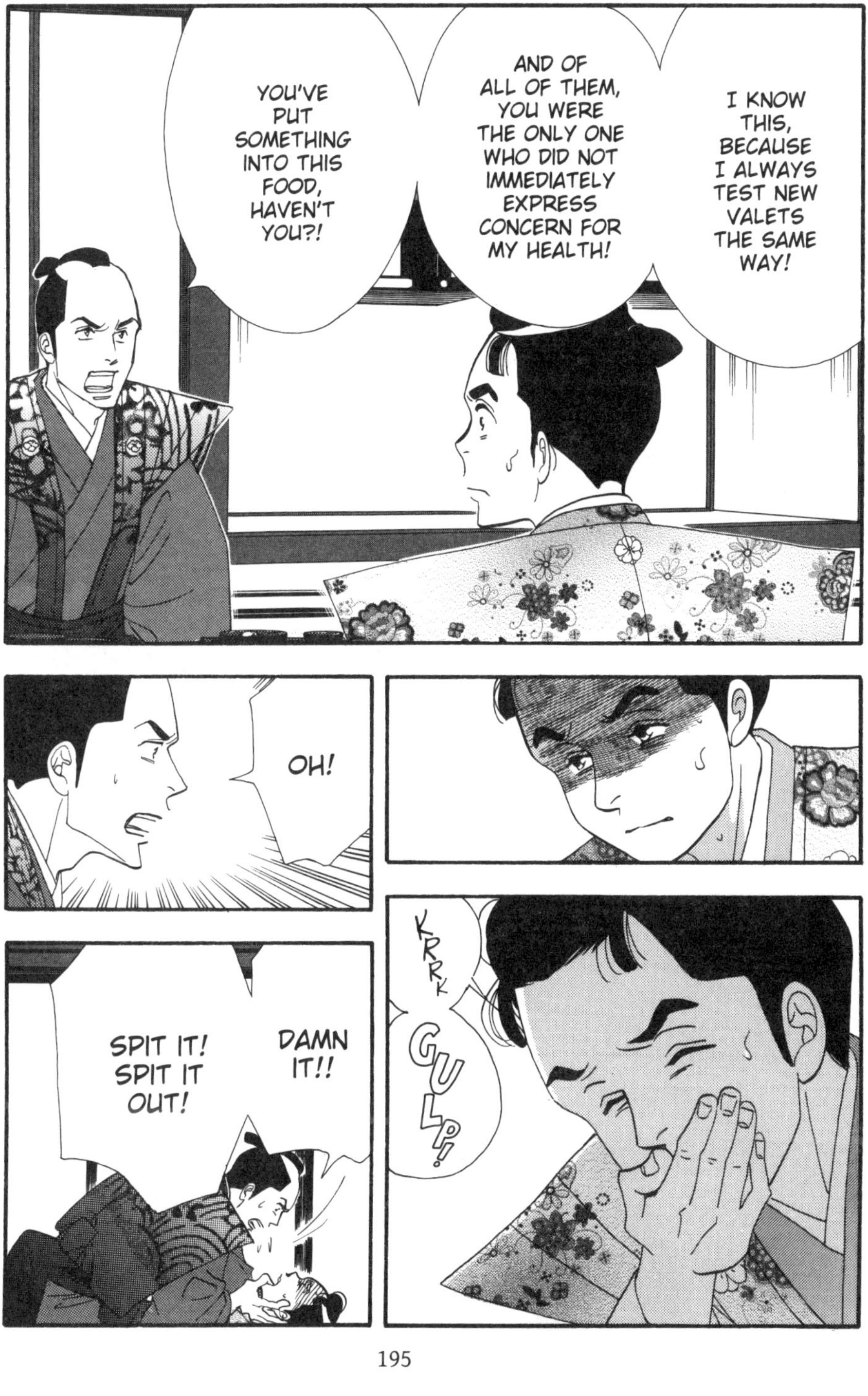
I KNOW THIS, BECAUSE I ALWAYS TEST NEW VALETS THE SAME WAY!
AND OF ALL OF THEM, YOU WERE THE ONLY ONE WHO DID NOT IMMEDIATELY EXPRESS CONCERN FOR MY HEALTH!
YOU'VE PUT SOMETHING INTO THIS FOOD, HAVEN'T YOU?!
OH!
KRRRK
GULP!
DAMN IT!!
SPIT IT! SPIT IT OUT!

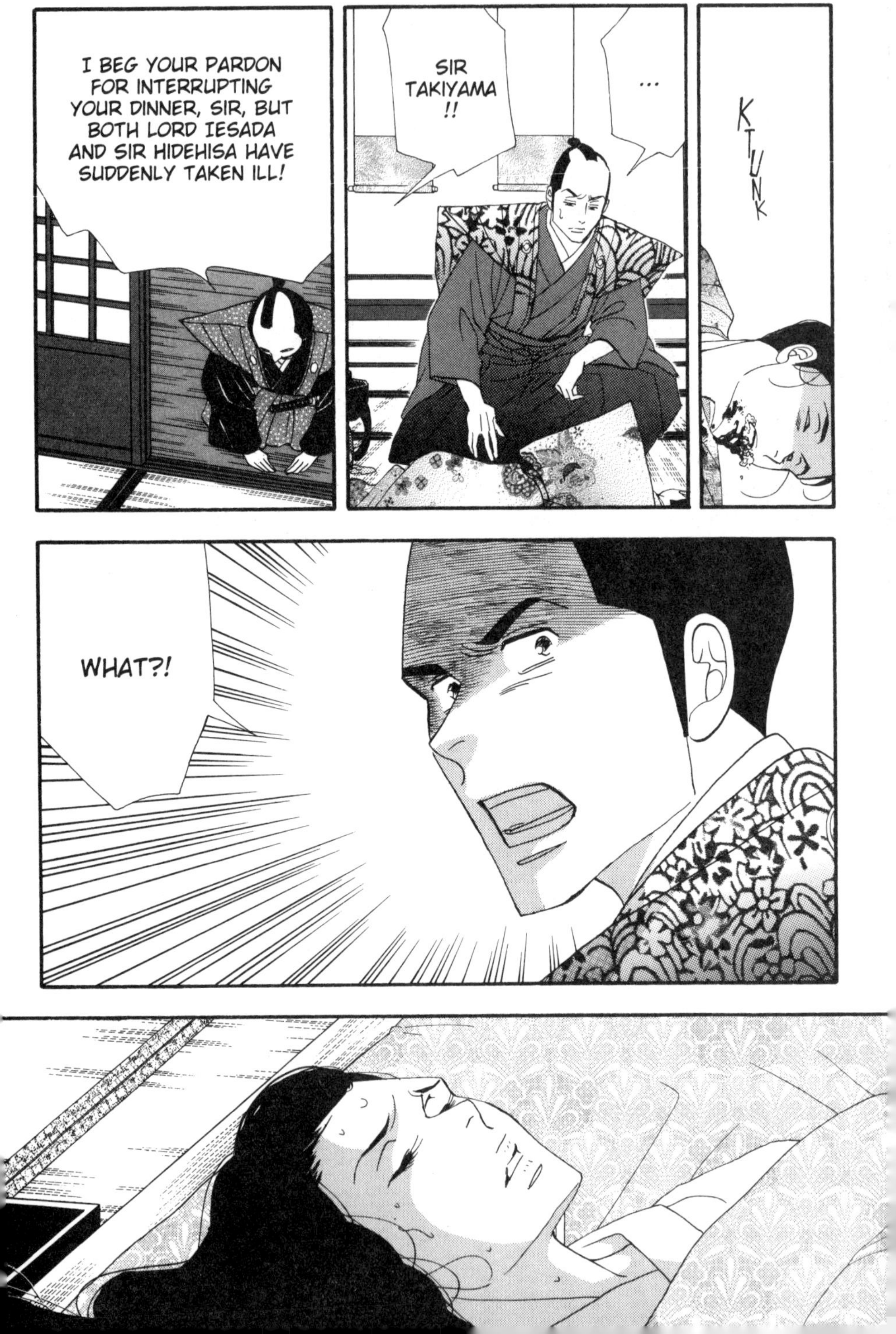
KTUNK
...
SIR TAKIYAMA !!
I BEG YOUR PARDON FOR INTERRUPTING YOUR DINNER, SIR, BUT BOTH LORD IESADA AND SIR HIDEHISA HAVE SUDDENLY TAKEN ILL!
WHAT?!

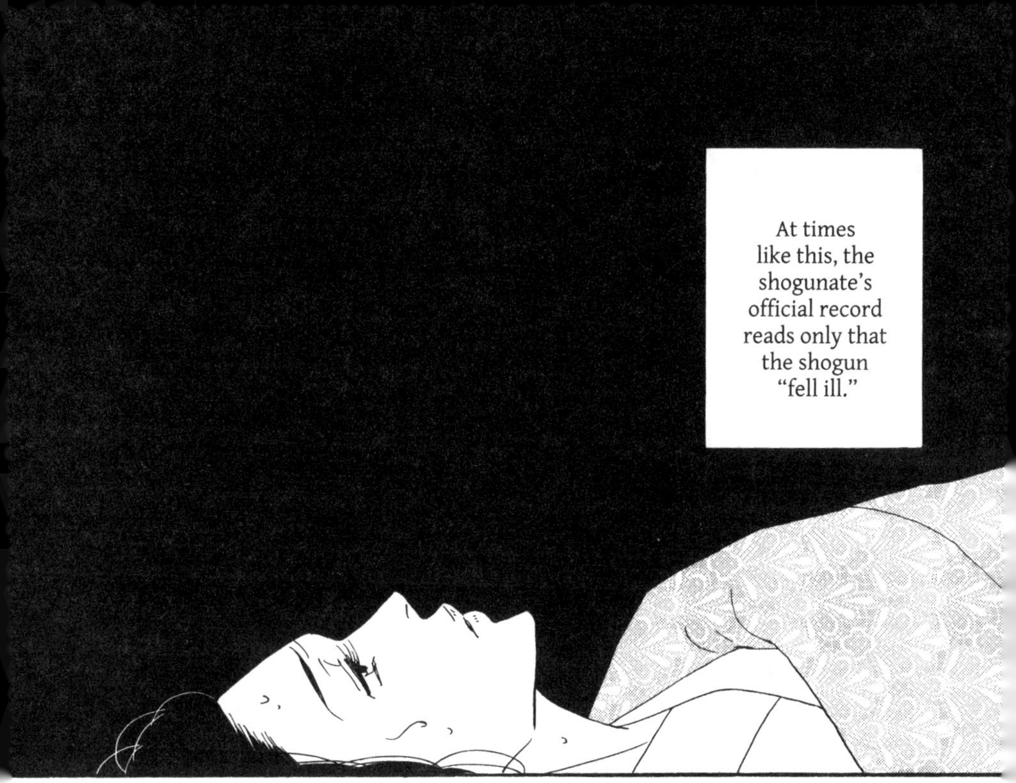
At times like this, the shogunate's official record reads only that the shogun "fell ill."

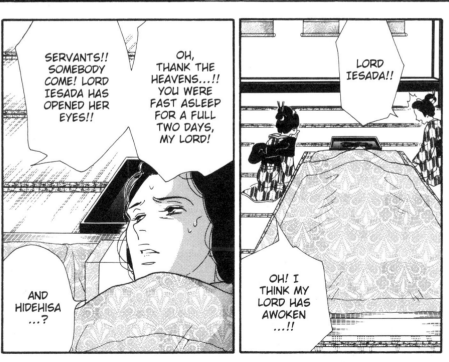

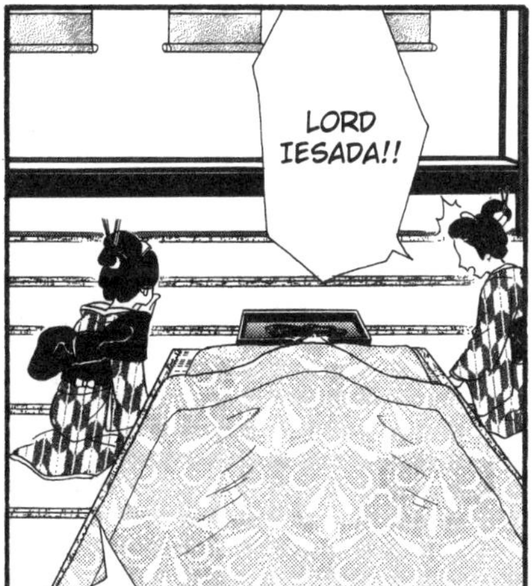
LORD IESADA!!
OH! I THINK MY LORD HAS AWOKEN ...!!

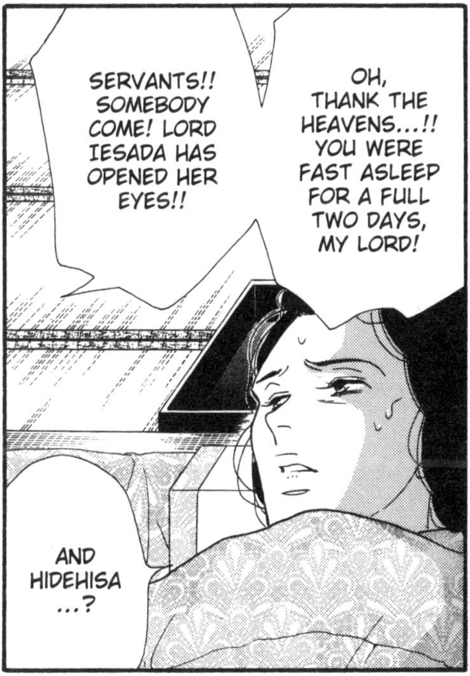
OH, THANK THE HEAVENS...!! YOU WERE FAST ASLEEP FOR A FULL TWO DAYS, MY LORD!
SERVANTS!! SOMEBODY COME! LORD IESADA HAS OPENED HER EYES!!
AND HIDEHISA ...?

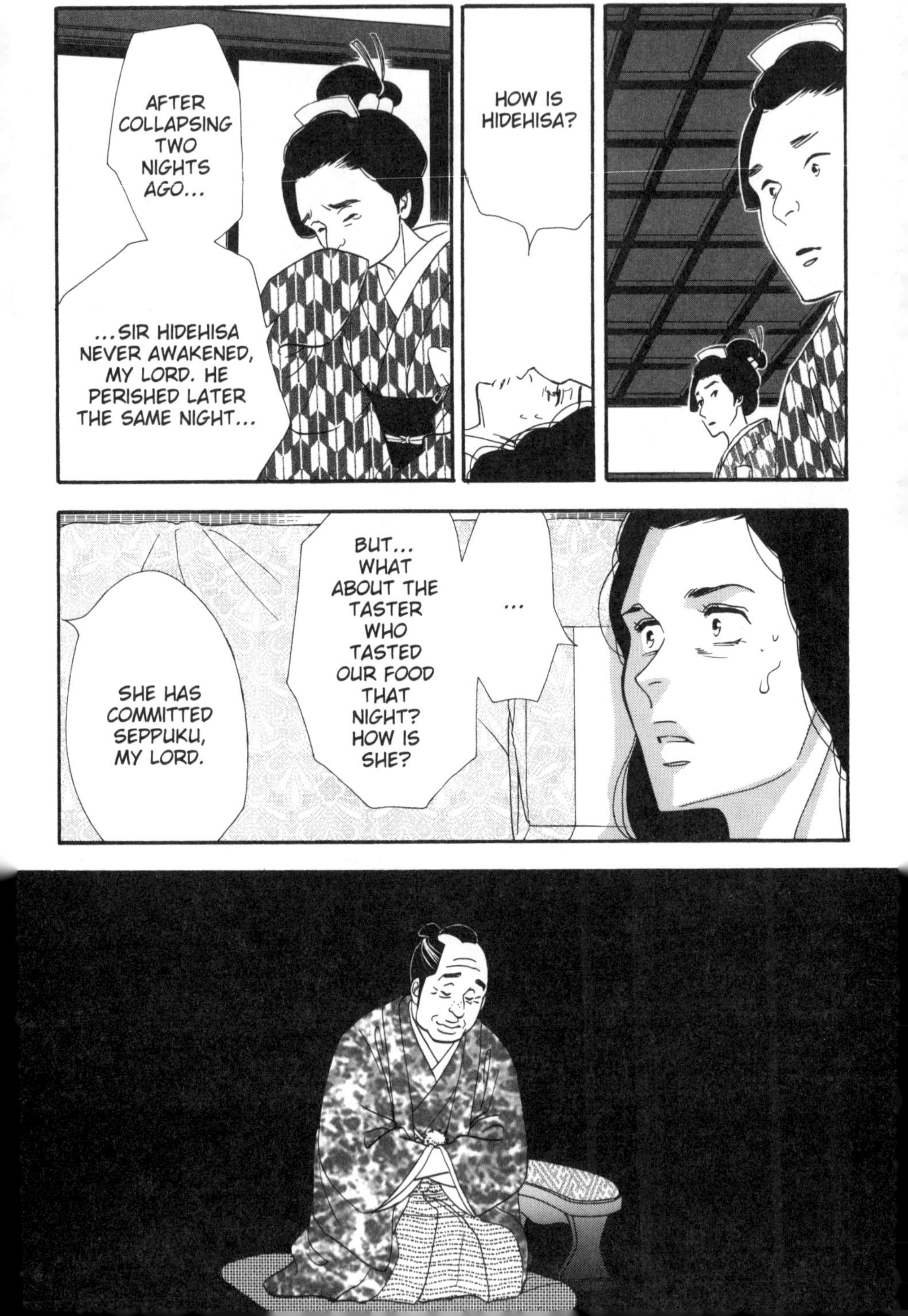
HOW IS HIDEHISA?
AFTER COLLAPSING TWO NIGHTS AGO...
...SIR HIDEHISA NEVER AWAKENED, MY LORD. HE PERISHED LATER THE SAME NIGHT...
...
BUT... WHAT ABOUT THE TASTER WHO TASTED OUR FOOD THAT NIGHT? HOW IS SHE?
SHE HAS COMMITTED SEPPUKU, MY LORD.

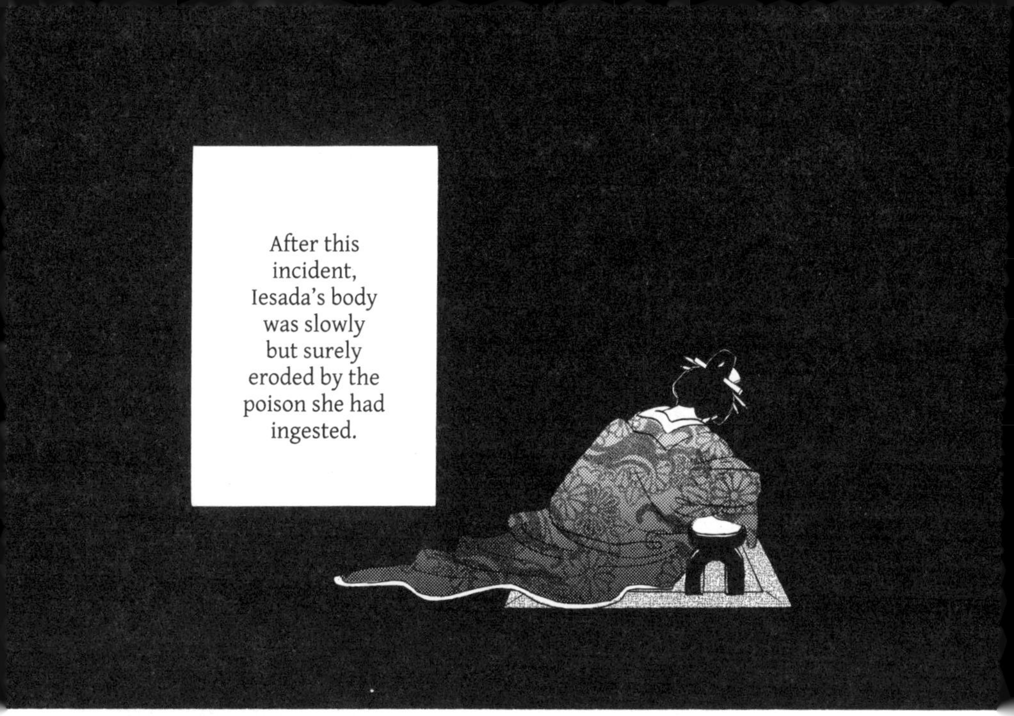
After this incident, Iesada's body was slowly but surely eroded by the poison she had ingested.

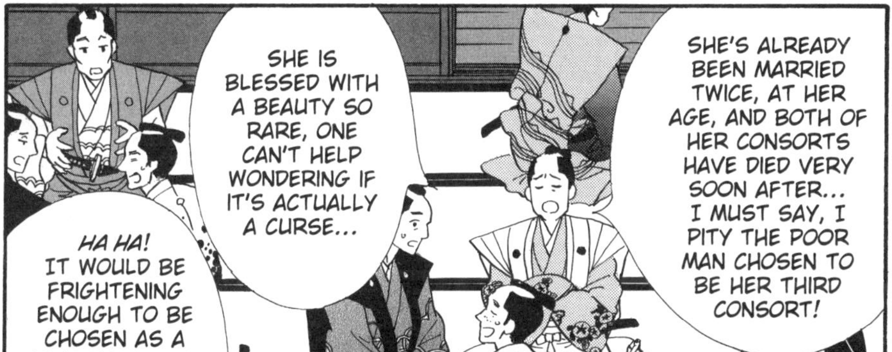
SHE'S ALREADY BEEN MARRIED TWICE, AT HER AGE, AND BOTH OF HER CONSORTS HAVE DIED VERY SOON AFTER... I MUST SAY, I PITY THE POOR MAN CHOSEN TO BE HER THIRD CONSORT!
SHE IS BLESSED WITH A BEAUTY SO RARE, ONE CAN'T HELP WONDERING IF IT'S ACTUALLY A CURSE...
HA HA! IT WOULD BE FRIGHTENING ENOUGH TO BE CHOSEN AS A CONCUBINE—LET US KEEP OUR HEADS DOWN AND PRAY SHE DOES NOT NOTICE US!

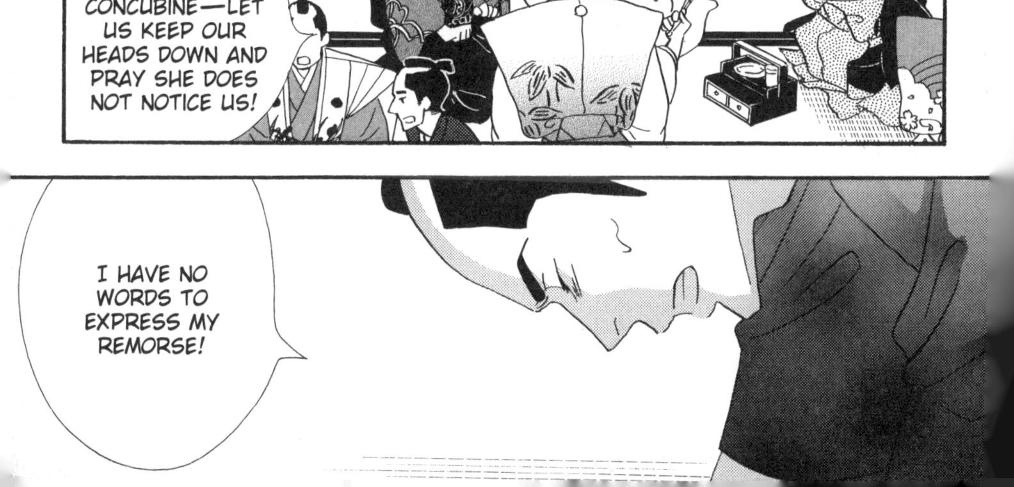
I HAVE NO WORDS TO EXPRESS MY REMORSE!

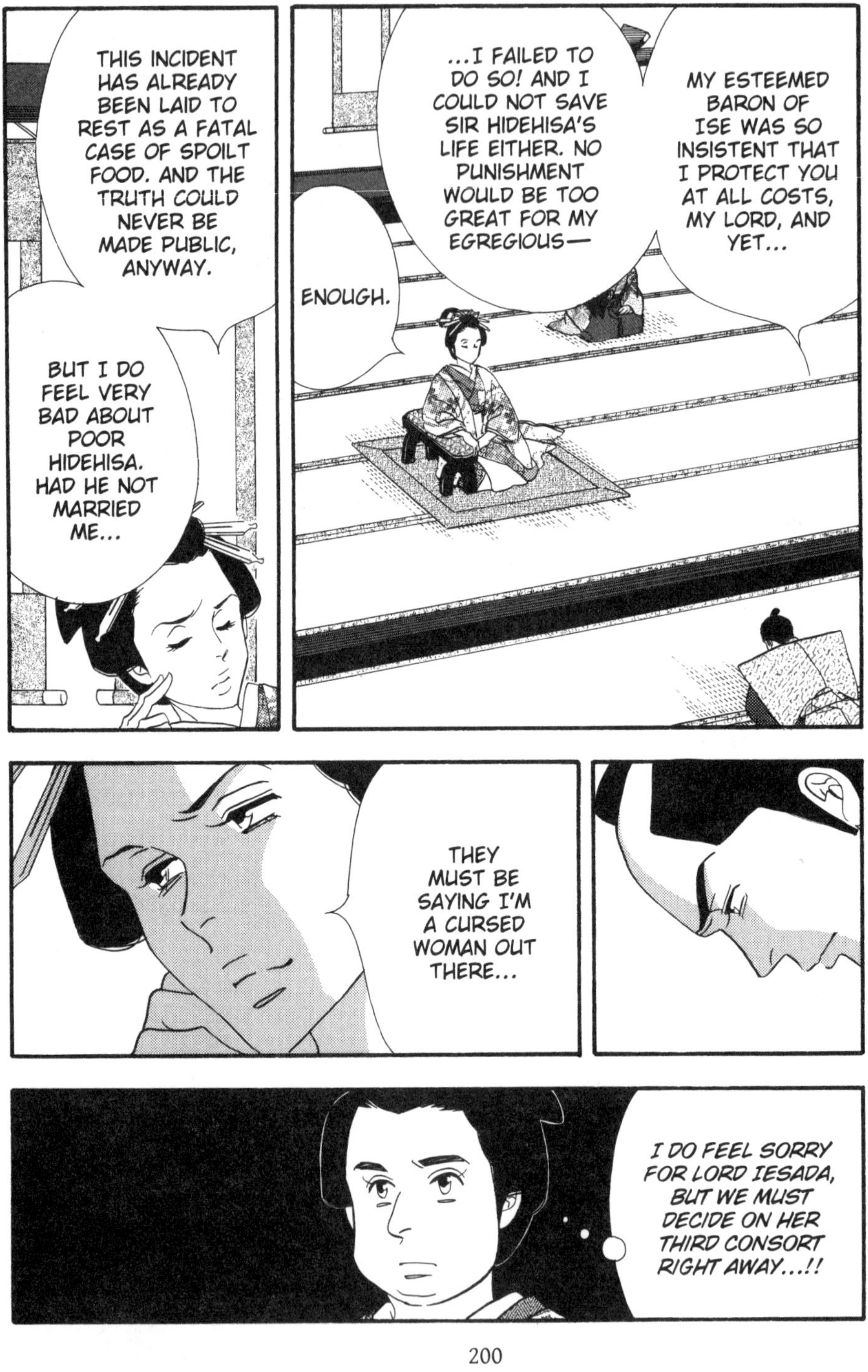
MY ESTEEMED BARON OF ISE WAS SO INSISTENT THAT I PROTECT YOU AT ALL COSTS, MY LORD, AND YET...
...I FAILED TO DO SO! AND I COULD NOT SAVE SIR HIDEHISA'S LIFE EITHER. NO PUNISHMENT WOULD BE TOO GREAT FOR MY EGREGIOUS—
ENOUGH.
THIS INCIDENT HAS ALREADY BEEN LAID TO REST AS A FATAL CASE OF SPOILT FOOD. AND THE TRUTH COULD NEVER BE MADE PUBLIC, ANYWAY.
BUT I DO FEEL VERY BAD ABOUT POOR HIDEHISA. HAD HE NOT MARRIED ME...
THEY MUST BE SAYING I'M A CURSED WOMAN OUT THERE...
I DO FEEL SORRY FOR LORD IESADA, BUT WE MUST DECIDE ON HER THIRD CONSORT RIGHT AWAY...!!

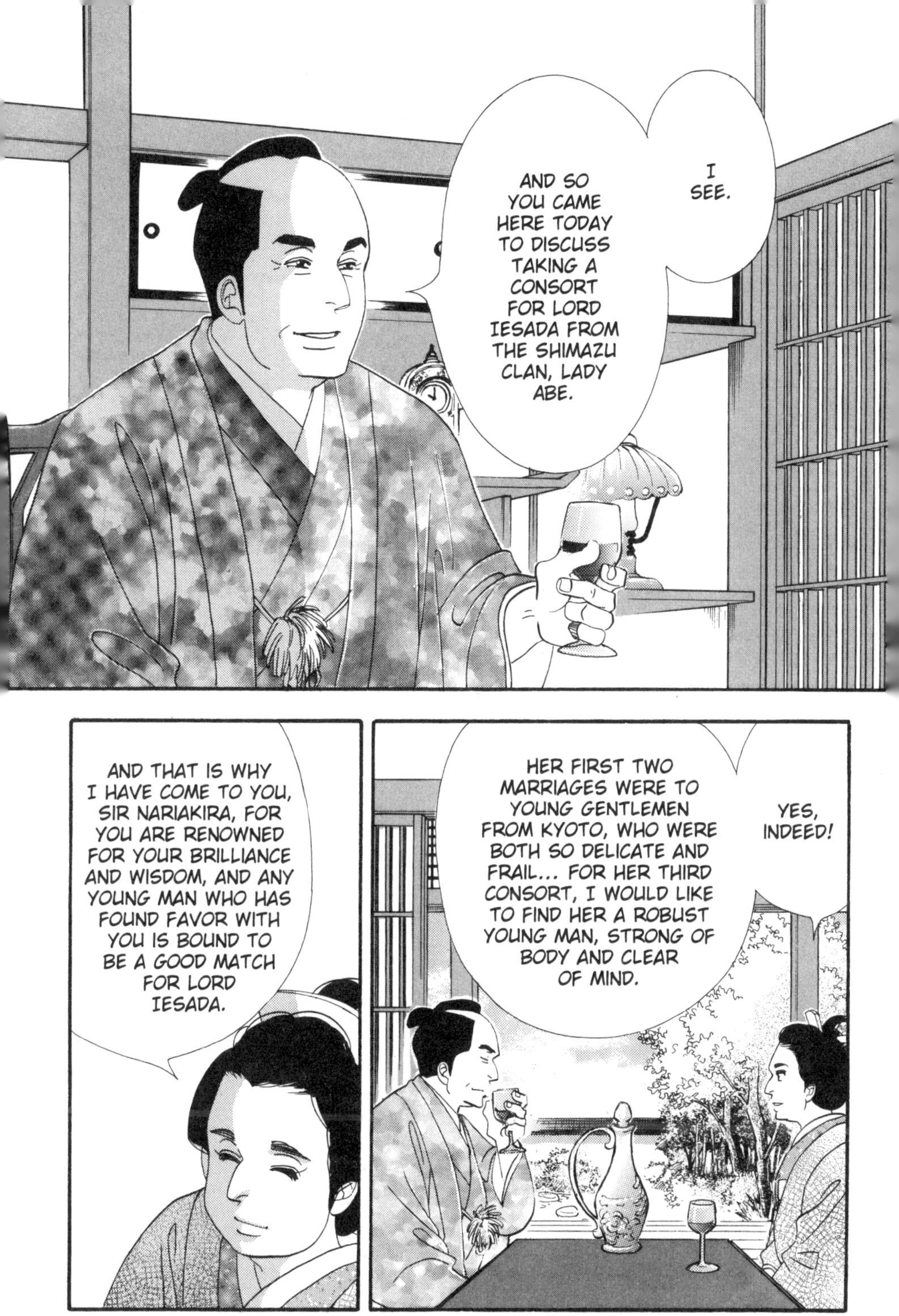
I SEE.
AND SO YOU CAME HERE TODAY TO DISCUSS TAKING A CONSORT FOR LORD IESADA FROM THE SHIMAZU CLAN, LADY ABE.
HER FIRST TWO MARRIAGES WERE TO YOUNG GENTLEMEN FROM KYOTO, WHO WERE BOTH SO DELICATE AND FRAIL... FOR HER THIRD CONSORT, I WOULD LIKE TO FIND HER A ROBUST YOUNG MAN, STRONG OF BODY AND CLEAR OF MIND.
YES, INDEED!
AND THAT IS WHY I HAVE COME TO YOU, SIR NARIAKIRA, FOR YOU ARE RENOWNED FOR YOUR BRILLIANCE AND WISDOM, AND ANY YOUNG MAN WHO HAS FOUND FAVOR WITH YOU IS BOUND TO BE A GOOD MATCH FOR LORD IESADA.

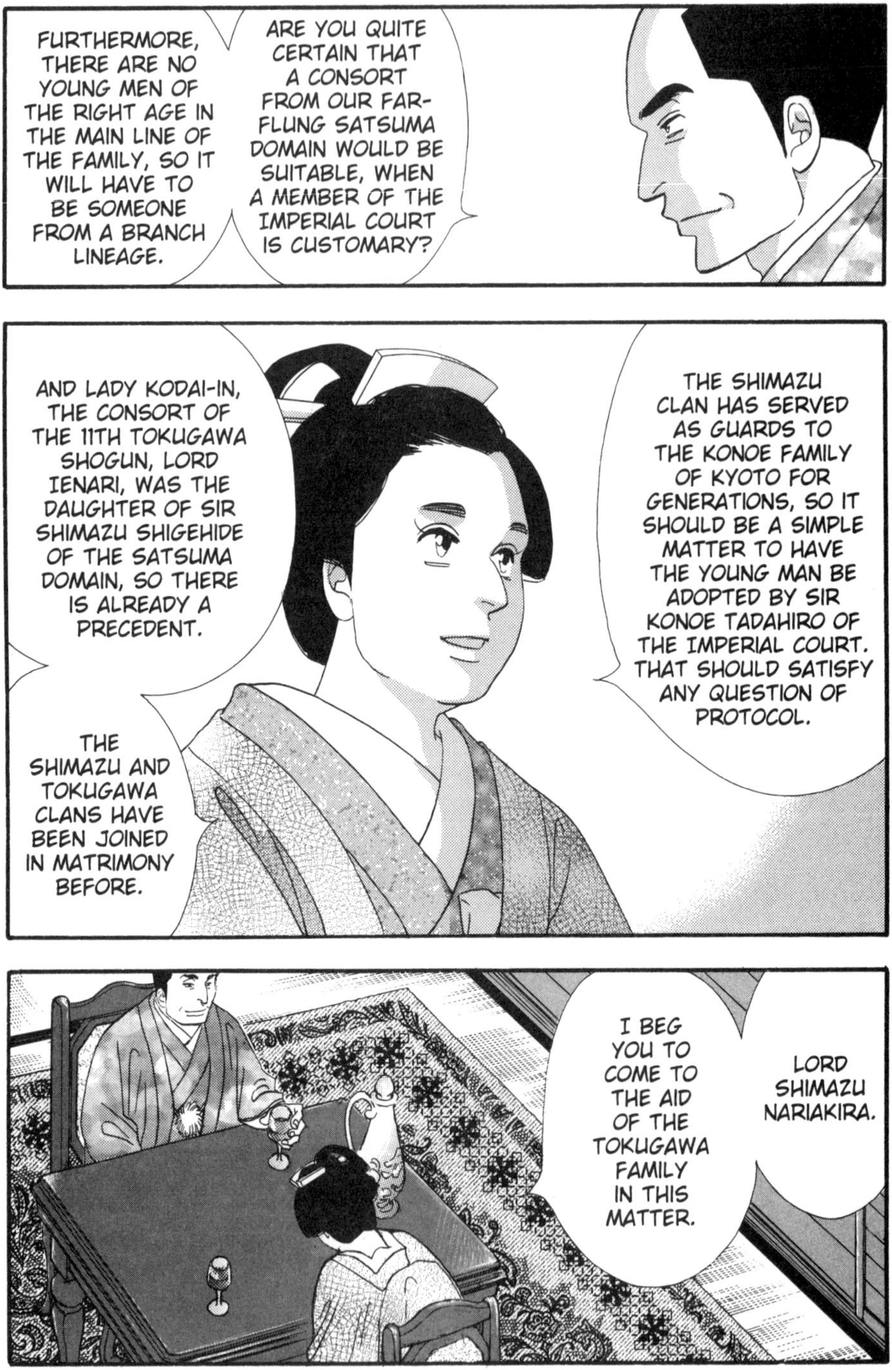
ARE YOU QUITE CERTAIN THAT A CONSORT FROM OUR FAR-FLUNG SATSUMA DOMAIN WOULD BE SUITABLE, WHEN A MEMBER OF THE IMPERIAL COURT IS CUSTOMARY?
FURTHERMORE, THERE ARE NO YOUNG MEN OF THE RIGHT AGE IN THE MAIN LINE OF THE FAMILY, SO IT WILL HAVE TO BE SOMEONE FROM A BRANCH LINEAGE.
THE SHIMAZU CLAN HAS SERVED AS GUARDS TO THE KONOE FAMILY OF KYOTO FOR GENERATIONS, SO IT SHOULD BE A SIMPLE MATTER TO HAVE THE YOUNG MAN BE ADOPTED BY SIR KONOE TADAHIRO OF THE IMPERIAL COURT. THAT SHOULD SATISFY ANY QUESTION OF PROTOCOL.
AND LADY KODAI-IN, THE CONSORT OF THE 11TH TOKUGAWA SHOGUN, LORD IENARI, WAS THE DAUGHTER OF SIR SHIMAZU SHIGEHIDE OF THE SATSUMA DOMAIN, SO THERE IS ALREADY A PRECEDENT.
THE SHIMAZU AND TOKUGAWA CLANS HAVE BEEN JOINED IN MATRIMONY BEFORE.
LORD SHIMAZU NARIAKIRA.
I BEG YOU TO COME TO THE AID OF THE TOKUGAWA FAMILY IN THIS MATTER.

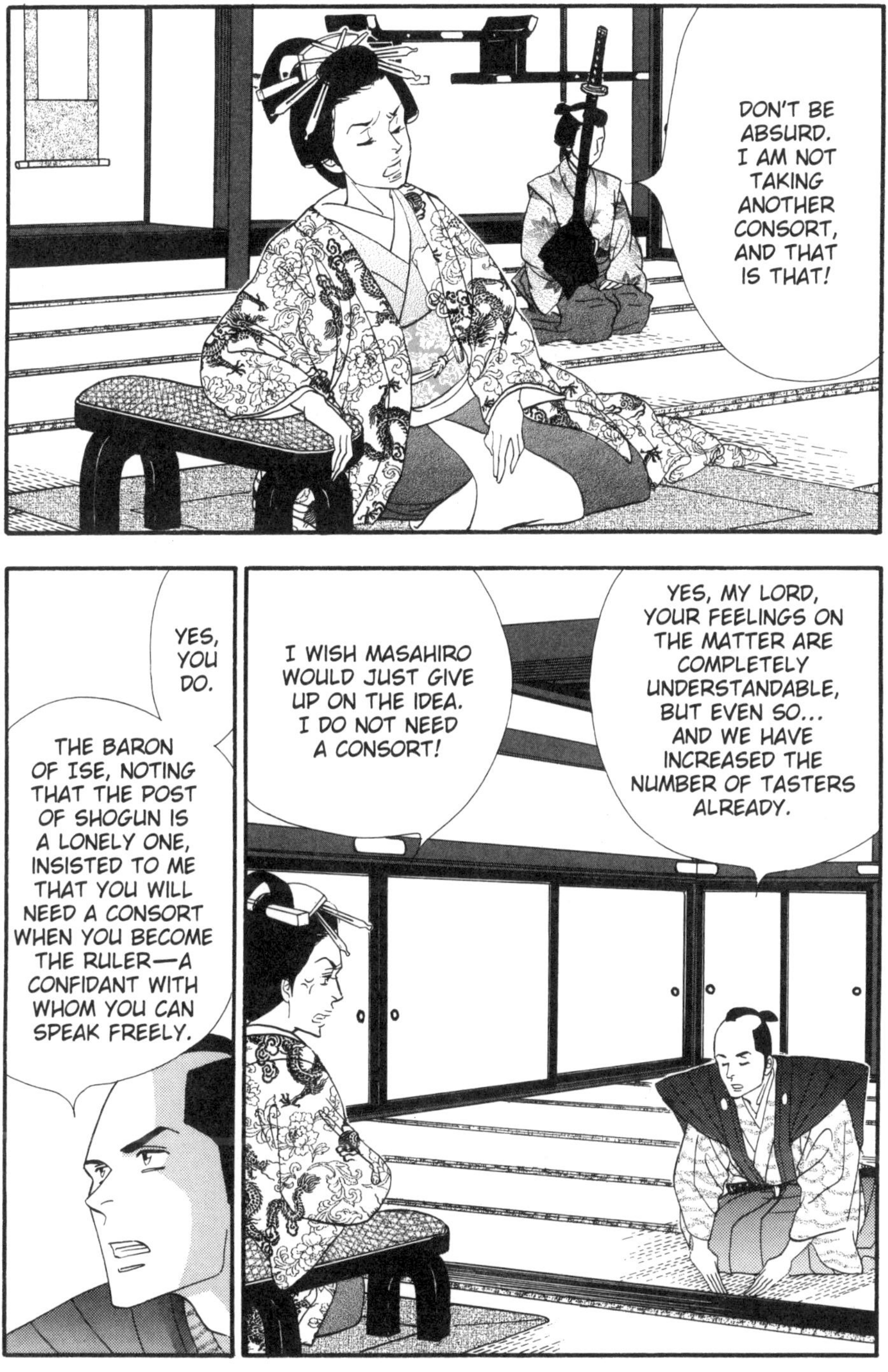
DON'T BE ABSURD. I AM NOT TAKING ANOTHER CONSORT, AND THAT IS THAT!
YES, MY LORD, YOUR FEELINGS ON THE MATTER ARE COMPLETELY UNDERSTANDABLE, BUT EVEN SO... AND WE HAVE INCREASED THE NUMBER OF TASTERS ALREADY.
I WISH MASAHIRO WOULD JUST GIVE UP ON THE IDEA. I DO NOT NEED A CONSORT!
YES, YOU DO.
THE BARON OF ISE, NOTING THAT THE POST OF SHOGUN IS A LONELY ONE, INSISTED TO ME THAT YOU WILL NEED A CONSORT WHEN YOU BECOME THE RULER—A CONFIDANT WITH WHOM YOU CAN SPEAK FREELY.

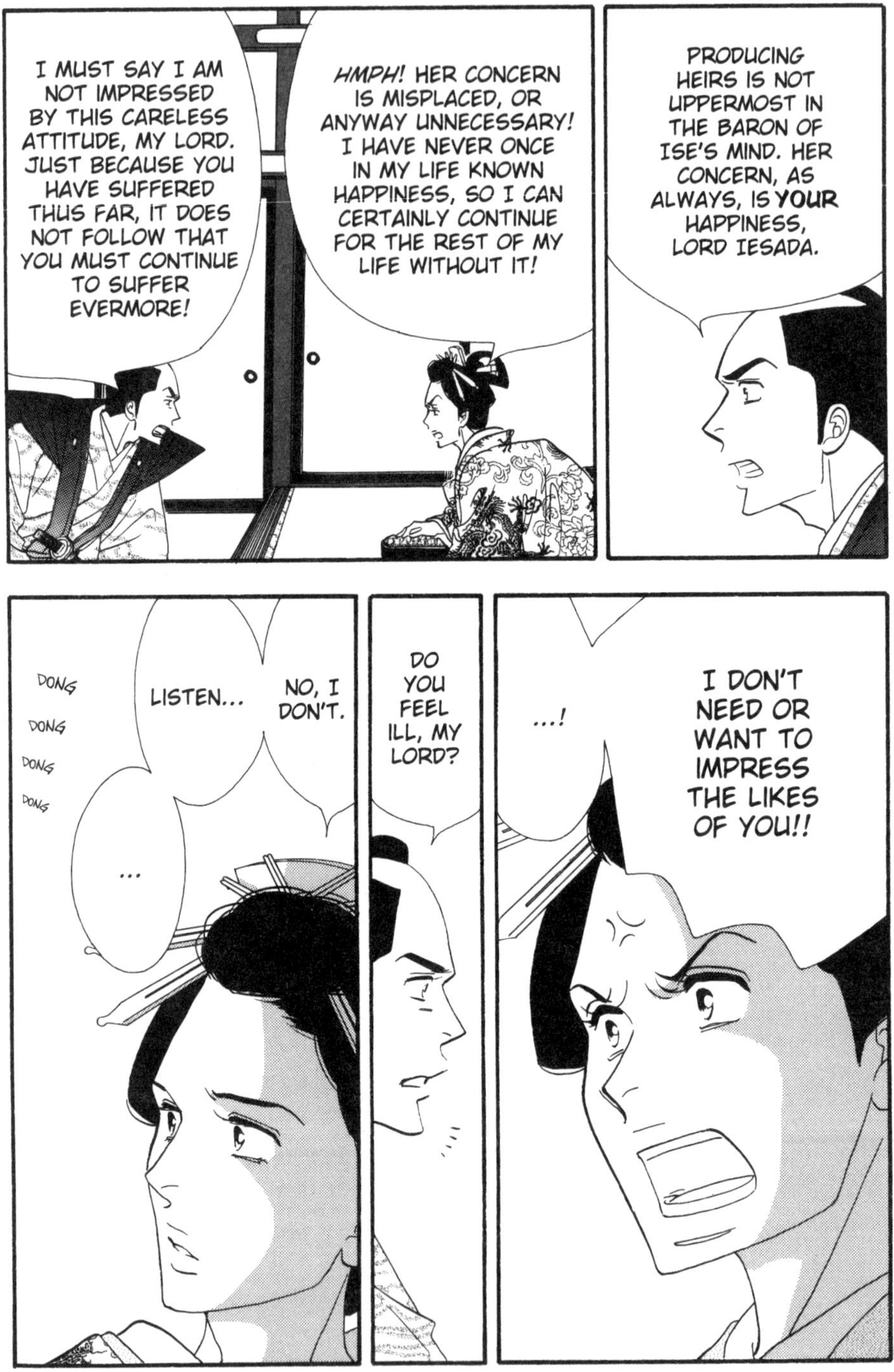
PRODUCING HEIRS IS NOT UPPERMOST IN THE BARON OF ISE'S MIND. HER CONCERN, AS ALWAYS, IS **YOUR** HAPPINESS, LORD IESADA.
HMPH! HER CONCERN IS MISPLACED, OR ANYWAY UNNECESSARY! I HAVE NEVER ONCE IN MY LIFE KNOWN HAPPINESS, SO I CAN CERTAINLY CONTINUE FOR THE REST OF MY LIFE WITHOUT IT!
I MUST SAY I AM NOT IMPRESSED BY THIS CARELESS ATTITUDE, MY LORD. JUST BECAUSE YOU HAVE SUFFERED THUS FAR, IT DOES NOT FOLLOW THAT YOU MUST CONTINUE TO SUFFER EVERMORE!
...!
I DON'T NEED OR WANT TO IMPRESS THE LIKES OF YOU!!
DO YOU FEEL ILL, MY LORD?
NO, I DON'T.
LISTEN...
DONG
DONG
DONG
DONG
...

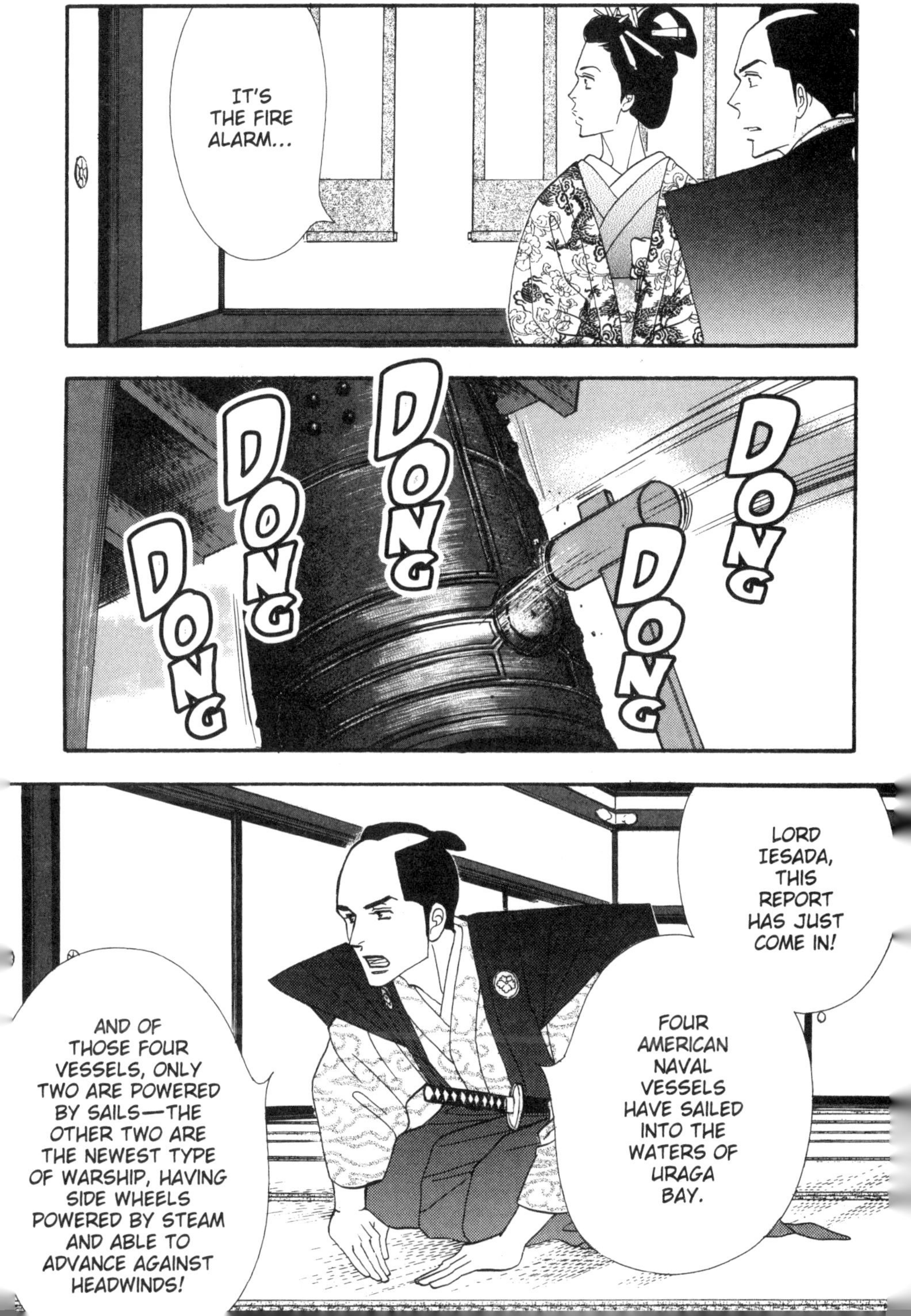
IT'S THE FIRE ALARM...
DONG
DONG
DONG
DONG
DONG
LORD IESADA, THIS REPORT HAS JUST COME IN!
FOUR AMERICAN NAVAL VESSELS HAVE SAILED INTO THE WATERS OF URAGA BAY.
AND OF THOSE FOUR VESSELS, ONLY TWO ARE POWERED BY SAILS—THE OTHER TWO ARE THE NEWEST TYPE OF WARSHIP, HAVING SIDE WHEELS POWERED BY STEAM AND ABLE TO ADVANCE AGAINST HEADWINDS!

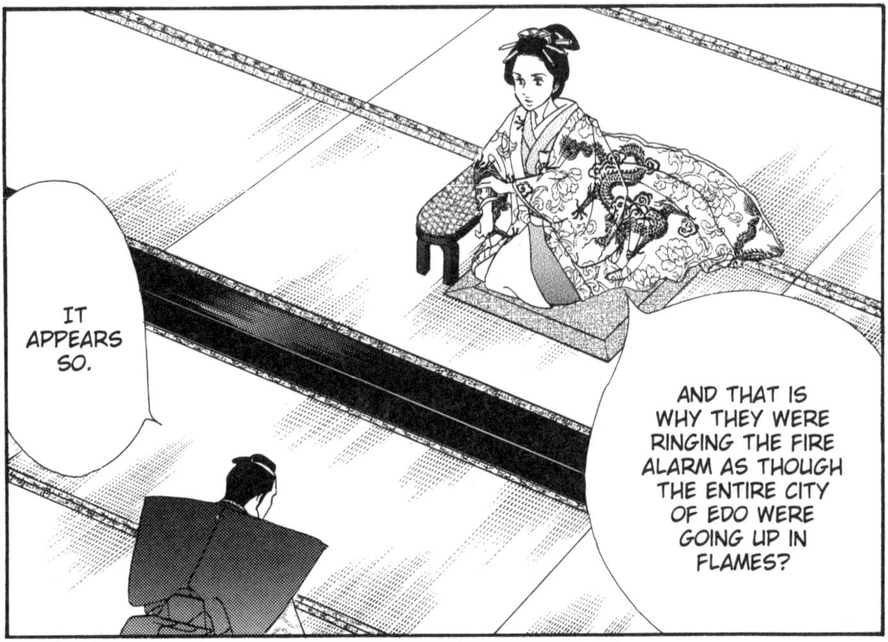
AND THAT IS WHY THEY WERE RINGING THE FIRE ALARM AS THOUGH THE ENTIRE CITY OF EDO WERE GOING UP IN FLAMES?
IT APPEARS SO.

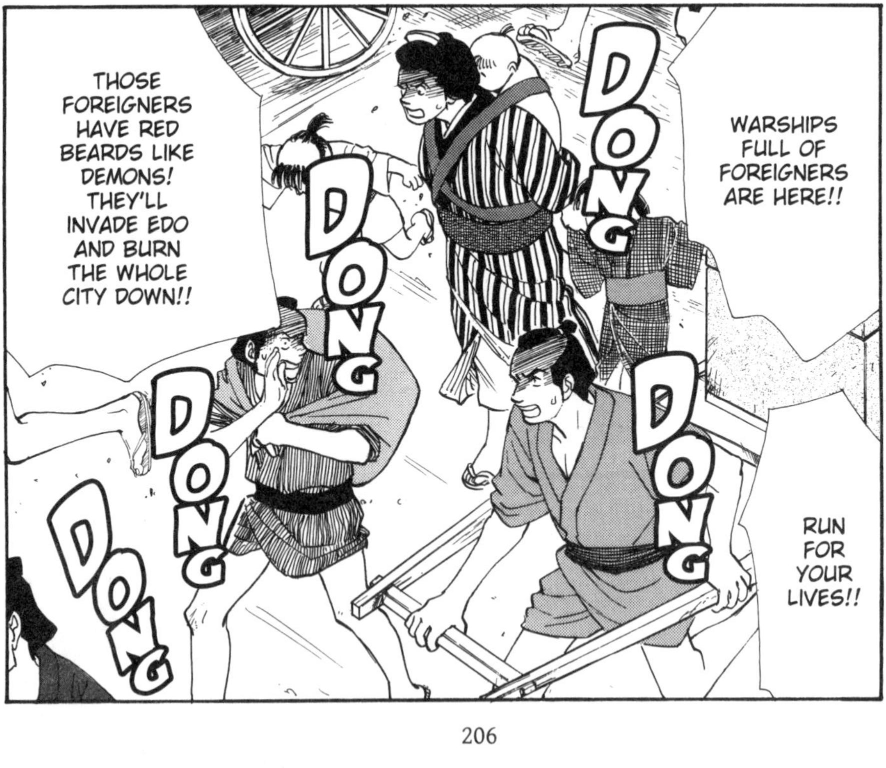
WARSHIPS FULL OF FOREIGNERS ARE HERE!!
DONG
THOSE FOREIGNERS HAVE RED BEARDS LIKE DEMONS! THEY'LL INVADE EDO AND BURN THE WHOLE CITY DOWN!!
DONG
RUN FOR YOUR LIVES!!
DONG
DONG
DONG

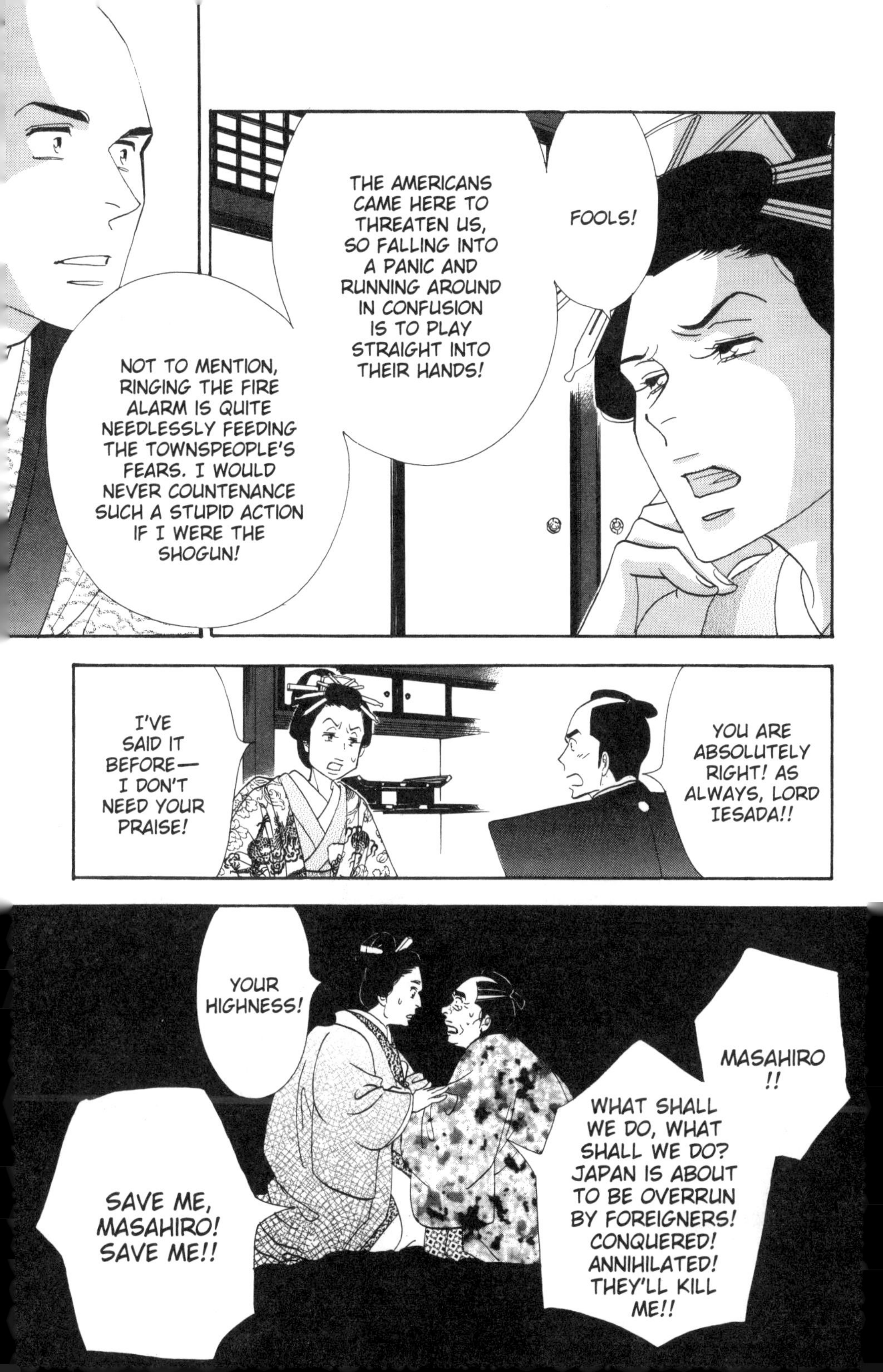
FOOLS!
THE AMERICANS CAME HERE TO THREATEN US, SO FALLING INTO A PANIC AND RUNNING AROUND IN CONFUSION IS TO PLAY STRAIGHT INTO THEIR HANDS!
NOT TO MENTION, RINGING THE FIRE ALARM IS QUITE NEEDLESSLY FEEDING THE TOWNSPEOPLE'S FEARS. I WOULD NEVER COUNTENANCE SUCH A STUPID ACTION IF I WERE THE SHOGUN!
YOU ARE ABSOLUTELY RIGHT! AS ALWAYS, LORD IESADA!!
I'VE SAID IT BEFORE—I DON'T NEED YOUR PRAISE!
MASAHIRO!!
WHAT SHALL WE DO, WHAT SHALL WE DO? JAPAN IS ABOUT TO BE OVERRUN BY FOREIGNERS! CONQUERED! ANNIHILATED! THEY'LL KILL ME!!
YOUR HIGHNESS!
SAVE ME, MASAHIRO! SAVE ME!!

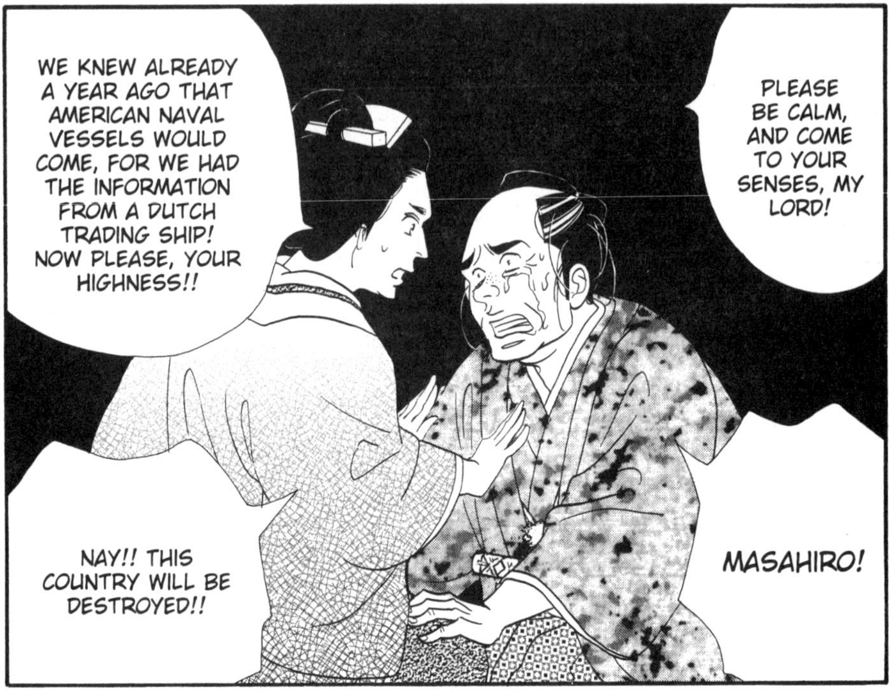
PLEASE BE CALM, AND COME TO YOUR SENSES, MY LORD!
WE KNEW ALREADY A YEAR AGO THAT AMERICAN NAVAL VESSELS WOULD COME, FOR WE HAD THE INFORMATION FROM A DUTCH TRADING SHIP! NOW PLEASE, YOUR HIGHNESS!!
MASAHIRO!
NAY!! THIS COUNTRY WILL BE DESTROYED!!
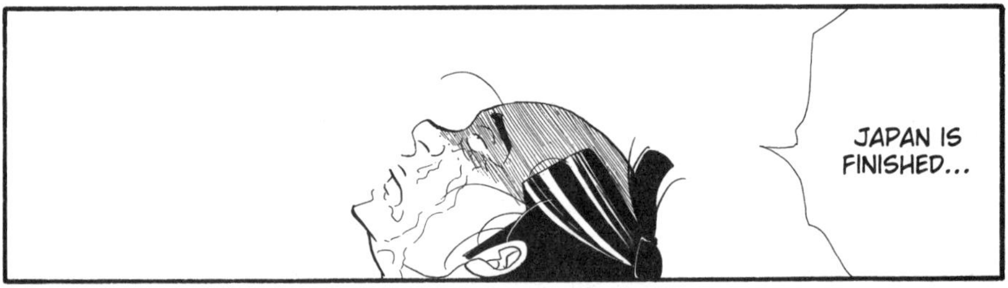
JAPAN IS FINISHED...
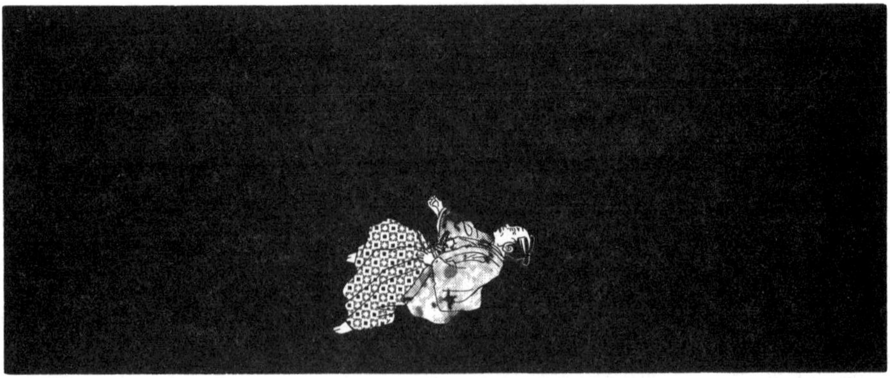

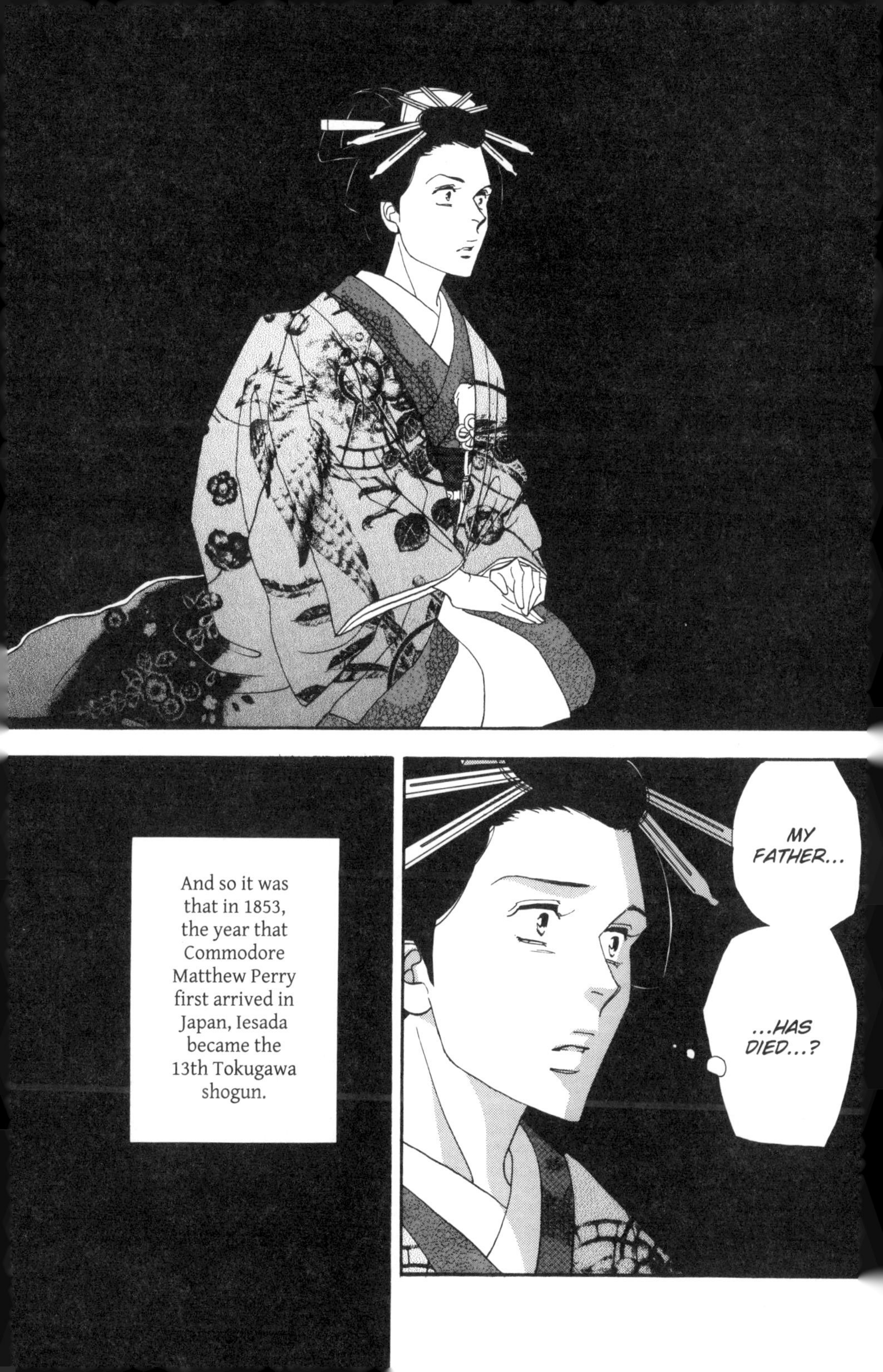
MY FATHER...
...HAS DIED...?
And so it was that in 1853, the year that Commodore Matthew Perry first arrived in Japan, Iesada became the 13th Tokugawa shogun.

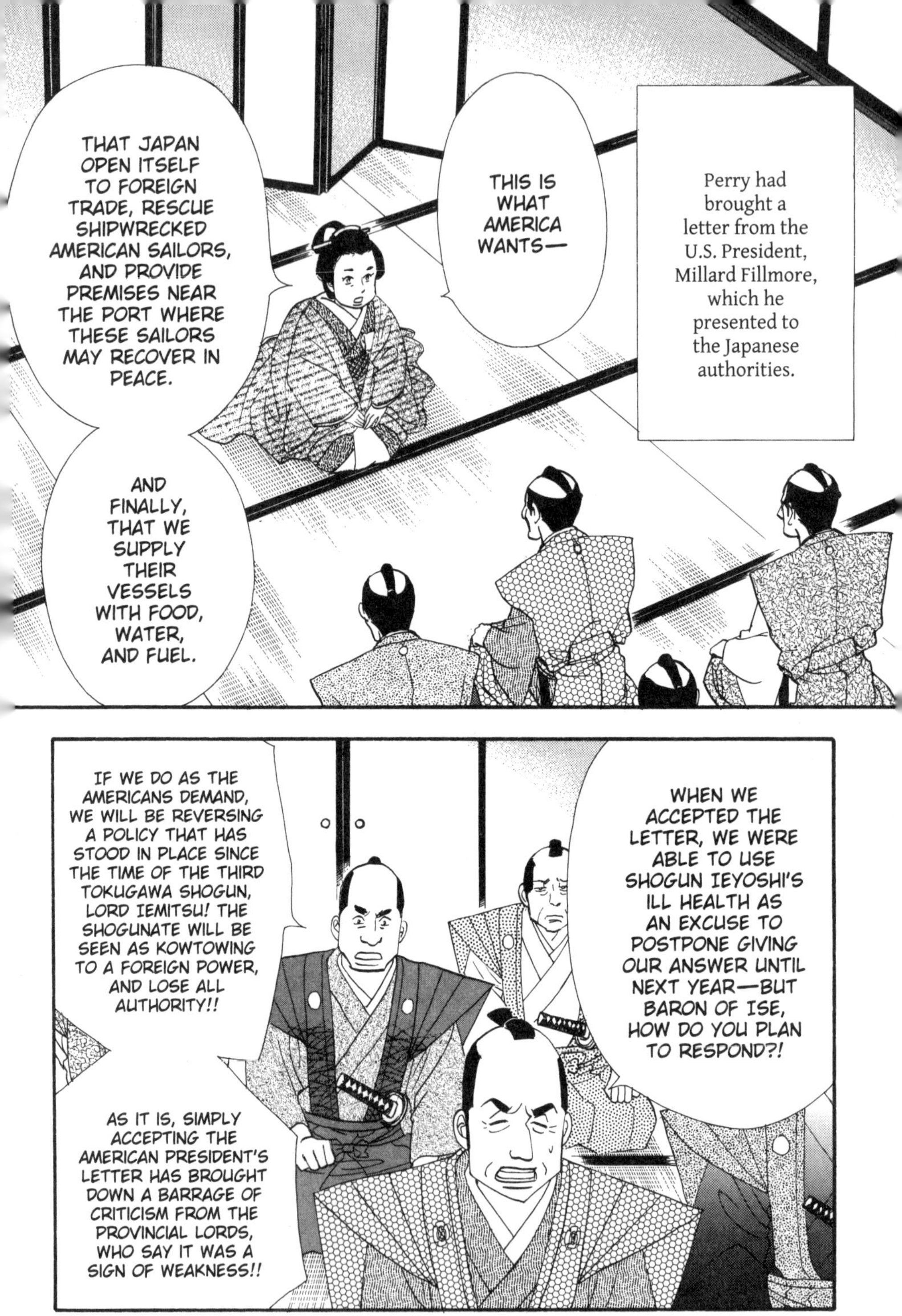

Perry had brought a letter from the U.S. President, Millard Fillmore, which he presented to the Japanese authorities.
THIS IS WHAT AMERICA WANTS—
THAT JAPAN OPEN ITSELF TO FOREIGN TRADE, RESCUE SHIPWRECKED AMERICAN SAILORS, AND PROVIDE PREMISES NEAR THE PORT WHERE THESE SAILORS MAY RECOVER IN PEACE.
AND FINALLY, THAT WE SUPPLY THEIR VESSELS WITH FOOD, WATER, AND FUEL.
WHEN WE ACCEPTED THE LETTER, WE WERE ABLE TO USE SHOGUN IEYOSHI'S ILL HEALTH AS AN EXCUSE TO POSTPONE GIVING OUR ANSWER UNTIL NEXT YEAR—BUT BARON OF ISE, HOW DO YOU PLAN TO RESPOND?!
IF WE DO AS THE AMERICANS DEMAND, WE WILL BE REVERSING A POLICY THAT HAS STOOD IN PLACE SINCE THE TIME OF THE THIRD TOKUGAWA SHOGUN, LORD IEMITSU! THE SHOGUNATE WILL BE SEEN AS KOWTOWING TO A FOREIGN POWER, AND LOSE ALL AUTHORITY!!
AS IT IS, SIMPLY ACCEPTING THE AMERICAN PRESIDENT'S LETTER HAS BROUGHT DOWN A BARRAGE OF CRITICISM FROM THE PROVINCIAL LORDS, WHO SAY IT WAS A SIGN OF WEAKNESS!!

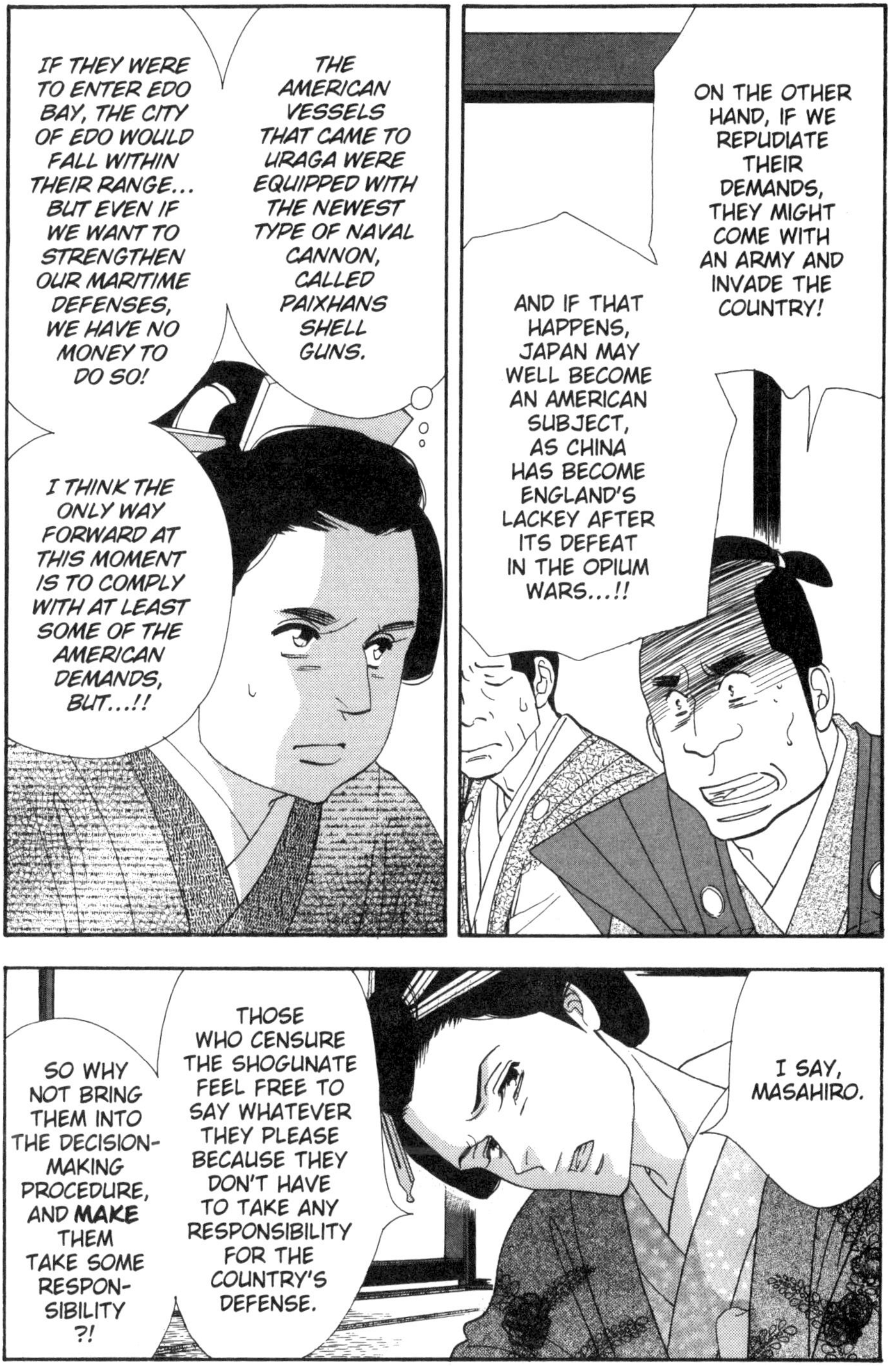
ON THE OTHER HAND, IF WE REPUDIATE THEIR DEMANDS, THEY MIGHT COME WITH AN ARMY AND INVADE THE COUNTRY!
AND IF THAT HAPPENS, JAPAN MAY WELL BECOME AN AMERICAN SUBJECT, AS CHINA HAS BECOME ENGLAND'S LACKEY AFTER ITS DEFEAT IN THE OPIUM WARS...!!
THE AMERICAN VESSELS THAT CAME TO URAGA WERE EQUIPPED WITH THE NEWEST TYPE OF NAVAL CANNON, CALLED PAIXHANS SHELL GUNS.
IF THEY WERE TO ENTER EDO BAY, THE CITY OF EDO WOULD FALL WITHIN THEIR RANGE... BUT EVEN IF WE WANT TO STRENGTHEN OUR MARITIME DEFENSES, WE HAVE NO MONEY TO DO SO!
I THINK THE ONLY WAY FORWARD AT THIS MOMENT IS TO COMPLY WITH AT LEAST SOME OF THE AMERICAN DEMANDS, BUT...!!
I SAY, MASAHIRO.
THOSE WHO CENSURE THE SHOGUNATE FEEL FREE TO SAY WHATEVER THEY PLEASE BECAUSE THEY DON'T HAVE TO TAKE ANY RESPONSIBILITY FOR THE COUNTRY'S DEFENSE.
SO WHY NOT BRING THEM INTO THE DECISION-MAKING PROCEDURE, AND **MAKE** THEM TAKE SOME RESPONSIBILITY ?!

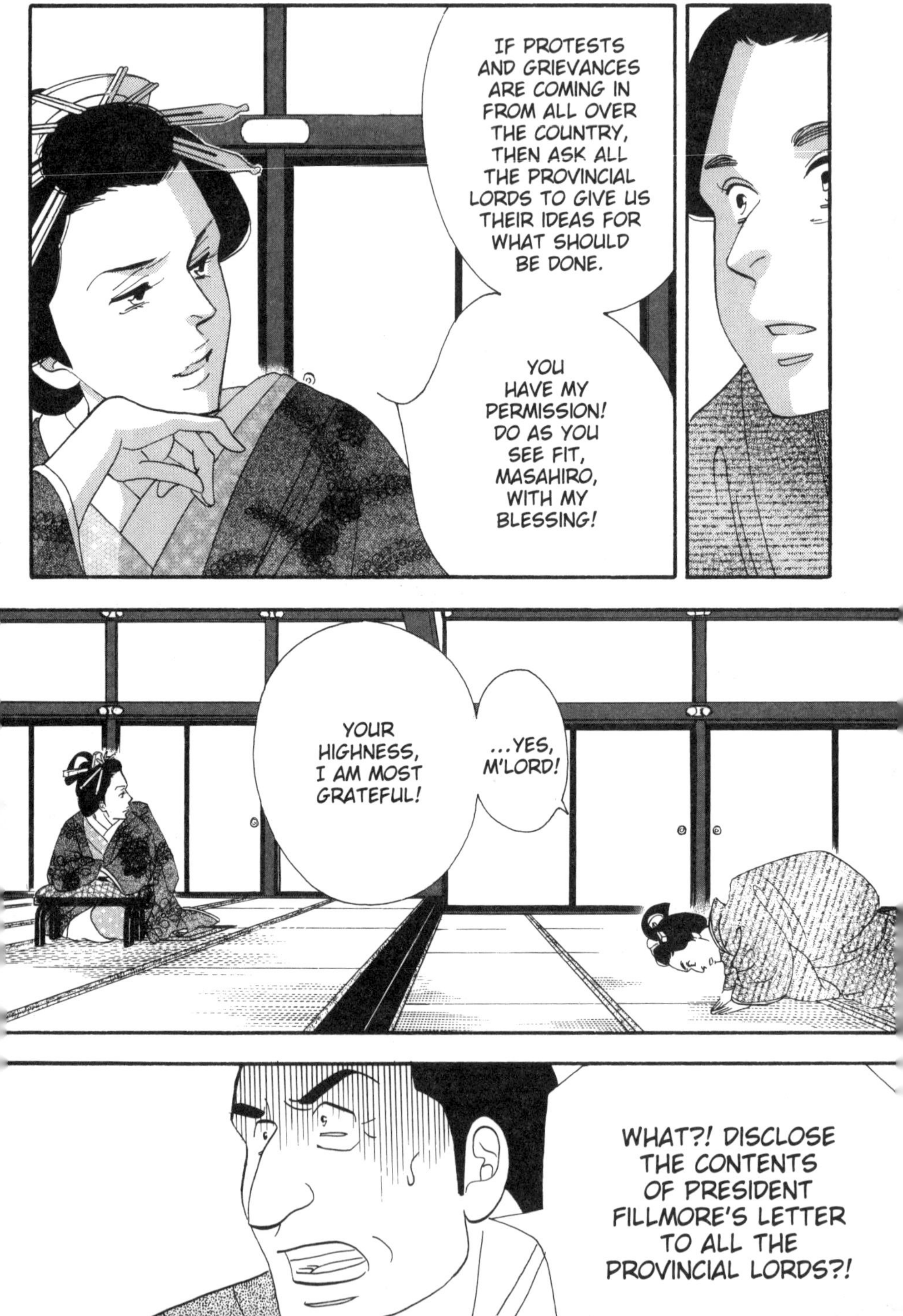
IF PROTESTS AND GRIEVANCES ARE COMING IN FROM ALL OVER THE COUNTRY, THEN ASK ALL THE PROVINCIAL LORDS TO GIVE US THEIR IDEAS FOR WHAT SHOULD BE DONE.
YOU HAVE MY PERMISSION! DO AS YOU SEE FIT, MASAHIRO, WITH MY BLESSING!
...YES, M'LORD!
YOUR HIGHNESS, I AM MOST GRATEFUL!
WHAT?! DISCLOSE THE CONTENTS OF PRESIDENT FILLMORE'S LETTER TO ALL THE PROVINCIAL LORDS?!

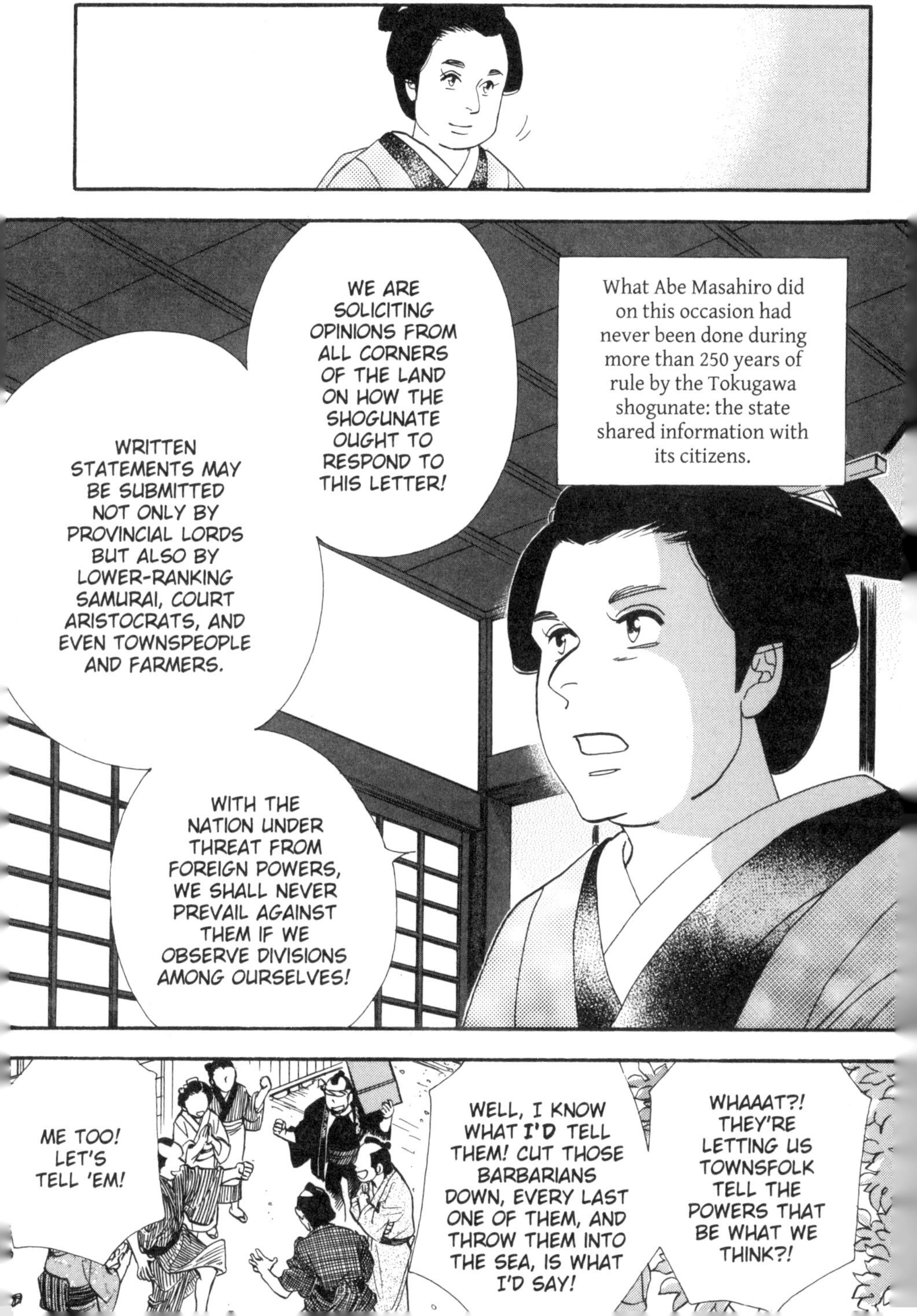
What Abe Masahiro did on this occasion had never been done during more than 250 years of rule by the Tokugawa shogunate: the state shared information with its citizens.
WE ARE SOLICITING OPINIONS FROM ALL CORNERS OF THE LAND ON HOW THE SHOGUNATE OUGHT TO RESPOND TO THIS LETTER!
WRITTEN STATEMENTS MAY BE SUBMITTED NOT ONLY BY PROVINCIAL LORDS BUT ALSO BY LOWER-RANKING SAMURAI, COURT ARISTOCRATS, AND EVEN TOWNSPEOPLE AND FARMERS.
WITH THE NATION UNDER THREAT FROM FOREIGN POWERS, WE SHALL NEVER PREVAIL AGAINST THEM IF WE OBSERVE DIVISIONS AMONG OURSELVES!
WHAAAT?! THEY'RE LETTING US TOWNSFOLK TELL THE POWERS THAT BE WHAT WE THINK?!
WELL, I KNOW WHAT **I'D** TELL THEM! CUT THOSE BARBARIANS DOWN, EVERY LAST ONE OF THEM, AND THROW THEM INTO THE SEA, IS WHAT I'D SAY!
ME TOO! LET'S TELL 'EM!

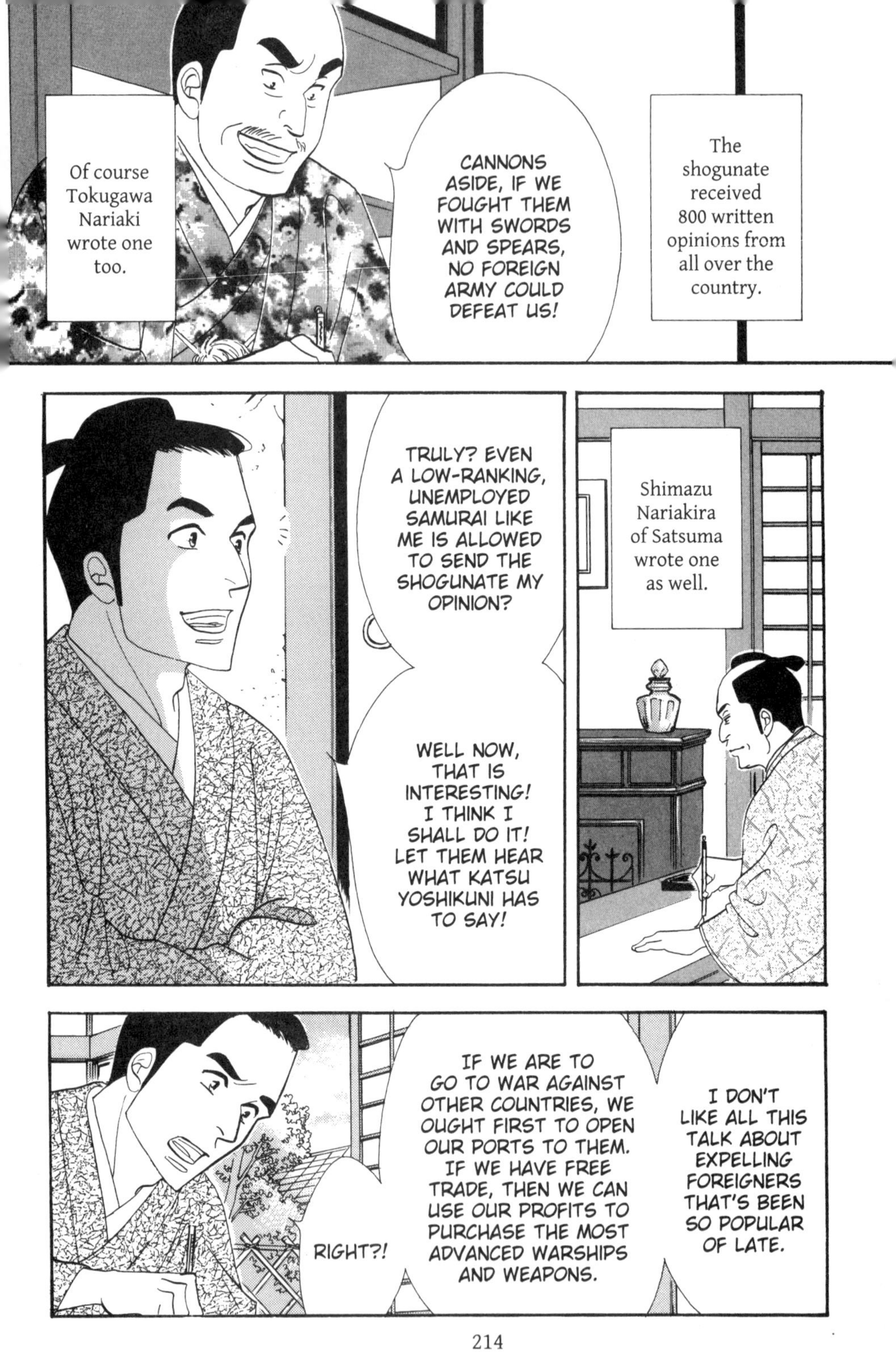
The shogunate received 800 written opinions from all over the country.
CANNONS ASIDE, IF WE FOUGHT THEM WITH SWORDS AND SPEARS, NO FOREIGN ARMY COULD DEFEAT US!
Of course Tokugawa Nariaki wrote one too.
Shimazu Nariakira of Satsuma wrote one as well.
TRULY? EVEN A LOW-RANKING, UNEMPLOYED SAMURAI LIKE ME IS ALLOWED TO SEND THE SHOGUNATE MY OPINION?
WELL NOW, THAT IS INTERESTING! I THINK I SHALL DO IT! LET THEM HEAR WHAT KATSU YOSHIKUNI HAS TO SAY!
I DON'T LIKE ALL THIS TALK ABOUT EXPELLING FOREIGNERS THAT'S BEEN SO POPULAR OF LATE.
IF WE ARE TO GO TO WAR AGAINST OTHER COUNTRIES, WE OUGHT FIRST TO OPEN OUR PORTS TO THEM. IF WE HAVE FREE TRADE, THEN WE CAN USE OUR PROFITS TO PURCHASE THE MOST ADVANCED WARSHIPS AND WEAPONS.
RIGHT?!

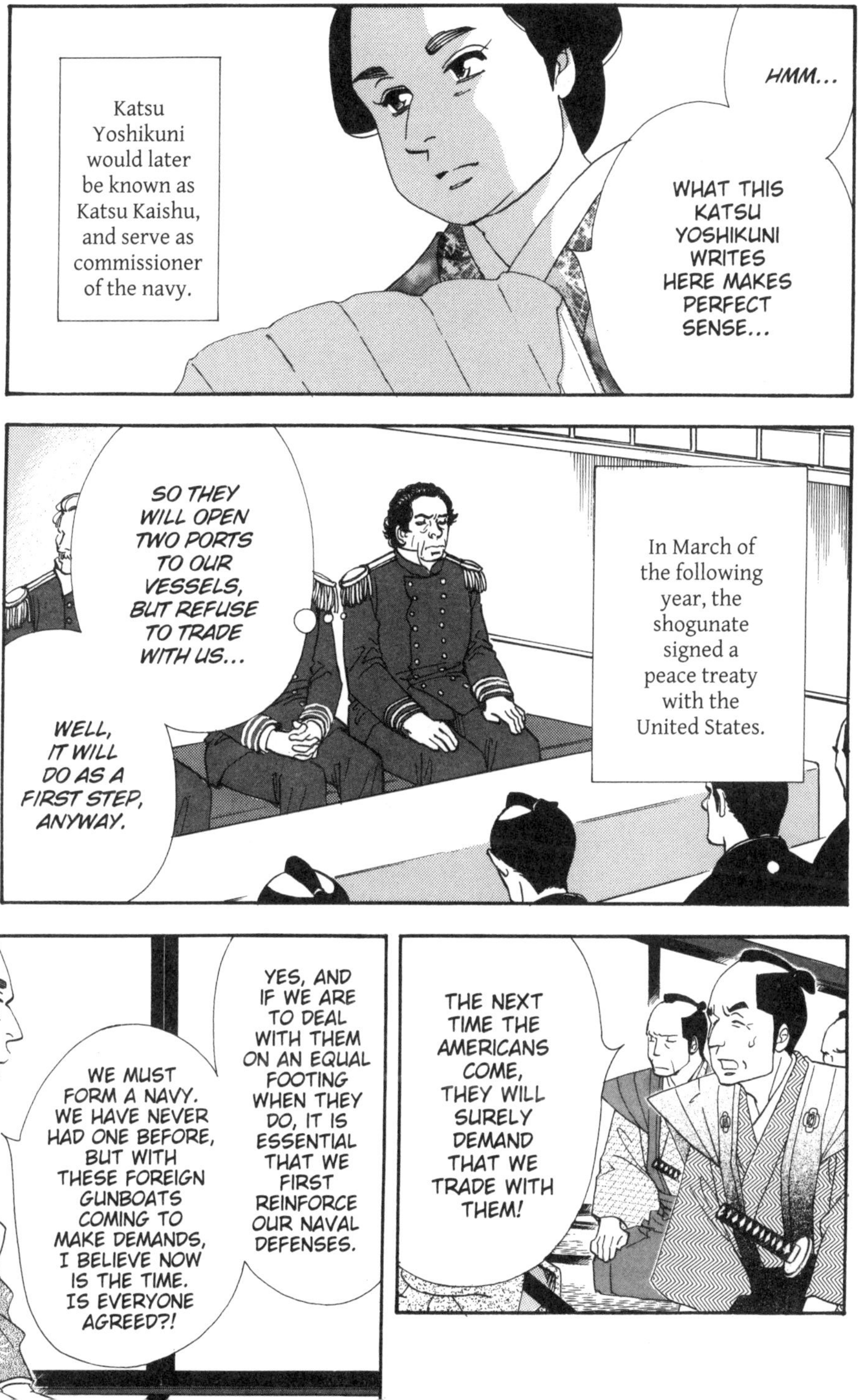
HMM...
WHAT THIS KATSU YOSHIKUNI WRITES HERE MAKES PERFECT SENSE...
Katsu Yoshikuni would later be known as Katsu Kaishu, and serve as commissioner of the navy.
In March of the following year, the shogunate signed a peace treaty with the United States.
SO THEY WILL OPEN TWO PORTS TO OUR VESSELS, BUT REFUSE TO TRADE WITH US...
WELL, IT WILL DO AS A FIRST STEP, ANYWAY.
THE NEXT TIME THE AMERICANS COME, THEY WILL SURELY DEMAND THAT WE TRADE WITH THEM!
YES, AND IF WE ARE TO DEAL WITH THEM ON AN EQUAL FOOTING WHEN THEY DO, IT IS ESSENTIAL THAT WE FIRST REINFORCE OUR NAVAL DEFENSES.
WE MUST FORM A NAVY. WE HAVE NEVER HAD ONE BEFORE, BUT WITH THESE FOREIGN GUNBOATS COMING TO MAKE DEMANDS, I BELIEVE NOW IS THE TIME. IS EVERYONE AGREED?!

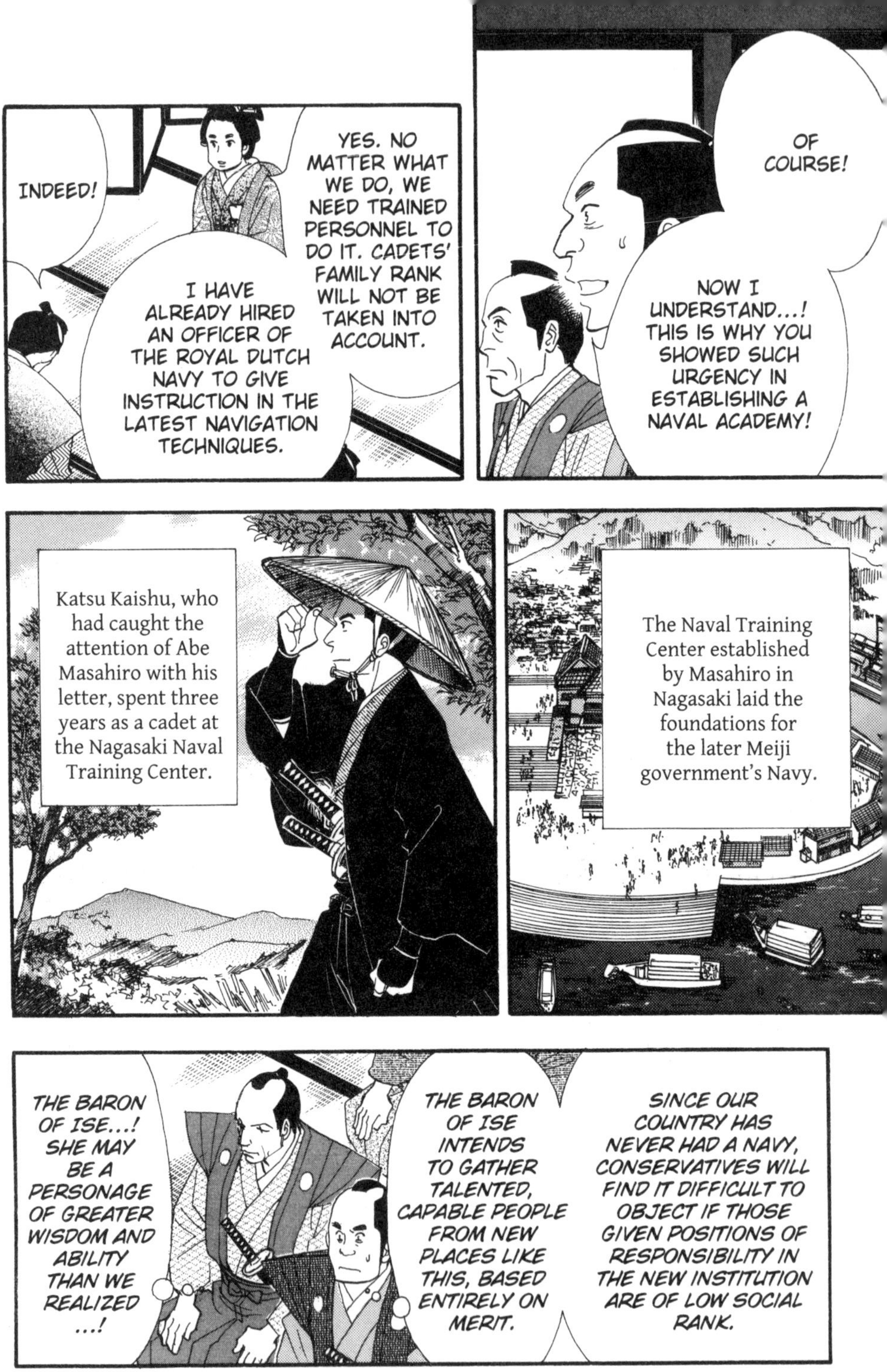
OF COURSE!
NOW I UNDERSTAND...! THIS IS WHY YOU SHOWED SUCH URGENCY IN ESTABLISHING A NAVAL ACADEMY!
YES. NO MATTER WHAT WE DO, WE NEED TRAINED PERSONNEL TO DO IT. CADETS' FAMILY RANK WILL NOT BE TAKEN INTO ACCOUNT.
INDEED!
I HAVE ALREADY HIRED AN OFFICER OF THE ROYAL DUTCH NAVY TO GIVE INSTRUCTION IN THE LATEST NAVIGATION TECHNIQUES.
The Naval Training Center established by Masahiro in Nagasaki laid the foundations for the later Meiji government's Navy.
Katsu Kaishu, who had caught the attention of Abe Masahiro with his letter, spent three years as a cadet at the Nagasaki Naval Training Center.
SINCE OUR COUNTRY HAS NEVER HAD A NAVY, CONSERVATIVES WILL FIND IT DIFFICULT TO OBJECT IF THOSE GIVEN POSITIONS OF RESPONSIBILITY IN THE NEW INSTITUTION ARE OF LOW SOCIAL RANK.
THE BARON OF ISE INTENDS TO GATHER TALENTED, CAPABLE PEOPLE FROM NEW PLACES LIKE THIS, BASED ENTIRELY ON MERIT.
THE BARON OF ISE...! SHE MAY BE A PERSONAGE OF GREATER WISDOM AND ABILITY THAN WE REALIZED...!

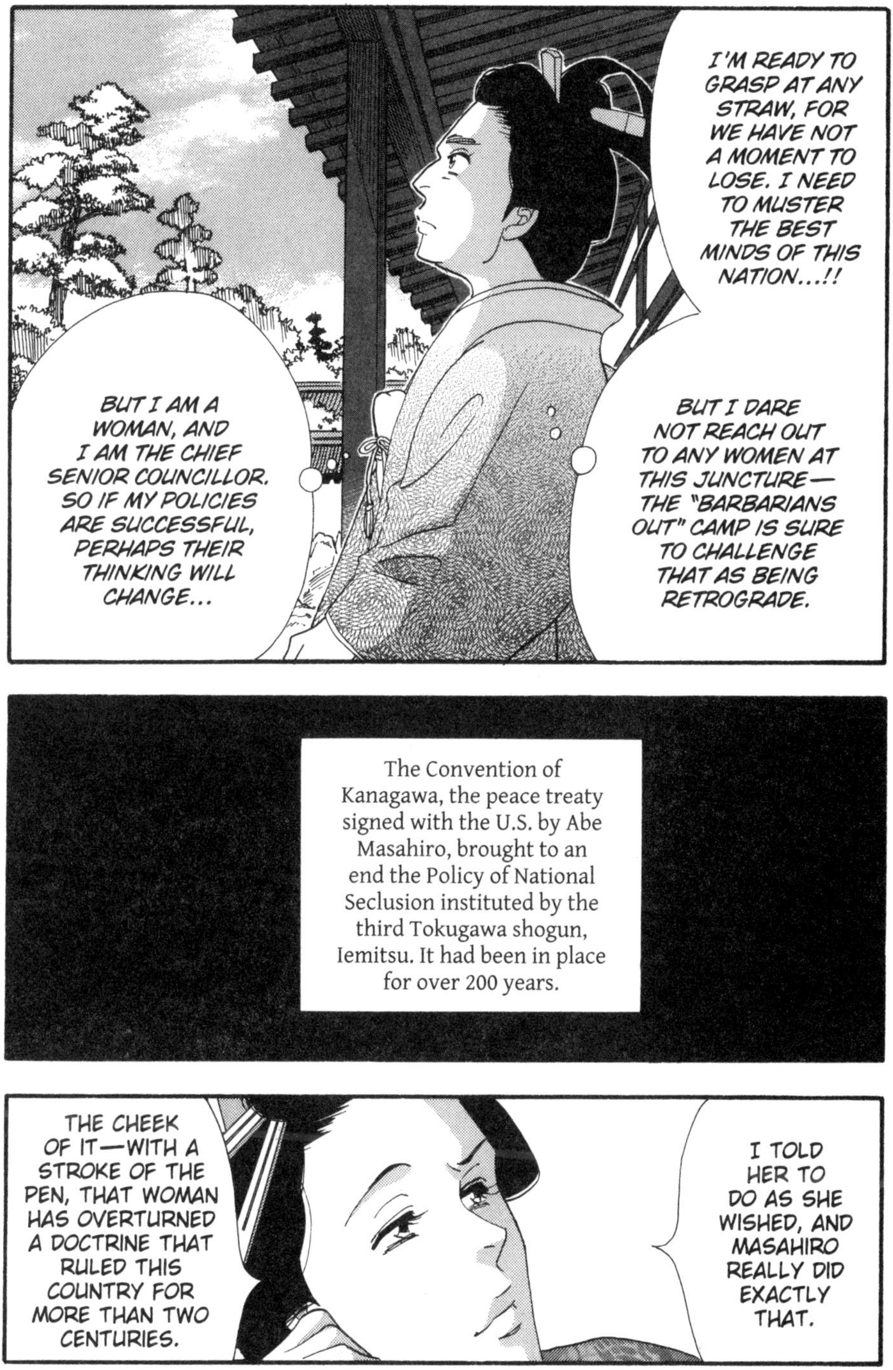
I'M READY TO GRASP AT ANY STRAW, FOR WE HAVE NOT A MOMENT TO LOSE. I NEED TO MUSTER THE BEST MINDS OF THIS NATION...!!
BUT I DARE NOT REACH OUT TO ANY WOMEN AT THIS JUNCTURE—THE "BARBARIANS OUT" CAMP IS SURE TO CHALLENGE THAT AS BEING RETROGRADE.
BUT I AM A WOMAN, AND I AM THE CHIEF SENIOR COUNCILLOR. SO IF MY POLICIES ARE SUCCESSFUL, PERHAPS THEIR THINKING WILL CHANGE...
The Convention of Kanagawa, the peace treaty signed with the U.S. by Abe Masahiro, brought to an end the Policy of National Seclusion instituted by the third Tokugawa shogun, Iemitsu. It had been in place for over 200 years.
I TOLD HER TO DO AS SHE WISHED, AND MASAHIRO REALLY DID EXACTLY THAT.
THE CHEEK OF IT—WITH A STROKE OF THE PEN, THAT WOMAN HAS OVERTURNED A DOCTRINE THAT RULED THIS COUNTRY FOR MORE THAN TWO CENTURIES.

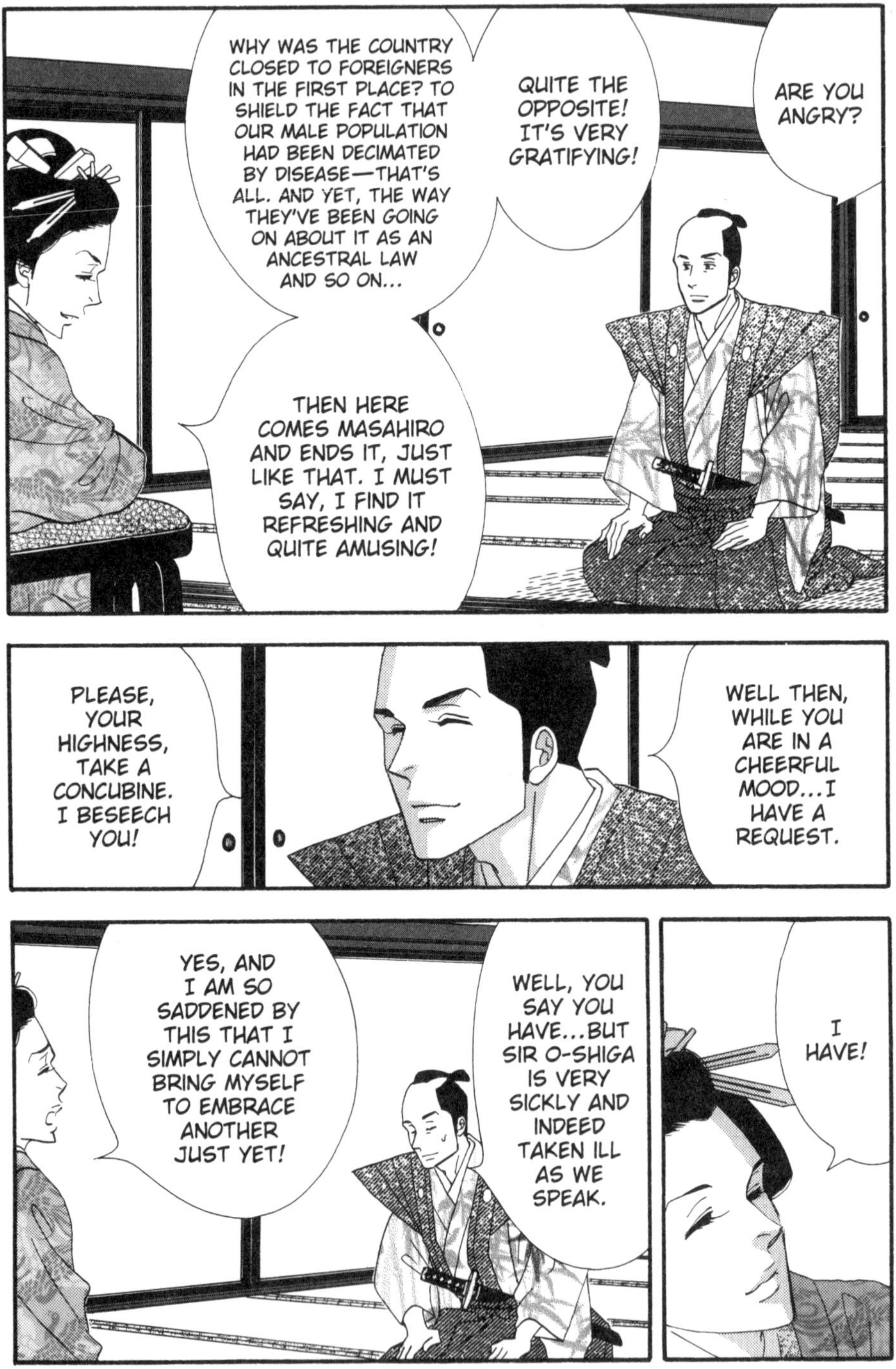
ARE YOU ANGRY?
QUITE THE OPPOSITE! IT'S VERY GRATIFYING!
WHY WAS THE COUNTRY CLOSED TO FOREIGNERS IN THE FIRST PLACE? TO SHIELD THE FACT THAT OUR MALE POPULATION HAD BEEN DECIMATED BY DISEASE—THAT'S ALL. AND YET, THE WAY THEY'VE BEEN GOING ON ABOUT IT AS AN ANCESTRAL LAW AND SO ON...
THEN HERE COMES MASAHIRO AND ENDS IT, JUST LIKE THAT. I MUST SAY, I FIND IT REFRESHING AND QUITE AMUSING!
WELL THEN, WHILE YOU ARE IN A CHEERFUL MOOD...I HAVE A REQUEST.
PLEASE, YOUR HIGHNESS, TAKE A CONCUBINE. I BESEECH YOU!
I HAVE!
WELL, YOU SAY YOU HAVE...BUT SIR O-SHIGA IS VERY SICKLY AND INDEED TAKEN ILL AS WE SPEAK.
YES, AND I AM SO SADDENED BY THIS THAT I SIMPLY CANNOT BRING MYSELF TO EMBRACE ANOTHER JUST YET!

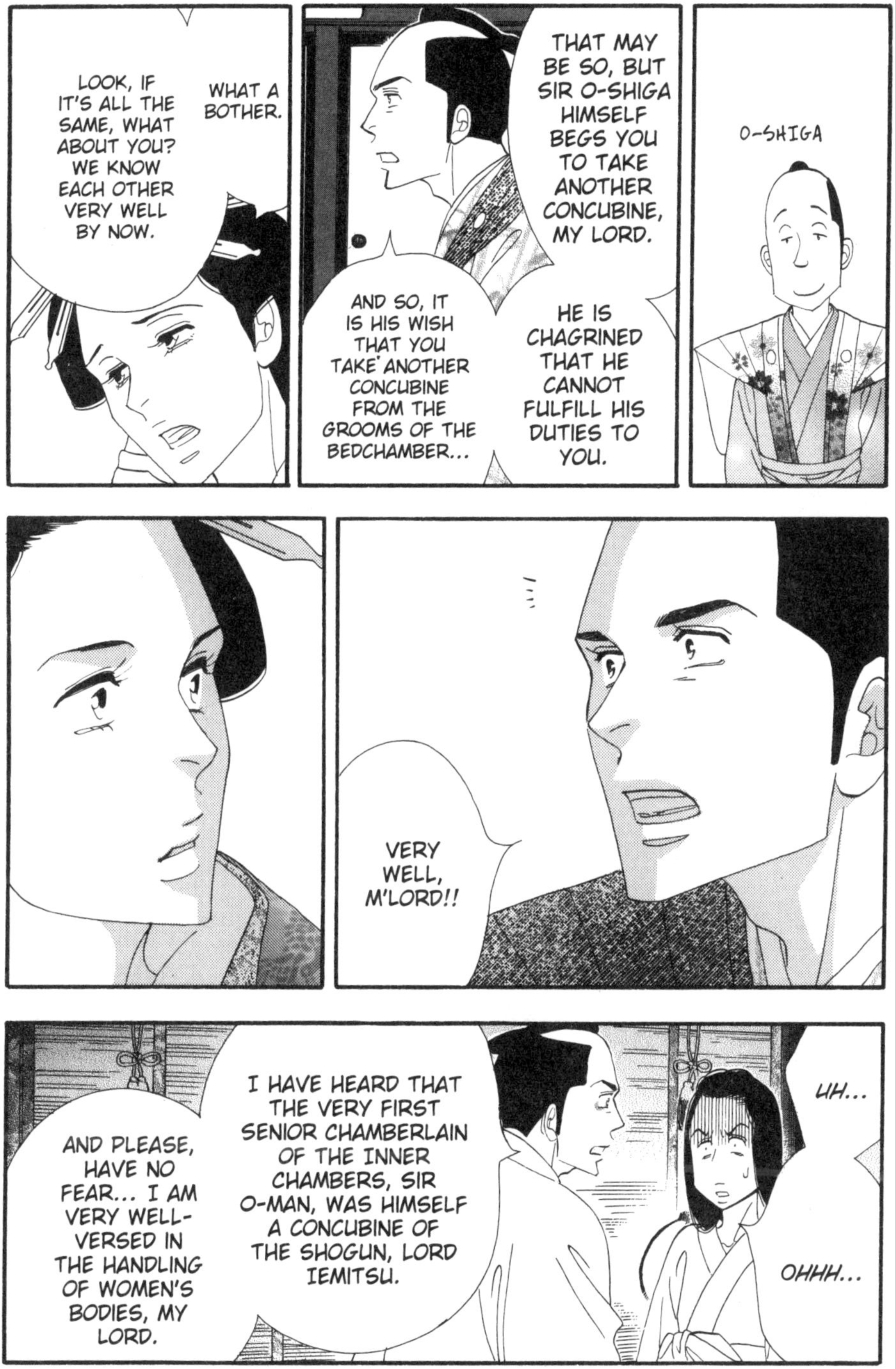
O-SHIGA
THAT MAY BE SO, BUT SIR O-SHIGA HIMSELF BEGS YOU TO TAKE ANOTHER CONCUBINE, MY LORD.
HE IS CHAGRINED THAT HE CANNOT FULFILL HIS DUTIES TO YOU.
AND SO, IT IS HIS WISH THAT YOU TAKE ANOTHER CONCUBINE FROM THE GROOMS OF THE BEDCHAMBER...
WHAT A BOTHER.
LOOK, IF IT'S ALL THE SAME, WHAT ABOUT YOU? WE KNOW EACH OTHER VERY WELL BY NOW.
VERY WELL, M'LORD!!
UH...
I HAVE HEARD THAT THE VERY FIRST SENIOR CHAMBERLAIN OF THE INNER CHAMBERS, SIR O-MAN, WAS HIMSELF A CONCUBINE OF THE SHOGUN, LORD IEMITSU.
OHHH...
AND PLEASE, HAVE NO FEAR... I AM VERY WELL-VERSED IN THE HANDLING OF WOMEN'S BODIES, MY LORD.

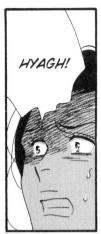

MY LORD...
HYAGH!
MY LORD?
...I'M FINE!
IT'S ALL RIGHT, TAKIYAMA. CONTINUE!
WITH YOU I WON'T BE AFRAID. I SHALL GET ACCUSTOMED TO IT, IN TIME!

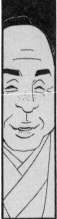

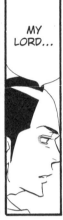

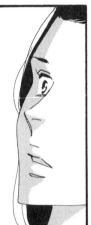

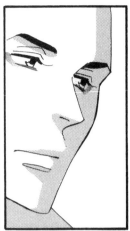

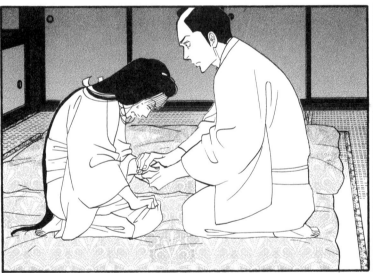

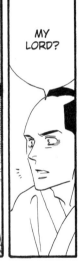

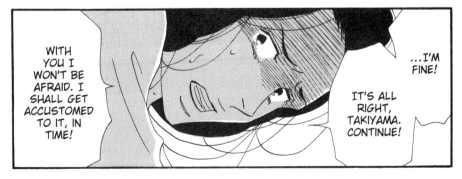

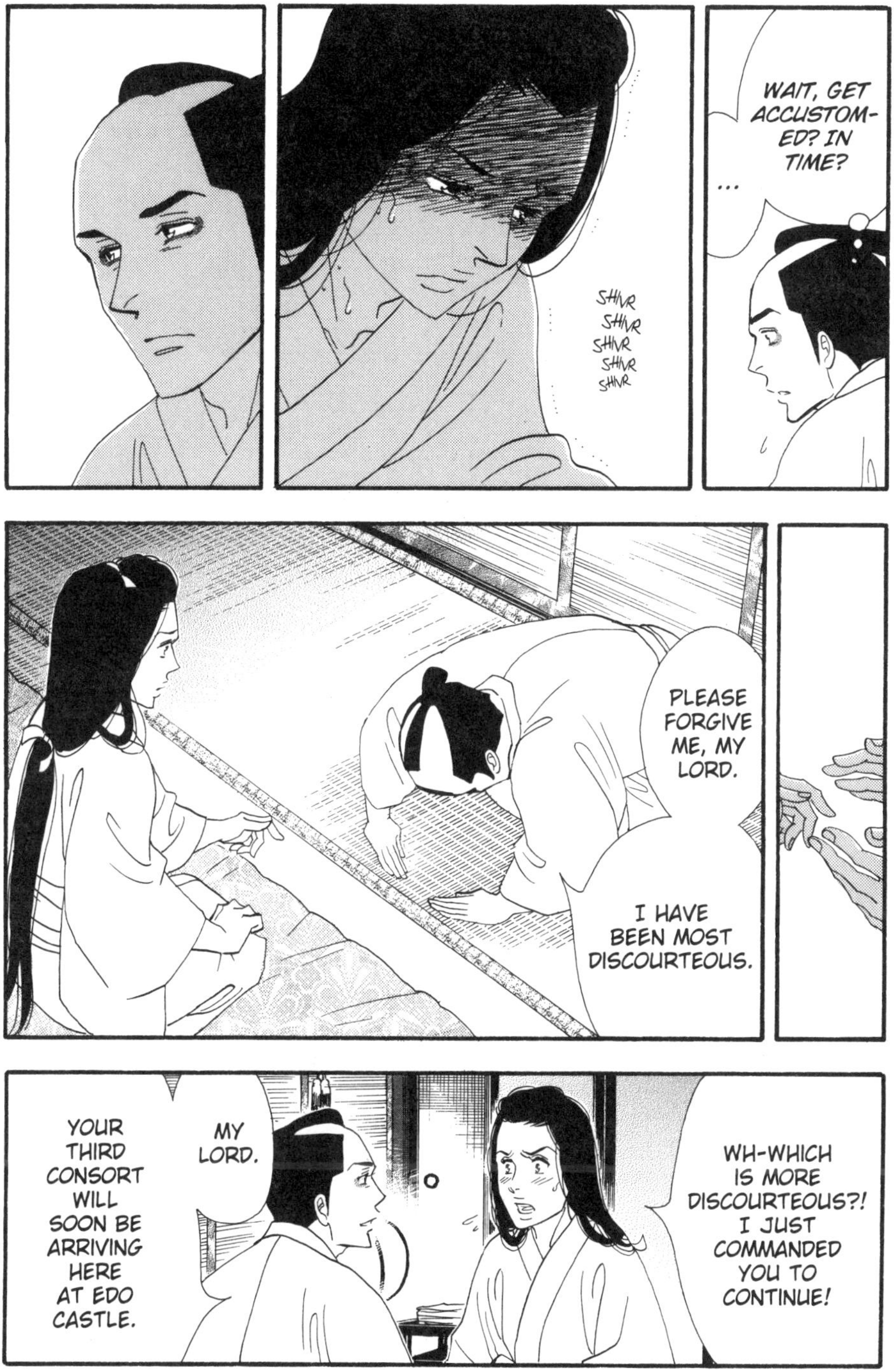
WAIT, GET ACCUSTOM-ED? IN TIME?
...
SHIVR SHIVR SHIVR SHIVR SHIVR
PLEASE FORGIVE ME, MY LORD.
I HAVE BEEN MOST DISCOURTEOUS.
WH-WHICH IS MORE DISCOURTEOUS?! I JUST COMMANDED YOU TO CONTINUE!
MY LORD.
YOUR THIRD CONSORT WILL SOON BE ARRIVING HERE AT EDO CASTLE.

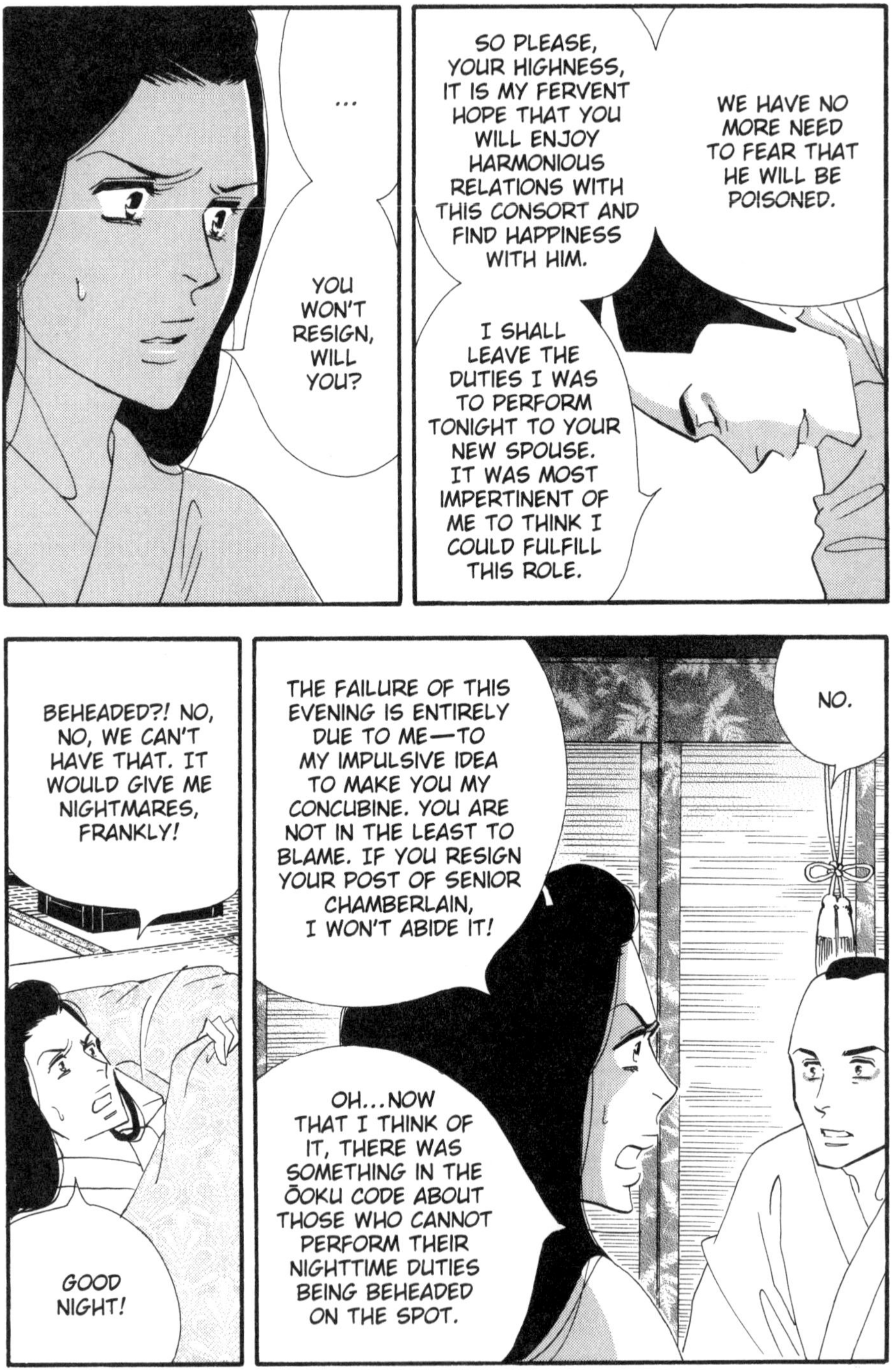
WE HAVE NO MORE NEED TO FEAR THAT HE WILL BE POISONED.
SO PLEASE, YOUR HIGHNESS, IT IS MY FERVENT HOPE THAT YOU WILL ENJOY HARMONIOUS RELATIONS WITH THIS CONSORT AND FIND HAPPINESS WITH HIM.
I SHALL LEAVE THE DUTIES I WAS TO PERFORM TONIGHT TO YOUR NEW SPOUSE. IT WAS MOST IMPERTINENT OF ME TO THINK I COULD FULFILL THIS ROLE.
...
YOU WON'T RESIGN, WILL YOU?
NO.
THE FAILURE OF THIS EVENING IS ENTIRELY DUE TO ME—TO MY IMPULSIVE IDEA TO MAKE YOU MY CONCUBINE. YOU ARE NOT IN THE LEAST TO BLAME. IF YOU RESIGN YOUR POST OF SENIOR CHAMBERLAIN, I WON'T ABIDE IT!
OH...NOW THAT I THINK OF IT, THERE WAS SOMETHING IN THE ŌOKU CODE ABOUT THOSE WHO CANNOT PERFORM THEIR NIGHTTIME DUTIES BEING BEHEADED ON THE SPOT.
BEHEADED?! NO, NO, WE CAN'T HAVE THAT. IT WOULD GIVE ME NIGHTMARES, FRANKLY!
GOOD NIGHT!

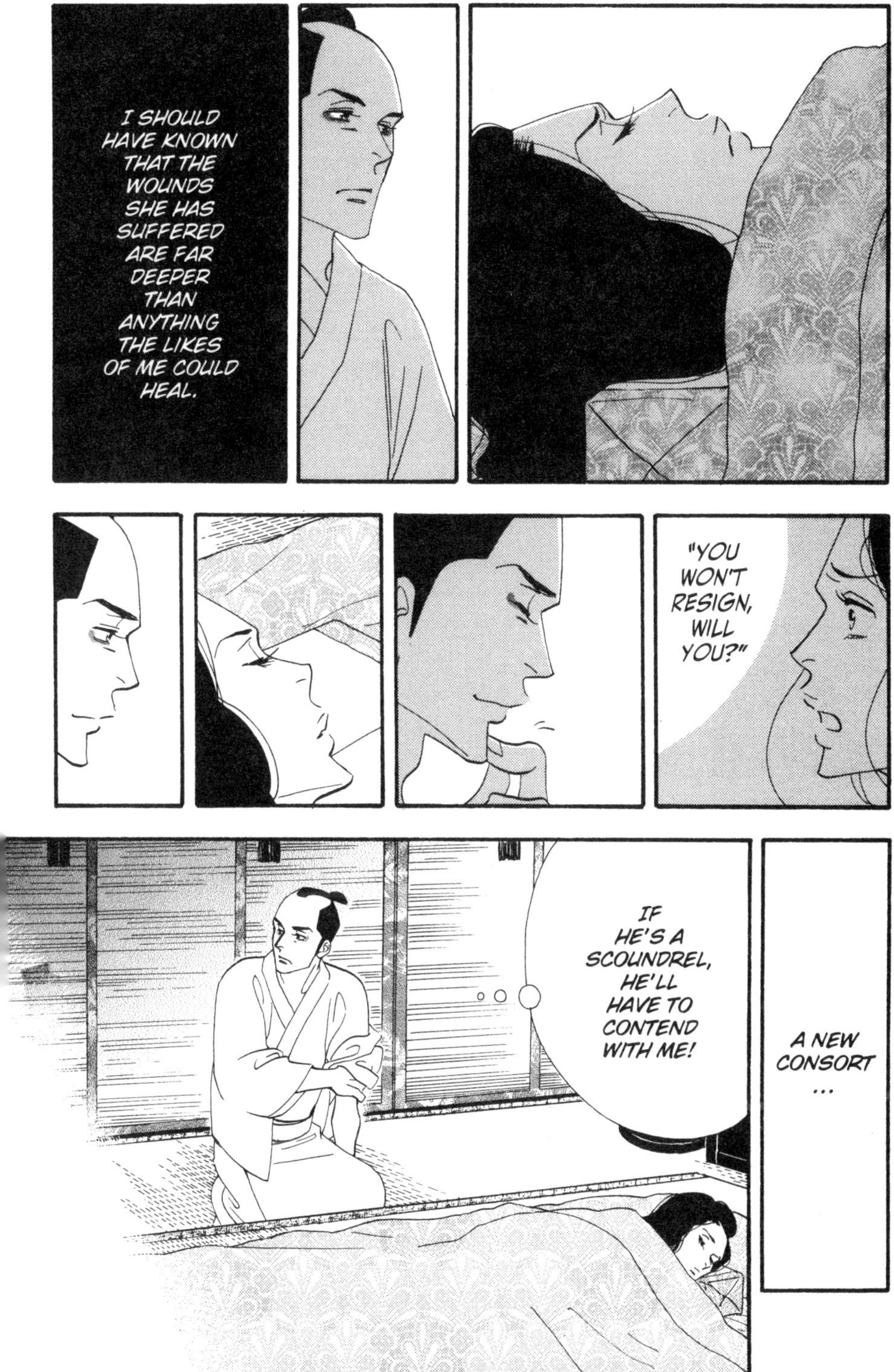
I SHOULD HAVE KNOWN THAT THE WOUNDS SHE HAS SUFFERED ARE FAR DEEPER THAN ANYTHING THE LIKES OF ME COULD HEAL.
"YOU WON'T RESIGN, WILL YOU?"
A NEW CONSORT ...
IF HE'S A SCOUNDREL, HE'LL HAVE TO CONTEND WITH ME!

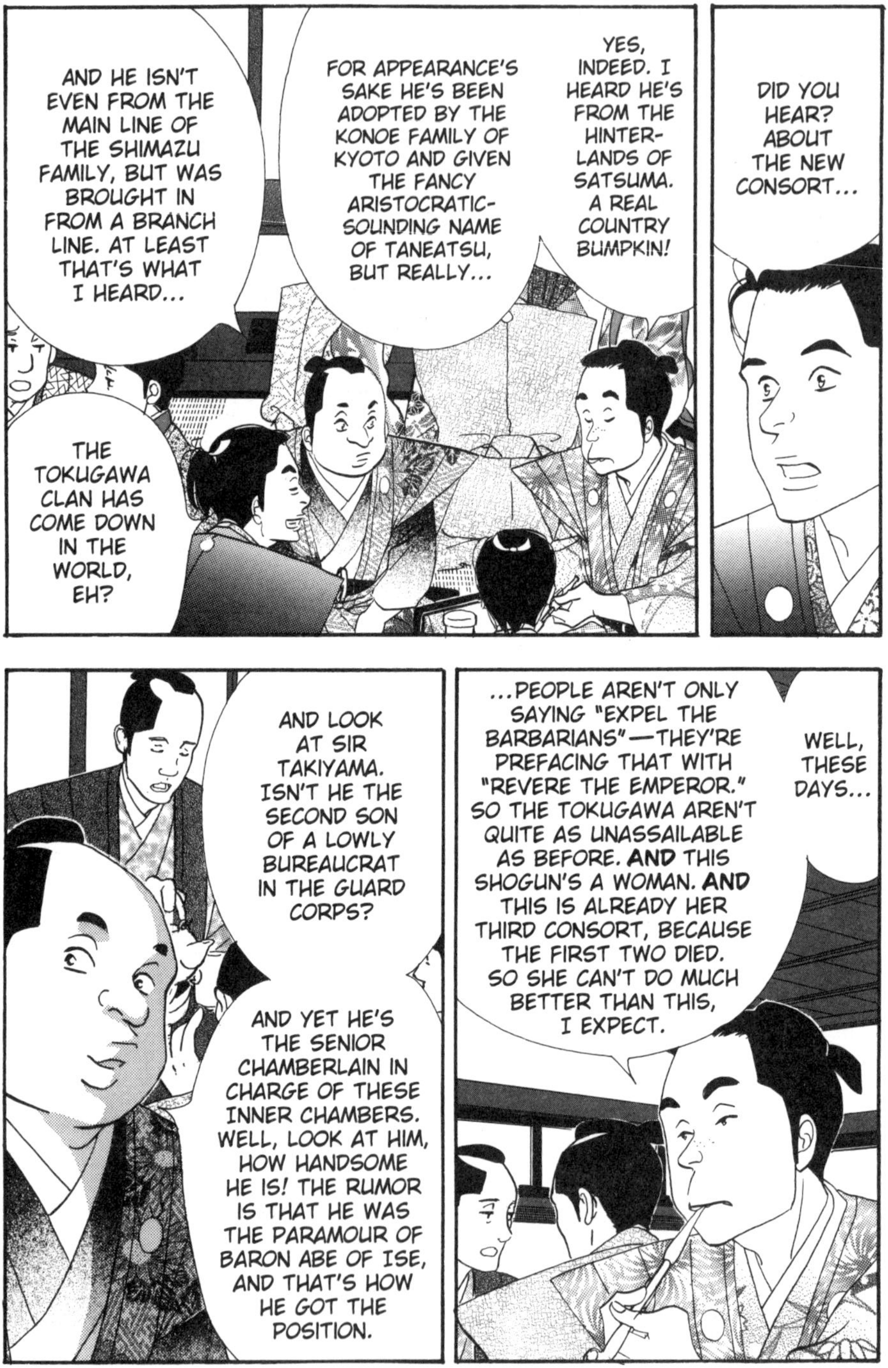
DID YOU HEAR? ABOUT THE NEW CONSORT...
YES, INDEED. I HEARD HE'S FROM THE HINTER-LANDS OF SATSUMA. A REAL COUNTRY BUMPKIN!
FOR APPEARANCE'S SAKE HE'S BEEN ADOPTED BY THE KONOE FAMILY OF KYOTO AND GIVEN THE FANCY ARISTOCRATIC-SOUNDING NAME OF TANEATSU, BUT REALLY...
AND HE ISN'T EVEN FROM THE MAIN LINE OF THE SHIMAZU FAMILY, BUT WAS BROUGHT IN FROM A BRANCH LINE. AT LEAST THAT'S WHAT I HEARD...
THE TOKUGAWA CLAN HAS COME DOWN IN THE WORLD, EH?
WELL, THESE DAYS...
...PEOPLE AREN'T ONLY SAYING "EXPEL THE BARBARIANS"—THEY'RE PREFACING THAT WITH "REVERE THE EMPEROR." SO THE TOKUGAWA AREN'T QUITE AS UNASSAILABLE AS BEFORE. **AND** THIS SHOGUN'S A WOMAN. **AND** THIS IS ALREADY HER THIRD CONSORT, BECAUSE THE FIRST TWO DIED. SO SHE CAN'T DO MUCH BETTER THAN THIS, I EXPECT.
AND LOOK AT SIR TAKIYAMA. ISN'T HE THE SECOND SON OF A LOWLY BUREAUCRAT IN THE GUARD CORPS?
AND YET HE'S THE SENIOR CHAMBERLAIN IN CHARGE OF THESE INNER CHAMBERS. WELL, LOOK AT HIM, HOW HANDSOME HE IS! THE RUMOR IS THAT HE WAS THE PARAMOUR OF BARON ABE OF ISE, AND THAT'S HOW HE GOT THE POSITION.

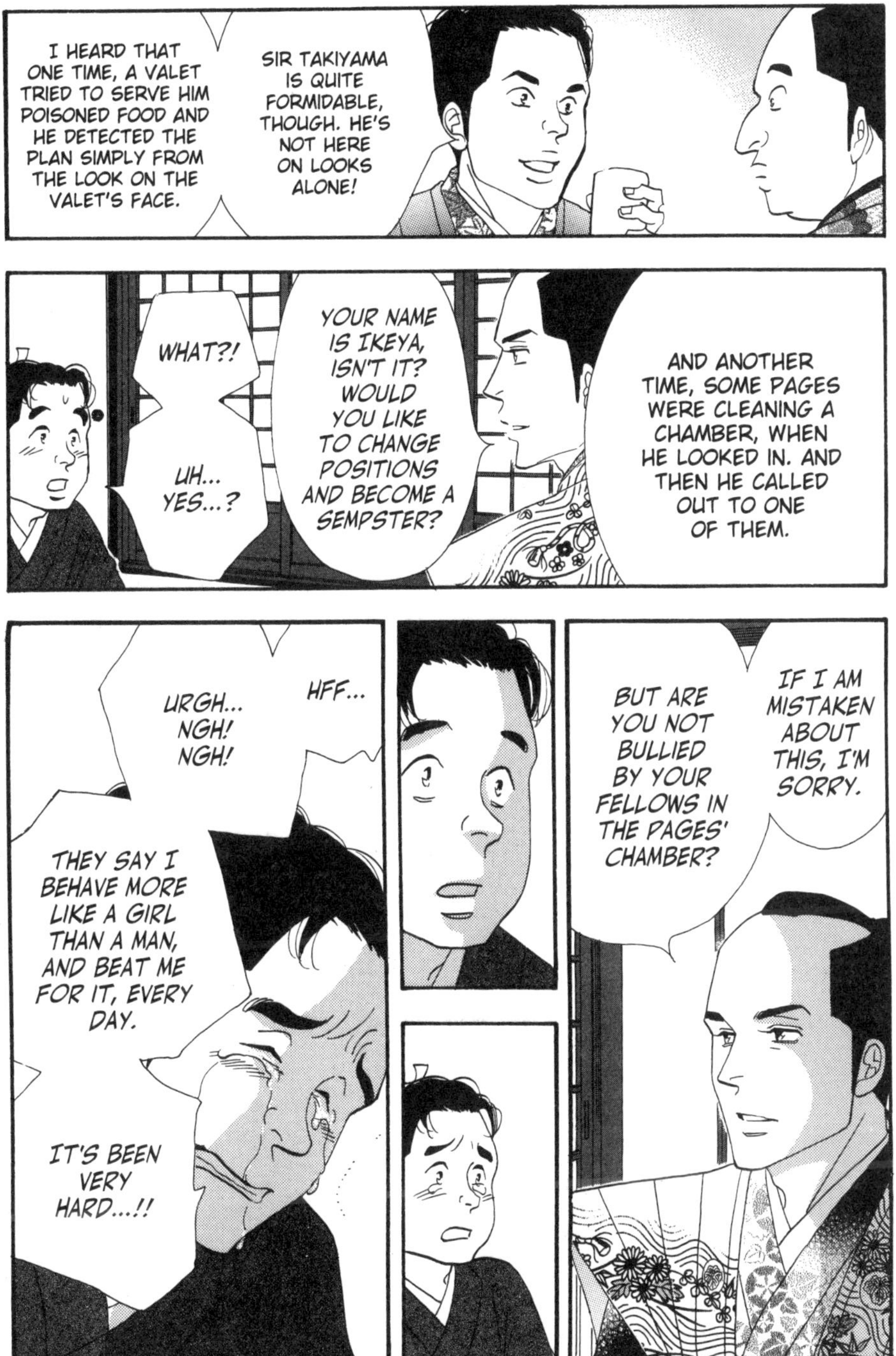
SIR TAKIYAMA IS QUITE FORMIDABLE, THOUGH. HE'S NOT HERE ON LOOKS ALONE!
I HEARD THAT ONE TIME, A VALET TRIED TO SERVE HIM POISONED FOOD AND HE DETECTED THE PLAN SIMPLY FROM THE LOOK ON THE VALET'S FACE.
AND ANOTHER TIME, SOME PAGES WERE CLEANING A CHAMBER, WHEN HE LOOKED IN. AND THEN HE CALLED OUT TO ONE OF THEM.
YOUR NAME IS IKEYA, ISN'T IT? WOULD YOU LIKE TO CHANGE POSITIONS AND BECOME A SEMPSTER?
WHAT?!
UH... YES...?
IF I AM MISTAKEN ABOUT THIS, I'M SORRY.
BUT ARE YOU NOT BULLIED BY YOUR FELLOWS IN THE PAGES' CHAMBER?
HFF...
URGH... NGH! NGH!
THEY SAY I BEHAVE MORE LIKE A GIRL THAN A MAN, AND BEAT ME FOR IT, EVERY DAY.
IT'S BEEN VERY HARD...!!

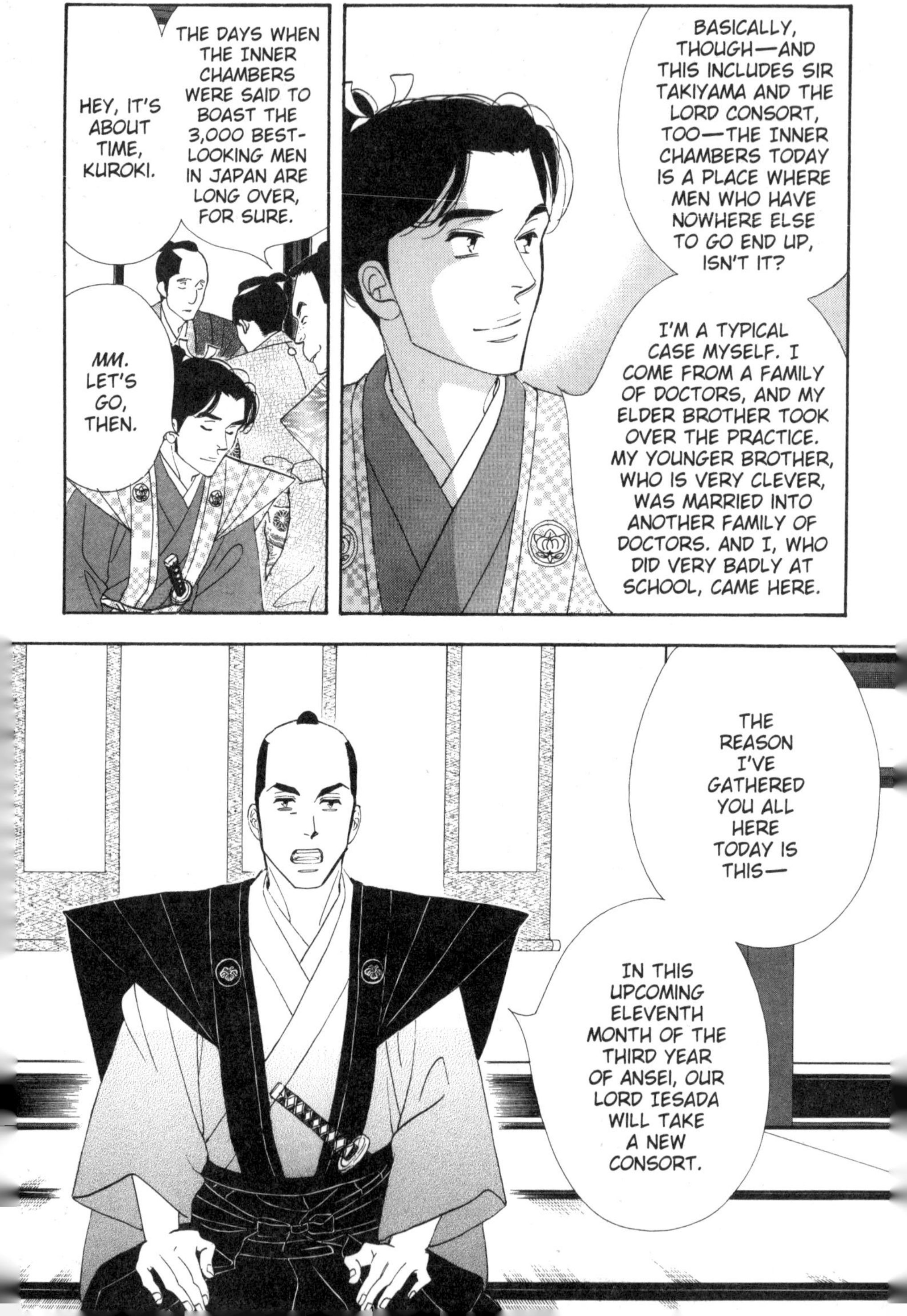
BASICALLY, THOUGH—AND THIS INCLUDES SIR TAKIYAMA AND THE LORD CONSORT, TOO—THE INNER CHAMBERS TODAY IS A PLACE WHERE MEN WHO HAVE NOWHERE ELSE TO GO END UP, ISN'T IT?
I'M A TYPICAL CASE MYSELF. I COME FROM A FAMILY OF DOCTORS, AND MY ELDER BROTHER TOOK OVER THE PRACTICE. MY YOUNGER BROTHER, WHO IS VERY CLEVER, WAS MARRIED INTO ANOTHER FAMILY OF DOCTORS. AND I, WHO DID VERY BADLY AT SCHOOL, CAME HERE.
THE DAYS WHEN THE INNER CHAMBERS WERE SAID TO BOAST THE 3,000 BEST-LOOKING MEN IN JAPAN ARE LONG OVER, FOR SURE.
HEY, IT'S ABOUT TIME, KUROKI.
MM. LET'S GO, THEN.
THE REASON I'VE GATHERED YOU ALL HERE TODAY IS THIS—
IN THIS UPCOMING ELEVENTH MONTH OF THE THIRD YEAR OF ANSEI, OUR LORD IESADA WILL TAKE A NEW CONSORT.

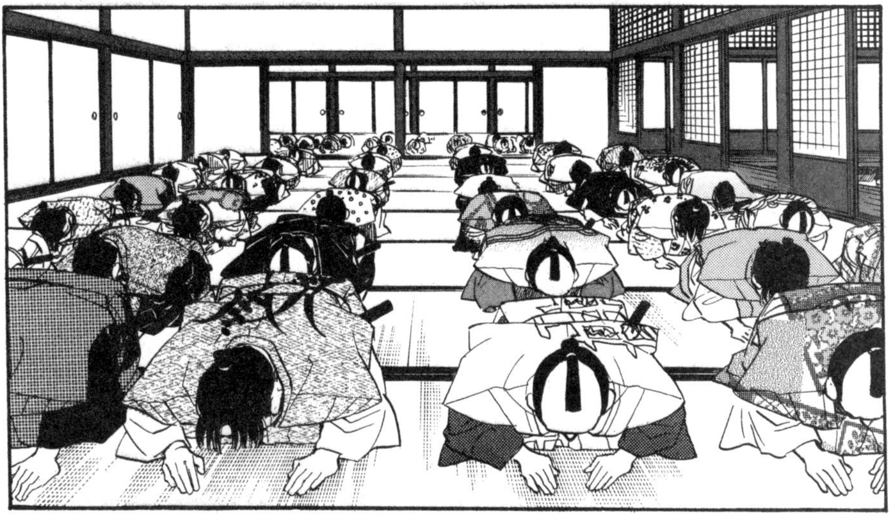

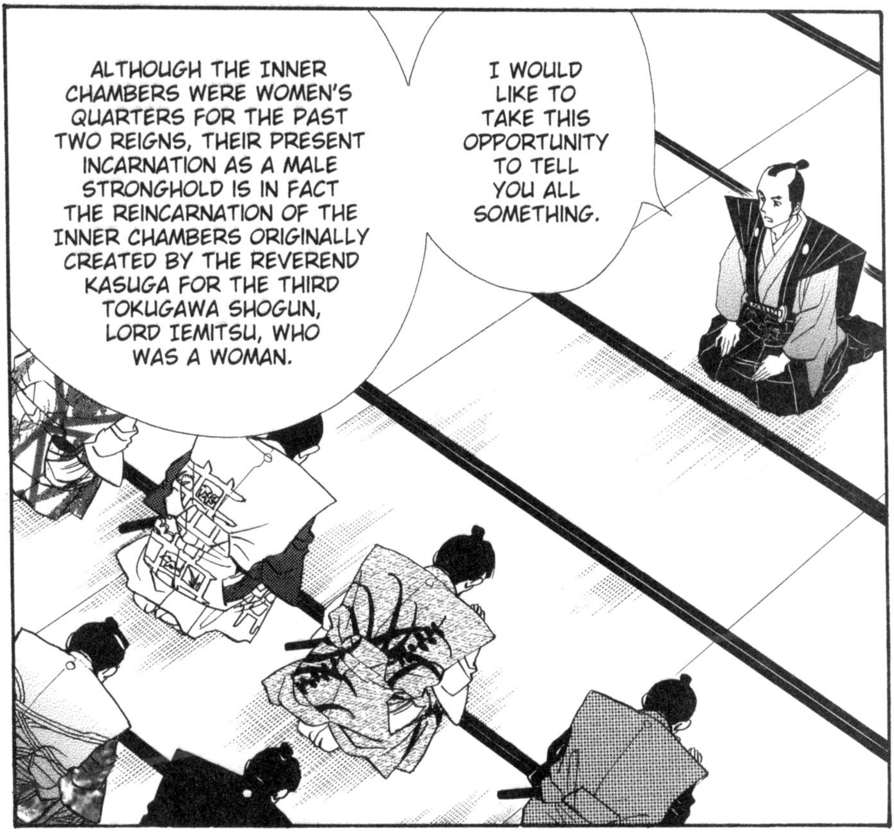
I WOULD LIKE TO TAKE THIS OPPORTUNITY TO TELL YOU ALL SOMETHING.
ALTHOUGH THE INNER CHAMBERS WERE WOMEN'S QUARTERS FOR THE PAST TWO REIGNS, THEIR PRESENT INCARNATION AS A MALE STRONGHOLD IS IN FACT THE REINCARNATION OF THE INNER CHAMBERS ORIGINALLY CREATED BY THE REVEREND KASUGA FOR THE THIRD TOKUGAWA SHOGUN, LORD IEMITSU, WHO WAS A WOMAN.

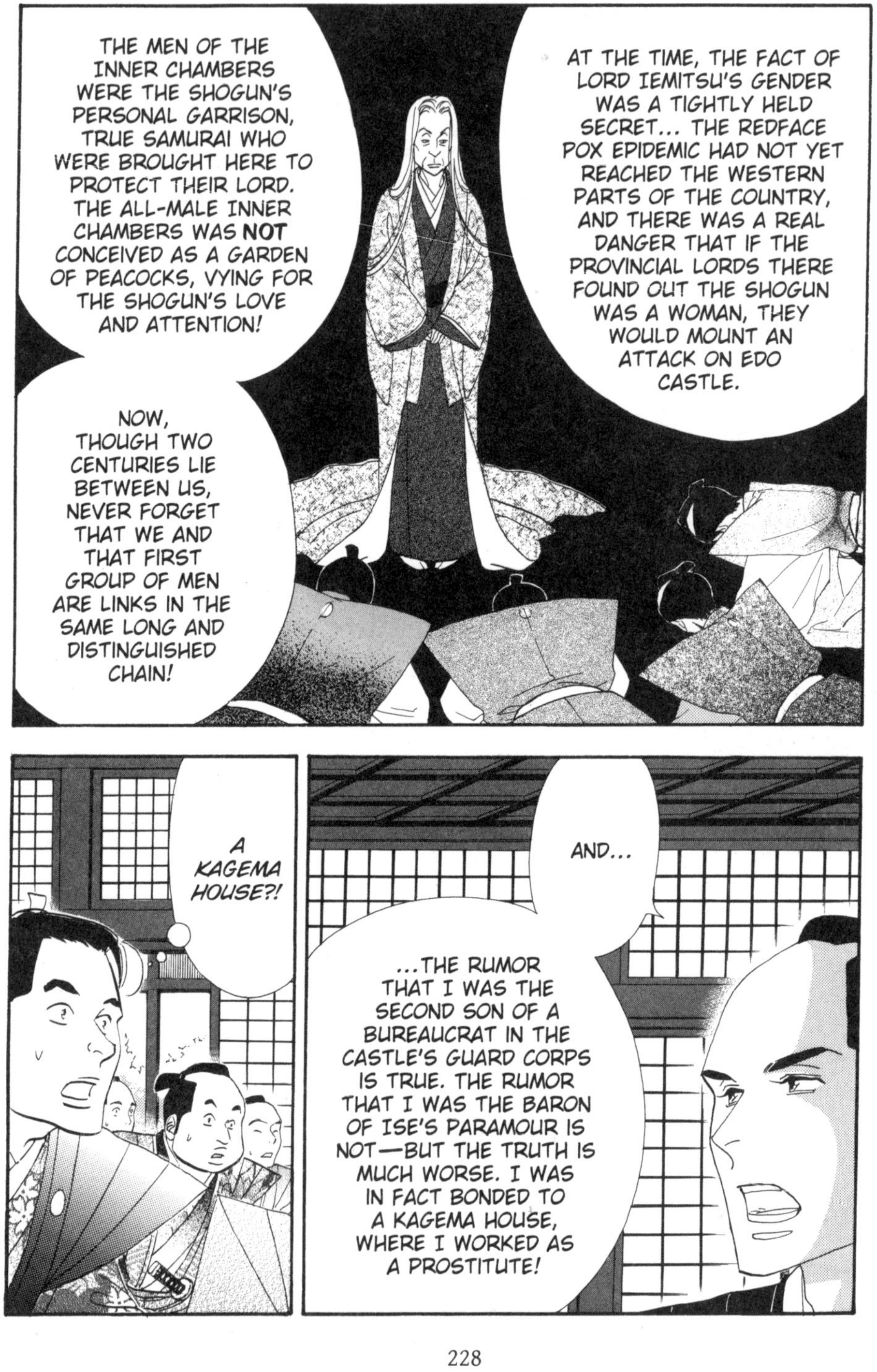
AT THE TIME, THE FACT OF LORD IEMITSU'S GENDER WAS A TIGHTLY HELD SECRET... THE REDFACE POX EPIDEMIC HAD NOT YET REACHED THE WESTERN PARTS OF THE COUNTRY, AND THERE WAS A REAL DANGER THAT IF THE PROVINCIAL LORDS THERE FOUND OUT THE SHOGUN WAS A WOMAN, THEY WOULD MOUNT AN ATTACK ON EDO CASTLE.
THE MEN OF THE INNER CHAMBERS WERE THE SHOGUN'S PERSONAL GARRISON, TRUE SAMURAI WHO WERE BROUGHT HERE TO PROTECT THEIR LORD. THE ALL-MALE INNER CHAMBERS WAS **NOT** CONCEIVED AS A GARDEN OF PEACOCKS, VYING FOR THE SHOGUN'S LOVE AND ATTENTION!
NOW, THOUGH TWO CENTURIES LIE BETWEEN US, NEVER FORGET THAT WE AND THAT FIRST GROUP OF MEN ARE LINKS IN THE SAME LONG AND DISTINGUISHED CHAIN!
AND...
...THE RUMOR THAT I WAS THE SECOND SON OF A BUREAUCRAT IN THE CASTLE'S GUARD CORPS IS TRUE. THE RUMOR THAT I WAS THE BARON OF ISE'S PARAMOUR IS NOT—BUT THE TRUTH IS MUCH WORSE. I WAS IN FACT BONDED TO A KAGEMA HOUSE, WHERE I WORKED AS A PROSTITUTE!
A KAGEMA HOUSE?!

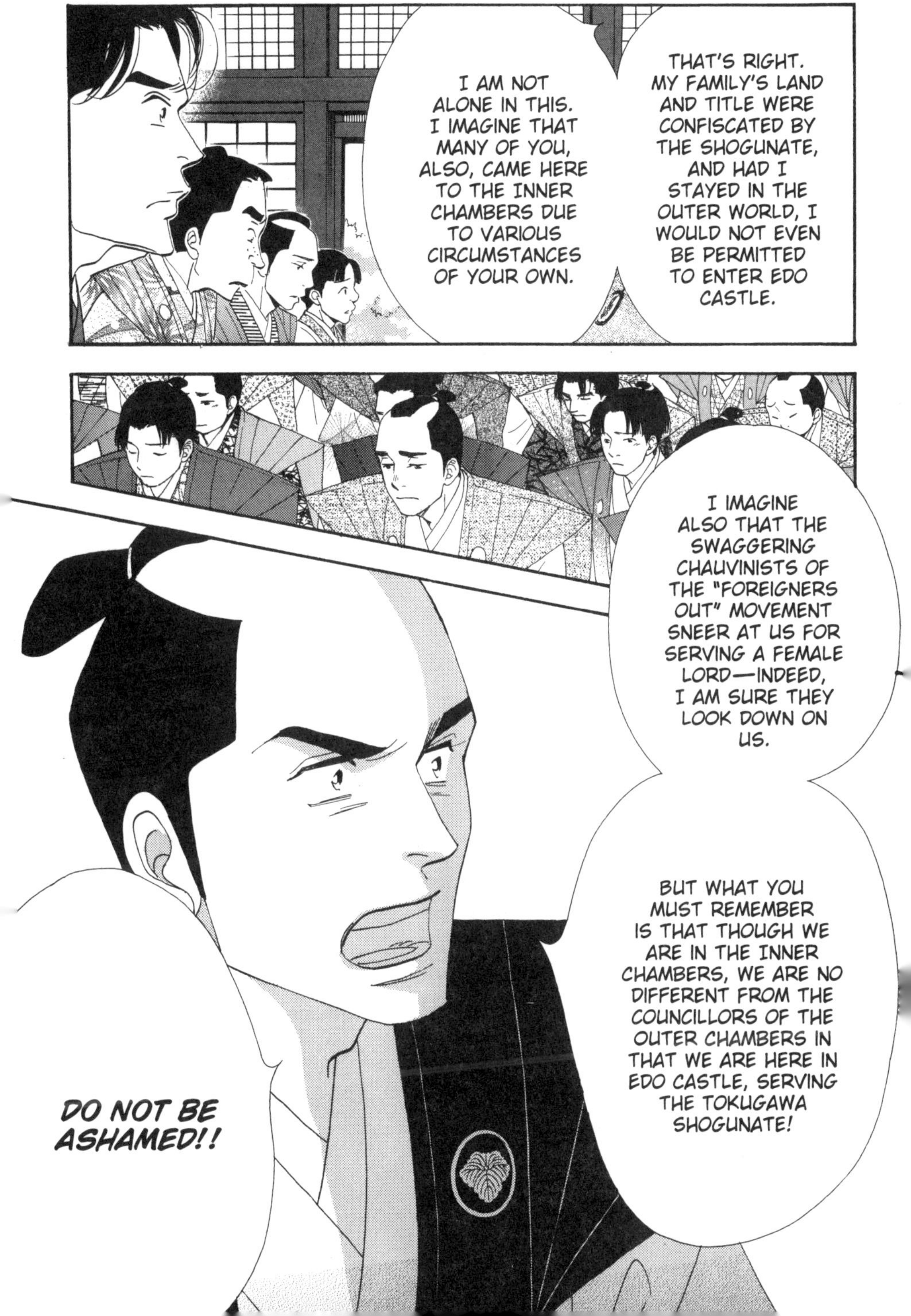
THAT'S RIGHT. MY FAMILY'S LAND AND TITLE WERE CONFISCATED BY THE SHOGUNATE, AND HAD I STAYED IN THE OUTER WORLD, I WOULD NOT EVEN BE PERMITTED TO ENTER EDO CASTLE.
I AM NOT ALONE IN THIS. I IMAGINE THAT MANY OF YOU, ALSO, CAME HERE TO THE INNER CHAMBERS DUE TO VARIOUS CIRCUMSTANCES OF YOUR OWN.
I IMAGINE ALSO THAT THE SWAGGERING CHAUVINISTS OF THE "FOREIGNERS OUT" MOVEMENT SNEER AT US FOR SERVING A FEMALE LORD—INDEED, I AM SURE THEY LOOK DOWN ON US.
BUT WHAT YOU MUST REMEMBER IS THAT THOUGH WE ARE IN THE INNER CHAMBERS, WE ARE NO DIFFERENT FROM THE COUNCILLORS OF THE OUTER CHAMBERS IN THAT WE ARE HERE IN EDO CASTLE, SERVING THE TOKUGAWA SHOGUNATE!
DO NOT BE ASHAMED!!

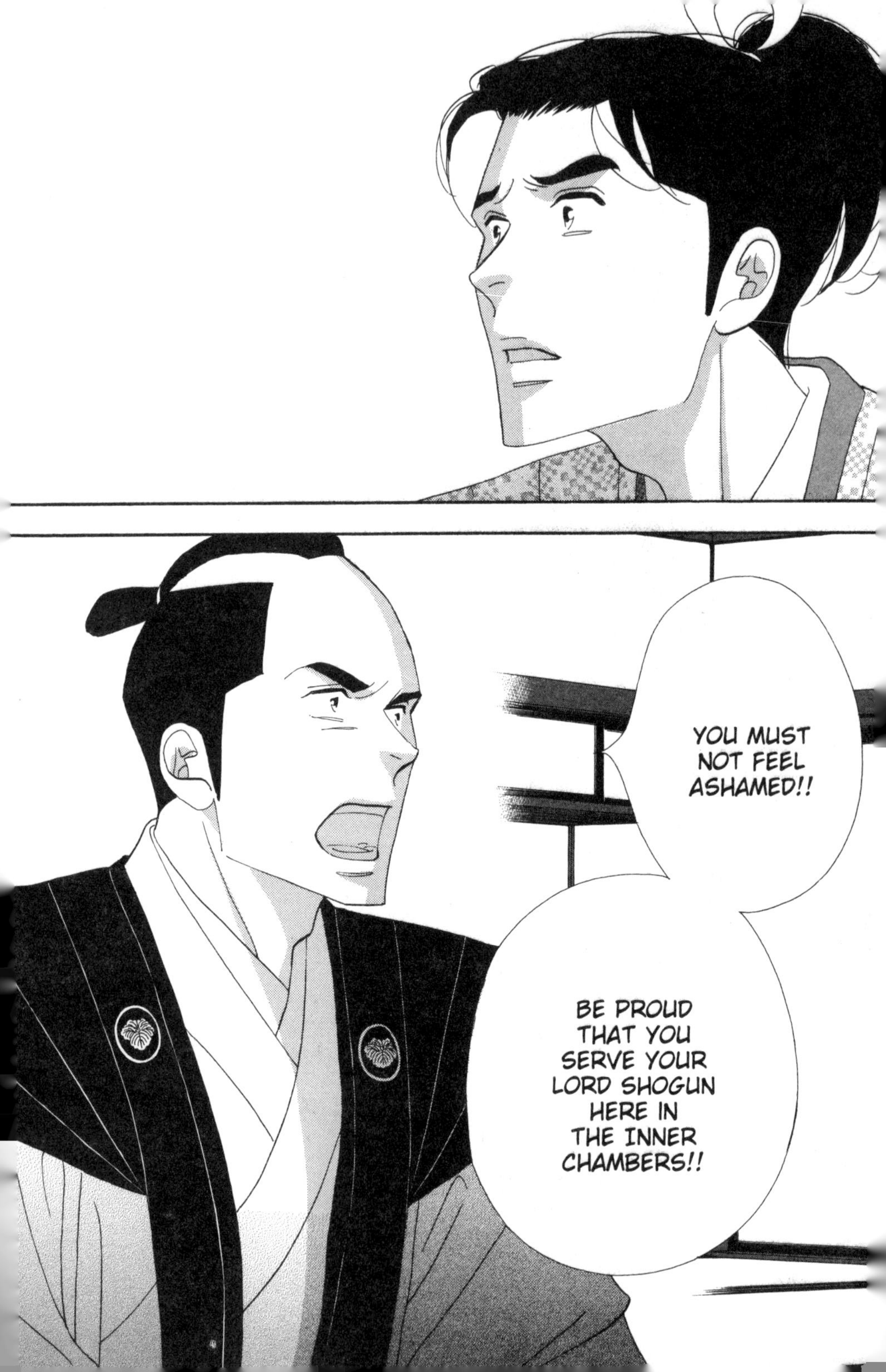
YOU MUST NOT FEEL ASHAMED!!
BE PROUD THAT YOU SERVE YOUR LORD SHOGUN HERE IN THE INNER CHAMBERS!!

SIR TAKI-YAMA...

SHWA

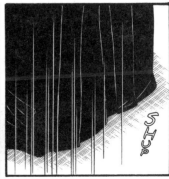

SHUP

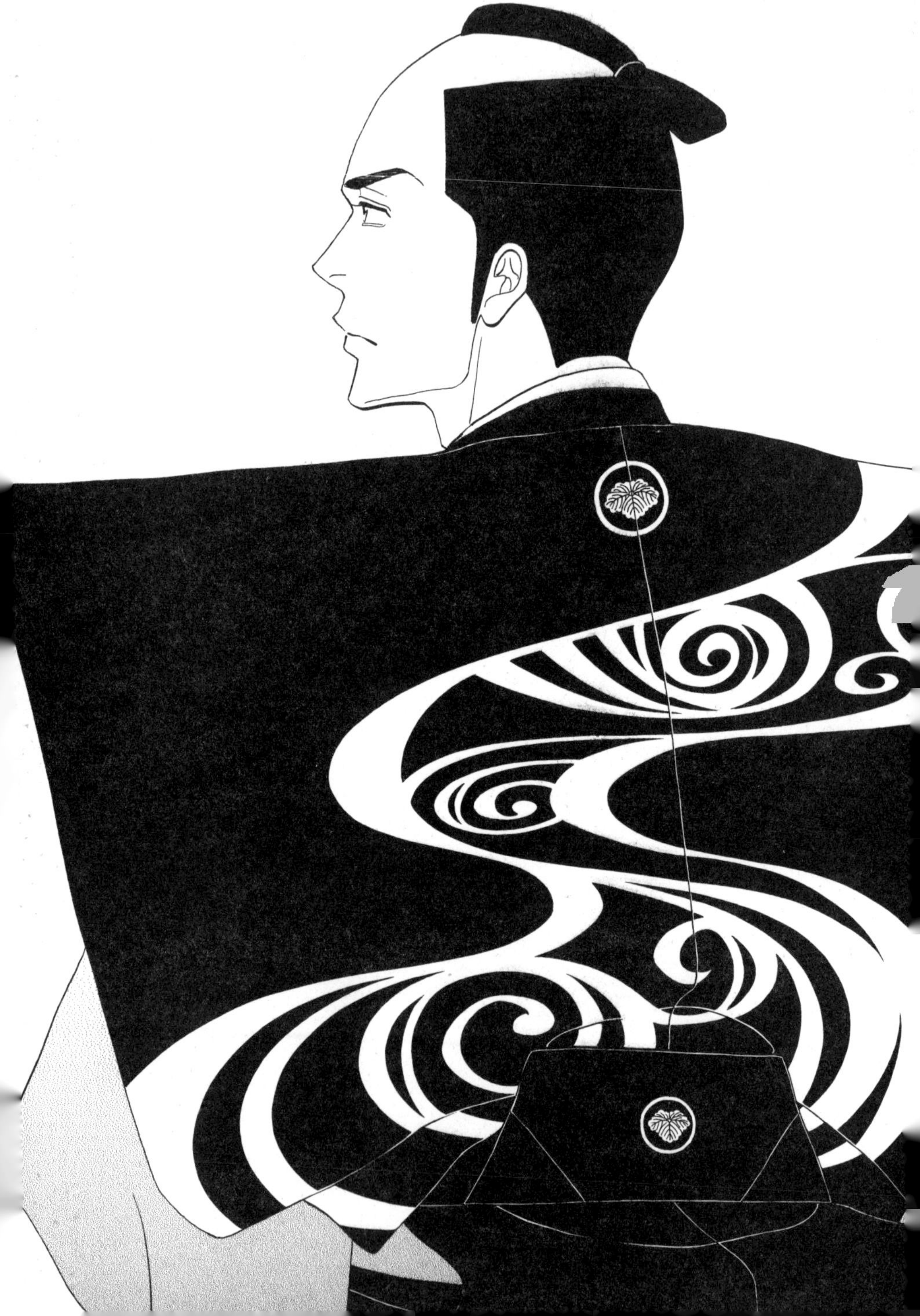

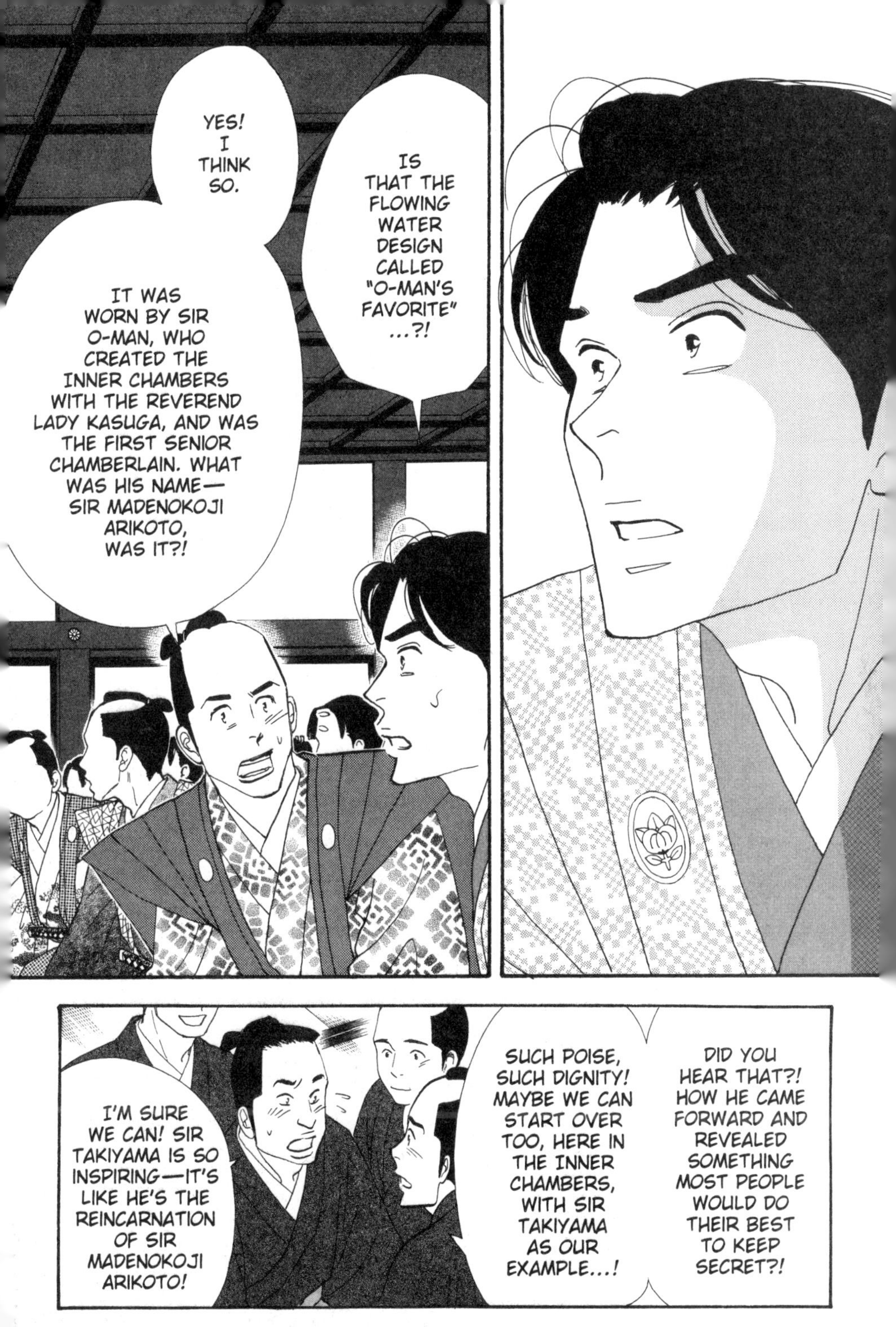
IS THAT THE FLOWING WATER DESIGN CALLED "O-MAN'S FAVORITE"...?!
YES! I THINK SO.
IT WAS WORN BY SIR O-MAN, WHO CREATED THE INNER CHAMBERS WITH THE REVEREND LADY KASUGA, AND WAS THE FIRST SENIOR CHAMBERLAIN. WHAT WAS HIS NAME—SIR MADENOKOJI ARIKOTO, WAS IT?!
DID YOU HEAR THAT?! HOW HE CAME FORWARD AND REVEALED SOMETHING MOST PEOPLE WOULD DO THEIR BEST TO KEEP SECRET?!
SUCH POISE, SUCH DIGNITY! MAYBE WE CAN START OVER TOO, HERE IN THE INNER CHAMBERS, WITH SIR TAKIYAMA AS OUR EXAMPLE...!
I'M SURE WE CAN! SIR TAKIYAMA IS SO INSPIRING—IT'S LIKE HE'S THE REINCARNATION OF SIR MADENOKOJI ARIKOTO!

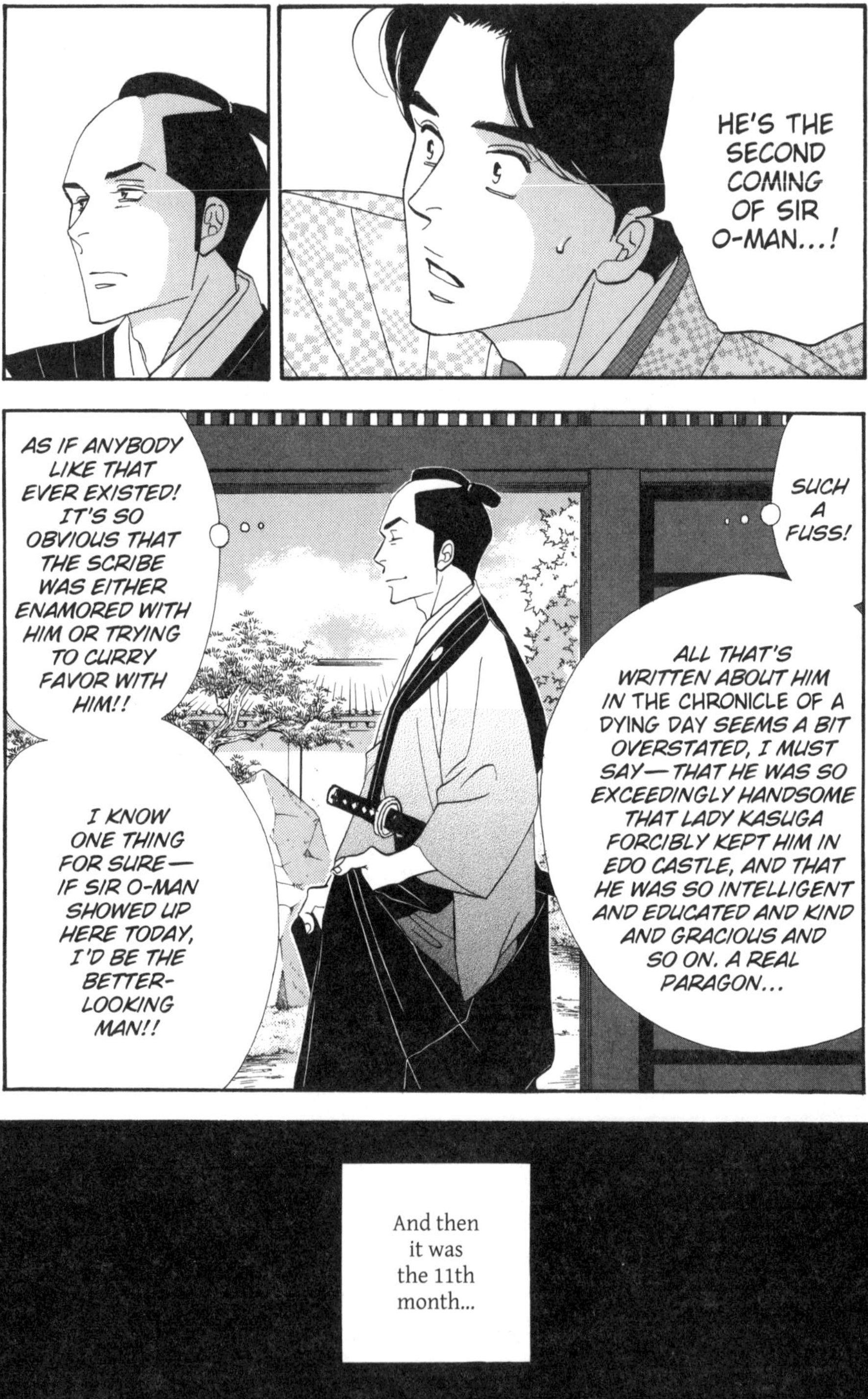
HE'S THE SECOND COMING OF SIR O-MAN...!
SUCH A FUSS!
ALL THAT'S WRITTEN ABOUT HIM IN THE CHRONICLE OF A DYING DAY SEEMS A BIT OVERSTATED, I MUST SAY—THAT HE WAS SO EXCEEDINGLY HANDSOME THAT LADY KASUGA FORCIBLY KEPT HIM IN EDO CASTLE, AND THAT HE WAS SO INTELLIGENT AND EDUCATED AND KIND AND GRACIOUS AND SO ON. A REAL PARAGON...
AS IF ANYBODY LIKE THAT EVER EXISTED! IT'S SO OBVIOUS THAT THE SCRIBE WAS EITHER ENAMORED WITH HIM OR TRYING TO CURRY FAVOR WITH HIM!!
I KNOW ONE THING FOR SURE—IF SIR O-MAN SHOWED UP HERE TODAY, I'D BE THE BETTER-LOOKING MAN!!
And then it was the 11th month...

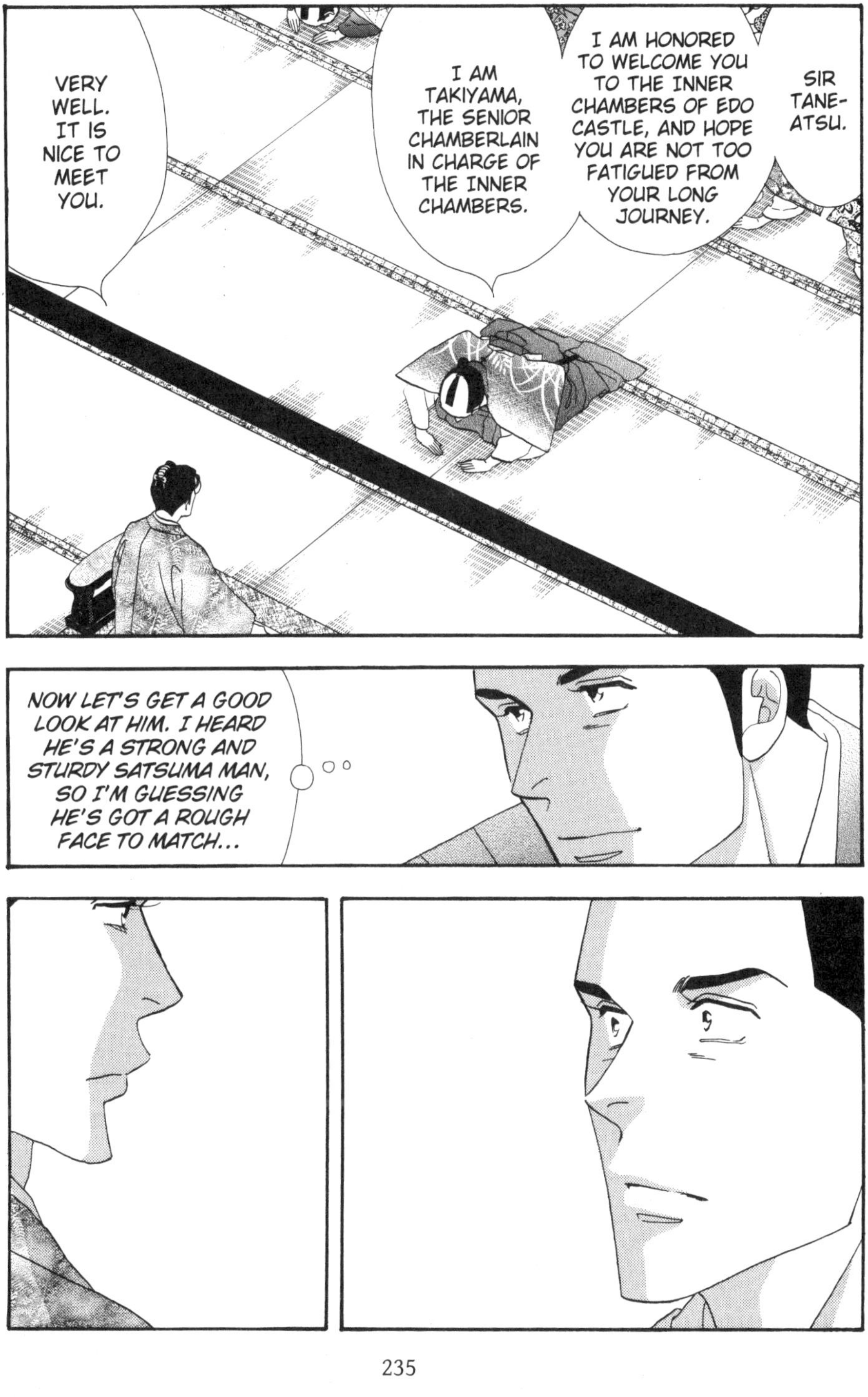
SIR TANE-ATSU.
I AM HONORED TO WELCOME YOU TO THE INNER CHAMBERS OF EDO CASTLE, AND HOPE YOU ARE NOT TOO FATIGUED FROM YOUR LONG JOURNEY.
I AM TAKIYAMA, THE SENIOR CHAMBERLAIN IN CHARGE OF THE INNER CHAMBERS.
VERY WELL. IT IS NICE TO MEET YOU.
NOW LET'S GET A GOOD LOOK AT HIM. I HEARD HE'S A STRONG AND STURDY SATSUMA MAN, SO I'M GUESSING HE'S GOT A ROUGH FACE TO MATCH...

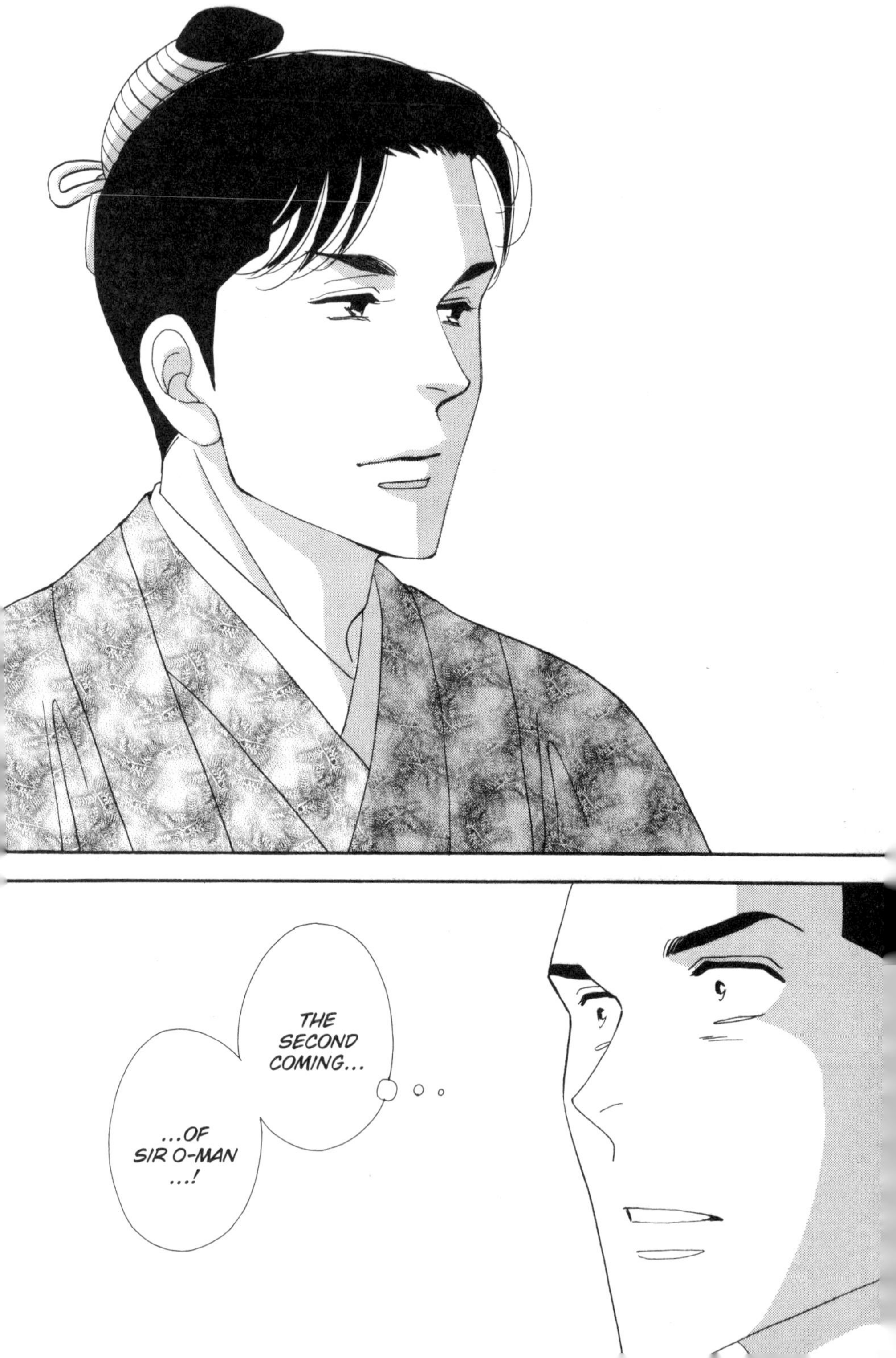
THE SECOND COMING...
...OF SIR O-MAN ...!

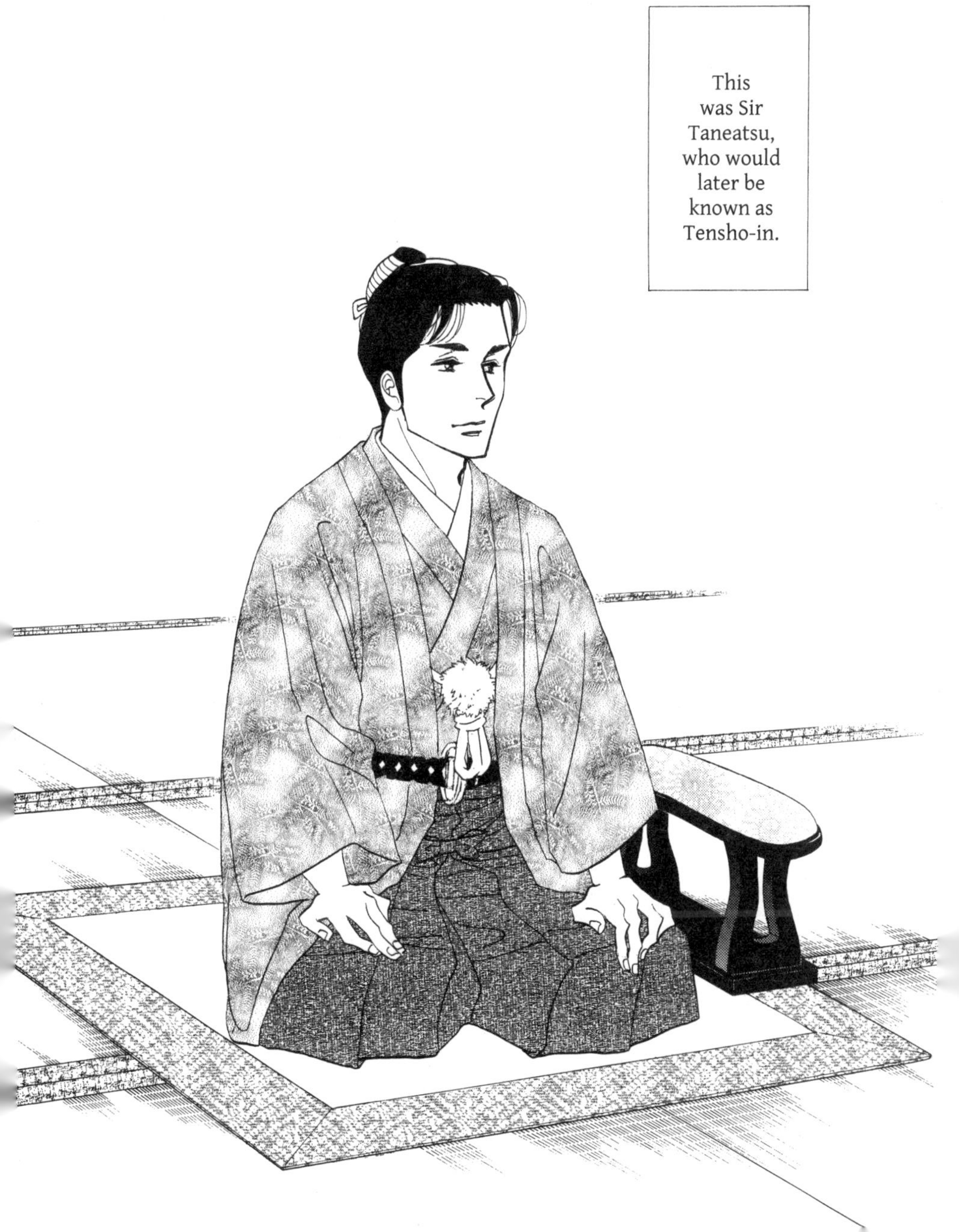
This was Sir Taneatsu, who would later be known as Tensho-in.

Ōoku

⬡ THE INNER CHAMBERS

Ōoku: The Inner Chambers

VOLUME 13 · END NOTES

by Akemi Wegmüller

Page 9, panel 1 · SIR TAKECHIYO
Tokugawa Ieyasu's childhood name. Ieyasu founded the Tokugawa shogunate in 1600.

Page 12, panel 5 · THE VOICES...
He is singing part of the Noh play *Takasago*.

Page 19, panel 1 · PANEL SETTING
This is the changing room of a public bathhouse, which in those days was not segregated between men and women.

Page 20, panel 2 · MERCHANT SHIP REPORT
Dutch and Chinese merchant vessels arriving in Nagasaki Harbor were required to provide reports to the Tokugawa Shogunate on world events.

Page 35, panel 2 · IENARI'S REIGN
The Bunka and Bunsei eras, 1804–1830.

Page 37, panel 2 · "THE MASTER SAID..."
He is quoting from the *Analects of Confucius*.

Page 53, panel 2 · YOSHI-CHO
Area around today's Ningyo-cho district of Nihonbashi in Tokyo's Chuo ward.

Page 54, panel 2 · KAGEMA
Kagema are male prostitutes. Actors often doubled as kagema, and vice versa, which is why they congregated near the theaters.

Page 62, panel 3 · WOMEN'S LANGUAGE
Onna kotoba in Japanese, it refers to a vocabulary and speech pattern associated with women and girls.

Page 63, panel 3 · YOSHIWARA
The pleasure quarters, originally located near what is today Nihonbashi in central Tokyo and eventually moved to the outskirts of the city. The area was walled off from the rest of the city, and the courtesans were restricted to its confines.

Page 115, panel 1 · OGYU SORAI'S *POLITICAL DISCOURSE*
A secret memorandum about the political and economic situation in Japan, written around 1727, which started to circulate in the 1750s.

Page 133, panel 3 · CASTELLA
A sponge cake of Portuguese origin, originally brought into Japan through Nagasaki.

Page 137, panel 2 · MONME
A measure of weight equivalent to 3.75 grams.

Page 175, panel 3 · KUZU TEA
Made by adding hot water to the powdered root of kuzu, a starchy plant similar to arrowroot, and used medicinally. The starch content keeps the liquid hot for much longer than ordinary teas, and it is favored as a warming drink in winter, often sweetened and flavored with ginger or yuzu.

CREATOR BIOGRAPHY

FUMI YOSHINAGA

Fumi Yoshinaga is a Tokyo-born manga creator who debuted in 1994 with *Tsuki to Sandaru* (*The Moon and the Sandals*). Yoshinaga has won numerous awards, including the 2009 Osamu Tezuka Cultural Prize for *Ōoku*, the 2002 Kodansha Manga Award for her series *Antique Bakery* and the 2006 Japan Media Arts Festival Excellence Award for *Ōoku*. She was also nominated for the 2008 Eisner Award for Best Writer/Artist.